What's on the CD

The CD included with this second edition of the *A+: Core Module Study Guide* contains a valuable software tool that will help you prepare for the A+ Core Module exam. An installation interface is designed to run automatically when you place the CD in your Windows 95 or Windows NT 4 or later machine. If it doesn't run automatically, you can access and install the files on the CD through a user-friendly graphical interface by running the **CLICKME.EXE** file located in the root directory.

Minimum System Requirements: 486/100MHz, 16MB RAM, 2× CD-ROM, SoundBlaster-compatible soundcard, 640×480 256-color display, Windows 95/NT 4 or later.

A+ Core Module Test Prep Program

Test your knowledge with this custom program that contains all of the review questions found in the *A+: Core Module Study Guide.* You can choose to test yourself chapter by chapter or randomly. Click the Install Study Guide button on the autorun CD interface screen to install the test prep program on your hard disk, or run the **SETUP.EXE** program from the CD's StudyGuide folder. Once installation is complete, you can run the program by choosing the A+ Core Study Guide program icon in the Programs folder of your Start menu.

Please consult the **README.TXT** file located in the root directory for more detailed information on the CD contents.

During installation of the test engine, you may be prompted to allow the program to update certain system files. The files referred to are Microsoft DLL files and should not pose a threat to your system; however, as a precaution you may wish to back up your system files prior to installing this program. In some instances, you may need to reboot your computer before the new files can take effect. After rebooting, you will need to reaccess the CD interface before completing the program installation.

D1402491

A+: Core Module Study Guide

A+: Core Module Study Guide

2nd Edition

David Groth

SYBEX®

San Francisco • Paris • Düsseldorf • Soest

Associate Publisher: Guy Hart-Davis
Contracts and Licensing Specialist: Adrienne Crew
Acquisitions & Developmental Editor: Neil Edde
Editors: James A. Compton, Doug Robert
Technical Editors: Ted Harwood, Jon R. Hansen
Book Designer: Kris Warrenburg
Graphic Illustrators: Andrew Benzie, Tony Jonick, Elizabeth Creegan, Terry Keaton, Joel Bavagboli, Kristof Chemineau
Desktop Publisher: Maureen Forys, Happenstance Type-O-Rama
Production Coordinator: Charles Mathews
Indexer: Ted Laux
Companion CD: Rick Sawtell, Molly Sharp, Ginger Warner
Cover Designer: Design Site
Cover Illustration: Design Site

Screen reproductions produced with Collage Complete.

Collage Complete is a trademark of Inner Media Inc.

SYBEX is a registered trademark of SYBEX Inc.

TRADEMARKS: SYBEX has attempted throughout this book to distinguish proprietary trademarks from descriptive terms by following the capitalization style used by the manufacturer.

The CD Interface music is from GIRA Sound AURIA Music Library © GIRA Sound 1996.

The author and publisher have made their best efforts to prepare this book, and the content is based upon final release software whenever possible. Portions of the manuscript may be based upon pre-release versions supplied by software manufacturer(s). The author and the publisher make no representation or warranties of any kind with regard to the completeness or accuracy of the contents herein and accept no liability of any kind including but not limited to performance, merchantability, fitness for any particular purpose, or any losses or damages of any kind caused or alleged to be caused directly or indirectly from this book.

Library of Congress Card Number: 98-85671
ISBN: 0-7821-2344-9

Manufactured in the United States of America

10 9 8 7 6 5 4 3 2 1

*Dedicated to my wife Linda and
to the geek in all of us.*

ACKNOWLEDGMENTS

I have never really known how a movie star feels when accepting an Academy Award, until now. There are so many people to thank, and so little space. I'll begin by thanking my wife. She tirelessly edited glossary inserts, listened to my rants about the books, and gave me a "swift kick" when and where I needed it.

Then there's my Dad, who always told me that "You've gotta do what you've gotta do." Thanks, Dad. And Mom, for encouraging me to do whatever I wanted to, as long as I did the "have to's" first.

To my contributing writers: Your tireless work and patience made my life easier. Yes, I asked a lot, but I think you'll be proud to have your names here, in print. Who says you should never go into business with your friends?

Christel Fritz, MCT, CTT, A+: Christel is also a technical instructor at Corporate Technologies. She currently teaches several Microsoft classes as well as the A+ curriculum. Many people have commented on the way she explains things very clearly (Christel Clear?). She wrote the chapters on PC architecture, networks, and safety. They turned out wonderfully, in my humble opinion.

Patti Heisler: Patti is currently the Training Manager at Corporate Technologies. She wrote the chapter on customer service. She has worked in the customer service industry for several years. Whenever I deal with customers, I think of the way Patti would do it. She is calm, patient, and professional with every customer. For this reason, I humbly begged her to write that chapter and I think it turned out exceptionally well.

Editors Doug Robert and Jim Compton have turned my chicken scratchings into a professional study guide. I can't thank these gentlemen enough, for without them, I would not be writing this acknowledgment. Many thanks also to Ted Harwood and Jon Hansen for double-checking the technical accuracy and relevance of the materials, to Andrew Benzie for creating the art from my sometimes less-than-clear sketches and photographs, and to Maureen Forys and Charles Mathews for taking all the pieces and turning them into a book that is not only useful but good looking as well. Thanks also to Rick Sawtell for programming the Test Prep program for the companion CD, and to Ginger Warner and Molly Sharp for producing the CD.

Finally, I would like to thank you, the reader, for purchasing this book. I firmly believe that the A+ Study Guide is the best study guide available today for the A+ Certification exams. I hope that you get out of it as much as I put into it.

CONTENTS AT A GLANCE

TABLE OF CONTENTS

INTRODUCTION: THE A+ CERTIFICATION PROCESS

The A+ Certification tests are sponsored by the Computing Technology Industry Association (CompTIA) and supported by several of the computer industry's biggest vendors (for example, Compaq, IBM, and Microsoft). This book was written to provide you with the knowledge you need to pass the first of the two exams for the A+ Certification, the *Core Module exam*. (The second is a combination Windows/DOS exam.) A+ Certification gives employers a benchmark for evaluating their employees' knowledge. When an applicant for a job says "I'm A+ Certified," the employer can be assured that the applicant knows the fundamental computer service concepts. For example, an A+ Certified technician should know the difference between the different types of hard disk subsystems and how to configure them.

This book was written at an intermediate technical level: we assume that you already know how to *use* a personal computer and its basic peripherals, such as modems and printers, but recognize that you may be learning how to *service* some of that computer equipment for the first time. The exam itself covers basic computer service topics as well as some more advanced issues, and it covers some topics that anyone already working as a technician, whether with computers or not, should be familiar with. The exam is designed to test you on these topics in order to certify that you have enough knowledge to fix and upgrade some of the most widely used types of personal desktop computers.

We've included review questions at the end of each chapter to give you a taste of what it's like to take the exam. If you're already working as a technical service or support person, we recommend checking out these questions first, to gauge your level of knowledge of the subject. You can use the book mainly to "fill in the gaps" in your current computer service knowledge. You may find, as many service technicians have, that being well-versed in all the technical aspects of the equipment is not enough to provide a satisfactory level of support—you must also have "customer relations" skills. The exam recognizes the need for such skills (even though the questions in that area don't actually count towards your score), so we devote an entire chapter to that topic.

If you can answer 80 percent or more of the review questions correctly for a given chapter, you can probably feel safe moving on to the next chapter. If you're unable to answer that many correctly, reread the chapter and try the questions again. Your score should improve.

WARNING   DON'T just study the questions and answers—the questions on the actual exam will be different from the practice ones included in this book. The exam is designed to test your knowledge of a concept or objective, so use this book to learn the objective *behind* the question.

What Is A+ Certification?

The A+ Certification program was developed by the Computer Technology Industry Association (CompTIA) to provide an industry-wide means of certifying the competency of computer service technicians. The "A+ Certified" diploma, which is granted to those who have attained the level of knowledge and troubleshooting skills that are needed to provide capable support in the field of personal computers, is similar to other certifications in the computer industry. For example, Novell offers the Certified Novell Engineer (CNE) program to provide the same recognition for network professionals who deal with its NetWare products, and Microsoft has its Microsoft Certified Service Engineer (MCSE) program. The theory behind these certifications is that if you need to have service performed on any of their products, you would sooner call a technician who has been certified in one of the appropriate certification programs than you would just call the first "expert" in the phone book.

The A+ Certification program was created to offer a wide-ranging certification, in the sense that it is intended to certify competence with personal computers from many different makers/vendors. There are two tests required to become A+ Certified. You must pass the A+ Certification *Core Module*, which covers basic computer concepts, hardware troubleshooting, customer service, and hardware upgrading. You must also pass the specialty exam covering the DOS and Windows operating environments (the *DOS/Windows Module*). You don't have to take the Core Module and the Specialty Module at the same time; you have 90 days from the time you pass one test to pass the second. The "A+ Certified" diploma is not awarded until you've passed the second test.

NOTE The tests have been updated as of July 31, 1998. If you passed one of the previous version's exams before July 30, 1998 but have not yet passed the other exam, you must take both of the *updated* tests in order to receive A+ Certification. (In other words, the 90-day window for successfully passing both of the previous version's exams closed as of July 30, 1998.)

NOTE The Macintosh Specialty exam offered as an alternative to the DOS/Windows exam prior to July 31, 1998 is no longer offered.

Benefits of A+ Certification

Why should you get A+ Certified? There are several good reasons. The CompTIA "Candidate's Information" packet lists five major benefits: It demonstrates proof of professional achievement, it increases your marketability, it provides greater opportunity for advancement in your field, it is increasingly found as a requirement for some kinds of advanced training, and it raises customer confidence in your and your company's services.

It's Proof of Professional Achievement

The A+ Certification is quickly becoming a status symbol in the computer service industry. Organizations that contain members of the computer service industry are recognizing the benefits of A+ certification and are pushing for their members to become certified. And more people every day are putting the emblem of the "A+ Certified Technician" on their business cards.

It Increases Your Marketability

A+ Certification makes an individual more marketable to a potential employer. Also, that individual may be able to receive a higher base salary, because the employer won't have to spend as much money on vendor-specific training.

What Is an AASC?

More service companies are becoming A+ Authorized Service Centers (AASCs). This means that over 50 percent of the technicians employed by that service center are A+ Certified. At the time of the writing of this book, there are over 1,400 A+ Authorized Service Centers in the world. Customers and vendors alike recognize that AASCs employ the most qualified service technicians. Because of this, an AASC will get more business than a non-authorized service center. Also, because more service centers want to reach the AASC level, they will give preference in hiring to a candidate who is A+ Certified than one who is not.

It Provides Opportunity for Advancement

Most raises and advancement are based on performance. A+ certified employees work faster and more efficiently, thus making them more productive. The more productive an employee is, the more money they will make for their company. And of course, the more money they make for the company, the more valuable they will be to the company, so if an employee is A+ certified, their chances of getting promoted will be greater.

It Fulfills Training Requirements

A+ Certification is recognized by most major computer hardware vendors, including (but not limited to) IBM, Hewlett-Packard, Apple, and Compaq. Some of these vendors will apply A+ Certification toward prerequisites in their own respective certification programs. For example, an A+ Certified technician is automatically given credit towards HP laser printer certification without having to take prerequisite classes and tests. This has the side benefit of reducing training costs for employers.

It Raises Customer Confidence

As the A+ Certified technician moniker becomes more well-known among computer owners, more of them will realize that the A+ technician is more qualified to work on their computer equipment than a non-certified technician is.

How to Get A+ Certified

A+ Certification is available to anyone who passes the tests. You don't have to work for any particular company. It's not a secret society. It is, however, an elite group. In order to become A+ Certified you must do two things:

- Pass the A+ Certification *Core Module* exam (the focus of this book).

- Pass the A+ Certification *Operating System Specialty* exam (DOS/Windows).

You don't have to take both exams at the same time; you have 90 days from the time you pass one test to pass the second.

The exams are administered by Sylvan Prometric and can be taken at any Sylvan Prometric Testing Center. If you pass both exams, you will get a certificate in the mail from the CompTIA saying that you have passed, as well as a lapel pin and business card. To find the Sylvan Prometric training center nearest you, call (800) 755-EXAM (755-3926).

To register for the tests, call Sylvan at (800) 77-MICRO (776-4276). You'll be asked for your name, Social Security number (an optional number may be assigned if you don't wish to provide SSN), mailing address, phone number, employer, when and where (i.e., which Sylvan testing center) you want to take the test, and your credit card number (arrangement for payment must be made at the time of registration).

NOTE   Note that although you can save money by arranging to take more than one test at the same seating, there are no other discounts—for example, if you have to take a test more than once in order to get a passing grade, you have to pay both times.

It is possible to pass these tests without any reference materials, but only if you already have the knowledge and experience that come from reading about and working with personal computers. Even experienced service people, however, tend to have what you might call a 20/80 situation with their computer knowledge—they may use 20 percent of their knowledge and skills 80 percent of the time, and have to rely on manuals or guesswork or phone calls for the rest. By covering all the topics that are tested by the exam, this book can help you to refresh your memory concerning topics that until now you might have only seldom used. (It can also serve to fill in gaps that, let's admit, you may have tried to cover up for quite some time.) Further, by treating all the issues that the exam covers, i.e., problems you may run into in the arenas of PC service and support, this book can serve as a general field guide, one that you may want to keep with you as you go about your work.

> **NOTE**   In addition to reading the book, you might consider practicing these objectives through an internship program. (After all, all theory and no practice make for a poor technician.) Companies that offer training programs are listed in Appendix C.

The A+ Core Module Exam Objectives

As mentioned previously, there are two tests required to become A+ Certified: the Core Module exam and the Operating System Specialty exam. This book covers the Core Module only. Look for a second book in this series to cover the DOS/Windows Operating System Specialty exam.

The following are the areas (or "domains" according to CompTIA) in which you must be proficient in order to pass the A+ Core Module exam.

1. Installation, Configuration and Upgrading

This content area deals with the installation , configuration and upgrading of common computer Field Replaceable Units (FRU's). Most technicians spend a lot of time performing these operations. To that end, CompTIA has made sure that questions from this content area will make up 30 percent of the exam. The bulk of this information is contained in the first six chapters.

- 1.1: Identify basic terms, concepts, and functions of system modules, including how each module should work during normal operation. (Chapters 2, 4, 5)

- 1.2: Identify basic procedures for adding and removing field replaceable modules. (Chapter 7)

- 1.3: Identify available IRQs, DMAs, and I/O addresses and procedures for configuring them for device installation. (Chapter 7)

- 1.4: Identify common peripheral ports, associated cabling, and their connectors. (Chapter 1)

- 1.5: Identify proper procedures for installing and configuring IDE/EIDE devices. (Chapter 4)

- 1.6: Identify proper procedures for installing and configuring SCSI devices. (Chapter 4)

- 1.7: Identify proper procedures for installing and configuring peripheral devices. (Chapter 6)

- 1.8: Identify concepts and procedures relating to BIOS. (Chapter 2)

- 1.9: Identify hardware methods of system optimization and when to use them. (Chapter 3)

2. Diagnosing and Troubleshooting

Before a technician can install or upgrade a component, he or she must determine which component needs to be replaced. A technician will normally use the skills addressed by the diagnosing and troubleshooting content areas to make that determination. Questions about these two topics together make up 20 percent of the exam.

- 2.1: Identify common symptoms and problems associated with each module and how to troubleshoot and isolate the problems. (Chapter 12)

- 2.2: Identify basic troubleshooting procedures and good practices for eliciting problem symptoms from customers. (Chapter 11)

3. Safety and Preventive Maintenance

Most people don't think of computer service as a dangerous job. Most often, safety precautions are taken to prevent damage to the components. In actuality, there are a few components that can cause severe injury. This topic also covers maintenance and cleaning of computer components. Questions about these topics constitute 10 percent of the exam. Safety and preventive maintenance procedures are covered mostly in Chapter 10.

- 3.1: Identify the purpose of various types of preventive maintenance products and procedures, and when to use/perform them. (Chapter 10)

- 3.2: Identify procedures and devices for protecting against environmental hazards. (Chapter 10)

- 3.3: Identify the potential hazards and proper safety procedures relating to lasers and high-voltage equipment. (Chapter 10)

- 3.4: Identify items that require special disposal procedures that comply with environmental guidelines. (Chapter 10)

- 3.5: Identify ESD (Electrostatic Discharge) precautions and procedures, including the use of ESD protection devices. (Chapter 10)

4. Motherboards, Processors, and Memory

Several of the items in these content areas give people the most problems (for example, learning the differences between all the different types of processors). We will discuss those issues in depth in their respective chapters: Chapter 2 contains information about motherboards and processors; Chapter 3 covers memory.

- 4.1: Distinguish between the popular CPU chips in terms of their basic characteristics. (Chapter 2)

- 4.2: Identify the categories of RAM (Random Access Memory) terminology, their locations, and physical characteristics. (Chapter 3)

- 4.3: Identify the most popular type of motherboards, their components, and their architecture (e.g., bus structures and power supplies). (Chapter 5)

- 4.4: Identify the purpose of CMOS (Complementary Metal-Oxide Semiconductor), what it contains, and how to change its basic parameters. (Chapters 2 and 7)

5. Printers

As I was writing this book, I asked A+ Certified technicians what they thought was the hardest part of the Core Module exam. With a single, resounding voice they all said "Printers!" For this reason, I have tried to make the printer section as comprehensive as possible. Although there are only three objectives here, and the questions on printers make up 10 percent of the test, I have dedicated an entire chapter (Chapter 8) to printer components and operation to make sure that this area won't give you any problems.

- 5.1: Identify basic concepts, printer operations, and printer components. (Chapter 8)

- 5.2: Identify care and service techniques and common problems with primary printer types. (Chapters 8 and 12)

- 5.3: Identify the types of printer connections and configurations. (Chapter 8)

6. Portable Systems

As of summer 1998 this area is new to the A+ curriculum. Portable computers are growing in popularity daily. To that end, CompTIA included this content area to ensure that technicians are experienced in the unique service concepts that portable systems introduce. Questions from this area make up 5 percent of the number of exam questions on the Core Module exam.

- 6.1: Identify the unique components of portable systems and their unique problems. (Chapters 2 and 5)

7. Basic Networking

With the explosion of the Internet into the service world, the line between a service technician and networking technician has blurred. Frequently, computers that come in for service have problems that are related to their networking hardware. An A+ Certified technician should know how both the hardware and software components of networking can affect the operation of the computer. CompTIA has put basic networking concepts on the latest revision of the A+ Core Module exam and they make up 5 percent of the total exam questions. The majority of Chapter 9 is dedicated to networking.

- 7.1: Identify basic networking concepts, including how a network works. (Chapter 9)

- 7.2: Identify procedures for swapping and configuring network interface cards. (Chapter 9)

- 7.3: Identify ramifications of repairs on the network. (Chapter 9)

8. Customer Satisfaction

Customer satisfaction is an extremely important aspect of any technician's job. When customers aren't satisfied, they don't come back. And, as we all know, repeat business is what makes a business successful. The customer satisfaction content area comprises 10 percent of the number of exam questions. However, even though you are tested on customer satisfaction, the questions don't count towards your final pass/fail score. Your percentage correct in this area will be noted on the score report that prints out after the exam so you will know how well you did in this area. Customer satisfaction is discussed in detail in Chapter 11.

- 8.1: Differentiate effective from ineffective behaviors as these contribute to the maintenance or achievement of customer satisfaction. (Chapter 11)

Good Luck!

You should now have a good understanding of the A+ Certification process. For the latest pricing on the exams and updates to the registration procedures, call Sylvan Prometric at (800) 755-EXAM (755-3926) or (800) 77-MICRO (776-4276). If you have further questions about the scope of the exams or related CompTIA programs, refer to the CompTIA site on the World Wide Web. They're at the following address:

http://www.comptia.org/

Tips for Taking the A+ Exams

Here are some general tips for taking your exam successfully:

- Arrive early at the exam center so you can relax and review your study materials, particularly tables and lists of exam-related information.

- Read the questions carefully. Don't be tempted to jump to an early conclusion. Make sure you know *exactly* what the question is asking.

- Don't leave any unanswered questions. Unanswered questions are scored against you.

- When answering multiple-choice questions you're not sure about, use a process of elimination to get rid of the obviously incorrect questions first. This will improve your odds if you need to make an educated guess.

- Because the hard questions will eat up the most time, save them for last. You can move forward and backward through the exam.

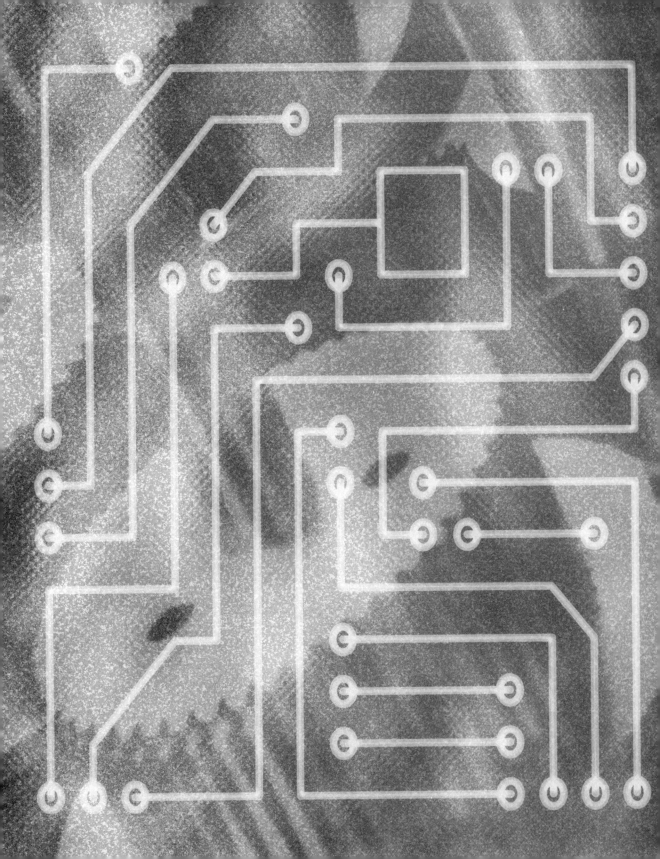

CHAPTER
ONE

Basic Computer Service Concepts

Objectives

- Identify common peripheral ports, associated cabling, and their connectors.

- Recognize the functions and effective use of common hand tools.

- Identify ESD precautions and procedures, including the use of ESD protection devices.

The computers of today are very complex devices. Each computer contains hundreds of individual components, and these components work together to perform specific functions inside the computer. In this chapter we will discuss the most common components and their functions. We'll also explain a few of the basic electronics concepts needed to service the microcomputer hardware of today. The topics are categorized as follows:

- Microcomputer electronic components
- The physics of electronics
- Tools of the trade
- Electrostatic discharge

The material in this chapter is very introductory and is included to make sure we have all our bases covered. If you are already familiar with this material, skim through the chapter and answer the review questions at the end of the chapter.

Microcomputer Electronic Components

Many of the components found in computers today are basically the same as what you'd find in almost every major household appliance. Most of these components have been used since the late 1960s. For example, every television set contains resistors and transistors. Automobiles today actually contain small computers that monitor the speed of the car and make adjustments to the fuel mixture accordingly. These computers contain many of the same components as your home computer.

Analog vs. Digital

Before we discuss electronic components we must define the words *analog* and *digital*, for we will be using these words throughout our discussions of computer technology.

Today's computer components use digital signals, which means these signals contain values that are discrete. Analog signals, on the other hand, change values over time. Consider the difference between two common types of light switches: a standard light switch and a dimmer switch. The standard light switch has only two values: on and off. As a rule, at any one time the switch will be in either one position or the other. This is similar to digital electrical signals, which have discrete values (like on and off). By way of comparison, the dimmer switch starts at *off*, but can be changed gradually to stronger and stronger intensities, up to the full *on* setting. At any one instant, a dimmer switch can have a setting almost anywhere between on and off. This is similar to an analog electrical signal, which may be on or off or somewhere in between.

Vacuum Tubes—The Old Days...

Today's computer components are the products of previous generations of trial and error. Each generation improves upon the previous era. The grandfather of today's computer components is the *vacuum tube* (Figure 1.1).

FIGURE 1.1:

A vacuum tube

The vacuum tube is really nothing more than a switch. A small voltage at one pole switches a larger voltage at the other poles on or off. Since information in a computer is represented as *binary* (ones and zeros), switches are ideal—because they too have only two positions, 1 or 0.

The first electronic computers contained cabinets full of vacuum tubes. There were several problems with this. First of all, the tubes utilized a heating element in order to facilitate the flow of electrons between the poles. These heating elements had to be "warmed up" in order to function properly. Thus, it took several minutes to turn the computer on. Also, with several tubes in the same cabinet, the elements would generate quite a bit of heat. Unfortunately, heat shortens the life of electronic components—so each computer usually had a room full of air conditioning equipment just for keeping the tubes cool! Even so, the average temperature in these computers was greater than 100 degrees Fahrenheit.

Second, the vacuum tubes were very bulky. Computers like the ENIAC often took up enough cabinets to fill an entire floor of a building, with the computer in one room and the air conditioning equipment in the one next to it.

Transistors—Turn Them On

If the vacuum tube is the grandfather, then the *transistor* is the parent of today's electronic components. Transistors (Figure 1.2) work in basically the same manner as vacuum tubes. A small voltage applied to one pole controls a larger voltage on the other poles. The difference between a transistor and a vacuum tube is that a transistor uses a sandwich of silicon instead of tube filled with gas to do the switching. Silicon falls into a family of elements that are neither conductor nor insulator; they're called *semiconductors*. This type of element will be either a conductor *or* an insulator depending on some condition. In the case of transistors, an electrical current will cause the silicon to be a conductor.

FIGURE 1.2:

A transistor

Transistors overcame most of the limitations of vacuum tubes. They generate very little heat, and they are much smaller than vacuum tubes. With transistors, computers could be made that fit into a single room. As manufacturing techniques have become more precise, transistors have gotten smaller and smaller. Today, five million transistors can fit into an area smaller than a thumbnail.

Resistors—Keeping Electricity at Bay

Another component that is commonly used in computers is the *resistor*. As its name suggests, it resists the flow of electricity. The electricity is dissipated in the form of heat. There are two types of resistors: fixed resistors and variable resistors.

Fixed Resistors

Fixed resistors are used when we need to reduce the current by a certain amount. Fixed resistors are easily identified by their size and shape (see Figure 1.3). Their resistance level is indicated by means of colored bands painted on the resistor.

FIGURE 1.3:

A fixed resistor

NOTE   Fixed resistors are color coded to identify their resistance values. There are two reasons why they are color coded rather than having their values printed right on their bodies. First, the resistors are only 3/4" long. Second, they're cylindrical. In other words, it is rather difficult to print on them (and they are difficult to read at that size anyway).

If you ever need to replace a resistor, you must replace it with a resistor of the same *resistance level*. The resistance level can be determined by reading the values of the colored bands. Each colored band stands for a number:

- The first two bands represent the digits of a two-digit number.

- The third band represents a multiplier.

- The presence or absence of a fourth band represents a margin-of-error factor (commonly called the resistor's *tolerance range*).

For example, say you have a resistor with the following colors (reading from left to right): red, orange, and brown. Checking the values as listed in Table 1.1, we see that red represents the number 2; orange represents the number 3; and brown represents a multiplier of 10. The resistance is 23 times 10, which equals 230. Resistance is expressed in *ohms*, so you could express the value as 230Ω. But don't forget the tolerance value for the resistor. Since there is no fourth band in this example, the tolerance range for this value is plus or minus 20% (as noted at the bottom of Table 1.1); the true resistance of the resistor is thus somewhere between 184Ω and 276Ω.

Table 1.1 gives the colors and their associated values. Remember to always read the colors from left to right. ("Left" on a resistor is the side that has the three colored bands on it.)

TABLE 1.1: Standard Color Codes for Resistors

Color	1st Band (Left Digit)	2nd Band (Right Digit)	3rd Band (Multiplier)
Black	0	0	1
Brown	1	1	10
Red	2	2	100
Orange	3	3	1,000
Yellow	4	4	10,000
Green	5	5	100,000
Blue	6	6	1,000,000
Violet	7	7	10,000,000
Gray	8	8	100,000,000
White	9	9	N/A

Note: Be sure to look for a fourth band. **If there is no fourth band**, it means the tolerance level of the resistor is not very good—it's between plus or minus 20% of the value indicated by the other bands. **If there is a fourth band**, it will be either silver or gold. Silver represents a tolerance of ±10%. Gold represents a tolerance of ±5%.

Pay special attention to the note at the bottom of the table. Tolerance bands indicate how well the resistor holds to its rated value. As we mentioned in the previous example, if there is no fourth band, the resistor has a tolerance of plus or minus 20%. That's pretty bad. In electronics, you usually need things to be very close (like a tolerance of less than 5%). A silver band indicates a 10% variation, and a gold band indicates a 5% variation. Remember, though, this range indicates the *maximum* variation—it's possible that the resistor might be right on with its resistance value. For example, say you have the color sequence brown, green, orange, silver. The resistance would be indicated as 15 × 1,000, or 15,000Ω (you can also express it as 15kΩ)—and it may very well be that this particular resistor *is* able to resist currents up to precisely that strength. However, to be safe, you need to take into account the maximum deviation from this value, which would be indicated by the fourth band color (silver in this example, which represents a ±10% variation), so this resistor might have a value of as little as 13,500Ω (13.5kΩ) or as much as 16,500 (16.5kΩ).

Variable Resistors

The variable resistor is also called a *rheostat* or *potentiometer*. The most common use in a computer for a variable resistor is for a volume control or brightness control. The resistance is varied between the center pole and either of the end poles (see Figure 1.4). It can be used to vary resistance directly from zero to infinity by hooking the target to one pole and the source to the center pole. Or, we can use a variable resistor to slowly vary from one source to another by hooking each source to a pole and the target to the center pole.

FIGURE 1.4:

A variable resistor

Sometimes resistors are placed together into an assembly that is commonly referred to as a *resistor pack*. These resistor packs are used in some drive systems to terminate (stop) the signals being sent on the drive cable. When they perform this function, we call them *terminators*. We will discuss this type of resistor more in later chapters.

Capacitors—Storing a Charge for Later

Another commonly used component is the *capacitor*. A capacitor is used to store electrical charge. Typically used in power supplies and in timing circuits, these items are rarely the cause of failure in a system, because all they do is store a charge and release it. Capacitors in a computer can be easily identified because they usually look like small metal cans or small disks with two connectors (Figure 1.5).

FIGURE 1.5:

A capacitor

> **WARNING** *Do not touch a charged capacitor!* They can hold charges of thousands of volts and can cause serious injury. Stay away from them even when power has been removed. They can retain a charge for hours after power has been removed.

Integrated Circuits (ICs)— Welcome to the 1980s

With today's manufacturing techniques, it is possible to put all of these components together into circuits that perform certain functions. In the 1970s, you might have hooked up several components on boards called circuit boards. Starting in the 80s, components were etched into pieces of silicon no larger than a dime. In order to get this small item onto a circuit board, the silicon wafer is placed into a package that has pins coming out of it. These pins are wired with tiny copper or gold wiring directly to the silicon chip. This package comes in several forms, but is generally called an *integrated circuit chip* or *IC*.

NOTE When we say "chip" in the computer business today, we often mean the package that the silicon wafer is housed in, not the wafer itself. From now on, when we use the word "chip," we are referring to the IC.

There are several types of ICs, but we will only cover the most commonly used types.

Dual Inline Package

The most common package for an IC is the *Dual Inline Package*, or *DIP*. DIPs contain two rows of pins and are usually black with markings on top indicating their manufacturer and purpose. Figure 1.6 shows a Dual Inline Package IC. DIPs are commonly seen being used as memory chips, although this design is being used less and less.

FIGURE 1.6: A Dual Inline Package IC

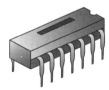

Quad Small Outline Package

The *Quad Small Outline Package* (*QSOP*—also called a "surface mount") is among the most commonly used types of chips today. Figure 1.7 shows an example of a QSOP package. This design has the advantage of being very compact.

> **NOTE**
>
> Most chip manufacturers use a technology called VLSI, or Very Large Scale Integration. The idea is to integrate the functions of several small chips into one, usually larger, chip. Most often, these VLSI chips are of the QSOP type.

FIGURE 1.7:

A Quad Small Outline Package IC

Single Inline Package

When a circuit needs to be removable, there are several ways of designing it. One of the first ways was with the *Single Inline Package* (*SIP*). SIPs are characterized by a small circuit board with several small pins coming out of it (see Figure 1.8); the SIPs are plugged into corresponding holes or mounts in a circuit board. SIPs are not used much anymore, primarily because of the tendency of the pins to break. SIPs were often used for memory modules.

FIGURE 1.8:

A Single Inline Package IC

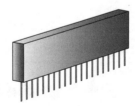

Pin Grid Array Package

Finally, when a circuit or component doesn't have to be removed often, and it contains a large number of transistors, typically you use a *PGA* and a *ZIF* (Figure 1.9). PGA stands for *Pin Grid Array*, describing the array of pins used to connect the chip to the circuit board. ZIF is a type of socket (ZIF stands for *Zero Insertion Force*, which describes how easy it is to place a chip in this kind of socket) that works with PGA chips to allow them to be mounted on a circuit board.

FIGURE 1.9:

PGA Package and a ZIF socket

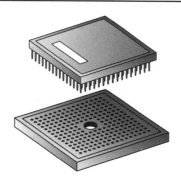

And Now for the Real World...

In the past, computer service required an electronics degree, or at the very least a working knowledge of every component. Today, it is very labor intensive to troubleshoot an individual resistor or capacitor. Typically, the technician will troubleshoot a particular module or FRU (Field Replaceable Unit). Troubleshooting the logic board, hard disk, power supply, or monitor is easier than finding out which particular IC or resistor is causing the problem. This makes repair easier, faster, and cheaper. Also, it makes it easier for people to become technicians, since they don't need to have electronics degrees.

It should be noted, however, that electronics experience makes troubleshooting a particular FRU easier.

Miscellaneous Components

There are a few types of hardware components that don't fit well into any of the categories we've already defined. These include *jumpers*, *DIP switches*, and *connectors*.

Jumpers

Jumpers were developed as a way of allowing a particular device option (like which *interrupt* is being used—see Chapter 5) to be both user settable and semipermanent without requiring the user to own a chip "burner." Jumpers consist of a row of pins and a small plastic cap with metal inserts. The cap can be moved by the user to cover different pairs of pins. The cap completes a circuit between those two pins, thus selecting one of the possible configuration options for that device (see Figure 1.10).

FIGURE 1.10:

Jumpers and their use

A jumper (above left) can be used to make a connection between various pairs of pins in an array of pins. On some devices you may need to jumper multiple pairs, using several jumpers. This arrangement of six pins offers eight different jumper settings.

You'll often see devices with just three pins. These are common for devices that require only two settings, like on and off, or enabled and disabled.

Some cards or circuit boards have several jumpers—so when you go to configure that device, you will need to select the appropriate jumpering option. To find out which pins have to be jumpered in order to select different configuration options, consult the documentation of the device.

If you don't have the documentation, you may have to try all the different jumpering combinations to see if you can get the device configured properly:

- With a six-pin device (as shown in the top part of Figure 1.10), you have eight possible settings: all unjumpered, left pair jumpered, middle pair jumpered, right pair jumpered, left and middle pairs jumpered, left and right pairs jumpered, middle and right pairs jumpered, and all jumpered. This arrangement is common for setting the ID number or other configuration setting of a SCSI device.

- With a three-pin device (as shown in the bottom part of the figure), you are usually only concerned with setting the device to an active or inactive status. Any one of the options shown in the bottom of Figure 1.10 may mean "on"; one of the others would then be the "off" setting. (The third, perhaps in this case represented by the all-unjumpered configuration on the left, may mean "let Plug-and-Play determine the setting.")

Dual Inline Package (DIP) Switches

Jumpers are fine for single settings, but what if you have a number of settings that have to be user settable and semipermanent? You could use several jumpers, but in larger numbers, they were difficult to work with. Someone came up with the idea of using several *really* small switches and to have the pattern of their ons and offs represent the different settings. These switches are known as DIP switches, and can either be rocker-type or sliding-type (see Figure 1.11).

FIGURE 1.11:

DIP switches

"Slide-type" DIP switch

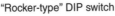

"Rocker-type" DIP switch

If you look carefully at Figure 1.11, you will notice that there is a little "1" imprinted on one side of the switches. When a rocker switch is depressed on that side, it is considered *on*. By comparison, when the nub of a sliding switch is sticking *up* on the side with the "1" marking, *that* indicates *on*. (Some DIP switches, by the way, are marked with a "0" to indicate the side that is the *off* position for the switch.)

Since these switches are so small, it is often easier to set them with a pen, probe, or small screwdriver than it is to set them with your fingers. If you do use your fingers, you may notice that you move more than just the switch you were intending to move.

Connectors

The last type of component that we'll discuss includes the numerous types of connectors found outside the computer. The most common type, the DB connectors, are typically designated with "DB-*n*," with the letter *n* being replaced by the number of connectors. DB connectors are usually shaped like a trapezoid, as you can see in the various end-on views in the following three-page figure (Figure 1.12). The nice part about these connectors is that they will only go on in one orientation. If you try to connect them upside down or try to connect a male connector to another male connector, the connectors just won't go together and the connection can't be made.

FIGURE 1.12:

Common PC connectors

25-pin male: generally a serial port.

25 female: a parallel port.

9 male is serial. 25 female is, again, parallel.

EGA: 9-pin female, two RCA connectors, DIP switches.

A video (9 female) and parallel port (25 female). Probably a monochrome/ printer adapter.

9 female with a single RCA connector: probably CGA (Color Graphics Adapter).

Video? That's a good guess when you see a female 9-pin. But when you see a lone female 9-pin, it may be a Token-Ring LAN board.

Fifteen pins in three rows indicates VGA (Video Graphics Array) and graphics accelerators.

**FIGURE 1.12:
(CONTINUED)**

Common PC
connectors

A BNC connector helps
give this away as an
Ethernet LAN board.
Here, the female 15-pin
connector is for Thick
Ethernet cable, not games.

A 10baseT Ethernet card has
an RJ-45 connector with a few
LEDs. Some combination
Ethernet boards include BNC
and 15-pin connectors, too.

Two RJ-11 phone jacks:
an internal modem.

Joysticks and standard Ethernet
(Thicknet) use 15-pin connectors.
This may be a game card or an
Ethernet LAN board.

Not all mice use a 9-pin
serial connection; PS/2s use
a round 6-pin mouse port.

A round port with nine
holes identifies this as a
bus mouse interface card.

FIGURE 1.12:
(CONTINUED)

Common PC
connectors

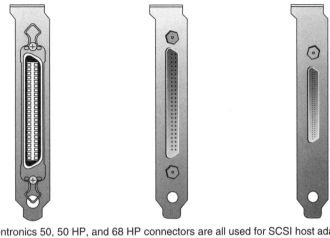

Centronics 50, 50 HP, and 68 HP connectors are all used for SCSI host adapters.

| Sound cards typically have a joystick port, volume control, and audio input/output jacks. | Playback-only sound cards have headphone output jacks, line-out jacks, and volume control. | Interface cards for add-in CD-ROM drives have two audio output jacks for speakers. |

Another type, the DIN-*n* connectors, again with the *n* being replaced by the number of connectors, are usually circular. DIN connectors were developed in Germany and became popular in the USA because of their small size.

For communications, there is another type, following the RJ-*n* specifications. It's a rather strange-looking connector, with a tab on the bottom and small brass connectors on top. These connectors are easy to identify—just look at the connectors on your telephone. The connector on the end of the cord that runs from the phone to the wall is an RJ-11 connector. The connector on the end of the cable that runs from your handset to your phone is the smaller, RJ-12 connector. You may have seen the type of network cable that uses an RJ-45 connector, which looks about twice as big as an RJ-11 connector.

Finally, the most unique type of connector is the Centronics connector. The 36-pin Centronics connector is used on your parallel printer cable (one end has a DB-25 connector, the other a 36-pin Centronics connector).

NOTE DB-*n* connectors are also known as D-Shell or D-Sub connectors. The terms may be used interchangeably.

Connector identifications are often given with male or female designations—*DB-9 male*, for example. Table 1.2 indicates the common uses of various connectors.

TABLE 1.2: PC Connectors

Connector	Number of Pins or Sockets	Male or Female	Common Applications
DB-9	9 pins	Male	Serial port
DB-9	9 sockets	Female	EGA/CGA video port (Might also be a Token Ring adapter port)
DB-15	15 sockets	Female	If there are three rows of five, it's probably a VGA/SVGA video adapter. If it's one row of eight and one row of seven, it might be a network transceiver port or, more commonly, a joystick port.

Continued on next page

TABLE 1.2 CONTINUED: PC Connectors

Connector	Number of Pins or Sockets	Male or Female	Common Applications
DB-25	25 pins	Male	Serial port
DB-25	25 sockets	Female	Most often a parallel port. On Macintoshes, however this type of connector is used for the external SCSI bus.
RJ-11	4 pins	Male	Telephone wall jack phone cord
RJ-12	4 pins	Male	Telephone handset cord
RJ-45	8 pins	Male	10Base-T Ethernet cable
Centronics36	36 pins	Male	Parallel cable
Centronics 50	50 pins	Male	SCSI connector
DIN-6	6 sockets	Female	PS/2 mouse port
DIN-8	8 sockets	Female	Macintosh printer connector
DIN-9	9 sockets	Female	Bus mouse port

The Physics of Electronics

Every technician should have a basic understanding of certain physics concepts. I'm sure some of you are saying "Oh, no—not physics!" Before you get upset, however, there are only four main concepts that we have to discuss. Also, this material is not on the test, so if you don't want to read it, or if you already know it, feel free to skip ahead to the next section in this chapter.

Electricity Defined

Let's start by defining electricity. Electricity is the flow of electrons from one molecule of a substance to another. In order for electrons to flow, an element must have free electrons. Elements such as copper, iron, and zinc have free electrons, thus making them good conductors of electricity. All computer components use electricity to function.

Conductors vs. Non-Conductors

A question I always ask my class is "Does water conduct electricity?" The standard answer is *Yes*—but technically that's an incorrect answer. I'm setting them up, I admit, but it gets them thinking. Here's the scoop. If I use a multimeter (a device used to measure voltages and resistances in electronic components) to test the resistance in a bowl of pure (meaning distilled and de-ionized) water, I will get a reading of infinite resistance (meaning very little, if any, electricity is flowing through that bowl of water). When I follow up, then, with the question "If water doesn't conduct electricity, can I take a bath with my radio?", the answer is "Not if you don't want to get a permanent 1970s hairdo!" Why? Because the water you take a bath in *does* conduct electricity. What's happening here?

The answer is that the water you take a bath in, wash dishes in, even drink, contains impurities. It is these impurities that conduct electricity. The electrons hop from each molecule of impurity to another. The bottom line is that most metals conduct electricity, and this includes salts of metals that dissolve in water—for example, sodium chloride (table salt). Therefore, water in its *naturally occurring state* (i.e., with the impurities) *is* a conductor.

A *conductor* is any material that conducts electricity (allows it to flow readily). Copper metal is an example of a great conductor. Conversely, a *non-conductor* is a material that inhibits the flow electricity. Paper, rubber, and most organic materials are generally considered to be non-conductors.

Dynamic vs. Static Electricity

The electricity that comes from the wall is one of two types of electricity. That kind of electricity is usually just called electricity. For the purposes of our discussion, we'll call *it dynamic electricity*, because it is constantly moving. The other type is *static electricity*. This is the type of electricity that exists when electrons build up on a surface. For example, if you walk across a shag carpet with smooth soled shoes in the winter, a lot of electrons are picked up from the carpet and transferred to your body—and they remain there and collect to build up a sizable charge. This charge is a *static* charge, meaning it doesn't move or flow like dynamic electricity. You'll know you're carrying this charge when you go to touch a metal doorknob, because you'll feel a jolt or a "zap." This happens because when you come into contact with a surface that has a different charge than the one you're carrying, electrons will be transferred from your body (or to it, depending on which surface has fewer electrons). The surface with fewer electrons will receive electrons in a burst that evens out the charge between the two objects. This burst is the "zap" you feel when you touch a metal doorknob.

This is important because one of these types of electricity will operate the components of an electronic circuit, and the other will destroy it. Even though the amperage of static electricity is low compared to the amperage of dynamic electricity, *static electricity destroys electronic components*.

Electromagnetic Theory

Finally, electricity and magnetism have been proven to be directly related. If you run an electric current through a wire, it will produce a magnetic field around that conductor. The direction of the current flow determines the direction of the magnetic field.

There is a common trick to remember the relationship between the directions. It's called the "right hand rule." If you make a "thumbs up" sign with your right hand and point your thumb in the direction of the current flow in the wire, the other fingers will curl in the direction of the magnetic field. Figure 1.13 illustrates this trick.

FIGURE 1.13:

The "Right Hand Rule"

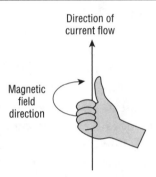

Direction of current flow

Magnetic field direction

Electromagnetic theory also says that if you intersect a magnetic field with a conductor, you will induce an electric current in the wire. Using the "right hand rule," you can see that if the magnetic field is in the direction of the fingers, then a current will be induced in the direction of the thumb. This is important because in electronics, you often have signals traveling in wires next to each other. As signals travel on the wire, they will induce spurious signals in the wires next to it. After a distance, these signals can overcome the actual signals in the adjoining wires. This problem is called *crosstalk*, and can be a real problem in data communications over distances longer than three meters (ten feet).

Another physics-related concept is the transfer of heat. Heat is the enemy of electronic components. As the temperature increases, the longevity and reliability of the component decreases. Some processors (most notably the Pentium family of processors) produce temperatures in excess of 100° F. To reduce the heat, you use a very specialized device known as a *heat sink* (Figure 1.14). This device works by a process known as conduction. It works a lot like the way the fins on an air-cooled engine work. The device is made out of a heat-conducting metal, such as aluminum. As air moves throughout the inside of the computer, it will pass over the fins of the heat sink, cooling them. The heat will move towards the cooler area of the metal, thus drawing it away from the components.

FIGURE 1.14:

A heat sink

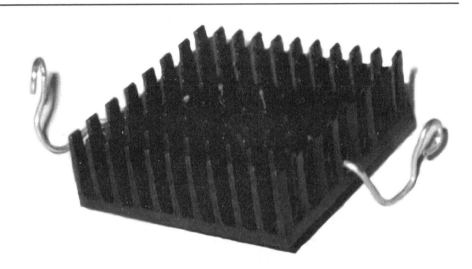

Numbering Systems

Computers have often been called "number crunchers." But what numbers do they actually "crunch"? There are several different types of numbering systems in use in the computer industry today. The three major ones used by computers are decimal (base 10), binary (base 2), and hexadecimal (base 16).

Decimal Numbers

We've all used decimal numbers before. Decimal numbers are the numbers you learned to count with when you were young. The word *decimal* comes from the Latin word *decem*, meaning ten. There are ten digits in this counting system—0,1,2,3,4,5,6,7,8, and 9.

The only time you use decimal numbers with respect to computers is when you are trying to explain things in real-world terms. Because we have used this counting system all our lives, I won't devote a lot of space to it here. Everyone knows how big 5,690 is, but do many people understand how large 5FA3 is?

Binary Numbers

Why do we need more than one numbering system? Wouldn't it be easier if computers operated in decimal mode like we do? The truth is that it is easier to store numbers as combinations of two digits, or *binary numbers*, than it is to store them as decimal digits. This is because every computer contains hundreds of thousands of transistors that are nothing more than simple switches, and these switches have only two positions: on and off. Computers are designed to store information as patterns of ons and offs, which are represented in binary as ones and zeros, respectively.

Before we can discuss the details of the binary numbering system, you must understand a couple of things. First of all, the binary numbers 0 and 1 are not the same as they are in the decimal number systems. Instead, they are just placeholders. They could just have easily been called A and B. Second, we use a few special words to categorize binary numbers:

- A single digit—an individual 0 or 1—is called a *bit*.

- Eight bits associated together are called a *byte*.

- Multiple bytes associated together are usually called a *word*.

Binary numbers can have any number of digits, but because we're using binary, the number of digits will typically be a multiple of 2.

The Magic Number...

If there were such a thing as a magic number in computer science, that number would surely be the number 8, which is the number of bits in a byte. Because bytes are the real building blocks of computer information, most numbers and sizes reported by the computer are evenly divisible by 8. Notice that hexadecimal has sixteen characters (16 characters = 2 times the magic number of 8).

Counting In Binary

Let's talk a little about how to count in binary.

You should recall that in a base 10 number system, each position signifies a power of 10. Since binary is base 2, all the number positions signify powers of 2. In all modern numbering systems, however, the *first* position is always reserved for numbers to the power of *zero*. This means you have to remember that when we talk about an 8-bit (binary) number, the highest position in the number is for values to the 7th power of 2, not the 8th power of 2. Table 1.3 shows the positions used in an 8-bit counting system.

TABLE 1.3: 8-Bit Binary Positions

Position	8	7	6	5	4	3	2	1
Power of 2	2^7	2^6	2^5	2^4	2^3	2^2	2^1	2^0
Decimal value of a 1 in this position	128	64	32	16	8	4	2	1

The rightmost bit in a binary number (the digit in the 2^0 position) is called the *Least Significant Bit*, or *LSB*. The leftmost bit in a binary number (its actual power of 2 depends, of course, on how many bits are in the word) is called the *Most Significant Bit*, or *MSB*. So, in the binary number 10001000, the LSB is 0 and the MSB is 1.

Converting Binary to Decimal

Since binary numbers contain only 1's and 0's, and the 0's equal zero no matter what position they're in, you really only have to worry about the 1's. When trying to convert a binary number, such as 10001001, to a decimal number, all you need to do is look at the positions of the 1's. As in base 10, you read the digits from MSB (left) to LSB (right). In this number, you have 1's in the 2^7, 2^3, and 2^0 positions, which means you have decimal values of 1×128, 1×8, and 1×1, respectively. When you add these numbers together, you get the decimal equivalent: 137.

A number that is all 1's would be the highest value you could have in a binary number; in an 8-bit binary word it equals the decimal number 255. It would be calculated like so:

(1×128) + (1×64) + (1×32) + (1×16) + (1×8) + (1×4) + (1×2) + (1×1) = 255

You could use the technique above to determine the decimal value of any 8-bit binary number, by substituting 0's for 1's wherever appropriate. For example, the decimal value of the binary word 01101010 is calculated as follows:

(0×128) + (1×64) + (1×32) + (0×16) + (1×8) + (0×4) + (1×2) + (0×1) = 106

Hexadecimal Numbers

Binary numbering systems are very easy to understand. However, it is very inefficient to represent large numbers with strings of 1's and 0's. It is more efficient to use the hexadecimal (often simply called "hex") numbering system. Hexadecimal is base 16; it uses the decimal numbers 0 through 9 and the letters A through F to represent the sixteen numbers. When counting in hex, you count from 0 to 9 the regular way, but instead of 10, which we're used to expressing with two digits in our common decimal number system, you use *A*. For the value of 11 we use *B*, for 12 we use *C*, and so on through *F* for the value of 15 (see Table 1.4). Although hex numbers are easily recognized by the fact that they combine letters and numbers, it is also common to see a subscript $_{16}$ or an *h* after the number to designate it as a hex number.

TABLE 1.4: Decimal, Binary, and Hex Equivalents

Decimal Number	Binary Number	Hex Number
0	0000	0
1	0001	1
2	0010	2
3	0011	3
4	0100	4
5	0101	5
6	0110	6
7	0111	7
8	1000	8
9	1001	9
10	1010	A
11	1011	B
12	1100	C
13	1101	D
14	1110	E
15	1111	F

And Now for the Real World...

When you were a kid, the teacher first showed you how to do math the long way. Later, you found out how to use a calculator to figure out the problems faster. As with so many things, in computer service, anything you can do to make the service call go faster will save the customer money. (Still, you *should* know how to do it the old-fashioned way, since you may not always have access to a calculator.)

Windows comes with a tool that can help you convert decimal numbers to hex or binary numbers. That tool is the Windows Calculator. When set to scientific mode, it is a great tool for doing the conversions.

To convert a decimal number to binary, start by running Calculator; in Windows 9x you can find it on the Start menu's Accessories folder. Set it to scientific mode by going to the View menu and selecting Scientific. Then, in the calculator's display box, type in the decimal number you want to convert. To convert the number to binary, click the button next to the word *Binary*. To convert it to hex, just click the button next to *Hex*.

The hexadecimal system works as follows: A binary number is broken up into groups of four bits. If the number of bits in the binary number is not an even multiple of 4—that is, if there aren't enough bits to make complete groups of four each—enough 0's are added to the left of the MSB to make a complete 4-bit group. Why break the binary number into 4-bit elements? Because a single hexadecimal digit can stand for any one of the sixteen values that could possibly be represented by any 4-bit binary number. Each group of four bits is then converted from its binary value to its equivalent hexadecimal digit.

For example, if you have the binary number 01001101 (decimal number 77), you would break this 8-bit word into two groups. The first group (0100) would translate to 4 in hex, and the second group (1101) translates to D. So, this 8-bit binary number would convert to the two-digit hex number 4D. A 32-bit binary number like 01001010010010100001110000101101 converts to 4A4A1C2D (a *much* shorter number, in terms of the number of digits used to represent it).

Tools of the Trade

Behind every great technician is an even greater set of tools. Your troubleshooting skills alone can get you only so far in diagnosing a problem; you also need some troubleshooting tools. And once the problem has been identified, yet a different set of tools needs to be used—to fix the problem.

There are two major types of tools: hardware and software. We'll cover the hardware category first. (We should note here that there are very few questions on the test about this material; it is only being included for background and reference information.)

Hardware Tools

Hardware tools are those tools that are "hard," meaning you can touch them, as opposed to software tools, which cannot be touched. There are several different kinds of hardware tools used in PC service today. We will discuss the most commonly used ones in this section.

Screwdrivers

The tool that can most often be found in a technician's toolkit is a set of screwdrivers. Most of the larger components in today's computers are mounted in the case with screws. If these components need to be removed, you must have the correct type of screwdriver available. There are three major types: flat blade, Phillips, and Torx.

Flat Blade Screwdrivers   The first type is often called a flat blade screwdriver or flathead screwdriver, though most people simply refer to it as a "standard" screwdriver (Figure 1.15). The type of screw that this screwdriver is used to remove is not used much anymore. (Primarily because the screw head was easily damaged.)

FIGURE 1.15:

A flat-bladed screw-driver and screw

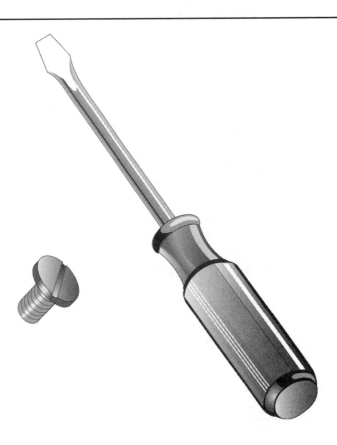

WARNING   I strongly advise against using a flathead screwdriver to *pry* anything open on a computer. Computers are usually put together very well; and if it seems that you need to pry something apart, it's probably because there's still a screw or fastener holding it together somewhere.

Phillips Screwdrivers   The most commonly used type of screwdriver for computers today is the Phillips driver (Figure 1.16). Phillips-head screws are used because they have more surfaces to turn against and thus reduce the risk of damaging the head of the screw. More than 90% of the screws in most computers today will be Phillips-head screws.

FIGURE 1.16:

A Phillips screwdriver and screws

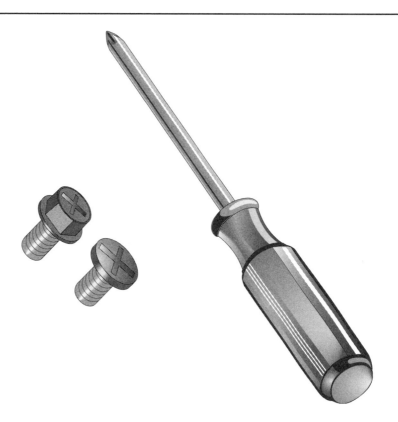

NOTE   Phillips screwdrivers come in different sizes, identified by numbers. The most common size is a #2 Phillips. It is important to have a few different-sized screwdrivers available. If the wrong size is used (for example, a Phillips driver that is too pointed or too small), it can damage the head of the screw.

The Torx Screwdriver   The last type of screwdriver that is important is for working with those maddening little screws that are found on Compaq and Apple computers (as well as on later GM car dashboards). Of course, I'm talking about the Torx screwdriver (Figure 1.17). The Torx type of screw has the most surfaces to turn against and therefore has the greatest resistance to screw head damage. It is becoming more popular since people like its clean, technical look.

FIGURE 1.17:

A Torx screwdriver and screw

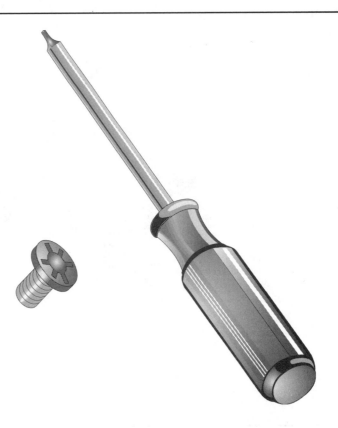

The sizes of Torx drivers are given with the designation T-*xx*, where the *xx* is replaced with a number from 1 through 20. The most common sizes are T-10 and T-15; though for some notebook computers you will need to have much smaller Torx drivers on hand.

TIP   Several screwdrivers are available with changeable tips, like bits for a drill. The advantage is that these screwdrivers can easily change from a flat blade to a Phillips to a Torx just by changing the bits in the driver. The bits are usually stored in the handle of this type of screwdriver.

WARNING   Although it may seem convenient, don't use a multiple-bit driver that is magnetized. Magnetism and computers don't make good friends. The magnetism can induce currents in conductors and burn out components without the technician's knowledge. It could also erase magnetic disk storage media.

Needle-Nose Pliers

Another great tool to have in your toolkit is a set or two of needle-nose pliers (Figure 1.18). They are great for grasping connectors or small screws when your hands are too big. If a needle-nose is still too big for the job, a standard pair of tweezers will work as well.

IC Pullers

When removing ICs from their mounting sockets, it is inadvisable to use your fingers. First of all, a static discharge could damage the pins. Also, if you pull the chip out unevenly, you may bend or break some of the pins. A pair of pliers would be even worse for this task since they multiply the force exerted by your hands into a force that can easily crush a component. It is better to use a specialized tool called a *chip puller* (Figure 1.19). This tool is usually made of spring steel and is shaped like the letter U. It has fingers at the ends of the "U" that are designed to be slipped between the chip and socket. All the technician has to do is pull up on the tool, and it will exert equal force on the different sides of the IC, thus safely removing the chip.

FIGURE 1.18:

A pair of needle-nose pliers

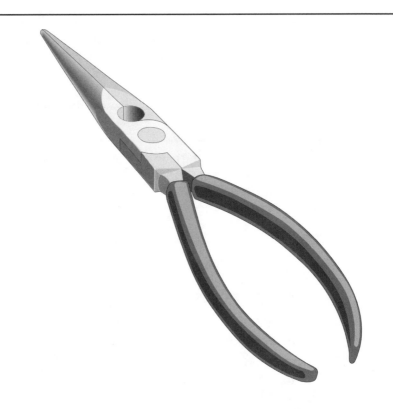

FIGURE 1.19:

An IC puller

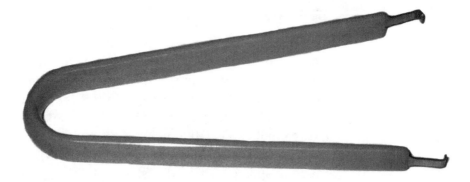

WARNING BE CAREFUL WHEN USING AN IC PULLER. It is possible to remove the socket as well as the chip if you pull hard enough. You may also damage the motherboard permanently.

Flashlight

Another handy tool to have is a small flashlight. You'll know how especially handy it is when you're crawling around under a desk looking for a dropped screw or trying to find a particular component in a dark computer case. Mag-Lite makes a powerful small flashlight that runs on two AA batteries. It also fits well into a toolkit. Also, Polaroid just came out with a very bright pocket flashlight to show off its new five-year batteries.

Compressed Air

When you work on a computer, typically you'll first remove the case. While the cover is off, it is a good idea to clean the computer and remove the accumulated "dust bunnies." These clumps of dust and loose fibers obstruct airflow and cause the computer to run hotter, thus shortening its life. The best way to clean out the dust is with clean, dry, compressed air. If you work for a large company, they will probably have a central air compressor as a source for compressed air. If an air compressor is not used, cans of compressed air are available, but they can be expensive—especially if several are needed. In any case, be sure to bring the computer outside before squirting it with compressed air.

Soldering Iron

One tool that is used less and less in the computer service industry is the soldering iron. You might use one occasionally to splice a broken wire; otherwise you won't have much need for it.

NOTE   The soldering iron isn't used much any more because most components have been designed to use "quick disconnect" connectors to facilitate easy replacement.

Traditionally, the soldering iron was used to connect electronic components to circuit boards. The most common iron used in electronic applications is one with a narrow tip rated at 15 to 20 watts. Generally, the component was heated with the iron, then rosin-core solder (*not* acid-core) was applied to the component. The solder melted, and, flowing into the joint, joined the component to the circuit board.

Wire Strippers

When soldering, it is a good idea to have a combination wire cutter/stripper available to prepare wires for connection. Stripping a wire simply means to remove the insulation from the portion that will be involved in the connection. The one shown in Figure 1.20 is a good example of a tool that does both. However, the technician must be careful not to cut the wire when stripping it.

FIGURE 1.20:

A combination wire cutter/stripper

Multimeters

The final hardware device we will discuss is the multimeter (see Figure 1.21). It gets its name from the fact that it is a combination of several different kinds of testing meters, including an ohmmeter,

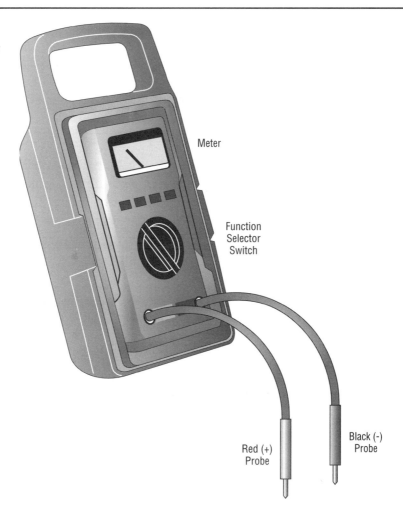

Meter

Function
Selector
Switch

Red (+)
Probe

Black (-)
Probe

ammeter, and voltmeter. In trained hands, it can help detect the correct operation or failure of several different types of components.

The multimeter consists of a digital or analog display, two probes, and a function selector switch. This rotary switch not only selects the function being tested, but also the range that the meter is set to. If you're measuring a battery using an older meter, you may have to set the range selector manually (to a range close to, but greater than,

1.5 volts). Newer meters, especially the digital ones, will automatically set their ranges appropriately.

WARNING   NEVER connect a non-auto-ranging meter to an AC power outlet to measure voltage. This action will most surely result in permanent damage to the meter mechanism, the meter itself, or both.

When measuring circuits, it is very important to have the meter hooked up correctly so that the readings are accurate. Each type of measurement may require that the meter be connected in a different way. In the following paragraphs, we will detail the most commonly used functions of the multimeter, and how to make measurements correctly with them.

Measuring Resistance with a Multimeter   Resistance is the electrical property most commonly measured in troubleshooting components. Measured in ohms, resistance is most often represented by the Greek symbol Omega (Ω). A measurement of infinite resistance indicates that electricity cannot flow from one probe to the other. If a multimeter is used to measure the resistance in a segment of wire and the result is an infinite reading, there is a very good chance that the wire has a break in it somewhere between the probes.

To measure resistance, the multimeter must first be set to measure ohms. This is done either through a button on the front, or through the selector dial. (Assume for the rest of this book that we are using newer *auto-ranging* multimeters.) Then the component to be measured must be connected properly between the probes (see the following note and Figure 1.22). The meter will then display the resistance value of the component being measured.

WARNING   DO NOT test resistance on components while they are mounted on a circuit board! The multimeter applies a current to the component being tested. That current may also flow to other components on that board, thus damaging them.

FIGURE 1.22:

Connecting a multi-
meter to measure
resistance

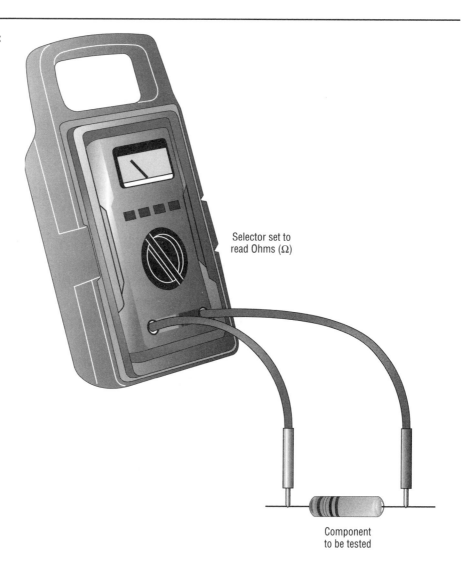

Selector set to
read Ohms (Ω)

Component
to be tested

Measuring Voltage with a Multimeter There is a similar
procedure to follow when measuring voltage, but with two major
differences. First, when measuring voltage, you must be sure
you connect the probes to the power source correctly: with DC
voltage, the + must connect to the positive side and the – to the
negative. (The position doesn't matter with AC voltage.) Second,

you must change the selector to VDC (Volts DC) or VAC (Volts AC), whichever is appropriate, to tell the meter what you are measuring. (See Figure 1.23.) It should be noted that these settings protect the meter from overload. If you piug a meter into a power supply while it's still set to measure resistance, it may blow the meter.

FIGURE 1.23:

Connecting a multimeter to measure voltage

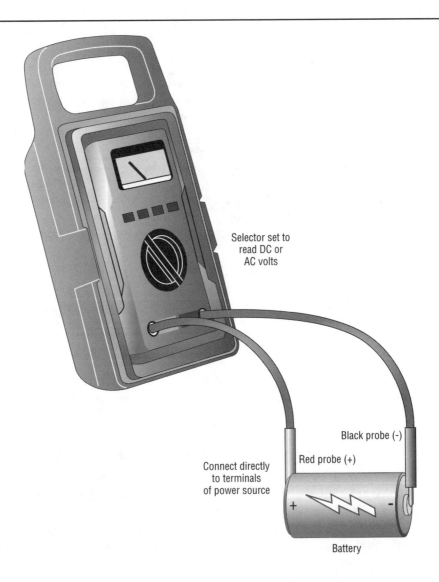

Selector set to read DC or AC volts

Black probe (-)

Red probe (+)

Connect directly to terminals of power source

+ -

Battery

And Now For the Real World...

If you ask farmers what is the most valuable tool in their toolbox, the answer is almost always "Duct tape." It is said that anything can be fixed with enough duct tape. Unfortunately, computers generally are not easily fixed with duct tape.

There *is* a tool that is invaluable when working on a computer. It can be bought from different tool vendors and is often given away at trade shows. That tool is known as a "tweaker" (pictured below). It is a screwdriver that is shaped like a pen and is about the same size. It has a Phillips screwdriver on one end and a flat-blade screwdriver on the other, and will clip easily into a shirt pocket.

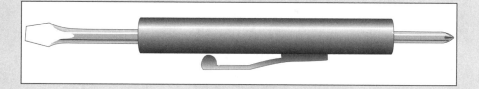

I have been able to fix several computers in a pinch with nothing more than a tweaker. I recommend that each technician run out and buy or find one immediately.

Measuring Current with a Multimeter The final measurement that is commonly made is that of current, in Amperes (amps). Again, the procedure is similar to those used for the other measurements. A major difference here is that when you connect an ammeter to measure the current that a circuit is drawing, you must connect the ammeter in series with the circuit being measured. Figure 1.24 illustrates the proper connection of a multimeter to measure current.

FIGURE 1.24:

Connecting a multi-meter to measure current

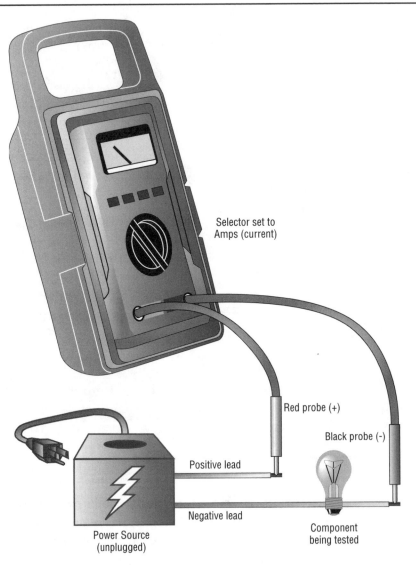

Selector set to
Amps (current)

Red probe (+)

Black probe (-)

Positive lead

Negative lead

Power Source
(unplugged)

Component
being tested

Connect meter in series
with the circuit being tested

Software Tools

Hardware tools are used when major failures have occurred. However, a great portion of problems aren't related to a failing component, but are due to malfunctioning or incorrectly configured hardware. You can use software diagnostics programs to troubleshoot some hardware problems. There are also programs available (usually from the component manufacturers) for configuring hardware, which relieves some or all of the task of setting jumpers or DIP switches. Finally, there are programs for testing the operation of other programs. In this section we'll look briefly at two of the most important types of software tools.

Bootable Disks

The very best software diagnostic tool for DOS machines is a bootable floppy disk: a disk that has been formatted with a version of DOS and made bootable. It belongs in every technician's bag of essentials. You create a bootable disk by typing **FORMAT A: /S** with a blank floppy in the A: drive. Diagnostic and configuration programs can also be copied onto this disk and be run without the possibility of software conflicts. The advantage to this approach is that when the computer boots from a DOS bootable floppy disk, it doesn't have any drivers loaded that might conflict with your diagnostics. Your diagnostics can thus get real information. Also, if the machine boots successfully with a bootable disk, but won't boot normally without it, this tells you that the motherboard, RAM, and major components are probably okay—which means that the problem may be the hard disk, a corrupt OS (operating system), or a device driver conflict. From this point, you can narrow the problem down.

Software Diagnostics

On the one hand are several software tools that examine the hardware, report its configuration, and identify any errors it finds.

Programs like CheckIt Pro, QAPlus, and Microsoft's MSD (Microsoft Diagnostics) work in this manner. On the other hand are programs that serve mainly as reference materials. For example, some manufacturers distribute CD-ROMs that contain all of the reference material concerning their brand of computer equipment. (Toshiba, for instance, distributes a set of CD-ROMs to authorized service centers on a quarterly basis, with parts ordering information, troubleshooting flowcharts, exploded diagrams, and FRU replacement information. All of it is searchable. A very handy tool, indeed.)

Electrostatic Discharge (ESD)

ESD stands for electrostatic discharge. ESD happens when two objects of dissimilar charge come in contact with one another. The two objects exchange electrons in order to standardize the electrostatic charge between the two objects. This charge can, and often does, damage electronic components.

The likelihood that a component will be damaged increases with the increasing use of Complementary Metal Oxide Semiconductors (CMOS) chips, because these chips contain a thin metal oxide layer that is hypersensitive to ESD. The previous generation's Transistor-Transistor Logic (TTL) chips are actually more robust than the newer CMOS chips since they don't contain this metal oxide layer. Since most of today's ICs are CMOS chips, there is more of a concern with ESD lately.

When you shuffle your feet across the floor and shock your best friend on the ear, you are discharging static electricity into the ear of your friend. The lowest static voltage transfer that you can feel is around 3,000 volts (it doesn't electrocute you because there is extremely little current). A static transfer that you can *see* is at least 10,000 volts! Just by sitting in a chair, you can generate around 100 volts of static electricity. Walking around wearing synthetic materials can generate around 1,000 volts. You can easily generate around 20,000 volts (!) simply by dragging your smooth-soled shoes across a shag carpet in the winter. (Actually, it doesn't have to be winter to run this danger. It can occur in any room with very low *humidity*. It's just that heated rooms in wintertime are generally of very low humidity.)

It would make sense that these thousands of volts would damage computer components. However, a component can be damaged with as little as 80 volts! That means, if your body has a small charge built up in it, you could damage a component without even realizing it.

Symptoms of ESD damage may be subtle, but they can be detected. When I think of ESD, I always think of the same instance. A few years ago, I was working on an Apple Macintosh. This computer seemed to have a mind of its own. I would troubleshoot it, find the defective component, and replace it. The problem was that as soon as I replaced the component, it failed. I thought maybe the power supply was frying the boards, so I replaced both at the same time, but to no avail.

I was about to send the computer off to Apple when I realized that it was winter. Normally this would not be a factor, but winters where I live (North Dakota) are extremely dry. Dry air promotes static electricity. At first I thought that my problem couldn't be that simple, but I was at the end of my rope. So, when I received my next set of new parts, I grounded myself with an anti-static strap for the time it took to install the components, and prayed while I turned on the power. Success!! The components worked as they should, and a new advocate of ESD prevention was born.

Anti-Static Wrist Strap

The silver lining to the cloud described in my story above is that there are measures you can implement to help contain the effects of ESD. The first, and easiest, one to implement is the anti-static wrist strap, also referred to as an ESD strap. The ESD strap works by attaching one end to an earth ground (typically the ground pin on an extension cord) and the other end is wrapped around your wrist. This strap grounds your body and keeps them at a zero charge. Figure 1.25 shows the proper way to attach an anti-static strap.

WARNING An ESD strap is a specially designed device to bleed electrical charges away *safely*. It uses a 1-megaohm resistor to bleed the charge away slowly. A simple wire wrapped around your wrist will not work correctly, and could electrocute you!

FIGURE 1.25:

Proper ESD strap connection

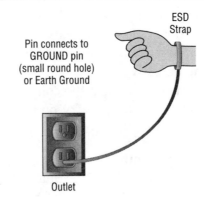

ESD Strap

Pin connects to
GROUND pin
(small round hole)
or Earth Ground

Outlet

WARNING There is only one situation where you should not wear an ESD strap. If you wear on while working on the inside of a monitor, you increase the chance of getting a lethal shock.

Anti-Static Bags for Parts

Anti-static bags are important tools to have at your disposal when servicing electronic components, because they protect the sensitive electronic devices from stray static charges. The bags are designed so that the static charges collect on the outside of the bags, rather than on the electronic components. These bags can be obtained from several sources. The most direct way to acquire anti-static bags is to simply go to an electronics supply store and purchase them in bulk. Most supply stores will have several sizes available. Perhaps the easiest way to obtain them, however, is to simply hold on to the ones that come your way. That is, when you purchase any new component, it usually comes in an anti-static bag. Once you have installed the component, keep the bag. It may take you a while to gather a sizable collection of bags if you take this approach, but eventually you will have a fairly large assortment.

ESD Static Mats

It is possible for a device to be damaged by simply laying it on a bench top. For this reason, you should have an ESD mat in addition to an ESD strap. This mat drains excess charge away from any item coming in contact with it (See Figure 1.26). ESD mats are also sold as mouse/keyboard pads to prevent ESD charges from interfering with the operation of the computer. ESD charges can cause a computer to hang, reboot, or generally cause problems.

FIGURE 1.26:

Proper use of an ESD static mat

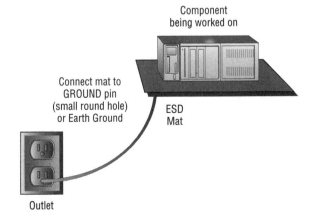

Component being worked on

Connect mat to GROUND pin (small round hole) or Earth Ground

ESD Mat

Outlet

Modifying the Relative Humidity

Another preventive measure that can be taken is to maintain the relative humidity at around 50 percent. Be careful not to increase the humidity too far—to the point where moisture starts to condense on the equipment! Also, make use of anti-static spray, which is available commercially, to reduce static buildup on clothing and carpets. In a pinch, a solution of dilute fabric softener sprayed on these items will do the same.

With regard to the components, vendors have methods of protecting them in transit from manufacture to installation. Vendors press the pins of ICs into anti-static foam to keep all the pins at the same potential. Also, circuit boards are shipped in anti-static bags, discussed above. However, keep in mind that unlike anti-static mats, anti-static bags do not "drain" the charges away, and they should never be used in the place of an anti-static mat.

At the very least, you can be mindful of the dangers of ESD and take steps to reduce its effects. Beyond that, you should educate yourself about those effects so you know when ESD is becoming a major problem.

NOTE   If an ESD strap or mat is not available, it is possible to discharge excess static voltage by touching the metal case of the power supply. However, the power supply *must be plugged into a properly grounded outlet* for this to work as intended. Because it's plugged in, extra caution should be taken so that you don't get electrocuted. Also, continuous contact should be maintained to continuously drain excess charge away. As you can see, it would be easier to have an anti-static wrist strap.

Review Questions

1. What is the resistance rating of a resistor with the markings (from left to right) red, brown, yellow, gold?

   A. 2100 Ω ±5%

   B. 21000 Ω ±5%

   C. 210000 Ω ±5%

   D. 2100000 Ω ±5%

2. If there are no ESD straps available, one can be fashioned from copper wire and duct tape. True or false?

   A. True

   B. False

3. When measuring resistance, the component can be measured while still installed on the circuit board. True or false?

   A. True

   B. False

4. Convert the following binary number to decimal: 10110101

   A. 10110101

   B. 181

   C. 192

   D. none of the above

5. Convert this hexadecimal number to its binary equivalent: A73F

   A. 1010011100111111

   B. 1010

   C. 1010001010010101

   D. 0100001001001100

   E. 10101011

6. ESD stands for:

    A. Every Single Day

    B. Electric System Degradation

    C. Electrosilicon Diode

    D. Electrostatic Discharge

    E. none of the above

7. When connecting an ESD strap to an extension cord, you must connect it to:

    A. the "hot" pin

    B. the "negative" pin

    C. the "Ground" pin

    D. all of the above

8. The following components are found in today's microcomputers (circle all that apply):

    A. vacuum tubes

    B. resistors

    C. transistors

    D. dilithium crystals

    E. capacitors

9. Convert the following decimal number to binary: 219

    A. 11011011

    B. 11101101

    C. 11111111

    D. 00101001

    E. none of the above

10. How many bits are represented by a single hexadecimal digit?

    A. 1

    B. 2

    C. 4

    D. 8

11. This type of IC package has two rows of pins, one on each side of the package.

    A. QSOP

    B. DIP

    C. SIP

    D. PGA

    E. ZIF

12. This type of IC package is usually surface mounted and used for VLSI applications.

    A. QSOP

    B. DIP

    C. SIP

    D. PGA

    E. ZIF

13. The best method of preventing ESD damage is:

    A. anti-static mat

    B. anti-static spray

    C. anti-static wrist strap

    D. anti-static thinking

14. This type of screw was chosen because of its relative immunity to head damage and for its "high-tech" look.

    A. Phillips-head

    B. flathead

    C. normal

    D. Torx

15. How many volts does it take to damage a CMOS-based IC?

    A. 1

    B. 100

    C. 1000

    D. 10,000

16. What is the Least Significant Bit (LSB) of the number 10100010?

    A. 0

    B. 1

17. ICs are best removed with needle-nose pliers. True or false?

    A. True

    B. False

18. What is the maximum resistance of a resistor with the following markings: red, brown, red?

    A. 2100 Ω

    B. 2020 Ω

    C. 2520 Ω

    D. 420 Ω

19. A male DB-25 port is most likely a:

    A. parallel port

    B. serial port

    C. joystick/game port

    D. network port

20. Which of the following components can be used to configure an adapter card? (Choose all that apply.)

    A. software

    B. male DB-25 port

    C. jumpers

    D. transistors

    E. none of the above

21. Does pure water conduct electricity? (Choose one.)

    A. Yes

    B. No

22. Which port(s) are used for serial ports? (Choose all that apply.)

    A. RJ-11

    B. DB-9

    C. Centronics 36

    D. DB-25

    E. none of the above

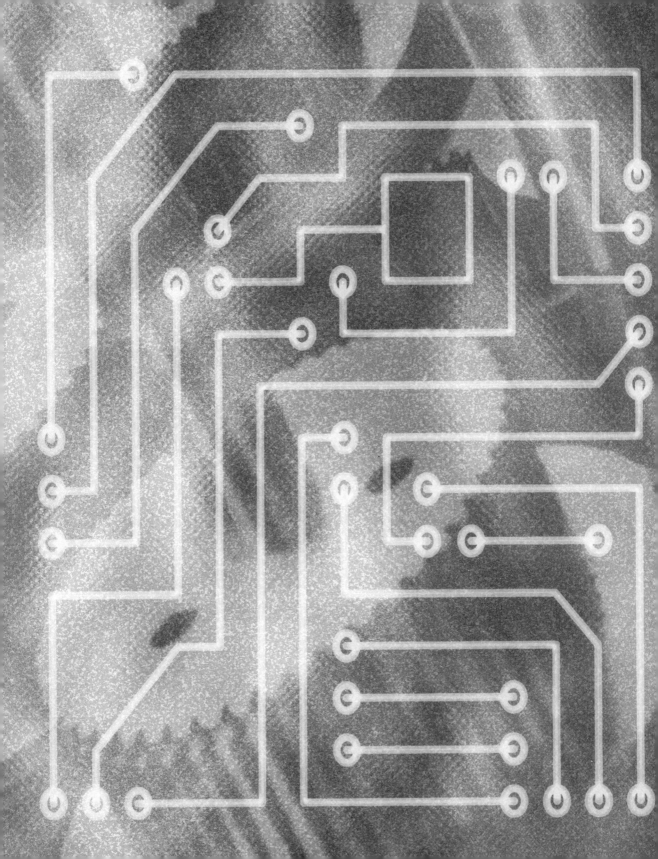

CHAPTER

TWO

PC Architecture

Objectives

■ Identify basic terms, concepts, and functions of system modules, including how each module should work during normal operation.

■ Identify concepts and procedures relating to BIOS.

■ Distinguish between the popular CPU chips in terms of their basic characteristics.

■ Identify the purpose of CMOS, what it contains, and how to change its basic parameters.

■ Identify the unique components of portable systems and their unique problems.

Fundamentally, a computer is a lot like the human body. The human body contains a brain, organs to help the body function properly, and skin to protect the internal organs. And everything works together to create a fully functional human being. Well, the microcomputer has analogous components to create a fully functional machine.

The aim of this chapter is simply to take a quick look inside the computer, identify the main components, give a little historical background, and discover how everything works together. We'll cover each of the topics again in more detail later in this book, but this chapter will serve as a useful overview. In this chapter, you'll be introduced to the following components:

- System boards
- CPUs
- BIOS
- Memory
- Storage
- Input/output devices
- Interfaces
- Display systems
- Power systems
- Portable systems

The System Board

The spine of the computer is the *system board*, otherwise known as the *motherboard* (and less commonly referred to as the *planar board*). This is the olive green or brown fiberglass sheet that lines the bottom of the computer. Figure 2.1 shows a typical system board, as seen from above. It is on this sheet that all other components are attached. On the system board you will find the CPU, underlying circuitry, expansion slots, video components, RAM slots, and a variety of other chips.

FIGURE 2.1:

A typical system board

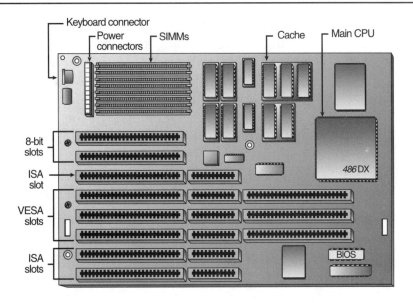

There are two major types of system boards: integrated and non-integrated. Let's discuss the nonintegrated system boards first.

Nonintegrated system boards have each major assembly installed in the computer as expansion cards. The major assemblies we're talking about here are items like the video circuitry, disk controllers, and accessories. Nonintegrated boards can be easily identified because each expansion slot is usually occupied by one of the components we just mentioned.

Integrated system boards are called that because most of the components that would otherwise be installed as expansion cards are integrated into the motherboard circuitry. Integrated system boards were designed for their simplicity. Of course, there's a drawback to this simplicity. When one component breaks, you can't just replace the component that's broken; the whole motherboard must be replaced. Although they are cheaper to produce, they are more expensive to repair.

Nonintegrated system boards are also classified by their form factor (design): AT or ATX. The AT system boards are the same as the motherboards found in the original IBM AT. The processor, memory, and expansion slots are all in line with each other. Because of advances in technology, the same number of components that were on the original AT motherboard were later compressed into a smaller area. This configuration is known as the *"baby" AT* configuration (see Figure 2.2).

FIGURE 2.2:

A "baby" AT motherboard

The "baby" AT is still the most commonly used design, but it has some fundamental problems. Because the processor and memory were in line with the expansion slots, only one or two full-length cards could be used. Also, the processor was far from the power supply's cooling fan and would therefore tend to overheat unless a heat sink or processor fan was directly attached to it. To overcome the limitations of the "baby" AT design, the ATX motherboard was designed. The ATX has the processor and memory slots at right angles to the expansion cards (see Figure 2.3). This puts the processor and memory in line with the fan output of the power supply, allowing the processor to run cooler. And, because those components are not in line with the expansion cards, you can install full-length expansion cards in an ATX motherboard machine.

FIGURE 2.3:

An ATX motherboard

The CPU

The role of the CPU, or central processing unit, is to control and direct all the activities of the computer using both external and internal buses (see the subsection titled "The Bus" later in this topic). It is a processor chip consisting of an array of *millions* of transistors.

CPUs are generally square, with transistors arranged in a Pin Grid Array (PGA). Prior to 1981, chips were found in a rectangle with two rows of 20 pins known as a Dual Inline Package (DIP). (See Figure 2.4.) There are still integrated circuits that use the DIP form factor. However, this form factor isn't used for PC CPUs anymore.

FIGURE 2.4:

DIP and PGA

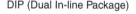

DIP (Dual In-line Package)   PGA (Pin Grid Array)

CPU Manufacturers

The market leader in the manufacture of chips is Intel Corporation. Intel's competition includes Motorola, Advanced Micro Devices (AMD), Cyrix, and IBM. At first, Intel shared its designs with other manufacturers, but with the introduction of the 80386 model in 1985 it ceased licensing to other manufacturers.

Motorola chips are used primarily in Apple Macintosh systems. Their physical construction and the instructions used to operate them are significantly different from Intel's. This is one reason why software written for Macintosh systems is incompatible with software written for Intel systems. In fact, Motorola was ahead of Intel with the development of its processors. However, they missed out on a huge opportunity when they refused to allow others to license their design. Intel was able to capture a huge market by sharing its processor designs, and the result is that the majority of business machines today are IBM-compatibles.

Motorola Processors

Motorola introduced its first commercially viable processor in 1979, with a 32-bit address bus and a 16-bit data bus. The 68010, introduced in 1982, added virtual memory support. It also included a 3-instruction cache, which enabled subroutines to react faster. In 1984, Motorola created its first 32-bit chip, enabling access to as much as 4 gigabytes (4 GB) of RAM and floating point processing capabilities. Demand-paged memory came in 1987 with the 68030, and in 1989 the 68040 was introduced. Table 2.1 provides a list of Motorola processors up to and including the 68040 to summarize the history of the Motorola processor.

Motorola also produces RISC (Reduced Instruction Set Computing) chips, designed in a consortium with other manufacturers and discussed later in this chapter.

TABLE 2.1: The Motorola Family of Processors

Processor	Year Added	New Features
68000	1979	32-bit address bus, 16-bit data bus
68010	1982	Virtual memory support, 3-instruction cache
68020	1984	32-bit data bus, accesses up to 4 GB of RAM, allows floating points
68030	1987	Demand-paged memory
68040	1989	Increased speed over the 68030

Intel Processors

When the first PC was introduced, IBM decided to go to the chip manufacturer Intel for a CPU. The Intel family of processors started with the 8080, which found only limited use in the computer industry. The 8088 was rectangular, using a DIP array of its 40 pins. It originally ran at 4.77 MHz with 29,000 transistors. It was used primarily in the IBM PC.

Next came the 8086 with a 16-bit external data bus; however, the processor used an 8-bit bus for compatibility with older systems.

After the 808*x* series came the 80*x*86 series, otherwise known simply as Intel's *x86 series*. The 80286 was the first to implement the PGA (Pin Grid Array) as described earlier in this section. It ran hotter than the 8088, with speeds from 6 MHz to 20 MHz. Both internal and external bus structures were 16 bits wide, and it could physically address up to 16 MB of RAM.

80386   Intel introduced the 80386 in 1985. With 250,000 transistors, the 80386 represented a new generation for processors, because it was the first Intel *x*86 processor that used both a 32-bit data bus and a 32-bit address bus. The situation with the 386 was unique because up until this point Intel would license its technology to other manufacturers. As we mentioned earlier, with the 386 Intel decided to stop licensing. Not to be outdone, the other manufacturers like AMD and Cyrix came up with a chip they called the 386SX. This chip still operated internally at 32 bits (just like the full-blown 386) but had only a 16-bit external data path and a 16-bit address bus. In order to compete on the same ground, Intel then renamed its 386 to the 386DX and introduced its own version of the 386SX.

The 386SX had a 16-bit data path, while the 386DX had a 32-bit data path. Overall the 386 ranged in speed from 16 MHz to 33 MHz, used up to 4 GB of memory (except the SX, which can only support 16 MB of memory), supported multitasking, and was significantly faster than the 286.

80486   Intel introduced the 486DX in 1989. This processor boasted 1.25 million transistors, 32-bit internal and external data path, 32-bit address bus, an 8K on-chip cache, and an integrated math coprocessor. In 1991 Intel introduced the 486SX, as a cheaper version of the 486 processor. The only difference between the 486DX and the 486SX was that the internal math coprocessor is disabled on the SX. To add the math coprocessor to the chip, it was necessary to purchase a 487SX chip and insert in into the math coprocessor slot. Interestingly enough, this was basically a 486DX chip that, once installed, would simply disable the on-board 486SX chip and take over all processing functions from the SX chip.

The 80486 operated at a maximum speed of 33 MHz. To overcome this limitation, Intel came up with a technology known as *clock doubling*. This worked by allowing a chip to run at the bus's rated speed externally, but running the processor's *internal* clock at twice the speed of the bus. For example, they designed a chip that ran at 33 MHz externally and 66 MHz internally. This chip was known as the 486DX2.

Then someone came up with idea that if you can double the clock speed, why not triple it? And so you were handed the clock-tripled 486DX not long after the 486DX2 came into production. These chips were called DX4 chips (don't ask me why; they just were).

The Pentium and Pentium Pro   Intel introduced the Pentium processor in 1993. This processor has 3.1 million transistors using a 64-bit data path, 32-bit address bus, 16K on-chip cache, and comes in speeds from 60 MHz to 200 MHz. It is basically a combination of two 486DX chips in one, larger chip. The benefit to this two-chips-in-one architecture is that each chip can execute instructions independently of the other. This is a form of *parallel processing* that Intel calls *superscalar*. Pentiums require special motherboards, because they run significantly hotter than previous processors. They also require the use of a heat sink on top of the processor to absorb and ventilate the heat. (The designers said that the processor would typically generate heat to the tune of 185° Fahrenheit!)

Interestingly enough, when Intel first introduced the Pentium, it came in two versions: 60 MHz and 66 MHz. They were essentially the same chip; the only difference being that the 60MHz version didn't quite pass the 66MHz quality-control cut. Although they were not rated for 66 MHz; the designers found that if they could slow them down a bit (to 60 MHz), they ran just fine.

After the initial introduction of the Pentium came the Pentium Pro, designed to meet the needs of today's server. It runs at speeds around 200 MHz, in a 32-bit operating system environment using "dynamic execution." Dynamic execution performs out-of-order guesses to execute program codes.

Pentium II and Beyond   At the time this book is being written, the fastest Intel processor available is the Pentium II. The Pentium II was formerly code-named "Klamath" during its development. Speeds for this processor range from 233 MHz to over 400 MHz.

The unique thing about the Pentium II is that it uses a Single Edge Connector (SEC) to attach to the motherboard instead of the standard PGA package. The processor is on a card that can be easily replaced. Simply shut off the computer, pull out the old processor card and insert a new one.

Table 2.2 lists a few of the upcoming processor technologies Intel plans to release.

TABLE 2.2: Upcoming Intel Processor Code Names and Descriptions

Code Name	Description
Deschutes	Expected in early 1998 at a clock speed of 333 MHz, with subsequent processors reaching 450 MHz by the end of the year. Both 66Mhz and 100MHz system bus options are expected.
Katmai	Expected in mid-1998 with an enhanced MMX (MMX2) that contains more 32-bit instructions.
Willamette	Expected in late 1998 with increased speed and 100MHz system bus. Enhanced 3-D geometry and parallel capabilities are also expected.
Merced	The next-generation Intel architecture. Expected in the 1998-1999 time frame, it introduces the 64-bit IA-64 instruction set jointly designed by Intel and HP, which runs *x*86 and PA-RISC software natively. Clock speeds are expected to go to 600 MHz and beyond.
Flagstaff	Expected in 2000, using two chips for the processor.

Overdrive and MMX—The Need for Speed   Intel's 486 Overdrive processor was designed for 486 users who wanted to give their machines Pentium performance without having to pay the price for a full Pentium chip. Installing an Overdrive chip is simply a matter of replacing the existing CPU with the Overdrive CPU. Once installed, the Overdrive runs at approximately two and a half times the motherboard's bus speed. For example, if you have a motherboard with a bus speed of 33 MHz, the Overdrive processor will run at approximately 83 MHz. Of course, there are tradeoffs to taking the Overdrive approach as opposed to making the step up to a conventional Pentium chip. First, Overdrive processors are only 32-bit processors, whereas Pentiums are completely 64-bit. Second, the Overdrive ran at least as hot as a conventional Pentium, so you had to make sure the system's ventilation could withstand the additional heat.

Another major change was the introduction of MMX technology. This version of the Pentium processor added three new features:

- It includes 57 new instructions for better video, audio, and graphic capabilities.

- It features Single Instruction Multiple Data (SIMD) technology, which enables one instruction to give instructions to several pieces of data rather than a single instruction per piece of data.

- Its cache was doubled to 32 KB.

NOTE   For more information on MMX technology, check out Intel's Web site, HTTP:\\www.intel.com.

Summary of Intel Processors   Table 2.3 provides a summary of the history of the Intel processors.

TABLE 2.3: The Intel Family of Processors

Chip	Year Added	Data Bus Width (in bits)	Address Bus Width (in bits)	Speed (in MHz)	Transistors	Other Specifications
8080	1974	8	8	2	6,000	Used only in appliances
8086	1978	16	20	5–10	29,000	Internal bus ran at 8 bits
8088	1979	8	20	4.77	29,000	
80286	1982	16	24	8–12	134,000	First to use PGA
386DX	1985	32	32	16–33	275,000	
386SX	1988	32	24	16–20	275,000	
486DX	1989	32	32	25–50	1.2 million	8 KB of level 1 cache
486SX	1991	32	32	16–33	1.185 million	Math coprocessor disabled
487SX	1991	32	32	16–33	1.2 million	Math coprocessor for 486SX computers
486DX2	1991	32	32	33–66	2.0 million	
486DX4	1992	32	32	75–100	2.5 million	
Pentium	1993	32	32	60–166	3.3 million	Superscalar
Pentium Pro	1995	64	32	150–200	5.5 million	Dynamic execution
Pentium Pro II	1997	64	64	233–300	7.5 million	32 KB of level 1 cache, dynamic execution, and MMX technology

Intel "Clones"

There are more than just Intel and Motorola processors out there. Among the so called Intel "clones" were chips made by Cyrix, Advanced Micro Devices, and IBM. In 1994, IBM and Motorola got together to introduce the *Reduced Instruction Set Code* (*RISC*)

PowerPC. PowerPC stands for Performance Optimization With Enhanced RISC. It supports a limited set of instructions but can process faster, up to three instructions per cycle. It is also very small and produces very little heat, so it is an ideal choice for portables. Digital Equipment Corporation's Alpha processor is based on the RISC technology as well, with speeds from 225 MHz to 500 MHz. The Alpha was designed primarily for high-end servers running 64-bit applications. Another manufacturer, Silicon Graphics, developed its own processor based on the RISC processor and called it the MIPS. It is able to execute four instructions per cycle running at over 200 MHz with a 64K on-chip cache. Although RISC-based processors can find instructions faster, they cannot run applications written for Intel processors—they can only run applications and operating systems written for RISC.

And Now for the Real World...

The surest way to determine which CPU your computer is using is to open the case and view the numbers stamped on the CPU. You might be able to get an idea without opening the case, however, because many manufacturers indicate the type of processor by using a model number that contains some combination of numbers for the processor type and speed. For example, a Whizbang 466 could be a 486 DX 66MHz computer. Similarly, a 75MHz Pentium computer might be labeled Whizbang 575.

Another way to determine a computer's CPU is to save your work, exit any programs, and restart the computer. As the computer returns to its normal state, watch closely. You should see a notation that tells you what chip you are using. If you are using MS-DOS, you can also run Microsoft Diagnostics to view the processor type (that is, unless your computer has a Pentium, in which case it will report a very fast 486).

Processor Performance Issues

Don't forget, there's more to a chip than what meets the eye. There are several factors that affect the performance of a processor. Among them are availability of a math coprocessor, clock speed, internal cache memory, and supporting circuitry.

Math Coprocessor

The math coprocessor is used to improve the processor's number-crunching speed. It does not, however, increase the speed of simple additions and subtractions. What it does is increase the speed of calculations that involve floating decimal point operations (like calculations for algebra and statistics). Since the introduction of the 486, the math coprocessor has been built into the processor. CPU models that preceded the 486 can add a math coprocessor as an option. (There is a special slot for it next to the CPU.)

Clock Speed

The clock speed is the frequency with which a processor executes instructions. This frequency is measured in millions of cycles per second, or megahertz (MHz). There is actually a "clock" of sorts within the CPU. This clock signal is generated by a quartz crystal, which vibrates as electricity passes through it, thereby generating a steady pulse to every component synchronized with the signal. A system cycle is generated by this pulse (called a clock "tick"), which sends a signal through the processor telling it to perform another operation. To transfer data to and from memory, an 8086 computer needed four cycles plus "wait states." Wait states allow the processor to wait for the slower speed RAM that was used in 8086-based computers. Generally speaking, the higher the MHz value, the faster the PC will be.

Internal Cache

An internal cache memory is a storage area for frequently used data and instructions. It requires a small amount of physical RAM that can keep up with the processor. It uses this RAM for storage. The processor contains an internal cache controller that integrates the cache with the CPU. The controller stores frequently accessed RAM locations to provide faster execution of data and instructions. Therefore, a larger cache leads to the perception of a faster CPU.

The Bus

Finally, the processor's ability to communicate with the rest of the system's components relies on the supporting circuitry. The system board's underlying circuitry is called the bus. Although this is not the bus used to get to the mall or the football game, the idea is similar: the computer's bus moves information into and out of the processor and other devices. A bus allows all devices to communicate with each other. The bus consists of several components, including the external bus, the data bus, and the address bus.

The External Bus (System Bus)   The external bus is also referred to as the *system bus* or *expansion bus*. The expansion bus is a bus system that allows the processor to talk to another device. It is known as an external bus system because it is outside of the processor. The devices are connected through expansion cards and slots. (An expansion card is a removable circuit board that expands the capability of the computer.) We will cover bus types in more detail in Chapter 5.

The Data Bus   The data bus is used to send and receive data. The larger the bus width, the more data that can be transmitted (and, therefore, the faster the bus).

NOTE   The data bus and address bus are independent of each other, but for better performance larger data buses require larger address buses. The data bus width indicates how much data the chip can move through at one time, and the size of the address bus indicates how much memory a chip can handle.

Data in a computer is transferred digitally. A single wire carries 5 volts to indicate a 1 data bit or carries zero volts to indicate a 0 data bit. Remember, computers use the binary system to transmit information. The greater number of wires allows more bits to be transmitted at the same time. For example, a 16-bit data bus width has sixteen wires to transmit data, and a 32-bit data chip can transmit twice the amount of data as a 16-bit chip. A good comparison would be to the highway system. A single lane for traffic allows only one car through at a time whereas two lanes allows twice the amount of traffic to pass through at one time.

Be careful not to assume that data flows at the same speed within the processor as it does outside of the processor. Some Intel processors have an internal data bus that is greater than the external data bus. The 8088 and 80386SX are good examples of this. They are designed with an internal bus that has twice the width of the external bus. This provides for backwards compatibility with other processors that do not support a wider bus.

The Address Bus   The address bus also contains a set of wires to carry information in and out of the processor, but the information the address bus sends is addressing information used to describe memory locations. This location is used for data being sent or retrieved. The address bus carries a single bit of information, representing a digit in the address, along each wire. The size of the address bus corresponds to the number of address locations. The larger the address bus, the more memory address locations that can be supported. The more memory address locations a processor can address, the more RAM a processor can use.

As an analogy, we can compare the address bus to the address of a house or its house number. If the house numbers for a street were limited to two digits, then the street could have only 100 addresses (00 to 99). For an address bus, which communicates in binary language, a limit of two digits would give four addresses (00, 01, 10, and 11). Thus, the larger the address bus, the more combinations of 0 and 1 that would be permitted to pass through at one time. Take a look back to Table 2.2. A 286 processor has a 24-bit address bus width. Using binary theory, this translates to a little over 16 million locations, which means it allows access to as much as 16 MB of RAM. Using similar calculations, a 386DX with a 32-bit address bus will allow access up to 4 GB of RAM.

NOTE   For more information on bus types, see Chapter 5.

The BIOS

BIOS stands for Basic Input/Output System. The BIOS communicates between the computer and devices. The BIOS is usually stored in ROM. It was created by IBM to act as a translator to run the same operating systems on different hardware platforms. When the operating system needs to access a piece of hardware, it would now ask the BIOS, rather than just taking control of the hardware. The use of BIOS prevented programs from fighting over hardware. As long as the operating system (such as DOS) uses the BIOS for its hardware requests, it can run on different hardware platforms. The BIOS creates a standard reference point for many different types of hardware.

There are three major companies that manufacture ROM BIOS software:

- **Phoenix**: Phoenix was the pioneer who developed BIOS in the first place. Their BIOS software supports user-defined hard drive types and 1.44MB floppy disk drives.

- **American Megatrends International (AMI)**: AMI BIOS has been very popular. AMI not only added a more extensive diagnostic program, but, more than that, AMI produced its own system board. This provided guaranteed reliability between BIOS and computer.

- **Award**: Award is the next largest manufacturer of BIOS software. Award took its production one step further by allowing other companies that purchase their BIOS to make modifications as needed to the software.

> **NOTE**   For more information on the three ROM BIOS manufacturers, check out their Web sites, at `http://www.ptltd.com`, `http://www.megatrends.com`, and `http://www.award.com`, respectively.

Sometimes, hardware vendors will want to include new types of hardware the processor was never designed to talk to. In that case, a "BIOS upgrade" may have to be performed. A BIOS upgrade is the process by which the BIOS software is upgraded to a newer version. There are two ways of doing this: A PROM upgrade, or by "flashing" the EEPROM. Upgrading the PROM is as simple as removing the BIOS chip on the motherboard (while the computer is off, of course) and replacing it with a new BIOS chip that contains the new version of the BIOS. "Flashing" the BIOS involves using a special piece of software to upload the new BIOS software to the BIOS EEPROM. This software can be downloaded from the BIOS manufacturer or ordered through the mail. Once the "flashing" is complete, the computer is rebooted and the new BIOS is functional.

WARNING NEVER TURN OFF A COMPUTER DURING A BIOS "flash" UPGRADE! The computer won't come back up because it doesn't have the software to boot itself. Wait for the "flash" to complete, then reboot the computer (many times the software used to "flash" the BIOS EEPROM will do this for you automatically).

Memory

"More memory, more memory, I don't have enough memory!" Today, memory seems to be one of the most popular, easy, and inexpensive ways to upgrade a computer. As the computer's CPU works, it stores information in the computer's memory. The rule of thumb is, the more memory a computer has, the faster it will operate. In this brief section I'll outline the three major types of computer memory. (Memory will also be covered in more detail in Chapter 3.)

DRAM: DRAM is dynamic random-access memory. This is actually the "RAM" that most people are talking about when they mention RAM. When you expand the memory in a computer, you are adding DRAM chips. The reason you use DRAM to expand the memory in the computer is because it's cheaper than any other type of memory. Dynamic RAM chips are cheaper to manufacture than other types because they are less complex. "Dynamic" refers to the chips' need for a constant update signal (also called a "refresh" signal) in order to keep the information that is written there.

SRAM: The "S" in SRAM stands for static. Static random-access memory doesn't require the refresh signal that DRAM does. The chips are more complex and are thus more expensive. However, they are also faster. DRAM access times come in at 80 nanoseconds (ns) or more; SRAM has access times of 15 to 20 ns. SRAM is often used for cache memory.

ROM: ROM stands for read-only memory. It is called read-only because it can't be written to. Once the information has been written to the ROM, it can't be changed. ROM is normally used to store the computer's BIOS, because this information normally does not change. The system ROM in the original IBM PC contained the Power-On Self Test (POST), basic input-output system (BIOS), and cassette BASIC. Later IBM computers and compatibles include everything but the cassette BASIC. The system ROM enables the computer to "pull itself up by its bootstraps," or "boot" (start the operating system).

CMOS: CMOS is a special kind of memory that holds the BIOS configuration settings. CMOS memory is powered by a small battery so the settings are retained when the computer is shut off. The BIOS will read information like which hard drive types are configured for this computer to use, and which drive(s) should it search for boot sectors and so on. CMOS memory is usually NOT upgradable.

Storage

What good is a computer without a place to put everything? Storage media hold the data being accessed, as well as the files the system needs to operate, and data that needs to be saved. When everything is done and information needs to be kept, where should it be kept? The many different types of storage differ in terms of their capacity (how much they can store), access time (how fast the computer can access the information), and the physical type of media being used.

Hard Disk Systems

For permanent storage and quick access, the hard disk systems are used (Figure 2.5). Hard disks reside inside the computer and can hold more information than other forms of storage. The hard disk system contains three critical components: the controller, the hard disk, and the host adapter. The controller controls the drive. It understands how the drive operates and sends signals to the various motors in the disk and receives signals from the sensors inside the drive. The drive is the physical storage medium. Hard disk systems store information on small disks (between three and five inches in diameter) stacked together and placed in an enclosure. Finally, the host adapter is the translator, converting signals from the hard drive and controller to signals the computer can understand. Some hard disk technologies incorporate the controller and drive into one enclosure. (For more information on disk types, see Chapter 4.)

FIGURE 2.5:

A hard disk system

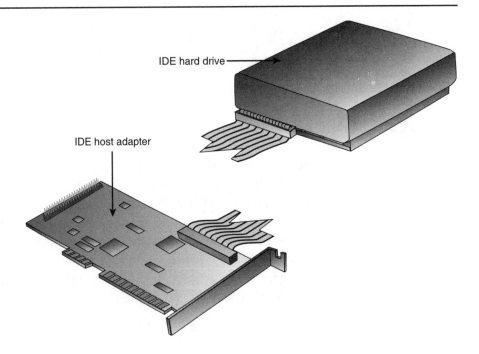

IDE hard drive

IDE host adapter

Floppy Drives

A floppy disk drive is a magnetic storage medium that uses a floppy diskette made of a thin plastic encased in a protective casing. The floppy disk itself (or "floppy," as it is often called) enables the information to be transported from one computer to another very easily. The down side of a floppy disk drive is its limited storage capacity. Whereas a hard drive can store hundreds of megabytes of information, most floppy disks were designed to store only in the vicinity of one megabyte. Table 2.4 shows the five different floppy disk drives that you may run into, with five corresponding diskette sizes supported in PC systems. (Note that the drives that offer anything less than 1.2 MB are increasingly rare, as most computers today do not carry the 5¼" size.)

TABLE 2.4: Floppy Diskette Capacities

Floppy Drive Size	Number of tracks	Capacity
5¼"	40	360 KB
5¼"	80	1.2 MB
3½"	80	720 KB
3½"	80	1.44 MB
3½"	80	2.88 MB

CD-ROM Drives

CD-ROM stands for Compact Disk Read-Only Memory. The compact disk is virtually the same as those used in CD players. The CD-ROM is used to store data for long-term storage. It can hold about the same amount of data as a hard disk system, but CD-ROMs are read-only, meaning that once information is written to a CD, it can't be erased or changed. Also, the time to access the information is a lot slower than access to data residing on a hard drive. Why, then, is it so popular? Mainly because it makes a great software distribution medium. Programs are always getting larger and larger, and are requiring more and more disks to install them. So, instead of installing a program using 100 floppy disks (a real possibility, believe me), you can use a single CD—because it can hold approximately 650 megabytes. (A second reason they are so popular is that CD-ROMs have been standardized across platforms, with the ISO 9660 standard.)

Other Storage Media

There are many additional types of storage available for PCs today. However, most of them are not covered on the A+ exam, so we'll just discuss them briefly here. Among the other types of storage are ZIP drives, tape backup devices, and optical drives.

ZIP Drives and Jaz Drives

Iomega's ZIP and Jaz drives are detachable, external hard disks that are used to store a large volume (around 100 MB for the ZIP, 1 and 2 GB for the Jaz) of data on a single, floppy-sized disk. The drives connect to either a parallel port or a special interface card. The major use of ZIP and Jaz drives is for transporting large amounts of data from place to place. This used to be accomplished with several floppies.

Tape Backup Devices

Another form of storage device is the tape backup. Tape backup devices can be installed internally or externally and use a magnetic tape medium instead of disks for storage. They hold much more data than any other medium, but are also much slower. They are primarily used for archival storage. With hard disks, it's not "if they fail," it's "when they fail." So, you must back up the information onto some other storage medium. Tape backup devices are the most common choice in larger enterprises and networks, because they can hold the most data and are the most reliable over the long term.

Optical Drives

The final type of storage is the optical drive. Optical drives work by using a laser rather than magnetism to change the characteristics of the storage medium (typically an aluminum-coated plastic disk). Optical drives are used for the same applications as ZIP drives. However, optical drives can store more information and have slower access times than ZIP drives.

Input/Output

Putting information into the computer involves more than just turning it on. You need a keyboard, mouse, or some other type of input device. Output devices take data from the computer and translate it to some other usable form. An A+ technician must be able to troubleshoot and fix problems with these types of devices.

Input Devices

The most important device of any computer system is the keyboard. In fact, on Macintosh systems, if a keyboard is not hooked up the computer will not start. Actually, on any computer if a keyboard is not attached, there isn't a whole lot one can do with the computer. (It becomes a good doorstop.) On computers that do run without a keyboard (i.e., most PCs), if the keyboard is missing an error message will occur at startup (usually a "301 – Keyboard

Missing" error). It is the basic component used to enter information or data to the processor and storage device, so it's very important to have it connected. A standard 101-key keyboard has four separate areas:

Standard alphanumeric keys: These include the large or separately located Shift, Backspace, Tab, Enter, and Caps Lock keys.

Function keys: These are placed horizontally along the top of the keyboard, with the Escape key in the top left corner.

Numeric keypad: This set of keys has been separated to the right of the typing, cursor, and screen controls. This allows a user who is familiar with a calculator to perform with the same accuracy and speed.

Cursor and screen controls: These have also been separated, and include the Home, End, Page Up, Page Down, and Insert and Home keys. The directional keys are placed below the Home, End, Page Up, and Page Down keys.

Another device involved in the input of data is the mouse (or, generically, the *pointer device*, since many people use trackballs or touchpads instead of mice). The mouse changes the position of a pointer on the screen relative to the position of the mouse. It is used to select menu options and other items within Graphical User Interfaces (GUIs).

Other input devices include digitizing tablets, light pens, and touch screens. *Digitizing tablets* are most often used by artists and draftspersons. They comprise a flat "drawing" pad and a pen or plotter that interacts with electronic sensors in the pad. As the user moves the pen or plotter over the pad, the position of the pen or plotter is communicated to the computer. *Light pens* are an interactive pointing device. Attached to the computer, light pens have a photodetector in the tip that tracks the phosphors that blink on the screen. Pressing the light pen to the screen is the same as clicking a mouse button. *Touch screens* are probably the most prevalent of the non-keyboard/non-mouse input devices. They can be seen anywhere from the gift registry at the local department store to the information kiosks in shopping malls.

Output Devices

An output device gives the user a means to receive reports, communications, or the results of calculations. The most common output devices are printers, modems, and of course display systems (monitors). These devices are connected to ports in the back of the computer. The ports are either a parallel port with a standard female DB-25 connector or a serial port with a standard male DB-9 connector.

Printers

A printer is a device that converts signals from the computer into paper documents. Most printers are electromechanical devices that put either ink or toner on the paper to form the images. There are three main types of printers: dot-matrix, ink-jet, and laser.

Dot-Matrix Printers   Dot-matrix printers are the oldest type of printer, as well as the simplest. This type of printer uses an array of pins to strike an inked ribbon, which in turn makes a pattern of dots on the paper. The patterns of dots ultimately form letters and images. Dot-matrix printers are easy to use as well as very inexpensive. However, they are relatively slow and very noisy (as anyone who has tried to talk on the phone while using one can attest). The best dot-matrix printers are only "near letter quality" (letter quality is the quality found with a typewriter). They are still in use because they are the only printer that can print on carbon copy forms (invoices, receipts, etc.). Because the pins on dot-matrix printers actually strike the paper, they can make simultaneous copies when used with pressure-sensitive forms or carbon paper.

Ink-Jet Printers   Ink-jet printers spray the ink on the page instead of using an inked ribbon. The major advantages of ink-jet printers are their low cost, increased image quality, and ability to use colored ink and a variety of paper styles and sizes. However, they aren't very fast (though admittedly they are faster than dot-matrix), and the ink needs to be replaced as it runs out, which is often. Additionally, if the printer is not used for a long period of time, the ink can dry out, making the printer unusable until the ink is replaced. For these reasons, they are widely used with home computers and are not often found in offices.

Laser Printers   The laser printer is the most sophisticated type of printer. A laser jet printer uses lasers, electric charges, and toner (a black carbon substance similar to the lead in a pencil) to create images on paper. Laser printers have the highest image quality and speed when compared to dot-matrix and ink-jet printers. They can print at a speed of several pages per minute, which is similar to the speed of photocopiers. Laser printers are more expensive than the other types of printers. They take up more space, and their consumables (like toner) are more expensive than those used by other types of printers. However, they are very popular in offices where high capacity and quality are priorities.

NOTE   For more information on printers, see Chapter 8.

Display Systems

Another important tool to use with computer systems is the monitor. It would be a little difficult to perform a calculation without being able to see the result; indeed, it's useful just to see what was input.

The first display systems were nothing more than fancy black-and-white TV monitors called CRTs (Cathode Ray Tubes). These displays were usually run from a video adapter that could also be connected to a television set. As computer technology developed, the demand for high-quality displays also developed. Soon after, technologies such as VGA, EGA, CGA, and XGA were developed and far outpaced the former CRT technology. However, each of these technologies uses some of the same concepts as the original CRT.

Modems

Modems (MODulator/DEModulators) are the devices that computers use to talk to one another over phone lines. They can be considered a type of output device because they move data out of the computer to another device. Modems work by converting digital signals (binary 1's and 0's) into analog signals (tones over a phone line), and vice versa. Modems are added to a computer either as an external device or as an expansion card installed inside the computer. Internal modems are usually less expensive than external modems, but external modems are easier to troubleshoot than internal modems because you can see the lights that indicate what is happening. For more information on modems, see Chapter 6.

Interfaces

Computers need ways of exchanging information with printers and other devices. These ways are called *interfaces*. There are two major types of interfaces available on computers today: parallel and serial. They differ primarily in the speed of transfer and method of connection. Let's examine each of the these interfaces in detail.

Parallel Interface

The most popular type of interface available on computers today is the parallel interface. Parallel communications take the "interstate approach" to data communications. Everyone knows that interstate travel is faster, normally. This is mainly because you can fit multiple cars going the same direction on the same highway by using multiple lanes. On the return trip, you take a similar path, but on a completely separate road. The *parallel interface* transfers data eight bits at a time over eight separate transmit wires inside a parallel cable (one bit per wire). Normal parallel interfaces use a DB-25 female connector on the computer to transfer data to peripherals.

The most common use of the parallel interface is printer communication, and there are three major types, Standard, Bidirectional, and Enhanced Parallel Ports. Let's look at the differences between the three.

"Standard" Parallel Ports

The "standard" parallel port is a parallel port that only transmits data OUT of the computer. It cannot receive data (except for a single wire carrying a "Ready" signal). This is the parallel port that came with the original IBM PC, XT, and AT. This port can transmit data at 150KB/second and is commonly used to transmit data to printers. This technology also has a maximum transmission distance of 10 feet.

Bidirectional Parallel Ports

As its name suggests, the bidirectional parallel port has one important advantage over standard parallel ports: it can both transmit and receive data. These parallel ports are capable of interfacing with devices like external CD-ROM drives and external parallel port backup drives (ZIP, Jaz, and tape drives). Most computers made since 1994 have a bidirectional parallel port.

Enhanced Parallel Ports

As more and more people started using their parallel ports for interfacing with devices other than printers, they started to notice that the speed wasn't good enough. Double-speed CD-ROM drives had a transfer rate of 300 KBps, but the parallel port could only transfer data at 150 KBps, thus limiting the speed a computer could retrieve data from an external device. To solve that problem, the Institute of Electrical and Electronics Engineers (IEEE) came up with a standard for enhanced parallel ports, called IEEE 1284. The 1284 standard provided for greater data transfer speeds and the ability to send memory addresses as well as data through a parallel port. This allowed the parallel port to theoretically act as an extension to the main bus. In addition, these ports would be backward compatible with the "standard" and bidirectional ports.

There are two implementations of IEEE 1284, ECP parallel ports and EPP parallel ports. An *Enhanced Capabilities Port* (ECP port) was designed to transfer data at high speeds to printers. It uses a DMA channel and a buffer to increase printing performance. An *Enhanced Parallel Port* (EPP port) increases bidirectional throughput from 150 KBps to anywhere from 600 KBps to 1.5 MBps.

Serial Interface

If parallel communications are similar to taking the interstate, then serial communications are similar to taking a country road. In serial communications, each bit of data is sent one after another (single-file, if you will) down one wire, and returns on a different wire in the same cable. There are two main types of serial interfaces available today: Standard and the Universal Serial Bus (USB).

Standard Serial

Almost every computer made since the original IBM PC has at least one serial port. They are easily identified because they have either a DB-9 male or DB-25 male port. Standard serial ports have a maximum data transmission speed of 57 Kbps and a maximum cable length of 50 feet.

Universal Serial Bus (USB)

Most newer computers (those built after 1997) have one or two flat ports in place of one DB-9 serial port. These ports are Universal Serial Bus (USB) ports and they are used for connecting multiple (up to 127) peripherals to one computer through a single port (and use of multi-port peripheral "hubs"). USB supports data transfer rates as high as 1.5 MBps.

Power Systems

The computer's components would not be able to operate without power. The device in the computer that provides this power is the power supply (Figure 2.6). A power supply converts 110 volt AC current into the four voltages that a computer needs to operate. These are +5 volts DC, −5 volts DC (ground), +12 volts DC, and −12 volts DC (ground). By the way, you may frequently see "volts DC" abbreviated as "VDc."

WARNING Power supplies contain transformers and capacitors which carry LETHAL amounts of current. They are not meant to be serviced. DO NOT attempt to open them or do any work on them.

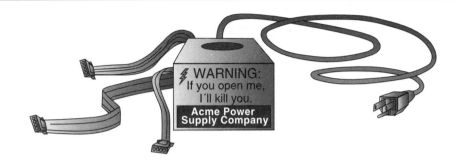

FIGURE 2.6:

A power supply

Power Supply Connectors

A power supply has three types of connectors used to power the various devices within the computer (Figure 2.7). Each has a different appearance and way of connecting to the device. Additionally, each type is used for a specific purpose.

Floppy Drive Power Connectors

The first type are called *floppy drive power connectors* because they are most commonly used to power floppy disk drives. This type of connector is smaller and flatter than any of the other types of power connectors. (These connectors are also called *Berg* connectors.)

System Connectors

The next type of power connector is called the *system connector*. There are only two of these, labeled P8 and P9. They connect to the motherboard and deliver the power that feeds the electronic components on it. These connectors have small tabs on them that interlock with tabs on the power connector on the motherboard.

If there are two connectors, you must install them in the correct fashion. To do this (on most systems) place the connectors side by side with their black wires together. Then push the connectors onto the receptacle on the motherboard.

FIGURE 2.7:

Standard power supply power connectors

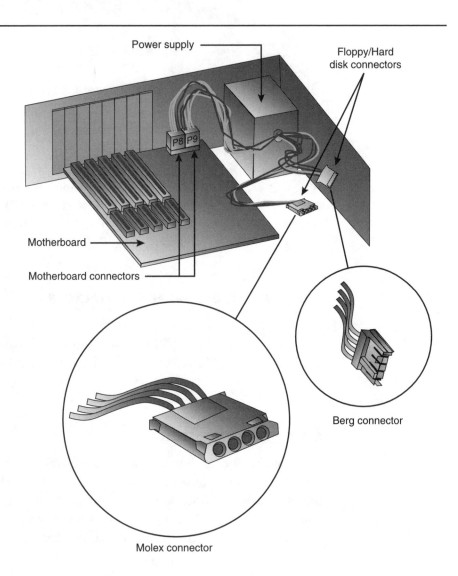

> **TIP**
>
> While it's easy to remove this type of connector from the motherboard, the tabs on the connector make it difficult to reinstall it. Here's a hint: Place the connector at a right angle to the motherboard's connector, interlocking the tabs in their correct positions. Then tilt the connector to the vertical position. The connector will slide into place very easily.

Standard Peripheral Power Connector

The last type of connector is the *standard peripheral power connector*. This type of connector is usually used to power different types of internal disk drives. (This type of connector is also called a *Molex* connector.)

Specialized Power Devices

Unfortunately, it's rare for the power that comes out of the wall (what we normally call *line power*) to be consistently 110 V, 60 Hz. It may be of a slightly higher or lower voltage, it may cycle faster or slower, there may occasionally no power, or the worst, a 5000V spike may come down the power line from a lightning strike and fry the expensive electronic components of your computer and its peripherals.

There are three main classes of power problems that technicians have to deal with: power quality problems, problems where too much power is coming out of the wall, and problems where there is not enough. Almost every outlet has at least one of these problems. Let's examine each of these problems in detail.

Power Quality Problems and Solutions

The first type of power problem exists when the power coming out of the wall has a different frequency than normal (60 Hz is considered "normal"). This type of problem manifests itself when stray electromagnetic signals get introduced into the line. This interference is called Electromagnetic Interference (EMI) and is usually caused by the electromagnetic waves emitted by the electric motors in appliances. Additionally, televisions and other electronic devices (including the computers themselves) can produce a different type of interference, called Radio Frequency Interference (RFI), which is really just a higher-frequency version of EMI. However, RFI is produced by ICs and other electronic devices. If your power lines run near a powerful radio broadcast antenna or factory, they can both introduce noise into your power.

To solve these problems, companies like BEST Power Systems and APC make accessories called *line conditioners*. The function of these devices is to produce "perfect" power of 110V/60Hz. These devices will remove most of the stray EMI and RFI signals from the incoming power. They will also reduce any power overages down to 110 V.

Power Overage Problems and Solutions

The most common type of power problem that causes computer damage is power overages. As the name suggests, these problems happen when too much power comes down the power lines. There are two main types of overage problems: spikes and surges. The primary difference between the two is the length of time the events last. A *spike* is a power overage condition that exists for an extremely short period of time (a few milliseconds at the most). *Surges*, on the other hand, last for much longer (up to several seconds). Spikes are usually the result of faulty power transformer equipment at power substations. Surges can come from both power equipment and lightning strikes.

A common misconception is that a power strip can protect your computer from power overage problems. Most power strips (the ones that cost less than $15.00) are nothing more than multiple outlets with a circuit breaker. There are real "surge protectors," but they usually cost upwards of $25.00. These devices have MOSFET semiconductors that sacrifice themselves in the case of a power overage. But even these aren't perfect. They are rated in terms of clamping speed (how long it takes to go from the overvoltage to zero volts) and clamping voltage (at what voltage the MOSFET shorts out). The problem is that by the time the clamping voltage is reached, some of the overvoltage has gotten through to the power supply and damaged it. After a time, the power supply will be damaged permanently.

Realistically, having "surge protector" is better than not having one, but not by much. It's better to use a line conditioner that can absorb the overvoltage than to use a circuit breaker.

Undervoltage Power Problems and Solutions

Undervoltage problems don't cause damage to hardware, usually. More often, they cause the computer to shut down completely (or at the very least, to reboot), thus losing any unsaved data in memory. There are three major types of undervoltage problems: sags, brownouts, and blackouts.

A sag is a momentary drop in voltage, lasting only a few milliseconds. Usually, you can't even tell one has occurred. Your house lights won't dim or flicker (well, actually they will, but it's too fast for you to notice). But your computer will react strangely to this sudden drop in power. Have you ever been on the "up" side of a see-saw and had someone jump off the other end? You were surprised at the sudden drop, weren't you? Your computer will experience the same kind of disorientation when the power drops immediately to a lower voltage. A computer's normal response to this kind of "disorientation" is to reboot itself.

You've probably experienced one of the other two power undervoltage problems: brownouts and blackouts. A *brownout* occurs when voltage drops below 110 volts for a second or more. Brownouts are typically caused by an immediate increase in power consumption in your area and the lag time it takes for your power provider to respond by increasing production. You might notice when brownouts occur, because the lights in your home will dim, but not go out, then go back to full brightness a second or two later. You might also notice because your computer will reboot or the screen will flicker. While writing this section, I have counted two brownouts (luckily, my computer hasn't rebooted, so the voltage drop probably wasn't too bad).

Everyone has experienced a blackout. A *blackout* occurs when the power drops from 110 volts to zero volts in a very short period of time. It is a complete loss of power for anywhere from a few seconds to several minutes. They are typically caused by a power failure somewhere in your area. Sometimes there are backup systems available, but it may take anywhere from a couple of seconds to several minutes to get power available in your area again.

There are two different hardware solutions to power undervoltage condition: the SPS and the UPS. They each take a different approach to keeping the power at 110 V. In both cases you plug the units into the wall, then plug your computer equipment into the SPS or UPS. Let's look at the SPS first. SPS stands for *Standby Power Supply*. It's called that because there is a battery waiting to take over power production in case of a loss of line voltage. The SPS contains sensors which constantly monitor the line voltage and a battery with a step-up transformer. While conditions are normal, the line voltage charges the internal battery. When the line voltage drops below a preset threshold (also called the *cutover* threshold—i.e. 105 V), the sensors detect that and switch the power from the wall to the internal battery. When the power comes back above the threshold, the sensors detect the restoration of power and switch the power source back to the line voltage.

The main problem with SPSes is that they take a few milliseconds to switch to the battery. During those few milliseconds, there is NO voltage to the computer. This lack of voltage can cause reboots or crashes (rather like a brownout). An SPS is great for preventing against blackouts, but it does little for brownouts and sags. The better choice for undervoltage problems would be the *Uninterruptible Power Supply* or UPS. The UPS works similarly to an SPS, but with one important difference. The computer equipment is always running off the battery. While the line voltage is normal, the battery gets charged. When power fluctuates, only the charging circuit is affected. The battery continues to provide power to the equipment uninterrupted. Because the equipment is constantly operating off the battery, the UPS also acts as a kind of line conditioner.

There is one main problem with UPSes, however—the quality of power they provide. Batteries provide DC power, and computer power supplies run on AC power. Inside the UPS is a power inverter that converts the DC into AC. However, it isn't perfect. AC power produces 60Hz sine waveform, whereas the inverter produces a square wave. A computer's power supply will accept these square waveforms, but it doesn't like them (see Figure 2.8). Even though this problem exists, UPS manufacturers are using more sensitive inverters that can more closely approximate the sine wave. So, a UPS should be put on every piece of computer equipment where data loss would be a problem (in other words, almost every piece of computer equipment).

FIGURE 2.8:

A comparison between line power and UPS-supplied power

Normal Line Power

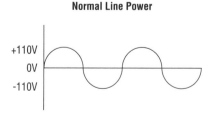

UPS Line Power

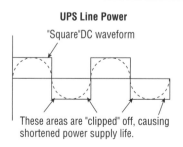

WARNING Never plug a laser printer or copier into a UPS! The large surge of power they draw when they first get turned on can burn out the inverter and battery. These devices can draw close to 15 amps when they first turn on.

Portable Computer Systems

If miniaturization trends continue, we will all soon be able to have a computer with the power of a current mainframe contained in a wristwatch or other piece of jewelry. To that end, many people have embraced the current crop of portable systems. A *portable computer* is any computer that contains all the functionality of a desktop computer system, but is portable. Most people's definition of portable is defined in terms of weight and size. Just so that we can discuss things on the same level, let's define portable as under 20 pounds and smaller than an average desktop computer case.

Most portable computers fall into one of three categories: "luggable," laptop, or PDA. "Luggable" computers were the first truly portable computers, although some of their owners would beg to differ with me. Compaq computer made some of the first "luggable computers."

Laptop computers were the next type of portable computer. They contain a built-in keyboard, pointing device, and LCD screen in a clamshell design. They are also called "notebook" computers because they resemble large notebooks. Most portable computers in use today are laptop computers.

The final type of portable computer, and one that has really taken off recently, is the palmtop computer (also known as a Personal Digital Assistant, or PDA). These computers are designed to keep the information you need close to you so you have access to it whenever you need it. There are two different approaches to the PDA. Pen-based assistants are basically small digital notepads that use a stylus and handwriting interpretation software to perform operations. The Apple Newton and 3Com Pilot are two examples of this type of PDA.

The other type of PDA is known as a Handheld PC (HPC). These are basically "shrunken" laptops. The HPCs run an operating system from (who else?) Microsoft known as Windows CE. Windows CE is basically Windows 95 "shrunken" to fit into the limited RAM of the HPC. Instead of using a mouse to point to the icons and menus in Windows CE, the HPCs use a stylus on the touch-sensitive screen.

Portable Computer Accessories

Since portable computers have unique characteristics as a result of the portability, they have unique accessories as well. First of all, portable computers can use either of two power sources: batteries or AC power. There are many different sizes and shapes of batteries, but most of them are either Nickel-Cadmium (NiCad) or Nickel Metal Hydride (NiMH). Both of these perform equally well as batteries, but NiCad batteries can only be recharged a finite number of times. After a time, they develop a "memory" and must be recharged on a special "deep charging" machine. NiMH batteries don't normally develop a memory and can be recharged many times. The problem with NiMH batteries is that they're a little more expensive.

TIP   Some of the palmtop computers can use either type of battery, but some vendors like Hewlett-Packard took a more common-sense approach: they designed it to use standard AA batteries.

Most notebook computers are also able to use AC power with a special adapter that converts AC power into DC power (called an AC adapter). These can be integrated into the notebook (as on some Compaq notebooks) or as a separate "brick" with a cord that plugs into the back of the laptop.

The final accessory that is unique to portable computers is the docking station. A docking station allows a portable computer to function as a desktop computer when it is attached to it (or "docked"). The docking station usually contains interfaces and expansion ports and bays that the laptop can only use when it is "docked."

Review Questions

1. Which computer component contains all the circuitry necessary for *all* components or devices to communicate with each other?

    A. system board

    B. adapter card

    C. hard drive

    D. expansion bus

2. Clock speeds are measured in _____.

    A. ohms

    B. volts

    C. megahertz

    D. milliseconds

3. A monitor was originally called a CRT. True or false?

   A. True

   B. False

4. Which of the following is the most important input device?

   A. mouse

   B. digitizing tablet

   C. keyboard

   D. printer

5. Access time refers to what?

   A. revolutions per unit of time

   B. difference between the time data is requested and received

   C. latency

   D. the time it takes to create an Access database

6. What is the maximum amount of data that can be stored on a 5¼" floppy disk?

   A. 360 KB

   B. 1.2 MB

   C. 320 KB

   D. 720 KB

7. The system board is also called _____.

   A. a fiberglass board

   B. a planar board

   C. a bus system

   D. an IBM system board XR125

8. The _____ is used to store frequently accessed data and instructions.

   A. hard drive

   B. RAM

   C. internal cache memory

   D. ROM

9. This processor was introduced with 1.2 million transistors and a 32-bit internal and external data path.

   A. 386SX

   B. 486DX

   C. 486DX2

   D. Pentium

10. This processor had the math coprocessor disabled.

    A. 286

    B. 486SX

    C. 486DX

    D. 387SX

11. What are the four voltages produced by a common PC's power supply?

12. Which power device would be best to attach to your computer if you were having power problems?

    A. Surge Protector

    B. UPS

    C. Line Conditioner

    D. SPS

13. If you wanted to connect a LapLink cable (a parallel data transfer cable) so that you could upload and download files from a computer, which type of parallel port(s) does your computer need to have?

   A. Standard

   B. Bidirectional

   C. EPP

   D. ECP

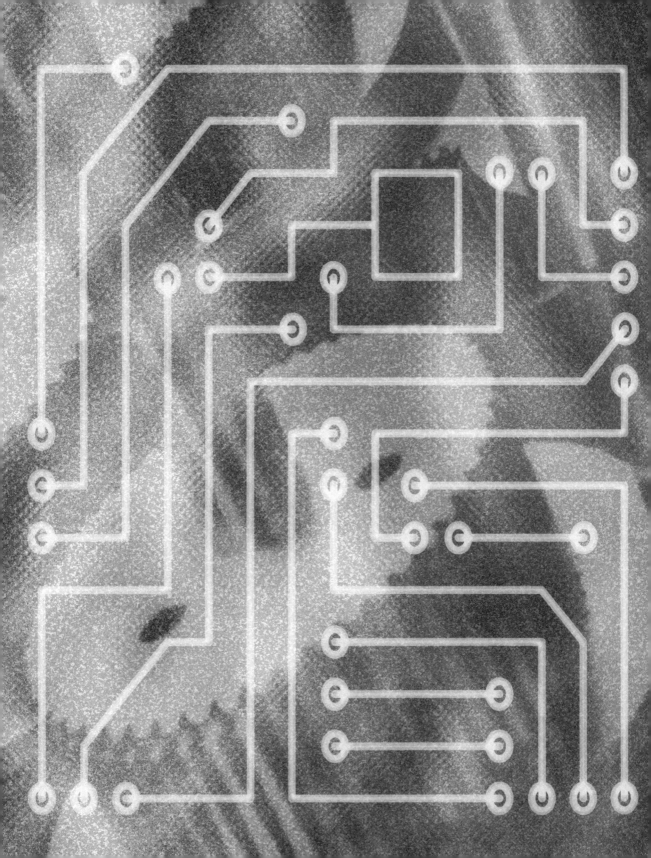

CHAPTER
THREE

3

PC Memory Architecture

Objectives

- Identify hardware methods of system optimization and when to use them.

- Identify the categories of RAM (Random Access Memory) terminology, their locations, and physical characteristics.

The most commonly misunderstood concept in PC maintenance is memory. Often confused with hard disk space, memory gives a computer its "work area." The computer uses this work area to store program instructions and data that it's working with.

In this chapter, we'll present the various types of memory that are used by PCs today. We'll also discuss approaches to recognizing problems that may be related to or solved by changing the memory settings in a customer's computer. The topics fall into the following categories:

- Physical vs. logical memory
- Conventional memory
- Reserved memory
- Expanded memory
- Extended memory
- Memory optimization
- Memory troubleshooting

Physical Memory

The most important component in the computer is the memory system. When we say the word memory, we are most often referring to Random Access Memory or RAM. However, there are other types of memory. We will discuss them all in this chapter.

Physically, memory is a collection of integrated circuits (ICs) that store data and program information as patterns of 1's and 0's (on and off states) in the chip. Most memory chips require constant power (also called a constant *refresh*) to maintain those patterns of 1's and 0's. If power is lost, all those tiny switches revert back to the off position, effectively erasing the data from memory. Some memory types, however, do not require refresh.

There are as many types of memory as there are IC types. Let's take a look at each type in detail.

SRAM

One type of memory is known as Static Random Access Memory (SRAM). It is called *static* because the information doesn't need a constant update (refresh). SRAM stores information as patterns of transistor ons and offs to represent binary digits. This type of memory is physically bulky and somewhat limited in its capacity. It can generally store only 256K bits per IC. The original PC and XT, as well as some notebook computer systems, use SRAM chips for their memory.

Most new computers are moving away from SRAM, to the newer, more efficient type of memory known as DRAM.

DRAM

Dynamic Random Access Memory (DRAM) was an improvement over SRAM. DRAM uses a different approach to storing the 1's and 0's. Instead of transistors, DRAM stores information as charges in very small capacitors. If a charge exists in a capacitor, it's interpreted as a 1. The absence of a charge will be interpreted as a 0.

Because DRAM uses capacitors instead of switches, it needs to use a constant refresh signal to keep the information in memory. DRAM requires more power than SRAM for refresh signals, and therefore is mostly found in desktop computers.

DRAM technology allows several memory units, called *cells*, to be packed with very high density. Therefore, these chips can hold very large amounts of information. Most PCs today use DRAM.

EDO RAM   In the last couple of years, a new type of RAM has become popular. EDO (Extended Data Out) RAM increases performance by eliminating memory wait states. It's usually a bit more expensive than regular DRAM, but it will increase performance about 10%.

ROM

Read-Only Memory (ROM) is used to store information permanently for easy and quick retrieval. This type of memory chip contains transistors that are manufactured permanently in the on or off position. This is the main reason why this type is called "Read Only" memory. Once these transistors have been set, they can't be changed. Because these switches are permanently in these positions, accessing the information contained in ROMs is extremely fast.

ROMs are expensive to develop and manufacture. They are mainly used for very specialized purposes, such as storing information about how a device needs to operate. A computer's BIOS is typically stored on a type of ROM chip.

PROM

For purposes more general than those required by ROM, a type of ROM chip was developed called the Programmable ROM (PROM). The PROM is a ROM that is first manufactured with all of its circuits as logical 0's (that is, with all switches on); then, when the PROM is to be programmed, the connections that need to be set to 1 are destroyed, using a high voltage electrical pulse. This makes the settings permanent.

EPROM

The main disadvantage to ROM is that it can't be changed once it has been manufactured. To resolve this, IC developers came up with

Erasable Programmable Read Only Memory (EPROM). EPROMs are erasable and able to be reprogrammed, making them more flexible than ROMs. They work by storing binary information as electrical charges deposited on the chip. These electrical deposits are *almost* permanent. They will stay until dislodged by a special-frequency ultraviolet light shined through a small window (see Figure 3.1). Exposure to this light returns the chip to its blank state. The chip can then be completely reprogrammed. These chips are usually easily identified by their small, circular windows. Some older computers like the IBM PC or XT used EPROMs for their BIOS information.

FIGURE 3.1:

A typical EPROM

WARNING The windows in EPROM chips are used during the erasure process. When you open a computer case, make sure they are covered with a small piece of opaque material (part of self-adhesive mailing label works well) to prevent light (either sunlight or light from fluorescent lamps) from inadvertently erasing these chips.

EEPROM

It is very inconvenient to remove an IC every time it needs to have the software it contains upgraded. It can be a real pain, and *can* be dangerous. A way was needed to permit erasing of these chips "on the fly" while still maintaining their capability of keeping information intact once power is removed. Electrically Erasable PROM (EEPROM) chips were designed to solve this problem. They can be erased by sending a special sequence of electric signals to the chip while it is still in the circuit. These signals then erase all or part of the chip.

Although it might seem a good idea to use this type of chip for the main memory in a computer, it would be very expensive. The primary use of this type of chip is for BIOS information; you'll see CMOS BIOS chips in most computers. The CMOS memory keeps the computer's BIOS settings while the computer is turned off. These special EEPROM chips keep their information by means of a small battery. Although the battery's charge lasts for several years, it *will* eventually lose its ability to keep the CMOS settings. It's easy to tell when this is happening, though: the computer begins to lose its ability to keep BIOS settings when powered off.

NOTE   Because the BIOS settings can eventually be lost when the CMOS battery finally loses its charge, we encourage all technicians (and PC owners in general) to record their BIOS settings (on paper, or save them to a floppy) so that they may be reset if you have to replace the CMOS battery. The BIOS settings are available from the computer's Setup program, which is accessible by a special key or key combination during startup. Some computers use the Delete key, one of the function keys, or Esc; others use Ctrl+Alt+Esc.

Memory Chip Package Types

The memory chips themselves come in many different types of packages. The ones most frequently encountered are discussed in the following sections.

Dual Inline Package (DIP)

The first type of memory chip package is dual inline package (DIP) memory (Figure 3.2), so called because the individual RAM chips use the DIP-style package for the memory IC. Older computers such as the IBM AT arranged these small chips like rows of caskets in a small memory "graveyard." There are typically eight chips in one of these rows, although there may be nine. If data is written to memory eight bits at a time, why the ninth chip? The answer is that the ninth chip is used for *parity*, a kind of error-checking routine (see the sidebar on the next page).

FIGURE 3.2:

A DIP memory chip

Every time a person wanted to add memory to a computer, they had to go to a computer or electronics store and buy a *tube* of RAM. These tubes typically contained eight to sixteen of these chips. The markings on the chips indicated their speed and size. A marking of AB256-80 means a 256-Kilobit chip that has an access time of 80 ns. The size was commonly given in bits or Kilobits (Kb). If the chips you put in were 256Kb chips and you put in eight of them (or nine, depending on the system), you would have added 256 Kilobytes (256 KB) of RAM.

These chips were used with computers based on the 8086, 8088, and 80286 processors. The problem with the 286 processor and memory was that the processor was faster then the memory. The memory would get overrun with requests from the processor, causing serious performance problems. To solve this problem, manufacturers introduced *wait states* into their RAM. A wait state causes the processor to wait one or more clock cycles, allowing the RAM to catch up. A wait state of zero means that the processor and the memory are equally matched in speed.

Parity: How Does It Work?

Parity is a simple form of error checking used in computers and telecommunications. Parity works by adding an additional bit to a binary number and using it to indicate any changes in that number during transmission. There are two types of parity: even and odd.

- *Even parity* works by counting the number of 1's in a binary number and, if that number is odd, adding an additional 1 to guarantee that the total number of 1's is even. For example, on the one hand, the number 11101011 has an even number of 1's, so the sending computer would assign a 0 to the parity bit. On the other hand, the number 01101101 has five 1's, and so would have a 1 in the parity bit position to make the total number of 1's even. If, in the second number, the computer had checked the parity position after transmission and had found a 0 instead, it would have asked the processor to resend the last bit.

- *Odd parity* works in a similar manner. But, instead of guaranteeing that the total number of ones is even, it guarantees that the total is an odd number.

Parity works well for detecting single-bit errors (where one bit has changed its value during transmission). But if the transmission is extremely garbled, two bits might be switched at the same time. If that were the case, the value for parity would still be valid; as a consequence, the sender would not be asked to retransmit. That's why transmissions that really need to be reliable often use another method of error checking called a *checksumming*.

Checksumming works as follows: when the sender is ready to transmit a unit of data, it runs a special algorithm against the binary data and computes what is known as a *checksum*. The sender then appends this checksum to the data being transmitted and sends the whole data stream to its intended recipient. The recipient decodes the entire data stream and runs a similar algorithm against the data portion. The recipient compares the value that it computed to the value contained in the received checksum. If the values are different, it rejects the data and asks the sender to retransmit it.

Continued on next page

Most error checking done today uses checksumming, unless only a basic communication check is required. For example, parity is used in the case of modem communications, because these transfers are relatively slow to begin with. If modems used checksumming instead of parity, modem communications would be too slow to be a viable means of telecommunication. That's why it is necessary to set the parity to even or odd when setting up modem communications.

Single Inline Memory Module (SIMM)

The next type of RAM packaging that is commonly seen in computers is called the Single Inline Memory Module (SIMM). SIMMs were developed because DIPs took up too much "real estate" on the logic board. Someone got the idea to put several of the DIP chips on a small circuit board and then make that board easily removable. A couple of versions (there are many configurations) are shown in Figure 3.3.

FIGURE 3.3:

Single Inline Memory Modules (SIMMs)

30-pin SIMM

72-pin SIMM

The first SIMMs had nine small DIP chips on them and took up less room than before, because four of them could be installed in the same space as one row of the older DIP memory chips. In order to accomplish this, the SIMMs are installed very close to each other at approximately a 45° angle. This design was also meant to prevent "chip creep"—whereby the chips that have been placed in sockets on the board start to slowly move out of their sockets (caused by the repeated heating and cooling of the system board).

TIP   An old technician's trick: If an older computer (PC or XT) is having strange, irreproducible problems, open the case and reseat all socketed chips by pressing them down securely in their sockets. Most of the time, that will solve the problem. If it does, then the problem was caused by "chip creep."

Most memory chips are 32-bit; so are several of the processors. You have a problem, however, when you have 32-bit memory chips and a 64-bit processor. To solve this, you must either install the SIMMs in pairs (always installing multiples of two—this is especially true for Pentium computers) or change to a DIMM installation (discussed next).

Dual Inline Memory Module (DIMM)

The final type of memory package is known as a DIMM, or Dual Inline Memory Module. DIMMs are dual-sided memory chips that hold twice as many chips as a SIMM. (And, except for the fact that they have chips on both sides, they look just like a SIMM.) Generally, the DIMMs you'll run into will have either 72 or 168 pins. Some DIMMs are 32-bit, but more and more are 64-bit and only have to be installed one at a time in Pentium-class computers.

Specialized Memory Types

There are four major specialized applications for memory besides main memory.

Video RAM

Video memory (also called video RAM or VRAM) is used to store image data for processing by the video adapter. The more video memory an adapter has, the better the quality of image that it can display. Also, more VRAM allows the adapter to display a higher resolution of image.

Windows RAM (WRAM)

Windows RAM (WRAM) is a specialized memory for Windows accelerator cards. Developed by Samsung, it is similar to video RAM, except that it's much faster. While information is being read from one set of WRAM addresses to draw the screen, other information can be written to another set of addresses. This is faster than normal VRAM, where all addresses can only be either read from or written to. This ability of WRAM to be read from or written to simultaneously is called *dual-ported* memory.

Portable Memory

The memory styles for portable computers are many and varied. Each portable computer manufacturer comes up with their own specification for portable memory. Installing memory in a laptop usually involves removing a specially attached panel on the bottom of the laptop and installing the memory in the slot that is under the removed panel. Then, you can replace the panel.

TIP   Since each laptop's memory could potentially install in completely different ways, check with the manufacturer of your laptop to determine how to upgrade the memory.

Cache Memory

When a CPU goes to get either its program instructions or data, it always has to get them from main memory. However, in some systems, there is a small amount of very fast SRAM memory, called *cache memory*, between the processor and main memory, that is used to store the most frequently accessed information. Since it's faster than main memory and contains the most frequently used information, cache memory will increase the performance of any system.

There are two types of cache memory: on-chip (internal) and off-chip (external). Internal cache memory is found on Intel Pentium, Pentium Pro, and Pentium II processors, as well as on other manufacturer's chips. The original Pentium contains two 8KB-on-chip caches, one for program instructions and the other for data. External cache memory is typically either a SIMM of SRAM or a separate expansion board that installs in a special processor-direct bus.

TIP

To get the most out of cache memory, if you have the option of installing an external cache card onto your motherboard, do it. It can give you as much as a 25% boost in speed.

Logical Memory

Now that we have discussed the different types of physical memory, we need to talk about the logical types of memory. *Logical memory* is the way the physical memory is "put together" for the operating system. In order to use the physical memory installed in a computer, we need to organize it in some logical manner. Most people don't understand this concept. Let's reduce that number by at least one right now.

There is a model that helps us understand the way that memory is laid out. This model is actually called the "MS-DOS memory map." It was not created all at once, but has evolved over time. The first computers to run DOS were based on the Intel 8088 processor. That processor could only access a maximum of 1 MB (1,024 KB) of memory. So, the first memory map looked like the one illustrated in Figure 3.4. This map allows us to describe how the memory is being used. It is important to remember that this memory map is also called a *stack*, because for purposes of visualizing concepts the memory blocks are stacked on top of one another.

FIGURE 3.4:

The MS-DOS memory map

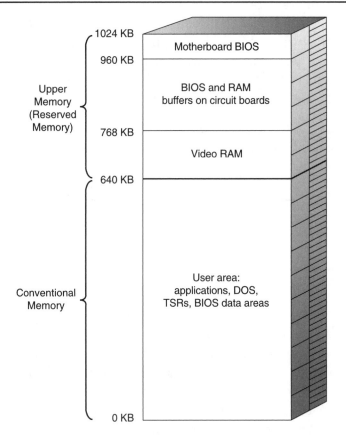

The memory map's first 1024 KB is divided up into sixteen blocks of 64 KB each. We will be describing the purpose of each of these blocks in the sections that follow.

The sixteen 64KB blocks are further divided into four "pages" of 16 KB each. This division allows us to look in a more detailed way at how an application is using memory. Memory is allocated by the processor to those applications or devices that request it. When you need to refer to these blocks you can refer to them either by their block number (block 1, block 2, and so on), or you can refer to them as a range of hexadecimal addresses. The hexadecimal method is the most common way, since that is how the computers refers to them. These addresses are typically five-digit hex addresses, primarily because the largest five-digit hex address is FFFFF (1,048,575 decimal, corresponding to 1,048,575 bytes, or 1 MB). Table 3.1 gives the blocks, their ranges in bytes, and their ranges in hexadecimal addresses.

TABLE 3.1: Memory Addresses in the MS-DOS Memory Map

Block #	Byte Range	Hex Range
1	0 to 63 KB	00000 to 0FFFF
2	64 to 127 KB	10000 to 1FFFF
3	128 to 191 KB	20000 to 2FFFF
4	192 to 255 KB	30000 to 3FFFF
5	256 to 319 KB	40000 to 4FFFF
6	320 to 383 KB	50000 to 5FFFF
7	384 to 447 KB	60000 to 6FFFF
8	448 to 511 KB	70000 to 7FFFF
9	512 to 575 KB	80000 to 8FFFF

Continued on next page

TABLE 3.1 CONTINUED: Memory Addresses in the MS-DOS Memory Map

Block #	Byte Range	Hex Range
10	576 to 639 KB	90000 to 9FFFF
11	640 to 703 KB	A0000 to AFFFF
12	704 to 767 KB	B0000 to BFFFF
13	768 to 831 KB	C0000 to CFFFF
14	832 to 895 KB	D0000 to DFFFF
15	896 to 959 KB	E0000 to EFFFF
16	960 to 1024 KB	F0000 to FFFFF

In most utilities that scan memory to find its contents, you will see memory addresses listed as hex addresses. The table above will be valuable when you're determining where a particular program or driver is resident in memory.

Conventional Memory

The first type of memory, represented as the first 640 KB in the memory map, is called "conventional memory," as highlighted in Figure 3.5. It takes the first ten blocks (00000 to 9FFFF). This type of memory is used for running programs, loading the operating system files, and loading *drivers* (see sidebar). With the old 8086 chip, this area was dedicated for user applications and data. Conventional memory turned out to be the Achilles' heel for a DOS-based system, as almost all DOS applications are written to be backward compatible, so they must support conventional memory.

FIGURE 3.5:

The conventional
memory area

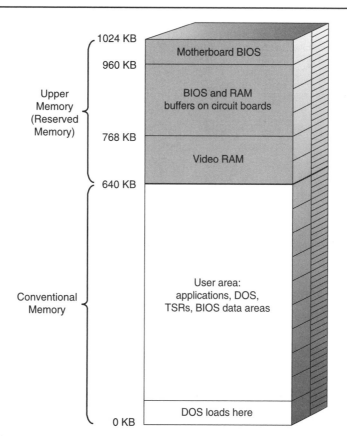

Device Drivers and Conventional Memory

Device drivers are small pieces of software that are loaded to allow the computer to talk to hardware devices. Drivers control and understand these hardware devices. For example, if you want DOS to be able to use a sound card, a driver needs to be loaded for it. When you load a driver, it is allocated memory from the conventional memory area. The problem is that your applications use this area to run in. If you have too many drivers loaded, you may not have enough conventional memory to run your programs. We will address this problem later in this chapter, in the section titled "Memory Optimization."

The first block (the first 64 KB) is used for loading the DOS operating system files into memory. Also, this area contains any memory allocated to DOS disk buffers (specified by the BUFFERS= parameter in the CONFIG.SYS file). Additionally, DOS uses this area to load additional memory drivers (EMM386.EXE and HIMEM.SYS). Finally, any memory that DOS needs for system operations (input/output buffers, the processing of interrupts, and so on) is also allocated from this first 64 KB area.

Besides DOS itself and drivers, there are often programs that are loaded into conventional memory and then keep a portion of themselves there after they've been terminated. This behavior can be pretty handy, as programs like e-mail software can be called up more quickly when parts of them are still located in memory. These programs are called *Terminate and Stay Resident* (*TSR*) programs. The following are a few examples of TSRs:

- Anti-Virus programs, since they need to stay in memory constantly

- Disk Caching programs (for example, SMARTDRIVE.EXE)

- Network protocol stacks

All of these types of programs may want to take up more memory than is available. Therefore, the developers came up with more types of memory.

Reserved Memory

If an 8088 can access 1 MB of RAM, why can't you use all of it to run programs? The answer is that some devices in the computer also need RAM. Some RAM is reserved for use by some devices in the computer to store data so it can be accessed directly by the processor. This area of RAM, called "reserved memory" or "upper memory," consists of the remaining six blocks—the upper 384 KB—in the MS-DOS memory map. It is highlighted in Figure 3.6.

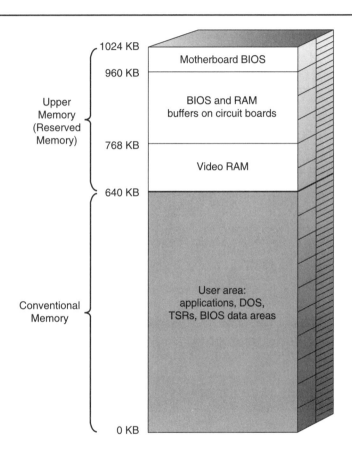

A unique characteristic of reserved memory is that various sections of this memory area are typically allocated for special purposes. Table 3.2 lists the common uses for the reserved memory blocks and the addresses they occupy.

TABLE 3.2: Reserved Memory Block Usage

Address Range	Standard Usage	Notes
A0000 to BFFFF (128 KB)	Video RAM	Varies according to type of video adapter used.
C0000 to CFFFF (64 KB)	Available	Adapter ROMs sometimes mapped here; can also be used for EMS page frame.
D0000 to FFFFF (192 KB)	Available	Adapter ROMs may also be mapped here.
E0000 to FFFFF (128 K)	System ROMs	BIOS and BIOS "echo" may also be mapped here.

The first two blocks of reserved memory are usually used for accessing video RAM. When a computer needs to send information to the display, it writes it to this area. The adapter has its own memory mapped into this area. This area is only 128 KB large, but some video cards have more than 1 MB on them. How can the computer fit 1 MB into a 128 KB area? It does this through a technique known as *paging*. Paging works by taking a portion of that 1 MB and accessing it by swapping it into this reserved area as data needs to be written to it.

Here's an example of how this might work: Say the processor has a large graphic to draw on the screen. It makes a call to the video card and says "Hey, I've got some video for you," then starts writing to the video area in reserved memory. When this area is full, the video card "swaps" those full blocks for empty ones from the memory on the card. The video card takes the instructions from the "full" blocks and uses them to draw the picture on the screen. Table 3.3 shows the most commonly used memory addresses for video cards.

TABLE 3.3: Commonly Used Video Card Memory Addresses

Video Card	Memory Address Range
Monochrome Display Adapter (MDA)	B0000 to B1000 (4 KB)
Color Graphics Adapter (CGA)	B8000 to BC000 (16 KB)
Enhanced Graphics Adapter (EGA)	A0000 to BFFFF (128 KB)
Video Graphics Adapter (VGA)	A0000 to BFFFF (128 KB)
Super Video Graphics Adapter (SVGA)	A0000 to BFFFF (128 KB)
Other VGA cards (super, accelerated, others)	A0000 to BFFFF (128 KB)

In addition to the video adapter, other adapter cards may use the reserved memory area in the same way. These adapter cards are configured to use a particular range of memory in this area, typically in the area from C0000 to DFFFF. This area is used to map ROM memory addresses in Upper Memory. Additionally, some LAN cards have buffers that are mapped into this area.

Finally, the area from D0000 to DFFFF is most often used for mapping the BIOS ROM information, and a copy of it called the BIOS "shadow." This is done so that a processor can access BIOS information when it needs to. Some BIOSes have the ability to shut off the "shadow," thus freeing up 64 KB of Upper Memory.

The important concept to remember is that when you're configuring adapter cards, you can't let these memory ranges overlap. If they do overlap, you'll find that either one or the other card will work (not both), or *neither* will work. It's guaranteed, though, that the computer won't work properly.

Expanded Memory

When programs evolved and grew to the point where they were bumping up against the 640 KB conventional-memory barrier, three vendors—Lotus, Intel, and Microsoft—came up with a technology to circumvent this limitation. The technology they came up with was expanded memory, or *EMS*, for *Expanded Memory System*. (It's also called LIM memory in honor of its creators.)

EMS worked by using the same type of paging technology that video cards use. Expanded memory is divided up into 16KB chunks called *pages* that are swapped into a special memory address space in reserved memory four pages at a time. The area in reserved memory that is used to hold these pages is called the *expanded memory page frame* (or *page frame*, for short—see Figure 3.7). This area normally occupies a full 64KB block in the memory map and is created when the expanded memory driver is loaded.

In the case of the original expanded memory, the actual memory was installed on a special hardware board installed in the computer, and the driver that was loaded was actually a hardware driver for the board. Incidentally, the reason that all three companies got involved is rather unique. Intel developed one of the first expanded memory boards, called the AboveBoard, that was used by people who wanted to make larger spreadsheets with Lotus 1-2-3, which ran primarily under MS-DOS (made by Microsoft). Expanded memory can be utilized on any computer from the 8088-based PC to the Pentium and higher. Depending on the motherboard you were using, you could install as much as 32 MB of memory to be used as expanded memory.

Today, computers are capable of emulating expanded memory through software, since very few programs today use expanded memory. (Most use the next type of memory we're going to describe, *extended memory*.) The EMS emulator is a software driver called EMM386.EXE. You load it in the CONFIG.SYS file by adding the following line:

```
DEVICE=C:\DOS\EMM386.EXE
```

FIGURE 3.7:

Expanded memory

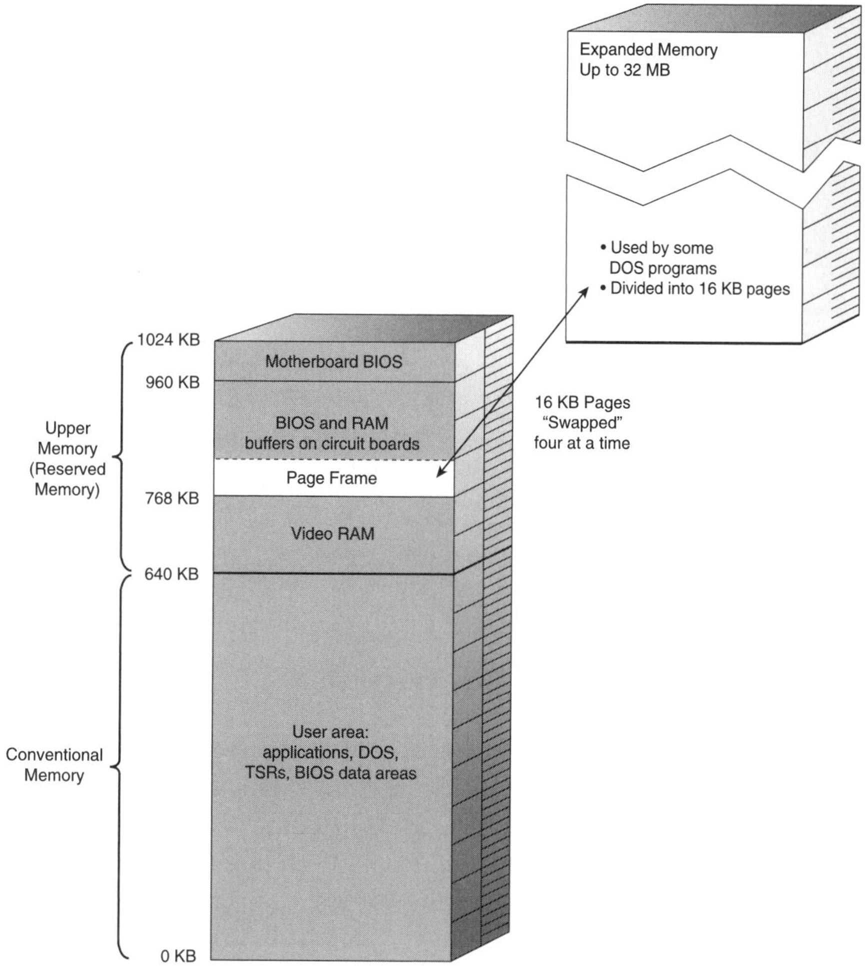

This driver also allows DOS drivers and TSR programs to be loaded into the unused portions of reserved memory by adding a second line:

```
DEVICE=C:\DOS\EMM386.EXE
DOS=UMB
```

This has the benefit of freeing up conventional memory for use by your programs and is a key concept to *memory optimization* (which will be discussed later in this chapter). If you don't need expanded memory capability, you can change these lines to turn off EMS, but keep the ability to load drivers and TSRs into *upper memory blocks* (free areas in reserved memory, also called *UMBs*). To do this, your CONFIG.SYS file must have these lines:

```
DEVICE=C:\DOS\EMM386.EXE NOEMS
DOS=UMB
```

NOTE   The EMS emulator (EMM386.EXE) and the DOS=UMB command were first available in MS-DOS version 5.0 (which came out in 1991). If you're trying to optimize memory on a machine that is running an earlier version of DOS, your first step should be to install the latest version of DOS.

Extended Memory

With the introduction of the 286 processor, things changed dramatically for PC memory. This processor (and all processors since then) had the capability of accessing up to 16 MB of RAM (current processors can access up to 4 GB of RAM). The problem was that DOS was written for the old 8086 processor, and that processor could access only 1 MB of RAM. In order to allow DOS programs to use all this memory, DOS would have to be rewritten to support the new processor. If this was done, the new version of DOS would not support old programs, since the old programs would not run above 1 MB. Computer buyers don't like it when they buy programs that are made obsolete with the introduction of new technology. So the chip manufacturers came up with an idea to allow their new technology to be introduced.

To do this, the processor would use two different operating modes: real mode and protected mode. In *real mode*, the 286 (and above) would operate like an 8086 (only faster) and could access only 1 MB of RAM. To access memory above 1 MB, the processor would have to switch to *protected mode*. It is called protected mode because each program that is running is protected from other programs that may be misbehaving and taking memory away from it. For DOS programs to use this memory, a program was written to *extend* DOS for those programs that can take advantage of it. This program is called a *DOS extender*.

An example of a DOS extender is the memory driver HIMEM.SYS; it allows certain programs to switch the processor to protected mode and access the memory above 1 MB. It is loaded by adding the following line to the CONFIG.SYS file:

```
DEVICE=HIMEM.SYS
```

Once HIMEM.SYS is loaded, DOS can "see" the memory above 1 MB. This memory is what is referred to as *extended memory*.

Additionally, when HIMEM.SYS is loaded, DOS can place the majority of itself into the first 64 KB of extended memory. This first 64 KB is called the *High Memory Area* or *HMA*. In order to load DOS into the HMA, you modify the CONFIG.SYS with the following two lines:

```
DEVICE=HIMEM.SYS
DOS=HIGH
```

You may have noticed that the last line is analogous to the DOS=UMB line in the last section. It is possible to have both of these lines in the CONFIG.SYS to get the greatest amount of conventional memory available, although it is easier to do them both at once, like so:

```
DEVICE=HIMEM.SYS
DEVICE=EMM386.EXE
DOS=HIGH,UMB
```

Basically, DOS can't use extended memory without the help of these extenders. However, there are several operating systems that can. These include OS/2, UNIX, and Windows NT. Programs written for these non-DOS operating systems are able to take advantage of the benefits of the 286 (and above) processor, including multitasking and access to all the memory the processor can address.

NOTE   Windows 3.*x* (that is, Windows 3.1 and Windows 3.11) relies on DOS's extenders in order to use extended memory. (That's because, unlike Windows 95 and Windows NT, Windows 3.*x* is not an operating system in its own right. It is a GUI running on top of DOS.)

With all of the different types of memory, you end up with a DOS memory map that looks like the one in Figure 3.8. With so many different types of memory, it is easy to get them confused. Most often, expanded and extended are juxtaposed. The easiest way to remember the difference is that expanded memory is paged and extended is not.

And Now for the Real World...

Most people don't understand the MS-DOS memory map. That's okay; most people don't need to. However, it is an invaluable tool for the PC technician. Several programs report problems with memory addresses in hexadecimal. This helps us understand which programs were fighting when the error occurred. Also, in order to keep most PCs running efficiently, you must get as much conventional memory as possible. To do this, it is very important you understand the different types of memory, their addressing, and how they work together in a PC.

FIGURE 3.8:

The Complete MS-DOS memory map

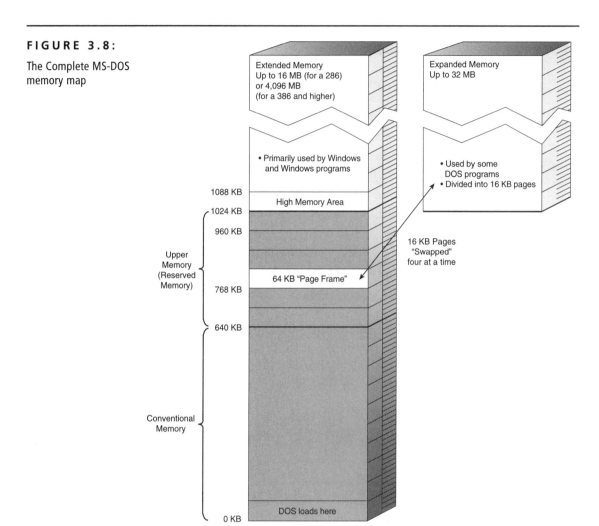

Memory Optimization

Because of the small amount of conventional memory available, the increasing number of drivers that need to be loaded, and the increasing size of the programs you need to run, it is very common to not have enough conventional memory. When people talk about memory optimization, they usually mean making as much conventional memory available as possible.

Memory optimization is one of the most important skills a technician can have. With the number of DOS applications that exist, the need for a technician to know how to optimize memory will continue to be valuable. In general, your DOS-based PCs will run best with the most possible conventional memory available. Ideally, we're talking in the neighborhood of 600 KB or more free.

Step One: Determining How Much Memory You Have Available

We already understand what conventional memory is, but in order to optimize it, you must first make the determination whether or not memory optimization is needed. For DOS systems, you use the MEM.EXE program. This program allows us to determine how memory is being utilized within DOS. The syntax for the MEM command is as follows:

MEM <option>

The available options are described in Table 3.4. If you execute the command without an option, the MEM command shows how much of each type of memory is installed, as shown in Figure 3.9.

NOTE In IBM's PC-DOS, the QCONFIG.EXE program gives some of the same information as the MS-DOS MEM.EXE program, as well as information regarding fixed disks.

FIGURE 3.9:

A report from the MS-DOS MEM command when executed without any options

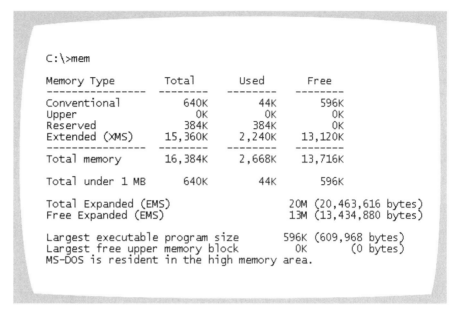

```
C:\>mem

Memory Type        Total      Used       Free
----------------   --------   --------   --------
Conventional         640K        44K       596K
Upper                  0K         0K         0K
Reserved             384K       384K         0K
Extended (XMS)    15,360K     2,240K    13,120K
----------------   --------   --------   --------
Total memory      16,384K     2,668K    13,716K

Total under 1 MB     640K        44K       596K

Total Expanded (EMS)                  20M (20,463,616 bytes)
Free Expanded (EMS)                   13M (13,434,880 bytes)

Largest executable program size       596K (609,968 bytes)
Largest free upper memory block         0K       (0 bytes)
MS-DOS is resident in the high memory area.
```

TABLE 3.4: MEM.EXE Command-Line Options

Option	Description
/?	The *help switch*. It gives basic information on the syntax of the MEM command and its usage. It shows all the switches listed in this table and their usage.
/C	The *classify switch*. When executed, gives an output similar to the one following this table.
/D	The *debug switch*. It details the usage of the first 640 KB of memory (conventional memory). This switch is helpful in finding out the memory addresses of the various programs that are loaded. (Remember that MEM itself is also a program and should be listed.) An example report of MEM /D is shown a couple of pages after from this table.
/F	The *free memory switch*. Shows all the free memory blocks in the first 640 KB and their starting addresses. Also useful in optimizing memory.
/M <module>	The *module switch*. Shows the starting addresses of the data, program, and free memory allocated to the module you specify.
/P	The *pause switch*. When used in conjunction with the other switches, /P displays the output of the command one page at a time. When a page is displayed, the display will pause until a key is pressed. The same effect can be accomplished by piping the command's results into the MORE command (i.e., using MEM <option>|MORE).

A Report from the MEM /C Command

The following is the output of the MEM /C command:

```
Modules using memory below 1 MB:

Name         Total           Conventional      Upper Memory
--------     ----------------   ----------------  ----------------
SYSTEM       48,880  (48K)     10,592  (10K)     38,288  (37K)
HIMEM         1,168   (1K)      1,168   (1K)          0   (0K)
EMM386        4,320   (4K)      4,320   (4K)          0   (0K)
WIN           3,696   (4K)      3,696   (4K)          0   (0K)
--------        288   (0K)        288   (0K)          0   (0K)
vmm32       102,064 (100K)        448   (0K)    101,616  (99K)
COMMAND       7,456   (7K)      7,456   (7K)          0   (0K)
IBMIDECD     10,848  (11K)          0   (0K)     10,848  (11K)
IFSHLP        2,864   (3K)          0   (0K)      2,864   (3K)
DOSKEY        4,688   (5K)          0   (0K)      4,688   (5K)
Free        627,120 (612K)    627,120 (612K)         0   (0K)


Memory Summary:

Type of Memory      Total          Used           Free
----------------   -----------   -----------   -----------
Conventional        655,360        28,240        627,120
Upper               158,304       158,304              0
Reserved            393,216       393,216              0
Extended (XMS)   32,347,552        95,648     32,251,904
----------------   -----------   -----------   -----------
Total memory     33,554,432       675,408     32,879,024

Total under 1 MB    813,664       186,544        627,120

Largest executable program size          627,104  (612K)
Largest free upper memory block                0    (0K)
MS-DOS is resident in the high memory area.
```

A Report from the MEM /D Command

The following is the output of the MEM /D command:

```
Conventional Memory Detail:

Segment           Total         Name          Type
-------      ----------------   -----------   --------
 00000         1,024  (1K)                    Interrupt Vector
 00040           256  (0K)                    ROM Communication Area
 00050           512  (1K)                    DOS Communication Area
 00070         1,424  (1K)   IO               System Data
                             CON              System Device Driver
                             AUX              System Device Driver
                             PRN              System Device Driver
                             CLOCK$           System Device Driver
                             A: - C:          System Device Driver
                             COM1             System Device Driver
                             LPT1             System Device Driver
                             LPT2             System Device Driver
                             LPT3             System Device Driver
                             CONFIG$          System Device Driver
                             COM2             System Device Driver
                             COM3             System Device Driver
                             COM4             System Device Driver
 000C9         5,120  (5K)   MSDOS            System Data
 00209         7,632  (7K)   IO               System Data
               1,024  (1K)                    Relocated EBIOS data
               1,152  (1K)   XMSXXXX0         Installed Device=HIMEM
               4,304  (4K)   $MMXXXX0         Installed Device=EMM386
                 544  (1K)                    Sector buffer
                 512  (1K)                    BUFFERS=50
 003E6            80  (0K)   MSDOS            System Program
 003EB            32  (0K)   WIN              Data
 003ED           288  (0K)   --------         Data
 003FF           256  (0K)   WIN              Environment
 0040F         3,408  (3K)   WIN              Program
 004E4            48  (0K)   vmm32            Data
 004E7           400  (0K)   vmm32            Program
```

```
00500              288    (0K)   COMMAND      Data
00512            5,728    (6K)   COMMAND      Program
00678            1,440    (1K)   COMMAND      Environment
006D2              288    (0K)   MEM          Environment
006E4           90,464   (88K)   MEM          Program
01CFA          536,656  (524K)   MSDOS        -- Free --
```

Upper Memory Detail:

Segment	Region	Total		Name	Type
0C95C	1	51,968	(51K)	IO	System Data
		10,832	(11K)	IBMCD001	Installed Device=IBMIDECD
		2,848	(3K)	IFSHLP	Installed Device=IFSHLP
		464	(0K)		Block device tables
		4,736	(5K)		FILES=85
		256	(0K)		FCBS=4
		26,800	(26K)		BUFFERS=50
		2,816	(3K)		LASTDRIVE=`
		3,072	(3K)		STACKS=9,256
0D60C	1	272	(0K)	vmm32	Data
0D61D	1	4,688	(5K)	DOSKEY	Program
0D742	1	101,344	(99K)	vmm32	Data

Memory Summary:

Type of Memory	Total	Used	Free
Conventional	655,360	28,240	627,120
Upper	158,304	158,304	0
Reserved	393,216	393,216	0
Extended (XMS)	32,347,552	95,648	32,251,904
Total memory	33,554,432	675,408	32,879,024
Total under 1 MB	813,664	186,544	627,120

```
Memory accessible using Int 15h                 0    (0K)
Largest executable program size           627,104  (612K)
```

```
Largest free upper memory block                    0     (OK)
MS-DOS is resident in the high memory area.

XMS version  3.00; driver version  3.95
```

Step Two: Making the Optimization Changes

Once you have determined how much conventional memory you have available (and in all likelihood found that you need to optimize your conventional memory), you must then determine how to best optimize it. If you have installed DOS with the default installation, you will have the CONFIG.SYS file shown here:

```
DEVICE=C:\DOS\HIMEM.SYS
Files=40
Stacks=9,256
SHELL=C:\DOS\COMMAND.COM /E:1024
```

The first procedure you can perform that will increase available conventional memory is to add the DOS=HIGH line to CONFIG.SYS. This has the effect of moving DOS to the HMA, thus freeing up the first 64 KB block (minus a small amount to keep HIMEM.SYS and a few smaller files in conventional memory).

The next thing you can do is load some or all of your device drivers and TSRs into Upper Memory. This is also called loading them "high," which is a misnomer since you aren't loading them into the HMA, but rather into the Upper Memory area (simply the other name for reserved memory, which I guess is *higher* than conventional memory, but still, it's not in the area typically referred to as the High Memory Area—oh, well, I didn't come up with it). This is accomplished by doing three things:

1. Add DEVICE=C:\DOS\EMM386.EXE and DOS=UMB in your CONFIG.SYS so that DOS can manage the UMBs (upper memory blocks, discussed earlier in this chapter).

2. Make sure that you have some free UMBs. This can be done with the MEM /C command, which, in its "Memory Summary" portion (the bottom half of its report), shows the amount of Upper Memory available for UMBs (the row labeled "Upper") and the amount of Upper Memory that is already being used (the row labeled "Reserved").

3. Add something to each command that loads a driver or TSR so that it loads into the Upper Memory area.

The command that you use to load a driver into the Upper Memory area is the DEVICEHIGH=<drivername> command. You use this command in the same manner as the DEVICE= command in CONFIG .SYS. When you replace each DEVICE= line in your CONFIG.SYS with a DEVICEHIGH= command, the driver will attempt to load into the Upper Memory area. You can see whether this is successful by using the MEM /C command to show how much of the driver is loaded into Upper Memory. The driver will be displayed, along with a number in the "Upper Memory" column (in the top portion of the report) if it successfully loaded into Upper Memory. Additionally, if you have drivers loaded from the AUTOEXEC.BAT, you use the LOADHIGH <drivername> (or LH, for short) to load that driver or TSR into a UMB.

Additionally, you should check to see if you have a program that uses expanded memory. If you don't, you can place the NOEMS line after C:\DOS\EMM386.EXE in the CONFIG.SYS. This frees up the 64 KB area being used by the page frame so it can be used for UMBs.

These memory optimization "tricks" are easy enough, but most users don't want or need to know memory optimization theory. So, both Microsoft and IBM included intelligent memory optimization utilities with their DOS operating systems (starting with version 6 of each one). The programs are MEMMAKER (by Microsoft) and RAMBOOST (by IBM). These utilities already know the theory behind memory optimization and can examine the system and determine how best to optimize the system. Each accomplishes the same ends by different means. MEMMAKER scans the CONFIG.SYS and AUTOEXEC.BAT and adds DEVICEHIGH and LOADHIGH statements to optimize memory. RAMBOOST, on the other hand, is a TSR that is constantly running. Any time you make a change to your CONFIG .SYS or AUTOEXEC.BAT, RAMBOOST detects the change, automatically reboots the computer, and automatically rearranges the drivers in Upper Memory to give the best possible memory configuration. It saves all its information to a file known as RAMBOOST.INI.

> **NOTE** For more information regarding RAMBOOST or MEMMAKER, please refer to their respective user manuals.

One caution about MEMMAKER, though, is that it isn't as "smart" as we would like it to be. For example, if you had the following CONFIG.SYS:

```
DEVICE=C:\DOS\HIMEM.SYS
DEVICE=C:\DOS\EMM386.EXE
FILES=50
BUFFERS=9,256
DEVICE=C:\SB16\CTMMCD.SYS
```

MEMMAKER might optimize it to read like so:

```
DEVICE=C:\DOS\HIMEM.SYS
DEVICE=C:\DOS\EMM386.EXE NOEMS
FILES=50
BUFFERS=9,256
DOS=UMB
DEVICEHIGH=C:\SB16\CTMMCD.SYS
```

The memory usage would be more efficient after MEMMAKER had run, but there is one glaring problem. Where is DOS=HIGH,UMB? If MEMMAKER had included this statement, it would have freed up a 64KB block of conventional memory, but it didn't include it. So, while it's good at general optimization, MEMMAKER can't beat an intuitive technician with a good grasp of memory theory.

Another factor in memory optimization is the *order* in which drivers are loaded into memory. When optimizing memory, sometimes you run into a situation where you only need one or two kilobytes more of conventional memory and you've done all you can to get the most available conventional memory. The final "trick" in your bag is to change the order in which the drivers load. To do this, you load the driver that needs the most memory first. Then the next largest, and so on. Think of it this way, when you build a wall, do you put the smallest stones down first, then the largest? Or, do you put the biggest first, then the smallest? Obviously, you do the latter so that your wall is stable.

Memory Troubleshooting

Very rarely does anything go wrong with the memory in a PC. However, you need to have background knowledge of *possible* memory problems in case they do occur.

It is very easy to tell when a memory error occurs, because a computer malfunctions seriously with bad memory. With a memory error, the computer will do one of two things. If the computer is already running, it will report the error and stop the program. If the error occurs during the POST (power on self-test) memory countup, the computer will not start at all. The reason the computer stops in both cases is that the computer needs reliable memory in order to function. If the computer knows the memory is unreliable, it knows it might write a 1 to memory and read back a 0. And it knows that would be bad.

There are two types of memory problems: hard errors and soft errors. We'll discuss these in reverse order.

Soft Memory Errors

Soft errors occur once and disappear after the computer is rebooted. They are usually caused by power fluctuations or single bit errors. The symptoms are typically unexplained problems with software, and are not reproducible. Soft errors are like gnats: annoying little things you wish you could kill, but they don't stay in one place long enough for you to do so. However, if these errors increase in frequency, it usually indicates a hard memory error is about to occur.

Hard Memory Errors

Hard memory errors are related to a hardware failure and *are* reproducible. When a hard memory error occurs, the computer might issue either a "Parity Error" or a "201 BIOS Error" or issue a series of beeps (upon startup). For example, if you are using AMI BIOS, and the computer issues 1 long and 3 short beeps on startup (other BIOSes will use different beep codes), you have a hardware-related memory error. A table of BIOS error codes is included in Chapter 12.

To solve a hard memory error, you must replace some memory chips. The question is always one of money. Since most computers have more than one memory chip, you must determine which chip(s) or SIMM(s) need to be replaced. One way to do this is to systematically replace one chip at a time until the memory error goes away. It may be easiest, however, to simply replace all the memory at one time, especially if memory prices stay low.

TIP Some BIOSes have beep or error codes that indicate which chip has failed. In that case, use the manual that comes with the motherboard to determine which chip is causing the error (assuming there is a manual available). Another good argument for having documentation available.

Review Questions

1. RAM is short for _____:

    A. Readily Accessible Memory

    B. Recently Affected Memory

    C. Random Access Memory

    D. Read And Modify

2. When you turn off a computer, the information in ROM is erased. True or false?

    A. True

    B. False

3. When you turn off a computer, the information in RAM is erased. True or false?

    A. True

    B. False

4. Which of the following types of memory are erasable? (Circle all that apply.)

    A. RAM

    B. SRAM

    C. ROM

    D. PROM

    E. EPROM

    F. EEPROM

5. DRAM uses banks of transistors to store patterns of ones and zeros. True or false?

    A. True

    B. False

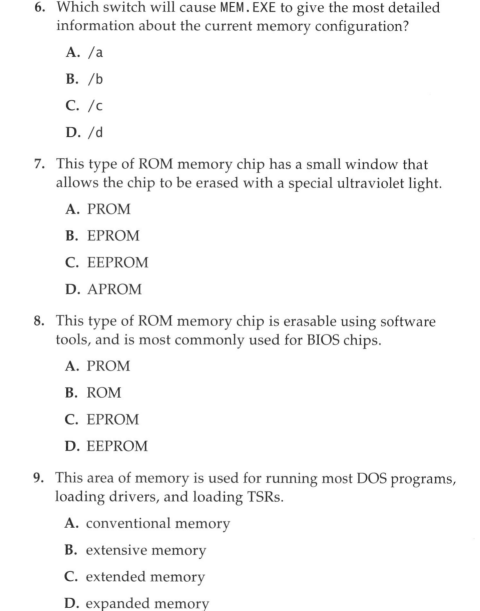

6. Which switch will cause MEM.EXE to give the most detailed information about the current memory configuration?

   A. /a

   B. /b

   C. /c

   D. /d

7. This type of ROM memory chip has a small window that allows the chip to be erased with a special ultraviolet light.

   A. PROM

   B. EPROM

   C. EEPROM

   D. APROM

8. This type of ROM memory chip is erasable using software tools, and is most commonly used for BIOS chips.

   A. PROM

   B. ROM

   C. EPROM

   D. EEPROM

9. This area of memory is used for running most DOS programs, loading drivers, and loading TSRs.

   A. conventional memory

   B. extensive memory

   C. extended memory

   D. expanded memory

10. Which of these processors was the first to access more than 1 MB of RAM?

    A. 8088

    B. 8086

    C. 80286

    D. 80386

    E. 80486

11. Which processor(s) can access as much as 4 GB of RAM? (Circle all that apply.)

    A. 8088

    B. 8086

    C. 80286

    D. 80386

    E. 80486

    F. Pentium

12. If you are transmitting the 8-bit binary number 11010010 and are using even parity, the parity bit would be _____.

    A. 1

    B. 0

    C. None

    D. A

13. Modem communications most often use the following type of error-checking routine.

    A. parity

    B. error correction

    C. addition

    D. checksumming

14. A memory chip has markings of 45256–40. The last 2 digits after the dash mean an access time of _____.

    A. 4 ms

    B. 4 ns

    C. 40 ms

    D. 40 ns

    E. 400 ns

15. Which of the following indicate(s) a hard memory error? (Circle all that apply.)

    A. 201 BIOS Error

    B. 301 BIOS Error

    C. 1 long beep, 3 short beeps

    D. 2 long beeps, 2 short beeps

    E. Parity Error

16. RAMBOOST is the IBM PC-DOS functional equivalent to MS-DOS MEMMAKER. True or false?

    A. True

    B. False

17. The first thing you can do to increase the available conventional memory is:

    A. load all device drivers into UMBs

    B. add `DOS=HIGH` to the `CONFIG.SYS`

    C. remove DOS

    D. rearrange the loading order of the drivers

18. If you don't need expanded memory, you can free up 64 KB of reserved memory that can be used for UMBs by putting the following parameter after `C:\DOS\EMM386.EXE` in the `CONFIG.SYS` to disable expanded memory and remove the page frame.

    A. NOEXT

    B. NOEXP

    C. NOPAGE

    D. NOEMS

19. Memory optimization programs are not always the best way of optimizing memory. True or false?

    A. True

    B. False

20. Which driver must be loaded in the `CONFIG.SYS` to give DOS access to extended memory?

    A. `C:\DOS\EXTMEM.SYS`

    B. `C:\DOS\UPPMEM.SYS`

    C. `C:\DOS\MEMORY.SYS`

    D. `C:\DOS\EMM386.EXE`

    E. `C:\DOS\HIMEM.SYS`

21. LIM memory is another name for which type of memory?

    A. conventional memory

    B. extended memory

    C. expanded memory

    D. CMOS memory

22. Which command(s) displays the list of all programs in memory and stops the display after one page, waiting for user input? (Circle all that apply.)

   A. MEM /C /P

   B. MEM /C |MORE

   C. MEM /PC /USER

   D. MEM /D /P

   E. MEM /C

23. What is the hexadecimal range for conventional memory?

   A. A0000 to 7FFFF

   B. 00000 to A0000

   C. 00000 to 9FFFF

   D. 00000 to A0000

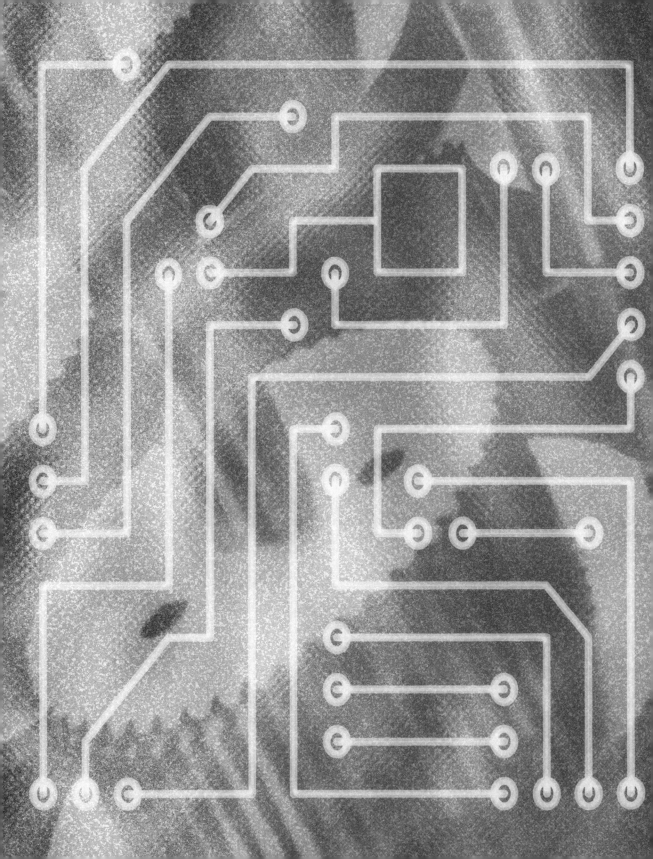

CHAPTER
FOUR

Disk System Architecture

Objectives

- Identify proper procedures for installing and configuring IDE/EIDE devices.

- Identify proper procedures for installing and configuring SCSI devices.

- Identify basic terms, concepts, and functions of system modules, including how each module should work during normal operation.

All information needs to be stored somewhere. It's a simple fact of life. At your office, you may have letters, contracts, etc., that need to be stored somewhere to make them easily accessible and retrievable. This storage space needs to be large enough to hold as much information as possible, but it should also be organized for easy access to that information. Although some people simply use the top of the desk for storing documents in piles, the best solution for storing paper documents at most offices is a filing cabinet.

With computers, you have various types of electronic information to store, including data files, application files, and configuration files. In this chapter, we will explain the following A+ exam topics related to information storage:

- Storage types
- Floppy disk systems
- ST-506 and ESDI disk systems
- IDE disk systems
- Small Computer Systems Interface (SCSI)

Storage Types

In this section, I will give a detailed description of each type of disk storage, starting with a brief overview of punch card and tape storage, then moving into the different types of disks, tips on how to configure them, and their different troubleshooting techniques.

Punch Cards and Tape

Originally, computer information was contained in memory and printed to punch cards. When you wanted to retrieve the data, you ran the punch cards back into a special reader and the information was read back into memory and could then be used. This proved to be a very limited storage medium in terms of capacity and ease of retrieval. A single page of data could take several pages of punch cards. Also, the punch card order was very important. The cards had to be put into the reader in the correct order, or the program wouldn't run correctly. Hopefully you kept the cards in their correct order—God forbid you dropped them on the floor or had some jokester shuffle your punch cards.

Then one day, someone discovered that computer signals could be recorded with a tape recorder. When the tape was played back into the computer, the information was retrieved. This was a much more efficient storage system than punch cards. Since the tape only moved in one direction and was a single, long tape (rather than several punch cards) it reduced the possibility of getting the information out of sequence, and made it easier to access the information. We've all seen movies where the computer room has massive cabinets with reels of tape moving back and forth. What you might not know is that several early personal computer systems (such as the TRS-80, the Tandy Color Computer, and the Apple II) came with cassette tape storage devices to load and store programs and data.

The major limitations of tape were in speed and precision. Tape was slow to store programs and data. Also, it was slow to access information, because of the linear nature of tape. Tape devices are described as *sequential storage* devices. With these types of devices, if a piece of information is located at the end of a tape, you have to "fast forward" through all the other information to get to the data you need. Also, the early tape mechanisms didn't have very good position locators or stepper motors. It was quite possible to start reading a tape after the information you needed had already begun, causing you to miss the start of the program or data and making it unusable.

Despite its drawbacks for most tasks you might want to undertake with a computer, magnetic tape in various forms is still a great medium for "backing up" your system—that is, recording some or all of the information stored on your hard disk and putting the recording away, in case of hard disk catastrophe. Why is tape, which is not recommended for other types of information storage, recommended so often for backups? In part, it's because of the sheer amount of data it can store. Some of the cheaply available tape media of today can hold more than 4 GB, and the media are easily movable, removable, and insertable into their respective recorder/playback drives. Moreover, the relatively low speed of recording or playing back a backup tape is not a significant consideration for most users, as it would be with other computer tasks. Most users know that they are simply performing a safety measure when they utilize a backup, so they schedule their backups to be carried out automatically when no one is using the computer anyway.

Disk Drives

To overcome the limitations of magnetic tape, magnetic disk systems were developed. Rotating stacks of disks were coated with a special substance that was sensitive to magnetism. As the disk rotated, the particles in the substance could be polarized (magnetized), indicating a 1. The unpolarized areas would indicate 0's. (We will discuss the way information is stored on a disk in the next section.) This technology is the cornerstone behind most current disk storage types and hasn't changed much since its inception. These types of disk systems store data in nonlinear format, and are called *random access* storage devices, in contrast to tape's *sequential access* methods. The data can be accessed no matter where it is located on the disk, because the read/write head can be exactly positioned over the requested data without having to "fast forward" through the data that was stored before it.

There are two major types of disk systems—*fixed* and *removable*. Let's cover fixed disks first.

Fixed Disk Drives

Also known as *hard disks* and *hard drives*, fixed disks actually contain several disks called *platters*, stacked together and mounted through their centers on a small rod called a *spindle* (see Figure 4.1). The disks are rotated about this rod at a speed between 2,000 and 10,000 RPM. As they rotate, one or more *read/write heads* float approximately 10 microinches (about 1/10th the width of a human hair) above the disk surfaces and make, modify, or sense changes in the magnetic positions of the coatings on the disks. Several heads are moved together as one unit by an *actuator arm*. There is usually one head for each side of a platter. This entire mechanism is enclosed in a hard disk case. These disks are called fixed disks because the mechanism is not designed to be removed. The disk platters, though perfectly free to revolve at high RPM, are otherwise fixed in place.

FIGURE 4.1:

A fixed disk

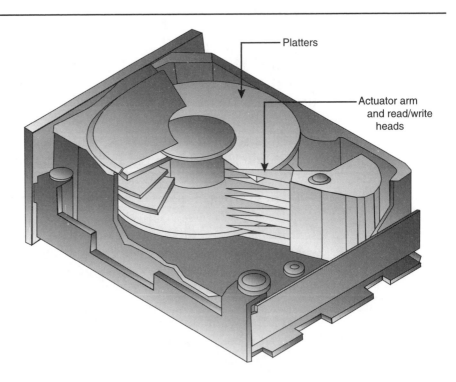

Platters

Actuator arm
and read/write
heads

Disk Organization

We must have a way of organizing this disk into usable sections. It's done by first dividing up the platters into sections like a pie, and then further dividing this area into concentric circles, called *tracks* (see Figure 4.2). Tracks are numbered from the outside (track 0) to the inside (track 902 on a 903-track hard disk). A disk *sector* is the part of a track that falls in a particular section of the "pie slice" on the disk.

FIGURE 4.2:

Disk organization

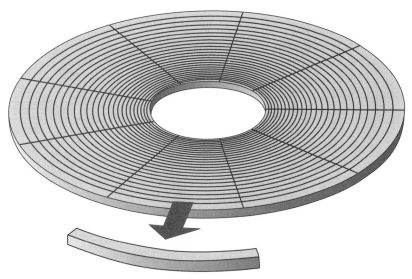

1 sector of 1 track

If you can visualize several tracks stacked together vertically (the same tracks on each disk), you might describe that collection of tracks as a *cylinder*. In fact, that's how tracks are referred to when discussing the organization of disk information, because when information is read from or written to a disk, the heads read or write a sector-sized division of a track a whole stack at a time, from top to bottom (see Figure 4.3). In other words, the disks' tracks aren't treated as individual tracks on single disks; they're treated as cylinders. This amounts to quite a bit of information read or written at one time. The precise amount of information that is read at once depends on the number of cylinders, heads, and sectors, or what we call *drive geometry*.

FIGURE 4.3:

Hard drive geometry

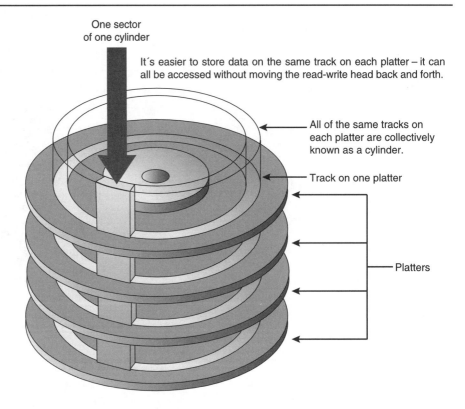

One sector
of one cylinder

It's easier to store data on the same track on each platter – it can all be accessed without moving the read-write head back and forth.

All of the same tracks on each platter are collectively known as a cylinder.

Track on one platter

Platters

Disk Specifications

When a fixed disk is rated, it has several qualities that are given as specifications. Size, or capacity, is just one of the properties given. Size is determined by drive geometry. Let's quantify this by giving some values to each variable. Let's say we have 903 cylinders, 12 heads (6 platters—one head per side, two sides to each platter), and 63 sectors per track. A typical fixed disk has 512 bytes per sector (that's 0.5 KB/sector). The capacity of the hard disk would be 341,334 KB, or 333 MB (903 cyl × 12 heads × 63 sectors/track × 0.5 KB/sector). These values are commonly given on the outside of a fixed disk.

Another quality that is used to gauge the performance of an individual drive is *seek time*. This value, commonly given in milliseconds (ms), is how long it takes the actuator arm to move from rest to the position where the read/write head will access information. Additionally, because the platters rotate, once the read/write is in position it may take a few milliseconds for the target sector to move under the read/write head. This delay is known as the *latency* factor. Latency values are given in milliseconds (ms).

Because the faster a drive spins, the lower the average latency values, drives are also rated with a *spin speed*. Spin speeds are an indication of how fast the platters are spinning. They are stated in revolutions per minute (RPM); higher RPM values mean faster speeds and lower latency values. For example, if a disk has a spin speed of 5,000 RPM, it will be rotating at 83.34 revolutions per second. One rotation will take 1/83.34 seconds, or 11.9 ms. This value would represent the largest possible delay (i.e., the disk head is in position just after the required sector moved past it). However, disk latency values are actually only *average latency* values, because latency values are not constant. The target sector could be close, or it could be far away. So in our example we take the largest possible latency (11.9 ms) and smallest possible latency (0 ms) and average them to get the average latency: (11.9 ms + 0)/2 = 5.95 ms.

The two factors, seek time and latency, make up the drive's *access time*. Put simply, the average seek time plus the average latency equals the drive's access time. The smaller the access time value is, the faster the drive.

Read/Write Processes

Now that we know how the drive functions and how the drives are rated, let's discuss the most important topic: how the drive stores the information. At the most basic level, the disk works by making *flux transitions* with an electromagnet in the read/write head to store information on the disk surface. A flux transition is the presence or absence of a magnetic field in a particle of the coating on the disk. As the disk passes over an area, the electromagnet is energized to cause the material to be magnetized in a small area. The process by which binary information is changed into flux transition patterns is called *encoding*.

There are many ways of converting 1's and 0's to flux transitions. The simplest way is to interpret the presence of a flux transition as a 1, and the absence as a 0. Since this was the most obvious choice, the first hard disks (ST-506, ESDI types) used this method of encoding, known as Frequency Modulation (FM) and its cousin Modified FM (MFM). This worked well until techniques for increasing the track/cylinder density became almost too successful. What happened was that tracks would be placed so tightly together that at higher speeds, the read/write heads would affect not only the track immediately under the head, but the adjacent ones as well.

To solve this problem, a technology known as *Run Length Limited* (*RLL*) was developed, which spaced the 1's farther apart using a special code for each byte. This method turned out to be more efficient for large drives than for small ones. RLL encoding also introduced *data compression*, a set of technologies that increased the amount of data that could be stored on the drive. Most of today's drives (IDE, SCSI, and so on) use a form of RLL encoding.

With this new type of encoding, much more data could be transferred to the computer at once, but this created a new problem. The interface would sometimes get bogged down, and would stop reading in order to "catch up." This was a problem because during this pause, the platters were still rotating and the read/write heads could skip a whole bunch of sectors. To solve this problem, disk designers developed a technology known as *interleaving*.

A Question of Interleaves

Although interleaving may come up on the A+ Certification exam, the topic is almost irrelevant with the hard drives available in the last few years, because the hardware technology has improved so much. Here's what you need to know for the test.

Interleaving involves skipping sectors to write the data, instead of writing sequentially to every sector. This evens out the data flow and allows the drive to keep pace with the rest of the system. Interleaving is given in ratios. If the interleave is 2:1, the disk skips 2 minus 1, or 1 sector, between each sector it writes (it writes to one sector, skips one sector, then writes to the next sector following). Most drives today use a 1:1 interleave, since today's drives are very efficient at transferring information. A 1:1 ratio means that the drive writes to one sector and then simply goes to the immediate next sector (skipping 1 minus 1 sectors, or 0 sectors). A 1:1 interleave ratio really means that the drive has no interleave at all.

To make it easier for the operating system to manage the storage space, the information encoded on the drive is written to groups of sectors known as *clusters*. A cluster is made up of up to 64 sectors grouped together (the actual number of sectors included in a cluster varies with the size of the hard disk). When the operating system is storing information, it writes it to a particular cluster instead of to an actual sector, because it's more efficient for the operating system to keep track of clusters than sectors. The file that contains the information about where the tracks and sectors on the disk are located is known as the *file allocation table*, or *FAT*. It is contained in the outermost track (track 0) of the disk.

Why Is the FAT on Track 0?

Because advances in disk technology are constantly increasing the number of tracks, even on disks of the same size (i.e., the designers are always striving to increase the track density), if the FAT were located on the inside track, it might be in a slightly different position on one disk than on another. Also, because the outside track (track 0) is so easily accessible, the FAT is placed there so that the computer can use a simple routine to locate its operating system and disk information. Moreover, this routine never needs to change.

Formatting the Disks to Prepare Them for Use

To create the FAT, a machine at the factory performs a procedure known as a *low-level format*. This procedure organizes the disk into sectors and tracks. Once the sectors and tracks have been created, the low-level format procedure makes the FAT file and records in it the positions of the new sectors and tracks. Additionally, during this procedure, the low-level format procedure meticulously checks the disk's surface for defects. If any are found, the locations of these "bad spots" are entered into the FAT as well, so that the operating system knows not to store any information in those locations.

When an operating system is installed, it will do a *high-level format* (or operating system format) and create its own separate FAT that keeps track of where clusters are located and which files are located in which clusters. These two FAT technologies are applicable to all types of drives.

Removable Media Drives

Another type of drive system is *removable media* drives. Removable drives use technologies similar to fixed disk (fixed media) drives, except the storage medium is removable. The obvious advantage is that removable media multiplies the usefulness of the drive. With a hard disk, when the disk is full, the only two things you can do to increase space are to delete some information or get a larger drive. With removable media drives, you can remove the full disk and insert a blank one. Other than the ZIP and Jaz drives discussed in Chapter 2 (and other than removable hard drives themselves), there are numerous categories of removable media drives covered on the test, as discussed in the rest of this section.

Floppy Disk Drives   The type of removable media drive that is the most often described is the floppy disk drive. It is called that because the original medium was flexible. Floppy disks are like fixed disks, but they have only one "platter" encased in a plastic shell. There are several types of floppy disk drives available in many different capacities (Figure 4.4 shows a 1.44MB $3\frac{1}{2}$" drive), and we will discuss them in the sections to come.

FIGURE 4.4:

A floppy disk drive

A floppy drive has either one or two read/write heads. Each head moves in a straight line on a track over the disk, rather than using an angular path as with fixed disk systems. When the disk is placed into the drive, a motor engages the center of the disk and rotates it. This action moves the tracks past the read/write heads.

CD-ROM Drives   Another type of removable media drive is the CD-ROM drive (see Figure 4.5). These drives are slightly different from other storage media in several ways. First of all, they have a different way of reading information than magnetic media disk drives. Because CD-ROM drives use laser light to read the information from the media, they are described as *optical* drives.

FIGURE 4.5:

A CD-ROM drive

When reading information from a CD, the drive is basically reading a lot of *pits* and *lands* (lands are the spaces between the pits) in the disk surface. The pits are etched into the CD at production time. The laser reflects off the CD's surface and onto a sensor. The sensor detects the pattern of pits and lands as the disk rotates and translates them into patterns of 1's and 0's. This binary information is fed to the computer that is retrieving the data.

Another difference between magnetic media and CD-ROM drives is that CD-ROM drives are read-only devices (CD-ROM stands for Compact Disc–*Read-Only* Memory). The only way of writing to a CD-ROM is during manufacture time, where the pits are "burned" into the substrate of the disk. Once written, they cannot be erased.

The reason CD-ROMs are so popular, even though they can't be written to, is their large capacity (greater than 500 MB) and easy access. They are a great choice for archival storage. Most often used for software distribution, they have really taken off in the past few years as the speed of CD-ROM drives has increased.

NOTE   Recordable and rewritable CD devices are becoming available; but strictly speaking, they are not CD-ROMs. Technically, these new devices are called *rewritable compact discs*.

Finally, a CD-ROM disc has a single track that runs from the center to the outside edge, exactly the reverse of the groove on a record.

A CD-ROM uses basically the same technology as the audio compact discs in use in most homes today. When a CD-ROM is placed into a CD-ROM drive, a motor spins the CD at a specific rate. A laser is then activated that reads the CD. Because of these basic similarities, there are several compatibilities between the different compact disc technologies. For example, it is possible to play audio CDs in a computer's CD-ROM drive. Also, some computer CDs have audio tracks on them and are made to be used in either type of CD drive (home audio or computer).

This compatibility is possible because of *standards*. Standards are put together by committee (*"de jure* standards") or simply to recognize a standard that's already in practice (*"de facto* standards"). CD-ROM standards are put together by several groups, the largest of which is the International Standards Organization (ISO) which has defined several standards. Table 4.1 shows the most popular CD standards and their respective applications. The compact disc standards are given as colors of books (I don't know why, they just are).

TABLE 4.1: Compact Disc Standards

CD Standard	Application	ISO Name (If any)
Red Book	Audio CDs	CD-Audio
Yellow Book	Data Storage (CD-ROM)	ISO 9660
Green Book	CD-I (Interactive CD)	N/A
Orange Book	Write-Once CD and Magneto-Optical	N/A
White Book	CD-I Bridge	N/A

Optical Disk Drives   Another type of disk is the optical disk. An optical disk is much like a CD-ROM, except that optical disks can be read from and written to (like fixed disks, except the media are similar to CD-ROM disks and thus a laser is used). The upside is that optical disks are removable and can hold lots of information. The downside is that they are expensive and are still slower than fixed disks.

Tape Drives   The final type of removable media drive is a tape drive (see Figure 4.6). The tape cartridge uses a long polyester ribbon coated with magnetic oxide wrapped around two spools. As the tape unwinds from one spool, it passes by a read/write head in the drive that retrieves or saves the information. It then proceeds to the other spool where it is kept until needed again.

FIGURE 4.6:

A tape drive

Tape media are great for large capacity storage, but they are agonizingly slow. The best application for tape media is for backup purposes. Current tape technology uses 4mm or 8mm Digital Audio Tape (DAT) for its storage medium. With this technology it is possible to store up to 16 GB of data on a single tape.

Disk Theory

With all of these storage technologies available, there are many to choose from. Which one is the best? The answer is: It depends. Each type of storage has its own benefits and drawbacks. Each type of storage is ideally suited to a different application. To help understand this, a model has been developed to define the different types of storage. This model is called the "storage pyramid" and shows the relationship between the types of storage and their benefits (see Figure 4.7).

FIGURE 4.7:

The "storage pyramid"

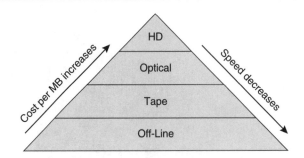

As you can see, at the bottom of the pyramid the storage types have the largest capacity, but the slowest access times. Additionally, those types have the cheapest cost per megabyte.

Floppy Disk Systems

There are four major types of floppy disk drives in use today. They are usually identified by the size of the media they use and the capacity of that media. We'll cover each one and its associated configuration and troubleshooting issues. But, before we do, let's discuss the four components of a floppy drive subsystem: the disk (also called the medium), the drive, the controller, and the cable.

The Medium

The floppy disk, as we have already mentioned, is the removable medium on which information is stored in a floppy disk system. There are two major types in use today, the 5$\frac{1}{4}$" "floppy" disk and the 3$\frac{1}{2}$" "diskette" (sometimes incorrectly called a "hard floppy" or even a "hard disk"). Both are shown in Figure 4.8.

F I G U R E   4 . 8 :

A 5¼″ floppy disk and
a 3½″ diskette

5¼″ Floppy Disk   The $5^1/4$″ floppy disks are made from a poly-ester disk coated with iron oxide and a flexible outer covering. The disk has a large hole in the center, called the *drive hole,* that is used by the motor in the disk drive to spin the disk. In addition, there is also a $1^1/2$″ oval window cut into the case to allow the read/write heads access to the disk media. A small round hole cut into the disk shell next to the drive hole lines up with an even smaller hole cut into the disk media. When this smaller hole spins past the slightly larger hole in the shell, it allows a light to shine all the way through the disk system. In this way, the floppy drive can tell how fast the disk is rotating by how many times in a second that hole appears.

Finally, there is a notch cut in one side of the disk. This notch is called the *write-protect* tab. When a disk is inserted into a floppy drive, a small lever places itself into this notch. When the lever is in the notch, the disk can be written to. You can disable writing to the disk (or "write protect" the disk) by covering this hole.

The $5^1/4$″ disks have almost completely disappeared in the last few years, replaced by the $3^1/2$″ format; and most newer comput-ers no longer include $5^1/4$″ drives.

3½″ Diskette   The other type of floppy disk media is not really "floppy" at all. Some people mistakenly call it a "hard disk." Its real name is a $3^1/2$″ *diskette* (to differentiate it from a full-grown "disk," I suppose). The $3^1/2$″ diskettes are also made from a polyester disk coated with a layer of iron oxide. This disk is enclosed in a durable, plastic case. This was an improvement over the $5^1/4''$ variety, since the $5^1/4''$ floppies were easily creased or damaged. Also, the $3^1/2''$ diskettes have a metal shutter over the media access window. Again, this was an improvement over $5^1/4''$ media since people often grasped the disks inadvertently by this edge of the disk, pressing their fingers onto the media and thus contaminating the disk, making the disk difficult to read.

Finally, the $3^1/2''$ disks use a notch with a sliding plastic tab over it to write protect the disk. This is also better than $5^1/4''$ disks, because the write-protect notch in the other disks was covered with a type of tape that could come loose in the drive and cause gum-ups.

The Drives

The next item we need to discuss is the floppy disk drives themselves. There are three items we need to discuss regarding the drives: media size, form factor, and capacity.

Media Size   Since we just discussed media size in our discussion of the media, I'll just refer you to the previous paragraphs and continue on. I do want to make one note, however. You can't put a $5^1/4''$ diskette into a $3^1/2''$ drive. Or vice versa. I know some of you are saying "Thank you, Captain Obvious, for that enlightening bit of minutia." However, it has become apparent to me that not everyone seems to know this fundamental rule, as I am constantly pulling folded-up $5^1/4''$ disks out of $3^1/2''$ drives.

Form Factors   There are three main types of *form factors*, or drive styles, available today. A form factor usually just means the physical dimensions and characteristics. Today's floppy disk drives use either the full-height, half-height, or combo form factors. *Full-height* drives were the only ones available for the first PCs. The drives were large and bulky and usually lower in capacity than today's drives. Half-height drives take up only half the space (vertically) of full-height drives. (Captain Obvious?)

The final form factor is becoming more popular as space becomes a premium in computer cases. The *combination form factor* (or *combo*, for short) contains both 1.2 MB 5$\frac{1}{4}$″ and 1.44 MB 3$\frac{1}{2}$″ drives in a half-height enclosure. This has the obvious advantage of having both drives in the space for one.

Capacity   The final topic we need to discuss about the drives is their capacity. The capacities range from 360 KB to 1.44 MB in various form factors. Table 4.2 details the range of capacities available today, their associated form factors, the number of sides used, and the "density" of the disk. Some disks use only one side of the media, while others use both sides. The density of a disk determines how closely the sectors and tracks can be packed. Notice how the combination of all three items relates to the capacity.

WARNING   You may have heard that even though some floppy disks and diskettes are rated as *single-sided*, in fact *both* sides of a disk are *always* coated with media. Some people have taken this bit of industry knowledge and decided that it means you can actually store information on both sides of a single-sided disk. DON'T DO IT. Even though the disk *might* be able to be formatted, that doesn't mean the data will stay on the disk. If the disk was rated as single-sided at the factory, you can be assured that the testing process determined that there were problems on the other side of the disk. Spend the extra 20 cents and get a disk rated for the drive you are using.

WARNING   The same holds true for formatting a low-density disk in a high-density drive and then using it in a low-density drive. These low-density disks aren't designed to have the information packed as tightly as the high-density drives save it.

TABLE 4.2: Disk Capacities

Capacity	Form Factor	Density	Sides
180 KB	5¼" FH	Single	Double
360 KB	5¼" FH	Double	Double
720 KB	3½" HH	Double	Double
1.2 MB	5¼" FH or HH	High	Double
1.44 MB	3½" HH	High	Double

The Controller

The next item we need to discuss is the floppy disk controller (Figure 4.9). This is the circuit board installed in a computer that translates signals from the CPU into signals that the floppy disk drive can understand. Often, the floppy controller is integrated into the same circuit board that houses the hard disk controller. Or, even better, the controller might be integrated into the motherboard in the PC. Some people might like this approach, but from a technician's standpoint, it's a nightmare. Imagine having to tell the customer that the reason their floppy drive doesn't work is because their motherboard needs to be replaced at a cost of $1100! Wouldn't it be nicer to tell them that you need to replace the $22 floppy disk controller board?

A floppy controller is not a complicated device. The early controllers were large expansion boards that usually contained an Intel 8272 or Zilog 765 controller chip. At the time of the writing of this book, you can buy a card that contains the floppy controller, two serial interfaces, parallel and game interface ports, and disk interface for about $35.00.

FIGURE 4.9:

A floppy controller
with cable

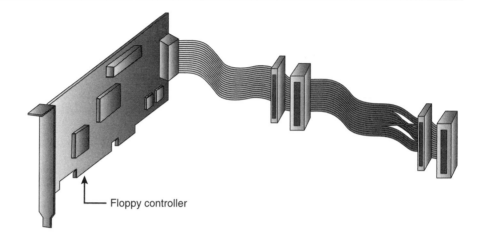

Floppy controller

The Cable

The last topic on our list of prerequisites is the floppy drive cable
(shown above in Figure 4.9). This cable is made up of a 34-wire ribbon cable and three connectors. One of these connectors attaches to
the controller. The other two connect to the drives (one for drive
A:, the other for drive B:). You can attach up to two floppy drives
to a single controller. These connectors are specially made so that
they can be attached to the drives in only one way.

Additionally, you might think that with 34 wires the data would
be transmitted in a parallel manner (8 bits at a time), but it isn't. Data
is transmitted one bit at a time, serially. This makes floppy transfers slow, but usually the serial data transfer isn't the bottleneck.

The cable also has a red stripe running down one side, as shown
in the detailed version of Figure 4.10. This stripe indicates which
wire is for pin #1 on the controller and on the drive(s). This pin is
usually marked with a small *1* or a white dot on the controller.
When connecting the drives to the controller, you need to make

sure that the red stripe is oriented so the wire it represents is connected to pin #1 on the drive and pin #1 on the controller. Also, you connect the drive that is going to be drive A: *after* the twist in the floppy cable for most ISA floppy systems (very important).

FIGURE 4.10:

A typical floppy cable

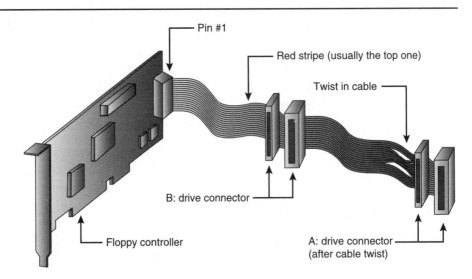

Pin #1

Red stripe (usually the top one)

Twist in cable

B: drive connector

Floppy controller

A: drive connector
(after cable twist)

WARNING A common technician's trick to remember how to connect floppy drives is to say "Point the red stripe towards the power cable." The problem is that this trick doesn't work with every brand of floppy drive. It could be considered a general "rule of thumb," but not a "rule to live by."

Installation and Configuration

Now that we've covered the basics, let's talk about installation, configuration and troubleshooting. Installing floppy drives is no big trick. The first step is to connect the cable to the drive as per the aforementioned instructions. Then, install the drive in the computer by physically mounting it in the computer case and connecting the power cable. Finally, you connect the cable from the drive to the controller as we discussed already.

With regular diskette drives, when connecting the cable to the drives, you connect the B: drive to the connector before the twist in the cable and the A: drive to the connector after the twist.

NOTE   One unique situation crops up if you have a Compaq Deskpro. These computers have twists before each of the drives as well as reversing the position. The first drive on the cable, for Deskpros, is the A: drive, the second drive is the B:. Finally, Deskpros will sometimes have a tape drive connected after the B: drive on the same cable to the last connector on the cable. This tape drive must be one specially made for a Deskpro.

Troubleshooting the floppy drive is also relatively simple. The most common problem after installation is a drive light that refuses to go out. This is caused by having the floppy drive cable upside down on one side. As you already know, most floppy cables are keyed so that they go on in only one direction. However, in some systems, the floppy cable might not be keyed, so this is a distinct possibility. Just remember which way the red stripe goes!

In addition to the cable position, you must also set the drive type and size of the floppy drive in the CMOS setup. This is done so that the computer will know what drives are attached. If this information is wrong, most computers will detect that the wrong drive type is selected and will give an error during boot up.

Another problem you can troubleshoot is sporadic read/write problems. More often than not, these are caused by a dirty drive. If this is the problem, it can be fixed with a floppy-disk head-cleaning kit. Another cause might be a bad floppy disk. Floppies have a finite number of uses in them and they *can* go bad. (I know this will come as a shock to some people who think their data is safe forever on a floppy disk.) This problem can be fixed by copying the data (if possible) from the old disk to a new one.

Also, don't forget to check the obvious things like disconnected floppy cable, power not plugged in, or the disk isn't inserted properly. Any one of these can cause problems that most people just assume can't be the problem because it's too obvious.

Enough about floppies; let's talk about the disks that have a little more backbone: the hard disks. In the next section, we'll discuss the early hard disk drive interface technologies.

ST-506 and ESDI Disk Systems

The first types of fixed disk technologies we're going to talk about are the ST-506 and ESDI technologies. They have many similarities, so we'll group them together in this section. We'll discuss their technologies as well as the installation and configuration issues that arise from their design.

ST-506 Systems

Early hard disks were relatively dumb devices. They had no ability to control themselves. In order to use them, computers had to use special circuit boards called *controllers* installed in them that interpreted commands from the CPU and told the hard drive what to do. The controller would send commands to the hard drive—how far to move the read/write heads, where the data was located, and so on. Once the disk was positioned, it would send the data back to the controller. The controller would interpret the data and send it on to the CPU.

One of the first hard disk interfaces was developed by a company known as Shugart Associates (now Seagate Technologies). It was developed for use on their ST-506 5 MB drive. This drive used MFM encoding, transferred data serially, and so was basically a very large floppy drive. It worked well, but was pitifully slow by today's standards.

Subsequently, the company developed a similar interface for their ST-412 10 MB hard drive. This new revision could transfer data at a blazing 7.5 Mbits/sec and used RLL encoding. This latter interface and drive were the drive system of choice for the then-fledgling IBM PC. As the "PC" gained in popularity, so did the interface. Many drives after that used the same basic technology and were subsequently called ST-506/412 type drives (or ST-506 drives for short). Figure 4.11 shows a typical ST-506 drive and interface card.

The identifying characteristic for this type of drive interface is the two cables going from the controller to the disk drive: one 20-wire ribbon cable for data and a wider 34-wire ribbon cable for control information. Also, typically the disks are physically very large and bulky. Finally, the disks couldn't support more than 16 heads. If you see one with a rating of more than 16 heads, it probably isn't an ST-506 drive. With all these methods, it shouldn't be too difficult to identify one, if you ever run across it.

In addition to being large and bulky, ST-506 drives and their interfaces were very inefficient at transferring data. When the controller needed the disk to read data from a particular sector, it had to send the drive *exact* instructions on how to get there. It couldn't just say where the data was and "go get it," it could only send one command at a time, like move over 1 sector, move down 1 cylinder. For example, if the read/write heads were at cyl 3, sector 20, and the computer needed to read a cluster of data that started at cyl 4, sector 42, the controller had to send 23 commands to get the read/write heads in position (1 command to move up a cylinder, and 22 commands to move from sector 20 to sector 42).

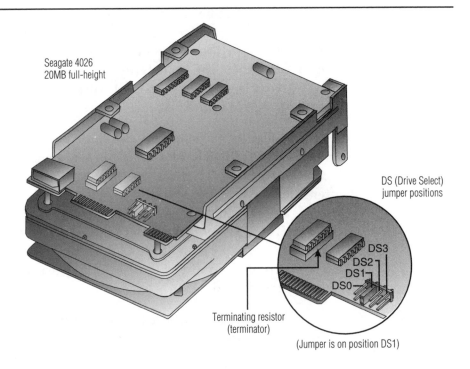

FIGURE 4.11:

ST-506 drive and interface

Seagate 4026
20MB full-height

DS (Drive Select)
jumper positions

DS3
DS2
DS1
DS0

Terminating resistor
(terminator)

(Jumper is on position DS1)

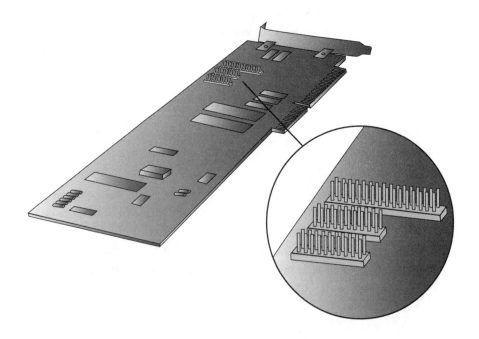

ESDI Systems

ST-506 was great for a while, but as drives grew, the technology didn't. Vendors (and customers) started to get frustrated, so they decided to do something about it. They decided to develop an interface with many similarities while correcting some of the glaring problems. The interface technology they came up with was the Enhanced Small Device Interface or ESDI.

ESDI's first improvement was to improve upon the data transfer rate. Whereas ST-506 could only transfer data at 7.5 Mbps, ESDI could transfer at a much improved 24 Mbps. This was one of the features that made ESDI a favorite choice for server drives.

Another limitation overcome by ESDI was capacity, since ST-506 could only support 16 heads. ESDI could support more heads (up to 256) and the controller could get that information right from the drive, rather than having to configure the controller for the number of cylinder, heads, and sectors that the drive had.

Installation and Configuration

Installing either of these drive systems is rather complex, by today's standards. As with any drive system, it needs to be installed in a carrier of some kind, then have the cables connected. After that, you need to mount the drive and carrier in the computer and connect the power cables. Finally, you need to configure the drives for the system. It is the first and last items that cause problems: cabling and configuration. Since the cabling and configuration are almost identical in both ST-506 and ESDI drive systems, we'll discuss them together.

Cabling for ST-506/ESDI drives is fairly easy; you just need to use two cables: one for data and one for the control signals. When connecting them, however, you need to follow a few rules (Figure 4.12).

1. Connect one end of the control cable (the wider, 34-wire cable) to the disk controller.

2. Connect the first drive to the connector at the end of the cable.

3. Connect the second drive, if you have one, to the connector in the middle of the cable.

4. Connect the data cable (the narrower, 20-wire cable) to the controller and drives.

> **NOTE** It should be noted that the cable used to connect floppy disks together is not the same as the control cable in an ST-506/ESDI disk system (even though they have the same number of wires).

FIGURE 4.12:

ST-506/ESDI disk connection

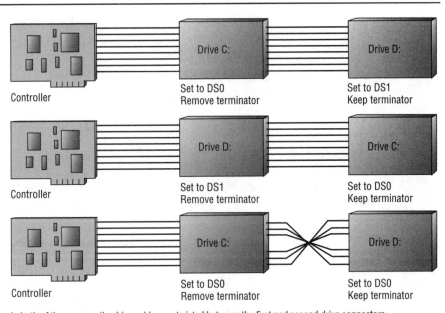

In both of these cases, the drive cables are twisted between the first and second drive connectors.

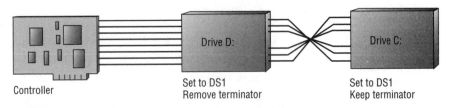

When configuring ST-506/ESDI drives for use with their controller, you must use jumpers to select their drive position. As you saw in Figure 4.11, there is a special "drive select" jumper on the back of an ST-506/ESDI drive that tells the controller how to talk to that drive. How you set that jumper depends upon where the disk is in the chain and what type of cable you are using (a straight cable or a cable with a twist between the two drive connectors). See Table 4.3 for the correct combination of settings for the position of the drive and cable type. There is a terminator that will need to be placed on the drive, depending on these settings. The following table is very general. Check the documentation with each controller/drive combination for the exact settings for your particular combination.

TABLE 4.3: ST-506/ESDI Configuration Information

IF you want the drive to be:	and the cable type:	THEN the drive position should be:	and the drive terminator should be:	and the drive should be jumpered to be:
1st	Has no twist	End of cable	In place	Drive 0
2nd	Has no twist	Middle	Removed	Drive 1
1st	Has a twist	End of cable	In place	Drive 1
2nd	Has a twist	Middle	Removed	Drive 1

Once the drive has been installed, the system needs to be told how many cylinders, heads, and sectors the drive has. You do this by a process known as low-level formatting (or "low-leveling" for short). The manufacturers decided to put the routine in to accomplish this in a special address in the BIOS. To access it, you use the DOS DEBUG.EXE program. A person would think that there should some utility program you could use, but these drives were around when there were very few utility programs available for PCs.

To execute it, you just type DEBUG at the command prompt, like so:

```
C:\>DEBUG
```

This will then drop us into the program debugger and present us with a dash (–) as a prompt. At this point you need to tell the debugger to go to that address and run the program it finds there with the parameters you specify. The program is located at address C800. You start a low-level format by typing the following at the "–" prompt.

```
g=c800:5
```

The number 5 shown in the above command tells the program what type of drive controller you are using. Most Western Digital and Seagate controllers work with a 5. Other controllers may require a different number. Again, check the documentation to be sure.

WARNING Whenever you low-level format a ST-506/ESDI drive, make sure it is installed in the computer in the position it's going to be in when the computer is operating. These drives are not as accurate as current technologies, so tipping the drive on its side after low-level formatting can move the heads slightly out of alignment. Just enough to prevent reads and writes.

After installing, configuring, and "low-leveling" a drive, you can then format it for the operating system you are using (also called a high-level format) and install the operating system on it.

IDE Disk Systems

ST-506 and ESDI drives were great drive systems in their day, but by the time the IBM AT computer came out, drive sizes were increasing beyond the capabilities of existing technologies to utilize them. The only way out was to use a technology called SCSI (pronounced "scuzzy," it stands for Small Computer System Interface—which we discuss in the next section). While it was technologically superior, it was also, at the time, quite expensive. Two companies, Compaq and Western Digital, saw this problem and developed an alternative to SCSI.

Their idea was that if they could develop a cheap, flexible drive system, people would buy it. They were more right than they realized. That solution, known as Integrated Drive Electronics (IDE) because its major feature was a controller located right on the disk, is one of the most popular drive interfaces on the market today.

In this section, we'll discuss the theory behind IDE drive systems, as well as their configuration and installation issues.

IDE Technologies

The idea for IDE (also known as AT Attachment interface or ATA) was a simple one: put the controller right on the drive itself and use a relatively short cable to connect the drive/controller to the system (Figure 4.13). This had the benefits of decreasing signal loss (thus increasing reliability) and making the drive easier to install.

In addition, since the controller was integrated into the same assembly as the drive, the only board that needed to be installed in the computer was an adapter that converted signals between the motherboard and the drive/controller. The board is normally called a pass-through or paddle board. (This board is often, incorrectly, called a controller. The term is incorrect because the paddle board is often integrated with a floppy controller, two serial ports, a game port, and a parallel port. In fact, this combination is normally called a multifunction interface board.) With some of today's systems, the IDE adapter is integrated into the motherboard.

FIGURE 4.13:

An IDE drive and interface

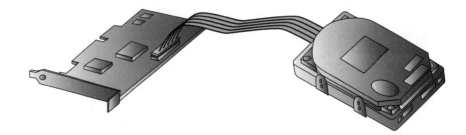

IDE drives, in addition to being relatively simple to install, also can support drives of up to 528 MB. A new technology developed in the last few years, enhanced IDE (EIDE) can support drives of several gigabytes. Also, these newer drives have data transfer rates greater than 10 Mbps.

The main limitation to IDE is that it supports only two drives (or four if you're using EIDE). In order to add more drives, you must use a different technology, like SCSI.

Installation and Configuration

Installation and configuration of IDE and EIDE devices is much easier than ST-506 and ESDI systems. The basic steps for installing them are the same: mount the drive in the carrier, connect the cable to the drive, install the drive in the computer, and configure the drive. However, IDE's cabling and configuration issues are less complex. For example, you only have a single, 40-pin cable to connect the drives to the computer. (And no, there aren't any twists in this cable.) Cabling is just a matter of connecting the drive(s) to the cable and plugging the cable into the paddle board (Figure 4.14). This is made easier because the majority of the IDE cables today are keyed so that they only plug in one way. If you happen to get one of the cables that isn't keyed, just use the red stripe trick (as discussed earlier in this chapter, under "Floppy Drive Systems").

FIGURE 4.14:

IDE cable installation

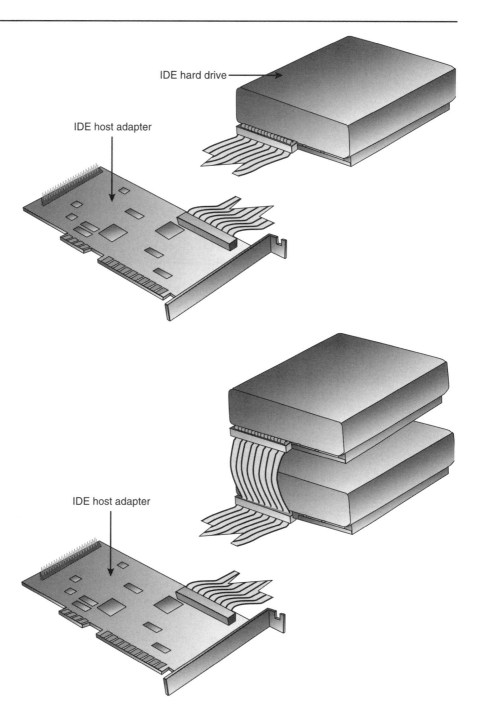

IDE hard drive

IDE host adapter

IDE host adapter

You may also want to note that some IDE drives come with only a two-connector cable, as shown at the top of Figure 4.14. If you need three connectors (for installing a second drive, as in the bottom of the figure), you may have to go to your local electronics supplier and get one.

The one situation that does complicate matters is when you have two (or more) drives in an IDE/EIDE system. Remember that an IDE drive has the controller *mounted on the drive*. If you had two drives connected, which controller would be talking to the computer and sending data back and forth? The answer is: only one of them. When you install a second drive, you need to configure it so that the controller on one drive is active and the other drives use the controller on this drive for their instructions. You do this by setting the first drive to be the *master* and the others to be *slaves*. As you might suspect, the master is the drive whose controller is used by the other drives (the slaves).

You implement the master/slave setting by jumpering a set of pins. There are several different configurations of these pins, so I'll just detail the most common. As always, check your documentation to determine which method your drive uses.

The first type is the simplest. There are two sets of pins, one labeled "master/single," the other labeled "slave" (Figure 4.15). If you have one drive, you jumper the master side and leave the slave side jumper off. If you have two drives, you jumper the master side only on the first drive (at the end of the cable), and jumper the slave side only on the other drive(s). A variant of this type uses no jumpers on either to indicate just one drive in the system.

The other type commonly in use has three sets of pins with each pin labeled 1 through 6. These six pins are arranged in three rows of two with one set labeled "master," another set labeled "slave," and the third set with no label. With one drive installed, you leave all jumpers off. With two drives installed, you set the first drive

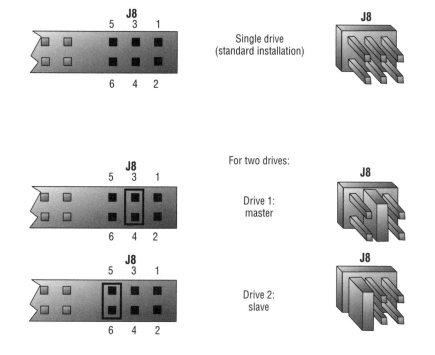

FIGURE 4.15:

Master/Slave jumpers

(usually located at the end of the cable) to *master* by jumpering the two pins labeled "master," then set the second drive to *slave* by jumpering the two pins labeled "slave."

WARNING If you have two drives in your system and both are set to *master*, or both are set to *slave*, neither drive will work. In the first case (two masters), they will be fighting each other for control of the disks. In the latter case (two slaves), the disks won't know where to get their instructions from.

Once you have the cable installed and the drives configured as either master or slave, you must tell the computer that the drives exist and what their drive geometry is. You do this by entering the BIOS's *CMOS setup program* (or the disk-based BIOS setup program for older computers). This setup program modifies the computer's settings in the CMOS memory that stores the configuration information for that computer. It is accessed by a special key or key combination at startup. Some BIOSes use Del, Esc, or one of the function keys; others use Ctrl+Alt+Esc. It should be noted that some of the newer BIOSes will auto-detect the type of drive installed in the system and automatically configure these parameters. With this type of system you only need to accept these parameters and reboot.

Since each machine is different, we'll just talk in general terms. Once you have the disks installed, you enter the setup program and go to the "Fixed Disk" area and enter the appropriate numbers for the number of cylinders, heads, and sectors that the drives have. You then save these values and reboot the machine. At this point the system should recognize that there is at least one drive in the system.

WARNING This is the point where IDE drives take a drastic turn from ST-506/ESDI system. With the older (that is, the ST-506/ESDI) systems, you would normally low-level format them. *YOU DO NOT LOW-LEVEL FORMAT IDE (or SCSI) DRIVES*. IDE drives are low-leveled at the factory and should never be redone. They use a special utility to perform this delicate procedure. Performing a low-level format on an IDE or SCSI drive will render your drive unreliable, at the least. (And will thus compound any problems you may have already been having.) At the worst, it will make the drive completely useless by overwriting sector translation information. Once you have the drive installed and recognized by the computer, low-leveling is not necessary.

Now that your drive is installed, you can then proceed to format it for the operating system you have chosen. Then, finally, you can install your operating system of choice.

And Now for the Real World...

IDE was such a popular hard disk interface that some people have adapted CD-ROM and tape devices to operate on IDE-type interfaces as well. Granted, it should be noted that an "IDE" CD-ROM may or may not coexist peacefully with an IDE hard disk. The former may reduce the performance of the latter. In some of the new Compaq computers, for example, they have included a second IDE bus for the CD-ROM (it is labeled specifically for that purpose).

Small Computer Systems Interface (SCSI)

The last type of disk subsystem is probably the most flexible and the most robust. Conversely, it's probably the most complex. In this section we'll discuss the theory behind the Small Computer Systems Interface (SCSI), the different types of SCSI, and configuration and installation issues.

As already mentioned, SCSI (pronounced "scuzzy") stands for Small Computer Systems Interface. It was a technology developed in the early 80s and standardized by the American National Standards Institute (ANSI) in 1986. The standard, which is known as ANSI document X3.131-1986, specifies a universal, parallel, system-level interface for connecting up to eight devices (including the controller) on a single, shared cable (called the *SCSI bus*). One of the many benefits of SCSI is that it is a very fast, flexible interface. You can buy a SCSI disk and install it in a Mac, a PC, a Sun workstation, or a Whizbang 2000, assuming they make a SCSI host adapter for it. SCSI systems are also known for their speed.

At its introduction, SCSI supported a throughput of 5 MB/sec (five to ten times faster than previous buses).

SCSI devices can be either internal or external to the computer. If they are internal, they use a 50-pin ribbon cable (similar to the 40-pin IDE drive cable). If the devices are external, they use a thick, shielded cable with Centronics-50 or male DB-25 connectors on it. These devices aren't always disk drives. Scanners and some printers also use SCSI because it has a *very* high data throughput.

SCSI works by assigning a unique device number (often called a SCSI "address") to each device on the SCSI bus (also sometimes call the SCSI "chain"). These numbers are configured either through jumpers or DIP switches. When the computer needs to send data to the device, it sends a signal on the wire "addressed" to that number. A device called a *terminator* (technically a *terminating resistor pack*) must be installed at both ends of the bus to keep the signals "on the bus." The device then responds with a signal that contains the device number that sent the information and the data itself.

This information is sent back to the *SCSI adapter*, which operates somewhat like a controller and somewhat like a paddle board. The adapter is used to manage all the devices on the bus as well as send and retrieve data from the devices.

The adapter doesn't have to do as much work as a true controller because the SCSI devices are "smart" devices; they contain a circuit board that can control the read/write movement. It can also receive signals like, "Get this information and give it to me." When a device receives a command like that, it is smart enough to interpret the signal and return the correct information.

Types of SCSI

The original implementation of SCSI was just called "SCSI" at its inception. However as new implementations came out, this was referred to as "SCSI-1." This implementation is characterized by its 5 MBps transfer rate, its Centronics-50 or DB-25 female connectors, and its 8-bit bus width. SCSI-1 also had some problems. Some devices wouldn't operate correctly on the same SCSI bus as other devices. The problem here was mainly that the ANSI SCSI standard was so new that each vendor might choose to implement it differently. These differences would be the primary source of conflicts.

After a time, the first major improvement to SCSI-1 was introduced. Known as SCSI-2 (ANSI Standard document X3.131-1994), it improved SCSI-1 by allowing for more options. These options produced several subsets of SCSI-2, each having its own name and characteristics. But the most obvious change from SCSI-1 is that SCSI-2 now used a higher-density connector (see Figure 4.16). Also, SCSI-2 is backward-compatible with SCSI-1 devices.

FIGURE 4.16:

A SCSI-2 connector

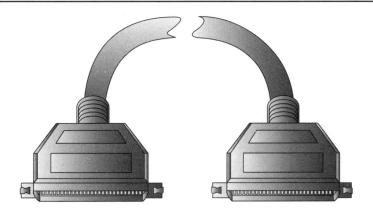

The first improvement that was designed into SCSI-2 was a wider bus. The new specification specified both 8-bit and 16-bit buses. The larger of the two specifications is known as Wide SCSI-2 because it's wider (Captain Obvious rides again). It improved data throughput for large data transfers. Another important change was to improve upon the now-limiting 5 MBps transfer rate. The Fast SCSI-2 specification allowed for a 10 MBps transfer rate, thus allowing transfers twice as fast as SCSI-1.

The final option was to combine both of these options into a blazingly fast technology known as SCSI-2 Fast-Wide. It combined the speed of Fast SCSI-2 with the bus width of Wide SCSI-2 to produce a transfer rate of 40 MBps!

Finally, there is a new SCSI standard currently being proposed to the ANSI. That proposed standard is SCSI-3. You may have already seen some devices claiming to be SCSI-3 devices. Technically, the SCSI-3 standard is not out yet, so the devices really couldn't be SCSI-3 devices. The truth is that the companies just incorporated *some* of the proposed feature subsets into their drives and adapters. One of the proposed feature sets is known as Fast-20 SCSI (also known to some as "Ultra SCSI"). Basically this is a faster version of Fast SCSI-2 operating at 20 MBps.

There are other proposed SCSI implementations, like Apple's FireWire, Fiber Channel, and IBM's SSA, all offering speeds in the hundreds of MBps range. It will be an interesting next few months.

SCSI Device Installation and Configuration

Installing SCSI devices is rather complex, but you still follow the same basic steps as mentioned with the other types of drives (refer back to the previous types of hard disk interfaces if you're still unclear). The main issues with installing SCSI devices are cabling, termination, and addressing.

We'll discuss termination and cabling together because they are very closely tied together. There are two types of cabling: internal and external.

- Internal cabling uses a 50-wire ribbon cable with several keyed connectors on them. These connectors are attached to the devices in the computer (the order is unimportant), with one connector connecting to the adapter.

- External cabling uses thick, shielded cables run from adapter to device to device in a fashion known as *daisy-chaining* (see Figure 4.17). Each device has two ports on it (most of the time). When hooking up external SCSI devices, you run a cable from the adapter to the first device. Then you run a cable from the first device to the second device. Then from the second to the third, and so on.

FIGURE 4.17:

A "daisy chain"

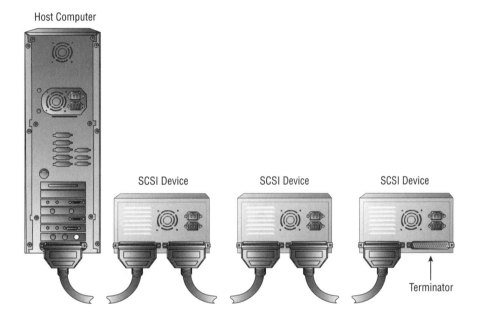

Because there are two types of cabling devices, you have three ways of connecting them. The methods differ by where the devices are located and whether or not the adapter has the terminator installed. The guide to remember here is that *both ends* of the bus must be terminated.

1. The first situation we'll discuss is where you have internal devices only (Figure 4.18). When you have only internal SCSI devices, you connect the cable to the adapter and to

every SCSI device in the computer. You then install the terminating resistors on the adapter and on the last drive in the chain only. All other terminating resistors are removed.

NOTE Some devices and adapters don't use terminating resistor packs, but instead use a jumper or DIP switch to activate or deactivate SCSI termination on that device. (Where do you find out what type your device uses? In the documentation, of course.)

FIGURE 4.18:

Cabling internal SCSI devices only

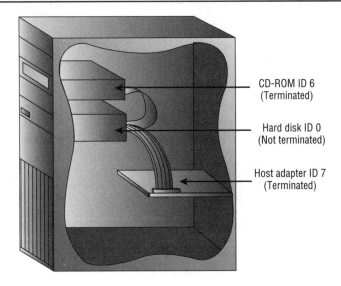

CD-ROM ID 6 (Terminated)

Hard disk ID 0 (Not terminated)

Host adapter ID 7 (Terminated)

2. The next situation is where you have external devices only (Figure 4.19). By external devices, I mean each with its own power supply. You connect the devices in the same manner as with internal devices, but in this method you use several very short (less than 0.5 meters) "stub" cables to run between the devices in a daisy-chain (rather than one, long cable with several connectors). The effect is the same. The adapter and the last device in the chain (the one with only one stub cable attached to it) must be terminated.

FIGURE 4.19:

Cabling external SCSI
devices only

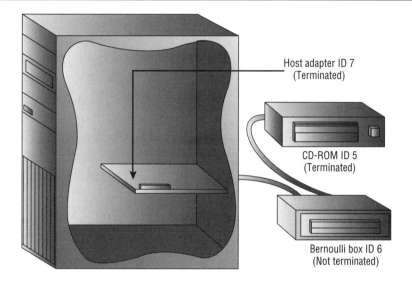

Host adapter ID 7
(Terminated)

CD-ROM ID 5
(Terminated)

Bernoulli box ID 6
(Not terminated)

3. Finally, there's the hybrid situation where you have both internal and external devices (Figure 4.20). Most adapters have connectors for both internal and external SCSI devices—if yours doesn't have both, you'll need to see if anybody makes one that will work with your devices. For adapters that do have both types of connectors, you connect your internal devices to the ribbon cable and attach the cable to the adapter. Then, you daisy-chain your external devices off the external port. Finally, you terminate the last device on each chain, leaving the adapter *unterminated.*

| NOTE | Even though the third technique described above is the technically correct way to install termination for the hybrid situation (where you have both internal and external devices), some adapter cards still need to have terminators installed (for instance, Adaptec AHA-1542's). If you set up both internal and external devices and none of them work, you might have one of these adapters. Try enabling termination on it to see if that fixes the problem. |

FIGURE 4.20:

Cabling internal and
external SCSI devices
together

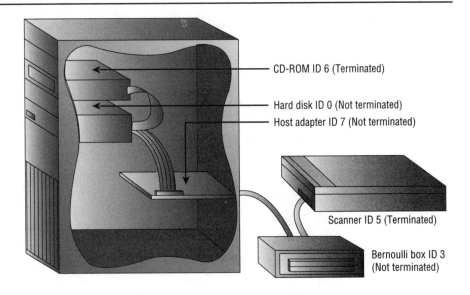

CD-ROM ID 6 (Terminated)

Hard disk ID 0 (Not terminated)
Host adapter ID 7 (Not terminated)

Scanner ID 5 (Terminated)

Bernoulli box ID 3
(Not terminated)

Now that you have them all correctly connected together, you
need to assign each device a unique SCSI ID number. This number can be assigned by jumper (with internal devices), or with a
rotary switch (on external devices). You start by assigning your
adapter an address. This number can be any number from 0 to 7
on an 8-bit bus, 0 to 15 on a 16-bit bus and 0 to 31 on a 32-bit bus,
as long as no other device is using that ID.

At our office, we have an 8-bit bus, so we normally set our
adapter to 7 if we're using regular PC SCSI. This is because on PC
SCSI, the higher the number, the higher the priority. If two devices
request the bus at the same time, the device with the higher priority wins. However, if we were running PS/2 SCSI, the opposite
would hold true (lower numbers, higher priority). So on PS/2s
we would set our adapter to 0.

Every other device can be set to any number as long as it's not in use. However, there are some recommendations that are commonly accepted by the PC community. Remember that these are guidelines, not rules.

- Generally speaking, give slower devices higher priority so they can access the bus whenever they need it.

- Set the bootable (or first) hard disk to ID 0.

- Set the CD-ROM to ID 3.

Now that we've got the devices cabled together and terminated correctly, you have to get the PC to recognize the SCSI adapter and its devices. The good news is that you don't have to modify the PC's CMOS settings. As a matter of fact, because SCSI devices are intelligent, you tell the PC that there is no disk installed and let the adapter handle the controlling of the devices. You have two other ways of getting the PC to recognize the SCSI devices.

- If the device is going to be bootable, then you must set the card to be "BIOS enabled," meaning that the card has its own BIOS extension that will allow the PC to recognize the device without a software driver. The downside to this method is that the adapter must be configured to use an area in reserved memory for its BIOS. However, in a machine with only SCSI devices, it's the most efficient method.

- The other method, in case you haven't guessed it, is to load a driver in the operating system for the adapter. This method only works if you are booting from some other, non-SCSI device. If you must boot from the SCSI drive, you must use the previous method. This method is commonly used when the only SCSI device attached to the computer is a scanner or CD-ROM drive.

NOTE Generally speaking, it's a bad idea to mix SCSI with any other disk technology. The only way you can make mixing work is to have the SCSI disks be secondary storage devices. It will degrade the performance of your system, however, since the boot files will be located on the first hard disk (the non-SCSI one). It will not work to have it the other way around (SCSI first, other disks second), because in that situation their BIOSes will conflict as to who is the "boss."

Now that you have the drive installed and talking to the computer, we're almost done. At this point you can high-level format the media and install the operating system.

WARNING Remember the note about low-level formatting IDE and SCSI drives—DON'T DO IT!

TIP If there are problems, double-check the termination and ID numbers. If everything looks correct, try changing ID numbers one at a time. SCSI addressing is one of those areas that is a "voodoo" art. Some things that should work don't, and some things that shouldn't work do.

Review Questions

1. When installing a second ST-506 drive to a cable without a twist in it, the drive select jumper should be set to _____.

   A. Drive 0

   B. Drive 1

   C. Drive 2

   D. Drive 3

2. What are the most most common sizes for floppy drives? (Circle all that apply.)

    A. $3^{1}/_{4}''$

    B. $3^{1}/_{2}''$

    C. $5^{1}/_{4}''$

    D. $5^{1}/_{2}''$

3. How many devices can SCSI-1 support (including the controller)?

    A. 8

    B. 7

    C. 1

    D. 9

4. Which kind of device is connected to the last connector on a Compaq Deskpro?

    A. Drive A:

    B. Drive B:

    C. Drive C:

    D. tape drive

5. The device that converts signals from an IDE drive into signals the CPU can understand is called a _____.

    A. controller

    B. host bus adapter

    C. bus

    D. paddle board

6. Which implementation of SCSI has a transfer rate of 20 MB/sec?

   A. Fast SCSI-2

   B. Fast-Wide SCSI-2

   C. SCSI-3

   D. Ultra SCSI

7. Suppose you have an internal SCSI hard drive and two external devices: a scanner and a CD-ROM drive. The scanner is the last device on the chain. Which device(s) should be terminated? (Circle all that apply.)

   A. hard disk

   B. scanner

   C. CD-ROM drive

   D. host bus adapter

8. The process known as _____ converts binary information into patterns of magnetic flux on a hard disk's surface.

   A. fluxing

   B. warping

   C. encoding

   D. decoding

9. What is the name for the areas that a typical hard disk is divided into like the wedges in a pie?

   A. tracks

   B. sectors

   C. clusters

   D. spindles

10. How do you low-level format an IDE drive?

   A. Enter the DEBUG.EXE program and enter g=c800:5 at the "–" prompt.

   B. Run LOWLEVEL.COM.

   C. Execute FORMAT.COM.

   D. You don't; it's done at the factory.

11. How do you low-level format an ST-506/ESDI drive?

   A. Enter the DEBUG.EXE program and enter g=c800:5 at the "–" prompt.

   B. Run LOWLEVEL.COM.

   C. Execute FORMAT.COM.

   D. You don't; it's done at the factory.

12. How do you low-level format a SCSI drive?

   A. Enter the DEBUG.EXE program and enter g=c800:5 at the "–" prompt.

   B. Run LOWLEVEL.COM.

   C. Execute FORMAT.COM.

   D. You don't; it's done at the factory.

13. Which of the following must be done when installing SCSI devices? (Circle all that apply.)

   A. Terminate the first and last devices in the chain.

   B. Set unique SCSI ID numbers.

   C. Connect the first device to the connector before the twist.

   D. Set every device on the same SCSI channel to the same SCSI ID number.

14. "Low-leveling" a disk drive means _____.

    A. Installing the drive in the bottom of the computer

    B. Getting a disk drive ready for the installation of an operating system

    C. Organizing the disk into sectors and tracks

    D. Organizing the disk into clusters and FATs

15. You have just replaced the floppy drive in a PC. Upon turning the computer on, you discover you can't boot to the floppy drive. The drive light turns on during power-up and stays lit until you turn the computer off. What should you do to solve this problem?

    A. Change the drive type in the CMOS setup.

    B. Reverse the floppy drive cable.

    C. Remove the terminating resistor on the floppy drive.

    D. Move the floppy drive to the end of the floppy cable.

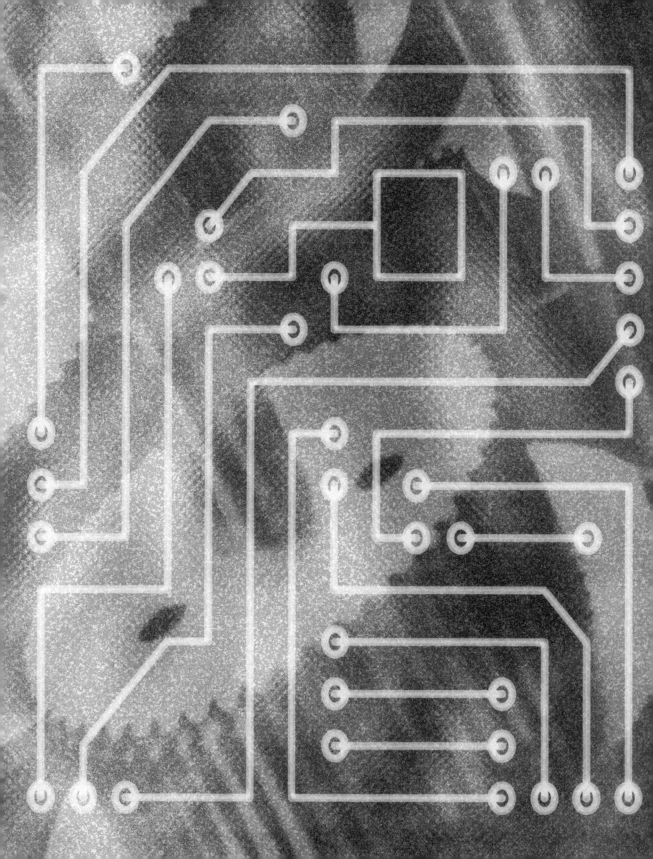

CHAPTER

FIVE

5

PC Bus Architectures

Objectives

- Identify basic terms, concepts, and functions of system modules, including how each module should work during normal operation.

- Identify the most popular type of motherboards, their components, and their architecture (e.g., bus structures and power supplies).

- Identify the unique components of portable systems and their unique problems.

So far, we have discussed many key components in the average PC. However, we haven't talked about the way information travels between these components. In this chapter we will cover the following A+ exam topics related to information flow:

- Expansion bus components

- The 8-bit expansion bus

- The Industry Standard Architecture (ISA) bus

- The Micro Channel Architecture (MCA) bus

- The Extended ISA (EISA) bus

- VESA Local Bus (VL-Bus)

- Peripheral Component Interconnect (PCI)

- PCMCIA

Additionally, we'll discuss the identification, installation, and configuration issues associated with each.

What Is a Bus?

Exactly what is a bus? A bus is a set of *signal pathways* that, as we have already alluded to, allows information and signals to travel between components inside or outside of a computer. There are three types of buses inside a computer: the *external bus*, the *address bus*, and the *data bus*.

The *external bus* allows the CPU to talk to the other devices in the computer and vice versa. It is called that because it's *external* to the CPU. When the CPU wants to talk to that device, it uses the *address bus* to do that. It will select the particular memory address that the device is using and write to that address using the address bus. When the device wants to send information back to the microprocessor, it uses the *data bus*.

In this chapter we are going to talk primarily about the most common type of external bus—the expansion bus.

Expansion Bus Features

The expansion bus allows the computer to be expanded using a modular approach. Whenever you need to add something to the computer, you plug specially made circuit boards into the connectors (also known as expansion "slots") on the expansion bus. The devices on these circuit boards are then able to communicate with the CPU and are semi-permanently part of the computer.

The Connector, or "Slot"

The connector slots are made up of several tiny copper "finger slots," the row of very narrow channels that grab the fingers on the expansion circuit boards. These finger slots connect to copper pathways on the motherboard. Each set of pathways has a specific function. One set of pathways provides the voltages needed to power the expansion card (+5, +12, and ground). Another set of pathways makes up the data bus, transmitting data back to the processor. A third set makes up the address bus, allowing the device to be addressed through a set of I/O addresses. Finally, there are other lines for different functions like interrupts, DMA channels, and clock signals.

Interrupt Lines

Interrupts are special lines directly to the processor that a device uses to get the attention of the CPU when it needs to. It's rather like the cord you use when you're a passenger on an actual bus, to signal the driver when you need to get off at the next stop. Just as you would use the "stop requested" cord to send a signal when you need the bus driver's attention, a computer device uses the *interrupt request* (*IRQ*) line to get the attention of the CPU.

There are several interrupt request lines in each type of bus. Lines 0 and 1 (corresponding to IRQ 0 and IRQ 1, respectively) are used by the processor for special purposes. The other lines are allocated to the various pieces of hardware installed in the computer. Not every line is used. In an average PC, there is usually at least one free IRQ line. When you configure a device for a computer, you must tell it which IRQ to use to get the attention of the processor. If two devices use the same IRQ line, the processor will get confused and neither device will work.

DMA Channels

Another feature of the bus is the ability to allow devices to bypass the processor and write their information directly into main memory. This feature is known as *Direct Memory Access* or *DMA*. Each type of bus has a different number of channels that can be used for DMA. If two devices are set to the same DMA channel, neither device will write information to memory correctly; thus neither device will work.

I/O Addresses

Each bus type has a set of lines used to allow the CPU to send instructions to the devices installed in the bus's slots. Each device is given its own unique communication line to the CPU. These lines are called *input/output* (*I/O*) *addresses* and function a lot like unidirectional mailboxes. If I want to send an invitation for people to come to a party, I write a message and address it to the mailbox of the person I want to invite. When the person receives the message, they read it and return some information, perhaps via some other method (like a phone call). The I/O addresses (also called *I/O ports* or *hardware ports*) work in a similar fashion. When the CPU wants a device to do something, it sends a signal to a particular I/O address telling the device what to do. The device then responds via the data bus or DMA channels.

Clock Signals

Finally, each computer has a built-in metronome-like signal called a *clock signal*. There are two types: the *CPU clock* and the *bus clock*. The former dictates how fast the CPU can run; the latter indicates how fast the bus can transmit information. (In the first PCs, the CPU clock was also the clock for the bus.) The speed of the clocks is measured in how fast they "tick," and is given in millions of cycles per second, or Megahertz (MHz). The bus or the CPU can only perform an operation on the occurrence of a tick signal. Think of the clock signal as a type of metronome that keeps the processor "in time."

Bus Mastering

With DMA channels, a device can write directly to memory. But what if a device needs to read or write directly to another device (like the hard disk)? For this purpose, bus designers came up with *bus mastering*. This is a feature that allows a device to distract the CPU for a moment, "take control" of the bus, and read from or write information to the device. This feature can greatly improve performance of the device. Some buses can use several bus mastering devices. The more bus mastering devices, the faster the bus can operate.

Now that we have discussed the basic expansion bus concepts, we will now use these concepts to describe each of the different types of buses.

The 8-Bit Expansion Bus

The first type of expansion bus we're going discuss is the 8-bit bus. It is also sometimes known as "You know, the first PC bus." When the first PC was developed with the Intel 8088, it only had eight data lines running from the processor to the expansion connectors. Each line carried one bit of data. Thus was born the *8-bit bus*. This was the most common name given to this particular bus. Some other names include the IBM PC bus, the XT bus, and the "slow bus." (Okay, that last one is a name *I* gave it, but it's true, don't you think?)

Information and Identification

The 8-bit bus is characterized by having a maximum bus clock speed of 4.77 (approximately 5) MHz, eight interrupts (of which six could be used by expansion devices), four DMA channels, and one large connector with 62 tiny "finger slots" (channels) along the sides. See Figure 5.1.

FIGURE 5.1:

The 8-bit bus connector

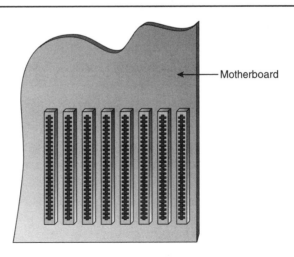

It is very rare to find an 8-bit bus in today's computer. If there are any, it's usually just one: an 8-bit slot for a single 8-bit expansion card (Figure 5.2). The expansion cards for this size bus are easily identifiable, as they have only one connector. Also, when these cards came out, VLSI had not taken off yet, so if you find an 8-bit card it will usually be packed with resistors and other large electronics components.

FIGURE 5.2:

An 8-bit bus expansion card

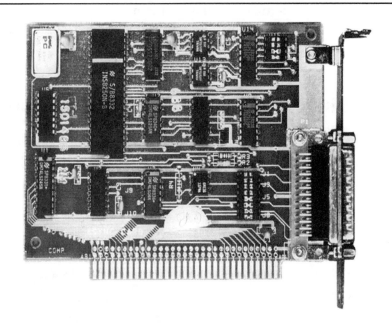

The 8-bit bus died out about the same time that the 8-bit processors fell by the wayside. It wasn't efficient to try to shoehorn 32 bits or more into a bus that can only accept 8 bits at a time. Even so, some manufacturers tried to accomplish just that, by placing a 386 chip on a motherboard with an 8-bit bus. What normally happened in that situation is that the computer divided the 32-bit signal into four 8-bit "chunks." It was a lot like trying to run lunchtime city freeway traffic down a side street. Every car could get through, just a lot more slowly. Also, since most processors run at quite a bit faster than 4.77 MHz, it was like putting the speed limit on that side street at 4.77 MPH instead of 55 MPH. Just a bit poky, don't you think?

Also, in the 8-bit bus, there were only eight interrupts and four DMA channels, most of which were being used. It made expansion of the 8-bit bus relatively difficult, as there were very few choices to set expansion cards to. Tables 5.1 and 5.2 show the default uses for the eight IRQ lines and four DMA channels.

TABLE 5.1: 8-Bit Bus Default IRQ Assignments

IRQ Line	Default Assignment
IRQ 0	System Timer
IRQ 1	Keyboard
IRQ 2	Available
IRQ 3	COM 2
IRQ 4	COM 1
IRQ 5	Hard Disk Controller
IRQ 6	Floppy Controller
IRQ 7	LPT1

TABLE 5.2: 8-Bit Bus Default DMA Channel Assignments

DMA Channel	Default Assignment
DMA 0	Dynamic RAM Refresh
DMA 1	Hard Disk Controller (XT)
DMA 2	Floppy Controller
DMA 3	Available

Bus Configuration

Configuring your devices involves assigning system resources (that is, DMA channels, IRQs, and I/O addresses) that aren't being used by other devices. Configuration of the 8-bit bus is relatively complex, primarily because there is only one IRQ (IRQ 2) and one DMA channel available (DMA 3). With so few system resources available, you have to decide which components will use each of the limited resources. One way to do it is to free up a resource by disabling a device that you won't be using at the same time as the device you need to work with.

Each card must be separately configured to operate with the computer, according to the instructions that come with the card. You set the configuration on each card using jumpers and DIP switches so that the settings are the way you want them. The first step in the procedure is to take the case off the computer. Then, you configure the card using the aforementioned jumpers. After that, you install the card in a free slot (assuming you have one). Finally, you boot the computer and install the software drivers to activate the card. If all was successful, the drivers will load without incident. If a conflict exists, you must repeat the entire procedure, changing one setting at a time until you get the correct setting: one that doesn't conflict with any other devices. A tedious process, to be sure.

We will cover expansion card installation in detail in Chapter 8.

The Industry Standard Architecture (ISA) Bus

The biggest shortcoming of the 8-bit bus was that it was only eight bits wide. The design of the IBM AT processor specified a processor with a 16-bit data path. A new bus was needed for this processor since the old bus would cause the "traffic jam" scenario described earlier. The new bus design was a 16-bit bus; it was given the same name as the computer it was designed for: the "AT bus." It was also known as the Industry Standard Architecture (ISA) bus.

Information and Identification

The ISA bus is easily identifiable by the presence of the small bus connector behind the 8-bit connector, as shown in Figure 5.3. This additional connector adds several signal lines to make the bus a full 16-bit bus. The other connector is a regular 8-bit bus connector. The ISA bus has eight more interrupts than the 8-bit bus and four additional DMA channels. Also, this bus can operate at nearly twice the speed of the older, 8-bit bus (ISA can run at 8 MHz, and "Turbo" models can run as fast as 10 MHz reliably). Finally, this bus can use one bus-mastering device, if necessary.

FIGURE 5.3:

An ISA bus connector

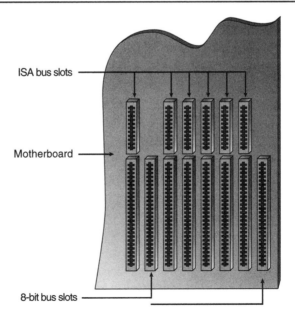

ISA bus slots

Motherboard

8-bit bus slots

ISA expansion cards use a connector similar to the 8-bit bus, but with the additional connector for the 16-bit data and address lines (Figure 5.4).

FIGURE 5.4:

An ISA bus expansion card

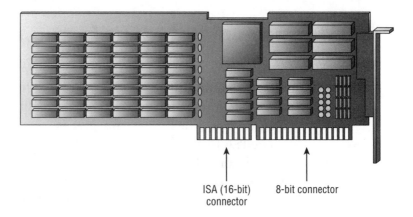

ISA (16-bit)   8-bit connector
connector

One interesting thing about the ISA bus is that it is backwards compatible with the older, 8-bit bus. ISA bus slots are basically 8-bit slots with the extra signal lines required to make them 16-bit on a second connector. Expansion cards made for the PC's 8-bit bus can be inserted into ISA slots and they will function properly. There is one exception, however. Some 8-bit cards have a "skirt" extending below the bus slot. This skirt will not allow the 8-bit card to be inserted all the way into the ISA slot. It is for this reason that you will sometimes have 8-bit slots mixed in with ISA slots on the same motherboards.

A major problem soon cropped up, however. When CPU speed outpaced the 8MHz bus speed (like the early Compaqs with their 12MHz 286 processor), the computer could not use the ISA bus, because that bus ran at 8 MHz and the processor ran faster. Putting a 12MHz processor in this type of system would limit it to only run at 8 MHz, thus negating any benefits received from a faster processor.

The solution was to dissociate the CPU clock from the bus clock. This would allow the 12MHz processor to run at its rated speed, and let the 8MHz ISA bus run at its rated speed. When information needed to get transferred to a component on the ISA bus, it would get transferred at the 8MHz clock speed. But all other operations inside the processor happen at 12 MHz.

This works well, with one exception. Some boards (like memory expansion boards) *need* to run at the processor's speed. If you put memory in an ISA board and place it in an ISA bus along with a 33MHz processor, information will get transferred from memory to the processor at 8 MHz instead of 33 MHz! This is a serious performance degradation. Granted, you don't find many ISA memory boards, but the potential is there. Take heart, though. This problem has been solved in a few of the other bus types (those buses that are considered to be "local" buses).

Bus Configuration

Configuring expansion cards for use in ISA buses is a little less complex than configuring 8-bit buses, mainly because there are more choices available for interrupts and DMA channels. Tables 5.4 and 5.5 detail which interrupts and DMA channels are available in an ISA system.

TABLE 5.4: ISA Bus IRQ Defaults

IRQ	Default Assignment
IRQ 0	System Timer
IRQ 1	Keyboard
IRQ 2	Cascade to IRQ 9
IRQ 3	COM 2 & 4

Continued on next page

TABLE 5.4 CONTINUED: ISA Bus IRQ Defaults

IRQ	Default Assignment
IRQ 4	COM 1 & 3
IRQ 5	LPT2 (usually available)
IRQ 6	Floppy Controller
IRQ 7	LPT1
IRQ 8	Real Time Clock (RTC)
IRQ 9	Cascade to IRQ 2
IRQ 10	Available
IRQ 11	Available
IRQ 12	Bus Mouse port (available if not used)
IRQ 13	Math Coprocessor
IRQ 14	Hard Disk Controller Board
IRQ 15	Available

TABLE 5.5: ISA Bus DMA Channel Defaults

DMA Channel	Default Assignment
DMA 0	Available
DMA 1	Available
DMA 2	Floppy Controller
DMA 3	Available
DMA 4	2nd DMA controller
DMA 5	Available
DMA 6	Available
DMA 7	Available

Note that COM1 and COM3 as well as COM2 and COM4 share the same interrupt. The pairs are differentiated by using different I/O addresses for the different COM ports. This can work without conflict. The only problem is if you connect two devices that need to use an interrupt to the COM ports that use the same interrupts (for example, a mouse on COM1 and a modem on COM3). When this happens, the devices will work separately, but if you try to use both at the same time (for example, use the mouse while downloading a file with the modem), they will conflict and problems will occur.

The same procedures that are used to configure the 8-bit expansion cards are used to configure ISA cards. You need to configure the card for interrupts, memory addresses, DMA channels, and I/O ports. Again, this is done using jumpers and DIP switches.

One special case exists for interrupts when configuring them. You will notice that some interrupts are "cascaded" to each other. What this means is that in an ISA system, when the computer needs to access an interrupt higher than 9, it uses IRQ 2 to get to them. This method insures backward compatibility with 8-bit buses.

As the ISA bus and its expansion cards evolved, people got tired of setting all those jumpers and DIP switches. As the saying goes, "Build a better mousetrap and the world will beat a path to your door." Well, someone found a better way to configure ISA devices. They found that if they put the jumper positions into an EEPROM chip on the device, they could set them using a special software configuration program. Because of this ease of setting up the cards, most ISA cards today use this method of configuring their settings.

NOTE There is a special case with regard to configuring ISA buses. This case is the ISA "Plug and Play" bus. This bus consists of a standard ISA bus and a special set of BIOS extensions. These extensions examine the installed "Plug and Play" compatible cards at startup and set them to available settings. At least, that's the theory. The reality is that the only real "Plug and Play" bus is a inside a Macintosh computer. The main reason this technology fails with PCs is that it's still reliant on the old technology for compatibility. It's a good idea in theory, but in practice works very poorly. It's actually gotten a nickname in the computer service industry—"Plug and Pray."

The Micro Channel Architecture (MCA) Bus

Even though IBM developed the original 8-bit bus, and had a hand in developing ISA, through the early part of the 1980s it steadily lost its domination of the PC market. But IBM had an ace up its sleeve. It was developing a new line of computers call the PS/2 (Personal System 2). Along with the new computer, they were developing a new bus that was supposed to be better in every way than ISA. Their higher-end models (PS/2's numbered more or less sequentially from 50 to 80) were going to incorporate this new bus. This bus used a smaller, high-density connector and was known as Micro-Channel Architecture (MCA).

Information and Identification

MCA was a major step forward in bus design. First of all, it was available in either 16-bit or 32-bit versions. Second, it could have multiple bus mastering devices installed. Third, the bus clock speed is slightly faster (10 MHz instead of 8 MHz). And finally, it offered the ability to change configurations with software rather than jumpers and DIP switches.

The MCA bus connector is a high-density connector that looks similar to an ISA bus connector. However, the MCA bus connector has almost twice as many connectors in a smaller area and is segmented to provide for 16-bit, 32-bit, and video extension segments.

There are two easy ways to identify an MCA bus card. The first is by the connector on the card (see Figure 5.5). It looks like no other bus connector. The connectors on the card are spaced very close together. The second is the labeling on the connector. Most MCA cards (more than 80%) are made by IBM. When you take an MCA card out of the package, you will notice that on the top of the card are two *blue* handles. It's likely the handles will display the IBM logo. Even if the cards were made by other vendors, the handles will still more than likely be blue.

FIGURE 5.5:

An MCA bus expansion card

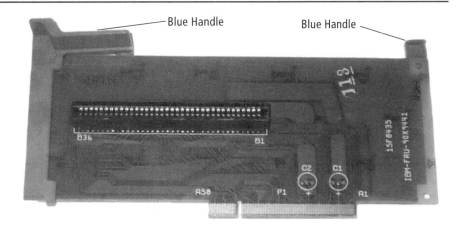

The MCA bus was a bold venture by IBM. They were hoping it would be *the* new standard for the PC bus. Unfortunately, it had a major drawback. It was *very* proprietary. Anyone who wanted to clone the MCA bus had to pay around five percent of their *gross*

receipts to IBM. While being one of the best technically, it was more expensive. And, it was incompatible with the established, ISA bus architecture. It was for these reasons that many system designers chose not to "hop on the MCA bandwagon," and implemented other bus choices instead.

Bus Configuration

As we have already mentioned, one of MCA's strengths is its ability to be configured by software. Installing an expansion card in an MCA slot still involves the same concepts as installing an ISA card. You must configure the card to use an available IRQ, DMA channel, memory address, and I/O ports. To configure the options on these cards you must use a *reference disk* and an *option diskette* after installing the device into the computer physically.

The reference disk is a special disk that is bootable and contains a program that is able to send special commands to bus devices to configure their parameters. This disk is included with the computer and is very special in that it only works with that model of MCA bus computer.

TIP   Don't lose the reference or option diskettes. You can't add new devices without it. Make a backup copy and use it to configure the system. Place the original in a safe place.

Every new MCA device you can install will come with an option diskette. An option diskette contains the device-specific configuration files for the device being installed. For example, if you are going to install a sound card, the option diskette will contain settings pertaining to how the sound card needs to communicate with the rest of the computer.

> **TIP**   Device-specific configuration files are also called ADF files, because their filenames have a .ADF extension.

Once you have a new device ready to be installed, you shut down the computer and install the board into the slot. Then, you boot the computer to the reference diskette. From the main menu, you select the option to configure the installed boards, then pick the slot number of the board you wish to configure. Since this is a new board, it will ask you to insert an option diskette with the configuration files on it. This is where you insert the option diskette that came with the card. The files particular to that device will be copied to the reference diskette so that the next time you need to change its settings, the files will be already on the reference diskette.

The Extended ISA (EISA) Bus

Since MCA was rather expensive and ISA was slowing down their systems, a few companies (mainly Olivetti, Compaq, AST, Tandy, WYSE, Hewlett-Packard, Zenith, NEC, and Epson, a.k.a. the "gang of nine") got together and came up with the Extended ISA or EISA. This bus took the best parts of the other buses and combined them into a 32-bit software-configurable bus. The best part was that 16-bit ISA cards were compatible with this new bus and the standard was open.

Information and Identification

There were several new, desirable features introduced with EISA. It took the best of MCA's features and added to them. As we have already mentioned, EISA has a 32-bit data path. Additionally, it had more I/O addresses, it allowed expansion cards to be set up using software, there was no need for interrupts or DMA channels, and it allowed for multiple bus-mastering devices. However, despite all these advances it still used the 8MHz clock speed of ISA (to ensure backward compatibility with ISA cards).

The bus slots (Figure 5.6) have both 16-bit and 32-bit finger slots. The 16-bit finger slots are staggered every other finger slot with the 32-bit finger slots. Also, the 16-bit finger slots are located toward the top of the connector and the 32-bit finger slots are buried deep within the connectors. The reason for all this staggering, burying, and arranging is that when you insert a 16-bit card, it will only go in halfway and make contact with the top (16-bit) connectors. But an EISA card (Figure 5.7), because of its longer fingers, will seat all the way into an EISA slot and make full contact with the deeper, 32-bit finger slots.

FIGURE 5.6:

An EISA bus connector

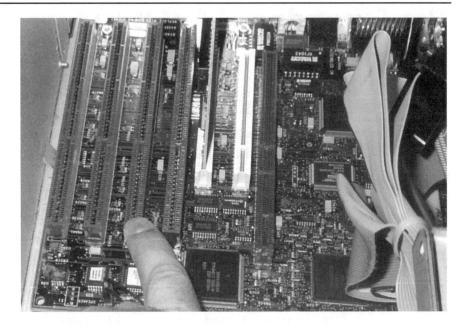

FIGURE 5.7:

An EISA bus
expansion card

Bus Configuration

Configuring an EISA bus is very similar to configuring an MCA bus, unless you install an ISA card into an EISA bus slot. If you do that, the configuration issues for ISA apply (including interrupts, DMAs, and so forth). If you are using only EISA cards, then the steps are quite different.

First of all, you must select a slot number to install the card into. Obviously, the slot must not have a card already installed in it. Second, you must install the card into one of the available slots. Third, you must boot the computer. When you do this, the computer will recognize that there is a new, unconfigured card in the bus slot (very much like a Plug-and-Play ISA bus without the auto-configuration). Then, you are given the choice to run the *EISA Configuration Utility* program (or *EISA Config* for short) or to continue and ignore the new information. If you choose the latter, the next time you boot, you will be asked again.

TIP   To access the EISA configuration program on a Compaq server, press <F10> when the flashing, white cursor appears in the upper right-hand corner of the screen at system startup. If the cursor doesn't appear, then the EISA configuration program was not installed onto the boot sector(s) of the first hard disk. Booting to the Compaq EISA Configuration Utility disk for the first time will assist you in this process.

If you choose to configure the bus, you must have the EISA Configuration Utility disk in the A: drive so that the computer can boot to it. During the boot process, it will detect which card has been installed and it will ask for a disk with the configuration files. These files are device-specific, have the extension .CFG, and can be downloaded from the particular vendors. Also, the .CFG files specific to the devices installed in that computer will be copied to the Configuration Utility disk so that that disk can be used to change the various parameters without having to have more than one disk.

Once booted, you will be running the EISA Config utility and can then pick which slot number the new card is using by selecting it from the menu. Once you are viewing this portion of the configuration screen, you can change any parameters you need to. After this has been done, you pick the option "Save the configuration information to the BIOS" and reboot the computer. The computer now knows about the card and what resources it's using.

The high-performance and ease-of-configuration benefits offered by EISA were taken advantage of mainly by Intel 80486 and newer processors. For quite some time, EISA buses were the primary expansion bus for servers; now however, they are quickly being replaced by the PCI bus (covered later in this chapter).

VESA Local Bus (VL-Bus)

The EISA bus had several major advantages, but it had one glaring problem: it had a maximum clock speed of 8 MHz. As processors got faster and faster, the 8 MHz limit was a major obstacle. What was needed was a bus that would run at the same clock speed as the processor. This type of bus is known as a "local" bus.

There are several different types of local buses. One type is a *bus slot*, usually called something like a "processor direct slot." It is used for adding higher-speed expansion cards, like memory or cache cards. And because it is a local bus slot, it runs at the processor's rated speed. It is usually a single connector, and it's very proprietary. Usually, only cards made by the computer's manufacturer will work in this slot.

Some companies took this idea and thought that they could speed up some components in the computer by putting them onto the local bus. In addition to the memory and cache cards, one of the first components to be put on the local bus was the video circuitry, since it could benefit from direct communication with the processor. Some manufacturers designed a special local-bus video card slot and designed special, high-performance cards for these slots. This approach became very popular and most companies adopted it. The problem with this approach is that the local-bus video card from one vendor would not work in a local bus slot from another vendor.

The Video Electronics Standards Association (VESA) was formed for this reason. This group made sure that cards made for one vendor's slot would work in another vendor's computer. As time passed, the slot design changed and was given a new name, the *VESA Local Bus slot* (and was also known variously as VL-Bus, VLB, or just VESA, after the group that came up with the standard).

This slot was a 32-bit addition to the ISA bus, and was therefore backward-compatible with it.

VLB has one major drawback in that it really is just a bigger ISA bus; namely, it still has the same limitations as ISA. Configuration is still done through jumpers and DIP switches, instead of special bus configuration programs. It's been called the "big ISA" bus, because that's what it is: just a 32-bit version of ISA.

Information and Identification

Identifying a VL-Bus slot is very easy, if you know what to look for. First of all, VESA designed this slot to be an extension of ISA. A VL-Bus slot is a regular ISA slot, with the 32-bit, local bus connector added to the ISA bus connector as a third bus connector (Figure 5.8). This connector was a high-density connector that had all of its lines running directly to the processor.

The VL-Bus expansion card is also easily identifiable. The card is a bit longer than an ISA card, and has one extra connector (the 32-bit, local connector). Figure 5.9 shows two typical VL-Bus expansion cards. These cards are typically used for video cards (as previously mentioned), SCSI host bus adapters, and multimedia expansion cards (sound cards, hard drive and CD-ROM controllers, and video input devices) because of the amount of throughput they need. Typically, you'll find no more than three VL-Bus connectors on a motherboard (mixed with other bus types). Any more than three, and the processor wouldn't be able to keep up with the bus transfers.

NOTE   Because of the three VL-Bus slot limitation, most vendors will mix VL-Bus slots and ISA slots (or EISA slots) on the motherboard. This approach gives the computer owner more choices for expansion.

FIGURE 5.8:

A VL-Bus connector

VL-Bus connectors

8-bit connectors   ISA (8-bit plus 16-bit) connectors   VESA (8-bit plus 16-bit plus local bus) connectors

Bus Configuration

There is very little new information we need to discuss about the configuration of VL-Bus devices. Primarily, they are ISA bus devices with an extra connector. When you configure a VLB card, you perform similar operations to ISA cards (moving jumpers, setting DIP switches, and so on). However, since the VL-Bus is a more modern bus, some of these cards are Plug-and-Play or, at the very least, software configurable.

FIGURE 5.9:

VL-Bus expansion cards. Top: A video card. Bottom: An IDE hard-drive controller.

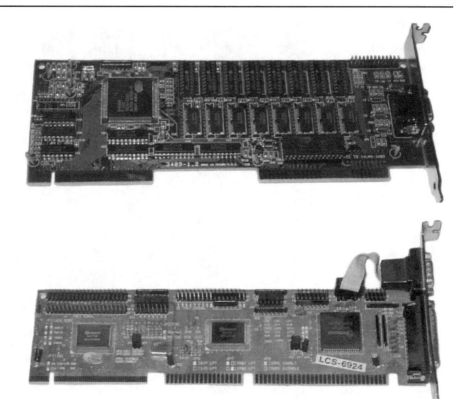

Peripheral Component Interconnect (PCI)

With the introduction of the Pentium-generation processors, all existing buses instantly became obsolete. Since the Pentiums were 64-bit processors and most buses were of the 16-bit or 32-bit variety, using existing buses would severely limit the performance of the new technology. It was primarily for this reason that the Peripheral Component Interconnect (PCI) bus was developed.

PCI has many benefits over other bus types. First of all, it supports both 64-bit and 32-bit data paths, so it can be used in both 486 and Pentium based systems. In addition, it is processor-independent. The bus communicates with a special "bridge circuit" that communicates with both the CPU and the bus. This has the benefit of making the bus an almost universal one. PCI buses can be found in PCs, Mac OS-based computers, and RISC computers. The same expansion card will work for all of them, you just need a different configuration program for each.

Another advantage to PCI over other buses is a higher clock speed. PCI (in its current revision) can run up to 33 MHz. Also, the bus can support multiple bus-mastering expansion cards. These two features give PCI a maximum bus throughput of up to 265 Mbps (with 64-bit cards).

The final two features of PCI that we should discuss are its backward-compatibility and software setup features. First of all, the PCI bus uses a chipset that works with PCI, ISA, and EISA. It is possible to have a PC that contains all these buses on the same motherboard. Also, the PCI cards are mostly Plug-and-Play. The cards will automatically configure themselves for IRQ, DMA, and I/O port addresses.

NOTE   In some systems today that are combination PCI and ISA, each PCI slot will be located right next to an ISA slot. When you put a card in that PCI slot, you disable the ISA slot and vice versa. Only one card will fit in a combination slot at a time.

Information and Identification

Identification of PCI bus slots is very simple. The finger slots in the bus (Figure 5.10) are very tightly packed together. This connector is usually white and contains two sections. There are two versions of the PCI bus that are found in today's system. The versions are differentiated by the voltages that they use. One uses +5.5 Vdc to power the expansion cards, the other uses +3.3 Vdc. When you look at the connectors for these buses, the only difference you'll see is the different placement of the *blocker* (called a "key") in each connector, so that a +3.3Vdc card can't be plugged into a +5.5Vdc bus slot and vice-versa.

FIGURE 5.10:

PCI bus connectors

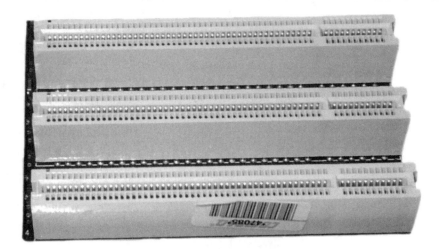

Bus Configuration

When you need to configure a PCI expansion card, you don't move jumpers or DIP switches, you run a configuration program (similar to MCA and EISA). When you install a new PCI card (see Figure 5.11) and reboot the computer, it will detect what device has been installed and present you with a list of options to configure (like IRQ, I/O, and DMA). You can then set these options from here rather than moving jumpers or DIP switches. After that, you reboot again and install the appropriate software so that the computer can use the device.

FIGURE 5.11:

A PCI expansion card

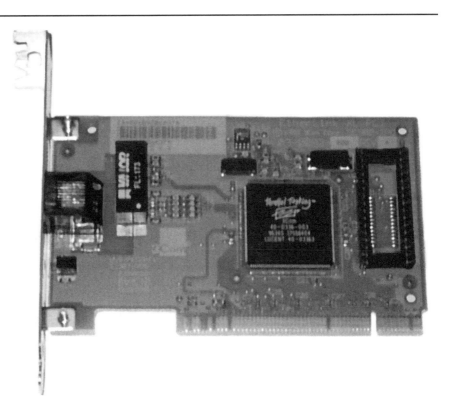

PCMCIA—What Does It Stand For?

The tongue-twister *PCMCIA* stands for Personal Computer Memory Card International Association. The bus was originally designed as a way of expanding the memory in a small, handheld computer. The PCMCIA was organized to provide a standard way of expanding portable computers. The PCMCIA bus has been recently renamed to *PC card* to make it easier to pronounce. The PC card bus uses a small expansion card (about the size of a credit card). While it is primarily used in portable computers, there are PC card bus adapters for desktop PCs. It was designed to be a universal expansion bus that could accommodate any device.

The first release of the PCMCIA standard (PCMCIA 1.0, the same used in that original handheld computer) only defined the bus to be used for memory expansion. The second release (PCMCIA 2.0) is the most common; it is in use throughout the computer industry and has remained relatively unchanged. PCMCIA 2.0 was designed to be backward-compatible with version 1.0, so memory cards can be used in the 2.0 specification.

Information and Identification

At the time of the writing of this book, PCMCIA's bus width is only 16 bits, but a 32-bit version is on the way. Also, PC cards support only one IRQ (a problem if you need to install two devices in a PC card bus that both need interrupts). PC cards also do not support bus mastering or DMA. However, because of its flexibility, PCMCIA has quickly become a very popular bus for all types of computers (not just laptops).

There are three major types of PC cards (and slots) in use today. Each has different uses and physical characteristics (see Figure 5.12). Coincidentally, they are called Type I, Type II, and Type III:

- Type I cards are 3.3mm thick and are most commonly used for memory cards.

- Type II cards are 5mm thick and are mostly used for modems and LAN adapters. This is the most common PC card type found today, and most systems have at least two Type II slots (or one Type III slot).

- The Type III slot is 10.5mm thick. Its most common application is for the PC card hard disks. Developers have been slowly introducing these devices to the market.

FIGURE 5.12:

PC card types by thickness

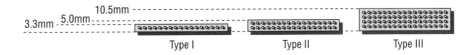

In addition to the card, there are two other components in the PC card architecture. The first one is the Socket Services software. This software is a BIOS-level interface to the PCMCIA bus slot. When loaded, it hides the details of the PC card hardware from the computer. This software can detect when a card has been inserted and what type of card it is.

The second component is the Card Services software. This software is the interface between the application and Socket Services. This is the software that tells the applications which interrupts and I/O ports the card is using. Applications that need to access the PC card don't access the hardware directly. Instead, they tell Card Services they need access to a particular feature and Card Services gets the appropriate feature from the PC card.

This dual-component architecture allows the PCMCIA architecture to be used in different types of computer systems (that is, not just Intel's). For example, the Apple laptop computers currently use PC cards for modems and LAN interface cards, and they are based on Motorola processors.

Bus Configuration

The process for installing a PC card is different than that for any of the other bus types, mainly because this type was designed to allow the cards to be "hot swapped"—inserted or removed while the computer is powered up. This is the only bus that allows this. However, see the following warning about taking advantage of this feature.

WARNING Even though you can remove a PC card while the power is on, YOU SHOULDN'T! If you remove a PCMCIA card while the system is up, realize that some software may not like having its hardware ripped out from underneath it. That software will then have no hardware to talk to and it may crash the system. (As for other expansion cards, NEVER remove them without shutting off the power to the computer first! If the power is on, you will certainly damage the card, the computer, or both.)

Installing a PC card is very straightforward. Just slip the card into an available slot, making sure the card type matches the slot type. Once the card is installed, you must install the software to use the card (Windows 95 will do this automatically).

You have a few items to note when installing and configuring PC cards. First of all, you must have the Card and Socket Services software installed before you try to physically install the card, so that the computer can manage the card's resources. Second, you may have a PC card bus that supports two Type II cards or one Type III. If you do have one of these buses, you can only have one or the other situation. If you have a Type II card installed, you can't install a Type III card without removing the existing Type II. Finally, PC cards are too small to have jumpers or DIP switches, so the hardware must be configured through a software configuration program.

And Now for the Real World...

Sometimes, there is not enough memory to load all the files for Card and Socket Services. In the DOS world, the software for Card and Socket Services loads in conventional memory (or in UMBs if you so choose). With many such DOS drivers being loaded, you many run out of conventional memory and not be able to run some DOS programs.

Continued on next page

To solve this, PC card manufacturers have come up with a piece of software called a PC Card "shim" that allows the card to be used like any other expansion card. In addition, it takes up less conventional memory. The only downside is that the shim might not be completely compatible with the system. Windows 95 incorporates this software as virtual device drivers, or VXDs.

A Summary of Bus Types

To round out this chapter (and to make it easier to jog your memory when you're reviewing for the exam), we've summarized some of the important points concerning bus types and their specifications (see Table 5.6).

TABLE 5.6: Summary of Bus Types

Bus Type	Bus Width (bits)	Maximum Speed (MHz)	Uses Bus Mastering?	Configuration
8-bit	8	4.77	N	Jumpers/DIP Switches
ISA	16	8 (10 for Turbo)	N	Jumpers/DIP Switches (Some cards are software configurable)
MCA	16 or 32	10	Y	Software—"Reference Disk"
EISA	32	8	Y	Software—"EISA Configuration Disk"
VL-Bus	32	Processor Speed	Y	Same as ISA
PCI	64	Processor Speed	Y	Software—"Plug-N-Play"
PC Card	16	33	N	Software—"PC Card & Socket Services"

Review Questions

1. PCMCIA expansion cards need the following software in order to operate (circle all that apply):

   A. Cardmember Services

   B. PC Card Services

   C. Modem Services

   D. Socket Services

2. ISA is an acronym for _____.

   A. InSide Architecture

   B. Industry Standard Architecture

   C. Industry Simple Architecture

   D. Internal Systems Architecture

3. EISA has a bus width of _____ bits.

   A. 32

   B. 16

   C. 64

   D. 8

4. PCI has a bus width of _____ bits.

   A. 32

   B. 16

   C. 64

   D. 8

5. ISA has a bus width of _____ bits.

    A. 32

    B. 16

    C. 64

    D. 8

6. MCA has a bus width of _____ bits. (Circle all that apply.)

    A. 32

    B. 16

    C. 64

    D. 8

7. Which of the following buses *require* a software configuration program to configure their settings? (Circle all that apply.)

    A. 8-bit bus

    B. ISA

    C. EISA

    D. MCA

    E. PCI

    F. PCMCIA

8. Which of the following buses *require* the use of jumpers and DIP switches to configure their settings? (Circle all that apply.)

    A. 8-bit bus

    B. ISA

    C. EISA

    D. MCA

    E. PCI

    F. PCMCIA

9. Which bus signal line allows a device to request the processor's attention?

   A. I/O address lines

   B. DMA address lines

   C. Clock address lines

   D. Interrupt Request (IRQ) address lines

10. Which bus signal line allows a device to send data directly to a computer's memory, bypassing the CPU?

    A. I/O addresses

    B. DMA address

    C. Clock addresses

    D. Interrupt Request (IRQ) addresses

11. Which bus signal line allows the CPU to send requests to the device to send data?

    A. I/O addresses

    B. DMA address

    C. Clock addresses

    D. Interrupt Request (IRQ) addresses

12. What is the maximum clock speed that an ISA Turbo bus can run reliably?

    A. 8 MHz

    B. 10 MHz

    C. 16 MHz

    D. 33 MHz

13. How many DMA channels are available in an 8-bit system?

    A. 1

    B. 4

    C. 8

    D. 16

14. You have just installed a sound card in a PC and it is not functioning correctly. (It produces no sound and it hangs the computer when it tries.) After checking the settings, you find that it is set to IRQ 7, DMA 1, I/O port 300. You suspect an IRQ conflict exists, so you check the other devices in the system. The system is using an ISA bus. Which device is it conflicting with? (Assume the computer is using default settings for all devices.)

    A. A network card

    B. COM1

    C. LPT1

    D. COM2

15. If you change the sound card in question #14 from IRQ 7 to IRQ 10, will a conflict still exist?

    A. Yes

    B. No

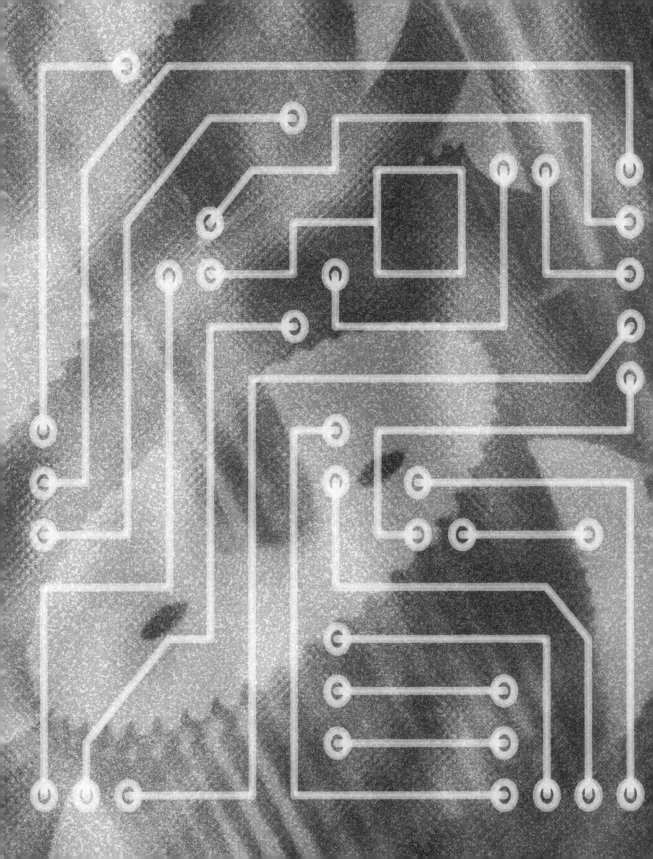

CHAPTER

SIX

6

Peripheral Devices

Objectives

- Identify proper procedures for installing and configuring peripheral devices.

- Identify basic concepts, printer operations, printer components, and field replaceable units in primary printer types.

Up to this point, we have discussed the main components of the average PC, how they work, and their service issues. But there are many kinds of components that are not directly a part of the PC. They are on the outside, or the periphery, of the computer's operations. For this reason they fall into the category of devices known as *peripherals*. In this chapter we will discuss the following topics:

- Input devices

- Output devices

- Computer display devices

- Other peripherals

In addition to discussing these devices, we will also discuss how to properly clean some of them.

TIP   Since printers are such complex peripherals (they're also the reason for the largest percentage of service calls), they are covered pretty extensively on the A+ exam. For the same reasons, we'll skip the details concerning printers in this overall peripherals chapter and instead devote an entire chapter to printers later in the book (Chapter 8). The topic of troubleshooting printer problems also comes in for detailed coverage in the chapter on Troubleshooting (Chapter 12).

Input Devices

Let's start this chapter off by talking about some of the most commonly used peripheral devices, those being input devices. As their name suggests, input devices exist so that human beings can communicate with the object we call a computer. These devices interpret the intentions of their users (via a keystroke or some other movement) to tell the computer to perform some action. Without them, the computer would be of little use to us.

Keyboards

Let's begin our discussion of input devices with the most common PC input device: the keyboard (Figure 6.1). This type of device translates keystrokes into letters or numbers. These letters are then interpreted and commands are performed, depending on what was being sent. With today's PCs, it is the most important input device. There are two major types of keyboards, mechanical keyswitch and capacitive.

Mechanical Keyswitch Keyboards

The first type of keyboard technology is the keyswitch type (Figure 6.2). This type works by using an individual switch for each key. When you press a key, a plunger under the key cap moves down and makes a connection between two signal lines coming from the keyboard controller in the keyboard. When the connection is made, the keyboard controller sends a signal to the computer, saying "Someone just typed an 'A'." When a key is released, a spring pushes the plunger back to its original position. On a typical keyswitch keyboard, there may be more than 100 individual keyswitches.

FIGURE 6.2:

How a keyswitch keyboard works

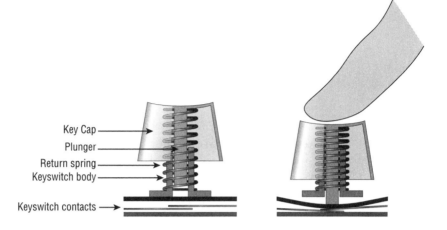

Key Cap
Plunger
Return spring
Keyswitch body

Keyswitch contacts →

There are a few benefits to this type of keyboard. First of all, they are simple to make. Thus, they are inexpensive. Also, they are simple to service. When a key goes bad, a technician can de-solder the broken keyswitch and solder in a new one.

Originally there were a few problems with this type of keyboard. The first keyboards had really "bouncy" springs. Sometimes, when a key was pressed and released quickly, the key would bounce, causing duplicate letters to appear on the screen. The first attempt at solving this problem was a mechanical one. The designers first tried to lessen the tension on the spring. That didn't work because the lessened tension increased the finger fatigue of the person typing.

Their second attempt worked better. They used an electronic technique that we call *debouncing*. It worked by having the keyboard controller constantly scan the keyboard for keystrokes. The controller registered only those keystrokes that were pressed for more than two scans, and it ignored all others (like those coming from a "bouncing" key). This technique worked and has been included in most keyboard controllers since then.

Capacitive Keyboards

The problem with keyswitch-based keyboards is that they are rather bulky. The mechanical keyswitches take up too much room to be used in laptops. Also, they require a certain minimum amount of power to operate, as each switch requires a certain amount of voltage.

The solution to these problems was to take the switch out of the key. One keyboard design placed two sheets of semi-conductive material separated by a thin sheet of Mylar inside the keyboard. This is one type of capacitive keyboard. When a key is pressed, the plunger presses down and a paddle connected to the plunger presses the two sheets of semi-conductive material together, changing the total capacitance of the two sheets. The controller can tell by the value returned which key was pressed. The controller then sends the results (called *scan codes*) to the computer, telling it what key to display.

This keyboard has the advantages of being less complex, more durable, and even cheaper than mechanical keyswitch keyboards. One disadvantage of these keyboards—although in some ways it is also an advantage—is that you can't repair them. This can be an advantage insofar as the price for a new one (less than $40 at the time of the writing of this book) is less than the labor to repair it (around $50).

Keyboard Connectors

Keyboards have to be connected to the computer somehow. They are connected through some type of connector (Captain Obvious strikes again). This connector carries the signals from the keyboard controller to the CPU. There are two major types, identified by the type of connector they use.

- DIN-5 connector (Figure 6.3). This is also called the standard, IBM PC, or XT/AT keyboard connector.

- Mini DIN-6 connector (Figure 6.4). This one is also called the PS/2 style connector since it was first used on the IBM PS/2. This style of keyboard connector has one main advantage: it's smaller.

FIGURE 6.3:

An IBM PC keyboard plug and connector

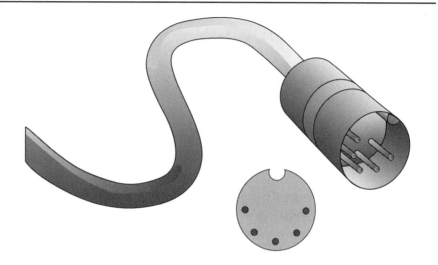

FIGURE 6.4:

A PS/2-style keyboard plug and connector

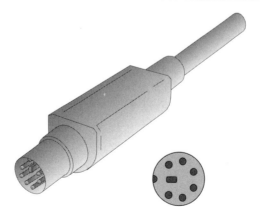

Cleaning Keyboards

I personally think everyone who drinks pop and eats potato chips near computers should have to clean a keyboard used by such a person. When the soda dries, it leaves the syrup behind, which is *almost* impossible to remove from the keyboard without disassembling the keyboard. Potato chip crumbs love to stick to this syrup and complicate matters.

The easiest way to clean a keyboard is to remove the keyboard from the computer and soak it with distilled, demineralized water as soon as the spill occurs. If the spill is allowed to dry, the contaminants will be much harder to remove and may require disassembly of the keyboard. Some people have even run their keyboards through the dishwasher (with soap and a heat-dry cycle) to clean them! This approach works when the local water supply doesn't contain very many contaminants. An easy way to tell if your water contains the type of contaminants that may be harmful to your keyboard is to look to see if water drips stain your sink; if so, your local water contains minerals or other other contaminants and the dishwasher will probably do more harm than good. In any case, make sure the keyboard is *completely* dry before using it.

The other way to clean your keyboard is to disassemble it completely and use special keyboard cleaners (available in most electronic supply stores) to clean the components. This approach works well when the keyboard is extremely dirty.

The only drawback to cleaning a keyboard is that, in terms of the time that you as a professional service technician would have to spend doing it, it usually costs more than a keyboard is worth. It's usually cheaper to replace a keyboard than to clean it.

Mice

For several years, operating systems were character-based. They displayed information on the screen in text format and people interacted with them using command words. Then, a couple of people at The Xerox Palo Alto Research Center (PARC), intrigued with the idea that computers should be "friendly" and easy to use, started working with a *Graphical User Interface*, or *GUI*, which used pictures to represent computer entities (like files, disks and so on). To interact with the pictures, a special device was introduced into the computer world. This device was the *mouse*. This device translates movements on a horizontal surface into movements of a pointer on the screen. There are two methods of making these translations: opto-mechanical and optical.

Mouse Types

The first type of mouse we'll discuss is the opto-mechanical type. This type of mouse contains a round ball that makes contact with two rollers—one for the X axis (the horizontal) and one for the Y axis (the vertical). Moving the mouse causes the ball to roll, and since the ball is in contact with the two rollers, causes them to turn. These rollers are connected to wheels with small holes in them (Figure 6.5). Each wheel rotates between the arms of a U-shaped optical sensor. The holes allow a light to shine through the wheel onto the optical sensor in flashes as the wheel turns. By the speed and patterns of the light pulses, the mouse can sense the speed and direction the mouse is moving and sends its interpretation of those movements to the computer and the mouse control software.

An optical mouse looks the same as any other computer mouse, except there is no mouse "ball." Instead, the optical mouse uses a special mouse pad and a beam of laser light (Figure 6.6). The beam of light shines onto the mouse pad and reflects back to a sensor in the mouse. The mouse pad has small lines crossing it that can reflect the light into the sensor in different ways. It is in this fashion that the optical mouse detects direction and speed of movements. This mouse *will not work* without the special mouse pad.

Now that we have discussed the different ways that mouse devices work, let's discuss the different ways of hooking them to a computer.

FIGURE 6.5:

An opto-mechanical mouse mechanism

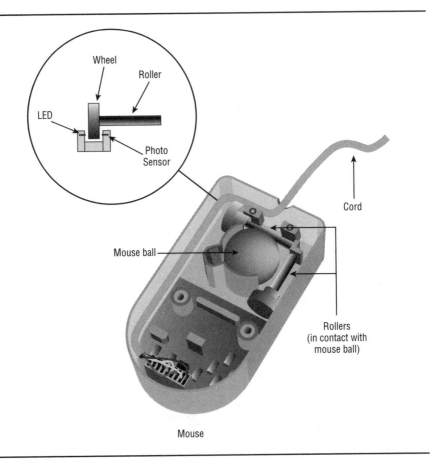

Mouse

FIGURE 6.6:

An optical mouse mechanism

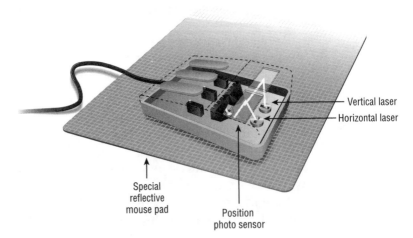

Mouse Interfaces

Just as there are many types of mice, there are several different ways of connecting them to a PC. There are three major types of mouse interfaces: serial, bus, and PS/2. Each one has its own installation and configuration issues. Let's discuss them, in order.

Serial Mouse Interface   The serial mouse was the first major type of mouse interface, mainly because it made the most sense: mice send position information in a stream of coordinates, and the interface that handles small, continuous streams of data best is the serial interface. All computers come with at least one serial port that the mouse could use with its female DB-9 connector. If the serial port was of the 25-pin variety, the user could plug the mouse's DB-9 connector into the adapter that was usually included with the mouse (Figure 6.7) to allow it to work. Also, installing the mouse was as simple as connecting the mouse to an available serial port and installing the mouse driver software. For these reasons, the serial mouse became very popular.

FIGURE 6.7:

A serial mouse DB-9–to–25-pin adapter

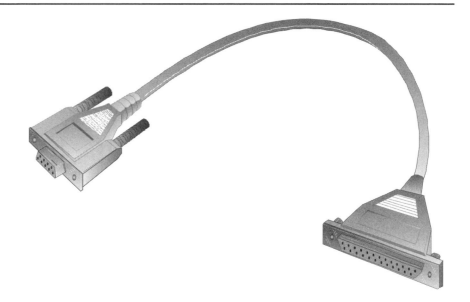

One disadvantage to the serial mouse is that it uses a COM port. If the computer had only one COM port, that was it—you couldn't use any other peripheral devices. Also, if you had another COM port but it was on a shared interrupt (see Chapter 5), that other COM port couldn't be used for another communication device (like a modem) as long as data was coming into the computer on the COM port being used by the mouse. So, in a manner of speaking, a serial mouse really takes up two COM ports. For example, since COM1 and COM3 both share Interrupt 4, when you put a mouse on COM1 you are also preventing the use of COM3.

Bus Mouse Interface   To some people, the serial interface was too bulky and cumbersome. For those people, a special mouse connector was developed: the small, round DIN-6 connector. This connector attached to a special, 8-bit interface card that was installed directly into the computer's bus. Thus, the signals traveled on a more direct path to the CPU. This type of mouse was called a *bus mouse* for these reasons (and since it was developed by Microsoft, primarily, it's also called the *MS bus mouse*). See Figure 6.8 for an example of a bus mouse connector.

FIGURE 6.8:

A bus mouse DIN-6 plug and connector

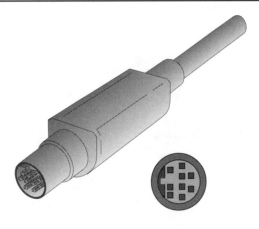

Although the bus mouse is a faster interface, speed isn't really an issue. The mouse signals didn't really overload the interface. The major advantage to a bus mouse, compared to a serial mouse, is that *it doesn't take up a COM port*. This allowed systems that were short on COM ports to add a mouse. The one downside was that the bus card does use an interrupt. (And, it can only use IRQ 2, 3, 4, or 5.)

Installing a bus mouse involved three steps. First, you installed the bus card to one of the possible IRQ choices. You might have to change the IRQs on a few devices to free up one of the possible choices for the bus mouse. Once that was accomplished, you could connect the mouse to the bus mouse port. Finally, you installed the driver software for the operating system you were using.

PS/2 Mouse Interface   The bus mouse is still around; however, it has evolved to be included on the motherboard of some of today's computers. This interface uses the same connector as the bus mouse, but, as already mentioned, it is not on a card, but rather is hard-wired to the motherboard. This interface was introduced with the IBM PS/2 series of computers, and was henceforth called the *PS/2 mouse interface* (see Figure 6.9). It's essentially the same mouse as the bus mouse, except that the bus mouse uses a special expansion card, whereas the PS/2 mouse port is integrated into the motherboard.

FIGURE 6.9:

A PS/2 mouse plug and connector

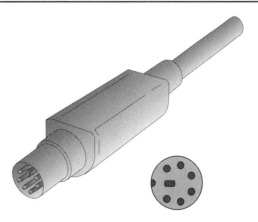

Installation of a PS/2 mouse is very easy. Just connect the mouse to the PS/2 mouse port. The interrupt has most likely been hardwired to IRQ 12 (check your documentation to be sure). Then you can install the mouse software and use the mouse.

Cleaning a Mouse

The largest problem with mechanical mice is that they contain moving parts. These moving parts don't like dirt and dust. The mouse is designed to move on a flat surface. Most often, the mouse ball picks up any dirt and dust and deposits it on the mouse rollers. When this dirt and dust combines with the oil from your skin, it forms a substance that sticks to the mouse rollers and forms a ring around the roller.

This ring around the roller causes the mouse to rattle as it moves across the mouse pad (mainly because the ring isn't completely even). If the ring builds up too far, it may actually wedge between the mouse ball and the roller and prevent the roller from rotating. If you've ever moved a mouse and the mouse pointer appeared to have hit an invisible "wall" in the middle of the screen (that is, the pointer won't move any farther in that direction no matter how much you move the mouse), your mouse more than likely has "ring around the roller."

There's nothing you can do to prevent this condition. It is possible, however to cure the symptoms. First, turn the mouse upside down and remove the mouse ball by rotating the retaining ring counterclockwise. Flip the mouse right side up and the mouse ball will drop out. Flip the mouse back over and locate the two rollers. The "ring around the roller" will be obvious. To clean the "gunk" from the rollers, I use a small eyeglass screwdriver. If the gunk won't come loose, I soak the deposits with a little isopropyl alcohol to loosen them. After cleaning the rollers, the mouse will perform better and the "phantom wall" will be gone.

Other Pointing Devices

Mice are the most popular pointing devices, but they are not the only type of pointing device in common use. Why is that? The answer I'll give is in the form of a question: Have you ever tried to draw a circle with a mouse? It's downright difficult. Also, mice are too bulky to be easily used on portable computers. These are some of the reasons why other pointing devices were designed.

Trackballs

A trackball is basically an opto-mechanical mouse turned upside down. Instead of moving the mouse on a table, we move the mouse ball (or, properly, the *trackball*), which otherwise remains stationary. The only other differences are that the trackball uses a bigger ball and the buttons are usually on the sides. Some manufacturers offer small, portable, clip-on versions of the trackball, which you can hold in your hand or clip onto the side of your laptop computer. Both are shown in Figure 6.10.

FIGURE 6.10:

Two kinds of trackballs: a typical desktop trackball and a portable trackball

Trackballs can be connected to a computer in the same ways as a mouse. More and more commonly, though, you'll see a trackball already installed into a laptop computer, right where your thumbs would hover (just below the spacebar). They fit well and the entire assembly doesn't have to move, just the trackball.

Since trackballs operate similarly to mice, they can be cleaned similarly. The trackball can be removed and rollers cleaned in exactly the same manner.

And Now for the Real World...

There is one laptop that does include a portable *mouse* built right into the body of the laptop. The Hewlett-Packard Omnibook has a small mouse that pops out of the side and can be used as a regular mouse. It's a nice compromise, and it really does work well.

Drawing Tablets

Another type of pointing device that is used with computers is the drawing tablet. These devices help solve the mouse-circle-drawing problem. To outward appearances, the tablet is just a flat piece of plastic covered with a rubberized coating. You use a pen-shaped tool called a *stylus* to "draw" on the surface. (Sometimes a mouse-shaped device known as a *puck* might be used.) As you can guess, if you do much typing at all, the drawing tablet is not really efficient as a pointing device, because you have to keep picking up the stylus to use it. But it is really efficient as a drawing tool. Graphic designers and Computer Aided Design (CAD) professionals use them to make their work easier, since they do quite a lot of drawing. Figure 6.11 shows a couple of typical drawing tablets.

FIGURE 6.11:

Drawing tablets: one with a stylus, one with a puck

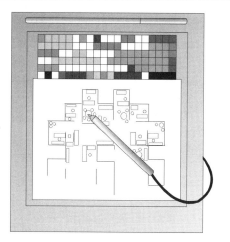

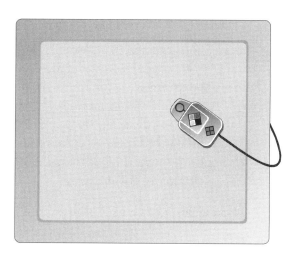

There are three major types of drawing tablets: electromagnetic, resistive, and acoustic. They differ primarily in the way that they work.

- Electromagnetic tablets have a grid of wires underneath the rubberized surface. The stylus contains a small sensor that is sensitive to electromagic fields. At timed intervals, an electromagnetic pulse is sent across the grid. The sensor in the stylus picks up these pulses. Since the pulses are timed, the stylus knows how long it takes to get from their point of origin in each direction to the stylus. The controller in the table then translates this information into a set of X and Y variables which are then sent to the computer. The computer then moves the pointer on the screen to the X and Y coordinates on the screen corresponding to the X and Y coordinates on the tablet.

- The resistive type of tablet has a special resistive surface under the rubberized coating instead of a grid of wires. This surface has a current induced from each of the X and Y coordinate sides. The current gets larger as it travels along one coordinate side. The puck detects these voltages and, depending on the position of the puck, will get different voltage readings from each side. These readings are translated into X and Y coordinate values, which are transmitted to the computer.

- The final type of drawing tablet in use today is the acoustic type. It works slightly differently than the other two models. The stylus or puck has a small spark generator inside it. There are also banks of small microphones on the X and Y axes. When the user presses a button on the stylus, it activates the spark. The sound of the spark is picked up on the X and Y microphones and the coordinates are translated into X and Y values for the computer.

To clean a drawing tablet, wipe the rubberized surface with a damp cloth (no detergents!). If there is a tough stain that the damp cloth won't remove, use a cloth dampened with denatured alcohol. After removing the stain, follow with water-dampened cloth to remove any residue.

Touch Screens

The last type of pointing device we'll discuss can be found in use at many department stores: the little informational "kiosks" with screens that respond to our touch and give us information on product specials or bridal registries. Instead of a keyboard and mouse, these computer screens have a film over them that is sensitive to touch. This technology is known as a *touch screen* (see Figure 6.12). With most of the interfaces in use on touch screens, touching a box drawn on the monitor does the same thing as double-clicking on that box with a mouse.

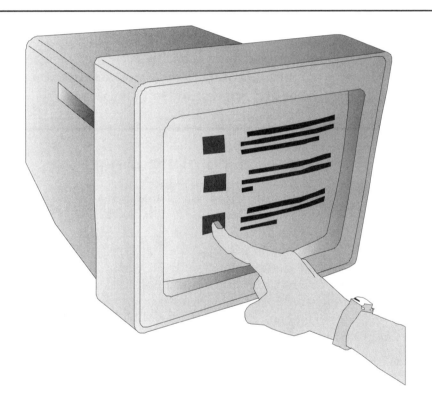

There are two major types of touch screens: optical and capacitive.

- Optical screens work like so: When a person uses their finger to touch the screen, they break light beams emanating in a grid from the sides of the screen (in front of the glass). Which light beams get broken indicates to the touch screen where the finger was, using an *X, Y* coordinate notation.

- Capacitive screens work just like capacitive keyboards. There are two clear, plastic coatings over the screen, separated by a thin layer of air. When we press the coatings together in a particular spot, the controller registers a change in the total capacitance of the two layers. Based on a table that relates capacitance values to position, the screen can relay X and Y coordinates to the computer.

Cleaning touch screens is usually just as easy as cleaning a regular monitor. With optical touch screens, the monitor *is*, in fact, a regular monitor. It can be cleaned with glass cleaner. However, if the screen has a capacitive coating, the glass cleaner may damage it. Instead, use a cloth dampened with water to clean the dirt, dust and fingerprints from the screen.

Other Types of Pointing Devices

There are some types of pointing devices that are not on the A+ exam. One example of these devices is the *touch pad*. It uses the capacitance method to translate position to *X, Y* coordinates. Its primary use is in notebook computers, since it takes up very little space and doesn't have to be moved. Another pointing device commonly seen on notebooks is the *finger mouse* (or *J-mouse*, because it sticks up next to the J key on the keyboard). This device looks like a small eraser sticking up from the middle of the keyboard. When you push this "eraser," the pointer on the screen moves in the same direction. Most people either love it or hate it.

These technologies have become popular in the last few years. So much, in fact, that some keyboard manufacturers have integrated these types of pointing devices into their keyboards.

Scanners

In addition to keyboards and pointing devices, there is another very common method of getting data into a computer. The *charge-coupled device* (CCD) was developed to allow light (and shades of light) to be converted into electrical pulses. This opened up the arena of input devices to allow a new breed of devices to input data to a computer. The largest class of these devices are scanners. *Optical scanners* (their full name) use CCDs and a light source to convert pictures into a stream of data.

Flatbed Scanners

The first type of scanner that was developed was the flatbed scanner. Named after the flat bed of glass that the item to be scanned would lie upon, they resemble the top half of a photocopier (Figure 6.13). Inside the scanner there is a motorized carriage, upon which is mounted a light source and a CCD. When you want to scan a picture into the computer, you place the item to be scanned face down on the glass that separates the item from the CCD. Then you use the software to indicate the start of the scan cycle. When this occurs, the software sends a signal to the scanner to begin scanning. The control board in the scanner turns on the light source and starts receiving data from the CCD. After scanning an entire line, the control board then tells the carriage to move down slightly so the CCD can scan the next line. The carriage moves slowly down the page and the CCD scans the page one line at a time. The controller then feeds this stream of image data to the scanning software, where it is assembled, line by line, together into a picture of the item.

Flatbed scanners are usually SCSI devices, therefore they need to be configured as any other SCSI device. (So remember the rules of addressing and termination, especially.) Sometimes, though, manufacturers include a special, proprietary interface card. In that case, configuration usually involves installing the card and simply connecting the scanner to the card with the cable provided. The downside is that this interface takes an additional IRQ address and can't be used for anything else (whereas SCSI can be used for disks and other devices). When configuring this card, use the configuration tips for the type of bus the card uses.

A dirty scanner bed (the big sheet of glass between the scanning CCD and the item being scanned) can cause image quality problems. Fingerprints show up as dark smudges in the scanned image. Since the scanner bed is simply glass, you can clean it with glass cleaner.

WARNING Be careful when handling flatbed scanners. Transporting them can be dangerous, since they contain a large sheet of glass. Also, never set anything sharp or heavy on the glass surface, because scratches will probably show up in the scanned image (and, besides, it could shatter and cut you).

Hand-Held Scanners

Hand-held scanners work exactly like flatbed scanners, with one exception. Instead of an all-in-one enclosure containing a carriage, controller, light source, and CCD, a hand-held unit is just the controller, CCD, and light source contained in a small enclosure with wheels on it (Figure 6.14). The carriage is your hand. To start scanning, you place the item to be scanned on a flat surface and place the scanner unit at the top. You tell the software you're ready to start scanning, and then press a "start" button on the scanner unit. This turns on the light source and tells the CCD to start receiving data. At the same time, you must move the scanner unit down the item being scanned. When you finish scanning, you release the start button.

FIGURE 6.14:

A hand-held scanner

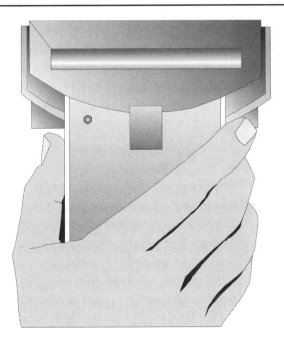

The major advantage of these scanners is that they produce adequate quality at less than half the price of a flatbed scanner. The major downside is that they are slow and the quality depends on how steady the hand of the operator is. They usually use a COM port or bidirectional parallel port instead of SCSI to transfer their data. They are limited in their quality, however, and generally should not be used in graphics work.

Output Devices

Since we have talked about how to get data *into* a computer, we must discuss ways of getting it *out*. To accomplish this, we use a class of devices known as output devices. There are two major categories: printers and computer displays.

Printers

Printers and their operation are the subject of Chapter 8 later in this book (and also about half of the troubleshooting chapter: Chapter 12), so we'll just briefly talk about the different types. There are four major types of printing devices used to get computer output into "hard" copy (paper copies). They are *impact, sprayed-ink, electrophotographic (EP)*, and *plotters*.

Impact

Impact printers work by striking a form through an inked ribbon onto the paper, similar to the way a printing press works. There are two major types of impact printers: *dot-matrix* and *daisy-wheel*. Dot-matrix printers press a set of pins through this ribbon in patterns corresponding to the characters to be produced. Daisy-wheel printers use a wheel that has all the letters of the alphabet on different spokes. The printer's controller rotates this wheel until the spoke holding the desired letter is in place. Then, a hammer behind the wheel strikes this letter onto the inked ribbon and the paper, thus making an image.

Dot-matrix printers sacrifice quality for speed, and thus produce a lower-quality image than the daisy-wheel printers. On the other hand, although daisy-wheel printers give letter-quality output, they cannot reproduce graphics. Dot-matrix printers can only achieve "near letter-quality," but are capable of printing graphics. In addition, daisy-wheel printers are, in general, noisier. They're also generally more expensive. (Of course, you'll find that some dot matrixes are noisier than some daisy wheels, and some are more expensive.)

Impact printers' primary use today is for printing multi-part carbon forms, since these forms require that something strike the page to make multiple copies. No other printing technology can handle multiple-part forms (unless they print multiple copies of the same form). The quality of printout is lower on daisy-wheel and dot-matrix printers than any other printing technology, so they are used when low-cost, fast printouts are needed and quality isn't an issue. A couple of typical impact printers are shown in Figure 6.15.

FIGURE 6.15:

Typical impact printers

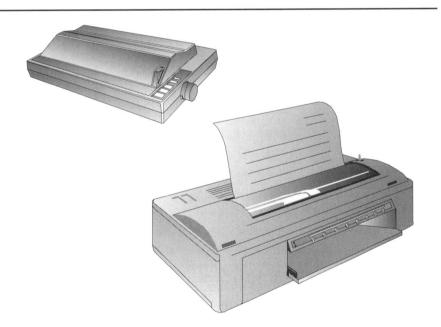

Sprayed-Ink

A sprayed-ink printer works as its name suggests. Ink is sprayed onto the page in the shape of the letters or images. There are a variety of sprayed-ink printers on the market, and they are all lumped together into this one category, but there are two basic types: ink-jet and bubble-jet. (As with the other printers mentioned in this chapter, we'll cover them in more detail in Chapters 8 and 12.) The quality of image is relatively good with both types of sprayed-ink printer; better than that produced by an impact printer but not quite as good as that produced by an electrophotographic printer (discussed next). The primary advantage to sprayed-ink printers is their cost. They can offer good output at a low cost (less than that of an electrophotographic printer). They have found a niche in the SOHO (Small Office, Home Office) market as a great printer for printing letters and other small documents.

A typical sprayed-ink printer is shown in Figure 6.16.

FIGURE 6.16:

A typical sprayed-ink printer

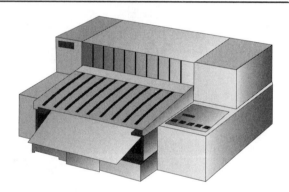

Electrophotographic (EP)

The name "electrophotographic (or EP) printer" suggests a complex image formation process. EP printers are actually more commonly known as *laser printers*, because they do use a laser (as well as high voltage and black carbon "toner") to form the image on the page. Because of their complexity, these printers have a relatively high cost associated with them (about twice the cost of a sprayed-ink or impact printer). But the complexity and cost have a benefit. The images produced by EP printers are of the very best quality, and they produce these images at higher speeds (most EP printers today print at least four pages per minute).

EP printers are often found in offices and publishing firms. It's rather interesting that the first EP printers to be sold (the Apple LaserWriter and the Hewlett-Packard LaserJet) sold for more than $4,000. Today you can buy an EP printer that produces output at more than twice their resolution and speed for about one eighth the cost.

A typical electrophotographic printer is shown in Figure 6.17.

FIGURE 6.17:

A typical electrophoto-graphic printer

Plotters

The last type of hard copy output device isn't really a printer at all. Printers make images one line at a time and move from top to bottom during the printing process. Plotters, on the other hand, draw the image like we would, with a pen. One shape at a time. Plotters are most often used with CAD software to produce blueprints or technical diagrams. Because these drawings require such large paper, it would be quite expensive to make a printer that can print on paper that wide. Because a plotter uses a pen (or several pens in a holder) on a cable carrier, it is easy (and relatively inexpensive) to make a very wide plotter.

A couple of typical plotters are shown in Figure 6.18.

FIGURE 6.18:

Typical plotters

Computer Display Systems

The second way of getting information out of a computer is to use a computer display. Display systems convert computer signals into text and pictures and display them on a TV-like screen. As a matter of fact, the first personal computers actually used television screens, since it was simple to develop that technology. There are several different types of computer displays in use today, including the TV. All of them use either the same *cathode ray tube* (*CRT*) technology found in television sets (almost every desktop monitor uses this technology) or the *liquid crystal display* (*LCD*) technology found on all laptop, notebook, and palmtop computers.

Display Concepts

There are several aspects of display systems that make each type of display different. But most display systems work the same. First, the computer sends a signal to a device called the *video adapter*—an expansion board installed in an expansion bus slot—telling it to display a particular graphic or character. The adapter then *renders* the character for the display—that is, it converts that single instruction into several instructions that tell the display device how to draw the graphic—and sends the instructions to the display device. The primary differences after that are in the type of video adapter we are using (monochrome, EGA/CGA, VGA, or SuperVGA) and the type of display (CRT or LCD).

Video Technologies

Let's first talk about the different types of video technologies. There are four major types: Monochrome, EGA/CGA, VGA, and SuperVGA. Each type of video technology differs in two major areas: the highest resolution it supports and the maximum number of colors in its "palette." Resolution depends on how many picture units (called *pixels*) are used to draw the screen. The more pixels, the sharper the image. The resolution is described in terms of the screen's dimensions, indicating how many pixels across and down are used to draw the screen. For example, a resolution of 1024×768 means 1024 pixels across and 768 pixels down were used to draw the pixel "grid." The video technology in this example would have used 786,432 ($1024 \times 768 = 786,432$) pixels to draw the screen.

Monochrome   The first video technology for PCs was *monochrome* (from the Latin *mono* meaning one and *chroma* meaning color). This black-and-white video (actually, they were green-and-white or amber-and-black) was just fine for the main operating system of the day, DOS. DOS didn't have any need for color. Thus, the video adapter was very basic. The first adapter, developed by IBM, was known as the Monochrome Display Adapter (MDA). It could display text, but not graphics, and used a resolution of 720×350 pixels.

The Hercules Graphics Card (HGC), introduced by Hercules Computer Technology, had a resolution of 720×350 and could display graphics as well as text. It did this by using two separate modes: a *text mode* that allowed the adapter to optimize its resources for displaying pre-drawn characters from its on-board library, and a *graphics mode* that optimized the adapter for drawing individual pixels for on-screen graphics. It could switch between these modes "on the fly." These modes of operation have been included in all graphics adapters since the introduction of the HGC.

EGA and CGA   The next logical step for displays was to add a splash of color. IBM was the first with color, with the introduction of the Color Graphics Adapter (CGA). CGA could display text, but it displayed graphics with a resolution of only 320×200 pixels with four colors. (It displayed a better resolution (640×200) with two colors—i.e., black and one other color.) After some time, people wanted more colors and higher resolution, so IBM responded with the Enhanced Graphics Adapter (EGA). EGA could display 16 colors out of a palette of 64 with a resolution of 320×200 or 640×350 pixels.

These two technologies were the standard for color until the IBM AT was introduced. This PC was to be the standard for performance, so IBM wanted a better video technology for it.

VGA   With the PS/2 line of computers, IBM wanted to answer the cry for "More resolution, more colors" by introducing its best video adapter to date, the Video Graphics Array (VGA). This video technology had a whopping 256 KB of video memory on board and could display 16 colors at 640×480 pixels, or 256 colors at 320×200 pixels. It became very widely used and has since become the standard for color PC video; it's the "starting point" for today's computers, as far as video is concerned. You can get better, but your computer should use this video technology at minimum.

One unique feature of VGA is that it's an analog board. This allows the 256 colors it uses to be chosen from various shades and hues of a palette of 262,114 colors. It sold well mainly because users could choose from almost any color they wanted (or at least one that was close).

SuperVGA   Up to this point, most video standards were set by IBM. IBM made them, everyone bought them, it became a standard. Some manufacturers didn't like this monopoly, and set up the Video Electronics Standards Association (VESA) to try to enhance IBM's video technology and make the enhanced technology a public standard. The result of this work was the enhancement known as Super VGA (SVGA). This new standard was indeed an enhancement, as it could support 256 colors at a resolution of 800×600 (the VESA standard), or 1024×768 pixels with 16 colors, or 640×480 with 65,536 colors.

XGA The final development in this tale of "keeping up with the Joneses" is that IBM introduced a new technology in 1991 known as the Extended Graphics Array (XGA). This technology was only available as an MCA expansion board, and not as an ISA or EISA board. It was rather like saying "So there. You won't let me be the leader, so I'll lead my own team." XGA could support 256 colors at 1024 × 768 pixels, or 65,536 colors at 640 × 480 pixels. It was a different design, optimized for GUIs like Windows or OS/2. Also, it was an *interlaced* technology, which means that, rather than scan every line one at a time to create the image, it scanned every other line on each pass, using the phenomenon known as "persistence of vision" to produce what appears to our eyes as a continuous image.

Table 6.1 details the various video technologies, their resolutions, and the color palettes they support.

TABLE 6.1: Video Display Adapter Comparison

Name	Resolutions	Colors
Monochrome Display Adapter (MDA)	720 × 350	mono (text only)
Hercules Graphics Card (HGC)	720 × 350	mono (text and graphics)
Color Graphics Adapter (CGA)	320 × 200 640 × 200	4 2
Enhanced Graphics Adapter (EGA)	640 × 350	16
Video Graphics Array (VGA)	640 × 480 320 × 200	16 256
Super VGA (SVGA)	800 × 600 1024 × 768	256 16
Extended Graphics Array (XGA)	800 × 600 1024 × 768	65,536 256

Monitors

As we have already mentioned, a monitor contains a CRT. But how does it work? Basically, a device called an *electron gun* shoots electrons towards the back side of the monitor screen (see Figure 6.19). The back of the screen is coated with special chemicals (called *phosphors*) that glow when electrons strike them. This beam of electrons scans across the monitor from left to right and top to bottom to create the image.

FIGURE 6.19:

How a monitor works

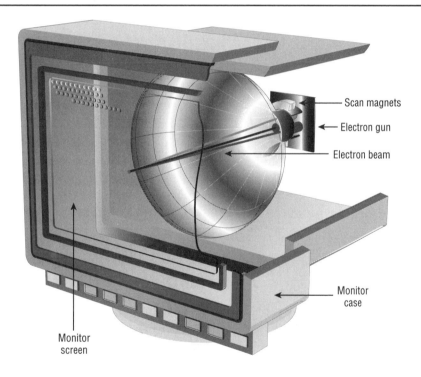

Scan magnets

Electron gun

Electron beam

Monitor case

Monitor screen

There are two ways of measuring a monitor's quality of image: dot pitch and refresh (scan) rate. A monitor's *dot pitch* is the shortest distance between two dots of the same color on the monitor. Usually given in fractions of a millimeter (mm), it tells how "sharp" the picture is. The lower the number, the closer together the pixels are, and thus, the sharper the image. An average dot pitch is 0.28mm. Anything smaller than 0.28mm is considered great.

A monitor's *refresh rate* (technically called the *vertical scan frequency*) specifies how many times in one second the scanning beam of electrons redraws the screen. The phosphors only stay bright for a fraction of a second, so they must constantly be hit with electrons to stay lit. Given in draws per second, or Hertz, it specifies how much energy is being put into keeping the screen lit. The standard refresh rate is 60 Hz for VGA. However, some monitors have a refresh rate of 72 Hz, which is much easier on the eyes (less flicker is perceived).

One note about monitors that may seem rather obvious: You must use a video card that supports the type of monitor you are using. For example, you can't use a CGA monitor on a VGA adapter.

NOTE To use a 72Hz monitor, your video card must also support the 72Hz refresh rate. Most video cards sold today support this faster 72Hz refresh rate, but are configured as 60Hz out of the box. If you intend on using the 72Hz rate, you must configure the card to do so. Check the documentation that came with the card for details on how to do this.

Liquid Crystal Displays (LCDs)

Portable computers were originally designed to be compact versions of their bigger brothers. They crammed all the components of the big, desktop computers into a small, suitcase-like box called (laughably) a *portable computer*. No matter what the designers did to reduce the size of the computer, the display remained as large as the desktop version's. That is, until an inventor found that when he passed an electric current through a semi-crystalline liquid, the crystals would align themselves with the current. It was found that by combining transistors with these liquid crystals, patterns could be formed. These patterns could represent numbers or letters. The first application of these *liquid crystal displays* (LCDs) was the LCD watch. It was rather bulky, but it was cool. I can't think of one kid I grew up with that didn't own at least one during my school years.

As the LCD elements got smaller, the detail of the patterns became greater until one day someone thought to make a computer screen out of several of these elements. This screen was very light compared to computer monitors of the day. Also, it consumed very little power. It could easily be added to a portable computer to reduce the weight by as much as 30 pounds! As the components got smaller, so did the computer, and the laptop computer was born.

There are two major types of LCD displays in use in laptops today: active matrix screen and passive matrix screen. Their main differences lie in the quality of the image. Both types, however, use some kind of lighting behind the LCD panel to make the screen easier to view.

Active Matrix   An active matrix screen works in a similar manner to the LCD watch. The screen is made up of several individual LCD pixels. A transistor behind each pixel, when switched on, activates two electrodes which align the crystals and turn the pixel dark. This type of display is very crisp and easy to look at.

The major disadvantage to an active matrix screen is that it requires large amounts of power to operate all the transistors in an active matrix screen. Even with the backlight turned off, the screen can still consume battery power at an alarming rate. Most laptops with active matrix screens can't operate on a battery for more than two hours.

Passive Matrix   Within the passive matrix screen, there are two rows of transistors: one at the top, another at the side. When the computer's video circuit wants to turn a particular pixel on (turn it black), it sends a signal to the X and Y coordinate transistors for that pixel, thus turning them on. This then causes voltage lines from each axis to intersect at the desired coordinates, turning the desired pixel black. Figure 6.20 illustrates this concept.

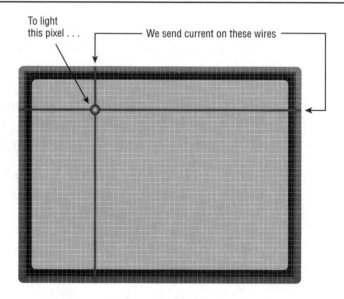

The main difference between active matrix and passive matrix is image quality. Since the computer takes a millisecond or two to light the coordinates for a pixel in passive matrix displays, the response of the screen to rapid changes is poor. An effect known as "submarining" is an example of this slow response time: if, on a computer with a passive matrix display, we move the mouse rapidly from one location to another, it will disappear from the first location and reappear in the new location without appearing anywhere in between.

In order to keep the quality of the image on an LCD the best, the screen must be cleaned often. Liquid crystal displays are typically coated with a clear, plastic covering. This covering commonly gets several fingerprints as well as a generous coating of dust. The best way to clean the LCD lens coating is to wipe it off occasionally with a damp cloth. This will ensure that the images stay crisp and clear.

Other Peripherals

In addition to all the input and output devices, we have a few categories of devices that are neither input nor output devices. Devices like multimedia devices (sound cards and CD-ROM drives) and modems don't fit well into any category, so we'll discuss them here.

Multimedia Devices

The first category of devices we'll discuss is multimedia devices. What is multimedia? The simplest answer is *multiple media*. That is, it's a way of communicating information using more than one form, using some combination of video, pictures, sound, and text. Several devices are included in the category, including CD-ROM drives, sound cards, speakers, and microphones. Multimedia systems have been assigned a standard, known as the MPC standard, which is discussed (under "multimedia personal computer") in Appendix B.

CD-ROM Drives

In Chapter 4, we discussed the way CD-ROM drives work. Let's talk a bit more about the format compatibility of CD-ROM drives. Because all CD-ROM drives work in more or less the same manner, the companies that manufactured them came up with standards to allow the various types of CD disks to work in the different drives made by different vendors. The International Standards Organization (ISO) came up with several standards that specify what type of information can be saved on a CD and how it's recorded.

The first CD standard, called the Red Book standard, is the standard for recording digital audio (audio CDs that you play in your home CD player). It specifies the recording level as 16-bit, 44.1KHz, and that the entire disk will have an index of the music tracks stored on it. The Yellow Book standard defines the main requirements for data storage on a CD-ROM. This standard supports both PC (ISO9660) and Mac (HFS) file system formats as well as file-system formats from other vendors (DEC and VMS).

The Green Book standard is primarily for CD-I (Compact Disk-Interactive) CDs. These disks have interactive functionality written right to the CD. Orange book is for the "writable" CDs that are only now becoming affordable for the common user.

Sound Cards

Just as there are devices to convert computer signals into printouts and video information, there are devices to convert those signals into sound. These devices are known as *sound cards*. There are many different manufacturers making sound cards, but the standard has been set by Creative Labs with their SoundBlaster series of cards. As a matter of fact, the MPC standards specify a SoundBlaster-compatible sound card.

When installing a sound card, usually we set the IRQ, DMA, and I/O addresses with software (although some of the older, ISA cards use jumpers). Table 6.2 details the default settings of a typical SoundBlaster sound card.

TABLE 6.2: Default SoundBlaster Configuration Settings

Parameter	Default Setting
IRQ	5
Sound Card I/O Address	220
DMA	1
MIDI port I/O Address	330

Musical Instrument Digital Interface

In addition to producing sound, sound cards have another capability that is often overlooked. The Musical Instrument Digital Interface (MIDI—usually pronounced "Middy") technology incorporated into most sound cards allows PCs to talk with (and in some cases, control) musical devices. With the addition of a special adapter cable that plugs into the game port on most sound cards, a PC can use external sound modules to produce sounds. MIDI technologies are used by most electronic keyboard players and professional musicians. However, you don't need to have an electronic keyboard or external sound module to play MIDI sounds. Most sound cards include a set of ICs that incorporate some of the sound-generating circuitry found in most electronic keyboards.

Communication Devices

In this section we will be discussing communication devices and the various types of cables they use. Before we can discuss them, however, we must explain the two major types of communication, synchronous and asynchronous.

Synchronous vs. Asynchronous Communications

When two computers want to communicate, they must first agree on the rules of communication. One of those rules concerns whether or not they are going to communicate using a synchronous or an asynchronous process. As the magician said when asked about his magic trick, "It's all in the timing." *Synchronous* communications use a clock signal that's separate from the data signal (either on a separate wire, or on a completely separate cable). Communication can only happen during a "tick" of the timing signal. Synchronous communications work great when large amounts of data must be moved around quickly. However, even if there's no data, the timing signal still gets sent, which wastes bandwidth on the transmission medium.

But what if the computers only had a little data to exchange? In this case, they might use *asynchronous* transmission methods. Asynchronous transmissions don't use a constant clock signal. Instead, they add special signaling bits to each end of the data (see Figure 6.21). The bit at the beginning of the information signals the start of the data and is known as the "start bit." The next few bits are the actual data that needs to be sent. Those bits are known as the "data bits." Finally, you have one or more "stop bits" that indicate that the data is finished. These special "frames" of information are transmitted at irregular intervals until all the information has been exchanged.

FIGURE 6.21:

An asynchronous data "frame"

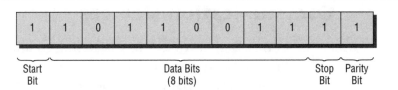

When configuring devices for asynchronous communication, both devices must agree on the number of data bits and stop bits, and on whether or not parity checking should be used. If both sender and receiver aren't set to the same values, communication can't take place. The values are usually set in the software of both the sending and receiving hardware.

Modems

Modems are devices used by computers to communicate over long distances. The word modem is actually a partial acronym; it stands for MOdulator-DEModulator. It got this name from the way it works. When a computer wants to send data, it uses a digital signal (fluctuations in voltage, representing 1's and 0's). The problem is that these signals can attenuate (decrease in strength) over long distances. For example, if you want to transmit the binary number 10110101 as a series of voltages, you might say to both computers, "A '1' is represented by a voltage of +5.0 volts, a '0' is any voltage less than that." If you try to transmit that number over a distance of only a few feet, +5.0 volts (representing the ones) will still be +5.0 volts when it comes out the other end of the wire. However, if you try to transmit that same number over a distance of a mile or more, after the first few hundred feet, the +5.0 voltages might drop to 4.5 volts, which of course is below +5.0 volts. This voltage will get lower as the distance gets longer. When the signals get to the other end, the number will be 00000000 because ALL the voltages will be less than +5.0 volts.

Analog signals, on the other hand, don't suffer from this problem because analog values are typically many values in a range, like sound waves. As a matter of fact, sound waves travel *very* well over long distances in wires. The sound waves are converted to pulses of voltages. Over long distances, the pulses get weaker, but the sound is just the same. It can be said, then, that analog signals are more reliable over longer distances.

Wouldn't it be great to have the best of both worlds? You can—with the modem. Modems convert digital signals into analog signals by using variations of tones to represent 1's and 0's (this is the MOdulation). The modem then sends these sounds over a phone line. At the other end, the tones are converted back into 1's and 0's (this is the DEModulation). Using two modems and a phone line, you transmit digital data through an analog medium.

The only downside to modems is that this process is relatively inefficient. Because modem communications are so sporadic, they use asynchronous communications, which have their overhead of start and stop bits. Also, today's phone lines are limited to a maximum throughput of 56 Kbps.

Bits vs. Baud

The most confusing terms used to describe modem speed are *bits-per-second* (or *bps*) and *baud*. Actually, it's a very easy distinction. The BPS value of a modem is how much data is being transmitted in one second. Baud is how many signal (tone) changes are happening in one second. Through a process known as encoding, several bits can be transmitted using only a few signal changes. Modern phone lines are limited to 9600 baud. If you increase the baud rate any higher, the modem on the other end starts to have difficulty distinguishing the individual tonal changes. However, with modern encoding techniques, it is possible to get up to 56 Kilobits-per-second (Kbps) transmitted with 9600 baud.

There are two types of modems: internal and external. Internal modems are installed as expansion cards inside a computer. External modems have their own power supplies and connect to an external COM port with a RS-232 cable. There are advantages and disadvantages to each.

Internal modems are usually smaller and cheaper than their external counterparts. However, they are more difficult to configure. You need to configure them to use an unused COM port. Table 6.3 lists the IRQ and I/O port addresses of the standard COM ports installed.

TABLE 6.3: Standard COM Port and IRQ Addresses

COM Port	IRQ Address	I/O address
COM1	4	3F8-3FF
COM2	3	2F8-2FF
COM3	4	3E8-3EF
COM4	3	2E8-2EF

External modems use an existing serial port, so they don't have the configuration problem with IRQs and I/O addresses. However, they don't interface directly with the computer's expansion bus, so data transfers may be slowed (especially if the modem is faster than 9600 bps). If this is the case, the serial port must use a higher-speed UART (Universal Asynchronous Receiver-Transmitter). The UART is the chip that manages the serial data that's moving in and out through the serial port. If the modem is 9600 bps or faster, you need to use a 16-bit UART (for example, the 16450 or 16550 model). Most computers come standard with 16550 UARTs so you don't have to worry about this. However, some older computers came with the old, 8-bit 8550 UART and may need to be upgraded.

And Now for the Real World...

An additional benefit to external modems is that the status lights on the modem are visible. Personally, I like to know when the modem has hung up or is transmitting data. Here's a quick little guide to the common abbreviations found next to the lights on a modem.

OH: (Off Hook) The modem is dialing or otherwise has the phone off the hook.

SD(TX): (Transmit Data) The modem is sending data.

RD(RX): (Receive Data) The modem is receiving data.

AA: (Auto Answer) The modem is set to automatically pick up after a few rings.

Cables

Cables are used to connect two or more entities together. They are usually constructed of several wires encased together in a rubberized outer coating. The wires are soldered to modular connectors at both ends. These connectors are used to allow the cables to be quickly attached to the devices they connect. A listing of common cable types used in PCs, their descriptions, their maximum effective lengths, and their most common uses is given in Table 6.4.

TABLE 6.4: Common PC Cable Descriptions

Application	1st Connector	2nd Connector	Max. Length
Null Modem	DB-9F	DB-9F	25 feet
Null Modem	DB-25F	DB-25F	25 feet
RS-232 (modem cable)	DB-9F	DB-25M	25 feet
RS-232 (modem cable)	DB-25F	DB-25M	25 feet
Parallel Printer	DB-25M	Centronics 36	10 feet
External SCSI Cable	Male Centronics 50	Male Centronics 50	10 feet (total SCSI bus length)
VGA Extension Cable	DB-15M	DB-15M	3 feet

WARNING It should be noted that some manufacturers have made cables that are much longer than the maximum length listed in the table. Although they might work, these cables may occasionally cause communication delays or dropouts and therefore should not be used. Using a 50-foot printer cable is *not* a good way to connect a computer to a printer 50 feet away. Unless you use low-capacitance cable (which might cost as much as $100), you're far better off moving the printer close enough to use a 10-foot printer cable!

One cable that deserves special mention is the *null-modem cable*. It is used to allow two computers to communicate with each other without using a modem. This cable has its transmit and receive wires crossed at both ends so when one entity transmits on its TD line, the other entity is receiving it on its RD line. The most popular application for a null modem cable is playing games, believe it or not. A null modem cable is required to play games like Doom and Descent in multi-player mode if you aren't playing them over a network or a modem connection. It does have more useful purposes, however. For example, there are some data transfer programs (like LapLink 3, from Traveling Software) that can transfer files over a null-modem cable between two computers. This can be very useful when upgrading computers.

Review Questions

1. "Debouncing" refers to:

    A. stopping a mouse ball from bouncing

    B. cleaning up keyboard signals and preventing multiple characters from a single keypress

    C. keeping the keyboard keyswitches from bouncing up and down

    D. making sure that service customers' checks don't bounce

2. COM1 shares an IRQ with which other COM port?

    A. COM1

    B. COM2

    C. COM3

    D. COM4

3. Which IRQ does COM1 share with the COM port in question 2?

    A. 4

    B. 2

    C. 3

    D. 10

4. What are the two major types of mice in use today?

   A. capacitive

   B. resistive

   C. optical

   D. opto-mechanical

5. You find a cable in a box of old computer parts. It has a DB-25F connector on both ends. What kind of cable is it most likely to be?

   A. printer cable

   B. modem cable

   C. null-modem cable

   D. VGA cable

6. Which type of computer communication uses a separate timing signal to dictate transmission times?

   A. synchronous

   B. asynchronous

   C. standard

   D. modem

7. What are the two major types of keyboards in use today?

   A. standard

   B. keyswitched

   C. capacitive

   D. resistive

8. If a display adapter is a VGA adapter in the standard configuration, which one of the following would be the default
resolution/color choice?

   A. 640 × 480 with 256 colors

   B. 640 × 480 with 16 colors

   C. 640 × 480 with 65,536 colors

   D. 1024 × 768 with 256 colors

9. Which of the following monitors has the highest resolution?

   A. VGA 640 × 480

   B. CGA 320 × 200

   C. SVGA 800 × 600

   D. XGA 1024 × 768

10. Which types of mouse interface technology use an interrupt
(other than the ones a PC is normally using)?

   A. bus

   B. PS/2

   C. serial

   D. Microsoft

11. Which type of signal degrades the most over longer
distances?

   A. serial

   B. analog

   C. digital

   D. parallel

12. What is the maximum length of a standard parallel printer cable?

    A. 6 feet

    B. 10 feet

    C. 25 feet

    D. 50 feet

13. Which type of scanner gives the best quality and highest resolution?

    A. flatbed

    B. hand-held

    C. photo

14. Which of the following types of output devices puts computer data on paper?

    A. modems

    B. monitors

    C. LCDs

    D. printers

15. Which type of output device has the highest resolution (and therefore the best quality)?

    A. impact printers

    B. sprayed-ink printers

    C. EP printers

    D. modems

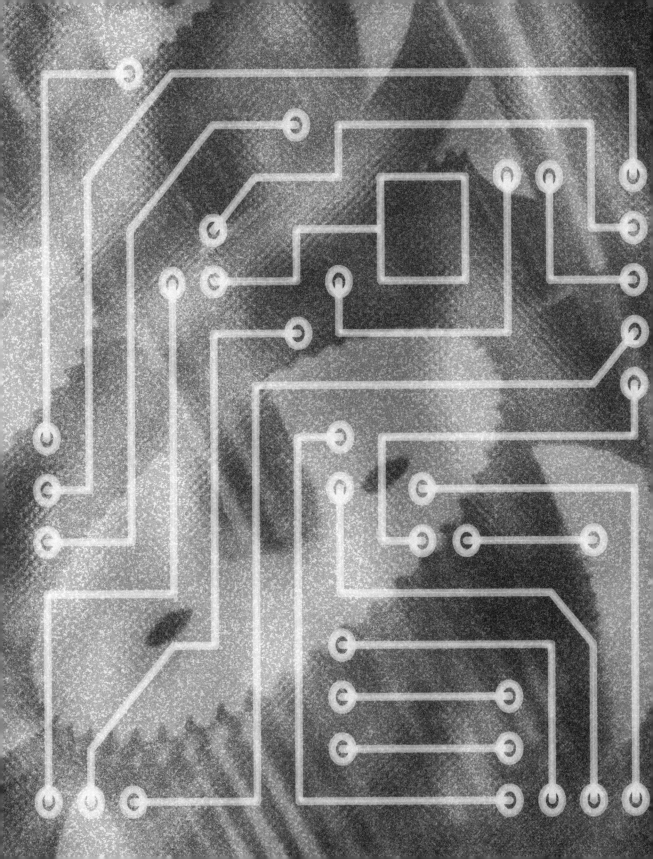

CHAPTER
SEVEN

7

Installation and Upgrades

Objectives

- Identify basic procedures for adding and removing field replace-able modules.

- Identify available IRQs, DMAs, and I/O addresses and procedures for configuring them for device installation.

- Identify the purpose of CMOS (Complementary Metal-Oxide Semiconductor), what it contains, and how to change its basic parameters.

At some point every computer will need to be upgraded. Upgrading usually means replacing old technology with new technology. An example of this would be replacing a slower, older modem with a faster, newer one. Upgrading usually involves adding a new component. This process consists of several basic steps, each of which must be carefully followed. In this chapter we will cover the following steps:

- Disassembly

- Inspection

- Installation and upgrades

- Reassembly

Disassembling the Computer

Disassembling a computer can be a complex operation. If you do it too quickly, you may lose parts or damage something. Further, you have to keep the reassembly process in mind as you're taking things apart, because everything you remove has to be put together again. Several steps need to be followed during the disassembly in order for the reassembly to be successful. People who take shortcuts through these steps often find themselves with "extra" parts and a computer that no longer functions.

Let's cover each step in detail, starting with the preparation of your work area.

Preparing Your Work Area

For any work you do on a computer, you must have an adequate workspace. This could mean any number of things. First, the work area must be flat. If it's not, small parts could roll around, possibly getting lost or damaged. Second, the area must be sturdy. A typical computer weighs about twenty-five pounds. Printers and other peripherals will add to that weight. Make sure the work surface you are using can support that weight. In addition, the area must be well lit, clean, and large enough to hold all pieces (assembled and disassembled) and all necessary tools. Figure 7.1 shows an adequate workspace for most computers.

FIGURE 7.1:

A typical computer workspace

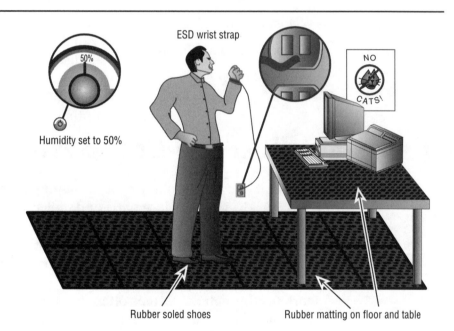

ESD wrist strap

50%

Humidity set to 50%

NO CATS!

Rubber soled shoes

Rubber matting on floor and table

Before you begin, make sure all necessary tools are available and in working order. It may help to lay out some of the more commonly used disassembly tools such as screwdrivers and nut drivers so they can be easily found (including several anti-static bags to place the removed components into). Also, make sure the documentation for the system you are working on is available (including owner's manuals, service manuals, and Internet resources). Two tools in particular that will be very handy aren't really tools in the traditional sense. They are, rather, timesavers. They are the *egg carton* and the *pen and notepad*. The egg carton is perfect for organizing screws and small parts that might otherwise end up in the "extra parts" pile. The pen and notepad should be used to record anything that may easily be forgotten, such as cable positions, DIP switch settings, and the location from which you removed the components.

The final guideline to preparing your work area is to set aside plenty of time to complete the task. To do this, estimate the time required to complete the entire task (disassembly, installation, reassembly, and testing), and then *double it*. Too often, a technician will start a "simple" job and underestimate the time needed to complete it. When they run out of time, they must come back later to complete the job. Because of this interruption, they may forget exactly where they left off. This can lead to the "extra parts" syndrome.

Once you've prepared your work area and gathered your tools, you're ready to begin the actual disassembly of the computer. The steps are basically the same for all brands and types of computers.

Disassembly Prerequisites

Let's start by fulfilling a few prerequisites—things you need to do before you even move the computer to your work area.

1. Shut down any running programs and turn the computer off.

2. Remove all cables (*especially the power cable*) that are attached to the computer. Remember that some cables use special screws to attach them to their ports.

WARNING That second step (removing all the cables before disassembling) is at least as important as the first. *DON'T ASSUME THAT THERE IS NO POWER TO THE COMPUTER JUST BECAUSE THE POWER SWITCH IS OFF!* Some new computers have a "low power mode" that, when active, makes the computer *appear* to be off. In truth, a computer in this mode is just idle and the video circuitry is shut off. If you disassemble the computer while it's plugged in or turned on, you could get *electrocuted*! Additionally, components could be damaged if inserted or removed while power is applied.

Additionally, you should remove any floppy disks from their respective drives to prevent damage to either the disk or the drive.

Finally, after checking once more to see that all the prerequisites have been dealt with, you can move the computer to the work surface.

Removing the Case Cover

Next, you are going to remove the computer's case cover. On many IBM-compatible PCs this is accomplished by removing some (but usually not all) of the screws at the back of the computer (see the warning following this paragraph) and *slowly* pulling the computer's case cover back and up to remove (see Figure 7.2). If you pull too fast, it is possible to damage cables that may be located close to the top of the case. If the case doesn't move, check to see that all the case cover screws were removed.

WARNING Don't just start removing *all* the screws at the back of the computer! Some of these screws hold vital components (like the power supply) to the case, and removing them will cause those components to drop into the computer. The computer's documentation should indicate which screws to remove in order to remove the case cover.

FIGURE 7.2:

Removing the case cover

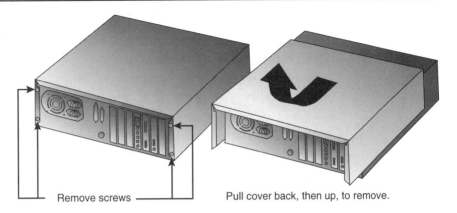

Remove screws ——————   Pull cover back, then up, to remove.

Some computers don't hold their cases on with screws, but use sliding tabs to hold the case on. (A great example of this is the Hewlett-Packard Vectra 5/75 low-profile PC.) Removing the case cover on these types of computers usually involves moving the tabs into their released position and sliding the case back and up. However, it's best to consult the computer's documentation for the exact details.

Removing the Expansion Cards

Once you have the case off, you will be able to see the inside of the computer. The next step in disassembly is to put on an anti-static wrist strap, plugging one end into the ground plug of an outlet. Then you can start to remove any expansion cards, mainly because they are the easiest things to remove at this point. There are four major steps in removing the expansion cards; to do this correctly you need to follow them in order:

1. Remove any internal or external cables or connectors. (You should already have removed the external ones in the prerequisite steps.) When you are removing a cable or connector, use your pen and notepad to diagram their installed positions. Also use the pen to make identifying marks on the cables to make sure they align correctly when reinstalled.

2. Remove any mounting screws that are holding the boards in place and place the screws somewhere where they won't be lost. If you don't have an egg carton, you can just put each screw back into its mounting hole as you remove each expansion board. Just make sure to screw them in all the way, not just a couple of turns.

3. Grasp the board by the top edge with both hands and *gently* "rock" it front to back (*NOT* side to side). Figure 7.3 clarifies this procedure. If the expansion board doesn't come out easily, don't force it. You may damage it. Check to see that the board is not being obstructed.

4. Finally, once the board is out, place it in an anti-static bag to help prevent ESD damage while the board is out of the computer. Place the board aside and out of the way before continuing.

Repeat the procedure for each card. At the same time, be sure to note which slot it came out of, since some bus types (EISA, MCA, and PCI) keep track of which slot expansion boards are installed in.

FIGURE 7.3:

Removing an expansion
board

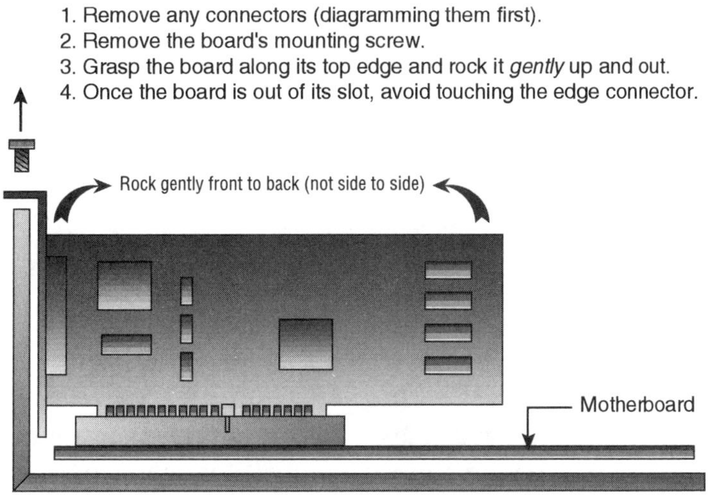

1. Remove any connectors (diagramming them first).
2. Remove the board's mounting screw.
3. Grasp the board along its top edge and rock it *gently* up and out.
4. Once the board is out of its slot, avoid touching the edge connector.

Rock gently front to back (not side to side)

Motherboard

Removing the Power Supply

The next component that can be removed is the power supply. You can easily access it with the expansion cards out of the way. Before you remove the power supply from the computer, however, you must do two things: disconnect the power supply connectors from the internal devices and remove the mounting hardware for the power supply.

Disconnecting the connectors from the devices is a very easy process. Before removing any power connectors, note their positions and connections on the notepad (and make any marks on them to indicate their installed positions). Then, simply grasp the connector (NOT THE *WIRES*) and gently wiggle it out of its receptacle. Then, proceed to the next connector. The system board and disk drives both use power connectors. Make sure all of them are removed, including (if they exist) the cable and connector that run to a power switch at the front of the case. Figure 7.4 illustrates these procedures.

FIGURE 7.4:

Removing power supply
connectors

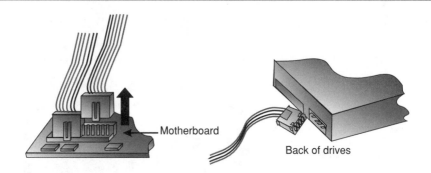

Motherboard

Back of drives

Once all the power supply connectors are disconnected from
their devices, you can remove the mounting hardware for the
power supply. In most PCs, you can detach the power supply
from the case by removing four screws (see Figure 7.5).

Some power supplies don't need to have screws removed;
instead, they are installed on tracks or into slots in the case and
only need to be slid out or lifted out.

FIGURE 7.5:

Removing power supply
screws

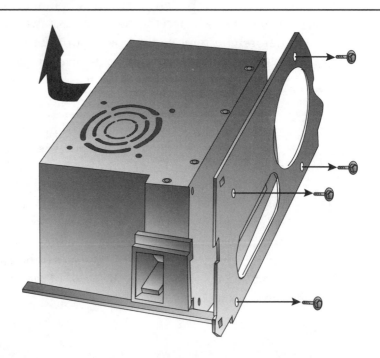

Removing the Disk Drives

Most disk drives are installed in IBM-compatible computers with "rails" that are attached to the drives with screws. These rails allow the drive to be slid into the computer's drive bays like a drawer. The drives are then secured with at least two screws on the sides (see Figure 7.6).

FIGURE 7.6:

Removing the hard drive

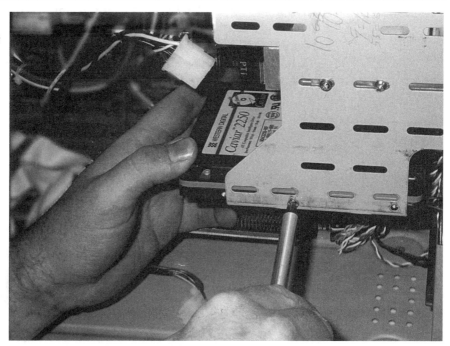

Most desktop computers (like Compaqs, IBM PS/2s, and Hewlett-Packards) use a special drive carrier that holds the drive in place and can be easily removed without tools. Consult the computer's documentation to see exactly how to remove this type of drive.

With most drives, however, you can just remove the mounting screws and slide the drive out.

Removing the Motherboard

All that's left in your computer is the motherboard (also known as the *logic board*). The only time the motherboard should need to be removed is when it needs to be upgraded or replaced. Otherwise, you should leave the motherboard in the PC's case to prevent either physical or ESD damage.

The motherboard is held away from the metal case using plastic spacers and is secured and grounded using mounting screws. To remove the motherboard, you must remove the screws holding the motherboard to the mounting brackets. Then, you must slide the motherboard to the side to release the spacers from their mounting holes in the case (see Figure 7.7).

FIGURE 7.7:

Removing the motherboard

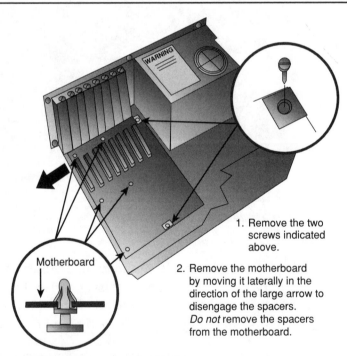

1. Remove the two screws indicated above.

2. Remove the motherboard by moving it laterally in the direction of the large arrow to disengage the spacers. *Do not* remove the spacers from the motherboard.

Motherboard

There are five spacers holding the motherboard off the case. A spacer is shown above, viewed from its side.

Installation and Upgrades

At some point, every computer will require the installation of a new component. Whether it's a new sound card, a memory upgrade, or the replacement of a failed component, installation is a procedure that every computer goes through in its lifetime. Throughout this section, we'll use the example of a sound card for our discussions.

The installation of new or replacement components in most computers is a simple process, if you follow a few, basic steps. These steps are very general, but should cover the installation of most components.

1. First, you must determine available resources. (If you're installing a Plug-and-Play component, you may not have to do this.)

2. Then, you need to configure the new devices, using the provided instructions. (Again, with Plug-and-Play you might not need to do this.)

3. After that, you can install the component and its supporting software.

4. Finally, you can test the component's operation.

Determining Available Resources

If this is the first time the particular component has been installed in this computer, you must determine if there are any available resources (IRQ channels, DMA channels, memory addresses, and so on). If the part you are installing is a replacement part, you simply set the jumpers or DIP switches the same as they were on the component you removed. (You did remember to diagram these settings, right?)

The best way to determine the PC's available resources is by using hardware configuration discovery utilities. These software programs talk to the PC's BIOS as well as the various pieces of hardware in the computer, and display which IRQ, DMA, and memory addresses are being used.

Microsoft includes a program with MS-DOS for this purpose. This program is called Microsoft Diagnostics (MSD or MSD.EXE). When you run it, it can display information about the computer's memory, I/O ports, IRQs that are being used, and many other PC resources that you want to see. Figure 7.8 shows the main menu that appears when you first run the program.

FIGURE 7.8:

Microsoft Diagnostics main menu

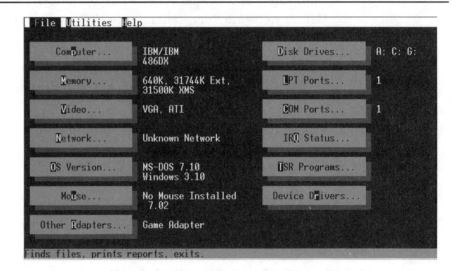

From the main menu, you can use the menu options to display information about the various resources. For example, if you want to find out if there are any IRQ channels available, you would press "Q" to bring up a screen similar to the one in Figure 7.9. (Your screen may show something different.)

As you can see, the computer in Figure 7.9 has IRQs 3, 5, 10, 11, 12, and 15 available. (You can tell because the "IRQ Status Detected" column indicates "No" for these IRQ channels.) If you were going to install a device that required an IRQ channel, you could set it to any of these channels and there should be no IRQ conflicts. You would perform the same procedure to find out if any of the other resources were available.

FIGURE 7.9:

MSD IRQ status screen

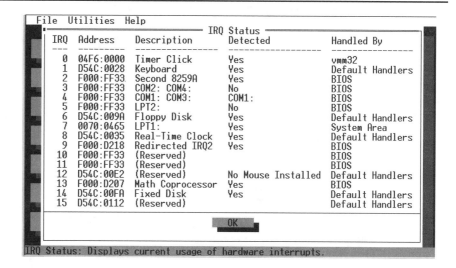

```
 File  Utilities  Help
                          IRQ Status
  IRQ  Address    Description      Detected             Handled By
  ---  -------    -----------      --------             ----------
   0   04F6:0000  Timer Click      Yes                  vmm32
   1   D54C:0028  Keyboard         Yes                  Default Handlers
   2   F000:FF33  Second 8259A     Yes                  BIOS
   3   F000:FF33  COM2: COM4:      No                   BIOS
   4   F000:FF33  COM1: COM3:      COM1:                BIOS
   5   F000:FF33  LPT2:            No                   BIOS
   6   D54C:009A  Floppy Disk      Yes                  Default Handlers
   7   0070:0465  LPT1:            Yes                  System Area
   8   D54C:0035  Real-Time Clock  Yes                  Default Handlers
   9   F000:D218  Redirected IRQ2  Yes                  BIOS
  10   F000:FF33  (Reserved)                            BIOS
  11   F000:FF33  (Reserved)                            BIOS
  12   D54C:00E2  (Reserved)       No Mouse Installed   Default Handlers
  13   F000:D207  Math Coprocessor Yes                  BIOS
  14   D54C:00FA  Fixed Disk       Yes                  Default Handlers
  15   D54C:0112  (Reserved)                            Default Handlers

                              OK

 IRQ Status: Displays current usage of hardware interrupts.
```

WARNING Don't rely completely on the report you get from MSD if you're running it under Windows (or Windows 95). In that situation, MSD simply gives the information that it gets from Windows. This may be somewhat incorrect and could prove to be a problem. For best results, run MSD in DOS only (or in MS-DOS mode under Windows 95). Actually, regardless of which operating system you're using, the operating system can "color" the performance of a software diagnostic program. For this reason, it's best to always *verify* the settings the program reports against the settings as published in your computer documentation and device manuals.

Besides addressing resources, there is one other resource you need to make sure is available: space. There must be adequate space in the computer for the device you are installing. If you are installing a disk drive, there must be an open disk bay available. If you are installing an expansion card (for example, a sound card), you must make sure that you have an open slot available. Also, in the case of computers that use multiple bus types (ISA/PCI for example), the available slot must be of the same type as the card being installed.

Configuring New Devices

Now that you know what resources are available, you can begin configuring the device. If you simply installed the device without configuring it, the device probably won't work (although you might get lucky and the default settings of the card will work). There are two major steps in the configuration: reading the instructions and setting the configuration of the device.

Reading the Instructions

The saying "If all else fails, read the directions" exists because most people assume they know how to do something, even if they've never done it before. This statement is especially true for service technicians. Most technicians think that if they've installed one sound card, they've installed them all. Even worse, they won't admit that they don't know how to repair something.

It is for this reason we have instructions. Of the two steps for configuring devices, this is the most important. Every component should come with instructions (although I have certainly found some components that require you to "guess" how to configure them). These instructions usually have diagrams that indicate where the jumpers or DIP switches are and what positions they need to be in to set the device so that it uses the resources you specify.

When looking through the instructions for this information, you need to find the section of the installation manual that deals with configuration (you may need to look in the index or table of contents to find it). Once you have found it, see if you can match the resources that you have to a set of jumper settings. For example, if you have IRQ 5 and I/O address 220 available, you need to see if your sound card can support those settings. If it can support them, find out which jumpers need to be moved. If it can't, you have to go back and pick a different set of available resources and repeat the process.

Setting the Configuration

Setting the configuration of a device usually involves following the instructions and moving jumpers and DIP switches.

These settings might be contained in a configuration table in the documentation. Examples of a sound card's configuration tables are shown in Tables 7.1 and 7.2. We'll assume that there are two sets of jumpers, one for the IRQ setting, another for the I/O address (labeled J1 and J2, respectively). Each set has five pairs of pins each.

TABLE 7.1: Sample IRQ Settings Table

IRQ	Jumper these pins on jumper J1
3	1
5 (default)	2
7	3
10	4
11	5

TABLE 7.2: Sample I/O Address Settings Table

I/O Address	Jumper these pins on jumper J2
220h (default)	1
240h	2
260h	3
280h	4
300h	5

If you knew that you had I/O address 220h available, and IRQ 5 available, you would know by the tables that you will have to jumper pin 1 on jumper J1, and pin 1 on jumper J2.

And Now for the Real World...

Most expansion cards made today don't use DIP switches or jumpers. Instead, they use a *software setup program*. When installing a new sound card that uses a software setup program, you only set one jumper: the one that controls the I/O address setting (which is usually set to 220h for sound cards). As long as it doesn't conflict with any other devices, the software setup program can be used.

Once you run the software setup program, it will present menu choices for each of the settings for that expansion card. You can use these menus to choose the IRQ, the DMA channel, and the memory addresses for the card.

Another type of configuration program that is used is the Plug-and-Play technology developed by several manufacturers, including Intel and Microsoft. This technology consists of a special BIOS that checks the configuration of every expansion card at startup. When a new card is inserted, the PC will detect that a change has occurred to the system and will configure the card to settings that, hopefully, do not conflict.

Plug-and-Play is a good idea, but the problem is that this technology doesn't work much of the time. More often than not, the settings the BIOS chooses *will* conflict, and these cards have no easy way of reconfiguring them. It has gotten the nickname "Plug-and-Pray" because of this aggravating "feature."

This problem manifests itself most often when the newer, Plug-and-Play cards are mixed with older, "legacy" expansion cards in the same computer. The term *legacy* usually applies to previous-generation hardware or software (i.e., older 8-bit and ISA cards). Generally speaking, legacy means older hardware or software.

To finish setting the configuration, you would change all jumpers or DIP switches to the settings you need. The board is now configured. Before continuing, double-check all jumper settings. They are easy to change while the device is still outside the computer.

Installing the Component

Now that your sound card is configured, you can finally mount the device into the computer. Mounting a device usually means attaching it to the computer's case with some kind of fastener and attaching the device to an interface. In this case, it means installing an expansion card into an expansion slot and securing it with a screw.

Most expansion cards can be inserted in the same way. First of all, make sure the power is off! This step is very important because if the power is applied and you try to install a card into a slot that has power, you will most likely destroy the card, the motherboard, or both!

Second, if the place you are installing the device has a *blank* (a piece of plastic or metal that covers that space where the device is going to go), remove it. Don't throw these blanks away. If you ever want to remove a component, you will need to replace the blank so that dirt, dust, and other contaminants can be kept out. I have a small box full of blanks that I keep handy, just in case I need them when removing components.

Next, align the connector on the bottom of the card with the connector on the motherboard and insert the card into its connector. You should feel a slight amount of resistance. Push the card firmly into place with an even pressure on the front and back of the card. Stop pushing when all of the card's connectors are making contact with the "fingers" in the expansion slot.

WARNING If the card doesn't go in easily, don't force it. You could break the card or the connector.

Finally, install the mounting screws to secure the device in place. In this case, you only have one screw to install, and it's located at the back of the computer. This screw will hold the metal tab on the expansion card to the computer's case. PS/2 computers have tabs that lock the board into place, so you can skip this step for PS/2 computers.

TIP Most people would begin to reassemble the computer at this point. However, you don't want to do that just yet. I've found that Murphy's Law applies quite often when installing computer components. So leave the case off while performing the next steps: installing the software and testing the component. If something goes wrong, you won't have to remove the case again to get at the component.

Install Software

I've got good news and bad news. The good news is that the new component is installed. The bad news is that it doesn't work yet. You have one thing left to do before the component will be fully functional. All components require some kind of software in order to function. You must install *software drivers* so that the operating system can communicate with the new hardware component. At the same time, other *utility software* is usually installed. These utilities are what the user uses to interact with the device.

In our case (continuing with our sound card example), you need to install the sound card drivers and software for the sound card you just installed. Find the disks that came with the sound card (they will probably be in a white envelope inside the sound card's box). Plug all the cords back in and turn the computer on. Insert the first disk into the A: drive and, depending on whether the program uses DOS or Windows, type one of the following on a command line:

- from a DOS prompt: type **A:INSTALL**
- from Windows 3.*x*, select File ➤ Run or from Windows 95 select Start ➤ Run, and then type **A:SETUP**

Your installation manual will tell you which you need to use. Follow the onscreen prompts and complete the software installation. When you've finished, you may need to reboot the computer.

Testing Components

The component should now be functional. To make sure that it's functioning properly, you need to test it. There are two ways to test components: through observation and by using software diagnostics.

Observation is the simplest method of testing. It involves observing the device and seeing if the device functions as it's supposed to. For example, if your sound card is installed properly, you should be able to hear sounds when you play your favorite games. Or, you should be able to play sound files with the utility that came with your sound card.

The other method of testing components is to run any diagnostics that may have come with the device. These are very simple software programs that are designed to test the functions of only that device. You can run these programs during the installation process, or later by running the diagnostic program.

These programs usually give their results in the form of pass/fail. For example, the diagnostic program will test the sound-generating capabilities of your sound card and return "pass" if the diagnostics found no problem with that aspect of the card. If there were problems, the diagnostics will return "fail" for the particular part of the sound card that wasn't functioning.

If your sound card is functioning normally, you can turn the computer off and put the covers back on.

NOTE   For more information on diagnostics, see Chapter 12, "Troubleshooting."

Reassembling the Computer

If you followed the steps under "Disassembing the Computer," you will have a computer case and several components laid out in front of you. This section deals with how to put this collection of parts together into a functioning computer. We'll cover the steps in reassembling the computer, as well as a few tips to make the job easier.

The basic rule to remember when reassembling anything is to reverse the steps you took when you took it apart. That sounds easy enough, but ask anyone who has ever taken a watch or clock apart how easy it actually is. Computers are simpler than watches, thankfully, and can be reassembled without too much trouble.

Installing the Motherboard

The first step in reassembly is sometimes optional. If you didn't remove the motherboard during disassembly, you can skip this step. Installing the motherboard involves positioning it in the case (as shown originally in Figure 7.7) and securing it with either screws or plastic circuit board fasteners.

Once the motherboard is secured in the case, you must connect the individual connectors that run to things like the reset switch and the turbo button (if present). Figure 7.10 details this step.

Reconnecting the cables

Installing the Disk Drives

The next step in the reassembly of the computer is the installation of the disk drives. This involves mounting the drives in the case and connecting the drive cables to the adapters.

Let's discuss installing the floppy drive(s) first. To install a floppy drive, place it into position and secure it with at least one screw in each side. Once you finish this, connect the appropriate connector on the floppy cable to the drive and the floppy controller. Remember to orient the cable so that the red wire in the floppy cable is positioned towards pin one. Also remember the rules for connecting floppy drives when more than one drive exists (i.e., when you have both an A: and a B: drive).

The installation of fixed disk drives follows basically the same procedure. With hard disks, position the drive (and its installation rails, if used), and secure it with at least one screw on each side. Once the drive is securely fastened to the case, connect the drive cable to the drive and to the disk adapter (or motherboard if your motherboard has an integrated disk adapter), remembering the "red wire guideline" mentioned above. Also, don't forget the rules for connecting disks to cables as mentioned in Chapter 4, "Disk System Architecture."

Configuring the CMOS

IDE hard disks get their configuration information from the BIOS' CMOS (Complementary Metal-Oxide Semiconductor) memory. CMOS contains settings that determine how the computer is configured. These settings are user-configurable and can be accessed through the *CMOS setup program* by pressing some key combination at startup (like Shift+F1 or Ctrl+Shift+Esc). For example, one setting in CMOS controls the boot sequence. The parameter is usually called "boot sequence" and can be set to either "A: C:" or "C: A:" (in most cases).

Every CMOS setup program is different and uses different commands for configuration. Usually, though, the CMOS setup program is menu driven and will present you with a list of settings that you can configure as well as the possible settings for them. When you're done configuring, you can press Esc and the CMOS setup program will ask you to press Enter to save the changes and reboot. After rebooting, the computer will operate with the modified settings.

TIP   During the system boot, the computer checks what hardware settings are in the CMOS versus what is actually installed in the computer. If they are different, the BIOS will issue a warning and usually bring you right to the CMOS setup screen.

If you run across a computer that doesn't automatically detect an IDE hard disk when you install it, you will have to run the CMOS setup program and change the hard disk definitions. These are usually shown as a series of numbers under columns like Cyl, Heads, and Sect. These columns and numbers correspond to the drive's cylinders, heads, and sectors (in other words, their geometry). By changing the numbers in these columns, you are changing what the BIOS "knows" about the hard disk. The numbers that must be entered in these columns can usually be found either on the back of the drive itself or in the documentation that came with the drive.

WARNING Changing the drive geometry without needing to can cause long-term data damage or loss.

Installing the Power Supply

At this point, you have the motherboard and disk drives installed. You can now install the power supply and provide power to these components. To install the power supply, hold the power supply in position and install the four mounting screws (if necessary). Then, connect the power connectors to each component (including the disk drives and motherboard) and make sure they are secure. Finally, make sure the power switch connector has been connected to the power supply.

When connecting the connectors labeled P8 and P9 to the motherboard, there is a hard way and an easy way. The hard way is to push the connectors straight down onto their pins. This takes considerable effort since the locking tabs are in the way. It's easier to position the connectors at a backwards tilt, as shown in Figure 7.11, and then slip them down into position. They slide on much easier and you won't damage anything (including yourself).

FIGURE 7.11:

Connecting power supply connectors P8 and P9

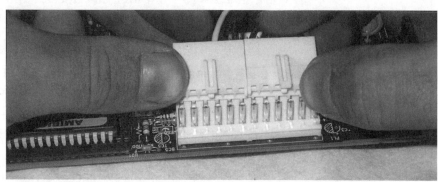

Installing the Expansion Cards

You are now ready to reinstall the expansion cards that you removed. To reinstall an expansion card, consult the diagram you made that shows the position of each expansion card and locate the slot for the card you are trying to install. Insert the card into its slot making certain that all of the card's connectors are making contact with the expansion slot. Other than that, reinstalling expansion boards is the same as installing new ones; see "Installing the Component" earlier in this chapter for instructions.

Installing the Case Cover

If everything is installed correctly, you should only have the case cover and case cover screws left to install. If you have other components left, you need to double-check your work. Go back and check to see that you haven't forgotten to install a component or mounting screw.

NOTE   The above reminder ("Check to see that you haven't forgotten to install a component") may seem unnecessary on the face of it, but I know that a large number of you, like most auto mechanics, will never have a completely clean workspace to start with. You probably have bits and pieces of other jobs sitting on the table you're working on right now. It's easy to lose track of which ones go with the current job and which ones you're holding onto for another project. So *do* strive to keep all the parts for one project at a time localized to just one area of your workspace; that way you'll be able to see easily whether you've finished the job or not.

When you are ready to install the case cover, position the computer on the work surface so that it won't move. Slide the case cover onto the computer so that it rests against its mounting tabs. Insert the mounting screws and tighten them so that the cover can't move. If the cover your computer uses has locking tabs, slide them into place so that the cover is secured.

Finally, hook up all the cables (keyboard, printer, power, and mouse) and make sure they are secured. When this is finished, you are ready to power up the computer. Turn on the computer and test your handiwork.

If it doesn't power up or work correctly, you will have to troubleshoot the problem. We will give you a few tips so that the chances of running into a problem are minimized.

NOTE   If these tips don't work, check Chapter 12, "Troubleshooting," for more steps.

General Reassembly Tips

There are several things that you can do to make your reassembly go smoother. While this is by no means a comprehensive list, it does outline the most common problems when reassembling a computer.

Read the directions. This is by far the most commonly ignored one. Everyone assumes that they know how to do something and they only read the instructions when they have problems. Besides offering the necessary warnings and guidelines, most instructions also contain a "Frequently Asked Questions" list (or FAQ) that provides answers to the most commonly asked questions. By reading the instructions before you start, you can avoid the most common pitfalls.

Take your time. The majority of disassembly/reassembly problems are caused by rushing. Rushing an installation may cause you to break components or to drop tools, which will cost you even more time. If you take your time, you will avoid these problems. Don't ever expect that a job will "just take ten minutes."

Check cables for proper orientation. A common problem when putting a computer back together is putting a cable on upside down (this frequently happens when installing cables for floppy drives). When this happens, the computer will get erroneous signals from the device. A rule of thumb for internal cables is to orient the cable so that the red wire is towards pin #1. A common indication that the floppy cable is on upside down is that the floppy light will be on constantly.

Make sure all connectors are secure. When installing any device, make sure that the connectors are secure. After installing a device, tug *lightly* on it to make sure that the connector isn't just "sitting" in the slot but is actually being grasped and held by it. If the connectors aren't secure, they can cause component failure or electrical shorts (which may destroy the component, the motherboard, or both).

Review Questions

1. Which of the following are important to consider when installing new expansion cards? (Circle all that apply.)

   A. ESD effects

   B. capacity of the hard disk

   C. position of expansion cards

   D. removing the cover

2. All case covers use three screws to hold them in. True or false?

   A. True

   B. False

3. During which disassembly step do you want to take notes?

   A. removing the case

   B. removing the expansion cards

   C. removing the power supply

   D. removing the disk drives

   E. removing the motherboard

   F. all of the above

4. You have just installed a new floppy drive. Upon powering up the computer, you discover that the floppy drive isn't working properly. The floppy drive light remains on as long as the computer is powered up. What should you check first?

   A. Floppy drive is in the wrong position on the floppy cable.

   B. Floppy cable is installed upside down.

   C. Floppy drive is defective.

   D. Floppy cable is defective.

5. What is the first step in installing a new device?

    A. disassembling the computer

    B. installing software

    C. removing the case

    D. reading the instructions

6. Which of the following can be used to determine the available resources on a computer before an upgrade or installation? (Circle all that apply.)

    A. MSD

    B. a visual examination of the computer

    C. reading the instructions

7. At this time, "Legacy" could correctly be used to refer to which types of expansion cards?

    A. 8-bit

    B. ISA

    C. MCA

    D. all of the above

8. A computer work area should contain which of the following? (Circle all that apply.)

    A. an oscilloscope

    B. assorted tools

    C. software

    D. anti-static wrist strap

9. The power supply motherboard connectors cannot be "pushed" vertically onto the motherboard receptacle. True or false?

    A. True

    B. False

10. What is the simplest method of testing a component?

    A. software diagnostics

    B. hardware diagnostics

    C. placing a multimeter across the power junction

    D. observing the component and seeing if it operates properly

11. Plug and Play cards don't work. True or false?

    A. True

    B. False

12. Anti-static bags should be used to store components when they are removed from a PC during service/disassembly. True or false?

    A. True

    B. False

13. Before you install a new device in a functioning computer, you should:

    A. disassemble the computer

    B. determine the computer's available resources

    C. install DOS

    D. install MSD

14. Removal of the motherboard is always required when disassembling a computer. True or false?

    A. True

    B. False

15. Which of the following is NOT a prerequisite to disassembling a computer?

    A. disconnecting the power cable

    B. shutting down the computer

    C. disconnecting the monitor and keyboard cables

    D. disassembling the power supply

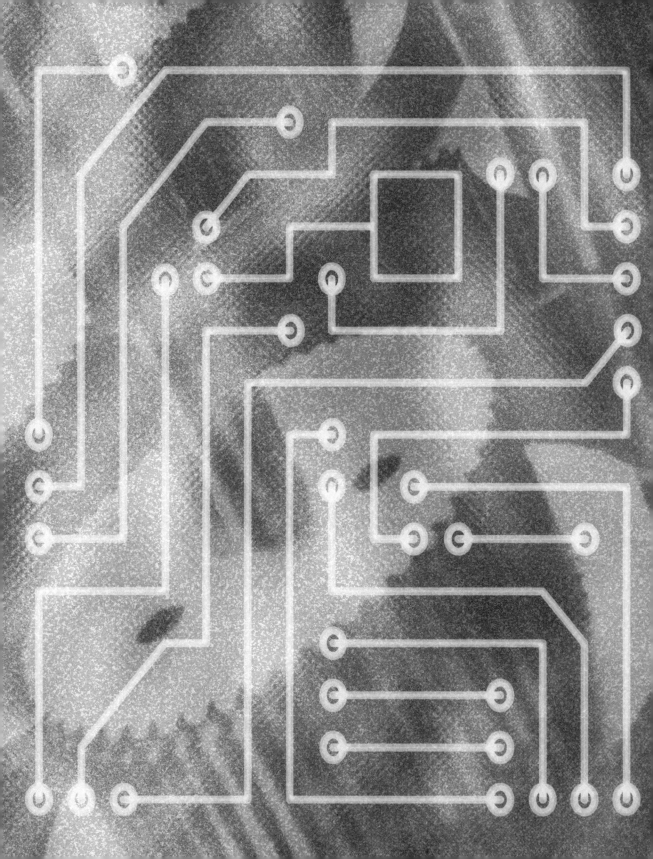

CHAPTER
EIGHT

How Printers Work

Objectives

- Identify basic concepts, printer operations, and printer components.

- Identify care and service techniques and common problems with primary printer types.

- Identify the types of printer connections and configurations.

Let's face it. We are a society dependent on paper. When we conduct business, we use different types of paper documents. Contracts, letters, and of course money, are all used to conduct business. As computers become the replacement for the paper ways of doing business, printers will become increasingly important.

Printers are electro-mechanical output devices that are used to put information from the computer onto paper. They have been around since the introduction of the computer. Other than the display monitor, the printer is the most popular peripheral purchased for a computer, since most people need to have paper copies of the documents they create.

In this chapter, we will discuss the details of each major type of printer. We will cover the following A+ exam topics:

- Impact printers
- Bubble-jet printers
- Laser printers (page printers)
- Interfaces and print media

TIP   Take special note of the section on laser and page printers. The A+ exams test these subjects in detail, so we'll cover them in as much detail.

Impact Printers

There are several categories of printers, but the most basic type is the category of printers known as *impact printers*. Impact printers, as their name suggests, use some form of impact and an inked ribbon to make an imprint on the paper. In a manner of speaking, typewriters are like impact printers. Both use an inked ribbon and an impact head to make letters on the paper. The major difference is that the printer can accept input from a computer.

There are two major types of impact printers: daisy-wheel and dot-matrix. Each type has its own service and maintenance issues.

Daisy-Wheel Printers

The first type of impact printer we're going to discuss is the *daisy-wheel* printer. These printers contain a wheel (called the daisy wheel because it looks like a daisy) with raised letters and symbols on each "petal" (see Figure 8.1). When the printer needs to print a character, it sends a signal to the mechanism that contains the wheel. This mechanism is called the *print head*. The print head rotates the daisy wheel until the required character is in place. An electromechanical hammer (called a *solenoid*) then strikes the back of the "petal" containing the character. The character pushes up against an inked ribbon which ultimately strikes the paper, making the impression of the requested character.

FIGURE 8.1:

A daisy-wheel printer mechanism

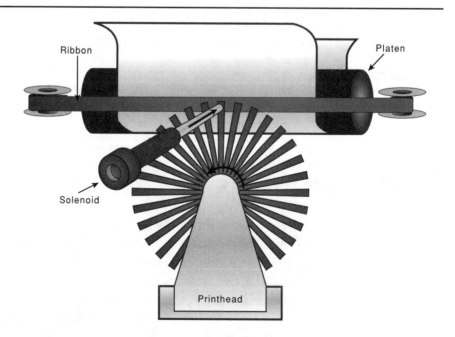

Daisy-wheel printers were one of the first types of impact printer developed. Their speed is rated by the number of *characters per second* (*cps*) they could print. The early printers could only print between two and four characters per second. Aside from their poor speed, the main disadvantage to this type of printer is that it makes a lot of noise when printing. So much, in fact, that special enclosures were developed to contain the noise.

The daisy-wheel printer has a few advantages, of course. First of all, because it is an impact printer, you can print on multipart forms (like carbonless receipts), assuming they can be fed into the printer properly. Second, it is relatively inexpensive, compared to the price of a laser printer of the same vintage. Finally, the print quality is comparable to a typewriter, because it uses a very similar technology. This typewriter level of quality was given a name: *Letter Quality* (*LQ*).

Dot-Matrix Printers

The other type of impact printer we're going to discuss is the dot-matrix printer. These printers work in a manner similar to daisy-wheel printers, except that instead of a spinning, character-imprinted wheel, the print head contains a row of "pins" (short sturdy stalks of hard wire). These pins are triggered in patterns that form letters and numbers as the print head moves across the paper (see Figure 8.2).

The pins in the print head are wrapped with coils of wire to create a solenoid. Also, the pins are held in the rest position by a combination of a small magnet and a spring. To trigger a particular pin, the printer controller sends a signal to the print head, which energizes the wires around the appropriate print wire. This turns the print wire into an electromagnet, which repels the print pin, forcing it against the ink ribbon, making a dot on the paper. It's the arrangement of the dots in columns and rows that creates the letters and numbers we see on the page. Figure 8.2 shows this process.

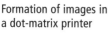

FIGURE 8.2:

Formation of images in a dot-matrix printer

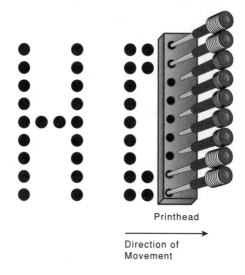

Printhead

Direction of Movement

The main disadvantage to dot-matrix printers is their image quality, which can be quite poor compared to the quality produced with a daisy-wheel. Dot-matrix printers use patterns of dots to make letters and images, and the early dot-matrix printers used only 9 pins to make those patterns. The output quality of such printers is referred to as "draft quality"—good mainly for providing your initial text to a correspondent or revisor. Each letter looked "fuzzy" because the dots were spaced as far as they could be while still being able to be perceived as a letter or image. As more pins were crammed into the print head (17-pin and 24-pin models were eventually developed), the quality increased, as the dots were closer together. Dot-matrix technology ultimately improved to the point where a letter printed on a dot-matrix printer was *almost* indistinguishable from typewriter output. This level of quality is known as Near Letter Quality (NLQ).

Dot-matrix printers are still noisy, but the print wires and print head are covered by a plastic dust cover, making them quieter than daisy-wheel printers. Also, dot-matrix printers use a more efficient printing technology, so the print speed is faster (typically in the range of 36 to 72 cps). Some dot-matrix printers (like the

Epson DFV series) can print at close to a page per second! Finally, because dot-matrix printers are also impact printers, they can also use multipart forms. Because of these advantages, dot-matrix printers quickly made daisy-wheel printers obsolete.

Bubble-Jet Printers

The next category of printer technology is one of the most popular in use today. This category of printers is actually an advanced form of an older technology known as ink-jet printers. Both types of printers spray ink on the page, but ink-jet printers use a reservoir of ink, a pump, and an ink nozzle to accomplish this. These printers were messy, noisy, and inefficient. Bubble-jet printers work much more efficiently.

Bubble-jet printers are very basic printers. There are very few moving parts. Every bubble-jet printer works in a similar fashion. First of all, every bubble-jet printer contains a special part called an ink cartridge (see Figure 8.3). This part contains the print head and ink supply, and it must be replaced as the ink supply runs out.

FIGURE 8.3:

A typical ink cartridge (size: approximately 3 inches by 1½ inches)

Inside this ink cartridge are several small chambers. At the top of each chamber is a metal plate and tube leading to the ink supply. At the bottom of each chamber is a small pinhole. These pinholes are used to spray ink on the page to form characters and images as patterns of dots (similar to the way a dot-matrix printer works, but with much higher resolution).

When a particular chamber needs to spray ink, an electric signal is sent to the heating element, energizing it. The elements heat up quickly, causing the ink to vaporize. Because of the expanding ink vapor, the ink is pushed out the pinhole and forms a bubble of ink. As the vapor expands, the bubble eventually gets large enough to break off into a droplet. The rest of the ink is pulled back into the chamber by the surface tension of the ink. When another drop needs to be sprayed, the process begins again.

Laser Printers (Page Printers)

Laser printers are referred to as page printers because they receive their print job instructions one page at a time (rather than receiving instructions one line at a time). There are three major types of page printers, those that use the Electrophotographic (EP) print process, those that use the Hewlett-Packard (HP) print process, and those that use the Light Emitting Diode (LED) print process. Each works in basically the same way, with slight differences.

Electrophotographic (EP) Laser Printer Operation

When Xerox and Canon developed the first laser printers in the late 1980s, they were designed around the Electrophotographic (EP) process (a technology developed by scientists at Xerox). This technology uses a combination of static electric charges, laser light, and a black powdery substance called *toner*. Printers that use this technology are called EP Process laser printers, or just *laser printers*. Every laser printer technology has its foundations in the EP printer process.

Let's discuss the basic components of the EP laser printer and how they operate so we can understand the way an EP laser printer works.

Basic Components

Any printer that uses the EP process contains eight standard assemblies. These assemblies are the toner cartridge, fusing assembly, laser scanner, high-voltage power supply, DC power supply, paper transport assembly (including paper-pickup rollers and paper-registration rollers), corona, and printer controller circuitry. Let's discuss each of the components individually, before we discuss how all the components work together to make the printer function.

The Toner Cartridge   The EP toner cartridge (Figure 8.4), as its name suggests, holds the toner. Toner is a black, carbon substance mixed with polyester resins (to make it "flow" better) and iron oxide particles (to make the toner sensitive to electrical charges). These two components make the toner capable of being attracted to the photosensitive drum and capable of melting into the paper. In addition to these components, toner contains a medium called the *developer (*also called the *carrier),* which "carries" the toner until it is used by the EP process. The toner cartridge also contains the EP print drum. This drum is coated with a photosensitive material that can hold a static charge when not exposed to light (but *cannot* hold a charge when it *is* exposed to light—a curious phenomenon, and one that EP printers exploit for the purpose of making images). Finally, the drum contains a cleaning blade that continuously scrapes the "used" toner off the photosensitive drum to keep it clean.

FIGURE 8.4:

An EP toner cartridge

SIDE VIEW

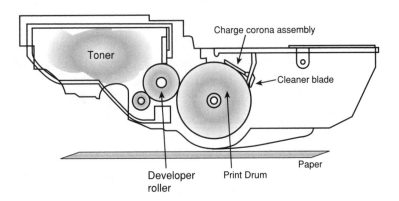

NOTE   In most laser printers, "toner cartridge" means an EP toner cartridge that contains toner and a photosensitive drum in one plastic case. In some laser printers, however, the toner and photosensitive drum can be replaced separately, instead of as a single unit. If you ask for a "toner cartridge" for one of these printers, all you will receive is a cylinder full of toner. Consult the printer's manual to find out which kind of toner cartridge your laser printer uses.

The Laser Scanning Assembly   As we mentioned earlier, the EP photosensitive drum can hold a charge if not exposed to light. It is dark inside an EP printer, except when the laser scanning assembly shines on particular areas of the photosensitive drum. When it does that, the drum discharges, but only in that area. As the drum rotates, the laser scanning assembly scans the laser across the photosensitive drum. Figure 8.5 shows the laser scanning assembly.

Side View

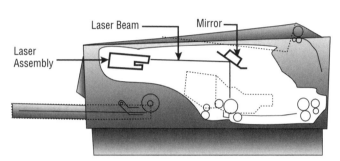

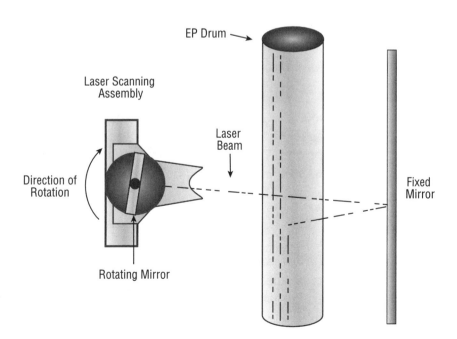

Laser light is damaging to human eyes. Therefore, it is kept in an enclosure and will operate only when the laser printer's cover is closed.

High-Voltage Power Supply (HVPS)   The EP process requires high-voltage electricity. The high-voltage power supply provides the high voltages that are used during the EP process. This component converts house AC current (120 volts, 60 Hertz) into higher voltages that the printer can use. This high voltage is used to energize both the corona wire and transfer corona wire.

DC Power Supply (DCPS)   The high voltages used in the EP process can't power the other components in the printer (the logic circuitry and motors). These components require low voltages, between +5 and +24 Vdc. The DC power supply converts house current into three voltages: +5 Vdc and –5 Vdc for the logic circuitry, and +24 Vdc for the paper transport motors. This component also runs the fan that cools the internal components of the printer.

Paper Transport Assembly   The paper transport assembly is responsible for moving the paper through the printer. It consists of a motor and several rubberized rollers that each perform a different function.

The first type of roller found in most laser printers is the *feed roller,* or *paper pickup roller* (Figure 8.6). This D-shaped roller, when activated, rotates against the paper and pushes one sheet into the printer. This roller works in conjunction with a special rubber pad to prevent more than one sheet from being fed into the printer at a time.

Another type of roller that is used in the printer is the registration roller (also shown in Figure 8.6). There are actually two registration rollers, which work together. These rollers synchronize the paper movement with the image formation process in the EP cartridge. These rollers don't feed the paper past the EP cartridge until the cartridge is ready for it.

FIGURE 8.6:

Paper transport rollers

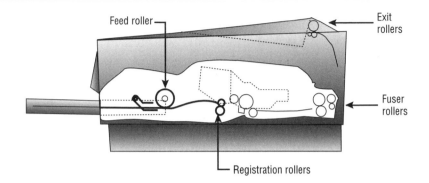

Both of these rollers are operated with a special electric motor known as an *electronic stepper motor*. This type of motor can accurately move in very small increments. This motor powers all of the paper transport rollers as well as the fuser rollers.

The Transfer Corona Assembly   When the laser writes the images on the photosensitive drum, the toner then sticks to the exposed areas (we'll cover this in the next section, "The EP Print Process"). How do you get the toner from the photosensitive drum onto the paper? Well, the *transfer corona assembly* (Figure 8.7) is charged with a high-voltage electrical charge. This assembly charges the paper, which pulls the toner from the photosensitive drum.

FIGURE 8.7:

The transfer corona assembly

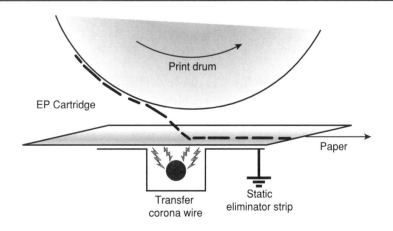

Included in the corona assembly is a *static-charge eliminator strip* that drains away the charge imparted to the paper by the corona. If you didn't drain away the charge, the paper would stick to the EP cartridge and jam the printer.

There are two types of corona assemblies, those that contain a *corona wire* and those that contain a *corona roller*. The corona wire is a small diameter wire that is charged by the high-voltage power supply. The wire is located in a special notch in the "floor" of the laser printer (underneath the EP print cartridge). The corona roller performs the same function as the corona wire, except for the fact that it's a roller rather than a wire. Because the corona roller is directly in contact with the paper, it supports higher speeds. It is for this reason that the corona wire isn't used in laser printers much any more.

Fusing Assembly   The toner in the EP toner cartridge will stick to just about anything, including paper. This is true because the toner has a negative static charge and most objects have a net positive charge. However, these toner particles can be removed by brushing any object across the page. This could be a problem if you want the images and letters to stay on the paper permanently!

To solve this problem, EP laser printers incorporate a device known as a *fuser* (Figure 8.8), that uses two rollers which apply pressure and heat to fuse the plastic toner particles to the paper. You may have noticed that pages from either a laser printer or a copier (which uses a similar device) come out warm. This is because of the fuser.

The fuser is made up of three main parts: a halogen heating lamp, a Teflon-coated aluminum fusing roller, and a rubberized pressure roller. The fuser uses the halogen lamp to heat the fusing roller to between 165°C and 180°C. As the paper passes between the two rollers, the pressure roller pushes the paper against the fusing roller, which melts the toner into the paper.

FIGURE 8.8:

The fuser

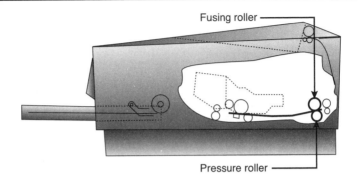

Fusing roller

Pressure roller

Printer Controller Circuitry   The final component in the laser printer we need to discuss is the *printer controller assembly*. This large circuit board converts signals from the computer into signals for the various assemblies in the laser printer, using the process known as *rasterizing*. This circuit board is usually mounted underneath the printer. The board has connectors for each of the types of interfaces, and cables to each assembly.

When a computer prints to a laser printer, it sends a signal through a cable to the printer controller assembly. The controller assembly formats the information into a page's worth of line-by-line commands for the laser scanner. The controller sends commands to each of the components telling them to "wake up" and start the EP print process.

Electrophotographic (EP) Print Process

The EP print process is the process by which an EP laser printer forms images on paper. It consists of six major steps, each for a specific goal. The steps are, in order:

1. Charging
2. Exposing
3. Developing

4. Transferring

5. Fusing

6. Cleaning

Before any of these steps can begin, however, the controller must sense that the printer is ready to start printing (toner cartridge installed, fuser warmed to temperature, and all covers are in place). Printing cannot take place until the printer is ready.

Step 1: Charging   The first step in the EP process is the *charging* step (Figure 8.9). In this step, a special wire (called a *charging corona*) within the EP toner cartridge (above the photosensitive drum) gets a high voltage from the HVPS. It uses this high voltage to apply a strong, uniform negative charge (–600 Vdc) to the surface of the photosensitive drum.

FIGURE 8.9:

The Charging step of the EP process

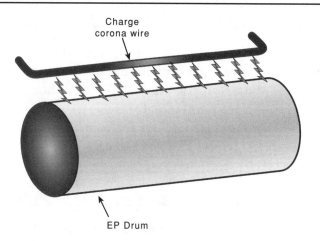

Charge corona wire

EP Drum

Step 2: Exposing   The next step in the EP process is the *exposure* step. In this step, the laser is turned on and "scans" the drum from side to side, flashing on and off according to the bits of information the printer controller sends it as it communicates the individual bits of the image. The areas where the laser "touches" severely reduce the photosensitive drum's charge from –600 Vdc to a slight negative charge (around –100 Vdc). As the drum rotates, a pattern of exposed areas is formed, representing the images to be printed. Figure 8.10 shows this process.

FIGURE 8.10:

The Exposure step of the EP process

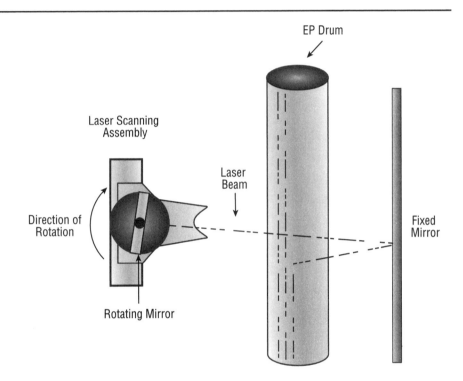

At this point, the controller sends a signal to the pickup roller to feed a piece of paper into the printer, where it stops at the registration rollers.

Step 3: Developing   Now that the surface of the drum holds an electrical representation of the image being printed, we need to convert its discrete electrical charges into something that can be transferred to a piece of paper. The EP process step that accomplishes this is the *developing* step (Figure 8.11). In this step, toner is transferred to the areas that were exposed in the exposure step.

The Developing step of the EP process

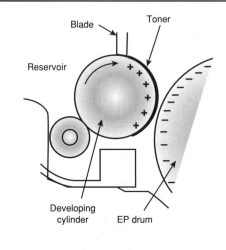

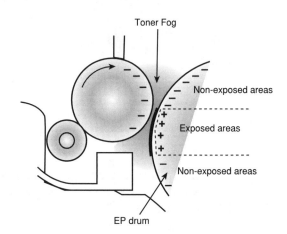

There is a metallic roller called the *developing roller* inside an EP cartridge that acquires a –600 Vdc charge (called a bias voltage) from the HVPS. The toner sticks to this roller because there is a magnet located inside the roller and because of the electrostatic charges between the toner and the developing roller. While the developing roller rotates towards the photosensitive drum, the toner acquires the charge of the roller (–600 Vdc). When the toner comes between the developing roller and the photosensitive drum, the toner is attracted to the areas that have been exposed by the laser (because these areas have a lesser charge, of –100 Vdc). The toner also is repelled from the unexposed areas (because they are at the same –600 Vdc charge, and like charges repel). This toner transfer creates a "fog" of toner between the EP drum and the developing roller.

The photosensitive drum now has toner stuck to it where the laser has written. The photosensitive drum continues to rotate until the developed image is ready to be transferred to paper in the next step, the transfer step.

Step 4: Transfer   At this point in the EP process, the developed image is rotating into position. The controller notifies the registration rollers that the paper should be fed through. The registration rollers move the paper underneath the photosensitive drum, and the process of transferring the image can begin, with the *transfer* step.

The controller sends a signal to the corona wire or corona roller (depending on which one the printer has) and tells it to turn on. The corona wire/roller then acquires a strong *positive* charge (+600 Vdc) and applies that charge to the paper. The paper, thus charged, pulls the toner from the paper at the line of "contact" between the roller and the paper, because the paper and toner have opposite charges. Once the registration rollers move the paper past the corona wire, the static-eliminator strip removes all charge from that "line" of the paper. Figure 8.12 details this step. If the strip didn't bleed this charge away, the paper would attract itself to the toner cartridge and cause a paper jam.

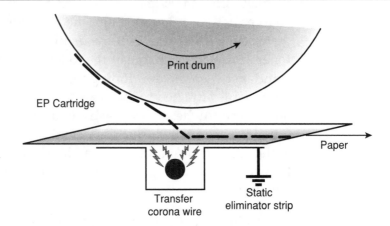

FIGURE 8.12:

The Transfer step of the EP process

The toner is now held in place by weak, electrostatic charges and gravity. It will not stay there, however, unless it is made permanent, which is the reason for the next step, the fusing step.

Step 5: Fusing In the next step, the *fusing* step, the toner image is made permanent. The registration rollers push the paper towards the fuser. Once the fuser grabs the paper, the registration rollers push for only a short time more. The fuser is now in control of moving the paper.

As the paper passes through the fuser, the 350°F fuser roller melts the polyester resin of the toner and the rubberized pressure roller presses it permanently into the paper (Figure 8.13). The paper continues on through the fuser and eventually exits the printer.

Once the paper completely exits the fuser, it trips a sensor that tells the printer to finish the EP process with the next step, the cleaning step.

Step 6: Cleaning Now that the image has been transferred to paper and permanently fixed to the page, the printer needs to clean up after itself. In the final step, a rubber blade inside the EP

FIGURE 8.13:

The Fusing step of the EP process

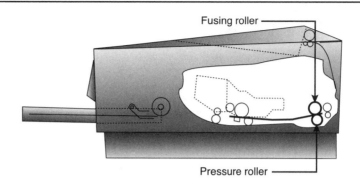

Fusing roller

Pressure roller

cartridge scrapes any untransferred toner into a used toner receptacle inside the EP cartridge and a fluorescent lamp discharges any remaining charge on the photosensitive drum (remember that the drum, being photosensitive, loses its charge when exposed to light). This step is called the *cleaning* step (Figure 8.14).

FIGURE 8.14:

The Cleaning step of the EP process

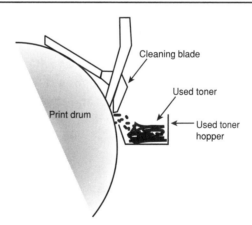

Cleaning blade

Used toner

Print drum

Used toner hopper

The EP cartridge is constantly cleaning the drum. It may take more than one rotation of the photosensitive drum to make an image on the paper. The cleaning step keeps the drum "fresh" for each use. If you didn't clean the drum, you would see "ghosts" of previous pages printed along with your image.

NOTE   The actual amount of toner removed in the cleaning process is quite small. The cartridge will run out of toner before the used toner receptacle fills up.

At this point, the printer can print another page and the EP process can begin again.

Summary of the EP Print Process   Figure 8.15 summarizes all the EP process printing steps. Let's sum up the EP print process. First, the printer places a uniform, negative, –600 Vdc charge on the photosensitive drum by means of a charging corona. The laser "paints" an image onto the photosensitive drum, discharging the image areas to a much lower voltage (–100 Vdc). The developing roller in the toner cartridge has charged (–600 Vdc) toner stuck to it. As it rolls the toner toward the photosensitive drum, the toner is attracted to (and sticks to) the areas of the photosensitive drum that the laser has discharged. The image is then transferred from the drum to the paper at its line of contact by means of the corona wire (or corona roller) with a +600 Vdc charge. The static-eliminator strip removes the high, positive charge from the paper, and the paper, now holding the image, moves on. The paper then enters the fuser where a fuser roller and the pressure roller make the image permanent. The paper exits the printer and the printer cleans the photosensitive drum.

HP LaserJet Operation

The largest manufacturer of laser printers is Hewlett-Packard. Their LaserJet series of printers outsell any other brand of laser or page printer on the market (at the time of the writing of this book). These printers are based on the EP print process, so they share most of the same basic components. There are some differences, however, both in the components and in the process. So we will detail the differences, where they exist. Otherwise you may assume that the HP and EP processes and components are the same.

FIGURE 8.15:

The EP print process

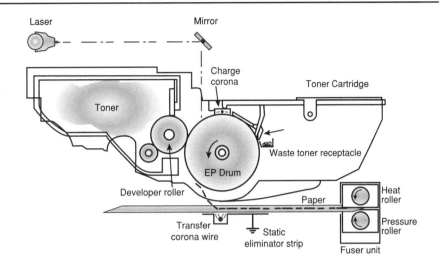

Basic Components

An HP LaserJet contains a toner cartridge, fusing assembly, laser scanner, high-voltage power supply, DC power supply, paper transport assembly (including paper pickup rollers and paper registration rollers), corona, and printer controller circuitry, just as in an EP laser printer. Because the HP is basically the same as an EP laser printer, we won't discuss them again. However, we will make a few, brief notes about the differences between the HP LaserJet components and EP laser printer components, when necessary.

First of all, the HP LaserJet toner cartridges contain the same parts (photosensitive drum, cleaning blade, developing roller, and toner), but the toner is charged differently. Also, the HP toner cartridges use a charging roller rather than a charge corona. Because of these differences, a LaserJet toner cartridge might not work in a generic EP process printer.

And Now for the Real World...

Apple LaserWriters and HP LaserJets use the same print engine, so some of the parts (including the toner cartridges) are interchangeable. For example, an Apple LaserWriter II uses the same toner cartridge as an HP LaserJet II. The HP cartridges are slightly cheaper than Apple-brand cartridges.

Also, the fusers and some of the rollers (pickup and registration) are the same and can be interchanged, if necessary.

Be careful, though, as not *every* component of these two types of printers is interchangeable. For example, the controller boards are completely different.

Additionally, HP LaserJet printers use a set of Light Emitting Diodes (LEDs) to erase the photosensitive drum during the cleaning stage of the HP process. Finally, the HP LaserJets use different polarities on the high voltages, but we will discuss those in the next section.

HP Print Process

Just as HP LaserJet components are very similar to EP laser printer components, the HP print process is similar to the EP print process. But, since we need to understand the HP process in detail, we cover the major differences between the EP process and the HP process.

TIP   The HP print process is covered heavily on the A+ exam. It is important to know the exact name of the different process steps as well as their order for the exam.

HP Step 1: Conditioning   In the *conditioning* step, the surface of the photosensitive drum in the toner cartridge is charged with a uniform negative charge to its surface by a charge roller. It gets this negative charge from the HVPS, just as in the EP process.

HP Step 2: Writing   In this step, areas of the print drum are selectively discharged to ground (0 Vdc, or zero charge) with a laser. When the laser light shines on the drum in a particular area, that small area is discharged to ground. As the beam is scanned across the surface of the drum (using a rotating mirror in the laser assembly and a beam reflector above the printer drum), the laser is repeatedly turned on and off, making patterns of discharge on the print drum. These patterns represent the image that you are printing.

HP Step 3: Developing   As the drum rotates, it passes by the developing roller. This roller has negatively charged toner stuck to it (using a small positive charge). The toner is attracted to the discharged areas of the drum and repelled from the other portions of the print drum. This develops the image on the drum. The image can then be transferred to the paper.

HP Step 4: Transferring   A strong positive charge is applied to the backside of the paper. This charge is strong enough to pull the toner from the print drum and transfer it to the paper. Usually HP LaserJets use a transfer roller to apply this charge. Immediately next to this item is a static-eliminator strip that removes the strong positive charge to prevent the paper from sticking to the negatively charged print drum.

HP Step 5: Fusing   Just as in the EP process, the fuser permanently bonds the toner to the paper in the *fusing* step. The fuser roller heats the paper and toner, and the pressure roller presses the toner into the paper. When the paper exits the fuser, a sensor tells the controller to feed another piece of paper.

HP Step 6: Cleaning Finally, in the *cleaning* step, any toner residue from a previous print image is removed by a cleaning blade and stored in the toner cartridge's waste toner receptacle. A set of Light Emitting Diodes (LEDs) totally exposes the drum and the process begins again.

Summary of the HP Print Process Let's sum up the HP print process. First, the printer places a uniform, negative charge on the photosensitive drum with a charging roller. The laser "paints" an image onto the photosensitive drum, discharging the areas to ground. The developing roller in the toner cartridge has negatively charged toner stuck to it. As the developing roller rotates, the toner sticks to the areas of the photosensitive drum that the laser has discharged. The image is transferred to the paper using the corona wire (or corona roller) with a strong, positive charge. The static-eliminator strip removes the high positive charge, and the paper moves on. The paper then enters the fuser, where a fuser roller and the pressure roller make the image permanent. The paper exits the printer, and the printer cleans the photosensitive drum by scraping the toner into the toner cartridge's waste receptacle; it also erases any residual charges by exposing the photosensitive drum to LEDs.

LED Page Printers

The final type of laser printer we're going to discuss is the LED page printer. This technology is primarily developed and used by Okidata and Panasonic. Since the A+ exam does not currently cover LED page printers, we will only discuss the differences between them and laser printers.

The two main differences between an LED page printer and a laser printer are the toner cartridges and the print process.

LED Page Printer Toner Cartridges

One problem with laser printers is that the toner usually runs out before the photosensitive drum needs to be replaced. But since they're both housed in the same replaceable unit, every time you replace the toner, you're also replacing the drum, whether it needs replacing or not. So, the designers of the LED page printers designed the photosensitive drum and toner to be separate, replaceable items.

NOTE   The main parts of the LED page printer toner cartridge are actually integrated into the printer. Additionally, the charging corona (or roller) and erasing lamps are integrated into the printer. These items cannot be replaced by the average user. An authorized service technician must remove them.

When replacing the photosensitive drum, you swing the photosensitive drum/toner cartridge out of the printer first. Then, you remove the drum from its carrier and install the new one (this also replaces the waste toner receptacle).

Filling the toner hopper is fairly easy. On most LED page printers, you place the new toner cartridge over the toner hopper and lock it in place. Between the new toner cartridge and the toner hopper is a lever and door. When the lever is slid over, it opens the door and allows the toner to fall through the opening. Once all the toner is out of the cartridge and hopper, the lever is slid back, closing the door. You can then remove the cartridge and throw it away.

The LED Page Printer Process

The LED page printer uses the same process as any other laser printer, with one major exception. It uses a row of small LEDs held very close to the photosensitive drum to expose it. Each LED is about the same size as the diameter of the laser beam used in laser printers. These printers are basically the same as EP process printers, except that in the exposure step they use LEDs instead of a laser.

There are several benefits of LED page printers over laser printers. First of all, because they use LEDs instead of lasers, these printers are much cheaper than a similar laser printer—they're about half the cost. Also, because the LEDs are very close to the drum, the whole printer is smaller—about two-thirds the size of a comparable laser printer. Finally, LEDs aren't as dangerous to the eye as lasers (you could probably damage your eyes if you stared at one long enough, but it's unlikely you'd do such a thing).

If they have so many advantages, why isn't everyone using them? Mainly because LED technology isn't as advanced as laser technology. The resolutions of LED page printers have yet to break the 800 dots-per-inch (dpi) mark. Another reason is that the toner system in an LED printer, while more efficient, is also messier. Because of its slight static charge, toner isn't easy to remove from surfaces.

WARNING   Never ship a printer anywhere with a toner cartridge installed! If the printer is a laser printer, remove the toner cartridge first. If it's an LED page printer, there is a method to remove the photosensitive drum and toner hopper (check your manual for details).

Printer Interfaces and Supplies

Besides understanding the printer's operation, for the exam you will need to understand how the printer talks to a computer and all the items involved in that process. Also, you must understand how the different types of print media affect the print process. These two concepts will complete our discussion of printers.

Interface Components

A printer's *interface* is the collection of hardware and software that allows the printer to communicate with a computer. Each printer has at least one interface, but some printers have several, in order to make them more flexible in a multiplatform environment. If a printer has several interfaces, it can usually switch between them "on the fly" so that several computers can print at the same time.

There are several components to an interface, including its *communication type* as well as the *interface software*. Each aspect must be matched on both the printer and the computer. For example, an HP LaserJet 4L only has a parallel port. Therefore, you must use a parallel cable as well as the correct software for the platform being used (e.g., a Macintosh HP LaserJet 4L driver if you connect it to a Macintosh computer).

Communication Types

When we say communication types, we're actually talking about the hardware technologies involved in getting the printed information from the computer to the printer. There are three major types: serial, parallel, and network.

Serial   When computers send data serially, they send it one bit at a time, one after another. The bits "stand in line" like people at a movie theater, waiting to get in. We've already discussed serial (asynchronous) communication in Chapter 6. Just as with modems, you must set the communication parameters (baud, parity, start and stop bits) on both entities—in this case the computer and its printer(s)—before communication can take place.

Parallel   When a printer uses parallel communication, it is receiving data eight bits at a time over eight separate wires (one for each bit). Parallel communication is the most popular way of communicating from computer to printer, mainly because it's faster than serial.

A parallel cable consists of a male DB-25 connector that connects to the computer and a male 36-pin Centronics connector that connects to the printer. Most of the cables are shorter than ten feet long.

WARNING Keep printer cable lengths to less than 10 feet. Some people try to run printer cables more than 50 feet. After 10 feet, communications can become unreliable due to crosstalk (which is described in Chapter 1).

Network   Some of the newer printers (primarily laser and LED printers) have a special interface that allows them to be hooked directly to a network. These printers have a *network interface card* (*NIC*) and ROM-based software that allow them to communicate with networks, servers, and workstations.

The type of network interface used on the printer depends on the type of network the printer is being attached to. For example, if you're using a token-ring network, the printer should have a token-ring interface.

Interface Software

Computers and printers can't talk to each other by themselves. They need interface software to translate software commands into commands that the printer can understand.

There are two factors to consider with interface software: the page description language and the driver software. The *page description language* determines how efficient the printer will be at converting the information to be printed into signals the printer can understand. The *driver software* understands and controls the printer. It is very important that you use the correct interface software for the printer you are using. If you use either the wrong page description language or the wrong driver software, the printer will print garbage, or possibly nothing at all.

Page Description Languages   A page description language works just as its name says it does. A page description language describes the whole page being printed. The controller in the printer interprets these commands and turns them into laser pulses (or pin strikes).

Life without a Page Description Language

The most basic page description language is no page description language. The computer sends all the instructions that the printer needs in a serial stream, like so: Position 1, print nothing; Position 2, strike pins 1 and 3; Position 3, print nothing. This type of description language works great for dot-matrix printers, but it can be very inefficient for laser printers. For example, if you wanted to print a page using a standard page description language and there was only one character on the page, there would be a lot of wasted signal for the "print nothing" commands.

Also, with graphics, the commands to draw a shape on the page are relatively complex. For example, to draw a square, the computer (or printer) has to calculate the size of the square and convert that into lots of "Strike pin *x*" (or "turn on laser") and "print nothing" commands. This is where the other types of page description languages come into the picture.

The first page description language was PostScript. Developed by Adobe, it was first used in the Apple LaserWriter printer. It made printing graphics fast and simple. PostScript works like so: The PostScript printer driver "describes" the page in terms of "draw" and "position" commands. The page is divided into a very fine grid (as fine as the resolution of the printer). When we want to print a square, a communication like the following might take place:

```
POSITION 1,42%DRAW 10%POSITION 1,64%DRAW10D% . . .
```

These commands tell the printer to draw a line on the page from line 42 to line 64 (vertically). In other words, a page description language tells the printer to draw a line on the page, gives it the starting and ending points, and that's that. Rather than send the printer the location of each and every dot in the line and an instruction at each and every location to print that location's individual dot, Post-Script can get the line drawn with fewer than five instructions. As you can see, PostScript uses more or less English commands. The commands are interpreted by the processor on the printer's controller and converted into the print control signals.

Another page description language is the Printer Control Language, or PCL. Currently in revision 5 (PCL 5), it was developed by Hewlett-Packard for their LaserJet series of printers as a competitor to PostScript. PCL works in much the same manner as PostScript, but it's found mainly in Hewlett-Packard printers (including their DeskJet bubble-jet printers). Other manufacturers use PCL, however. In fact, some printers support both page description languages and will automatically switch between them.

The main advantage to page description languages is that they move some of the processing from the computer to the printer. With text-only documents, they don't offer much benefit. However, with documents that have large amounts of graphics, or that use numerous fonts, page description languages make the processing of those print jobs happen much faster. This makes them an ideal choice for laser printers. However, other printers can use them as well (i.e., the aforementioned DeskJets, as well as some dot-matrix printers).

Driver Software   The *driver software* controls how the printer processes the print job. When you install a printer driver for the printer you are using, it allows the computer to print to that printer correctly (assuming you have the correct interface configured between the computer and printer).

When you need to print, you select the printer driver for your printer from a preconfigured list. The driver you select has been configured for the type, brand, and model of printer as well as which computer port it is hooked to. You can also select which paper tray the printer should use, as well as any other features the printer has (if applicable). Also, each printer driver is configured to use a particular page description language.

WARNING If the wrong printer driver is selected, the computer will send commands in the wrong language. If that occurs, the printer will print several pages full of garbage (even if only one page of information was sent). This "garbage" isn't garbage at all, but in fact the printer page description language commands printed literally as text instead of being interpreted as control commands.

Printer Supplies

Just as it is important to use the correct printer interface and printer software, you must use the correct printer supplies. These supplies include the *print media* (what you print on) and the *consumables* (what you print with). The quality of the final print job has a great deal to do with the print supplies.

Print Media

The print media is what you put through the printer to print on. There are two major types of print media, paper and transparencies. Of the two types, paper is by far the most commonly used.

Paper   Most people don't give much thought to the kind of paper they use in their printers. It's a factor that can have tremendous effect on the quality of the hard copy printout, however, and the topic is more complex than people think. For example, if the wrong paper is used, it can cause the paper to jam frequently and possibly even damage components.

There are several aspects of paper that can be measured; each gives an indication as to the quality of the paper. The first factor is composition. Paper is made from a variety of substances. Paper used to be made from cotton and was called *rag stock*. Paper can also be made from wood pulp, which is a cheaper way of making it. Most paper today is made from the latter or a combination of the two.

Another aspect of paper is the property known as *basis weight* (or simply "weight" for short). The "weight" of a particular type of paper is the actual weight, in pounds (*lb*), of 500 sheets of 17" × 22.5" paper made of that material. The most common weight used in printers is 20lb paper.

The final paper property we'll discuss is the *caliper* (or thickness) of an individual sheet of paper. If the paper is too thick, it may jam in feed mechanisms that have several curves in the paper path. (On the other hand, a paper that's too thin may not feed at all.)

These are just three of the categories that we use to judge the quality of the paper. Because there are so many different types and brands of printers as well as paper, it would be impossible to give the specifications for the "perfect" paper. However, the documentation for any printer will give specifications for the paper that should be used in that printer.

TIP   For best results with any printer, buy the paper that has been designated specifically for that printer by the manufacturer. It will be more expensive, but you won't have any problems related to having the wrong type of paper for the printer. Also, the print quality will be the best it could possibly be.

Transparencies   Transparencies are still used for presentations made with overhead projectors, even with the explosion of programs like PowerPoint (from Microsoft) and peripherals like LCD computer displays, both of which let you show a whole roomful of people exactly what's on your computer screen. Actually, though, PowerPoint still has an option to print "slides,"and you can use any program you want to print anything you want to a transparent sheet of plastic or vinyl for use with an overhead projector. The problem is, these "papers" are *exceedingly* difficult for printers to work with. That's why special transparencies were developed for use with laser and bubble-jet printers.

Each type of transparency was designed for a particular brand and model of printer. Again, check the printer's documentation to find out which type of transparency works in that printer. Don't use any other type of transparency!

WARNING   *NEVER* run transparencies through a laser printer without first checking to see if it's the type recommended by the printer manufacturer. The heat from the fuser will melt most other transparencies and they will wrap themselves around it. It is impossible to clean a fuser after this has happened. The fuser will have to be replaced. *Use ONLY the transparencies that are recommended by the printer manufacturer.*

Print Consumables

Besides print media, there are other things in the printer that run out and need to be replenished. These items are the *print consumables*. Most consumables are used to form the images on the print media. There are two main types of consumables in printers today: ink and toner. Toner is used primarily in laser printers. Most other printers use ink.

Ink   Ink is a liquid that is used to "stain" the paper. There are several different colors of ink used in printers, but the majority use some shade of black or blue. Both dot-matrix printers and bubble-jet printers use ink, but with different methods.

Dot-matrix printers use a cloth or polyester ribbon soaked in ink and coiled up inside a plastic case. This assembly is called a *printer ribbon* (or *ribbon cartridge*). It's very similar to a typewriter ribbon, except that instead of the two rolls you'd see on a typewriter, the ribbon is continuously coiled inside the plastic case. Once the ribbon has run out of ink, the ribbon must be discarded and replaced with a new one. Ribbon cartridges are developed closely with their respective printers. It is for this reason that ribbons should be purchased from the same manufacturer as the printer. The wrong ribbon could jam in the printer as well as cause adverse quality problems.

Bubble-jet cartridges actually have a liquid ink reservoir. The ink in these cartridges is sealed inside. Once the ink runs out, the cartridge must be removed and discarded. A new, full one is installed in its place. Because the ink cartridge contains ink as well as the printing mechanism, it's like getting a new printer every time you replace the ink cartridge.

Some bubble-jet printers have the ink cartridge and the print head in separate assemblies. In this way, the ink can be replaced when it runs out and the print head can be used several times. This works fine if the printer is designed to work this way. However, some people think they can do this on their integrated cartridge/print head system, using special ink cartridge refill kits. These kits consist of a syringe filled with ink and a long needle. The needle is used to puncture the top of an empty ink cartridge. The syringe is then used to refill the reservoir. Don't use these kits! See the warning on the following page.

WARNING DO NOT USE INK CARTRIDGE REFILL KITS! (The ones you see advertised with a syringe and a needle.) These kits have several problems. First, the kits don't use the same kind of ink that was originally in the ink cartridges. The new ink may be thinner, causing the ink to run out or not print properly. Also, the print head is supposed to be *replaced* around this same time. Just refilling it doesn't replace the print head. This will cause print quality problems. Finally, the hole the syringe leaves cannot be plugged and may allow ink to leak out. The bottom line is: *Buy new ink cartridges from the printer manufacturer*. Yes, they are a bit more expensive, but you will actually save money since you won't have any of the problems described above.

Toner   The final type of consumable we're going to discuss is toner. Each model of laser printer uses a specific toner cartridge. We've already discussed the different types of toner cartridges earlier in this chapter. The only note we have to make here is to check the printer's manual to see which toner cartridge it needs.

WARNING Just as with ink cartridges, always buy the exact model recommended from the manufacturer. That's because, just as with ink cartridges, the toner cartridges have been designed specifically for a particular model. Additionally, NEVER refill toner cartridges, for most of the same reasons we don't recommend refilling ink cartridges. The quality is poor and, besides, the fact that you're just refilling the toner means you're *not* replacing the photosensitive drum (which is usually inside the cartridge), and it might be that the drum *needs* to be replaced. Simply replacing the refilled toner cartridges with proper, name-brand ones has solved most laser printer quality problems I have run across. We keep recommending the right ones, but clients keep coming back with the refilled ones. But hey, we'll keep taking our clients' money to solve their quality problems, especially when all it involves is just a toner cartridge, the repeating of our advice to buy the proper cartridge next time, and the obligatory minimum charge for a half hour of labor, even though the job of replacing the cartridge takes all of five minutes!

Review Questions

1. The step in the EP print process that uses a laser to discharge selected areas of the photosensitive drum, thus forming an image on the drum.

    A. Writing

    B. Exposing

    C. Developing

    D. Discharging

2. The following is a list of the steps in the HP print process. Put them in the proper order in which they occur: ___, ___, ___, ___, ___, ___.

    A. Developing

    B. Writing

    C. Transferring

    D. Fusing

    E. Conditioning

    F. Cleaning

3. It is better to refill ink cartridges than to buy new ones. True or false?

    A. True

    B. False

4. Which voltage is used to transfer the toner to the paper in an EP process laser printer?

    A. +600 Vdc

    B. –600 Vdc

    C. +6000 Vdc

    D. –6000 Vdc

5. If the static-eliminator strip is absent (or broken) in either an EP process or HP LaserJet laser printer what will happen?

    A. Nothing. Both printers will continue to function normally.

    B. Nothing will happen in EP process printers, but HP LaserJet printers will flash a "−671 error."

    C. Paper jams may occur in both types of printers, because the paper may curl around the photosensitive drum.

6. Toner cartridges should be taken out and refilled with the correct toner when they run out of toner. True or false?

    A. True

    B. False

7. Which of the following are possible interfaces for printers? (Circle all that apply.)

    A. parallel

    B. mouse port

    C. serial

    D. network

8. Which laser printer component formats the print job for the type of printer being used?

    A. corona assembly

    B. DC power supply

    C. printer controller circuitry

    D. formatter software

9. Which of the following are page description languages?
   (Circle all that apply.)

   A. Page Description Language (PDL)

   B. PostScript

   C. PageScript

   D. Printer Control Language (PCL)

10. The basis weight is the weight in pounds of 500 sheets of
    what size of paper?

    A. 8.5" × 11"

    B. 11" × 17"

    C. 17" × 22.5"

    D. 8.5" × 17"

11. PostScript is most often used on dot-matrix printers. True or
    false?

    A. True

    B. False

12. Which type(s) of printers can be used with multipart forms?
    (Circle all that apply.)

    A. bubble-jet

    B. EP process laser printers

    C. HP process laser printers

    D. dot-matrix printers

13. LED page printers differ from EP process laser printers in
    which step?

    A. Exposing

    B. Charging

    C. Fusing

    D. Cleaning

    E. Developing

    F. Transferring

14. What part of both EP process and HP LaserJet process printers supplies the voltages for the charge and transfer corona assemblies?

    A. High-Voltage Power Supply (HVPS)

    B. DC Power Supply (DCPS)

    C. controller circuitry

    D. transfer corona

15. With HP LaserJet laser printers, the laser discharges the charged photosensitive drum to _____ Vdc.

    A. +600

    B. 0

    C. –100

    D. –600

16. With EP process laser printers, the laser discharges the charged photosensitive drum to _____ Vdc.

    A. +600

    B. 0

    C. –100

    D. –600

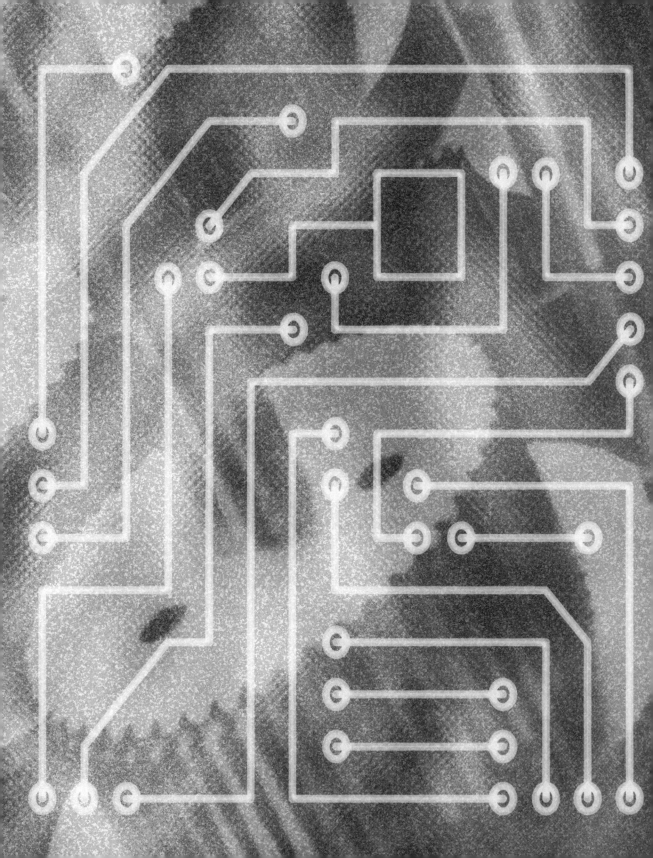

CHAPTER
NINE

Networks

Objectives

- Identify basic networking concepts, including how a network works.

- Identify procedures for swapping and configuring network interface cards.

- Identify ramifications of repairs on the network.

Imagine twenty years ago working in an office with little or no computer equipment. It's hard to imagine now, isn't it? One could say that we take for granted a lot of what we have gained in technology the past few decades. Now, imagine having to send a memo to everyone in the company. Back then we used interoffice mail; today we use e-mail. This is one form of communication that only became available due to the introduction and growth of *networks*.

This chapter focuses on the basic concepts surrounding how a network works, including the way it sends information and what it uses to send information. This information is covered only to a minor degree by the A+ certification exam. However, if you have interest in becoming a service technician this information will prove to be very useful, as you will in all likelihood find yourself asked to troubleshoot both hardware and software problems on existing networks. Included in this chapter is information on:

- What is a network?
- Network types
- Media types
- Connectivity devices

What Is a Network?

Stand-alone personal computers, first introduced in the late 1970s, gave users the ability to create documents, spreadsheets, and other types of data and save them for future use. For the small business user or home computer enthusiast this was great. For larger companies, however, it was not enough; for the larger the company, the greater the need to share information between offices, and sometimes over great distances. The stand-alone computer was not enough for the following reasons:

- Their small hard drive capacities were inefficient.

- To print, each computer required a printer attached locally.

- Sharing documents was cumbersome. People grew tired of having to save to a diskette, and then take that diskette to the recipient. (This procedure was called "sneakernet.")

- There was no e-mail. Instead, there was interoffice mail, which was not reliable, and frequently was not delivered in a timely manner.

To address these problems, *networks* were born. A network links two or more computers together to communicate and share resources. Their success was a revelation to the computer industry as well as businesses. Now, departments could be linked internally to offer better performance and an increase in efficiency.

You have heard the term "networking" in the business context, where people come together and exchange names for future contact and to give them access to more resources. The same is true with a computer network. A computer network allows computers to link to each other's resources. For example, in a network every computer would not need a printer connected locally to print. Instead, one computer would have a printer connected to it and allow the other computers to access this resource. Because they allow users to share resources, networks offer an increase in performance as well as a decrease in the outlay for new hardware and software.

LANs vs. WANs

Local area networks (LANs) were introduced to connect computers in a single office. *Wide area networks* (WANs) came to expand the LANs to include networks outside of the local environment and also to distribute resources across distances. Today, LANs can be seen in a lot of businesses, from small to large. WANs are becoming more widely accepted as businesses are becoming more mobile and as more of them are spanning across greater and greater distances. It is important to have an understanding of LANs and WANs as a service professional, because when you're repairing computers you are likely to come in contact with problems that are associated with the computer being connected to a network.

Local Area Networks (LANs)

The 1970s brought us the minicomputer, which was a smaller version of the mainframe. Whereas the mainframe used *centralized processing* (all programs ran on the same computer), the minicomputer used *distributed processing* to access programs across other computers. As depicted in Figure 9.1, distributed processing allows a user at one computer to use a program on another computer as a "back end" to process and store the information. The user's computer would be the "front end," performing the data entry. These allowed programs to be distributed across computers rather than centralized. This was also the first time computers used cable to connect rather than phone lines.

FIGURE 9.1:

Distributed processing

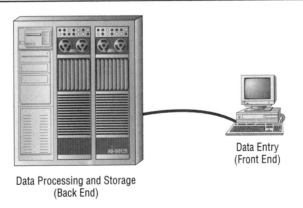

Data Processing and Storage
(Back End)

Data Entry
(Front End)

By the 1980s, offices were beginning to buy PCs in large numbers. Also, portables were introduced, allowing computing to become mobile. Neither PCs nor portables, however, were efficient in sharing information. As timeliness and security became more important, diskettes were just not cutting it. Offices needed to find a way to implement a better means to share and access resources. This led to the introduction of the first type of PC LAN: ShareNet, by Novell. LANs are simply the linking of computers to share resources within a closed environment. The first simple LANs were constructed a lot like Figure 9.2.

FIGURE 9.2:

A simple LAN

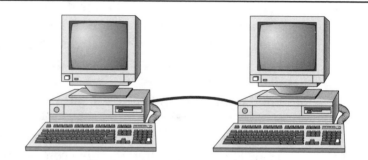

After the introduction of ShareNet, more LANs sprouted. The earliest LANs could not cover a great distance. Most of them could only stretch across a single floor of the office, and could support no more than 30 users. Further, they were still simple, and only a few software programs supported them. The first software programs that ran on a LAN were not capable of permitting more than one user at a time to use a program (this constraint was known as *file locking*). Nowadays, we can see multiple users accessing a program at one time, limited only by restrictions at the record level.

Wide Area Networks (WANs)

By the late 1980s, networks were expanding to cover ranges considered geographical in size and were supporting thousands of users. Wide area networks, or WANs, first implemented with mainframes at massive government expense, started attracting PC users as networks went to this whole new level. Businesses with offices across the country communicated as if they were only desks apart. Soon the whole world would see a change in its way of doing business, across not only a few miles but across countries. Whereas LANs are limited to single buildings, WANs are able to span buildings, states, countries, and even continental boundaries. Figure 9.3 gives an example of a simple WAN.

FIGURE 9.3:

A simple WAN

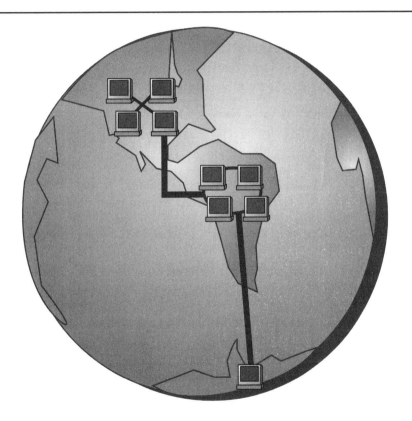

Networks of today and tomorrow are not limited anymore by the inability of LANs to cover distance and handle mobility. WANs play an important role in the future development of corporate networks worldwide. Although the primary focus of this chapter is LANs, we will feature a section on WAN connectivity. This section will briefly explain the current technologies and what you should expect to see in the future. If you are interested in more information on LANs or WANs, or plan on becoming a networking technician, check your local library resources or the Internet.

Primary Network Components

Putting together a network is not as simple as it was with the first PC network. You can no longer consider two computers cabled together a fully functional network. Today, networks consist of three primary components:

- Servers
- Clients or workstations
- Resources

No network would be complete without these three components working together.

Servers

Servers come in many shapes and sizes. Servers are a core component of the network, providing a link to the resources necessary to perform any task. The link it provides could be to a resource existing on the server itself or a resource on a client computer. The server is the "leader of the pack," offering directions to the client computers regarding where to go to get what they need.

Servers offer networks the capability of centralizing the control of resources, and can thus reduce administrative difficulties. They can be used to distribute processes for balancing the load on the computers and can thus increase speed and performance. They can also offer the departmentalizing of files for improved reliability. That way, if one server goes down then not all of the files are lost.

Servers perform several tasks. For example, servers that provide files to the users on the network are called file servers. Likewise, servers that host printing services for users are called print servers. (There are other tasks as well, such as remote access services, administration, mail, etc.) Servers can be *multi-purpose* or *single-purpose*. If they are multi-purpose, they can be both a file server (for example) and a print server at the same time. If the server is a single-purpose server, it is a file server only (for example) or print server only.

Another distinction we use in categorizing servers is whether they are *dedicated* or *nondedicated*:

Dedicated Servers These are assigned to provide specific applications or services for the network, and nothing else. Because a dedicated server is specializing in only a few tasks, it requires fewer resources from the computer that is hosting it than a nondedicated server might require. This savings in overhead may translate to a certain efficiency, and can thus be considered as having a beneficial impact on network performance.

Nondedicated Servers These are assigned to provide one or more network services *and* local access. A nondedicated server is expected to be slightly more flexible in its day-to-day use than a dedicated server. Nondedicated servers can be used not only to direct network traffic and perform administrative actions, but often to serve as a front-end for the administrator to work with other applications or services. The nondedicated server is not really what some would consider a true server, because it can act as a workstation as well as a server.

Many networks use both dedicated and nondedicated servers in order to incorporate the best of both worlds, offering improved network performance with the dedicated servers and flexibility with the nondedicated servers.

Workstations or Client Computers

Workstations are the computers that the users on a network do their work on, performing activities such as word processing, database design, graphic design, e-mail, and other office or personal tasks. Workstations are basically nothing more than an everyday computer, except for the fact that they are connected to a network that offers additional resources. Workstations can range from a diskless computer system to a desktop system. In network terms, workstations are also known as *client computers*. As clients, they are allowed to communicate with the servers in the network in order to use the network's resources.

It takes several items to make a workstation into a client. You must install a *network interface card* (NIC), a special expansion card that allows the PC to talk on a network. You must connect it to a cabling system that connects to another computer (or several other computers). And you must install some special software, called *client software*, which allows the computer to talk to the servers. Once all this has been accomplished, the computer will be "on the network."

To the client, the server may be nothing more than just another drive letter. However, because it is in a network environment, the client is able to use the server as a doorway to more storage or more applications, or through which it may communicate with other computers or other networks. To a user, being on a network changes a few things:

- They can store more information, because they can now store data on other computers on the network.

- They can now share and receive information from other users, perhaps even collaborating on the same document.

- They can use programs that would be too large for their computer to use by itself.

Network Resources

We now have the server to share the resources and the workstation to use them, but what about the resources themselves? A *resource* (as far as the network is concerned) is any item that can be used on a network. Resources can include a broad range of items, but the most important ones include:

- Printers and other peripherals
- Files
- Applications
- Disk Storage

When an office can purchase paper, ribbons, toner, or other consumables for only one, two, or maybe three printers for the entire office, the costs are dramatically lower than the costs for supplying printers at every workstation. Networks also give more storage space to files. Client computers are not always able to handle the overhead involved in storing large files, for example database files, because they are already heavily involved in the day-to-day work activities of the users. Since servers in a network can be dedicated to only certain functions, a server could be allocated to store all the larger files that are worked with every day, freeing up disk space on client computers. Similarly, applications (programs) no longer need to be on every computer in the office. If the server is capable of handling the overhead an application requires, the application could reside on the server and be used by workstations through a network connection.

NOTE   The sharing of applications over a network requires a special arrangement with the application vendor, who may wish to set the price of the application according to the number of users who will be using it. The arrangement allowing multiple users to use a single installation of an application is called a *site license*.

Being on a Network Brings Responsibilities

You are part of a community when you are on a network, which means that you need to take responsibility for your actions. First of all, a network is only as secure as the users who use it. You cannot just randomly delete files or move documents from server to server. You do not own your e-mail, so anyone in your company's management can choose to read it. Additionally, printing does not mean that if you send something to print now, that it will print immediately—yours may not be the first in line to be printed at the shared printer. Plus, if your workstation has also been set up to be a nondedicated server, you cannot turn it off.

Network Operating Systems (NOSes)

PCs use a disk operating system that controls the file system and how the applications communicate with the hard disk. Networks use a network operating system (NOS) to control the communication with resources and the flow of data across the network. The NOS runs on the server. Many companies offer software to start a network. Some of the more popular network operating systems at this time include Unix, Novell's IntranetWare, and Microsoft's Windows NT Server. Although several other NOSes exist, these three are the most popular.

Back in the early days of mainframes, it took a full staff of people working around the clock to keep the machines going. With today's NOSes, servers are able to monitor memory, CPU time, disk space, and peripherals, without a baby-sitter. Each of these operating systems allows processes to respond in a certain way with the processor.

With the new functionality of LANs and WANs, you can be sitting in your office in Milwaukee and carry on a real-time electronic "chat" with a coworker in France, or maybe print an invoice at the home office in California, or manage someone else's computer from your own, while they are on vacation. Gone are the days of disk-passing, phone messages left but not received, or having to wait a month to receive a letter from someone in Hong Kong. NOSes provide this functionality on a network.

Network Resource Access

Now that we have discussed the makeup of a typical network, let's discuss the way resources are accessed on a network. There are generally two resource access models: peer-to-peer and server-based. It is important to choose the appropriate model. How do you decide what type of resource model is needed? You must first think about the following questions.

- What is the size of the organization?

- How much security does the company require?

- What software or hardware does the resource require?

- How much administration does it need?

- How much will it cost?

- Will this resource meet the needs of the organization today and in the future?

- Will additional training be needed?

Networks today cannot just be put together at the drop of a hat. A lot of planning is required before implementation of a network to ensure that whatever design is chosen will be effective and efficient, and not just for today, but for the future as well. It is the forethought of the designer that will create the best network with the least amount of administrative overhead. In each network, it is important that a plan be developed to answer the above questions. The answers will help decide the type of resource model to be used.

Peer-to-Peer Networks

A peer-to-peer network is a network where the computers act as both workstations and servers. An example of a peer-to-peer resource model is shown in Figure 9.4.

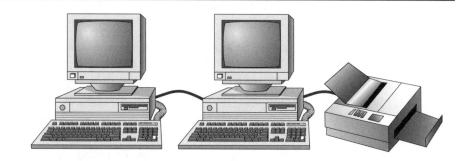

Peer-to-peer networks are great for small, simple, and inexpensive networks. In fact, this model can be set up almost immediately, with little extra hardware required. Windows 3.11, Windows 95, and Windows NT are popular operating system environments that support a peer-to-peer resource model.

There is no centralized administration or control in the peer-to-peer resource model. However, this very lack of centralized control can make it difficult to "administer" the network; for the same reason, it's not very secure. Moreover, since each computer is acting as both a workstation and server, it may not be easy to locate the resources. The person who is in charge of the file may have moved it without anyone's knowledge. Also, the users who work under this arrangement need more training, because they are not only users but also administrators.

Will this type of network meet the needs of the organization today and in the future? Peer-to-peer resource models are generally considered the right choice for companies where there is no expected future growth. For example, the business might be small, possibly an independent subsidiary of a specialty company, and has no plans on increasing its market size or number of employees. Companies that are expecting growth, on the other hand, should not choose this type of model. Although it could very well meet the needs of the company today, the growth of the company will necessitate making major changes over time. If a company chooses to set up a peer-to-peer resource model simply because it is cheap and easy to install, it could be making a costly mistake. The company's management may find that it will cost them more in the long run than if they had chosen a server-based resource model.

Server-Based Resource Model

The server-based model is better than the peer-to-peer model for large networks (say 25 users or more) that need a more secure environment and centralized control. Server-based networks use a dedicated, centralized server. All administrative functions and resource sharing are performed from this point. This makes it easier to share resources, perform backups, and support an almost unlimited number of users. It also offers better security. However, it does need more hardware than that used by the typical workstation/server computer in a peer-to-peer resource model. Additionally, it requires specialized software (the NOS) to manage the server's role in the environment. With the addition of a server and the NOS, server-based networks can easily cost more than peer-to-peer resource models. However, for large networks, it's the only choice. An example of a server-based resource model is shown in Figure 9.5.

Will this type of network meet the needs of the organization today and in the future? Server-based resource models are the desired models for companies that are continually growing or that need to initially support a large environment. Server-based networks offer the flexibility to add more resources and clients almost indefinitely into the future. Hardware costs may be more, but, with the centralized administration, managing resources becomes less time-consuming. Also, only a few administrators need to be trained, and users are only responsible for their own work environment.

FIGURE 9.5:

The server-based
resource model

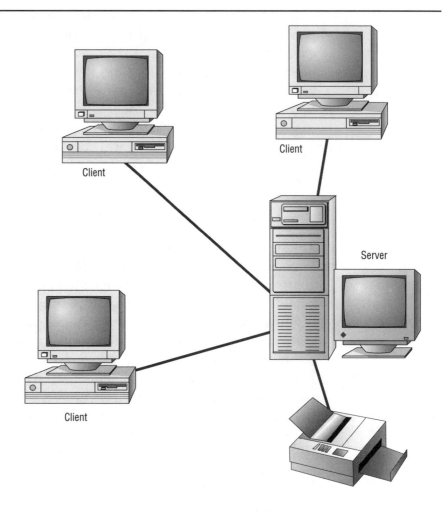

<table>
<tr><td>TIP</td><td>If you are looking for an inexpensive, simple network with very little setup required, and there is really no need for the company to grow in the future, then the peer-to-peer network is the way to go. If you are looking for a network to support many users (more than 25), strong security, and centralized administration, consider the server-based network your only choice.</td></tr>
</table>

Whatever you decide, be sure to take the time to plan. A network is not something you can just "throw together." You don't want to find out a few months down the road that the type of network you chose does not meet the needs of the company. This could be a timely and costly mistake.

Network Topologies

A *topology* is a way of "laying out" the network. Topologies can be either physical or logical. *Physical topologies* describe how the cables are run. *Logical topologies* describe how the network messages travel. Deciding which type of topology to use is the next step when designing your network.

You must choose the appropriate topology in which to arrange your network. Each type differs by its cost, ease of installation, fault tolerance (how the topology handles problems like cable breaks), and ease of reconfiguration (like adding a new workstation to the existing network).

There are five primary topologies (some of which can be both logical and physical topologies):

- Bus (can be both logical and physical)
- Star (physical only)
- Ring (can be both logical and physical)
- Mesh (can be both logical and physical)
- Hybrid (usually physical)

Each topology has its advantages and disadvantages. At the end of this section check out the table that summarizes the advantages and disadvantages of each one.

Bus

A bus is the simplest physical topology. It consists of a single cable that runs to every workstation like Figure 9.6. This topology uses the least amount of cabling, but also covers the shortest amount of distance. Each computer shares the same data and address path. With a logical bus topology, messages pass through the trunk, and each workstation checks to see if the message is addressed to itself. If the address of the message matches the workstation's address, the network adapter copies the message to the card's on-board memory.

Cable systems that use the bus topology are easy to install. You run a cable from the first computer to the last computer. All

FIGURE 9.6:

The bus topology

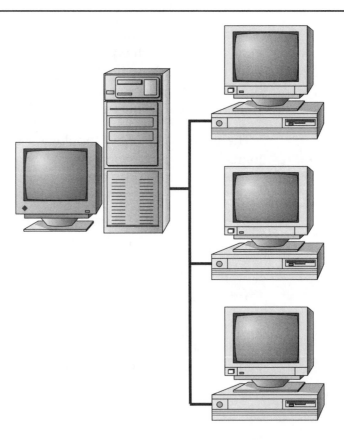

computers in between attach to the cable somewhere in between. Because of the simplicity of installation, and because of the low cost of the cable, bus topology cabling systems (like Ethernet) are the cheapest to install.

Although the bus topology uses the least amount of cabling, it is difficult to add a workstation. If you want to add another workstation, you have to completely reroute the cable and possibly run two additional lengths of it. Also, if any one of the cables breaks, the entire network is disrupted. Therefore, it is very expensive to maintain.

Star

A physical star topology branches each network device off of a central device called a *hub*, making it very easy to add a new workstation. Also, if any workstation goes down it does not affect the entire network. (But as you might expect, if the central device goes down the entire network goes down.) Some types of Ethernet and ARCNet use a physical star topology. Figure 9.7 gives an example of the organization of the star network.

Star topologies are easy to install. A cable is run from each workstation to the hub. The hub is placed in a central location in the office (for example, a utility closet). Star topologies are more expensive to install than bus networks, because there are several more cables that need to be installed, plus the cost of the hubs that are needed.

Ring

A physical ring topology is a unique topology. Each computer connects to two other computers, joining them in a circle creating a unidirectional path where messages move workstation to workstation. Each entity participating in the ring reads a message, then regenerates it and hands it to its neighbor on a different network cable. See Figure 9.8 for an example of a ring topology.

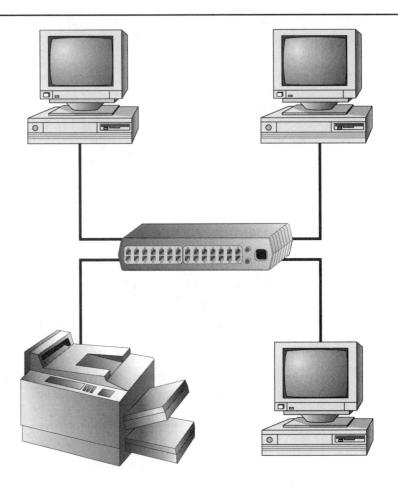

The ring makes it difficult to add new computers. Unlike a star topology network, the ring topology network will go down if one entity is removed from the ring. Physical ring topology systems don't exist much anymore, mainly because the hardware involved was fairly expensive and the fault tolerance was very low. However, one type of logical ring still exists: in IBM's Token Ring technology. We'll discuss this technology later in the "Network Architectures" section.

FIGURE 9.8:

FIGURE 9.8:

The ring topology

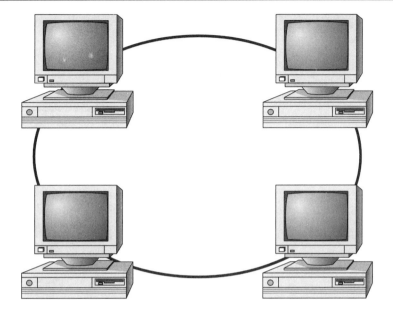

Mesh

The *mesh* topology is the simplest logical topology, in terms of data flow, but the most complex in terms of physical design. In this physical topology, each device is connected to every other device (Figure 9.9). This topology is rarely found in LANs, mainly because of the complexity of the cabling. If there are x computers, there will be $(x \times (x{-}1)) / 2$ cables in the network. For example, if you have five computers in a mesh network, it will use $5 \times (5{-}1)$ divided by 2, or 10 cables. This complexity is compounded when you add another workstation. For example, your five-computer, 10-cable network will jump to 15 cables just by adding one more computer. Imagine how the person doing the cabling would feel if you told them you had to cable 50 computers in a mesh network—they'd have to come up with $50 \times (50{-}1)$ divided by 2 = 1225 cables!

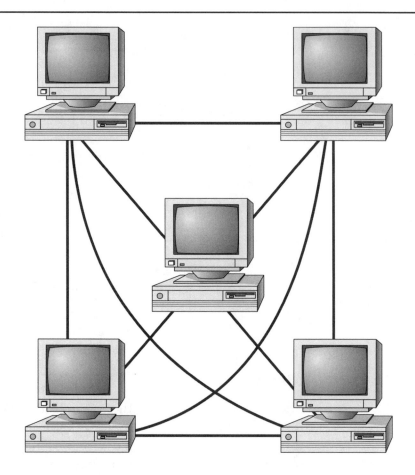

Because of its design, the physical mesh topology is very expensive to install and maintain. Cables must be run from each device to every other device. The advantage you gain from it is its high fault tolerance. With a logical mesh topology, however, there will always be a way of getting the data from source to destination. It may not be able to take the direct route, but it can take an alternate, indirect route. It is for this reason that the mesh topology is still found in WANs to connect multiple sites across WAN links. It uses devices called *routers* to search multiple routes through the mesh and determines the best path. However, the mesh topology does become inefficient with five or more entities.

Hybrid

The hybrid topology is simply a mix of the other topologies. It would be impossible to illustrate it, because there are many combinations. In fact, *most* networks today are not only hybrid, but heterogeneous (by heterogeneous I mean they include a mix of components of different types and brands). The hybrid network may be more expensive, on the one hand, than some types of network topologies, but, on the other hand, it takes the best features of all the other topologies and exploits them. Believe it or not, this is the most popular topology (second only to the star topology).

Summary of Topologies

Table 9.1 summarizes the advantages and disadvantages of each type of network topology. This table is a good study aid for the A+ exam. (In other words, memorize it!)

TABLE 9.1: Topologies—Advantages and Disadvantages

Topology	Advantages	Disadvantages
Bus	Cheap. Easy to install.	Difficult to Reconfigure. Break in bus disables entire network.
Star	Cheap. Easy to install. Easy to reconfigure. Fault tolerant.	More expensive than bus.
Ring	Efficient. Easy to install.	Reconfiguration difficult. Very expensive.
Mesh	Simplest. Most fault tolerant.	Reconfiguration extremely difficult. Extremely expensive. Very complex.
Hybrid	Gives combination of best features of each topology used.	Complex (less so than mesh, however).

Network Communications

You have chosen the type of network and arrangement, or topology. Now the computers need to understand how to communicate. Network communications take place using protocols. A *protocol* is a set of rules that govern communications. Protocols detail what "language" the computers are speaking when they talk over a network. If two computers are going to communicate, they both must be using the same protocol.

There are different methods used to describe the different protocols. We will discuss two of the most common, the OSI model and the IEEE 802 standards.

OSI Model

The International Standards Organization introduced the *Open Systems Interconnection (OSI)* model to provide a common way of describing network protocols. They put together a seven-layer model providing a relationship between the stages of communication, with each layer adding to the layer above or below it.

NOTE   This OSI model is just that: a model. It can't be implemented. You will never find a network that is running the "OSI protocol."

The theory with the OSI model is that as transmission takes place, the higher layers pass data through the lower layers. As the data passes through a layer, the layer will tack its information (also called a *header*) onto the end of the information being transmitted until it reaches the bottom layer. At this point, the bottom layer sends the information out on the wire.

At the receiving end, the bottom layer receives the information, reads its information from its header and removes its header from the information, and then passes the remainder to the next highest layer. This procedure continues until the topmost layer receives the data that the sending computer sent.

The OSI model layers from top to bottom are listed below. We'll *describe* each of these layers from bottom to top, however. After the descriptions, we'll summarize the entire model.

- Application layer
- Presentation layer
- Session layer
- Transport layer
- Network layer
- Data Link layer
- Physical layer

TIP   There are several acronyms that will help you remember the layers (as well as their order). For example, a popular one that indicates the layers from top to bottom is "All People Seem To Need Data Processing." One that indicates the layers from bottom to top is "People Design Networks To Send Packets Accurately." (There's also "Please Do Not Trust Sales People Always.")

Physical Layer   At the bottom of the OSI model is the *physical layer*. This layer describes how the data gets transmitted over a physical medium. It defines how long each piece of data is and the translation of each into the electrical pulses that are sent over the wires. It decides whether data travels unidirectionally or bidirectionally across the hardware. It also relates electrical, optical, mechanical, and functional interfaces to the cable.

Data Link Layer   The next layer is the data link layer. This layer arranges data into chunks called "frames." Included in these chunks is control information indicating the beginning and end of the data stream. This layer is very important because it makes transmission easier and more manageable as well as allowing for error checking within the data frames.

Network Layer   Addressing messages and translating logical addresses and names into physical addresses occurs at the network layer. The network layer is something like the traffic cop. It is able to judge the best network path for the data based on network conditions, priority, and other variables. This layer manages traffic through packet switching, routing, and controlling congestion of data.

Transport Layer   This layer signals "all clear" by making sure the data frames are error-free. It also controls the data flow and troubleshoots any problems with transmitting or receiving data frames. This layer's most important job is to provide error checking and reliable, end-to-end communications. Secondarily, it can also take several smaller messages and combine them into a single, larger message.

Session Layer   This layer allows applications on different computers to establish, use, and end a session. A session is one virtual "conversation." For example, all the procedures needed to transfer a single file make up one session. Once the session is over, a new process has begun. It enables network procedures such as identifying passwords, logons, and network monitoring. It can also handle recovery from a network failure.

Presentation Layer   This layer determines the "look," or format, of the data, network security, and file transfers. It performs protocol conversion and manages data compression. Data translation and encryption are handled at this layer. Also, the character set information is determined at this level. (The character set determines which numbers represent which alphanumeric characters.)

Application Layer   Finally, the *application layer* allows access to network services. This is the layer at which file services and print services operate. It also is the layer that workstations interact with. It also controls data flow and if there are errors, recovery.

Summary of OSI Model   Figure 9.10 shows the complete OSI model.

FIGURE 9.10:

OSI model and characteristics

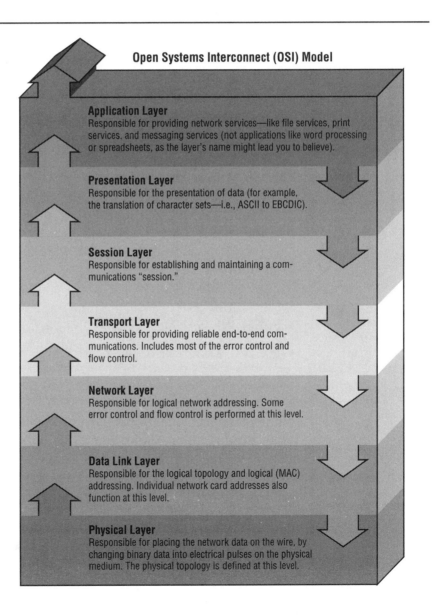

Open Systems Interconnect (OSI) Model

Application Layer
Responsible for providing network services—like file services, print services, and messaging services (not applications like word processing or spreadsheets, as the layer's name might lead you to believe).

Presentation Layer
Responsible for the presentation of data (for example, the translation of character sets—i.e., ASCII to EBCDIC).

Session Layer
Responsible for establishing and maintaining a communications "session."

Transport Layer
Responsible for providing reliable end-to-end communications. Includes most of the error control and flow control.

Network Layer
Responsible for logical network addressing. Some error control and flow control is performed at this level.

Data Link Layer
Responsible for the logical topology and logical (MAC) addressing. Individual network card addresses also function at this level.

Physical Layer
Responsible for placing the network data on the wire, by changing binary data into electrical pulses on the physical medium. The physical topology is defined at this level.

IEEE 802 Project Models

The Institute for Electrical and Electronics Engineers (IEEE) formed a subcommittee to create the 802 standards for networks. These standards specify certain types of networks, although not every network protocol is covered by the IEEE 802 committee specifications. This model breaks down into twelve categories, as listed below.

- 802.1 Internetworking
- 802.2 Logic Link Control
- 802.3 CSMA/CD LAN
- 802.4 Token Bus LAN
- 802.5 Token Ring LAN
- 802.6 Metropolitan Area Network
- 802.7 Broadband Technical Advisory Group
- 802.8 Fiber Optic Technical Advisory Group
- 802.9 Integrated Voice/Data Networks
- 802.10 Network Security
- 802.11 Wireless Networks
- 802.12 Demand Priority Access LAN

The IEEE 802 standards were designed primarily for enhancements to the bottom three layers of the OSI model. The IEEE 802 model breaks the Data Link layer into two sublayers: a Logical Link Control (LLC) sublayer and a Media Access Control (MAC) sublayer. In the logical link control sublayer, data-link communications are managed. The media access control layer watches out for data collisions, as well as assigning physical addresses.

We will focus on the two predominant 802 models that existing network architectures have been based on: 802.3 CSMA/CD and 802.5 Token Ring.

IEEE 802.3 CSMA/CD The 802.3 CSMA/CD model defines a bus topology network that uses a 50-ohm coaxial baseband cable and carries transmissions at 10 Mbps. This standard groups data bits into frames and uses the Carrier Sense Multiple Access with Collision Detection (CSMA/CD) cable access method to put data on the cable.

CSMA/CD specifies that every computer can transmit at any time. As sometimes happens, when two machines transmit at the same time, a "collision" takes place and no data can be transmitted for either machine. The machines then back off for a random period of time and try to transmit again. This process repeats until transmission takes place successfully. The CSMA/CD technology is also called "contention."

The only major downside to 802.3 is that with large networks (more than 100 computers on the same cable), the number of collisions increases to the point where there are more collisions than transmissions taking place.

An example of a protocol based on the IEEE 802.3 CSMA/CD standard is Ethernet.

NOTE   CSMA/CD and Ethernet are discussed in more detail later in this chapter.

IEEE 802.5 Token Ring The IEEE 802.5 standard specifies a physical star, logical ring topology that uses a token-passing technology to put the data on the cable. IBM developed this technology for their mainframe and minicomputer networks. IBM's name for it was Token Ring. The name stuck, and any network using this type of technology is called a Token Ring network.

In *token passing*, a special chunk of data called a *token* circulates through the ring from computer to computer. Any computer that has data to transmit must wait for the token. A transmitting computer that has data to transmit waits for a "free" token and takes it off the ring. Once it has the token, this computer modifies it in such a way that tells the computers who has the token. The transmitting computer then places the token (along with the data it needs to transmit) on the ring and it travels around the ring until it gets to the destination computer. The destination computer takes the token and data off the wire, modifies the token (indicating it has received the data), and places the token back on the wire. When the original sender receives the token back and sees that the destination computer has received the data, the sender modifies the token to set it "free." It then sends the token back on the ring and waits until it has more data to transmit.

The main advantage to the token-passing access method over contention (the 802.3 model) is that it eliminates collisions. Only workstations that have the token can transmit. It would seem that this technology has a lot of overhead and would be slow. But remember that this whole procedure takes place in a few milliseconds. This technology scales very well. It is not uncommon to have Token Ring networks based on the IEEE 802.5 standard reach hundreds of workstations on a single ring.

The story of the IEEE 802.5 standard is rather interesting. It's a story of "the tail wagging the dog." With all the other IEEE 802 standards, the committee either saw a need for a new protocol on its own or got a request for one. They would then sit down and hammer out the new standard. A standard created by this process is known as a *de jure* ("by law") standard. With the IEEE 802.5, however, everyone was already using this technology, so the IEEE 802 committee got involved and simply declared it a standard. This type of standard is known as a *de facto* ("from the fact") standard—a standard that was being followed without having been formally recognized.

Network Architectures

Network architectures define the structure of the network, including hardware, software, and layout. We differentiate each architecture by the hardware and software required to maintain optimum performance levels. The major architectures in use today are Ethernet, Token Ring, ARCNet, and AppleTalk.

Ethernet

The original definition of the 802.3 model included a bus topology using a baseband coaxial cable. From this model came the first Ethernet architecture. Ethernet was originally codeveloped by Digital, Intel, and Xerox and was known as *DIX Ethernet*.

Ethernet has several specifications, each one specifying the speed, communication method, and cable. The original Ethernet was given a designation of 10Base5. The "10" in Ethernet 10Base5 stands for the 10 Mbps transmission rate. "Base" stands for the baseband communications used. Finally, the "5" stands for the maximum distance of 500 meters to carry transmissions. This method of identification soon caught on, and as vendors changed the specifications of the Ethernet architecture, they followed the same pattern in the way they identified them.

After the 10Base5, came 10Base2 and 10BaseT. These quickly became standards in Ethernet technology. Many other standards (including 100BaseF, 10BaseF, and 100BaseT) developed since then. But those three are the most popular.

Ethernet 10Base2 uses thin coaxial cables and bus topology, and transmits at 10 Mbps, with a maximum distance of 200 meters. If that is the case, what does the Ethernet 10BaseT use? Actually, Ethernet 10BaseT uses twisted-pair cabling, transmitting at 10 Mbps, with a maximum distance of 100 meters, and physical star topology with a logical bus topology.

Token Ring

Token Ring networks are exactly like the IEEE 802.5 specification because the specification is based on IBM's Token Ring technology. Token Ring uses a physical star, logical ring topology. All workstations are cabled to a central device, called a *multistation access unit*, or *MAU*. The ring is created within the MAU by connecting every port together with special circuitry in the MAU. Token Ring can use shielded or unshielded cable and can transmit data at either 4 Mbps or 16 Mbps.

ARCNet (Attached Resource Computing Network)

A special type of network architecture that deserves mention is the Attached Resource Computer Network (ARCNet). Developed in 1977, it was not based on any existing IEEE 802 model. However, ARCNet is important to mention because of its ties to IBM mainframe networks and also because of its popularity. Its popularity comes from its flexibility and price. It is flexible because its cabling uses large trunks and star configurations, so if a cable comes loose or is disconnected, the network will not fail. Additionally, since it used cheap, coaxial cable, networks could be installed fairly cheaply.

Even though ARCNet enjoyed an initial success, it died out, as other network architectures became more popular. The main reason for this was its slow transfer rate of only 2.5 Mbps. Thomas-Conrad (a major developer of ARCNet products) recently developed a version of ARCNet that runs at 100 Mbps, but most people have abandoned ARCNet for other architectures. ARCNet is also not based on any standard, which makes it difficult to find compatible hardware from multiple vendors. Because of its speed and compatibility limitations, ARCNet is quickly being replaced in networks.

AppleTalk

Another architecture not based on any existing IEEE 802 models is AppleTalk. AppleTalk is a proprietary network architecture for Macintosh computers. It uses a bus, and typically uses either shielded or unshielded cable. There are a few things to note about AppleTalk, however.

First, AppleTalk uses a Carrier Sense-Multiple Access with Collision Avoidance (CSMA/CA) technology to put data on the cable. Unlike Ethernet, which uses a CSMA/CD method, this technology uses "smart" interface cards to detect traffic *before* it tries to send data. A CSMA/CA card will listen to the wire. If there is no traffic, it will send a small amount of data. If no collisions occur, it will follow that amount of data with the data it wants to transmit. In either case, if a collision does happen, it will back off for a random amount of time and try to transmit again.

A common analogy is used to describe the difference between CSMA/CD and CSMA/CA. Sending data is like walking across the street. With CSMA/CD you just cross the street. If you get run over, you go back and try again. With CSMA/CA you look both ways and send your little brother across the street. If he makes it, you can follow him. If either of you gets run over, you both go back and try again.

Another interesting point about AppleTalk is that it's fairly simple. Most Macintosh computers already include AppleTalk, so it is relatively inexpensive. It also will assign itself an address. In its first revision (Phase I), it allowed a maximum of 32 devices on a network. With its second revision (Phase II), it supports faster speeds and multiple networks with EtherTalk and TokenTalk. EtherTalk allows AppleTalk network protocols to run on Ethernet coaxial cable (used for Mac II). TokenTalk allows the AppleTalk protocol to run on a Token Ring network.

Network Media

We have taken a look at the types of networks, network architectures, and the way a network communicates. To bring networks together, we use several types of media. A medium is the material on which data is transferred one point to another. There are two parts to the medium, the network interface card and the cabling. The type of network card you use depends on the type of cable you are using, so let's discuss cabling first.

Cabling

When the data is passing through the OSI model and reaches the Physical layer, it must find its way onto the medium that is used to physically transfer data from computer to computer. This medium is *cables*. It is the network interface card's role to prepare the data for transmission, but it is the cable's role to properly move the data to its intended destination. It is not as simple as just plugging it into the computer. The cabling you choose must support both the network architecture and topology. There are four main types of cabling methods: twisted-pair cable, coaxial cable, fiber-optic cable, and wireless. We'll summarize all four cabling methods following the brief descriptions below.

Twisted-Pair

Twisted-pair is one of the most popular methods of cabling because of its flexibility and low costs. It consists of several pairs of wire twisted around each other within an insulated jacket, as shown in Figure 9.11. Twisted-pair is most often found in 10BaseT Ethernet networks, although other systems can use it.

FIGURE 9.11:

Twisted-pair cable

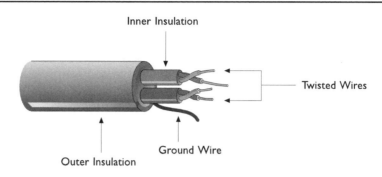

Twisted-Pair

We usually break twisted-pair cabling into two types: unshielded twisted-pair (UTP) and shielded twisted-pair (STP). UTP is simply twisted-pair cabling that is unshielded. STP is the same as UTP except that STP has a braided foil shield around the twisted wires (to decrease electrical interference).

UTP comes in five grades to offer different levels of protection against electrical interference.

- Category 1 is for voice-only transmissions, and is in most phone systems today.

- Category 2 is able to transmit data at speeds up to 4 Mbps. It contains four twisted pairs of wires.

- Category 3 is able to transmit data at speeds up to 10 Mbps. It contains four twisted pairs of wires with three twists per foot.

- Category 4 is able to transmit data at speeds up to 16 Mbps. It contains four twisted pairs of wires.

- Category 5 is able to transmit data at speeds up to 100 Mbps. It contains four twisted pairs of copper wire to give the most protection.

Each of these five levels has a maximum transmission distance of 100 meters.

Coaxial

The next choice of cable for most LANs would be coaxial cable. The cable consists of a copper wire surrounded by insulation and a metal foil shield, as shown in Figure 9.12. It is very similar to the cable used to connect cable television.

Coaxial cable is often called "Thinnet" or "Cheapernet." It comes in many thicknesses and types. The most common use for this type of cable is for Ethernet 10Base2 cabling.

FIGURE 9.12:

Coaxial cable

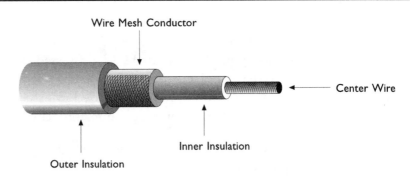

Coaxial

Fiber-Optic

Fiber-optic cabling has been called one of the best advances in cabling. It consists of a thin, flexible glass fiber surrounded by a rubberized outer coating (see Figure 9.13). It provides transmission speeds from 100 Mbps up to 1 Gbps and a maximum distance of several miles. Because it uses pulses of light instead of electric voltages to transmit data, it is completely immune from electric interference.

Fiber-optic cable has not become a standard in networks, however, because of its high cost of installation. Networks that need extremely fast transmission rates or transmissions over long distances, or that have had problems with electrical interference in the past, often use fiber-optic cabling.

FIGURE 9.13:

Fiber-optic cable

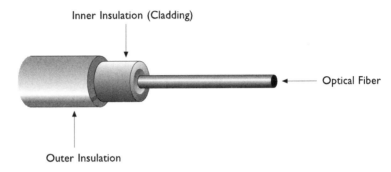

Inner Insulation (Cladding)

Optical Fiber

Outer Insulation

Fiber-Optic

Wireless Networks

One of the most fascinating cabling technologies today—and, actually, it's one that doesn't really *use* cable—is wireless. Wireless networks offer the ability to extend a LAN without the use of traditional cabling methods. Wireless transmissions are made through the air by infrared light, laser light, narrow-band radio, microwave, or spread-spectrum radio.

Wireless LANs are becoming increasingly popular as businesses are becoming more mobile and less centralized. You can see them most often in environments where standard cabling methods are not possible or wanted. However, they are still not as fast or efficient as standard cabling methods. Also, they are more susceptible to eavesdropping and interference than standard cabling methods.

Summary of Cabling Types

Each type of cabling has its own benefits and drawbacks. Table 9.2 details the most common types of cabling in use today.

TABLE 9.2: Cable Types

Characteristics	Twisted-Pair	Coaxial	Fiber-Optic	Wireless
Cost	Least	More than twisted-pair	Expensive	Most Expensive
Maximum Length	100 meters (328 ft)	185 meters (607 ft) to 500 meters (1640 ft)	>10 Miles	2 miles
Transmission Rates	10 Mbps to 100 Mbps	10 Mbps	100 Mps or more	10 Mbps
Flexibility	Most flexible	Fair	Fair	Limited
Ease of installation	Very Easy	Easy	Difficult	Somewhat difficult
Interference	Susceptible	Better than UTP, more susceptible than STP	Not susceptible	Susceptible
Special features	Often pre-installed; similar to wiring used in telephone systems	Easiest Installation	Supports voice, data, and video at highest transmission speeds	Very flexible
Preferred uses	Networks	Medium-size networks with high security needs	Networks of any size requiring high speed and data security	WANs and radio/TV communications
Connector	RJ-45	BNC-T and AUI	Special	Dish or Transceiver
Physical Topology	Star	Bus	Star (typically)	Bus or Star
Other Info	Five categories of quality	RG-58 and RG-59 family; also called Thinnet and Thicknet, respectively	Requires special training to configure	Most must comply with FCC regulations

The Network Interface Card (NIC)

The network interface card (NIC) provides the physical interface between computer and cabling. It prepares data, sends data, and controls the flow of data. It can also receive and translate data into bytes for the CPU to understand. It communicates at the Physical layer of the OSI model and comes in many shapes and sizes.

Different NICs are distinguished by the PC bus type and the network for which they are used. This section describes the role of the NIC and how to choose the appropriate one. The following factors should be taken into consideration when choosing a NIC:

- Preparing data
- Sending and controlling data
- Configuration
- Drivers
- Compatibility
- Performance

Preparing Data

In the computer, data moves along buses in parallel, as on a four-lane interstate highway. But on a network cable, data travels in a single stream, as on a one-lane highway. This difference can cause problems transmitting and receiving data, because the paths traveled are not the same. It is the NIC's job to translate the data from the computer into signals that can flow easily along the cable. It does this by translating digital signals into electrical signals (and in the case of fiber-optic NICs, to optical signals).

Sending and Controlling Data

For two computers to send and receive data, the cards must agree on several things. These include the following:

- The maximum size of the data frames

- The amount of data sent before giving confirmation

- The time needed between transmissions

- The amount of time needed to wait before sending confirmation

- The amount of data a card can hold

- The speed at which data transmits

If the cards can agree, then the sending of the data is successful. If the cards cannot agree, the sending of data does not occur.

In order to successfully send data on the network, you need to make sure the network cards are of the same type (i.e., all Ethernet, all Token Ring, all ARCNet, etc.) and they are connected to the same piece of cable. If you use cards of different types (for example, one Ethernet and one Token Ring), neither of them will be able to communicate with the other.

Configuration

The NIC's configuration includes things like a manufacturer's hardware address, IRQ address, Base I/O port address, and base memory address. Some may also use DMA channels to offer better performance.

Each card must have a unique hardware address. If two cards have the same hardware addresses, neither one of them will be able to communicate. For this reason, the IEEE committee has established a standard for hardware addresses, and assigns blocks of these addresses to NIC manufacturers, who then hard-wire the addresses into the cards.

Configuring a NIC is similar to configuring any other type of expansion card. The NIC usually needs a unique IRQ channel and I/O address, and possibly a DMA channel. Token Ring cards often have two memory addresses that must be excluded in reserved memory in order for them to work properly.

Drivers

In order for the computer to use the network interface card, it is very important to install the proper device drivers. These drivers communicate directly with the network redirector and adapter. They operate in the Media Access Control sublayer of the Data Link layer of the OSI model.

PC Bus Type

When choosing a NIC, use one that fits the bus type of your PC. If you have more than one type of bus in your PC (for example, a combination ISA/PCI), use a NIC that fits into the fastest type (the PCI in this case). This is especially important in servers, as the NIC can very quickly become a bottleneck if this guideline isn't followed.

NOTE   Refer back to Chapter 5, "PC Bus Architectures," to refresh your memory about the bus architectures mentioned in this discussion.

Performance

The most important goal of the network adapter card should be to optimize network performance and minimize the amount of time needed to transfer data packets across the network. There are several ways of doing this, including assigning a DMA channel, use of a shared memory adapter, and deciding to allow bus mastering.

If the network card can use DMA channels, then data can move directly from the card's buffer to the computer's memory, bypassing the CPU. A shared memory adapter is a NIC that has its own RAM. This feature allows transfers to and from the computer to happen much more quickly, increasing the performance of the NIC. Shared system memory allows the NIC to use a section of the computer's RAM to process data. Bus mastering lets the card take temporary control of the computer's bus to bypass the CPU and move directly to RAM. This is more expensive, but can improve performance by 20 to 70 percent. However, EISA and MCA cards are the only ones that support bus mastering.

Each of these features can enhance the performance of a network interface card. Most cards today have at least one, if not several, of these features.

Media Access Methods

You have put the network together in a topology. You have told the network how to communicate and send the data. You have also told it how to send the data to another computer. You also have the communications medium in place. The next problem you need to solve is how do you put the data *on* the cable? What you need now are the *cable access methods*, which define a set of rules for how computers put data on and retrieve it from a network cable. The four methods of data access are:

- Carrier-Sense Multiple Access with Collision Detection (CSMA/CD)

- Carrier-Sense Multiple Access with Collision Avoidance (CSMA/CA)

- Token Passing

- Polling

We'll discuss all of these in the following paragraphs.

Carrier-Sense Multiple Access with Collision Detection (CSMA/CD)

As we've already discussed, NICs that use CSMA/CD listen to or "sense" the cable to check for traffic. They compete for a chance to transmit. Usually if access to the network is slow, it means that there are too many computers trying to transmit, causing traffic jams.

Carrier-Sense Multiple Access with Collision Avoidance (CSMA/CA)

Instead of monitoring traffic and moving in when there is a break, CSMA/CA allows the computers to send a signal that they are ready to transmit data. If the ready signal transmits without a problem, the computer then transmits its data. If the ready signal is not transmitted successfully, the computer waits and tries again. This method is slower and less popular than CSMA/CD.

Token Passing

As previously discussed, token passing is a way of giving every NIC equal access to the cable. A special packet of data is passed from computer to computer. Any computer that wants to transmit has to wait until it has the token. It can then transmit its data.

Polling

An old method of media access that is still in use is polling. There aren't very many topologies that support polling anymore, mainly because it has special hardware requirements. This method requires a central, intelligent device (meaning that the device contains either hardware or software "intelligence" to enable it to make decisions) that asks each workstation, in turn, if it has any data to transmit. If the workstation answers "yes," the controller allows the workstation to transmit its data.

The polling process doesn't *scale* very well. That is, you can't take this method and simply apply it to any number of workstations. In addition, the high cost of the intelligent controllers and cards has made the polling method all but obsolete.

Connectivity Devices

It's the cabling that links computer to computer. Most cabling allows networks to be hundreds of feet long. But what if your network needs to be bigger than that? What if you need to connect your LANs to other LANs to make a WAN? What if the architecture you've picked for your network is limiting the growth of your network along with the growth of your company? The answer to these questions is found in a special class of networking devices known as *connectivity devices*. These devices allow communications to break the boundaries of local networks and let your computers talk to other computers in the next building, the next city, or the next country.

There are several categories of connectivity devices, but we are going to discuss the six most important and often used. They are:

- Repeaters
- Hubs
- Bridges
- Routers
- Brouters
- Gateways

These connectivity devices have made it possible to lengthen the distance of the network to almost unlimited distances.

Repeaters

Repeaters are very simple devices. They allow a cabling system to extend beyond its maximum allowed length by amplifying the network voltages so they travel farther. Repeaters are nothing more than amplifiers, and, as such, are very inexpensive.

Repeaters operate at the Physical layer of the OSI model. Because of this, repeaters can only be used to regenerate signals between similar network segments. I can, for example, extend an Ethernet 10Base2 network to 400 meters with a repeater. But I can't connect an Ethernet and Token Ring network together with one.

The main disadvantage to repeaters is that they just amplify signals. These signals not only include the network signals, but any noise on the wire as well. Eventually, if you use enough repeaters, you could possibly drown out the signal with the amplified noise. For this reason, repeaters are used only as a temporary fix.

Hubs

Hubs are devices used to link several computers together. They are most often used in 10BaseT Ethernet networks. They are also very simple devices. In fact, they are just multiport repeaters. They repeat any signal that comes in on one port and copy it to the other ports (a process that is also called *broadcasting*).

There are two types of hubs: *active* and *passive*. Passive hubs simply connect all ports together electrically and are usually not powered. Active hubs use electronics to amplify and clean up the signal before it is broadcast to the other ports. In the category of active hubs, there is also a class called "intelligent" hubs, which are hubs that can be remotely managed on the network.

Bridges

Bridges operate in the Data Link layer of the OSI model. They join similar topologies and are used to divide network segments. Bridges keep traffic on one side from crossing to the other. For this reason, they are often used to increase performance on a high-traffic segment.

For example, with 200 people on one Ethernet segment, the performance would be mediocre, because of the design of Ethernet and the number of workstations that are fighting to transmit. If you divide the segment into two segments of 100 workstations each, the traffic would be much lower on either side and performance would increase.

Bridges are not able to distinguish one protocol from another, because higher levels of the OSI model are not available to them. If it is aware of the destination address it is able to forward packets; otherwise a bridge will forward the packets to all segments. They are more intelligent than repeaters, but are unable to move data across multiple networks simultaneously. Unlike repeaters, bridges *can* filter out noise.

The main disadvantage to bridges is that they can't connect dissimilar network types or perform intelligent path selection. For that function, you would need a router.

Routers

Routers are highly intelligent devices that connect multiple network types and determine the best path for sending data. They can route packets across multiple networks and use routing tables to store network addresses to determine the best destination. Routers operate at the Network layer of the OSI model.

The advantage of using a router over a bridge is that routers can determine the best path that data can take to get to its destination. Like bridges, they can segment large networks and can filter out noise. However, they are slower than bridges because they are more intelligent devices; as such, they analyze every packet, causing packet forwarding delays. Because of this intelligence, they are also more expensive.

Routers are normally used to connect one LAN to another. Typically, when a WAN is set up, there will be at least two routers used.

Brouters

Brouters are truly an ingenious idea because they combine the best of both worlds—bridges and routers. They are used to connect dissimilar network segments and also to route only one specific protocol. The other protocols are bridged instead of being dropped. Brouters are used when only one protocol needs to be routed or where a router is not cost effective (like in a branch office).

Gateways

Gateways connect dissimilar network environments and architectures. Some gateways can use all levels of the OSI model, but frequently are found in the Application layer. It is there that gateways convert data and repackage it to meet the requirements of the destination address. This makes gateways slower than other connectivity devices, and costly. An example of a gateway would be the NT Gateway Service for NetWare that, when running on a Windows NT Server, can connect a Microsoft Windows NT network with a Novell NetWare network.

Review Questions

1. Which connectivity device transmits packets the fastest?

    A. gateway

    B. router

    C. brouter

    D. bridge

2. This IEEE 802 standard uses a bus topology and coaxial base-band cable, and is able to transmit at 10 Mbps.

    A. 802.4

    B. 802.3

    C. 802.2

    D. 802.1

3. _____ is immune to electromagnetic or radio-frequency interference.

    A. broadband coaxial cabling

    B. fiber-optic cabling

    C. twisted-pair cabling

    D. CSMA/CD

4. Printers, files, e-mail, and groupware can all be categorized as _____ .

    A. office equipment

    B. peer-to-peer networking

    C. resources

    D. protocols

5. This OSI layer signals "all clear" by making sure the data frames are error-free.

   A. Application layer

   B. Session layer

   C. Transport layer

   D. Network layer

6. This topology is the easiest to modify.

   A. Star

   B. Bus

   C. Ring

   D. Token

7. This is a routable protocol used by Unix clients.

   A. TCP/IP

   B. NetBEUI

   C. IPX

   D. XNS

8. The layer of the OSI model whose most important role is to provide error checking.

   A. Session layer

   B. Presentation layer

   C. Application layer

   D. Transport layer

9. Which type of cabling has the easiest installation?

    A. twisted-pair

    B. coaxial

    C. fiber-optic

    D. wireless

10. This is the type of media access method used by NICs that listen to or "sense" the cable to check for traffic, and send only when they hear that no one else is transmitting:

    A. Token Passing

    B. CSMA/CD

    C. CSMA/CA

    D. Demand Priority

11. A physical star topology consists of several workstations that branch off a central device called a _____ .

    A. repeater

    B. brouter

    C. router

    D. hub

12. A _____ links two or more computers together to communicate and share resources.

    A. server

    B. resource

    C. network

    D. client

13. This access method asks the other workstations for permission to transmit before transmitting.

   A. CSMA/CD

   B. CSMA/CA

   C. Token Passing

   D. Demand Priority

14. Offers total resistance to any electromagnetic or radio-frequency interference.

   A. twisted-pair cabling

   B. coaxial cable

   C. fiber-optic cabling

   D. wireless

15. Uses a thin baseband coaxial cable, bus topology, transmitting at 10 Mbps, with a distance up to 185 meters.

   A. Token Ring

   B. Ethernet 10BaseT

   C. Ethernet 10Base5

   D. Ethernet 10Base2

16. This topology uses the least amount of cabling, but also covers the shortest amount of distance.

   A. Bus

   B. Star

   C. Mesh

   D. Hybrid

17. This layer describes how the data gets transmitted over a physical medium.

    A. Session layer

    B. Data Link layer

    C. Physical layer

    D. Application layer

18. What is another name for IEEE 802.3?

    A. Logic Link Control

    B. Token Passing

    C. CSMA/CD LAN

    D. Token Ring LAN

19. This type of cabling looks similar to the cable used to connect cable television:

    A. twisted-pair

    B. coaxial

    C. fiber-optic

    D. wireless

20. These devices can switch and route packets across multiple networks and use routing tables to store network addresses to determine the best destination.

    A. brouters

    B. routers

    C. gateways

    D. bridges

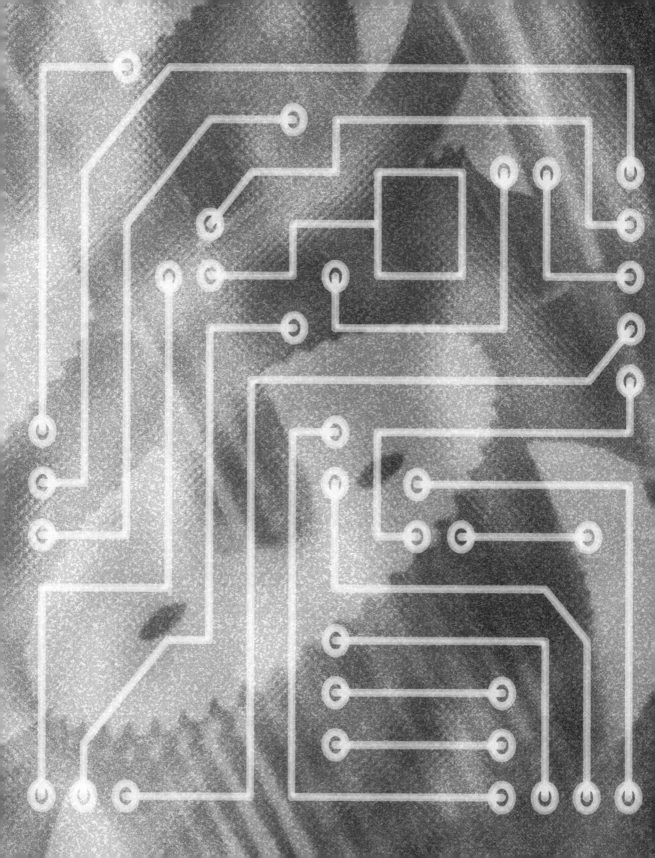

CHAPTER

TEN

Safety

Objectives

- Identify the purpose of various types of preventive maintenance products and procedures, and when to use/perform them.

- Identify procedures and devices for protecting against environmental hazards.

- Identify the potential hazards and proper safety procedures relating to lasers and high-voltage equipment.

- Identify items that require special disposal procedures that comply with environmental guidelines.

- Identify ESD (Electrostatic Discharge) precautions and procedures, including the use of ESD protection devices.

Besides needing to know what goes where and why—the subject of the preceding nine chapters—you need to know how to make your changes *safely*. Be careful when you go to open your computer; there are many hazards that you may or may not already be aware of, and any one of them could ultimately harm you or the components of the PC. Beyond the question of making repairs and upgrades safely, this chapter also addresses the problems of *ergonomics* when using the PC.

The topics covered in this chapter include:

- General service safety tips
- Proper disposal of computer parts
- Ergonomics
- Preventive maintenance

General Service Safety Tips

As a provider of a hands-on service (repairing, maintaining, or upgrading someone's computer), you need to be aware of some general safety tips, because, as already mentioned, if you are not careful you could harm yourself or the equipment. First, let's talk about playing it safe. Computers, display monitors, and printers can be dangerous if not handled properly. Perhaps the most important aspect of computers that you should approach with caution is the fact that they not only *use* electricity, they *store* electrical charge after they're turned off. This makes the power supply and the monitor pretty much off-limits to anyone but a trained electrical repair person. Also, the computer's processor and various parts of the printer run at extremely high temperatures, which could burn you if you try to handle them immediately after they've been in operation. Those are just two general safety measures that should be a concern. There are plenty more. When discussing issues of general computer safety, it is best to break down the subject of repairing and upgrading PCs into five general areas:

- The Computer
- The Power Supply
- The Printer
- The Monitor
- The Keyboard and Mouse

The Computer

If you have to open the computer to inspect or replace parts (as most of this chapter assumes you will), be sure to turn off the machine before you begin, and be sure to read the section below concerning the power supply.

The computer case is metal with sharp edges, so be careful when handling it. I cut myself once by jamming my fingers between the case and the frame when I was trying to force the case back on.

The Power Supply

Do not take the issue of safety and electricity lightly. If you were to remove the power supply from its case (and I don't recommend it), you would be taking a great risk. The current flowing through the power supply normally follows a complete circuit; when your body breaks that circuit, your body becomes a part of the circuit.

The two biggest dangers with power supplies are burning yourself and electrocuting yourself. These usually go hand in hand. If you touch a bare wire that is carrying current, you may get electrocuted. If a large amount of current passes through your body, it can cause your heart to stop, your muscles to seize, and your brain to stop functioning. In short, it can kill you. If there is a large enough current passing through the wire (and you), you can get severe burns as well. Electricity always finds the best path to ground. And, since we are basically bags of salt water (an excellent conductor of electricity), water will use us as a conductor if we are grounded. Because of the way electricity conducts itself (get it?), there are usually two burns that occur on electrical burn victims: the entry wound and exit wound.

The entry wound happens at the point of contact between conductor and person. It's rather gruesome. The current flowing through you has enough power to boil the water in the tissues it comes in contact with, essentially cooking you from the inside out. It isn't fun. As the electricity makes its way towards a ground, it sears the tissue on its way to whatever part of the body is closest to a ground. Then, at the point closest to a ground, the electricity bolts from the body, producing an exit wound. At this point, if I've done my job correctly, you should not like hearing this description. GOOD! This should encourage you to learn proper electrical safety so you may never have to experience the pain of electrical burns.

Fire Safety

Electrical fires don't happen often when repairing computers. You should, however, know how to extinguish one properly, should one occur. There are three major classes of fire extinguishers available, one for each type of flammable substance: A for wood and paper fires, B for flammable liquids, and C for electrical fires. The most popular type of fire extinguisher today is the multipurpose, or "ABC-rated" extinguisher. It contains a dry chemical powder that will smother the fire and cool it at the same time. For those fires that are electrical fires (which may be related to a shorted-out wire in a power supply) make sure the fire extinguisher will work for Class C fires. if you don't have an extinguisher that is specifically rated for electrical fires (type C), you can use an ABC-rated extinguisher.

Although it is possible to work on a power supply, it is NOT recommended. Power supplies contain several capacitors that can hold LETHAL charges *long after they have been unplugged*! It is extremely dangerous to open the case of a power supply. Besides, power supplies are inexpensive, so it would probably cost less to replace it than to try to fix it, and would be much safer.

Current vs. Voltage—Which Is More Dangerous?

When talking about power and safety, you will almost always hear the saying, "It's not the volts that kills you, it's the amps." That's mostly true. However, there is a need for some explanation of that expression.

The number of volts a power source has is its potential to do work. But, volts don't do anything by themselves. Current (or amperage—"amps") is the actual force behind the work being done by electricity. Here's an analogy to help explain this concept. Say you have two boulders, one 10 lbs and the other 100 lbs, each 100 feet off the ground, and you drop them. Which one would do more work? The obvious answer is the 100 lb boulder. They both have the same potential to do work (100 feet of travel), but the 100 lb boulder has more mass, thus more force. Voltage is analogous to the distance the boulder is from the ground, and amperage is analogous to the mass of the boulder.

This is why we can produce static electricity on the order of 50,000 volts and not electrocute ourselves. Even though this electricity has a great *potential* for work, it actually does very little work because the amperage is so low. This also explains why you can weld metal with only 110 volts. Welders use only 110 (sometimes 220) volts, but they also use anywhere from 50 to 200 amps!

The Printer

When I attempt to repair a printer I always imagine that there is a little monster in there trying to get me. This is because it always seems that I lose something in the printer as I am working on it, and it is usually screws. Have you ever had the problem of the missing sock? Well, I have the problem of the missing screws. It always seems that when I open a printer to do a repair there's a screw missing.

What else should you watch out for when repairing printers?

- When handling a toner cartridge from a laser printer or page printer, do not shake or turn the cartridge upside down. You will find yourself spending more time cleaning the printer and the surrounding area than you would have spent to fix the printer.

- Do not put any objects into the feeding system as the printer is running, in an attempt to clear the path.

- Laser jet printers generate a laser that is hazardous to your eyes. Do not look directly into the source of the laser.

- If it's an inkjet, do not try to blow in the ink cartridge to clear a clogged opening. That is, unless you like the taste of ink.

- Some parts of a laser printer (like the EP cartridge) will be damaged if touched. Your skin produces oils and has a small surface layer of dead skin cells. These substances can collect on the delicate surface of the EP cartridge and cause malfunctions. Bottom line: Keep your fingers out of where they don't belong!

The Monitor

Other than the power supply, one of the most dangerous components to try to repair is the monitor, or CRT. In fact, we recommend that you NOT try to repair monitors. To avoid the extremely hazardous environment contained inside the monitor—it can retain a high voltage charge for hours after it's been turned off—take it to a certified monitor technician or television repair shop. The repair shop or certified technician will know and understand the proper procedures to discharge the monitor, which involve attaching a resistor to the flyback transformer's charging capacitor to release the high-voltage electrical charge that builds up during use. They will also be able to determine whether the monitor can be repaired or needs to be replaced. Remember, the monitor works in its own extremely protective environment (the monitor case), and may not respond well to your desire to try to open it.

> **WARNING** The CRT is vacuum sealed. Be extremely careful when handling the CRT, because if you break the glass it will implode, which can send glass in any direction.

The Keyboard and Mouse

Okay, I know you are thinking, what danger could a keyboard or mouse cause? Well, I also pondered this, and as I dropped the keyboard on my foot and then tripped over the mouse cord, one danger came to mind.

Second, if you accidentally spill liquid on your keyboard, it could short circuit the keyboard. Keyboards don't function very well with half a can of cola in their innards!

Play It Safe with Common Sense

When you're repairing a PC, do not leave it unattended. Someone could walk into the room and inadvertently bump the machine, causing failure. Worse, they could step on any pieces lying around and get hurt. It is also not a good idea to work on the PC alone. If you should become injured, there should be someone around to help, if you need it. Finally, if you're fatigued, you may find it difficult to concentrate and focus on what you are doing. There are real safety measures related to repairing PCs, so the most important thing to remember is to pay close attention to what you are doing.

Electrostatic Discharge (ESD)

It is not only important to take care to avoid personal injury, it is important to take great care to prevent PC damage. The major cause of PC damage is *electrostatic discharge* (ESD). As mentioned in Chapter 1, ESD is the "shock" you feel after walking across a carpet and touching someone's hand. ESD is caused by static electricity transferring from one charged item (perhaps a person) to another item that is sensitive to the charge. It is very important to understand what causes ESD, the damage it can cause, and the methods used to prevent ESD from occurring.

TIP   The topic of ESD comes up in numerous questions on the exam.

What Causes ESD?

The static electricity that you generate every day creates ESD. I remember when I was younger how much fun it was to shuffle across a carpet and touch someone to see how much of a spark I could generate. Well, this "spark" is an electrostatic discharge, ESD. Static electricity is electricity at rest. Static electricity is also electrostatic *charge*. Electrostatic *dis*charge occurs when the electrostatic charge transfers from one charged entity to another that is sensitive to that charge. Figure 10.1 shows one example of how an electrostatic discharge occurs.

ESD can occur at many different levels, causing different degrees of damage. Here are some important facts about ESD:

- Computer components use 3 to 5 volts.

- The shock you *feel* when touching a doorknob on a dry winter day contains about 3,000 volts.

- If you can *see* a shock, it contains around 20,000 volts.

- A "carpet shock" can generate charges up to 30,000 volts.

FIGURE 10.1:

You can discharge 3,000 volts or more simply by touching a doorknob.

- Humans can only feel charges that are greater than 2,500 volts.

- Just shifting in a chair can generate 200 volts.

- A discharge as low as *30 volts* can destroy a computer device!

What this means is that *you can destroy a device without ever feeling a shock.* If you were to damage a computer component in this fashion, you might just assume that the component was bad from the factory, instead of suspecting the real cause. ESD damages are responsible for a large number of supposedly "DOA" (dead on arrival) components (components that in all probability worked fine before you touched them), and for many "no problems found" incident calls.

ESD is a result of natural processes, and therefore cannot be eliminated entirely. However, it is controllable. The first step to controlling ESD is to determine what materials can create the charge. There are three basic characteristics of materials that can generate static electricity.

- Insulative

- Static Dissipative

- Conductive

Insulative material does not allow the flow of electrons; thus it presents a high electrical resistance. Examples of insulative materials include mica and rubber. *Static dissipative* material allows the transfer of electrons to ground or other conductive objects. This material has a lower electrical resistance. An example of a static dissipative material would be the antistatic spray that is available for monitors. *Conductive* material allows a charge to flow through it easily; thus it presents a low electrical resistance. Metals are an example of a conductive material.

Environmental factors of dust and moisture contribute to ESD. If dust is allowed to build up, it is able to hold an electrical charge. If a room is dry, which is often the case in the winter months, this dryness will increase the ability of materials to hold a charge. The humidity level should be set to between 50% to 70% to prevent "dryness" from occurring.

What Damage Can ESD Create?

ESD can occur at many different levels, causing different degrees of damage. At the very least, an ESD shock can reboot the computer. In the worst case, it can destroy components. The degrees of damage include either *direct* or *latent*:

- Direct damage occurs immediately. This kind of damage is usually completely destructive. A component directly damaged is no longer usable and will need to be replaced.

- Latent damage doesn't happen immediately, but rather occurs over time. In this case, you will see intermittent errors followed by eventual failure of the component. This is probably more dangerous than direct damage in a way, because you will continue to use a latently damaged component without knowing it's damaged, and this could cause other components to fail.

What Practices Can Prevent ESD?

Even though it is impossible to stop ESD, you can minimize its effects. If you feel that you are at any risk for ESD, do not continue with the repair until you are certain that you are in a controlled environment. The following is a list of precautions to take before attempting to repair a piece of computer equipment. This information is also valid for repairs of any type of electrical equipment that may put you at risk of ESD.

- Don't wear clothes that contain synthetic materials. These clothes can transfer ESD charges from your skin when they rub against it.

- Use an ESD wrist strap *properly* to prevent ESD damage. Make sure it is securely connected to you *and* to an earth ground so that stray charges can be drained away.

- If you have no other means to remain grounded, go ahead and plug the computer into the wall outlet, keep the computer turned off, *and keep one hand on the frame of the computer while you're working on any parts that are still attached to the computer.* Obviously, this can cramp your abilities to perform the work the way you're used to working, so consider this a good reason to go out and buy an antistatic wrist strip. The frame of the computer is wired to the power supply's ground circuit. As long as you keep your hand on the frame, both you and the computer are at the same electronic potential, and no ESD transfers will take place.

WARNING If you are planning to use the method mentioned above, of plugging in the computer to stay grounded, make sure that there is no active current flowing through the computer. To do this, turn off the computer, and check the output of the power supply with a voltmeter.

- Keep electronic devices in their antistatic bags until they are ready for installation. The bags keep static electricity on the outside.

- Keep humidity levels between 50% and 70%.

- If adapter cards need removal, place some insulating material between the board and anything that could short.

The best protection against the effects of ESD is an *ESD workstation*. A good ESD protective workstation consists of a rubber mat and ESD wrist strap. An ESD wrist strap contains a resistor that provides protection in case the wire meets a charged object. An ESD mat is a special, rubberized surface that conducts static electricity away from the component being worked on.

Finally, a few words of wisdom: "A clean work environment is a happy work environment." Keep the work area free of dust and other contaminants that might conduct static electricity. Figure 10.2 is an example of what a good ESD-preventive environment would look like.

FIGURE 10.2:

The ESD-free environment

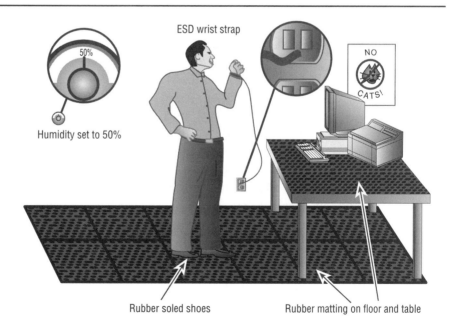

WARNING If you are working on high-voltage components, like monitors, DO NOT use an ESD strap! The strap provides such an easy path to ground it can actually do more harm than good.

Proper Disposal of Computer Parts

Remember all of those 386 and 486 computers that came out in the late 1980s and are now considered to be antiques? Where did they all go? Is there an "Old Computers Home" somewhere that is using these older computer systems for good purposes, or are they lying in a junkyard somewhere? Or could it be that I am not the only person who just cannot let go, with a stash of old computer systems and computer parts that lie in the deep dark depths of my basement?

Although it is relatively easy to put old machines away, thinking that you might be able to put them to good use again someday, it's really not realistic. Most computers are obsolete as soon as you buy them. And, if you have not used them recently, your old computer components will more than likely never be used again.

We recycle cans, plastic, newspaper, and even waste, so why not recycle computer equipment? Well, the problem is that most computers contain small amounts of hazardous substances (chemicals from monitor screens, chemicals from batteries, and noxious chemicals in the wiring). Some countries are exploring the option of recycling electrical machines, but most have still not enacted appropriate measures to enforce their proper disposal. However, there are a few things that we can do as consumers and environmentalists that can promote the proper disposal of our computer equipment:

- Check with the manufacturer. Some manufacturers will take back outdated equipment for parts (and may even pay you for them).

- Disassemble the machine and reuse the "parts" that are good.

- Check out businesses that can melt the components down for the lead or gold plating.

- Contact the EPA for a list of local or regional waste disposal sites that will accept used computer equipment.

- Check with local nonprofit or education organizations interested in using the equipment.

- Check out the Internet for possible waste disposal sites. Table 10.1 gives a few Websites that I came across on the Internet that deal with disposal of used computer equipment.

- Check with the EPA (www.epa.gov) to see if what you are disposing has an MSDS (Material Safety Data Sheet). These sheets contain information about the toxicity of a product and whether or not it can be disposed of in the trash. They also contain "lethal dose" information.

TABLE 10.1: Computer Recycling Web Sites

Site Name	Web Address
Computer Recycle Center	http://www.recycles.com/
Re-Compute	http://www.re-compute.com/
Re-PC	http://www.repc.com/

In addition to hardware recycling, there are also businesses that offer to recycle consumables, like ink cartridges or printer ribbons. However, although these businesses are doing us a favor in our quest to recycle, it might not be the best way to keep up with the recycle agenda. Why? Well, we don't recommend the use of recycled ink cartridges, because they may clog, the ink quality is not as good, or the small circuit board on the cartridge may be damaged. Similarly, recycled printer ribbons will lose their ability to hold ink after a while and don't last as long as a new ribbon. And, recycled toner cartridges don't operate properly after refilling.

Remember that recycling is a way to keep our environment clean and our landfills empty. If we can take one step to recycle or redistribute outdated computer equipment, we are one step closer to having a healthier environment. However, we should not have to sacrifice quality in the process.

NOTE   In particular, you should make a special effort to recycle *batteries*. Batteries contain several chemicals that are harmful to our environment and won't degrade safely. Batteries should not be thrown away, but rather recycled according to your local laws. Check with your local authorities to find out how batteries should be recycled.

Ergonomics

A PC's health is important, but so is the user's health. Good working conditions can prevent *repetitive strain injuries* (RSIs) in the future. RSIs are injuries that occur to your muscles and tendons, caused by the repetitive actions of work-related activities. A common cause of RSI when using computers comes from typing or mouse-clicking. These injuries are not usually instantaneous, but can occur over a period of time. The study of these injuries falls into an area called *ergonomics*, also known as *human engineering*, which proposes certain standards concerning the positioning and use of the body to promote a healthy work environment. This section takes a look at repetitive strain injuries and the ergonomics that can prevent them.

Risk of Repetitive Strain Injuries

Think about what parts of your body are used during computer operations. Those are the parts that are at risk for RSI. The body parts that are probably used the most include your fingers, wrists, elbows, arms, shoulders, back, and neck. Repetitive strain injuries (RSI) are caused by repeating small movements, uncomfortable body position, and lack of rest. The constant keystrokes or the moving of the mouse are the most prevalent causes of injuries to the arms, wrists, and shoulders.

Symptoms of RSI

Everyone who works on a computer is at risk of developing RSI. In fact, as I am sitting here I am thinking that after a couple more lines, I had better take a quick stretch because my wrists are starting to ache. The common repetitive strain injuries include Tendinitis, Tenosynovitis, and Carpal Tunnel Syndrome.

Tendinitis is the inflammation of tendons, which can lead to swelling and a loss of movement. *Tenosynovitis* is the inflammation of the sheath around the tendon, which can cause permanent damage. *Carpal Tunnel Syndrome* describes a host of symptoms caused mainly by a compression of the median nerve in the wrist.

Carpal Tunnel Syndrome is one of the most common of the symptoms of RSI, and is due in large part to the angle of the wrist when typing is in an unnatural or awkward position. The carpal tunnel is a tunnel of bone and ligament from the forearm to the hand and contains nine tendons and the median nerve. Repetitive bending of the wrist causes the median nerve to become compressed, which can lead to various symptoms, including the following:

- Aching, tenderness, pain, or swelling anywhere from the fingers to the head

- Tightness or discomfort in the hands, wrists, fingers, forearms, or elbows, neck and shoulders

- Numbness or soreness

- Loss of mobility in the hands, wrists, fingers

- Loss of ability to lift objects

- Pain that keeps you awake at night

These are just a few of the many related injuries that can occur. They normally don't occur instantaneously, and they can cause permanent damage, which may lead to the loss of movement or permanent disability.

Because of the serious nature of these injuries, it is important to watch out for the signals your body sends when something is not right. Although it is best to practice good work habits before an injury occurs, we don't always think about getting an injury until it happens. If at any point you feel any one of the symptoms listed, stop and take a break. During this break, it is a good idea to slowly move the body parts that hurt—move them through their full range of motion as much as you can, and get the blood circulating. This will let your tendons and muscles rest also. Don't just stop at the muscles that are hurting immediately—stretch your whole body, get up and walk around, and take it easy for ten minutes.

If you have persistent symptoms, see a doctor right away. Catching the problem early can avoid permanent damage to the muscles or tendons. Also avoid excessive computer usage (if possible). The bottom line is, if you don't change your computer habits, it won't matter what gadgets or splints the doctor gives you; the RSIs will not disappear without that primary change in behavior.

RSI Prevention

The best way to avoid injury is to take the proper steps to prevent it. These include taking frequent breaks, maintaining a good posture, and avoiding long durations of repetitive actions. It is not necessary to bang on the keyboard to type. It is better to maintain a more natural form. To protect yourself from RSI, it is important to follow certain guidelines:

- Adopt a more relaxed posture.

- Adjust your chair to a more natural position, as detailed in the next section.

- Adjust the keyboard and mouse to comfortable positions.

- Use wrist rests for both keyboard and mouse to support the tendons in the wrist while using these devices.

- Place the monitor at eye level.

- Keep the work area clean and adjusted so you do not have to make adjustments in your posture to answer the phone or do other simple tasks.

- Rest and stretch often.

Maintaining Good Posture

A natural posture is very important to a positive work environment. Imagine sitting at a piano and preparing to play: your feet are flat on the floor, your legs and back are at a ninety degree angle, your wrists are straight, your back is straight, and your forearms are parallel to the floor. Add to this a chairback that is positioned to support your lower back, and you have a picture of how you should be sitting to maintain good posture at the computer. If your wrists are bent and your back is not supported, this is a good sign that RSI injuries are in your future. If you need to move forward, bend, or move in any way that would be considered awkward, you are probably at risk for RSI. The best posture is a natural attentive posture. Figure 10.3 gives an example of the proper posture to use when working on your computer.

FIGURE 10.3:

Good posture for using a computer

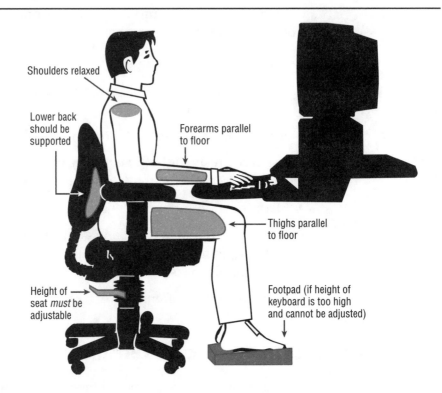

Shoulders relaxed

Lower back should be supported

Forearms parallel to floor

Thighs parallel to floor

Height of seat *must* be adjustable

Footpad (if height of keyboard is too high and cannot be adjusted)

Proper Chair Position

When choosing a computer chair, the most important quality it should have is that it should be adjustable. It should not be a couch or bed or lounge chair. It should roll easily along on the floor and be sturdy. It should allow you to move and shift frequently in order to answer the phone, reach for your file folders, or perhaps to turn and speak to a visitor. You should be able to get into and out of the chair and move it toward and away from your computer without having to "pick it up" to move it. Some of the more comfortable chairs include arm rests, adjustable back support, and a wider front edge to take the pressure away from your thighs. Many office supply stores market ergonomically correct chairs that offer these features. They may be expensive, but your health is worth it. After all, which costs more: a $300 chair or the medical costs of physical therapy and possible surgery to treat a repetitive strain injury? See Figure 10.3 for the proper height and adjustment for your chair.

Keyboard and Mouse Placement

The keyboard and mouse are also important to a positive work environment. Consider where the keyboard is placed and how that position affects your arms and wrists. It should be at just the right level to maintain a comfortable ninety degree angle of your biceps to your forearm. Since you're supposed to be sitting straight, this should also mean that your forearms are parallel to the floor. The mouse should also be placed at the same level as the keyboard to avoid awkward movements. If you cannot lower your keyboard and mouse to the proper height, at least adjust the height of your chair to bring yourself to the proper angles (and perhaps use a footrest if you have to raise your chair very far in order to match the height of the keyboard).

You should never have to "pound" the keyboard—it's called "touch typing," not "hammer typing." When using combination keystrokes use two hands instead of twisting one hand to find the right keys.

Microsoft's Natural™ ergonomic keyboard, as seen in Figure 10.4, is a strange looking keyboard, with the right and left halves of the keyboard set off at angles rather than all being aligned in one set of rows straight across the entire keyboard. This arrangement allows for a more comfortable typing position than the standard keyboard. This keyboard takes a little getting used to but can reduce the amount of strain on your tendons, muscles, fingers, arms, and wrists.

FIGURE 10.4:

Microsoft's Natural™ keyboard

If you notice that clicking your mouse causes you any kind of pain in your hand, wrist, or forearm, try another type of mouse, or even another type of pointing device entirely (for example, a touchpad or trackball). There are various models of each type of pointing device available; you just have to find the one that is most comfortable for you. Taking breaks to frequently stretch your arms and back can have a preventive effect on pains caused by too many "micro movements" such as those required in the keyboard and mouse work that so many workers engage in every day.

Monitor Placement

Remember the old adage that by eating carrots, your eyes will be stronger? When working with a monitor, it should be a requirement to have an ample supply of carrots nearby. The last time I went to the eye doctor I noticed that not only did the questionnaire I needed to fill out ask me if I worked on computers, but so did the optician. It is interesting that if you use computers, your eyes will weaken at a faster rate then normal due to the strain the monitor puts on them. The monitor should be one and a half to two feet away from your eyes. Also, it should be positioned in such a way that you do not have to look up. Is the top of the screen at eye level? (This is primarily true for 14″ and 15″ monitors. If it is a larger monitor, for example 17″ and larger, then the middle of the screen should be at eye level.) Paper documents or books that you are referring to while working at the computer should be placed in a holder at the same eye level and distance as the monitor, as seen in Figure 10.5. If you work near a window, position your entire work area to minimize the glare, and/or use glare screens to protect yourself from it.

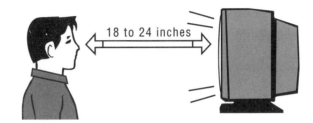

FIGURE 10.5:

Proper monitor distance

Work Environment

In an ideal world, we would have someone to clean our desks and organize our work areas. However, in the real world that just doesn't happen (unless we have a cleaning service). You need to take responsibility for your own work environment. This includes keeping the environment clean and avoiding overcrowding on the desk. If overcrowding occurs it becomes difficult to maintain a positive work environment that fosters good posture and ergonomics.

The phone should be within reach and set up in such a way that you do not have to put the receiver between your chin and shoulder to take a call. If you are using the phone a lot while working on the computer, you might need to invest in a speakerphone or headset.

There should also be ample space provided for your printer, speakers, desktop, monitor, and other accessories. By arranging your work environment to be conducive to a more natural and relaxed position, you decrease your chances of suffering a repetitive strain injury.

Rest Often

The most important thing to remember about RSI is that periods of rest will break the repetitive cycle. Every fifteen minutes or so a five minute break should be taken to stretch and let the blood circulate through the body. Every hour a longer fifteen minute break is needed to stretch your entire body and move the focus off of the computer. Try to arrange your work schedule in such a way that you can do filing, phoning, or some other aspect of your job besides computer work for short periods at more or less regular intervals throughout the day. It is also important to frequently move your eyes off of the monitor to avoid eye strain. Eye strain occurs because the optical muscles become fatigued due to extensive periods of continual eye focus. I often find that my eyes need a rest when I get headaches or experience blurring, or when my eyes simply feel tired. Taking breaks should offset these effects.

Preventive Maintenance Tips

There are several things you can do to keep your computer running at its best. Most of them are easy to do and should be done periodically to ensure that a service call isn't required. The following is a list of some of the things you can do to keep your computer from have "major surgery."

1. **Keep your keyboard and mouse clean.** Mice rollers can be cleaned with a swab dipped in isopropyl alcohol. Clean the

"gunk" off the rollers and the mouse won't skip across the screen. Clean the keyboard with compressed air and one of the "keyboard cleaners" available in any electronics supply house.

2. **Keep the inside of the computer clean.** Dust inside the computer acts like a blanket and can increase the operating temperature of some of the components. About once a month, open the computer's case and blow the dust out with compressed air (preferably outside, so the dust doesn't get everywhere inside).

3. **Defragment your hard disk only when needed.** Some people defragment their hard disks all the time (like once a day), thinking they'll get the best possible performance out of their computer. This just isn't the case. All that it does is put undue wear on hard disk mechanisms. Once a month is plenty if you are using your computer every day.

4. **Don't smoke near your computer.** Most people don't give this one enough attention. You have all heard what smoking does to your lungs. The computer is essentially "inhaling" the smoke you exhale through it's power supply (or in some cases, through other orifices). The smoke coats every component inside the computer with a black residue (the tar from the tobacco). This residue is slightly acidic and can eat away at the delicate electronics inside the computer. It is almost impossible to clean this residue from every surface.

5. **Make sure there is adequate airspace around the computer.** This is so the power supply fan can move air through the computer at the fastest possible rate. This moving air cools the components inside the computer. If there isn't air movement, cooling can't occur. The heat that the electronic components generate can damage them as well.

Review Questions

1. When you receive a shock from walking across the carpet, how many volts are generated?

   A. 2,500

   B. 30,000

   C. 10

   D. 5

2. ESD is caused by the discharge of static between you and sensitive computer components. True or false?

   A. True

   B. False

3. To prevent ESD, humidity should be kept right around

   _____ .

   A. 10%

   B. 20%

   C. 40%

   D. 50%

4. It is a good idea to take a short break every 15 minutes. True or false?

   A. True

   B. False

5. It is important not to leave your desk until the work is finished, no matter how long it takes. True or false?

   A. True

   B. False

6. ESD stands for:

   A. Electrostationary Static Discharge

   B. Electromagnetic Static Discharge

   C. Electrostatic Discharge

   D. Electrically Safe Discharge

7. When a battery in a laptop is bad, you should take it out and throw it away.

   A. True

   B. False

8. RSI stands for:

   A. Radix Strain Injury

   B. Repeating Simple Injury

   C. Ready Set Injury

   D. Repetitive Strain Injury

9. When working on PCs, it is a good idea to have the following available (circle all that apply):

   A. a blanket

   B. an ESD Strap

   C. a clean workspace

   D. all of the above

10. Which of the following items should be replaced rather than be serviced by a technician?

    A. computer

    B. hard disk

    C. keyboard

    D. power supply

11. Which class of fire extinguisher can be used to put out an electrical fire (computer fire)? (Circle all that apply.)

   A. A

   B. B

   C. C

   D. ABC (Multipurpose)

12. You should use an ESD strap when working on monitors, to prevent electrocution. True or false?

   A. True

   B. False

13. It's always best to use recycled computer parts. True or false?

   A. True

   B. False

14. Which of the following is *not* a good way to reduce the risk of Repetitive Strain Injuries (RSIs)?

   A. proper posture when sitting at the computer

   B. mounting your monitor in the desktop so you can see it when you look down.

   C. mounting your monitor at eye level

   D. proper use of a wrist rest

15. If improperly handled, CRT tubes can _____. (Circle all that apply.)

   A. shrink

   B. implode

   C. shock

   D. fall on your foot

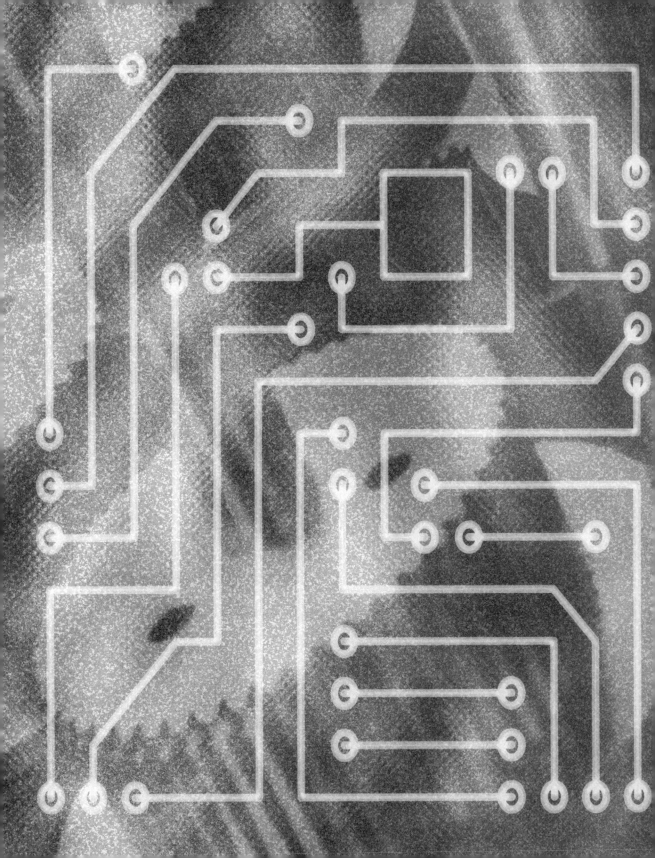

CHAPTER

ELEVEN

Customer Service

Objectives

- Differentiate effective from ineffective behaviors as these contribute to the maintenance or achievement of customer satisfaction.

- Identify basic troubleshooting procedures and good practices for eliciting problem symptoms from customers.

Most of us know better than to make the customer angry, and many of us have what it takes to practice good customer service. So why is it important to address this topic? Practicing customer service skills requires more knowledge and skills than what comes naturally to us. In the service industry, the level of standards has increased to the point where competition can break a business, even though that business may be providing good service. Customers know the difference between good and excellent customer service practices, and to be competitive, so should you. For this reason, this material is covered by the A+ core exam.

A customer can be anyone from a coworker to a large corporation. Common sense tells us that practicing good customer service helps businesses make a profit. Customer service is also an opportunity to improve business relations through solutions.

This chapter will cover the following customer service concepts:

- Identifying a customer

- Good vs. excellent customer service

- Why it pays to provide good customer service

Identifying a Customer

Some businesses call them clients, others call them customers or guests. Some businesses recognize internal and external customers. Any way you define it, a customer can be anybody.

Service professionals who practice good customer service recognize this well. Banks, for instance, started handing out suckers years ago to the children of people who do business with them. The banks realized that distressed parents appreciated the suckers to calm a crying child.

Part of your job as a service professional will involve trouble-shooting and making equipment repairs at the customer's site and making recommendations in person and over the telephone. For this reason, it is almost impossible for you to predict what you can expect and what type of customer you are dealing with. To do so is dangerously assuming.

Your customer's first impression of you will be the longest lasting impression; so of course, you will always want to make a good first impression. Once a bad impression is made, it is almost impossible to recover fully.

Impressions and Preconceptions

Even though customers formulate their impressions of you based on initial contact, you must be careful to withhold your impression of the customer. We often formulate a mistaken preconception of people and things based on the first impressions they make upon us.

One service professional had an interesting experience repairing an old, dot-matrix printer at a customer's site. The service professional ran all the diagnostics needed to solve the problem, repaired the printer, and tested the equipment to make sure it functioned consistently. By the time he finished, the secretary who had requested the repairs had gone to lunch, so the service professional explained his findings to a coworker located across the hall.

The coworker didn't even let the service professional complete his explanation when she became visibly upset and then yelled at him for fixing the wrong piece of equipment. The service professional stayed calm and listened to the coworker's story.

The coworker had been working to meet a deadline on a proposal worth $800,000 at the time her printer malfunctioned. As it happened, there were two printers that had broken down and, unknown to the coworker, the secretary had called two separate repair companies for service. The service professional had repaired the printer he was supposed to repair; the other repair shop's representative had simply not arrived yet. The printer used by the coworker, unfortunately, had a service agreement that specified that all repairs *must* be made by the other service center.

The service professional thought about the problem and asked the coworker about other printers in the building. He located a similar printer within the same building and found he was able to redirect her printouts to that printer through the network. She now had an alternate printer available so she could continue to work on her proposal while the other printer was being fixed.

Good vs. Excellent Customer Service

Studies have shown that customers who are unhappy with the service they receive will tell eleven people; customers who are happy with the service they receive will tell only four. In other words, more than twice the number of customers will hear about your bad service than those who hear about the good service you provide.

What the customer perceives as excellent service, good service, average service, and bad service is defined by each customer, and each customer has a different definition for each. What one customer thinks is average service might be considered bad service to another. What we can do as service professionals is to define for ourselves what the difference is between each of these categories and use the criteria to compare our service against our customers' expectations. The following is a simple guideline for distinguishing each level of service:

- **Excellent Service:** Above and beyond customer's expectations
- **Good Service:** Above customer's expectations

- **Average Service:** Meets customer's expectations

- **Bad Service:** Below customer's expectations

Each level of service can be viewed as a prerequisite to the one above it. Before we can provide excellent service we must understand what good service is. Even understanding what bad service is can help us define what average service is.

How do you learn what the customer's needs and expectations are? You need to ask them—it's as simple as that! However, there are more ways to collect information from the customer than just conversation. Listed below are several methods and some tips for getting the proper information from the customer. We suggest you use a combination of these methods to ensure you obtain complete information the first time.

- **Listen.** Active listening is much harder than you think. (See the "Two-Minute Listening Test" on the next page.) The customer should be allowed to speak entirely. We often start forming our responses before the customer is finished speaking. If we're doing that, we are not listening to the entire message.

- **Paraphrase.** Once the customer has spoken, repeat back to them the information they just gave you. "Let me repeat what you just said so I can make sure that I'm understanding you correctly: When you start your computer first thing in the morning, the indicator light on your printer is on, but when you send a document to the printer, the light turns off."

- **Speak slowly and calmly.** The customer may be anxious or under pressure, which tends to make them speak faster and with a higher pitch. This could cause a distraction in your ability to understand them. Because people unconsciously try to match the rate of the person with whom they are speaking, slowing your speech should have a calming effect. If this fails, ask them to speak more slowly.

- **Document.** When you are gathering information in person or over the telephone, indicate to the customer that you will need to write the information down. You should not try to write as the customer is speaking; it is easier to make a mistake or miss important information. Tell the customer, "I need just a moment to make sure I record all the information you just explained to me…. Okay, I'm ready now." Most companies have a standard form to fill out to help you collect complete information.

- **Ask questions.** Whenever a customer provides information in the form of a general statement, they haven't provided you with enough information, so you may need to pry it out of them. Example:

  "My printer doesn't work!"

  "Can you give me a better idea of what exactly isn't working? For instance, is there a problem getting the printer turned on, or is it having trouble printing? "

- **Don't interrupt.** Wait for a customer to finish speaking before offering a solution or asking additional questions. NEVER interrupt someone while they are describing a problem. They could interpret that action as rude and that you have a "know-it-all" attitude.

- **Check the customer files.** Your company might have information on file for the customer already. If you ask the customer if they've been serviced by your company and the customer replies that they haven't, look in your customer files anyway. (If you discover that the customer is on file, however, do *not* point this out to them. They will think you were out to prove them wrong.) If other service professionals have serviced this customer before, you can get a good idea of what level of service is expected, and this can help you solve a recurring problem faster.

Two-Minute Listening Test—An Exercise

You will need a partner for this exercise and someone to time the exercise for two minutes. The goal of this exercise is to demonstrate how difficult listening can be. When the exercise begins, one person will do nothing except listen and the other person will speak (about anything) for two minutes. In order to give full attention to the speaker, the listener should *not* make any verbal or non-verbal responses to the speaker while the exercise is in progress.

The listener will probably find it difficult to give undivided attention to the speaker. The speaker will probably find that the silence or lack of response feels uncomfortable. When the exercise is over, have the participants switch roles and repeat the exercise. That way, both partners will have a better understanding of just how difficult listening is, even in such a short amount of time.

Providing Bad Service

Many customers will not tell you when they have received bad service. Instead, they will tell others. A service professional would not intentionally provide bad service, but often it happens unknowingly. It can be very difficult to ascertain precisely what a customer's expectations are. It can also happen that their expectations are based on something that was unrealistic in the first place (for example, a cloudy memory of the extent of a warranty, or of how much was provided to them for free the last time they had a repair made). Once a service professional learns that a customer was unhappy with the service they received, a service professional will usually take the steps necessary to correct the situation with the customer; and sometimes management must intervene.

Customer complaints will usually come as no surprise. Sometimes things don't go as smoothly as you would have liked with a customer. When this happens, regardless of whether you think the customer will complain, tell your supervisor or manager immediately. Tell them about the situation privately and in person. If you must leave a voice mail or e-mail message, just explain that you need to speak to them regarding a situation with your customer rather than leaving the details of what happened. (This is to maintain confidentiality.) That way, if a complaint does result, the manager or supervisor is prepared to handle the situation and can have a solution ready for the customer.

Providing Average Service

Providing average service means you meet a customer's needs (by no means a bad thing) but not necessarily the customer's expectations, and don't go much further than that. The service professional should take caution here. For example, a service professional may have provided the customer with *good* service on a previous visit. The next service professional will be expected to provide that same level of service. Anything less could be perceived as bad service, rather than average service. If possible, research the customer's service history and ask your coworkers if they can tell you more about what to expect.

Keep in mind that coworkers have their own opinions about customers, and they may be different than your own. Some coworkers may find it intimidating or difficult to work with demanding customers, whereas you might have a higher level of expertise in this area and perhaps you find that working with difficult customers is a challenge you welcome. Likewise, your opinion of a customer can affect your coworkers' ability to work effectively with that customer. When disclosing information about a past experience with a customer, focus on the event and what was done to solve the problem. It is best to keep opinions to yourself.

Providing Good Service

This is the level of service that companies strive for. Companies that practice good service have standards, written or unwritten, they adhere to. These standards could be based on an industry code of ethics, certifications, company policies, corporate culture, any combination of these things, and more. The service professional who practices and provides good service understands the importance of all the following:

- Smiling, having a positive attitude

- Anticipating problems which could arise

- Being prepared for anything

- Focusing on the solution and not the problem

- Using (and remembering) the customer's name

- Always answering the telephone in a calm manner and friendly tone of voice (no matter what)

- Leaving a business card with the customer every time

- Using checklists to make certain nothing is forgotten

- Bringing more parts and tools to the customer's site than what is needed

- Establishing credibility with the customer

- Not using jargon (industry terminology) the customer won't understand

- Being on time

- Following up with the customer

- Keeping promises

- Teaching the customer so he or she can help themselves

- Being a role model for other service professionals

- Respecting the customer's values, opinions, time

- Making the customer feel important, not stupid
- Adding to your own fund of knowledge; keeping up to date on the latest information
- Using knowledge for solutions rather than power
- Knowing the difference between sympathy and empathy
- Never disclosing a negative opinion about your competition
- Saying thank you

Customers who receive good service will call again. They may recommend you or your company and you will eventually hear about it. Sometimes customers will write letters complimenting your work. Some will even express their appreciation with a gift. Even if you were only their hero/heroine for an hour, that is all it takes to make the job worthwhile. The more genuine your desire is to provide good service, the easier your job becomes.

Providing Excellent Service

Many companies who claim they provide excellent service really provide service that is average to good. This is because the opportunity that exists for excellent service is somewhat rare. Excellent service must first be based on good service. From this point one can extend oneself beyond the customer's expectations to provide excellent service. Actually, providing excellent service is not something you should expect you'll be able to do with every customer encounter. Excellent service is by definition out of the ordinary. Of course, the more skills and experience the service professional gains, the easier it becomes to provide excellent service.

Excellent service is what will give your company a renowned reputation and set you apart from your competition. Saturn Corporation and Wal-Mart are two companies who have long held the spotlight because of their excellent service stories. You probably even have stories of your own.

Once you've solved your customer's problem, what more is there that you can do? There's plenty. One method you can use to determine if the opportunity to provide excellent service exists is to sharpen your listening skills. When collecting information from the customer, be careful that you do not mentally discard the information they're giving you that has nothing to do with the problem you're there to solve. It could be enough information to help you move from providing good service to providing excellent service.

Here's one example. A service professional was casually speaking with an office manager about a presentation he was to give the next day. It was the office manager's first time using this special projector. The service professional remembered that a projector came in for repair that morning from the same company and wondered if it was the same one the office manager was planning to use. Sure enough, it was. No one had told the office manager about the projector being broken. The service professional knew of a sales representative back at the office who used the same type of projector for her sales presentations. The service professional contacted the sales representative who then loaned the projector to the office manager for his presentation.

Another method: When you're at the customer's site, be observant. Perhaps you are there to fix a printer and you notice that a coworker is having trouble centering text in his word processing program. By helping him with this problem, you will have provided service beyond expectations.

Know your limitations when providing excellent service. For example, if you see the coworker struggling to center text on their computer, don't attempt to help unless you are certain of the solution. Many service professionals get trapped with this. Furthermore, once the first problem gets solved, the question dam breaks. Be prepared for a flood of questions, as customers will think you have the answers to other questions as well.

A more foolproof way to provide excellent service is to point the customer toward a solution rather than provide the customer with the solution. If your company has other departments, suggest their services and have their business cards ready to hand out. In the word processing example above, one solution might be to call someone you know back at the office who would be knowledgeable with word processors and then ask them if they wouldn't mind speaking with your customer. If your company has a training department, this would be another solution.

Sometimes the solution might be in the hands of another company, and that other company could even be a competitor. But shouldn't it be *you* who's providing your customer with the solution? The answer in most cases is yes, of course. Before recommending a competitor, you must be 100% *certain* that you cannot provide your customer with the solution to their problem. If you're certain, you're not losing anything. And what the customer will see is your honesty and concern in finding a solution for them—ultimately, that is what the customer wants—and that referring them to your competitor is not a risk for you. (Moreover, you have now placed your competitor in the precarious position of having to provide this customer with even better service.) And it often happens that a competitor will begin sharing their customers with you as well.

Follow-up: A Valuable Tool

For those customers who complain about your service to everybody else except you, there is a special tool you can use to turn the complaint to your advantage. It's called follow-up. One primary purpose of follow-up is to control the flow of negative information. Another is quality control. Yet another reason to follow up is that it indicates to the customer that they are important to you and your company.

Follow-up channels the flow of information back to the company or the service professional. Think of how embarrassing it would be to learn from someone else that a customer thought your service was poor.

- If you plan to follow up with a customer yourself, the best way to approach the follow-up is to let the customer know you'd like to call them in a few days to see how things are working. Ask what day and times are best to reach them. Unexpected phone calls are not always convenient for the customer and can be perceived as pushy and intrusive. Once a promise is made to call the customer, it must not be broken or you will quickly destroy your credibility.

- Another option for follow-up is to survey the customer through an evaluation. Before leaving the customer's site, give them an evaluation along with a pre-addressed, postage-paid envelope. Customers like evaluations because they can provide you and your company with feedback when it is convenient for them. Plus, an evaluation gives them a locus of control. Customers need some type of mechanism to release not just negative feelings, but positive feelings too.

NOTE   The evaluation should be no more than one page long, should contain a variety of question types (open-ended, agree/disagree, and so on) and should take less than five minutes to complete. If the evaluation is constructed well, you will soon have a nice collection of suggestions on ways you can improve your service.

- A third follow-up option is to ask the manager or supervisor to make the call. Because the manager or supervisor was not initially involved with the service call, this method might not be as effective, but it can be helpful when you're too busy to make some calls yourself. Some companies try to disguise a sales call through a follow-up call. Customers aren't stupid; they see right through this. To the customer this behavior is very disappointing, if not irritating.

If the customer becomes angry, stay focused on the problem and try to brainstorm with that customer for a solution the customer can agree with. Avoid using the words "you" and "I" in the conversation, because in a situation that involves anger, these words can become the verbal equivalent of pointing your finger and assigning blame.

Finally, you will come across customers whom there is just no pleasing. This could be due to a conflict in personalities, and it might be time to ask another service professional to service this customer.

A skilled and educated service professional seeks a win/win solution (a solution where both the customer and the service professional win) every time. By establishing a set of standards for yourself in terms of customer service, you can gain more control over personal job satisfaction.

Why It Pays to Provide Good Customer Service

The whole reason we try to provide excellent customer service is to keep the customer coming back for more products and services. This does not mean fix their computer so that it will break down in three months and they will have to return for you to fix it again. It *does* mean fix it once, so that the same problem doesn't recur. Then, if the customer has a different problem, they won't hesitate to bring it to your company.

What does it cost to lose one customer? Before we can answer that question we need to understand that customers could be spending money in other departments besides our own. Therefore, if we are responsible for losing one customer, the other departments lose as well. Let's say one customer spends an average of about $1,000 a year. Let's also assume we lose that customer. Recalling the statistic cited at the beginning of this chapter, we remember that for every one customer lost, we could also lose eleven potential customers that the dissatisfied customer might have talked to. So, we might lose a possible $11,000. That's equivalent to half of someone's salary in an entry-level position. Of course, in real life, client revenues are not this simple. In many cases they're worse. For instance, when you consider that companies often land major contracts with large corporations, and that these contracts can represent a significant portion of the total revenue, then it's easy to see that losing one corporate customer can have a devastating effect, costing many people their jobs. Worse yet, smaller companies often get their start by landing a major contract; losing that one contract early in the game can thus be devastating to the business.

Most companies in the service business will rely on additional methods for maintaining financial health other than merely providing service on an as-needed basis. Service agreements and subcontracts from manufacturers are some examples. Recommending the services of other departments in the company is one way to expand a customer's business with your company. That way, even if they receive bad service from your department, the service they receive from another department may be enough to maintain them as a loyal customer.

Review Questions

1. You are at a customer's site to fix a paper jam in the customer's laser printer when you realize that you forgot a replacement part. You won't have time to run back to the office to pick up the part because you are due at another customer's site in 30 minutes. What should you do?

   A. Call the second customer and inform them of your possible late arrival and ask if they would like to reschedule (if necessary).

   B. Apologize profusely to the customer and go back to the office to get the part. Since the other customer has been a long-standing account, they won't mind waiting for you to finish this job correctly.

   C. Being on time is important with all customers. Put the printer back together and come back tomorrow. Hopefully, no one will need to use the printer until then.

   D. Call George, a service professional who works with one of your competitors. This is obviously a solution you cannot provide for your customer.

2. A customer arrives at your service window. He is angry because the modem he just had fixed by your company did not work when he brought it home and he had to drive 40 miles to bring it back to be fixed again. How should you handle this?

   A. The dumb cluck obviously doesn't know how a modem works so just explain it to him.

   B. Apologize. Question him on what he is doing to set up his modem, then point out what mistakes he is making with his procedures.

   C. Apologize. Ask him if he can explain in detail what the problem is. If he is still angry, ask the customer what he would like you to do about it.

   D. Apologize. Offer him a new modem, take him to lunch and give him a twenty-dollar bill for gas.

3. One of your coworkers, Bill, is on a coffee break when you receive a telephone call from one of his customers. You inform the customer that Bill is on a break and offer to ask him to return the call. The customer states that this is not acceptable and asks to speak with him immediately. When you informed Bill of the telephone call, Bill states that he is on a break and refuses to take the call. What should you do?

   A. Tell the customer that he can reach Bill if he calls back in 20 minutes.

   B. Tell the customer that Bill is not available but you would be happy to help him.

   C. Explain the situation to your manager or supervisor and ask them to take the call.

   D. Promise the customer that Bill will return his call shortly.

4. Your manager informs you that you will be taking over the Johnson account. You hear from the grapevine that the previous service professional had asked to be removed from the account. How will you approach the customer the next time you are called to service the account?

   A. Before arriving at the customer's site, ask your coworkers to provide you with as much detail as they can about the customer. The more information you have, the better prepared you will be.

   B. Ask your coworkers about what situations the service professional had been involved with and how those situations were resolved. Keep in mind that your coworker's opinions of the account may not necessarily be the same as your own.

   C. Call the secretary and ask her about the corporate culture there.

   D. Take the customer to lunch and introduce yourself as their new service professional. This is certain to impress them.

5. You've just come back to the office after having a tough service call. A sales representative at your company had promised the customer that the problem with their hard drive could be easily fixed when in fact you had to bring their hard drive back for repairs. The customer has stated his anger by saying that your company made a false promise to get his business and now it is too late to contact another service company. What should you do?

    A. Apologize. Keep the situation focused on the problem and its solution by telling the customer his options.

    B. Have a word with the sales representative's manager when you return.

    C. Inform your manager of the situation.

    D. all of the above

    E. A and C only

6. You are in the process of upgrading a software package on a customer's computer. Some strange things seem to be happening, so you decide to run an anti-virus program and discover the client has had a virus on the computer. You realize that you have an opportunity to provide excellent service by:

    A. Wiping out the virus and then finishing the upgrade.

    B. Selling the customer an anti-virus program.

    C. Informing the customer of the situation and letting them know that customer service is an opportunity to improve business relations through solutions.

    D. Offering to stay until you can determine a possible source of the virus so that it can be wiped out completely.

    E. Running the anti-virus program on another of the customer's computers. Once you get a feel of how far the virus may have spread, install the anti-virus program on their machines and bill the customer later. They will thank you for it.

7. Customer service is an opportunity to improve business relations through solutions. According to the material you just read, which of the following is *not* a solution that would provide an opportunity to improve a business relation?

   A. Offering the services of your competition.

   B. Following up with a customer.

   C. Fixing a problem without being told to do so.

   D. Saying thank you.

8. You have just diagnosed a print quality problem on a printer as being a defective ink cartridge. Upon further inspection, you notice that the ink cartridge has been refilled several times. This customer has told you that they constantly refill ink cartridges to save money. You know the refilled ink cartridges are causing this problem and will cause the owner to bring it back in a month for the same problem. What do you tell the customer when they pick up their computer?

   A. "Stop using the refilled ink cartridges. They're causing your problem."

   B. Explain to the customer that the money that they are saving on ink cartridges is being wasted on repeated service calls. Spending the extra couple of dollars on manufacturer-brand cartridges will actually save them more money on service calls.

   C. Nothing. It's money in the bank. They'll keep bringing it back for repairs.

9. It's 3:30 P.M. Your work day ends at 5:00. Your customer's business is open until 5:00 also. Your repair will take at least 2 more hours (possibly more). What should you do?

   A. Stay till 5:30 or so. Get the job done.

   B. Inform the customer that the job will take you past your closing time. Ask if they would like you to stay until the job is finished. If not, ask if they would like you to reschedule for the next available time.

   C. Inform the customer that the job will take you past their closing time. Ask if they would like you to stay until the job is finished. If not, ask if they would like you to reschedule for the next available time.

   D. Leave at 5:00. They're closed and you shouldn't stay past closing.

10. You have just hung up from a customer support phone call in which you had to walk a user through, step-by-step, the installation of Windows 95. You have spent two hours on the phone. What should you do next?

    A. Call back two days later and ask how the computer is operating.

    B. Don't return the customer's messages. They just want free help.

    C. Inform your manager.

    D. Bill the customer for two hours of phone support.

11. A customer is asking the unreasonable. They want your company to pay for a brand new computer even though the old one has only a small software problem. The problem has been narrowed down to a piece of software that the owner installed. They won't accept anything less than a new computer. What do you do?

    A. Give them a new computer.

    B. Fix the software problem and give the computer back.

    C. Explain that the software they installed is causing the problem. Show them that their software is causing the problem and offer to fix the problem for free.

    D. Cut your losses and give them their computer back. Do your best, however, to satisfy their needs, within reason.

12. The customer is always right. True or false?

    A. True

    B. False

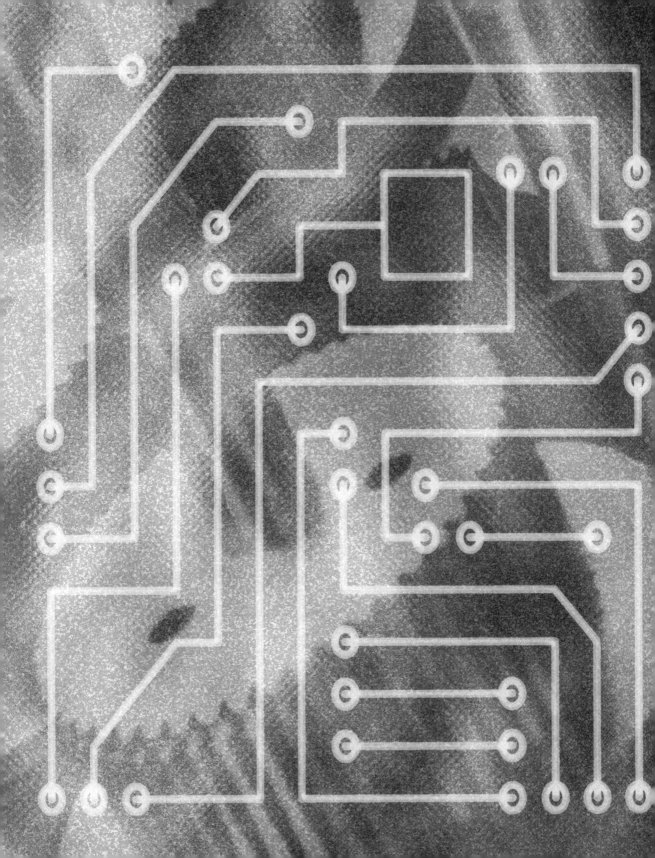

CHAPTER
TWELVE

Troubleshooting Techniques

Objectives

- Identify common symptoms and problems associated with each module and how to troubleshoot and isolate the problems.

- Identify care and service techniques and common problems with primary printer types.

Troubleshooting is the process of identifying a computer problem so that it can be fixed. Until you've had the opportunity to troubleshoot several computers with several different types of customers, the only way to gain the troubleshooting skills you will rely on as a certified technician is to learn from other people's experiences. In this chapter, I'll try to summarize for you some of the experience that my colleagues and I have gained over the course of our careers as service technicians, and I'll attempt to organize these experiences by providing you with guidelines and general tips for approaching the task of troubleshooting. This chapter will cover the following A+ troubleshooting topics in detail:

- Troubleshooting methodology

- Hardware troubleshooting

- Software troubleshooting

- Printer troubleshooting

TIP   Pay special attention to the last topic, Printer Troubleshooting, because there are quite a few questions on the exam that deal with printer problems.

Troubleshooting Resources

Just an artist has paintbrushes, paints, and a vision of how things should work together, a great troubleshooter has several tools to maker their job easier. And, like the artist's brushes, palette, and vision, a technician's resources can be put into service to accomplish a complex goal: the identification of a problem.

Intellectual Resources

Most technicians actually relish computer problems, because they know it's a chance to find a solution and maybe to brag to their colleagues. It can feel almost like being the first to discover a star or comet, although very seldom do you get to name a problem or its solution (like "The Roger Smith General Protection Fault Solution" or "The Dan Jones AUTOEXEC.BAT Conundrum"). Each time a technician solves a new problem, they know that if they ever run into that problem again, they'll be able to fix it easily (or at least have a starting point for troubleshooting).

The first major resource, then, that you can use for troubleshooting a problem is your own brain. Your brain can hold lots of information. We remember almost everything we're exposed to. For this reason, the best troubleshooters are usually the people who have been exposed to the most problems. They have seen several different types of problems and their solutions. Therefore, if they run into a particular problem, they may have seen it before and can quickly fix the problem.

Service documentation is another important intellectual resource, and we might point out that it's not used as often as it should be. As soon as a new product is released, several things are released at the same time (or very shortly thereafter). These include items like the owner's manual, the buyer's guide, and (most importantly) the service and replacement parts manuals. These books can be a valuable source of troubleshooting information. They can also contain replacement parts information, like which part(s) should be replaced when a particular component is found to be bad. Also, they usually contain exploded diagrams of the model being repaired.

The Internet, of course, has become an extremely valuable resource for troubleshooting. Almost every technology company now has a Web site. One feature of most such companies' Web sites is the "knowledge base" (many have a different name for this feature), an area that contains several pieces of information that the company knows can be very valuable to technicians working with its products. First of all, the knowledge base usually contains one or more Frequently Asked Questions (FAQ) files. The files are summaries of the questions (and answers) that technical support technicians get. Second, this is a good place to look for reports of "bugs" that have been discovered or suspected in the company's products. You may have to go to the company's support page (or some similarly purposed section of the Web site) to ask your question directly, or perform a search on the knowledge base or FAQ to determine if there's a specific question or problem that relates to your situation, but in many cases, a problem you're spending time trying to solve has already been solved by someone else, and reported.

Yet another intellectual resource that is seldom used, except in the most difficult cases, is a coworker. If you don't have the knowledge to troubleshoot or repair the component, a coworker might. (The reason this is the most seldom used is that people hate to admit that they don't know something. But as the saying goes, "The beginning of wisdom is 'I don't know'.")

Hardware and Software Resources

In addition to the intangible resources, you have other items you can use to troubleshoot the computer. These items fall into two categories: hardware and software.

There are several hardware resources you can use in the troubleshooting process. First, you have your computer toolkit. When troubleshooting, though, the only tools you should really need from the toolkit are the ones for removing the case, because most troubleshooting is done with the computer on and "as-is." After all, you need to see what's happening before you start making changes.

> **NOTE** See Chapter 1, *Basic Computer Service Concepts*, for more information on the tools used to service a computer.

Another example of a hardware resource is a *resource discovery expansion card*. These cards, when installed into any expansion slot, will tell you what resources are being used in the computer and will indicate any possible conflicts. Several companies make these cards.

Software Troubleshooting

This section deals with a canvas that the troubleshooting artist may have to paint often: software problems. More than half of all computer problems are software-related. The problems usually don't stem from the software itself, but rather the interaction of that software with other software that may be running on that machine. However, before you can start troubleshooting, you must determine if the problem is hardware related or software related. In order to determine the source of a problem (hardware or software), you have a few things you can do to narrow it down:

1. **In DOS/Windows computers, boot the computer "clean."** Booting it "clean" means starting the computer with no software drivers loading. The only things that should be in the AUTOEXEC.BAT or CONFIG.SYS (the two DOS configuration files) are the necessary memory managers and settings to get the computer up and running. Leave out sound card, CD-ROM, network, and other device drivers. You can also boot "clean" by using a bootable floppy disk (see the sidebar "Making a Bootable Diskette"). If the computer functions normally, then the problem is usually software related, although it could be a hardware problem and the device driver just enabled the device, causing the conflict to show itself.

2. **Check the operating system error messages.**   Every operating system has built-in error-detection routines. These routines are designed to intercept problems and notify the user. If there is a major problem, these routines will display an error message for the software or hardware component that caused the problem. For example, when you try to print to a printer connected to your primary parallel port (LPT1) and the system returns an error like "Error writing to device LPT1," that is more than likely a hardware-related problem because a hardware device was mentioned (or alluded to) in the error message.

3. **Uninstall and then reinstall the application that's having problems.**   This ensures that you have the correct version of all the application's components and that there are no missing files that may be required by the application. (For example, many applications today are intelligent enough to tell you when they're missing a necessary file to complete an operation—perhaps a spell-checker's dictionary files, or a library of programming objects, or even a file created by a coworker but stored in the wrong place on the network. The solution to this problem is very simple. If the missing file is a program file, reinstall that program from the original disks. Or, if the file is a data file, restore the data file from a backup.)

4. **Look for ways to repeat the problem.**   If it is a phantom problem, ask the user to help you out by finding a way to repeat the problem or looking for some type of pattern to the problem.

5. **Make sure you are using the latest patches.**   This is especially important with machines that are on a network; having a buggy *network client* (the software that communicates with the network server and network resources) can cause a host of strange application problems. Also, make sure that all the machines running on the network are using the latest bug fixes to the application itself. You should be able to obtain these by looking on the application company's Web site.

6. **Check the Internet.** This is related to the previous point. Often software publishers will post FAQs (Frequently Asked Questions) and have a searchable knowledge base on the Internet with useful resources for troubleshooting problems with their products.

7. **Compare and isolate.** It can be difficult to determine if an application problem is caused by the software or hardware. The best troubleshooting tools in this case are the twins comparison and isolation. Try comparing how the application behaves on the problem machine and on a machine that you know is working fine; then remove and/or replace hardware components from the two machines to eliminate possible causes and isolate the solution.

These indicators, along with your experience, should help you narrow the problem to either a hardware or software problem.

Making a Bootable Diskette

A DOS bootable diskette is a valuable tool for troubleshooting. The creation process is very simple. Insert a blank 1.44MB or 720KB diskette into your floppy drive and type the following at a DOS prompt:

```
FORMAT A: /S
```

(You can replace A: with the drive letter that represents your floppy drive.) The /S parameter instructs DOS to include the DOS "system files" on the floppy after formatting it. If the disk is already formatted, you can add the system files to a disk and make it bootable by typing the following at a DOS prompt:

```
SYS A:
```

When the computer is done, the "System Transferred" message will appear, telling you that the computer has finished making the disk bootable. This disk, when inserted before turning the computer on, will allow the computer to be booted because it contains the smallest portion of DOS necessary to start the computer.

DOS and Windows 9x offer several other ways of creating a bootable diskette.

DOS Troubleshooting

Troubleshooting DOS problems is a fundamental skill that most technicians get several chances to practice. Understanding and being able to modify the two main configuration files of DOS—AUTOEXEC.BAT and CONFIG.SYS—can solve most DOS problems.

NOTE   These topics apply to both MS-DOS and PC-DOS versions.

The DOS Configuration Files: CONFIG.SYS and AUTOEXEC.BAT

DOS is a simple operating system. It requires very few system resources to operate. It is also simple to operate. Unless you've damaged or misplaced part of DOS itself, you just type the command you want the computer to execute, and it does it. Despite the fact that it can take a lot of study to familiarize yourself with *all* the commands that DOS has to offer, you don't need to know very many of them to take advantage of its most useful capabilities. For these reasons, it stands as the most popular operating system of all time.

DOS uses two main configuration files, CONFIG.SYS and AUTOEXEC.BAT. Each file is a simple ASCII text file that contains commands and variables that set up the user environment in DOS.

- The CONFIG.SYS file is the main configuration file that DOS uses and, as such, it can be the source of several problems with DOS. The problems that are normally experienced are things like insufficient conventional memory, incorrect drivers loading, and not enough file handles. The CONFIG.SYS also has a detailed role in the logical mapping of the PC's memory. It loads memory drivers (like EMM386.EXE and HIMEM.SYS) as well as specifying the location of the DOS files (with statements like DOS=HIGH, UMB). It can also load device drivers by using lines that start with a "DEVICE=" statement.

- The AUTOEXEC.BAT, on the other hand, is a special batch file that executes automatically at system startup. This configuration file establishes the user environment and loads system drivers. Because it's a batch file, you can add statements to it that can automatically start other programs.

If either file becomes damaged or corrupt (with incorrect entries), the best two tools you have are the REM statement and backup files.

REM Statements

Let's say that the PC we're working on is inconsistently locking up. Further, let's say that you have already determined that the problem is software related, because when you boot "clean" with a boot diskette, the computer functions normally. This would mean that one of the statements in the CONFIG.SYS or AUTOEXEC.BAT is causing the problem.

NOTE The CONFIG.SYS and AUTOEXEC.BAT files are covered in more detail in the second book for the A+ exams, "A+ Certification DOS/Windows Exam Study Guide" (Sybex, 1998). Refer to this book for a detailed discussion of these two configuration files.

In order to solve the problem, you must remove (or change) the line that is causing the problem. However, first you must find the offending line. This can be accomplished through the use of REM statements. The REM command is short for *Remark*; by placing it at the beginning of any command line, you ensure that DOS will skip that line when running the file. The initial purpose for the REM command was to insert remarks or comments into batch files, so that the programmer or curious user could annotate what was going on in different sections of the file without requiring the computer to "run" the comment. However, you can also use it to *remove* suspect commands one at a time in order to test the effect of booting with and without them. By editing both the CONFIG.SYS and AUTOEXEC.BAT and "REMming out" one command at a time (and rebooting between each change), you can progressively eliminate statements that might be the cause of the problem.

TIP

There is another way to "step" through the CONFIG.SYS and AUTO-EXEC.BAT files to determine which line is causing the problem. During the boot process, press the F8 key when you see the words, "Starting MS-DOS." This will allow you to choose whether to execute a particular line in either of these files.

Let's take a look at a sample computer problem:

The computer is randomly locking up. The CONFIG.SYS and AUTOEXEC.BAT are as follows (the lines are numbered to facilitate our discussion here; the real files would not have the numbers):

CONFIG.SYS

```
1.DEVICE=C:\DOS\HIMEM.SYS
2.DEVICE=C:\DOS\EMM386.EXE
3.DOS=HIGH
4.FILES=40
5.BUFFERS=9,256
6.DEVICE=C:\SB16\DRV\CTSB16.SYS /UNIT=0 /BLASTER=A:220 I:5 D:1 H:5
7.DEVICE=C:\SB16\DRV\DRV\SBCD.SYS /D:MSCD001 /P:220
```

AUTOEXEC.BAT

```
1.@ECHO OFF
2.SET BLASTER=A220 I5 D1 T4
3.C:\DOS\MSCDEX.EXE /D:MSCD001
4.SET PATH=C:\DOS;C:\;C:\WINDOWS;C:\MOUSE
5.SET TEMP=C:\TEMP
6.C:\WINDOWS\SMARTDRV.EXE
```

When troubleshooting a software problem the first thing I always check is the non-DOS items in either configuration file. Lines 6 and 7 of the CONFIG.SYS and line 2 of the AUTOEXEC.BAT are from a recent sound card installation. To check if one of these drivers is the problem, always start by REMming out the non-DOS items. So, if you edit both the configuration files and REM out the non-DOS items, the CONFIG.SYS and AUTOEXEC.BAT will look like so:

CONFIG.SYS

```
1.DEVICE=C:\DOS\HIMEM.SYS
2.DEVICE=C:\DOS\EMM386.EXE
3.DOS=HIGH
4.FILES=40
5.BUFFERS=9,256
6.rem DEVICE=C:\SB16\DRV\CTSB16.SYS /UNIT=0 /BLASTER=A:220 I:5 D:1 H:5
7.rem DEVICE=C:\SB16\DRV\DRV\SBCD.SYS /D:MSCD001 /P:220
```

AUTOEXEC.BAT

```
1.@ECHO OFF
2.rem SET BLASTER=A220 I5 D1 T4
3.C:\DOS\MSCDEX.EXE /D:MSCD001
4.SET PATH=C:\DOS;C:\;C:\WINDOWS;C:\MOUSE
5.SET TEMP=C:\TEMP
6.C:\WINDOWS\SMARTDRV.EXE
```

If the computer boots and operates normally with this configuration, you can assume that the problem was related to one of the non-DOS entries—that is, a driver for a peripheral (if not the peripheral itself). It should be noted that REMming out the statements (as we did above) would cause the devices that the statements were intended to configure to not function at all. This is not a failure, but simply the way computers work.

Sherlock Holmes said it best: "When you have eliminated the impossible, whatever remains, no matter how improbable, must be the truth." In our example, the only device drivers were for the sound card, so it's probable that the sound card was configured improperly. If you had multiple device drivers in the configuration files, you would have to test each possibility separately to find out. Troubleshooting with REM statements is a process of elimination. One by one, you must eliminate the impossible, so that you can find the improbable.

Backups

Whenever you install drivers for a hardware device, the installation program will ask you if you want it to modify the CONFIG.SYS and AUTOEXEC.BAT for you, or if you would like to modify the files yourself. When the installation program modifies these files, it makes duplicates, or *backups*, of them just in case the drivers it installs cause problems. That way, if there *is* a problem, you can reboot using the backup files instead of the ones modified during the installation process.

To reboot using the backup files, first you need to rename the new CONFIG.SYS and AUTOEXEC.BAT (to anything other than those names). A good way to keep track of them is to replace the .SYS and .BAT filename extensions with your initials. Then you need to rename (to CONFIG.SYS and AUTOEXEC.BAT, of course) the backups that the installation process created.

Of course, before you can rename your backups to CONFIG.SYS and AUTOEXEC.BAT as directed above, you have to find them. Installation programs usually name the backup file for the CONFIG.SYS with a name like CONFIG.BAK or CONFIG.OLD, or, if you already have files with those names, by providing a numbered filename extension, like CONFIG.001 or CONFIG.002, etc. Similarly, they rename the backup file for the AUTOEXEC.BAT with a .BAK, .OLD, or numbered filename extension.

TIP   Since it's possible that over a matter of months a system will contain numerous backups from different installations, it can be very helpful to view the list of files according to date (in some listings this is given by clicking on the option named "Last Modified") to make it easy to find the most recently changed files—i.e., the configuration files created and modified by the problem installation.

Windows Troubleshooting

Windows problems are the most troublesome of all software-related problems, mainly because there are several components working together in Windows. If any of these components develops a problem or corruption, it can bring Windows to a screeching halt. There are three primary areas you can check for finding troubleshooting information in Windows: system resources, General Protection Faults, and the Windows configuration files.

> **NOTE** These topics apply to Windows 3.1, Windows 3.11, and Windows 95.

System Resources

When Windows runs out of memory, hard disk space, or both, we say it has run out of *system resources*. Windows 3.1 has an "About" window (select Help ➤About in the Windows Program Manager screen) that can be used to check the amount of available system resources (see Figure 12.1 for an example of the About window). For optimal Windows performance, the available system resources should be above 80%. If they are below 80% you will need to add RAM, disk space, or both.

You can check the system resources in Windows 95 by using the Resource Meter (available through the Start menu, under Programs ➤ Accessories ➤ System Tools, if you have installed the Microsoft Plus! pack). The resource meter will show up as a small bar graph on your Taskbar at the bottom of the screen. If you double-click the bar graph, it will bring up a screen that shows the available system resources (similar to the Windows 3.1 statistics). Figure 12.2 shows this window.

FIGURE 12.1:

Windows 3.1 system resources

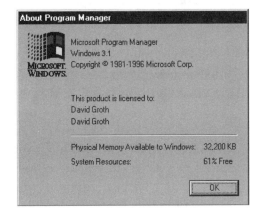

FIGURE 12.2:

Checking Windows 95 system resources

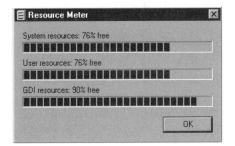

General Protection Faults

A misbehaving Windows program may overstep its bounds and try to take memory from another application. When it does this, Windows will halt the misbehaving program and display an error called a *General Protection Fault*, or *GPF*. This type of error is one of the most common Windows errors as well as the most frustrating. Such errors are generally the result of nonstandard programming. The programmer took shortcuts in their programming and left out the "safety nets" that would prevent a program from taking memory away from another, running program.

There is no way to make a system 100% GPF-free. You can, however, reduce the number of GPFs that occur by taking a couple of precautions. First of all, monitor your system resources carefully. When Windows starts running out of available memory, it means the programs that are running are tightly packed in memory. In a system with only a little space available, the likelihood is relatively great that a program will use another program's memory when it goes looking for more memory, and thus cause a GPF. (By way of comparison, when a program tries to take more memory in a system that has *plenty* of available memory, the chances are good that it will find memory that is *not* being used by some other program.) This underscores the guideline, "You can never have enough closet space or RAM."

Second, exercise some discipline, and use only the *released* versions of software—the retail version, the one available commercially. Software goes through three major steps of development: *Alpha*, *Beta*, and *Release*. In the Alpha release, the program is intended only for testing within the software company itself, and it may not include all the features that are intended to be included in the eventual release. Also, the software at this stage will still have many errors (called "bugs") that need to be worked out. The Beta release includes all the features that will be included in the Release version, as well as the installation program (often missing in the Alpha version), and is ready for consumer testing. The features may have changed significantly between Alpha and Beta, based on the feedback generated in-house by the Alpha testers and management. There may be numerous Alpha cycles before the software is ready for outside (i.e., Beta) testing; and Betas themselves frequently undergo numerous "builds" during a Beta cycle, as platform issues and bugs are found and addressed. By the final Beta, although some of the "loose ends" may need to be tightened up, the software is basically ready. When the software is released commercially ("Final Release"), the developers consider it to be more-or-less "bug-free." There may be a few, minor bugs that crop up after the initial release, but the software will be stable for use.

WARNING   NEVER use Alpha or Beta software on your computer. These software programs *are* buggy and *will* cause problems, as well as GPFs.

There are two ways of fixing the bugs that do appear after the initial release of the software. You can either use a "patch" (a type of software "Band-Aid" to fix the problem until the next release) on the software or wait until the next release of the software. Which brings us to our next tip: Try to avoid version 1.0 of any piece of software. Because this version is the first release, it will usually contain the most bugs. Wait until the software has been released for a few months and has gone through a few revisions before buying it and installing it on your computer. By Revision 1.2, most of the bugs have been worked out and the software can be considered stable.

How to Read the Version Numbers on Software

When reading the version number of most software titles, you can deduce a few things by the version number. The leftmost number in a version number indicates the *major release version*. Each major release introduces several new features and may completely change the way the software operates.

The first number to the right of the decimal point is the *revision number*. When a single feature (or small set of features) needs to be introduced, along with several bug fixes, a new revision of the software is released. Revision numbers increment until the software developers decide to release another major release.

Any numbers to the right of the revision number can be considered *patch levels*. When software is released with a second number to the right of a decimal point, it usually means that it is a bug-fix only. No new features would be released in this version.

Continued on next page

For example, let's examine the following revision number:

FURBLE 1.24

This would indicate that the software contains all the features of the first major release of the FURBLE program, and in addition is the second revision of that release, and the fourth patch at that level. This software should therefore be quite stable by this stage.

It also should be noted that some vendors (mainly Microsoft) have abandoned this convention in favor of naming the software with the year it was released (i.e. Windows 95, Office 97), etc. However, production schedules fall behind and sometimes software is released the following year.

Windows Configuration

When Windows 3.*x* programs are installed, their files are copied to the hard disk and entries are made into the Windows configuration files: the INI files and the System Registry. The entries that are made into these files control various settings and tell the program (or Windows itself) how to operate. Let's discuss each of them.

INI Files   Primarily used for Windows 3.*x* programs, INI files (short for initialization files) are made for each program as well as for Windows. When a new application is installed, the installation program will create an INI file that contains the new application's settings. INI files are text files that can be edited with any text editor, if necessary.

The three primary INI files that Windows uses are: SYSTEM.INI, WIN.INI, and PROGMAN.INI. Each of them should be backed up before changes are made. The SYSTEM.INI has settings for the drivers that Windows uses. It is probably the most critical of the three. Changes made to this file affect Windows' resource usage as well as resource availability.

The WIN.INI controls the Windows operating environment. There are entries for the programs that Windows starts automatically, screen saver settings, desktop color schemes, wallpaper, and system compatibility information. Changes made to this file can be critical (your screen might come up in a different color, for example), and you should take care when modifying the [Compatibility] section, as that could cause problems programs designed to run under older versions of Windows.

Finally, the PROGMAN.INI contains settings for the Program Manager. The settings control the number and file names of the program groups in the Program Manager. Changing these settings modifies which program groups appear in the Program Manager. You can also control Program Manager security (like what menu options appear or are grayed out in the Program Manager) by modifying the [Restriction] section.

TIP   If you delete the INI file of some programs, they will create a new one with the default settings.

A problem can be tracked to an INI file if a setting was made in a Windows 3.1 program and now the program doesn't function properly, or if it "GPFs" frequently. To solve this type of problem it is best to rename an old INI file to replace the corrupt one (like WINWORD.OLD to WINWORD.INI). Just like with DOS installation programs, Windows setup programs make backups of the configuration files they change and name them with .BAK or .OLD extensions or with number extensions (.001, .002, etc.). If you have a problem with a new INI file, you can rename one of the backups (preferably the most recent one) to the .INI extension to make *it* the active INI file.

The Registry   With the introduction of Windows 95, Microsoft did away with the practice of using several INI files to contain program configuration information. They introduced a special database called the Registry to provide a single common location for all configuration and program setting information. Every Windows 95 program, upon installation, will "register" itself so that Windows 95 knows about it. When other programs need information about what printers and devices are available in Windows 95, they query the Registry to get this information.

The Registry can be viewed and edited with REGEDIT.EXE. When you run this program, it presents the view shown in Figure 12.3. Each folder represents a section or "key" that contains specific information. It is within these keys that the settings for the Windows programs are kept.

FIGURE 12.3:

Viewing the Registry with REGEDIT.EXE

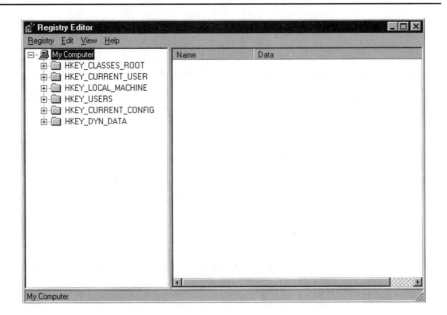

Generally speaking, you should not make changes to the Registry. Registry changes can be exceedingly complex, and are not covered on the A+ core exam, so we won't devote any more space to it here.

Hardware Troubleshooting

When you're troubleshooting hardware, there are a few common problems that any experienced technician should know about. These common problems usually have simple solutions. Knowing these problems (and their respective solutions) will make you a more efficient troubleshooter. Let's discuss a few of the most common hardware problems and their solutions.

POST Routines

The first item we're going to discuss isn't really a hardware problem, but a hardware troubleshooting aid. Every computer has a diagnostic program built into its BIOS called the *Power On Self-Test*, or *POST*. When you turn on the computer it executes this set of diagnostics. These tests go by pretty quickly, so we'll detail them here.

NOTE   The POST described below is typical of IBM-brand PCs; other manufacturers have similar POSTs, but they may differ in certain aspects.

---

1. **The processor is tested.**   POST runs checks on the CPU. If the tests fail, the system stops with no error message (usually).

2. **The ROMs are checked.**   POST computes a checksum for the BIOS ROMs. If the checksums do not match, the system halts with no error message.

3. **The DMA controller is tested.**   Again, if there are problems, the system halts.

4. **The Interrupt controller is checked.**   If there is a problem with this component, the system will give a long beep, then a short beep, then the system will stop.

5. **The system timing chip is tested.**   This is not the chip that tells time, but rather the chip that provides timing signals for

the bus and processor. If this chip fails, the system will give a long beep, then a short beep, then halt.

6. **The BASIC ROMs are tested (if they exist).** Most computers since the IBM AT have not included BASIC, so this step is usually not part of their POST routines. However, on older computers, if the ROMs fail the POST test, it does another long beep, then a short beep, and then halts.

7. **The video card is checked.** At this point the system runs the diagnostics for the video card. If it fails, the system issues one long beep and two short beeps and halts. If successful, the video ROM BIOS is copied into RAM and you will usually see a message about the type of video card that the computer is using.

8. **Expansion boards are initialized.** During this part of the POST routine, any expansion boards that need to can initialize and copy their ROMs into upper memory, if necessary.

9. **RAM is counted and tested.** The system tests and counts all RAM that's installed in the machine by writing a bit to each bit of memory. If a 1 is written and read back successfully, the counter increments. A failure during this portion of the POST will generate a "201 memory error" message on the screen. (Here's a free tip for you: Any POST error numbers starting with 2 are memory-related errors.)

10. **The keyboard is tested.** The keyboard controller is contacted and signals are sent to detect the presence of a keyboard. Checks for stuck keys are also made. If this test fails, a "301–Keyboard Failure" error is generated, along with a short beep. Some systems may halt, others may not. (Some systems also ask you to press <F1> ...which is kind of silly if the keyboard isn't working, huh?)

11. **The cassette interface is checked.** This is another POST routine only valid on IBM PCs and XTs. If the cassette interface doesn't work, a "131–Cassette Interface" error is generated. The system does not halt.

12. Test floppy drives. The floppy disk adapter is contacted and asked to activate the drive motors of any floppy disks, in order (A:, then B:). If there are problems, a "601 - Floppy Disk" error is generated and the system will try to load cassette BASIC (if it's present, on an IBM PC or XT).

13. Check resources and boot the computer. The POST routine queries any remaining devices (LPT ports, serial ports, etc.), makes a short beep, and then queries the disk drives looking for an operating system. If one is found on either a floppy drive or hard disk, it is loaded and the computer is functional. If an operating system can't be found, most systems will issue an "Operating system not found" error (or something to that effect).

The POST routines are a great tool for troubleshooting. They will usually give English descriptions of any problems that they find. Some BIOS POST routines may actually give suggestions on how to fix the problem (don't expect this kind of friendliness on an IBM AT, though; it only gives cryptic error codes). Tables 12.1 and 12.2 summarize the POST beep and error codes, respectively, most often seen on computers today.

TABLE 12.1: Common POST Beep Codes

Beep Code	Problem
No Beep, system dead	Power supply bad, system not plugged in, or power not turned on
Continuous beeps	Power supply bad, not plugged into motherboard correctly, or keyboard stuck
Repeating short beep	Power supply may be bad
1 short beep, nothing on screen	Video card failure
1 short beep, video present, but system won't boot	Bad floppy drive, cable, or controller
2 short beeps	Configuration error (on most PS/2 systems)
1 long, 1 short	System board bad
1 long, 2 short	Video card failure

TABLE 12.2: Common POST Error Codes

Error Number	Explanation
1**	Any number starting with 1 usually indicates a system board problem.
161	CMOS battery failure
164	Memory size error. Always happens after memory has been added. Running the BIOS setup program will allow the system to recognize the memory and the error should go away.
2**	Any number starting with 2 usually indicates a memory-related problem
201	Memory test failed. One or more portions of RAM were found to be bad. Any numbers following this error code may indicate which RAM chip is bad. See the computer's documentation for information on interpreting those codes.
3**	Any error number starting with 3 usually indicates a problem with the keyboard. Problems include a missing or malfunctioning keyboard, as well as stuck keys.
301	Keyboard error. Usually means a missing or malfunctioning keyboard or a key has been pressed too long during startup (are you resting your hand on the keyboard? is something leaning against one of the keys?). Also happens if a key remains depressed during the POST keyboard test.
4**	Monochrome video problems
5**	Color video problems
6**	Floppy disk system problems
601	Floppy disk error. Either the floppy adapter or the floppy drive failed. Check to see that the floppy cable isn't on upside down and that the power to the floppy drive(s) is hooked up correctly.
17**	Hard disk problems. The hard disk geometry might not be set correctly, or the disk adapter can't communicate with the hard disk.
1780	Drive 0 (C:) drive failure. The C: drive or controller isn't functioning. The disk might not be configured, or the adapter isn't installed correctly.
1781	Drive 1 (D:) drive failure. The D: drive or controller isn't functioning. The disk might not be configured, or the adapter isn't installed correctly.

Motherboard Problems

The motherboard's (or logic board's) functions are tested, for the most part, by the POST routines. The 1** errors and beep codes during startup indicate the biggest problems. So there are very few problems that don't show up in the POST. The occasional "phantom" problem does happen, however.

One problem that does happen becomes visible when the system constantly loses its clock. The time will reset to 12:00 on 12/01/83, for example. At the same time, you may start seeing "1780 – Hard disk failure" problems. When you try to reset the time, it will set correctly. But as soon as you turn off the computer and turn it back on, the time as been lost.

These symptoms indicate that the system's CMOS is losing the time, date, and hard disk settings (as well as several other system settings). The CMOS is able to keep this information when the system is shut off because there is a small battery powering this memory. Because it is a battery, it will eventually lose power and go dead.

NOTE   Some systems use a special chip called a "Dallas chip" to provide the same functionality as the CMOS, but, like the CMOS, it too will "die" eventually.

When the CMOS battery (or Dallas chip) is replaced, the system settings must be reset. But they will be retained when the power is shut off. Some people immediately think "system board problem" when the answer is a cheap little battery and ten minutes of labor. Because of the simplicity of this repair, most service professionals replace these batteries as a courtesy service for their customers. Consider it an "outpatient" repair.

Hard Disk System Problems

Hard disk system problems usually stem from one of three causes:

- The adapter is bad.
- The disk is bad.
- Or the two are connected incorrectly.

The first and last cause are easy to identify, because in either case the symptom will be obvious: the drive won't work. You simply won't be able to get the computer to communicate with the disk drive. (You can further narrow it down as to whether it's a configuration problem or not by checking to see if the drive is connected correctly. If it is, then the problem is usually a bad or misconfigured disk adapter.)

However, if the problem is a bad disk drive, the symptoms aren't as obvious. As long as the BIOS POST tests can communicate with the disk drive, they are usually satisfied. But the POST tests may not uncover problems related to storing information. For example, even with healthy POST results, you may find that you're permitted to save information to a bad disk, but of course when you try to read it back you get errors. Or, the computer may not boot as quickly as it used to because the disk drive can't read the boot information successfully every time. Bad disk drives could be the cause of the problems in both of these examples, but neither one of them would be indicated by a POST test. Keep in mind, then, that a successful POST test doesn't necessarily mean a "happy" computer.

In some cases, reformatting the drive can solve the problems described in the preceding paragraph. In other cases, reformatting only brings the drive back to life for a short while. The bottom line is, read and write problems usually indicate that the drive is "going south" and should be replaced soon. Never expect a "Band-Aid" type repair like reformatting to cover a "major trauma" problem like disk failure.

WARNING Never low-level format IDE or SCSI drives! They are low-leveled from the factory and you may cause problems by using low-level utilities on these types of drives.

Peripheral Problems

The biggest set of peripheral problems are those related to modem communications. The symptoms of these problems include the following:

- The modem won't dial.

- The modem keeps hanging up in the middle of my communications session.

- The modem spits out strange characters to my terminal screen.

If the modem won't dial, first check that it has been configured correctly, including its IRQ setting (as discussed in Chapter 7). If the configuration is correct, then the problem usually has to do with *initialization commands*. These are the commands sent to the modem by the communications program to "initialize" it. These commands tell it things like how many rings to wait before answering, how long to wait between when the last keystroke was detected and disconnecting, and at what speed to communicate.

For a while, each manufacturer had its own set of commands, and every communications program had to have settings for every particular kind of modem available. In particular, every program had commands for the Hayes line of modems (mainly because Hayes made good modems and their command language was fairly easy to program). Eventually, other modem manufacturers began using the "Hayes-compatible" command set. This set of modem initialization commands became known as the "Hayes command set." It is also known as the "AT command set," since each Hayes modem command started with the letters *AT* (presumably calling the modem to ATtention).

Each AT command does something different. The letters *AT* by themselves (when issued as a command) will ask the modem if it's ready to receive commands. If it returns "OK," that means that the modem is ready to communicate. If you receive "error," it means there is an internal modem problem that may need to be resolved before communication can take place.

Table 12.3 lists a few of the most common AT commands, their functions, and the problems that they can solve. These commands can be sent to the modem by opening a terminal program (such as the Windows Terminal or HyperTerminal (supplied with Windows 3.*x* and Windows 95, respectively), WINTERM.EXE, or Pro-COMM) and typing them in. All commands should return "OK" if they were successful.

> **NOTE**
>
> If you can't type anything, you either don't have the right COM port selected for the modem, or you have half-duplex mode enabled. To address this problem, you must enter "ATF1," then press <ENTER>. The modem should return the message "OK" and you will now be able to see your commands.

TABLE 12.3: Common "AT" Commands

Command	Function	Usage
AT	Tells the modem that what follows the letters "AT" is a command that should be interpreted.	Used to precede most commands.
ATDT *nnnnnnn*	Dials the number *nnnnnnn* as a tone-dialed number.	Used to dial the number of another modem if the phone line is set up for tone dialing.
ATDP *nnnnnnn*	Dials the number *nnnnnnn* as a pulse-dialed number.	Used to dial the number of another modem if the phone line is set up for rotary dialing.
ATA	Answers an incoming call manually.	Places the line off-hook and starts to negotiate communication with the modem on the other end.

Continued on next page

TABLE 12.3 CONTINUED: Common "AT" Commands

Command	Function	Usage
ATH0 (or +++ and then ATH0)	Tells modem to hang up immediately.	Places the line on-hook and stops communication. (Note: The "0" in this command is a zero, not the letter O.)
AT&F	Resets modem to factory default settings.	This setting works as the initialization string when others don't. If you have problems with modems hanging up in the middle of a session, or failing to establish connections, use this string by itself to initialize the modem.
ATZ	Resets modem to power-up defaults.	Almost as good as AT&F, but may not work if power-up defaults have been changed with S-registers.
ATS0-n	Waits n rings before answering a call.	Sets the default number of rings that the modem will detect before taking the modem off-hook and negotiating a connection. (Note: The "0" in this command is a zero, not the letter O.)
ATS6-n	Waits n seconds for a dial tone before dialing	If the phone line is slow to give a dial tone, you may have to set this register to a number higher than 2.
,	Pauses briefly	When placed in a string of AT commands, the comma will cause a pause to occur. Used to separate the number for an outside line (many businesses use 9 to connect to an outside line) and the real phone number (e.g. 9,555-1234).
*70 or 1170	Turns off call waiting	The "click" you hear when you have "call waiting" (a feature offered by the phone company) will interrupt modem communication and cause the connection to be lost. To disable call waiting for a modem call, place these commands in the dialing string like so: *70,555-1234. Call waiting will resume after the call is hung up.
CONNECT	Displayed when a successful connection has been made.	You may have to wait some time before this message is displayed. If this message is not displayed, it means the modem couldn't negotiate a connection with the modem on the other end of the line, due possibly to line noise.
BUSY	Displayed when the number dialed is busy.	If displayed, some programs will wait a certain amount of time and try again to dial.
RING	Displayed when the modem has detected a ringing line.	When someone is calling your modem, the modem will display this in the communications program. You would type "ATA" to answer the call.

If two computers can connect, but they both receive garbage to their screens, it's a good chance that both computers aren't agreeing on the communications settings. Settings like data bits, parity, stop bits, and compression must all agree in order for communication to take place. When both computers have different settings it's a lot like two people from different countries trying to communicate. They can meet and shake hands, but from there they can't communicate, because they are both speaking different languages.

Keyboard and Mouse Problems

Keyboards are simple devices. Therefore, they either work or they don't. There are rarely any "phantom" problems with keyboards. Usually, keyboard problems are environmental. They get dirty and the keys start to stick. This problem is easily avoided: DON'T EAT OR DRINK NEAR THE COMPUTER. It is my personal opinion that anyone who drinks near a computer keyboard should be made to clean one that has had a soft drink spilled in it. That person will never drink near a keyboard again. The liquid works its way into the plungers under the key caps, and, instead of drying, turns into a sticky, syrupy substance that doesn't easily wash away.

To clean a keyboard, it's best to use the keyboard cleaner sold by electronics supply stores. This cleaner foams up quickly and doesn't leave a residue behind. Spray it liberally on the keyboard and keys. Work the cleaner in between the keys with a stiff toothbrush. Blow the excess away with a strong blast of compressed air. Repeat until the keyboard functions properly. If you do have to clean a keyboard that's had a soft drink spilled on it, remove the key caps before you perform the cleaning procedure. It makes it easier to reach the sticky plungers.

TIP
A friend of mine told me about his way of cleaning keyboards: Remove the electronics and then place the keyboard in a dishwasher in the rinse cycle! Then, let them air dry. I wouldn't recommend this for some of the newer, capacitive keyboards. However, this will actually work for the older keyswitch keyboards (as long as the water isn't hard enough to leave residue inside the key switches or hot enough to melt the keys). Jet-Dry, anyone?

With mechanical keyboards, you can de-solder a broken key switch and replace it. However, most of the time, the labor to replace one key is more expensive than a new keyboard. New keyboards can be had for less than fifty bucks, so keep the one with the single malfunctioning key as a spare and replace it with a new one.

To clean the key caps on a keyboard, spray keyboard cleaner on a soft, lint-free cloth and rub it briskly onto the surface of each key. Be careful not to rub too hard; some of the cheaper keyboards use decals on their keys and you might rub them right off!

Display System Problems

Two types of video problems: No video and bad video. No video means that there is no image on the screen when the computer is powered up. Bad video means that the quality is sub-standard for the type of display system being used.

No Video

Any number of things can cause a blank screen. The first two are the most common: Either the power is off or the contrast or brightness is turned down. It's surprising how many people get stuck on that first one. I've gotten panicked phone calls (some even from experienced technicians) that go like this: "I can't get the monitor working!" or "I don't get any video on my screen!" Usually the technicians tell me they've even checked the video card's ROM address and changed it a couple of times just to be sure. I love this part.

Me: "Is it turned on?"

Them: (long pause) "Oh. Never mind." <click>

Or, if they verify that it's turned on:

Me: "Are the brightness and contrast turned down?"

Them: "Where do I check that?"

Me: "Can you see the knobs or buttons that have a picture of a sun on the one and a picture of a circle with half dark and half light on the other?"

Them: "Found 'em. Now what?"

Me: "Turn them one direction and then the other, and see if the screen gets brighter."

Them: "Okay. ...Oh! Wow! Cool! ...Sorry about that."

If they really did check the power as well as the brightness and contrast settings, then it's either a bad video card or blown monitor. An easy way to determine which one is to turn on the computer and monitor, then touch the monitor screen. The high voltage used to charge the monitor will leave a static charge on a working monitor, and it's a charge that can be felt. If there's no charge, there's a good chance the flyback transformer has blown and the monitor needs to be repaired. If there is a charge, the video card or cable are suspect.

TIP   This charge drains away fairly quickly after power-up, so this test only works immediately after power-up. Also, it's not a conclusive test, but it gives a good indication.

Bad Video

You may have seen a monitor that has a bad data cable. This is the monitor nobody wants because everything has a blue (or red, or green) tint to it and it gives everyone a headache. This monitor could also have a bad gun, but more often than not, the problem goes away if you wiggle the cable (indicating a bad cable).

You may have also seen monitors that are out of adjustment. Their pictures don't fill the screen (size adjustment), or the images "roll" (vertical or horizontal hold), or they are distorted (angle and pincushion adjustments). With most new monitors this is an easy problem to fix. Old monitors had to be partially disassembled to change these settings. New monitors have push-button control panels for changing these settings.

The earth generates a very strong magnetic field. This magnetic field can cause swirls and fuzziness in high-quality monitors. Most monitors have metal shields that can shield against magnetic fields. But eventually these shields can get "polluted" by taking on the same magnetic field as the earth, and the shield becomes useless. To solve this problem, these monitors have a built-in feature known as the "degauss" feature. This feature removes the effects of the magnetic field by creating a stronger magnetic field with opposite polarity that gradually fades to a field of zero. A special "degauss" button activates it. It only needs to be pressed when the picture starts to deteriorate. The image will shake momentarily during the degauss cycle, then return to normal.

TIP
The degauss feature should not be used every day. Once a month is usually sufficient if you are having color or clarity problems that get worse with time. You would only have to degauss every day if you lived in a place where high magnetic fields are a problem. If that's the situation you find yourself in, you might need to purchase a special, heavily shielded monitor for those conditions.

Miscellaneous Problems

There are a couple of problems that really don't fit well into any category but "Miscellaneous." So, we'll cover them here.

Dislodged Chips and Cards   The inside of your computer is a fairly harsh environment. The temperature inside the case of some Pentium computers is well over 100°F! When you turn your computer on, it heats up. Turn it off, it cools down. After several hundred cycles of this, some components can't handle the stress and start to move out of their sockets. This phenomenon is known as "chip creep" and can really be frustrating.

Chip creep can affect any socketed device, including ICs, RAM chips, and expansion cards. The solution to chip creep is simple. Open the case and reseat the devices. It's surprising how often this is the solution to "phantom" problems of all sorts.

Environmental Problems   I'll never forget the time I had to work on a computer that had been used on the manufacturing floor of a large equipment manufacturer. The computer and keyboard were covered with a black substance that would not come off (I later found out it was a combination of paint mist and molybdenum grease). There was so much diesel fume residue in the power supply fan it would barely turn. Also, the insides and components were covered with a thin, greasy layer of "muck." To top it all off, it *smelled terrible*!

Despite all this, the computer still functioned. However, it was prone to reboot itself every now and again. The solution was (as you may have guessed by now) to clean every component thoroughly and replace the power supply. The "muck" on the components was actually able to conduct a small current. Sometimes that current would go where it wasn't wanted and zap!—a reboot. Also, the power supply fan is supposed to partially cool the insides of the computer. In this computer, it was actually detrimental to the computer since it got its cooling air from the shop floor, which contained diesel fumes, paint fumes, and other chemical fumes. Needless to say, those fumes aren't good for computer components.

Computers are like human beings. They have similar tolerances to heat and cold (although computers like the cold better than we do). In general, anything comfortable to us is comfortable to a computer. They need lots of clean, moving air to keep them functioning. They don't, however, require food or drink (except maybe a few RAM chips now and again!). Keep food and drink away from the computer.

WARNING   The worst thing you can do is eat or smoke around your computer. The smoke particles contain tar that can get inside the computer and cause similar problems to what I've described above.

FRUs

When a component has been deemed to be "bad," it needs to be replaced. That's where the FRU comes in. FRU stands for *field replacement unit*.

FRUs can be individual parts (such as gears, springs, and shafts) or whole assemblies (like monitors, power supplies, and keyboards). In most cases you don't (or can't) replace individual parts. Most companies have gone to the strategy of using whole assemblies for FRUs. For example, you can't order a #2415 capacitor for a Compaq power supply from Compaq anymore. Instead you order a #A5123G power supply assembly. The individual assembly costs more, but there is less labor involved in replacing a whole power supply than a single capacitor, so it's actually cheaper for the customer as well as the service centers.

When you have determined that a particular component needs to be replaced, you will look in some kind of catalog (usually produced by the manufacturer) for the particular part number of the FRU that you need. These catalogs may also indicate the FRU's cost and shipping information. Some FRUs require an exchange of the old, broken component (called a "core" or "exchange" FRU). In this case, the catalog will indicate two prices: one for the FRU alone, another for the FRU with an exchange. The price of the single FRU is usually double (sometimes triple) the price of a core FRU.

Printer Troubleshooting

Other than the monitor, the most popular peripheral purchased for computers today is the printer. They are also the most complex peripheral, as far as troubleshooting is concerned. In this section, we will cover the most common types of printer problems you will run into. We will break the section into three areas, for the three different types of printers that exist.

Dot-Matrix Printer Problems

Dot-matrix printers are relatively simple devices. Therefore there are only a few problems that usually arise. We will cover the most common problems and their solutions here.

Low Print Quality

Problems with print quality are easy to identify. When the printed page comes out of the printer, the characters are too light or have dots missing from them. Table 12.4 details some of the most common print quality problems, their causes, and their solutions.

T A B L E   1 2 . 4 : Common Dot-Matrix Print-Quality Problems

Characteristics	Cause	Solution
Consistently faded or light characters	Worn-out print ribbon	Replace ribbon with a new, vendor-recommended ribbon.
Print lines that go from dark to light, dark to light as the print head moves across the page	Print ribbon advance gear slipping	Replace ribbon advance gear or mechanism.
A small, blank line running through a line of print (consistently)	Print head pin stuck inside the print head	Replace the print head.
A small, blank line running through a line of print (intermittently)	A broken, loose or shorting print head cable	Secure or replace the print head cable.
A small, dark line running through a line of print	Print head pin stuck in the "out" position	Replace the printhead. (Pushing the pin in may damage the print head).
Printer makes printing noise, but no print appears on page	Worn, missing, or improperly installed ribbon cartridge	Replace ribbon cartridge correctly.
Printer prints "garbage"	Cable partially unhooked, wrong driver selected, or bad printer control board (PCB)	Hook up cable correctly, select correct driver, or replace PCB (respectively).

Printout Jams inside the Printer (a.k.a. "The Printer Crinkled My Paper")

Printer jams are very frustrating because they always seem to happen more than halfway through your fifty-page print job, requiring you to take time to remove the jam before the rest of your pages can print. A paper jam happens when something prevents the paper from advancing through the printer evenly. Print jobs jam for two major reasons: an obstructed paper path and stripped drive gears.

Obstructed paper paths are often difficult to find. Usually it means disassembling the printer to find the bit of crumpled-up paper or other foreign substance that's blocking the paper path. A very common obstruction is a piece of the "perf"—the perforated sides of tractor-feed paper—that has torn off and gotten crumpled up and then lodged into the paper path. It may be necessary to remove the platen roller and feed mechanism to get at the obstruction.

TIP   Use extra caution when printing peel-off labels in dot-matrix printers. If a label or even a whole sheet of labels becomes misaligned or jammed, *DO NOT* roll the roller backwards to re-align the sheet. The small plastic paper guide that most dot-matrix printers use to control the forward movement of the paper through the printer will peel the label right off its backing if you reverse the direction of the paper. And once the label is free, it can easily get stuck under the platen, causing paper jams. A label stuck under the platen is almost impossible to remove without disassembling the paper feed assembly. If a label is misaligned, try realigning the whole sheet of labels *slowly* using the *feed roller,* with the power off, moving it in very small increments.

Stepper Motor Problems

A *stepper motor* is a motor that can move in very small increments. Printers use stepper motors to move the print head back and forth as well as to advance the paper (these are called the *carriage motor* and *main motor,* respectively). These motors get damaged when they are forced in any direction while the power is on. This includes moving the print head over to install a printer ribbon as well as moving the paper feed roller to align paper. These motors are very sensitive to stray voltages. And, if you are rotating one of these motors by hand, you are essentially turning it into a small generator, damaging it!

A damaged stepper motor is easy to detect. Damage to the stepper motor will cause it to lose precision and move farther with each "step." Lines of print will be unevenly spaced if the main motor is damaged (which is more likely). Characters will be "scrunched" together if the print head motor goes bad. In fact, if the motor is bad enough, it won't move at all in any direction. It may even make high-pitched squealing noises. If any of these symptoms show themselves, it's time to replace one of these motors.

Stepper motors are usually expensive to replace. They are about half the cost of a new printer! Damage to them is very easy to avoid, using common sense.

And Now for the Real World...

If I had a wish for the service department I worked in, I would wish that all the dot-matrix printers ever bought would be made by Okidata. Okidata dot-matrix printers are a technician's dream machine. With nothing but a flat-bladed screwdriver and your hands, you can completely disassemble an Okidata dot-matrix printer in less than ten minutes. Replacing parts on them is just as easy. All parts "snap" into place, including the covers. They also have an excellent reputation. If a customer asks you for a recommendation when buying a dot-matrix printer, you can't go wrong recommending an Okidata.

Bubble-Jet Printers

Bubble-jet printers are the most commonly sold printers for home use. For this reason, you need to understand the most common problems with bubble-jet printers so your company can service them effectively. Let's take a look at some of the most common problems with bubble-jet printers and their solutions.

Print Quality

The majority of bubble-jet printer problems are quality problems. Ninety-nine percent of these can be traced to a faulty ink cartridge. With most bubble-jet printers, the ink cartridge contains the print head and the ink. The major problem with this assembly can be described by "If you don't use it, you lose it." The ink will dry out in the small nozzles, blocking them if they are not used at least once a week.

An example of a quality problem is when you have thin, blank lines present in every line of text on the page. This is caused by a plugged hole in at least one of the small, pinhole ink nozzles in the print cartridge. Replacing the ink cartridge solves this problem easily.

WARNING Some people will try to save a buck by refilling their ink cartridge when they need to replace. If you are one of them, STOP IT! Don't refill your ink cartridges! Almost all ink cartridges are designed *not* to be refilled. They are designed to be used once and thrown away! By refilling them, you make a hole in them, and ink can leak out and the printer will need to be cleaned. Also, the ink will probably be of the wrong type, and print quality can suffer. Finally, a refilled cartridge may void the printer's warranty.

If an ink cartridge becomes damaged, or develops a hole, it can put too much ink on the page and the letters will smear. Again, the solution is to replace the ink cartridge. (You should be aware, however, that a very small amount of smearing is normal if the pages are laid on top of each other immediately after printing.)

One final print quality problem that does not directly involve the ink cartridge is when the print goes from dark to light quickly, then prints nothing. As we already mentioned, ink cartridges dry out if not used. That's why the manufacturers included a small suction pump inside the printer that "primes" the ink cartridge before each print cycle. If this "priming pump" is broken or malfunctioning, this problem will manifest itself and the pump will need to be replaced.

TIP   If the problem of the ink going from dark to light quickly and then disappearing ever happens to you, and you really need to print a couple of pages, try this trick I learned from a fellow technician: Take the ink cartridge out of the printer. Squirt some window cleaner on a paper towel and gently tap the print head against the wet paper towel. The force of the tap plus the solvents in the window cleaner should dislodge any dried ink, and the ink will flow freely again.

Paper Jams

Bubble-jet printers usually have very simple paper paths. Therefore, paper jams due to obstructions are less likely. They are still possible, however, so an obstruction shouldn't be overlooked as a possible cause of jamming.

Paper jams in bubble-jet printers are usually due to one of two things:

- A worn pickup roller

- The wrong type of paper

The pickup roller usually has one or two D-shaped rollers mounted on a rotating shaft. When the shaft rotates, one edge of the "D" rubs against the paper, pushing it into the printer. When the roller gets worn, it gets smooth and doesn't exert enough friction against the paper to push it into the printer.

If the paper used in the printer is too smooth, it causes the same problem. Pickup rollers use friction, and smooth paper doesn't offer much friction. If the paper is too rough, on the other hand, it acts like sandpaper on the rollers, wearing them smooth. Here's a rule of thumb for paper smoothness: Paper slightly smoother than a new one-dollar bill will work fine.

Laser and Page Printers

I've got good news and bad news. The bad news is that laser printer problems are the most complex, since the printer is the most complex. The good news is that most problems are easily identifiable and have specific fixes. Most of the problems can be diagnosed with knowledge of the inner workings of the printer and a little common sense. Let's discuss the most common laser and page printer problems and their solutions.

Paper Jams

Laser printers today run at copier speeds. Because of this, their most common problem is paper jams. Paper can get jammed in a printer for several reasons. First of all, feed jams happen when the paper feed rollers get worn (similar to feed jams in bubble-jet printers). The solution to this problem is easy: Replace the worn rollers.

TIP   If your paper feed jams are caused by worn pickup rollers, there is something you can do to get your printer working while you're waiting for the replacement pickup rollers. Scuff the feed roller(s) with a Scotch-Brite® pot-scrubber pad (or something similar) to roughen up the feed rollers. This trick only works once. After that, the rollers aren't thick enough to touch the paper.

Another cause of feed jams is related to the drive of the pickup roller. The drive gear (or clutch) may be broken or have teeth missing. Again, the solution is to replace it. To determine if the problem is a broken gear or worn rollers, print a test page, but leave the paper tray out. Look into the paper-feed opening with a flashlight and see if the paper pickup roller(s) are turning evenly and don't "skip." If they turn evenly, the problem is more than likely worn rollers.

Worn *exit rollers* can also cause paper jams. These rollers guide the paper out of the printer into the paper-receiving tray. If they are worn or damaged the paper may "catch" on its way out of the printer. These types of jams are characterized by a paper jam that occurs just as the paper is getting to the exit rollers. If the paper jams, open the rear door and see where the paper is. If the paper is very close to the exit roller, the exit rollers are probably the problem.

The solution is to replace all the exit rollers. You must replace all of them at the same time since even one worn exit roller can cause the paper to jam. Besides, they're cheap. Don't be cheap and skimp on these parts if you need to have them replaced.

And Now for the Real World...

I was in our local hospital ER recently having my hand looked at (I had cut it pretty badly on some glass). The receptionist who examined me asked me a few questions and filled out a report in the medical database on her computer. When she had finished asking me questions, she got up to get the printout from her laser printer.

I was shocked to see what she did next. When the paper starting coming out of the laser printer, she grabbed it and "ripped" it from the printer like you might do if the paper were in an old typewriter! The printer's exit rollers complained bitterly and made a noise that made me cringe. I don't know what hurt worse, my hand or my ears. She did this for every sheet of paper that she printed. I didn't say anything, since my health was of primary concern at the time.

Continued on next page

The following week I noticed a familiar laser printer come in for service from that very same hospital. As the technician started to work on it, I sauntered over and said, "I bet you twenty dollars it's the exit rollers." He said, "You're on!" Needless to say, I had a really good steak dinner that night with my wife.

I had a word with the person in charge of computer repair at that hospital the next day. They were surprised at what I had told them, but glad that I pointed it out. I saved them from many future repairs and they were very grateful. As far as I know, the ER receptionist doesn't rip the pages from the printer anymore, since we haven't seen that printer back in for service in a while.

Paper jams can actually be the fault of the paper. If your printer consistently tries to feed multiple pages into the printer, the paper isn't dry enough. If you live in an area with high humidity, this could be a problem. I've heard some solutions that are pretty far out, but that work (like keeping the paper in a Tupperware-type of airtight container, or microwaving it to remove moisture). The best all-around solution, however, is humidity control and to keep the paper wrapped until it's needed. Keep the humidity around 50% or lower (but above 25% if you can, in order to avoid problems with electrostatic discharge).

Finally, there is a metal, grounded strip called the static eliminator strip inside the printer that drains the corona charge away from the paper after it has been used to transfer toner from the EP cartridge. If that strip is missing, broken, or damaged the charge will remain on the paper and may cause it to stick to the EP cartridge, causing a jam. If the paper jams after reaching the corona assembly, this may be the cause.

Blank Pages

There's nothing more annoying than printing a ten-page contract and receiving ten pages of blank paper from the printer. Blank pages are a somewhat common occurrence in laser and page printers. Somehow, the toner isn't being put on the paper. There are three major causes of blank pages:

- The toner cartridge
- The corona assembly
- The high-voltage power supply (HVPS)

Toner Cartridge   As we have already discussed in Chapter 9, the toner cartridge is the source for most quality problems, since it contains most of the image-formation pieces for laser and page printers. Let's start with the obvious. A blank page will come out of the printer if there is no toner in the toner cartridge. I know it sounds simple, but some people think these things will last forever. It's very easy to check: just open the printer, remove the toner cartridge, and shake it. You will be able to hear if there's toner inside the cartridge. If it's empty, replace it with a known, good, manufacturer-recommended toner cartridge.

Another problem that crops up rather often is the problem of using refilled or reconditioned toner cartridges. During their recycling process, these cartridges may get filled with the wrong kind of toner (for example, one with an incorrect charge). This may cause toner to be repelled from the EP drum instead of attracted to it. Thus, there's no toner on the page because there was no toner on the EP drum to begin with. The solution once again is to replace the toner cartridge with the type recommended by the manufacturer.

A third problem related to toner cartridges happens when someone installs a new toner cartridge and forgets to remove the sealing tape that is present to keep the toner in the cartridge during shipping. The solution to this problem is as easy as it is obvious. Just remove the toner cartridge from the printer, remove the sealing tape, and reinstall the cartridge.

Corona Assembly   The second cause of the "blank page" problem is a damaged or missing corona wire. If there is a lost or damaged wire, the developed image won't transfer from the EP drum to the paper. Thus, no image appears on the printout. To determine if this is causing your problem, do the first half of the self-test (described later in this chapter). If there is an image on the drum, but not on the paper, you will know that the corona assembly isn't doing its job.

To check if the corona assembly is causing the problem, open the cover and examine the wire (or roller, if your printer uses one). The corona wire is hard to see, so you may need a flashlight. You will know if it's broken or missing just by looking (it will either be in pieces or just not there). If it's not broken or missing, the problem may be related to the HVPS.

The corona wire (or roller) is a relatively inexpensive part and can be easily replaced with the removal of two screws and some patience.

High-Voltage Power Supply (HVPS)   The HVPS supplies high-voltage, low-current power to both the charging and transfer corona assemblies in laser and page printers. If it's broken, neither will work properly. If the half self-test shows an image on the drum but none on the paper, and the corona assembly is present and not damaged, then the HVPS is at fault.

All Black Pages

Only slightly less annoying than ten blank pages is ten black pages. This happens when the charging unit (the charging corona wire or charging corona roller) in the toner cartridge malfunctions and fails to place a charge on the EP drum. Because the drum is grounded, it has no charge. Anything with a charge (like toner) will stick to it. As the drum rotates, all the toner will be transferred to the page and a black page is formed.

This problem wastes quite a bit of toner, but can be fixed easily. The solution (again) is to replace the toner cartridge with a known, good, manufacturer-recommended one. If that doesn't solve the problem, then the HVPS is at fault (it's not providing the high voltage that the charging corona needs to function).

Repetitive Small Marks or Defects

Repetitive marks occur frequently in heavily used (as well as older) laser printers. The problem may be caused by toner spilled inside the printer. It can also be caused by a crack or chip in the EP drum (this mainly happens with recycled cartridges). These cracks can accumulate toner. In both cases, some of the toner will get stuck onto one of the rollers. Once this happens, every time the roller rotates and touches a piece of paper, it will leave toner smudges spaced a roller circumference apart.

The solution is relatively simple: Clean or replace the offending roller. To help you figure out which roller is causing the problem, the service manuals contain a chart like the one in Figure 12.4. To use the chart, place the printed page next to the chart. Align the first occurrence of the "smudge" with the top arrow. The next smudge will line up with one of the other arrows. The arrow it lines up with tells which roller is causing the problem.

NOTE   Remember that the chart in Figure 12.4 is only an example. Your printer may have different size rollers (and thus need a different chart). Check your printer's service documentation for a chart like this. It is valuable in determining which roller is causing a smudge.

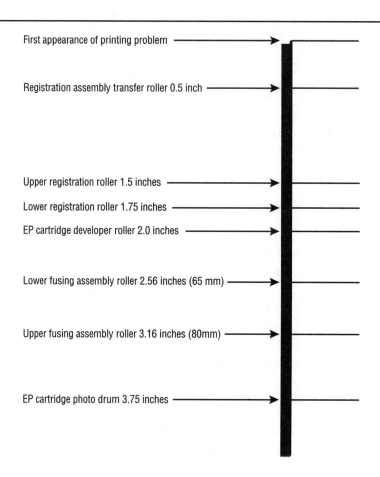

FIGURE 12.4:

Laser printer roller circumference chart

First appearance of printing problem

Registration assembly transfer roller 0.5 inch

Upper registration roller 1.5 inches

Lower registration roller 1.75 inches

EP cartridge developer roller 2.0 inches

Lower fusing assembly roller 2.56 inches (65 mm)

Upper fusing assembly roller 3.16 inches (80mm)

EP cartridge photo drum 3.75 inches

Vertical Black Lines on Page

A groove or scratch in the EP drum can cause the problem of vertical black lines running down all or part of the page. Since a scratch is "lower" than the surface, it doesn't receive as much (if any) of a charge as the other areas. The result is that toner will stick to it as though it were discharged. Since the groove may go around the circumference of the drum, the line may go all the way down the page.

Another possible cause of vertical black lines is a dirty charge corona wire. A dirty charge corona will prevent a sufficient charge from being placed on the EP drum. Since the EP drum will be almost zero, toner will stick to the areas that correspond to the dirty areas on the charge corona.

The solution to the first problem is, as always, to replace the toner cartridge (or EP drum if your printer uses a separate EP drum and toner). You can also solve the second problem with a new toner cartridge, but in this case that would be an extreme solution. It's easier to clean the charge corona with the brush supplied with the cartridge.

Vertical White Line on Page

Vertical white lines running down all or part of the page are relatively common problems on older printers, especially ones that don't see much maintenance. They are caused by some foreign matter (more than likely toner) caught on the transfer corona wire. The dirty spots keep the toner from being transmitted to the paper (at those locations, that is), with the result that streaks form as the paper progresses past the transfer corona wire.

The solution is to clean the corona wires. LaserJet Series II printers contain a small corona wire brush to help in this procedure. It's usually a small, green-handled brush located near the transfer corona wire. To use it, remove the toner cartridge and run the brush in the charge corona groove on top of the toner cartridge. Replace the cartridge and use the brush to brush away any foreign deposits on the transfer corona. Be sure to put it back in its holder when you're finished.

Image Smudging

If you can pick up a sheet from a laser printer, run your thumb across it, and have the image come off on your thumb, you have a fuser problem. The fuser isn't heating the toner and fusing it into the paper. This could be caused by a number of things—but all of them would be taken care of with a fuser replacement. For example, if the halogen light inside the heating roller has burned out, that would cause the problem. The solution is to replace the fuser. The fuser can be replaced with a rebuilt unit, if you prefer. Rebuilt fusers are almost as good as new fusers, and some even come with guarantees. Plus, they cost less.

TIP   The whole fuser may not need to be replaced. Fuser components can be ordered from parts suppliers and can be rebuilt by you. For example, if the fuser has a bad lamp, you can order a lamp and replace it in the fuser.

Another problem similar to this is when there are small areas of smudging that repeat themselves down the page. Dents or "cold spots" in the fuser heat roller cause this problem. The only solution is to replace either the fuser assembly or the heat roller.

"Ghosting"

"Ghosting" is what you have when you can see light images of previously printed pages on the current page. This is caused by one of two things: bad erasure lamps or a broken cleaning blade. If the erasure lamps are bad, the previous electrostatic discharges aren't completely wiped away. When the EP drum rotates towards the developing roller, some toner will stick to the slightly discharged areas. A broken cleaning blade, on the other hand, causes old toner to build up on the EP drum and consequently present itself in the next printed image.

Replacing the toner cartridge solves the second problem. Solving the first problem involves replacing the erasure lamps in the printer. Since the toner cartridge is the least expensive cure, you should try that first. Usually, replacing the toner cartridge will solve the problem. If it doesn't, you will then have to replace the erasure lamps.

Printer Prints Pages of Garbage

This has happened to everyone at least once. You print a one-page letter and ten pages of what looks to be garbage come out of the printer. This problem comes from one of two different sources: the print driver software or the formatter board.

Printer Driver The correct printer driver needs to be installed for the printer you have. For example, if you have a HP LaserJet III, then that is the driver you need to install. Once the driver has been installed, it must be configured for the correct page description language: PCL or PostScript. Most HP LaserJet printers use PCL (but can be configured for PostScript). Determine what page description your printer has been configured for and set the print driver to the same setting. If this is not done, you will get garbage out of the printer.

> **TIP** Most printers that have LCD displays will indicate that they are in Post-Script mode with a "PS" or "PostScript" somewhere in the display.

If the problem is the wrong driver setting, the "garbage" that the printer prints will look like English. That is, the words will be readable, but they won't make any sense.

Formatter Board The other cause of several pages of garbage being printed is a bad formatter board. This circuit board takes the information that the printer receives from the computer and turns it into commands for the various components in the printer. Usually problems with the formatter board produce wavy lines of print or random patterns of dots on the page.

It's relatively easy to replace the formatter board in a laser printer. Usually this board is installed underneath the printer and can be removed by loosening two screws and pulling the board out. Typically, replacing the formatter board also replaces the printer interface; another possible source of "garbage" printouts.

HP LaserJet Testing

Now that we've defined some of the possible sources of problems with laser printers, let's discuss a few of the testing procedures that you use with laser printers. We'll discuss HP LaserJet laser printers since they are the most popular types of laser printer, but the topics covered here can be applied to other types of laser printers as well.

When you troubleshoot laser printers, there are three tests you can perform on the printer to narrow down which assembly is causing the problem. (These tests are internal diagnostics for the printers and are included with most laser printers.) The three tests are the engine self-test, the engine half self-test, and the secret self-test.

Self-Tests   There are three significant printer "self-tests"—tests that the printer runs on its own (albeit when directed by the user). These are the engine self-test, the print engine half self-test, and the secret self-test.

- **Engine Self-Test:** The engine self-test tests the print engine of the LaserJet, bypassing the formatter board. This test will cause the printer to print a single page with vertical lines running its length. If an engine self-test can be performed, you will know that the laser print engine can print successfully. To perform an engine self-test, you must press the printer's self-test button, which is hidden behind a small cover on the side of the printer (see Figure 12.5). The location of the button varies from printer to printer, so you may have to refer to the printer manual. Using a pencil or probe, press the button and the print engine will start printing the test page.

FIGURE 12.5:

Print engine self-test button location. (Location may vary on different printers.)

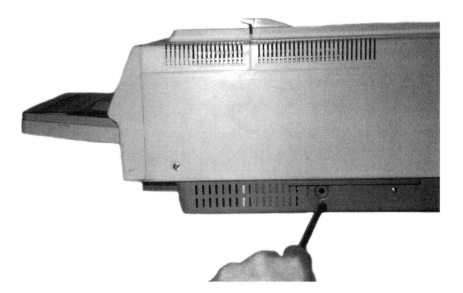

- **Half Self-Test:** A print engine half self-test is performed the same as the self-test, but you interrupt it halfway through the print cycle by opening the cover. This is useful in determining which part of the print process is causing the printer to malfunction. If you stop the print process and there is part of a developed image on the EP drum and part has been transferred to the paper, you know that the pickup rollers, registration rollers, laser scanner, charging roller, EP drum, and transfer roller are all working correctly. You can stop the half self-test at various points in the print process to determine the source of a malfunction.

- **Secret Self-Test:** To activate this test you must first put the printer into service mode. To accomplish this, you must first turn the printer on while simultaneously holding down the

On Line, Continue, and Enter buttons (that's the first secret part, because nobody knows it unless somebody tells them). When the screen comes up blank, release the keys and press, in order, Continue, then Enter. The printer will perform an internal self-test, then display "00 READY." At this point you are ready to initiate the rest of the secret self-test by taking the printer offline and pressing the Test button on the front panel and holding it until you see the "04 Self Test" message. When you see this message, release the Test button. This will cause the printer to print one self-test page. (If you want a continuous printout, then instead of releasing the Test button at the "04 Self Test" message, keep holding the Test button down until the message "05 Self Test" is displayed. The printer will print continuous self-test pages until you power off the printer or hit On Line, or until the printer runs out of paper.)

Error Codes   In addition to the self-tests, you have another tool for troubleshooting HP laser printers. Error codes are a way for the LaserJet to tell the user (and a service technician) what's wrong. Table 12.5 details some of the most common codes displayed on an HP LaserJet.

TABLE 12.5: HP LaserJet Error Messages

Message	Description
00 Ready	The printer is in standby mode and ready to print.
02 Warming Up	The fuser is being warmed up before the 00 Ready state.
05 Self-Test	Full self-test has been initiated from the front panel.
11 Paper Out	The paper tray sensor is reporting that there is no paper in the paper tray. Printer will not print as long as this error exists.
13 Paper Jam	A piece of paper is caught in the paper path. To fix, open the cover and clear the jam (including all pieces of the jam). Close the cover to resume printing. Printer will not print as long as this error exists.

Continued on next page

TABLE 12.5 CONTINUED: HP LaserJet Error Messages

Message	Description
14 No EP Cart	There is no EP cartridge (toner cartridge) installed in the printer. Printer will not print as long as this error exists.
15 Engine Test	An engine self-test is in progress.
16 Toner Low	The toner cartridge is almost out of toner. Replacement will be necessary soon.
50 Service	A fuser error has occurred. Most commonly caused by fuser lamp failure. Power off the printer and replace the fuser to solve. Printer will not print as long as this error exists.
51 Error	Laser scanning assembly problem. Test and replace, if necessary. Printer will not print as long as this error exists.
52 Error	The scanner motor in the laser scanning assembly is malfunctioning. Test and replace as per service manual. Printer will not print as long as this error exists.
55 Error	Communication problem between formatter and DC controller. Test and replace as per service manual. Printer will not print as long as this error exists.

Troubleshooting Tips for HP LaserJet Printers

There is a set of troubleshooting steps that are usually used by printer technicians to help them solve HP LaserJet printing problems. Let's detail each of them to bring our discussion of laser printer troubleshooting to a close.

1. **Is the exhaust fan operational?** This is the first component to receive power when the printer is turned on. If you can feel air coming out of the exhaust fan, this confirms that AC voltage is present and power is turned on, that +5 Vdc and +24 Vdc are being generated by the AC power supply (ACPS), and that the DC controller is functional. If there is no power to the printer (no lights, fan not operating), the ACPS is at fault. Replacement involves removing all printer covers and removing four screws. You can purchase new ACPS modules, but it is usually cheaper to replace it with a rebuilt unit.

TIP   If you are into electronics, you can probably rebuild the ACPS yourself simply and cheaply. It's usually the main rectifier that fails in these units; it can easily be replaced if you know what you're doing.

2. **Do the control panel LEDs work?**   This means that the formatter board can communicate with control panel. If the LEDs do not light, it could mean that the formatter board is bad, the control panel is bad, or the wires connecting the two are broken or shorting out.

3. **Does the main motor rotate at power up?**   Turn the power off. Remove the covers from the side of the printer. Turn the printer back on and carefully watch and listen for main motor rotation. If you see and hear the main motor rotating, this indicates that toner cartridge is installed, all photosensors are functional, all motors are functional, and the printer can move paper (assuming there are no obstructions).

4. **Does the fuser heat lamp light up after the main motor finishes its rotation?**   You will need to have the covers removed to notice. The heat lamp should light after the main motor rotation and stay lit until the control panel says "00 Ready."

5. **Can the printer perform an engine test print?**   A sheet of vertical lines indicates that the print engine works. This test print bypasses the formatter board and will indicate if the print problem resides in the engine or not. If the test print is successful, the engine can be ruled out as a source of the problem. If the test print fails, you will have to further troubleshoot the printer to determine which engine component is causing the problem.

6. **Can the printer perform a control panel self-test?**   This is the final test to ensure printer operation. If you can press the "Test Page" control panel button and receive a test printout, this means the entire printer is working properly. The only possibilities for problems would be outside the printer (i.e., interfaces, cables, and software problems).

Top Ten Troubleshooting Steps

Just as every artist has their own style, every technician has their own way to troubleshoot. Some people use their instincts; others use advice from other people. I have condensed the most common troubleshooting tips into a ten-step process. You try each step, in order. If that step doesn't narrow the problem down, you move on to the next step.

Step 1: Define the Problem

If you can't define the problem, you can't begin to solve it. You can define the problem by asking questions of the user. Here are a few questions to ask the user to aid in determining what exactly the problem *is*:

- **Can you show me the problem?**   This question is one of the best. It allows the user to show you exactly where and when they experience the problem.

- **How often does this happen?**   This question establishes whether or not this problem is a one-time occurrence (usually indicating a "soft" memory error or the like) that can be solved with a reboot, or whether the problem has a specific sequence of events that cause it to happen (usually indicating a more serious problem that may require software installation or hardware replacement).

- **Has any new software been installed recently?**   New software can mean incompatibility problems with existing problems. This is especially true for Windows programs. A new Windows program can overwrite a required DLL file with a newer version of the same name, which an older program may not find useful.

- **Have any other changes been made to the computer recently?**   If the answer is "Yes," ask if they can remember approximately when the change was made. Then ask them approximately when the problem started. If the two dates seem related, there's a good chance that the problem is related to the change. If it's a new hardware component, check to see that the hardware component was installed correctly.

Step 2: Check the Simple Stuff First

This step is the one that most experienced technicians overlook. Often, computer problems are the result of some simple problem. The technician will overlook them because they are so simple that they assume they *couldn't* be the problem. Some examples of simple problems are:

Is it plugged in?   And on *both ends*? Cables must be plugged in *on both ends* in order to function correctly. Cables can be easily tripped over and inadvertently pulled from their sockets.

Is it turned on?   This one seems the most obvious, but we've all fallen victim to it at one point or another. Computers and their peripherals must be turned on in order to function. Most have power switches that have LEDs that glow when the power is turned on.

Is the system ready?   Computers must be ready before they can be used. "Ready" means that the system is ready to accept commands from the user. An indication that a computer is ready is when the operating system screens come up and the computer presents you with a menu or a command prompt. If that computer uses a graphical interface, the computer is ready when the mouse pointer appears. Printers are ready when the "On Line" or "Ready" light on the front panel is lit.

Reseat chips and cables.   You can solve some of the strangest problems (random hang-ups or errors) by opening the case and pressing down on each socketed chip. This remedies the "chip creep" problem mentioned earlier in the book. In addition, you should also reseat any cables to make sure that they are making good contact.

Step 3: Check to See If It's User Error

One of the more common errors that technicians run into is the "EEOC error" (Equipment Exceeds Operator Capability). This error is common, but preventable. The indication that a problem is due to user error is when a user says they can't perform some very common computer task—i.e., "I can't print," "I can't save my file," "I can't run my favorite application," etc. As soon you hear these words, you should start asking questions of the user to determine if it is EEOC or a real problem. A good question to ask following their statement of the problem would be, "Were you *ever* able to perform that task?" If they answer no to this question, it means they are probably doing the procedure wrong—EEOC. If they answer yes, you must move on to another set of questions.

TIP   This doesn't mean you should assume "the user is always wrong." An attitude like that can come across on the phone, and in person, as arrogance.

Step 4: Reboot the Computer

It is amazing how often a simple computer reboot can solve a problem. Rebooting the computer clears the memory and starts the computer with a "clean slate." Whenever I perform phone support, I always ask the customer to reboot the computer and try again. If rebooting doesn't work, try powering down the system completely, and then powering it up again. More often than not, that will solve the problem.

Step 5: Determine If the Problem Is Hardware or Software Related

This step is an important one because it determines what part of the computer you should focus your troubleshooting skills on. Each part requires different skills and different tools.

To determine if a problem is hardware or software related, you could do a few things to narrow the problem down. For instance, does the problem manifest itself when you use a particular piece of hardware (a modem, for example)? If it does, the problem is more than likely hardware related.

This step relies on personal experience more than any of the other steps do. You will without a doubt run into several strange software problems. Each one has a particular solution. Some may even require reinstallation of the software or the entire operating system.

Step 6: If the Problem Is Hardware Related, Determine Which Component Is Failing

Hardware problems are pretty easy to figure out. If the modem doesn't work, and you know it isn't a software problem, it's pretty safe to say that the modem is probably the piece of hardware that needs to be replaced.

With some of the newer computers, several components are integrated onto the motherboard. If you troubleshoot the computer and find a hardware component to be bad, there's a good chance that the bad component is integrated into the motherboard (for example, the parallel port circuitry) and the whole motherboard must be replaced. An expensive proposition, to be sure.

Step 7: If the Problem Is Software Related, Boot "Clean"

If you are experiencing software problems, a common trouble-shooting technique with DOS-based computers is to boot "clean." This means starting the computer with a bootable diskette that uses a CONFIG.SYS and AUTOEXEC.BAT with no third-party drivers in it (for example, no drivers for sound card, CD-ROM, or network). If the software that's experiencing the problem is incompatible with something in these clean CONFIG.SYS or AUTOEXEC.BAT files, this will indicate it. Once you have determined that there's an incompatibility, you can further determine what your chances are for fixing the problem by using the "REM" techniques presented earlier in this chapter.

Step 8: Check Service Information Sources

As you may or may not have figured out by now, I'm fond of old sayings. There's another old saying that applies here: "If all else fails, read the instructions." The service manuals are your "instructions" for troubleshooting and service information. Almost every computer and peripheral made today has a set of service documentation in the form of books, service CD-ROMs, and Web sites. The latter of the three seem to be growing in popularity as more and more service centers get connections to the Internet. Refer to Appendix C, *Computer Service Information Web Sites*, for a list of some of the most useful ones.

Step 9: If It Ain't Broke...

When doctors take the Hippocratic oath, they promise to not make the patient any sicker than they already were. Technicians should take a similar oath. It all boils down to, "If it ain't broke, don't fix it." When you troubleshoot, make one change at a time. If the change doesn't solve the problem, change it back to its original state before making a different change.

Step 10: Ask for Help

If you don't know the answer, ask one of your fellow technicians. They may have run across the problem you are having and know the solution.

This solution does involve a little humility. You must admit that you don't know the answer. It is said that the beginning of wisdom is, "I don't know." If you ask questions, you will get answers, and you will learn from the answers. Making mistakes is valuable as well, as long as you learn from them.

TIP If you have no fellow technicians, get on the Internet and check out the technical "chat rooms." Appendix C of this book lists a number of sites on the Web that offer technical support and advice; some of them have chat rooms.

Summary

This book can give you the basic knowledge you need to be a good troubleshooter, but not the instinct you need to be a great one. There are very few people who have mastered the art of troubleshooting. The reason this is true is that troubleshooting *is* an art. And just as with any art, excellence comes only through experience. The best way to get experience is through reading, practice, and asking questions.

Review Questions

1. A customer complains that their hard disk is making lots of noise. After examining the computer and hearing the noise for yourself, you notice that the high-pitched noise seems to be coming from the fan in the power supply. Which component(s) should be replaced? (Choose all that apply.)

   A. hard disk

   B. power supply

   C. motherboard

   D. Nothing. This is a software problem.

2. When you try to turn the computer on, you notice that the computer won't activate. The monitor is blank and the fan on the power supply is not active. Turning the switch off and then back on makes no difference. What is the most likely cause of this problem?

   A. The computer is unplugged.

   B. The BIOS on the motherboard needs to be upgraded.

   C. The monitor is malfunctioning.

   D. Both the fan on the power supply and the video card are bad.

   E. The power supply is bad.

   F. none of the above

3. A laser printer is printing pages that are all black. Replacing the toner cartridge has no effect. What are some possible causes of this problem? (Choose all that apply.)

   A. The high voltage power supply (HVPS) is bad.

   B. The transfer corona assembly is damaged.

   C. The main motor assembly is bad.

    D. The laser scanner assembly is damaged.

    E. The EP cartridge is damaged.

    F. The printer has bad feed rollers.

4. What part of an HP LaserJet printer is malfunctioning if you receive a "50 Service" error?

    A. toner cartridge

    B. laser scanner assembly

    C. fuser

    D. AC power supply

5. A paper jam on a dot-matrix printer can be caused by:

    A. an obstructed paper path

    B. the wrong kind of paper

    C. a malfunctioning print head assembly

    D. the wrong ribbon is installed

6. A customer complains that they can't get their computer to work. When they turn it on, they get no video and a series of beeps. The beeps are in the sequence of one long beep, then two short beeps. You tell the customer to bring the machine in. Upon further examination you are able to reproduce the problem. What is your next step?

    A. Upgrade the PC's BIOS to the newest version.

    B. Replace the motherboard.

    C. Replace the video card.

    D. Replace the RAM.

    E. Upgrade the BEEP.COM file.

    F. Boot "clean" to a bootable floppy disk.

7. An HP LaserJet III printer isn't printing at all. The computer indicates that the "device on LPT1 isn't ready." You perform a service self-test on the printer and it prints the page of vertical lines with no problems. The front panel self-test doesn't work, however. Which component do you suspect is giving you the problem?

   A. fuser

   B. DC Controller

   C. AC Power Supply

   D. main motor

   E. formatter

   F. toner cartridge

   G. transfer corona

8. A "201" error at system startup means what?

   A. bad floppy drive

   B. bad system board

   C. bad hard disk system

   D. bad memory

   E. bad keyboard

9. Which Windows error is caused by an application being "greedy" and taking memory away from other programs?

   A. General System Error

   B. General Protection Fault

   C. System Fault

   D. Memory Protection Fault

10. A customer complains that the modem they are using is bad. When they try to connect to another computer, it connects, but it transmits and receives garbage. What do you do?

    A. Order a new modem for the customer.

    B. Change the initialization string to AT&F.

    C. Confirm that the data bits, parity, and stop bits are set the same on both ends.

    D. Confirm that both computers are using the same modem and software.

11. What two files are used by DOS to configure a computer?

    A. INI files

    B. AUTOEXEC.BAT

    C. CONFIG.BAT

    D. CONFIG.SYS

12. A computer is experiencing random reboots and "phantom" problems that disappear after reboot. What should you do?

    A. Tell the customer that it's normal for the computer to do that.

    B. Replace the motherboard.

    C. Boot "clean."

    D. Replace the power supply.

    E. Open the cover and reseat all cards and chips.

13. A bubble-jet printer produces output that is acceptable. But after an ink cartridge replacement, the ink smears and generally looks "heavier" than normal. What is the problem?

    A. The ink cartridge is bad from the factory.

    B. A refilled ink cartridge has been used.

    C. The printer's controller circuitry is bad.

    D. The paper is too thin.

    E. none of the above

14. A company that hires you to do service for them has just purchased a new laser printer. After two months and 3,000 copies, "ghosts" of previous pages appear on the printout. What action will solve the problem?

    A. Replace the toner cartridge.

    B. Replace the fuser.

    C. Replace the transfer corona assembly.

    D. Clean the transfer corona assembly.

    E. none of the above

15. What is the largest cause of computer problems?

    A. hardware failure

    B. software failure

    C. ESD

    D. technician inexperience

    E. user error

16. A user is getting a "301 error" when they turn on the computer. What is a possible cause?

    A. a virus on the boot sector of the hard disk

    B. user error

    C. dust and dirt on the power supply fan

    D. a book lying on the keyboard during system start up

17. A user calls you and reports that their computer is giving them a General Protection Fault in the program XXXX.EXE. What are some possible causes? (Choose all that apply.)

    A. The XXXX.EXE program is bad and should be replaced or "patched" (i.e., you should find and apply a bug fix).

    B. There is not enough memory in the computer.

    C. There is not enough hard disk space in the computer.

    D. all of the above

    E. none of the above

18. An HP LaserJet starts printing blank pages after you cleaned all of the internal parts. What is the most probable cause?

    A. You broke the transfer corona wire.

    B. There is no toner in the toner cartridge.

    C. The HVPS is not functioning.

    D. The fuser is still dirty.

19. What is the most probable cause of a defect that repeats itself on the page?

    A. bad toner cartridge

    B. bad fuser roller

    C. any dirty or scratched roller

    D. dirty or broken corona wire

    E. none of the above

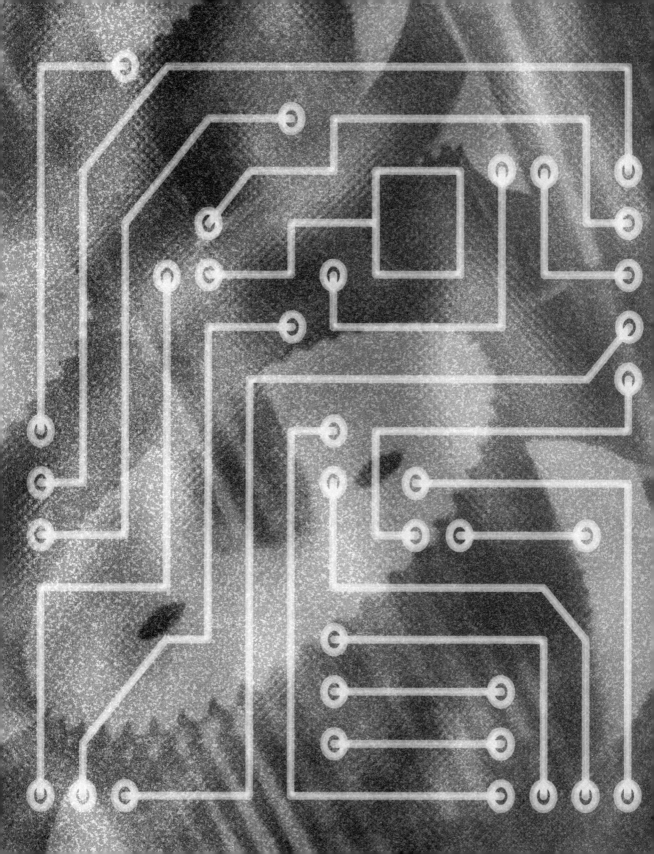

APPENDIX

A

Answers to Review Questions

Chapter 1
Basic Computer Service Concepts

1. What is the resistance rating of a resistor with the markings (from left to right) red, brown, yellow, gold?

   A. 2100 Ω ± 5%

   B. 21000 Ω ± 5%

   C. 210000 Ω ± 5%

   D. 2100000 Ω ± 5%

   Answer: C

2. If there are no ESD straps available, one can be fashioned from copper wire and duct tape. True or false?

   A. True

   B. False

   Answer: B

3. When measuring resistance, the component can be measured while still installed on the circuit board. True or false?

   A. True

   B. False

   Answer: B

4. Convert the following binary number to decimal: 10110101

   A. 10110101

   B. 181

   C. 192

   D. none of the above

   Answer: B

5. Convert this hexadecimal number to its binary equivalent: A73F
    A. 1010011100111111
    B. 1010
    C. 1010001010010101
    D. 0100001001001100
    E. 10101011
    Answer: A

6. ESD stands for:
    A. Every Single Day
    B. Electric System Degradation
    C. Electrosilicon Diode
    D. Electrostatic Discharge
    E. none of the above
    Answer: D

7. When connecting an ESD strap to an extension cord, you must connect it to:
    A. the "hot" pin
    B. the "negative" pin
    C. the "Ground" pin
    D. all of the above
    Answer: C

8. The following components are found in today's microcomputers (circle all that apply):
    A. vacuum tubes
    B. resistors
    C. transistors
    D. dilithium crystals
    E. capacitors
    Answer: B, C, E

9. Convert the following decimal number to binary: 219

    A. 11011011

    B. 11101101

    C. 11111111

    D. 00101001

    E. none of the above

    Answer: A

10. How many bits are represented by a single hexadecimal digit?

    A. 1

    B. 2

    C. 4

    D. 8

    Answer: C

11. This type of IC package has two rows of pins, one on each side of the package.

    A. QSOP

    B. DIP

    C. SIP

    D. PGA

    E. ZIF

    Answer: B

12. This type of IC package is usually surface mounted and used for VLSI applications.

    A. QSOP

    B. DIP

    C. SIP

    D. PGA

    E. ZIF

    Answer: A

13. The best method of preventing ESD damage is:

    A. anti-static mat

    B. anti-static spray

    C. anti-static wrist strap

    D. anti-static thinking

    Answer: C

14. This type of screw was chosen because of its relative immunity to head damage and for its "high-tech" look.

    A. Phillips-head

    B. flathead

    C. normal

    D. Torx

    Answer: D

15. How many volts does it take to damage a CMOS-based IC?

    A. 1

    B. 100

    C. 1000

    D. 10,000

    Answer: B

16. What is the Least Significant Bit (LSB) of the number 10100010?

    A. 0

    B. 1

    Answer: A

17. ICs are best removed with needle-nose pliers. True or false?

    A. True

    B. False

    Answer: B

18. What is the maximum resistance of a resistor with the following markings: red, brown, red?

    A. 2100 Ω

    B. 2020 Ω

    C. 2520 Ω

    D. 420 Ω

    Answer: C

19. A male DB-25 port is most likely a:

    A. parallel port

    B. serial port

    C. joystick/game port

    D. network port

    Answer: B

20. Which of the following components can be used to configure an adapter card? (Choose all that apply.)

    A. software

    B. male DB-25 port

    C. jumpers

    D. transistors

    E. none of the above

    Answer: A, C

21. Does pure water conduct electricity? (Choose one.)

    A. Yes

    B. No

    Answer: B

22. Which port(s) are used for serial ports? (Choose all that apply.)

    A. RJ-11

    B. DB-9

    C. Centronics 36

    D. DB-25

    E. none of the above

    Answer: B, D

Chapter 2
PC Architecture

1. Which computer component contains all the circuitry necessary for *all* components or devices to communicate with each other?

    A. system board

    B. adapter card

    C. hard drive

    D. expansion bus

    Answer: A

2. Clock speeds are measured in _____.

    A. ohms

    B. volts

    C. megahertz

    D. milliseconds

    Answer: C

3. A monitor was originally called a CRT. True or false?

    A. True

    B. False

    Answer: A

4. Which of the following is the most important input device?

    A. mouse

    B. digitizing tablet

    C. keyboard

    D. printer

    Answer: C

5. Access time refers to what?

    A. revolutions per unit of time

    B. difference between the time data is requested and received

    C. latency

    D. the time it takes to create an Access database

    Answer: B

6. What is the maximum amount of data that can be sotred on a 5¼″ floppy disk?

    A. 360 KB

    B. 1.2 MB

    C. 320 KB

    D. 720 KB

    Answer: B

7. The system board is also called _____.

    A. a fiberglass board

    B. a planar board

    C. a bus system

    D. an IBM system board XR125

    Answer: B

8. The _____ is used to store frequently accessed data and instructions.

   A. hard drive

   B. RAM

   C. internal cache memory

   D. ROM

   Answer: C

9. This processor was introduced with 1.2 million transistors and a 32-bit internal and external data path.

   A. 386SX

   B. 486DX

   C. 486DX2

   D. Pentium

   Answer: B

10. This processor had the math coprocessor disabled.

    A. 286

    B. 486SX

    C. 486DX

    D. 387SX

    Answer: B

11. What are the four voltages produced by a common PC's power supply?

    Answer: +5 VDc, –5 VDc, +12 VDc, –12 VDc

12. Which power device would be best to attach to your computer if you were having power problems?

    A. Surge Protector

    B. UPS

    C. Line Conditioner

    D. SPS

    Answer: B

13. If you wanted to connect a LapLink cable (a parallel data transfer cable) so that you could upload and download files from a computer, which type of parallel port(s) does your computer need to have?

 A. Standard

 B. Bi-directional

 C. EPP

 D. ECP

 Answer: B, C, D

Chapter 3

PC Memory Architecture

1. RAM is short for _____:

 A. Readily Accessible Memory

 B. Recently Affected Memory

 C. Random Access Memory

 D. Read And Modify

 Answer: C

2. When you turn off a computer, the information in ROM is erased. True or false?

 A. True

 B. False

 Answer: B

3. When you turn off a computer, the information in RAM is erased. True or false?

 A. True

 B. False

 Answer: A

4. Which of the following types of memory are erasable? (Circle all that apply.)

   A. RAM

   B. SRAM

   C. ROM

   D. PROM

   E. EPROM

   F. EEPROM

   Answer: A, B, E, F

5. DRAM uses banks of transistors to store patterns of ones and zeros. True or false?

   A. True

   B. False

   Answer: B

6. Which switch will cause MEM.EXE to give the most detailed information about the current memory configuration?

   A. /a

   B. /b

   C. /c

   D. /d

   Answer: D

7. This type of ROM memory chip has a small window that allows the chip to be erased with a special ultraviolet light.

   A. PROM

   B. EPROM

   C. EEPROM

   D. APROM

   Answer: B

8. This type of ROM memory chip is erasable using software tools, and is most commonly used for BIOS chips.

   A. PROM

   B. ROM

   C. EPROM

   D. EEPROM

   Answer: D

9. This area of memory is used for running most DOS programs, loading drivers, and loading TSRs.

   A. conventional memory

   B. extensive memory

   C. extended memory

   D. expanded memory

   Answer: A

10. Which of these processors was the first to access more than 1 MB of RAM?

    A. 8088

    B. 8086

    C. 80286

    D. 80386

    E. 80486

    Answer: C

11. Which processor(s) can access as much as 4 GB of RAM? (Circle all that apply.)

    A. 8088

    B. 8086

    C. 80286

    D. 80386

    E. 80486

    F. Pentium

    Answer: D, E, F

12. If you are transmitting the 8-bit binary number 11010010 and are using even parity, the parity bit would be _____.

   A. 1

   B. 0

   C. None

   D. A

   Answer: B

13. Modem communications most often use the following type of error-checking routine.

   A. parity

   B. error correction

   C. addition

   D. checksumming

   Answer: A

14. A memory chip has markings of 45256–40. The last 2 digits after the dash mean an access time of _____.

   A. 4 ms

   B. 4 ns

   C. 40 ms

   D. 40 ns

   E. 400 ns

   Answer: D

15. Which of the following indicate(s) a hard memory error? (Circle all that apply.)

   A. 201 BIOS Error

   B. 301 BIOS Error

   C. 1 long beep, 3 short beeps

   D. 2 long beeps, 2 short beeps

   E. Parity Error

   Answer: A, C, E

16. RAMBOOST is the IBM PC-DOS functional equivalent to MS-DOS MEMMAKER. True or false?

    A. True

    B. False

    Answer: A

17. The first thing you can do to increase the available conventional memory is:

    A. load all device drivers into UMBs

    B. add `DOS=HIGH` to the `CONFIG.SYS`

    C. remove DOS

    D. rearrange the loading order of the drivers

    Answer: B

18. If you don't need expanded memory, you can free up 64 KB of reserved memory that can be used for UMBs by putting the following parameter after `C:\DOS\EMM386.EXE` in the `CONFIG.SYS` to disable expanded memory and remove the page frame.

    A. `NOEXT`

    B. `NOEXP`

    C. `NOPAGE`

    D. `NOEMS`

    Answer: D

19. Memory optimization programs are not always the best way of optimizing memory. True or false?

    A. True

    B. False

    Answer: B

20. Which driver must be loaded in the CONFIG.SYS to give DOS access to extended memory?

    A. C:\DOS\EXTMEM.SYS

    B. C:\DOS\UPPMEM.SYS

    C. C:\DOS\MEMORY.SYS

    D. C:\DOS\EMM386.EXE

    E. C:\DOS\HIMEM.SYS

    Answer: E

21. LIM memory is another name for which type of memory?

    A. conventional memory

    B. extended memory

    C. expanded memory

    D. CMOS memory

    Answer: C

22. Which command(s) displays the list of all programs in memory and stops the display after one page, waiting for user input? (Circle all that apply.)

    A. MEM /C /P

    B. MEM /C |MORE

    C. MEM /PC /USER

    D. MEM /D /P

    E. MEM /C

    Answer: A, B. (D would also be acceptable, but /D gives more detailed info than the question requires.)

23. What is the hexadecimal range for conventional memory?

    A. A0000 to 7FFFF

    B. 00000 to A0000

    C. 00000 to 9FFFF

    D. 00000 to A0000

    Answer: C

Chapter 4
Disk System Architecture

1. When installing a second ST-506 drive to a cable without a twist in it, the drive select jumper should be set to _____.

    A. Drive 0

    B. Drive 1

    C. Drive 2

    D. Drive 3

    Answer: B

2. What are the most most common sizes for floppy drives? (Circle all that apply.)

    A. $3^1/_4$"

    B. $3^1/_2$"

    C. $5^1/_4$"

    D. $5^1/_2$"

    Answer: B, C

3. How many devices can SCSI-1 support (including the controller)?

    A. 8

    B. 7

    C. 1

    D. 9

    Answer: A

4. Which kind of device is connected to the last connector on a Compaq Deskpro?

    A. Drive A:

    B. Drive B:

    C. Drive C:

    D. tape drive

    Answer: D

5. The device that converts signals from an IDE drive into signals the CPU can understand is called a _____.

   A. controller

   B. host bus adapter

   C. bus

   D. paddle board

   Answer: D

6. Which implementation of SCSI has a transfer rate of 20 MB/sec?

   A. Fast SCSI-2

   B. Fast-Wide SCSI-2

   C. SCSI-3

   D. Ultra SCSI

   Answer: D

7. Suppose you have an internal SCSI hard drive and two external devices: a scanner and a CD-ROM drive. The scanner is the last device on the chain. Which device(s) should be terminated? (Circle all that apply.)

   A. hard disk

   B. scanner

   C. CD-ROM drive

   D. host bus adapter

   Answer: A, B

8. The process known as _____ converts binary information into patterns of magnetic flux on a hard disk's surface.

   A. fluxing

   B. warping

   C. encoding

   D. decoding

   Answer: C

9. What is the name for the areas that a typical hard disk is divided into like the wedges in a pie?

    A. tracks

    B. sectors

    C. clusters

    D. spindles

    Answer: B

10. How do you low-level format an IDE drive?

    A. Enter the DEBUG.EXE program and enter g=c800:5 at the "-" prompt.

    B. Run LOWLEVEL.COM.

    C. Execute FORMAT.COM.

    D. You don't; it's done at the factory.

    Answer: D

11. How do you low-level format an ST-506/ESDI drive?

    A. Enter the DEBUG.EXE program and enter g=c800:5 at the "-" prompt.

    B. Run LOWLEVEL.COM.

    C. Execute FORMAT.COM.

    D. You don't; it's done at the factory.

    Answer: A

12. How do you low-level format a SCSI drive?

    A. Enter the DEBUG.EXE program and enter g=c800:5 at the "-" prompt.

    B. Run LOWLEVEL.COM.

    C. Execute FORMAT.COM.

    D. You don't; it's done at the factory.

    Answer: D

13. Which of the following must be done when installing SCSI devices? (Circle all that apply.)

    A. Terminate the first and last devices in the chain.

    B. Set unique SCSI ID numbers.

    C. Connect the first device to the connector before the twist.

    D. Set every device on the same SCSI channel to the same SCSI ID number.

    Answer: A, B

14. "Low-leveling" a disk drive means _____.

    A. Installing the drive in the bottom of the computer

    B. Getting a disk drive ready for the installation of an operating system

    C. Organizing the disk into sectors and tracks

    D. Organizing the disk into clusters and FATs

    Answer: C

15. You have just replaced the floppy drive in a PC. Upon turning the computer on, you discover you can't boot to the floppy drive. The drive light turns on during power-up and stays lit until you turn the computer off. What should you do to solve this problem?

    A. Change the drive type in the CMOS setup.

    B. Reverse the floppy drive cable.

    C. Remove the terminating resistor on the floppy drive.

    D. Move the floppy drive to the end of the floppy cable.

    Answer: A, B

Chapter 5
PC Bus Architectures

1. PCMCIA expansion cards need the following software in order to operate (circle all that apply):

    A. Cardmember Services

    B. PC Card Services

    C. Modem Services

    D. Socket Services

    Answer: B, D

2. ISA is an acronym for _____.

    A. InSide Architecture

    B. Industry Standard Architecture

    C. Industry Simple Architecture

    D. Internal Systems Architecture

    Answer: B

3. EISA has a bus width of _____ bits.

    A. 32

    B. 16

    C. 64

    D. 8

    Answer: A

4. PCI has a bus width of _____ bits.

    A. 32

    B. 16

    C. 64

    D. 8

    Answer: C

5. ISA has a bus width of _____ bits.

   A. 32

   B. 16

   C. 64

   D. 8

   Answer: B

6. MCA has a bus width of _____ bits. (Circle all that apply.)

   A. 32

   B. 16

   C. 64

   D. 8

   Answer: A, B. (There are both 16 and 32 bit slots.)

7. Which of the following buses *require* a software configuration program to configure their settings? (Circle all that apply.)

   A. 8-bit bus

   B. ISA

   C. EISA

   D. MCA

   E. PCI

   F. PCMCIA

   Answer: C, D, E, F

8. Which of the following buses *require* the use of jumpers and DIP switches to configure their settings? (Circle all that apply.)

   A. 8-bit bus

   B. ISA

   C. EISA

   D. MCA

   E. PCI

   F. PCMCIA

   Answer: A only. (ISA buses can use either in special cases, but most often they use jumpers.)

9. Which bus signal line allows a device to request the processor's attention?

    A. I/O address lines

    B. DMA address lines

    C. Clock address lines

    D. Interrupt Request (IRQ) address lines

    Answer: D

10. Which bus signal line allows a device to send data directly to a computer's memory, bypassing the CPU?

    A. I/O addresses

    B. DMA address

    C. Clock addresses

    D. Interrupt Request (IRQ) addresses

    Answer: B

11. Which bus signal line allows the CPU to send requests to the device to send data?

    A. I/O addresses

    B. DMA address

    C. Clock addresses

    D. Interrupt Request (IRQ) addresses

    Answer: A

12. What is the maximum clock speed that an ISA Turbo bus can run reliably?

    A. 8 MHz

    B. 10 MHz

    C. 16 MHz

    D. 33 MHz

    Answer: B

13. How many DMA channels are available in an 8-bit system?

    A. 1

    B. 4

    C. 8

    D. 16

    Answer: A

14. You have just installed a sound card in a PC and it is not functioning correctly. (It produces no sound and it hangs the computer when it tries.) After checking the settings, you find that it is set to IRQ 7, DMA 1, I/O port 300. You suspect an IRQ conflict exists, so you check the other devices in the system. The system is using an ISA bus. Which device is it conflicting with? (Assume the computer is using default settings for all devices.)

    A. A network card

    B. COM1

    C. LPT1

    D. COM2

    Answer: C. (LPT1 uses IRQ 7 by default, which conflicts with the sound card setting.)

15. If you change the sound card in question #14 from IRQ 7 to IRQ 10, will a conflict still exist?

    A. Yes

    B. No

    Answer: B

Chapter 6
Peripheral Devices

1. "Debouncing" refers to:

    A. stopping a mouse ball from bouncing

    B. cleaning up keyboard signals and preventing multiple characters from a single keypress

    C. keeping the keyboard keyswitches from bouncing up and down

    D. making sure that service customers' checks don't bounce

    Answer: B

2. COM1 shares an IRQ with which other COM port?

    A. COM1

    B. COM2

    C. COM3

    D. COM4

    Answer: C

3. Which IRQ does COM1 share with the COM port in question 2?

    A. 4

    B. 2

    C. 3

    D. 10

    Answer: A

4. What are the two major types of mice in use today?

    A. capacitive

    B. resistive

    C. optical

    D. opto-mechanical

    Answer: C, D

5. You find a cable in a box of old computer parts. It has a DB-25F connector on both ends. What kind of cable is it most likely to be?

A. printer cable

B. modem cable

C. null-modem cable

D. VGA cable

Answer: C

6. Which type of computer communication uses a separate timing signal to dictate transmission times?

A. synchronous

B. asynchronous

C. standard

D. modem

Answer: A

7. What are the two major types of keyboards in use today?

A. standard

B. keyswitched

C. capacitive

D. resistive

Answer: B, C

8. If a display adapter is a VGA adapter in the standard configuration, which one of the following would be the default resolution/color choice?

A. 640×480 with 256 colors

B. 640×480 with 16 colors

C. 640×480 with 65,536 colors

D. 1024×768 with 256 colors

Answer: B

9. Which of the following monitors has the highest resolution?

   A. VGA 640 × 480

   B. CGA 320 × 200

   C. SVGA 800 × 600

   D. XGA 1024 × 768

   Answer: D

10. Which types of mouse interface technology use an interrupt (other than the ones a PC is normally using)?

    A. bus

    B. PS/2

    C. serial

    D. Microsoft

    Answer: A and B

11. Which type of signal degrades the most over longer distances?

    A. serial

    B. analog

    C. digital

    D. parallel

    Answer: C

12. What is the maximum length of a standard parallel printer cable?

    A. 6 feet

    B. 10 feet

    C. 25 feet

    D. 50 feet

    Answer: B

13. Which type of scanner gives the best quality and highest resolution?

    A. flatbed

    B. hand-held

    C. photo

    Answer: A

14. Which of the following types of output devices puts computer data on paper?

    A. modems

    B. monitors

    C. LCDs

    D. printers

    Answer: D

15. Which type of output device has the highest resolution (and therefore the best quality)?

    A. impact printers

    B. sprayed-ink printers

    C. EP printers

    D. modems

    Answer: C

Chapter 7
Installation and Upgrades

1. Which of the following are important to consider when installing new expansion cards? (Circle all that apply.)

    A. ESD effects

    B. capacity of the hard disk

    C. position of expansion cards

    D. removing the cover

    Answer: A, C

2. All case covers use three screws to hold them in. True or false?

   A. True

   B. False

   Answer: B

3. During which disassembly step do you want to take notes?

   A. removing the case

   B. removing the expansion cards

   C. removing the power supply

   D. removing the disk drives

   E. removing the motherboard

   F. all of the above

   Answer: F

4. You have just installed a new floppy drive. Upon powering up the computer, you discover that the floppy drive isn't working properly. The floppy drive light remains on as long as the computer is powered up. What should you check first?

   A. Floppy drive is in the wrong position on the floppy cable.

   B. Floppy cable is installed upside down.

   C. Floppy drive is defective.

   D. Floppy cable is defective.

   Answer: B

5. What is the first step in installing a new device?

   A. disassembling the computer

   B. installing software

   C. removing the case

   D. reading the instructions

   Answer: D

6. Which of the following can be used to determine the available resources on a computer before an upgrade or installation? (Circle all that apply.)

   A. MSD

   B. a visual examination of the computer

   C. reading the instructions

   Answer: A, C

7. At this time, "Legacy" could correctly be used to refer to which types of expansion cards?

   A. 8-bit

   B. ISA

   C. MCA

   D. all of the above

   Answer: D

8. A computer work area should contain which of the following? (Circle all that apply.)

   A. an oscilloscope

   B. assorted tools

   C. software

   D. anti-static wrist strap

   Answer: B, D

9. The power supply motherboard connectors cannot be "pushed" vertically onto the motherboard receptacle. True or false?

   A. True

   B. False

   Answer: A

10. What is the simplest method of testing a component?

    A. software diagnostics

    B. hardware diagnostics

    C. placing a multimeter across the power junction

    D. observing the component and seeing if it operates properly

    Answer: D

11. Plug-and-Play cards don't work. True or false?

    A. True

    B. False

    Answer: B

12. Anti-static bags should be used to store components when they are removed from a PC during service/disassembly. True or false?

    A. True

    B. False

    Answer: A

13. Before you install a new device in a functioning computer, you should:

    A. disassemble the computer

    B. determine the computer's available resources

    C. install DOS

    D. install MSD

    Answer: B

14. Removal of the motherboard is always required when disassembling a computer. True or false?

    A. True

    B. False

    Answer: B

15. Which of the following is NOT a prerequisite to disassembling a computer?

   A. disconnecting the power cable

   B. shutting down the computer

   C. disconnecting the monitor and keyboard cables

   D. disassembling the power supply

   Answer: D

Chapter 8
How Printers Work

1. The step in the EP print process that uses a laser to discharge selected areas of the photosensitive drum, thus forming an image on the drum.

   A. Writing

   B. Exposing

   C. Developing

   D. Discharging

   Answer: B

2. The following is a list of the steps in the HP print process. Put them in the proper order in which they occur: __, __, __, __, __, __.

   A. Developing

   B. Writing

   C. Transferring

   D. Fusing

   E. Conditioning

   F. Cleaning

   Answer: E, B, A, C, D, F

3. It is better to refill ink cartridges than to buy new ones. True or false?

 A. True

 B. False

 Answer: B

4. Which voltage is used to transfer the toner to the paper in an EP process laser printer?

 A. +600 Vdc

 B. −600 Vdc

 C. +6000 Vdc

 D. −6000 Vdc

 Answer: A

5. If the static-eliminator strip is absent (or broken) in either an EP process or HP LaserJet laser printer, what will happen?

 A. Nothing. Both printers will continue to function normally.

 B. Nothing will happen in EP process printers, but HP LaserJet printers will flash a "−671 error."

 C. Paper jams may occur in both types of printers, because the paper may curl around the photosensitive drum.

 Answer: C

6. Toner cartridges should be taken out and refilled with the correct toner when they run out of toner. True or false?

 A. True

 B. False

 Answer: B

7. Which of the following are possible interfaces for printers? (Circle all that apply.)

    A. parallel

    B. mouse port

    C. serial

    D. network

    Answer: A, C, D

8. Which laser printer component formats the print job for the type of printer being used?

    A. corona assembly

    B. DC power supply

    C. printer controller circuitry

    D. formatter software

    Answer: C

9. Which of the following are page description languages? (Circle all that apply.)

    A. Page Description Language (PDL)

    B. PostScript

    C. PageScript

    D. Printer Control Language (PCL)

    Answer: B, D

10. The basis weight is the weight in pounds of 500 sheets of what size of paper?

    A. 8.5″ × 11″

    B. 11″ × 17″

    C. 17″ × 22.5″

    D. 8.5″ × 17″

    Answer: C

11. PostScript is most often used on dot-matrix printers. True or false?

   A. True

   B. False

   Answer: B

12. Which type(s) of printers can be used with multipart forms? (Circle all that apply.)

   A. bubble-jet

   B. EP process laser printers

   C. HP process laser printers

   D. dot-matrix printers

   Answer: D

13. LED page printers differ from EP process laser printers in which step?

   A. Exposing

   B. Charging

   C. Fusing

   D. Cleaning

   E. Developing

   F. Transferring

   Answer: A

14. What part of both EP-process and HP LaserJet-process printers supplies the voltages for the charge and transfer corona assemblies?

   A. High-Voltage Power Supply (HVPS)

   B. DC Power Supply (DCPS)

   C. controller circuitry

   D. transfer corona

   Answer: A

15. With HP LaserJet laser printers, the laser discharges the charged photosensitive drum to _____ Vdc.

   A. +600

   B. 0

   C. −100

   D. −600

   Answer: B

16. With EP process laser printers, the laser discharges the charged photosensitive drum to _____ Vdc.

   A. +600

   B. 0

   C. −100

   D. −600

   Answer: C

Chapter 9

Networks

1. Which connectivity device transmits packets the fastest?

   A. gateway

   B. router

   C. brouter

   D. bridge

   Answer: D

2. This IEEE 802 standard uses a bus topology and coaxial baseband cable, and is able to transmit at 10 Mbps.

   A. 802.4

   B. 802.3

   C. 802.2

   D. 802.1

   Answer: B

3. _____ is immune to electromagnetic or radio-frequency interference.

   A. broadband coaxial cabling

   B. fiber-optic cabling

   C. twisted-pair cabling

   D. CSMA/CD

   Answer: B

4. Printers, files, e-mail, and groupware can all be categorized as _____.

   A. office equipment

   B. peer-to-peer networking

   C. resources

   D. protocols

   Answer: C

5. This OSI layer signals "all clear" by making sure the data frames are error-free.

   A. Application layer

   B. Session layer

   C. Transport layer

   D. Network layer

   Answer: C

6. This topology is the easiest to modify.

   A. Star

   B. Bus

   C. Ring

   D. Token

   Answer: A

7. This is a routable protocol used by Unix clients.

    A. TCP/IP

    B. NetBEUI

    C. IPX

    D. XNS

    Answer: A

8. The layer of the OSI model whose most important role is to provide error checking.

    A. Session layer

    B. Presentation layer

    C. Application layer

    D. Transport layer

    Answer: D

9. Which type of cabling has the easiest installation?

    A. twisted-pair

    B. coaxial

    C. fiber-optic

    D. wireless

    Answer: B

10. This is the type of media access method used by NICs that listen to or "sense" the cable to check for traffic, and send only when they hear that no one else is transmitting:

    A. Token Passing

    B. CSMA/CD

    C. CSMA/CA

    D. Demand Priority

    Answer: B

11. A physical star topology consists of several workstations that branch off of a central device called a _____.

    A. repeater

    B. brouter

    C. router

    D. hub

    Answer: D

12. A _____ links two or more computers together to communicate and share resources.

    A. server

    B. resource

    C. network

    D. client

    Answer: C

13. This access method asks the other workstations for permission to transmit before transmitting.

    A. CSMA/CD

    B. CSMA/CA

    C. Token Passing

    D. Demand Priority

    Answer: B

14. Offers total resistance to any electromagnetic or radio-frequency interference.

    A. twisted-pair cabling

    B. coaxial cable

    C. fiber-optic cabling

    D. wireless

    Answer: C

15. Uses a thin baseband coaxial cable, bus topology, transmitting at 10 Mbps, with a distance up to 185 meters.

    A. Token Ring

    B. Ethernet 10BaseT

    C. Ethernet 10Base5

    D. Ethernet 10Base2

    Answer: D

16. This topology uses the least amount of cabling, but also covers the shortest amount of distance.

    A. Bus

    B. Star

    C. Mesh

    D. Hybrid

    Answer: A

17. This layer describes how the data gets transmitted over a physical medium.

    A. Session layer

    B. Data Link layer

    C. Physical layer

    D. Application layer

    Answer: C

18. What is another name for IEEE 802.3?

    A. Logic Link Control

    B. Token Passing

    C. CSMA/CD LAN

    D. Token Ring LAN

    Answer: C

19. This type of cabling looks similar to the cable used to connect cable television:

A. twisted-pair

B. coaxial

C. fiber-optic

D. wireless

Answer: B

20. These devices can switch and route packets across multiple networks and use routing tables to store network addresses to determine the best destination.

A. brouters

B. routers

C. gateways

D. bridges

Answer: B

Chapter 10
Safety

1. When you receive a shock from walking across the carpet, how many volts are generated?

A. 2,500

B. 30,000

C. 10

D. 5

Answer: B

2. ESD is caused by the discharge of static between you and sensitive computer components. True or false?

A. True

B. False

Answer: B

3. To prevent ESD, humidity should be kept right around
   _____.
   A. 10%
   B. 20%
   C. 40%
   D. 50%
   Answer: D

4. It is a good idea to take a short break every 15 minutes. True or false?
   A. True
   B. False
   Answer: A

5. It is important not to leave your desk until the work is finished, no matter how long it takes. True or false?
   A. True
   B. False
   Answer: B

6. ESD stands for:
   A. Electrostationary Static Discharge
   B. Electromagnetic Static Discharge
   C. Electrostatic Discharge
   D. Electrically Safe Discharge
   Answer: C

7. When a battery in a laptop is bad, you should take it out and throw it away.
   A. True
   B. False
   Answer: B

8. RSI stands for:

   A. Radix Strain Injury

   B. Repeating Simple Injury

   C. Ready Set Injury

   D. Repetitive Strain Injury

   Answer: D

9. When working on PCs, it is a good idea to have the following available (circle all that apply):

   A. a blanket

   B. an ESD Strap

   C. a clean workspace

   D. all of the above

   Answer: B, C

10. Which of the following items should be replaced rather than be serviced by a technician?

    A. computer

    B. hard disk

    C. keyboard

    D. power supply

    Answer: D

11. Which class of fire extinguisher can be used to put out an electrical fire (computer fire)? (Circle all that apply.)

    A. A

    B. B

    C. C

    D. ABC (Multipurpose)

    Answer: C, D

12. You should use an ESD strap when working on monitors, to prevent electrocution. True or false?

    A. True

    B. False

    Answer: B

13. It's always best to use recycled computer parts. True or false?

    A. True

    B. False

    Answer: B

14. Which of the following is *not* a good way to reduce the risk of Repetitive Strain Injuries (RSIs)?

    A. proper posture when sitting at the computer

    B. mounting your monitor in the desktop so you can see it when you look down.

    C. mounting your monitor at eye level

    D. proper use of a wrist wrest

    Answer: B

15. If improperly handled, CRT tubes can _____. (Circle all that apply.)

    A. shrink

    B. implode

    C. shock

    D. fall on your foot

    Answer: B, C, D

Chapter 11

Customer Service

1. You are at a customer's site to fix a paper jam in the customer's laser printer when you realize that you forgot a replacement part. You won't have time to run back to the office to pick up the part because you are due at another customer's site in 30 minutes. What should you do?

   A. Call the second customer and inform them of your possible late arrival and ask if they would like to reschedule (if necessary).

   B. Apologize profusely to the customer and go back to the office to get the part. Since the other customer has been a long-standing account, they won't mind waiting for you to finish this job correctly.

   C. Being on time is important with all customers. Put the printer back together and come back tomorrow. Hopefully, no one will need to use the printer until then.

   D. Call George, a service professional who works with one of your competitors. This is obviously a solution you cannot provide for your customer.

   Answer: A

2. A customer arrives at your service window. He is angry because the modem he just had fixed by your company did not work when he brought it home and he had to drive 40 miles to bring it back to be fixed again. How should you handle this?

   A. The dumb cluck obviously doesn't know how a modem works so just explain it to him.

   B. Apologize. Question him on what he is doing to set up his modem, then point out what mistakes he is making with his procedures.

   C. Apologize. Ask him if he can explain in detail what the problem is. If he is still angry, ask the customer what he would like you to do about it.

   D. Apologize. Offer him a new modem, take him to lunch and give him a twenty-dollar bill for gas.

   Answer: C

3. One of your coworkers, Bill, is on a coffee break when you receive a telephone call from one of his customers. You inform the customer that Bill is on a break and offer to ask him to return the call. The customer states that this is not acceptable and asks to speak with him immediately. When you informed Bill of the telephone call, Bill states that he is on a break and refuses to take the call. What should you do?

   A. Tell the customer that he can reach Bill if he calls back in 20 minutes.

   B. Tell the customer that Bill is not available but you would be happy to help him.

   C. Explain the situation to your manager or supervisor and ask them to take the call.

   D. Promise the customer that Bill will return his call shortly.

   Answer: B

4. Your manager informs you that you will be taking over the Johnson account. You hear from the grapevine that the previous service professional had asked to be removed from the account. How will you approach the customer the next time you are called to service the account?

   A. Before arriving at the customer's site, ask your coworkers to provide you with as much detail as they can about the customer. The more information you have, the better prepared you will be.

   B. Ask your coworkers about what situations the service professional had been involved with and how those situations were resolved. Keep in mind that your coworker's opinions of the account may not necessarily be the same as your own.

   C. Call the secretary and ask her about the corporate culture there.

   D. Take the customer to lunch and introduce yourself as their new service professional. This is certain to impress them.

   Answer: B

5. You've just come back to the office after having a tough service call. A sales representative at your company had promised the customer that the problem with their hard drive could be easily fixed when in fact you had to bring their hard drive back for repairs. The customer has stated his anger by saying that your company made a false promise to get his business and now it is too late to contact another service company. What should you do?

   A. Apologize. Keep the situation focused on the problem and its solution by telling the customer his options.

   B. Have a word with the sales representative's manager when you return.

   C. Inform your manager of the situation.

   D. all of the above

   E. A and C only

   Answer: E

6. You are in the process of upgrading a software package on a customer's computer. Some strange things seem to be happening, so you decide to run an anti-virus program and discover the client has had a virus on the computer. You realize that you have an opportunity to provide excellent service by:

   A. Wiping out the virus and then finishing the upgrade.

   B. Selling the customer an anti-virus program.

   C. Informing the customer of the situation and letting them know that customer service is an opportunity to improve business relations through solutions.

   D. Offering to stay until you can determine a possible source of the virus so that it can be wiped out completely.

   E. Running the anti-virus program on another of the customer's computers. Once you get a feel of how far the virus may have spread, install the anti-virus program on their machines and bill the customer later. They will thank you for it.

   Answer: A

7. Customer service is an opportunity to improve business relations through solutions. According to the material you just read, which of the following is *not* a solution that would provide an opportunity to improve a business relation?

   A. Offering the services of your competition.

   B. Following up with a customer.

   C. Fixing a problem without being told to do so.

   D. Saying thank you.

   Answer: C

8. You have just diagnosed a print quality problem on a printer as being a defective ink cartridge. Upon further inspection, you notice that the ink cartridge has been refilled several times. This customer has told you that they constantly refill ink cartridges to save money. You know the refilled ink cartridges are causing this problem and will cause the owner to bring it back in a month for the same problem. What do you tell the customer when they pick up their computer?

   A. "Stop using the refilled ink cartridges. They're causing your problem."

   B. Explain to the customer that the money that they are saving on ink cartridges is being wasted on repeated service calls. Spending the extra couple of dollars on manufacturer-brand cartridges will actually save them more money on service calls.

   C. Nothing. It's money in the bank. They'll keep bringing it back for repairs.

   Answer: B

9. It's 3:30 P.M. Your work day ends at 5:00. Your customer's business is open until 5:00 also. Your repair will take at least 2 more hours (possibly more). What should you do?

   A. Stay till 5:30 or so. Get the job done.

   B. Inform the customer that the job will take you past your closing time. Ask if they would like you to stay until the job is finished. If not, ask if they would like you to reschedule for the next available time.

   C. Inform the customer that the job will take you past their closing time. Ask if they would like you to stay until the job is finished. If not, ask if they would like you to reschedule for the next available time.

   D. Leave at 5:00. They're closed and you shouldn't stay past closing.

   Answer: C

10. You have just hung up from a customer support phone call in which you had to walk a user through, step-by-step, the installation of Windows 95. You have spent two hours on the phone. What should you do next?

   A. Call back two days later and ask how the computer is operating.

   B. Don't return the customer's messages. They just want free help.

   C. Inform your manager.

   D. Bill the customer for two hours of phone support.

   Answer: A

11. A customer is asking the unreasonable. They want your company to pay for a brand new computer even though the old one has only a small software problem. The problem has been narrowed down to a piece of software that the owner installed.

They won't accept anything less than a new computer. What do you do?

    A. Give them a new computer.

    B. Fix the software problem and give the computer back.

    C. Explain that the software they installed is causing the problem. Show them that their software is causing the problem and offer to fix the problem for free.

    D. Cut your losses and give them their computer back. Do your best, however, to satisfy their needs, within reason.

Answer: D. (There are some customers who won't be satisfied no matter what you do, and you need to recognize that when it happens.)

12. The customer is always right. True or false?

    A. True

    B. False

Answer: B

Chapter 12
Troubleshooting Techniques

1. A customer complains that their hard disk is making lots of noise. After examining the computer and hearing the noise for yourself, you notice that the high-pitched noise seems to be coming from the fan in the power supply. Which component(s) should be replaced? (Choose all that apply.)

    A. hard disk

    B. power supply

    C. motherboard

    D. Nothing. This is a software problem.

Answer: B

2. When you try to turn the computer on, you notice that the computer won't activate. The monitor is blank and the fan on the power supply is not active. Turning the switch off and then back on makes no difference. What is the most likely cause of this problem?

   A. The computer is unplugged.

   B. The BIOS on the motherboard needs to be upgraded.

   C. The monitor is malfunctioning.

   D. Both the fan on the power supply and the video card are bad.

   E. The power supply is bad.

   F. none of the above

   Answer: A

3. A laser printer is printing pages that are all black. Replacing the toner cartridge has no effect. What are some possible causes of this problem? (Choose all that apply.)

   A. The high voltage power supply (HVPS) is bad.

   B. The transfer corona assembly is damaged.

   C. The main motor assembly is bad.

   D. The laser scanner assembly is damaged.

   E. The EP cartridge is damaged.

   F. The printer has bad feed rollers.

   Answer: A, E

4. What part of an HP LaserJet printer is malfunctioning if you receive a "50 Service" error?

   A. toner cartridge

   B. laser scanner assembly

   C. fuser

   D. AC power supply

   Answer: C

5. A paper jam on a dot-matrix printer can be caused by:

    A. an obstructed paper path

    B. the wrong kind of paper

    C. a malfunctioning print head assembly

    D. the wrong ribbon is installed

    Answer: A

6. A customer complains that they can't get their computer to work. When they turn it on, they get no video and a series of beeps. The beeps are in the sequence of one long beep, then two short beeps. You tell the customer to bring the machine in. Upon further examination you are able to reproduce the problem. What is your next step?

    A. Upgrade the PC's BIOS to the newest version.

    B. Replace the motherboard.

    C. Replace the video card.

    D. Replace the RAM.

    E. Upgrade the BEEP.COM file.

    F. Boot "clean" to a bootable floppy disk.

    Answer: C

7. An HP LaserJet III printer isn't printing at all. The computer indicates that the "device on LPT1 isn't ready." You perform a service self-test on the printer and it prints the page of vertical lines with no problems. The front panel self-test doesn't work, however. Which component do you suspect is giving you the problem?

    A. fuser

    B. DC Controller

    C. AC Power Supply

    D. main motor

    E. formatter

    F. toner cartridge

    G. transfer corona

    Answer: E

8. A "201" error at system startup means what?

    A. bad floppy drive

    B. bad system board

    C. bad hard disk system

    D. bad memory

    E. bad keyboard

    Answer: D

9. Which Windows error is caused by an application being "greedy" and taking memory away from other programs?

    A. General System Error

    B. General Protection Fault

    C. System Fault

    D. Memory Protection Fault

    Answer: B

10. A customer complains that the modem they are using is bad. When they try to connect to another computer, it connects, but it transmits and receives garbage. What do you do?

    A. Order a new modem for the customer.

    B. Change the initialization string to AT&F.

    C. Confirm that the data bits, parity, and stop bits are set the same on both ends.

    D. Confirm that both computers are using the same modem and software.

    Answer: C

11. What two files are used by DOS to configure a computer?

    A. INI files

    B. AUTOEXEC.BAT

    C. CONFIG.BAT

    D. CONFIG.SYS

    Answer: B, D

12. A computer is experiencing random reboots and "phantom" problems that disappear after reboot. What should you do?

    A. Tell the customer that it's normal for the computer to do that.

    B. Replace the motherboard.

    C. Boot "clean."

    D. Replace the power supply.

    E. Open the cover and reseat all cards and chips.

    Answer: E

13. A bubble-jet printer produces output that is acceptable. But after an ink cartridge replacement, the ink smears and generally looks "heavier" than normal. What is the problem?

    A. The ink cartridge is bad from the factory.

    B. A refilled ink cartridge has been used.

    C. The printer's controller circuitry is bad.

    D. The paper is too thin.

    E. none of the above

    Answer: B

14. A company that hires you to do service for them has just purchased a new laser printer. After two months and 3,000 copies, "ghosts" of previous pages appear on the printout. What action will solve the problem?

    A. Replace the toner cartridge.

    B. Replace the fuser.

    C. Replace the transfer corona assembly.

    D. Clean the transfer corona assembly.

    E. none of the above

    Answer: A

15. What is the largest cause of computer problems?

    A. hardware failure

    B. software failure

    C. ESD

    D. technician inexperience

    E. user error

    Answer: E

16. A user is getting a "301 error" when they turn on the computer. What is a possible cause?

    A. a virus on the boot sector of the hard disk

    B. user error

    C. dust and dirt on the power supply fan

    D. a book lying on the keyboard during system start up

    Answer: D

17. A user calls you and reports that their computer is giving them a General Protection Fault in the program XXXX.EXE. What are some possible causes? (Choose all that apply.)

    A. The XXXX.EXE program is bad and should be replaced or "patched" (i.e., you should find and apply a bug fix).

    B. There is not enough memory in the computer.

    C. There is not enough hard disk space in the computer.

    D. all of the above

    E. none of the above

    Answer: D

18. An HP LaserJet starts printing blank pages after you cleaned all of the internal parts. What is the most probable cause?

   A. You broke the transfer corona wire.

   B. There is no toner in the toner cartridge.

   C. The HVPS is not functioning.

   D. The fuser is still dirty.

   Answer: A

19. What is the most probable cause of a defect that repeats itself on the page?

   A. bad toner cartridge

   B. bad fuser roller

   C. any dirty or scratched roller

   D. dirty or broken corona wire

   E. none of the above

   Answer: C

APPENDIX

B

Computer Service and Support Dictionary

With this dictionary we're providing far more coverage than simply the topics that are covered by the A+ exam. This extensive listing of terms and descriptions covers just about every topic you may run into when providing support or service for users of personal computers, and we expect that you may find it so useful both on site and when researching solutions to persistent problems that you will keep it with your toolkit at all times.

Before you start skimming to your heart's content, permit us to point out a couple of things about the arrangement and treatment of terms in this dictionary. First, all the "numerical" entries (like "24-bit color") are listed before the alphabetical listing begins. Second, within the descriptions, we use *italics* to indicate cross references—terms that are further defined at their own place in the dictionary.

16-bit color   A method of representing a graphical image as a bitmap containing 65,536 different colors.

16-bit computer   Any computer that deals with information (*data*) 16 bits at a time. This description can be applied to:

- the *word* size of the *microprocessor* used in the computer. A 16-bit computer works with two *bytes* at a time.

- the width of the computer's data *bus*. A 16-bit data bus has 16 separate data lines.

A true 16-bit computer is one that meets both of these criteria. The *Macintosh* Plus and Macintosh SE, even though they are based on the 32-bit *Motorola 68000*, have a 16-bit data bus and are therefore considered to be 16-bit computers. The IBM PC/AT and other similar computers based on Intel's *80286* microprocessor are classified as 16-bit computers in terms of both the microprocessor word size and the width of the data bus.

24-bit color   A method of representing a graphical image as a bitmap containing 16,777,216 different colors.

24-bit video adapter   A video adapter that uses 24 bits to define the color used for an individual *pixel*. Each of the three color channels (red, green, blue) is defined by one 8-bit byte; this means that each channel can be defined in terms of 256 different intensities for each of the three primary colors. This adds up to a total of 16,777,216 different gradations of colors; probably at least as many as the human eye can distinguish.

3.5" disk   A *floppy disk*, originally developed by Sony Corporation, that encloses the recording media inside a rigid plastic jacket.

32-bit computer   Any computer that deals with information 32 bits at a time. This description can be applied to:

- the *word* size of the *microprocessor* used in the computer. A 32-bit computer works with 4 bytes at a time.

- the width of the computer's data *bus*. A 32-bit data bus has 32 separate data lines.

A true 32-bit computer is one that meets both of these criteria. The IBM PS/2 Model 80 is an example of a 32-bit computer, both in terms of the word size of the microprocessor used and the capacity of the data bus.

Some IBM-PC compatibles using the *Intel 80386SX* can take advantage of a 32-bit data word internally, but are limited to a 16-bit data bus. This kind of design takes advantage of much cheaper 16-bit components, leading to a lower overall system price, but also delivers slightly less performance.

386 enhanced mode   In *Microsoft Windows*, the most advanced and complex of the different operating modes. 386 enhanced mode lets Windows access the *protected mode* of the *80386* (or higher) processor for extended *memory management* and *multitasking* for both Windows and *non-Windows application* programs.

5.25" disk   A *floppy disk*, enclosed in a flexible 5.25" jacket, used in older IBM and IBM-compatible computers.

The 5.25" disk can contain either 360 KB or 1.2 MB of information, depending on the type of disk used. Because the disks are flexible, and because part of the recording surface is exposed through the read/write slot, 5.25" floppy disks should be handled with care, and always stored in their paper jackets when not in use. Also avoid exposure to temperature extremes.

6845   An early programmable video controller chip from *Motorola*, used in IBM's *Monochrome Display Adapter (MDA)* and *Color/Graphics Adapter (CGA)*. Because of the extensive use of the 6845, later and more capable video adapters like the *EGA* contained circuitry to emulate the functions of the 6845.

68000   A family of 32-bit *microprocessors* from *Motorola*, used in the *Macintosh* computers and many advanced workstations.

The 68000 uses a linear addressing mode to access memory, rather than the segmented addressing scheme used by popular microprocessors from *Intel*; this makes it more popular with programmers.

8-bit bus   The type of expansion bus that was used with the original IBM PC. The bus can transmit eight bits at a time.

8-bit color   A method of representing a graphical image as a bitmap containing 256 different colors.

8-bit computer   Any computer that deals with information 8 bits at a time. This description can be applied to the following items.

- The *word* size of the *microprocessor* used in the computer. An 8-bit computer works with 1 *byte* at a time.

- The width of the computer's *data bus*. An 8-bit data bus has 8 separate data lines.

An 8-bit computer is one that meets both criteria. The Apple IIe is an 8-bit computer, as it has both an 8-bit microprocessor and an 8-bit data bus. On the other hand, the IBM PC, PC/XT, and similar computers use the 8088 microprocessor with a 16-bit word size, but have only an 8-bit bus. This places them somewhere between an 8-bit and a 16-bit computer.

8080   An 8-bit *microprocessor*, introduced by *Intel* in April 1974, that paved the way for the *8086* family of microprocessors that followed. The 8080 contained 6,000 transistors, and was capable of 0.64 million instructions per second.

8086 A 16-bit *microprocessor* from *Intel*, first released in June 1978, available in speeds of 4.77 MHz, 8 MHz, and 10 MHz. The 8086 was used in a variety of early IBM-compatible computers as well as the IBM PS/2 Model 25 and Model 30. The 8086 contains the equivalent of 29,000 transistors, and can execute 0.33 million instructions per second.

8087 A *floating-point processor* from *Intel*, designed for use with the *8086* and *8088 CPU* chips. When supported by *application* programs, a floating-point processor can speed up floating-point and transcendental math operations by 10 to 50 times.

The 8087 conforms to the *IEEE* 754-1985 standard for binary floating-point operations, and is available in speeds of 5 MHz, 8 MHz, and 10 MHz.

8088 A 16-bit *microprocessor* from *Intel* released in June 1978 that was used in the first IBM PC, as well as the IBM PC/XT, Portable PC, PCjr, and a large number of IBM-compatible computers. The 8088 uses a 16-bit *data word*, but transfers information along an 8-bit *data bus*; the *8086* uses a 16-bit data word and a 16-bit data bus. Available in speeds of 4.77 MHz and 8 MHz, the 8088 is approximately equivalent to 29,000 *transistors*, and can execute 0.33 million instructions per second.

8514/A A *video adapter* from IBM, providing up to 256 colors or 16 shades of gray, on an interlaced display of 1,024 by 768 *pixels* in the highest resolution mode. The IBM monitor used with this adapter is also known as an 8514/A.

80286 Also called the 286. A 16-bit *microprocessor* from *Intel*, first released in February 1982, and used by IBM in the IBM PC/AT computer.

Since then it has been used in many other IBM-compatible computers.

The 80286 uses a 16-bit *data word* and a 16-bit *data bus*, uses 24 bits to address memory, and has the following modes:

• *Real mode* effectively limits performance to that of an 8086 microprocessor and can address 1 MB memory.

• *Protected mode* prevents an *application* program from stopping the operating system due to an inadvertent error and can address 16 MB of memory.

The 80286 is equivalent to approximately 134,000 *transistors*, and can execute 1.2 million instructions per second. The *floating-point processor* for the 80286 is the *80287*.

80287 Also called the 287. A *floating-point processor* from *Intel*, designed for use with the *80286 CPU* chip. When supported by *application* programs, a floating-point processor can speed up floating-point and transcendental math operations by 10 to 50 times.

The 80287 conforms to the *IEEE* 754-1985 standard for binary floating-point operations, and is available in clock speeds of 6, 8, 10, and 12 MHz.

80386DX Also called the 80386, the 386DX, and the 386. A full 32-bit *microprocessor* introduced by *Intel* in October 1985, and used in many IBM and IBM-compatible computers. Available in 16-, 20-, 25-, and 33-MHz versions, the 80386 has a 32-bit *data word*, can transfer information 32 bits at a time over the *data bus*, and can use 32 bits in addressing memory. It has the following modes:

• *Real mode* effectively limits performance to that of an 8086 microprocessor, and can address 1 MB of memory.

- *Protected mode* prevents an *application* program from stopping the operating system due to an inadvertent error, and can address 4 GB of memory.

- *Virtual 8086 mode* allows the operating system to divide the 80386 into several 8086 microprocessors, all running with their own 1-megabyte space, and all running a separate program.

The 80386 is equivalent to about 275,000 *transistors*, and can perform 6 million instructions per second. The floating-point processor for the 80386DX is the *80387*.

80386SX Also called the 386SX. A lower-cost alternative to the *80386DX microprocessor*, introduced by *Intel* in 1988. Available in 16-, 20-, 25, and 33-MHz versions, the 80386SX is an *80386DX* with a 16-bit data bus. This design allows systems to be configured using cheaper 16-bit components, leading to a lower overall cost. The *floating-point processor* for the 80386SX is the *80387SX*.

80387 Also called the 387. A *floating-point processor* from *Intel*, designed for use with the *80386 CPU* chip. When supported by *application* programs, a floating-point processor can speed up floating-point and transcendental math operations by 10 to 50 times.

The 80387 conforms to the *IEEE* 754-1985 standard for binary floating-point operations, and is available in speeds of 16, 20, 25, and 33 MHz.

80387SX Also called the 387SX. A *floating-point processor* from *Intel*, designed for use with the 16-bit data bus of the *80386SX CPU* chip

only. When supported by application programs, a floating-point processor can speed up floating-point and transcendental math operations by 10 to 50 times.

The 80387SX conforms to the *IEEE* 754-1985 standard for binary floating-point operations, and is available only in a 16-MHz version.

80486DX Also called the 486 or i486. A 32-bit *microprocessor* introduced by *Intel* in April 1989. The 80486 represents the continuing evolution of the *80386* family of microprocessors, and adds several notable features, including on-board *cache*, built-in *floating-point processor* and *memory management unit*, as well as certain advanced provisions for *multiprocessing*. Available in 25-, 33-, and 50-MHz versions, the 80486 is equivalent to 1.25 million *transistors*, and can perform 20 million instructions per second.

80486DX2 Also known as the 486DX2. A 32-bit *microprocessor* introduced by Intel in 1992. It is functionally identical to, and 100 percent compatible with, the 80486DX, but with one major difference; the DX2 chip adds what Intel calls speed-doubling technology—meaning that it runs twice as fast internally as it does with components external to the chip. For example, the DX2-50 operates at 50 MHz internally, but at 25 MHz while communicating with other system components, including memory and the other chips on the *motherboard*, thus maintaining its overall system compatibility. 50- and 66-MHz versions of the DX2 are available. The 486DX2 contains 1.2 million transistors, and is capable of 40 million instructions per second.

80486SX   Also called the 486SX. A 32-bit *microprocessor* introduced by *Intel* in April 1991. The 80486SX can be described as an *80486DX* with the *floating-point processor* circuitry disabled. Available in 16-, 20-, and 25-MHz versions, the 80486SX contains the equivalent of 1.185 million transistors, and can execute 16.5 million instructions per second.

80487   Also called the 487. A floating-point processor from *Intel*, designed for use with the *80486SX CPU* chip. When supported by *application* programs, a floating-point processor can speed up floating-point and transcendental math operations by 10 to 50 times.

The 80487 is essentially a 20MHz 80486 with the floating-point circuitry still enabled. When an 80487 is added into the coprocessor socket of a *motherboard* running the 80486SX, it effectively becomes the main processor, shutting down the 80486SX and taking over all operations.

The 80487 conforms to the *IEEE* 754-1985 standard for binary floating-point operations.

88000   A family of 32-bit *RISC* microprocessors from *Motorola*, introduced in 1988 and used in *workstations*. The 88000 chip set includes one 88100 *CPU*, and usually two 88200 *cache memory management units*. One of the units is used to cache *data*, the other to cache instructions. The 88100 CPU also includes a *floating-point processor*.

The 88000 is a true *32-bit computer*, with 32-bit internal registers, and a 32-bit data *bus*. Up to four chip sets can be configured to work together in a *multiprocessor* system.

9-track tape   A tape storage format that uses 9 parallel tracks on half-inch reel-to-reel magnetic tape. Eight tracks are used for data, and one track is used for *parity* information.

a-b box   A switching box designed to share a *peripheral* between two or more computers. It can be switched manually or under program control.

A: In *DOS, Windows,* and *OS/2,* the identifier used for the first *floppy disk drive*; the second floppy disk is designated as drive B:, while the first *hard disk* is known as drive C:. Unless instructed differently in the ROM-BIOS settings, the *operating system* always checks drive A: for startup (or *bootstrap*) instructions before checking the hard disk, drive C:.

ABIOS   Acronym for Advanced Basic Input/Output System. A set of *firmware* service routines built into the IBM PS/2 series of computers that use the Micro Channel Architecture (MCA) to support *multitasking operating systems* such as *OS/2.*

accelerator board   An add-in *printed circuit board* that replaces the main processor with a higher-performance processor, so you can upgrade your system without replacing monitor, case, keyboard, and so on.

Using an accelerator board can reduce upgrade costs substantially. However, there are other factors to consider, such as disk access time, in determining the overall performance of your system.

access mechanism   In a *floppy* or *hard disk drive,* the component that positions the *read/write* head over the surface of the disk, so that data can be read from or written to the disk.

access time   The period of time that elapses between a request for information from disk or *memory,* and the information arriving at the requesting device. Memory access time refers to the time it takes to transfer a character from memory to or from the processor, while disk access time refers to the time it takes to place the *read/write* heads over the requested data. *RAM* may have an access time of 80 nanoseconds or less, while *hard disk* access time could be 18 milliseconds or less.

active hubs   Types of network *hubs* that use electronics to amplify and clean up the signal before it is broadcast to the other ports.

active matrix   A type of *Liquid Crystal Display* that has a transistor for each pixel in the screen.

active partition   That part of the *hard disk* containing the *operating system* to be loaded when you start or restart the computer.

You can install two different operating systems (perhaps *DOS* and *OS/2*) on your hard disk, but each must be in its own separate area, or partition. Only one partition can be active at any given time, and to change from the DOS to the non-DOS partition, you may have to use the DOS *FDISK* command.

active-matrix screen   An *LCD* display mechanism that uses an individual transistor to control every *pixel* on the screen. Active-matrix screens are characterized by high contrast, a wide viewing angle, vivid colors, and fast screen refresh rates, and they do not show the streaking or shadowing that is common with cheaper LCD technology.

actuator arm   The device inside a hard disk drive that moves the read/write heads as a group in the fixed disk.

adapter   A *printed circuit board* that plugs into a computer's *expansion bus* to provide added capabilities. Common adapters for the PC include display adapters, memory expansion adapters, input/output adapters that provide serial, parallel, and games ports, and other devices such as internal *modems, CD-ROMs,* or network interface cards. One adapter can often support several different devices; for example, an input/output adapter may support one parallel port, a games or joystick port, and several serial ports. Some PC designs incorporate many of the functions previously performed by these individual adapters on the *motherboard*.

address

1. The precise location in *memory* or on disk where a piece of information is stored. Every *byte* in memory and every *sector* on a disk have their own unique addresses.

2. To reference or manage a storage location.

address bus   The electronic channel, usually from 20 to 32 separate lines wide, used to transmit the signals that specify locations in *memory*. The number of lines in the address bus determines the number of memory locations that the processor can access, as each line carries one bit of the address. An address bus of 20 lines (used in early Intel 8086/8088 processors) can access 1 MB of memory, one of 24 lines (as in the Intel 80286) can access 16 MB, and an address bus of 32 lines (as used by the Intel 80386, 80486, and later processors, or the Motorola 68020) can access over 4 GB.

advanced run-length limited encoding Abbreviated ARLL. A technique used to store information on a hard disk that increases the capacity of *run-length limited* (RLL) storage by more than 25 percent, and increases the data-transfer rate to 9 megabits per second.

algorithm   A formal set of instructions that can be followed to perform a specific task, such as a mathematical formula or a set of instructions in a computer program.

Alpha release   First phase of releasing software. In this phase the developers are aware that the software still has many errors that need to be delineated. The Alpha release is usually limited to people closely involved with the development process.

alphanumeric   Consisting of both letters and numbers.

Altair 8800   The first commercially successful microcomputer, based on the *Intel 8080*, introduced in 1975 by Micro Instrumentation Telemetry Systems of New Mexico. Over 10,000 were sold, mostly in kit form, and the Altair was packaged with the Microsoft MBASIC interpreter, written by Paul Allen and Bill Gates. The Altair 8800 had 256 bytes of memory, received input through a set of switches on the front panel, and displayed output on a row of LEDs.

alternating current   Abbreviated AC. An electrical current that reverses its polarity or direction of flow at regular intervals. AC is usually represented by a sine wave. In the United States, domestic wall plugs provide AC at 60 hertz, or 60 cycles per second.

America Online   One of the most popular and fastest-growing of the commercial *online services*, often abbreviated as AOL.

America Online provides a well-designed and easy-to-use service that includes a wide range of content, *e-mail* services, and basic Internet-access services. Many hardware and software vendors maintain software libraries and well-moderated technical-support *forums*.

American National Standards Institute   Abbreviated ANSI. A nonprofit organization of business and industry groups, founded in 1918, devoted to the development of voluntary standards. ANSI represents the USA on the International Standards Organization (ISO). In the PC world, ANSI committees have developed recommendations for the *C* programming language, as well as the *SCSI* interface and the *ANSI.SYS* device driver.

amperes   A unit of electrical current.

analog   Describes any device that represents changing values by a continuously variable physical property such as voltage in a circuit, fluid pressure, liquid level, and so on.

An analog device can handle an infinite number of values within its range. By contrast, a *digital* device can only manage a fixed number of possible values. For example, an ordinary mercury thermometer is an analog device and can record an infinite number of readings over its range. A digital thermometer, on the other hand, can only display temperature in a fixed number of individual steps.

analog-to-digital converter   Abbreviated ADC or A-D converter. A device that converts continuously varying *analog* signals into discrete *digital* signals or numbers.

Once analog signals have been converted into digital form, they can be processed, analyzed, stored, displayed and transmitted by computer. The key to analog-to-digital conversion lies in the amount of digital data created from the analog signal. The shorter the time interval between samples, and the more data recorded from that sample, the more closely the digital signal will reproduce the original analog signal. Many modern *sound boards* can sample and playback at up to 44.1 KHz using a *16-bit* analog-to-digital converter.

anonymous ftp   A method of accessing an *Internet* computer with the *ftp (file-transfer program)* which does not require that you have an *account* on the target computer system. Just log in to the Internet computer with the user name anonymous and use your *e-mail* address as your *password*.

anti-static bag   A bag designed to keep static charges from building up on the outside of a computer component during shipping. The bag will collect some of the charges, but does not drain them away as *ESD mats* do.

anti-static wrist strap (ESD strap)   A specially constructed strap worn as a preventive measure to guard against the damages of *ESD*. One end of the strap is attached to an earth ground and the other is wrapped around the technician's wrist.

anti-virus program   An *application* program you run to detect or eliminate a computer *virus* or *infection*. Some anti-virus programs are *terminate-and-stay-resident* programs that can detect suspicious activity on your computer as it happens, while others must be run periodically as part of your normal housekeeping activities.

applet   A small *application* program, limited in scope to one small but useful task. A calculator program or a card game might be called an applet.

AppleTalk   A network protocol developed by Apple Computer and included with all Macintosh computers.

application layer   The seventh, or highest, layer in the International Organization for Standardization's Open Systems Interconnection (ISO/OSI) model for computer-to-computer communications. This layer uses services provided by the lower layers, but is completely insulated from the details of the *network* hardware. It describes how *application* programs interact with the *network operating system*, including *database management, electronic mail*, and *terminal emulation* programs.

application program interface   Abbreviated API. The complete set of *operating system* functions that an *application* program can use to perform tasks such as managing files and displaying information on the computer screen.

An API is a complete definition of all the operating system functions available to an application program, and it also describes how the application program should use those functions.

In operating systems that support a *graphical user interface*, the API also defines functions to support *windows, icons, pull-down menus*, and other components of the interface.

In *network operating systems*, an API defines a standard method application programs can use to take advantage of all the network features.

application-specific integrated circuit Abbreviated ASIC. A computer chip developed for a specific purpose, designed by incorporating standard cells from a library, rather than designed from scratch. ASICs can be found in VCRs, microwave ovens, automobiles, and security alarms.

arbitration　The set of rules used to manage competing demands for a computer resource, such as *memory* or *peripheral* devices, made by multiple processes or users.

architecture　The overall design and construction of all or part of a computer, particularly the processor *hardware* and the size and ordering sequence of its *bytes*. Also used to describe the overall design of *software*.

ARCNet (Attached Resource Computing Network)　A simple network type, developed by the DataPoint Corporation, that uses a *token-bus* cable access method and a logical bus, physical star topology. It was very cheap; therefore, many networks used to use this technology.

array processor　A group of special processors designed to calculate math procedures at very high speeds, often under the control of another central processor. Some computers use array processors to speed up video operations or for fast floating-point math operations.

ASCII　Pronounced "askee." Acronym for American Standard Code for Information Interchange. A standard coding scheme that assigns numeric values to letters, numbers, punctuation marks, and control characters, to achieve compatibility among different computers and peripherals.

In ASCII each character is represented by a unique integer value. The values 0 to 31 are used for non-printing control codes, and the range from 32 to 127 is used to represent the letters of the alphabet and common punctuation symbols. The entire set from 0 to 127 is referred to as the standard ASCII character set. All computers that use ASCII can understand the standard ASCII character set.

The extended ASCII character set (from code 128 through code 255) is assigned variable sets of characters by computer hardware manufacturers and software developers, and is not necessarily compatible between different computers. The IBM extended character set includes mathematical symbols and characters from the PC line-drawing set.

ASCII character set　A character set that consists of the first 128 (from 0 to 127) *ASCII* characters. The second group of characters, from 128 to 255, is known as the *extended ASCII character set*.

ASCII file　A *file* that only contains text characters from the *ASCII character set*. An ASCII file contains letters, numbers, and punctuation symbols, but does not contain any hidden text-formatting commands. Also known as a *text file*, and ASCII text file.

Association for Computing Machinery Abbreviated ACM. A membership organization, founded in 1947, dedicated to advancing computer science through technical education of computing professionals and through technical publications. ACM also sponsors several *special interest groups (SIGs)*.

Association of PC User Groups   Abbreviated APCUG. A nonprofit affiliation of local PC User Groups, dedicated to fostering communications between *personal-computer user groups*, and acting as an information network between user groups and software publishers and hardware manufacturers.

asynchronous   Describes a type of communication that adds special signaling *bits* to each end of the data. The bit at the beginning of the information signals the start of the data and is known as the *start bit*. The next few bits are the actual data that needs to be sent. Those bits are known as the *data bits*. *Stop bits* indicate that the data is finished. Asynchronous communications have no timing signal.

asynchronous transmission   In communications, a method of transmission that uses *start bits* and *stop bits* to coordinate the flow of data so that the time intervals between individual characters do not have to be equal. *Parity* may also be used to check the accuracy of the data received.

AT command set   A set of standard instructions used to activate features on a *modem*. Originally developed by Hayes Microcomputer Products, the AT command set is now used by almost all modem manufacturers.

The code AT is short for ATtention, and precedes most of the modem commands. On a Hayes or Hayes-compatible modem, the ATDP (ATtention Dial Pulse) command initiates pulse (rather than touch-tone) dialing, while the ATDT (ATtention Dial Tone) command initiates touch-tone (rather than pulse) dialing.

ATA   The first IBM PC had no hard disk storage capability. When the 80286-based AT was developed, it included a hard disk as a major feature, and the hard disk *controller* interface (ATA or AT Attachment) became a de facto industry standard from that day to this. As PCs have grown up, however, the controller interface has also evolved, and we do mean evolution rather than revolution. Everything still leads back to that original interface, in one way or another. The children of ATA are now quite various and the family tree currently looks like this:

- **ATA** (AT Attachment) is the original interface and is the same as the Integrated Drive Electronics Interface (IDE) for disk drives. ATA (thus IDE) was designed as a way to integrate the controller onto the hard disk drive itself and to lower manufacturing costs, as well as making firmware implementations easier.

- **ATA-2** is an extension of ATA that was beefed up to include performance enhancing features such as fast PIO (programmed input/output) and DMA (Direct Memory Access) modes. The ATA-2 interface also got an improved Identify Drive command. This particular feature lets a hard drive tell the software exactly what its characteristics are, and is the basis for both Plug and Play hard drive technology and compatibility with any new version of the standard that may come down the road in the future.

- **ATAPI** (ATA Packet Interface) is a standard that is still being worked out. It has been designed for devices such as CD-ROMs and tape drives that plug into an ordinary ATA (IDE) port. The major benefit of ATAPI hardware is that it's cheap and it works on your current adapter. For CD-ROMs, ATAPI also uses fewer CPU resources than proprietary adapters, but is not otherwise any faster. For tape drives, ATAPI could potentially be both faster and more reliable than interfaces that are driven by the floppy drive controller.

- **Fast ATA** is what people are calling the technology and products that support the high-speed data transfers specified by ANSI-standardized Programmed Input/Output (PIO) Mode 3 and multi-word Direct Memory Access (DMA) Mode 1 protocols. Fast ATA enables the drive to transfer data at speeds as high as 13.3 MB/s.

- **Fast ATA-2** is like Fast ATA, but is a standard that will allow manufacturers to create products that support ANSI PIO Mode 4 and multi-word DMA Mode 2 protocols. With Fast ATA-2, we should be able to get data transfers as high as 16.6 megabytes/second.

attenuation   In communications, the decrease in power of a signal transmitted over a wire. Attenuation is measured in *decibels*, and increases as the power of the signal decreases. In a *local area network*, attenuation can become a problem when cable lengths exceed the stated network specification; however, the useful length of a cable can often be extended by the use of a *repeater*.

AUTOEXEC.BAT   A contraction of AUTO-matically EXECuted BATch. A special DOS batch file, located in the *root* directory of your startup disk, that runs automatically every time you start or restart your computer.

As with all batch files, the commands contained in AUTOEXEC.BAT are executed one by one just as if you had typed them at the system prompt. You don't have to use an AUTOEXEC.BAT file, but because most people use their computers in the same way each time, it is usually convenient to place startup commands in this file rather than have to remember to type them yourself every time. You can use any *DOS* command in AUTOEXEC.BAT, but it is most often used to establish the system path with the *PATH* command, the appearance of the system prompt with the *PROMPT* command, the system *environment* variables using one or more *SET* commands, and to load your favorite *terminate-and-stay resident* programs.

In *OS/2*, you can select any batch file to be used as the AUTOEXEC.BAT file for a specific DOS session; with careful use of this option, you can tailor specific environments for separate DOS sessions, each using a different AUTOEXEC file.

average latency   A measure of the speed of a hard disk. This value, given in milliseconds (ms) indicates the average time it takes to access a piece of information relative to the spinning of the hard disk platters. For example, a value of 7ms means that on average, once a disk read/write head is in the correct track to retrieve the information, it takes approximately 7ms for the information to rotate into the correct position.

B: In *DOS*, *Windows*, and *OS/2*, the identifier used for the second floppy disk drive; the first floppy disk is designated as drive *A:*, while the first hard disk is known as drive *C:*.

backbone   In communications, that portion of the network that manages the bulk of the *traffic*. The backbone may connect several different locations or buildings, and may also connect to other, smaller networks.

back-end processor   A secondary processor that performs one specialized task very effectively, freeing the main processor for other, more important work.

background noise   In communications, any unwanted signal that enters a line, channel, or circuit.

backplane   A *printed circuit board* containing slots or sockets, into which *expansion boards* are plugged.

backup   An up-to-date copy of all your *files* that you can use to reload your *hard disk* in case of an accident. It is an insurance against disk failure affecting the hundreds or possibly thousands of files you might have on your system hard disk, or on your local area network hard disk.

backward-compatible   Fully compatible with earlier versions of the same *application* program or computer system.

bad sector   An area on a *hard disk* or *floppy disk* that cannot be used to store data, because of a manufacturing defect or accidental damage. One of the tasks an *operating system* performs is finding, marking, and isolating bad sectors. Almost all hard disks have some bad sectors, often listed in the *bad track table*, as a result of the manufacturing process, and this is not usually

anything to worry about; the operating system will mark them as bad, and you will never even know that they are there.

bad track table   A list of the defective areas on a *hard disk*, usually determined during final testing of the disk at the factory. Some disk-preparation programs ask you to enter information from this list to reduce the time that a *low-level format* takes to prepare the disk for use by an *operating system*.

bandwidth   In communications, the difference between the highest and the lowest frequencies available for transmission in any given range.

In networking, the transmission capacity of a computer or a communications channel, stated in *megabits* or *megabytes per second*; the higher the number, the faster the data transmission takes place.

bank switching   A method of switching between two sets (or banks) of memory chips in a computer, only one of which can be active at a time. Because of the overhead involved in switching between banks, memory-intensive tasks can take much longer to perform using bank-switched memory than when using main memory. Bank-switched memory is often located on an *expansion card* plugged into an *expansion slot* on the *motherboard*.

basis weight   A measurement of the "heaviness" of paper. The number is the weight, in pounds, of 500 11" × 17" sheets of that type of paper.

batch file   An ASCII text *file* containing operating system commands and possibly other commands supported by the batch processor. The commands in the file are executed one line at a time, just as if you had typed them at the system prompt. You can include program names, operating system commands, batch language commands, and other variables in your batch files. Batch files are used to automate repetitive tasks; almost all DOS users place regularly-used setup commands in a batch file called *AUTOEXEC.BAT*, which executes every time the computer is started.

A DOS batch file must have the *file-name extension* .BAT, while an *OS/2* batch file has the extension .CMD.

baud   A measurement of data-transmission speed. Originally used in measuring the speed of telegraph equipment, it now usually refers to the data-transmission speed of a *modem* or other *serial* device.

baud rate   In communications equipment, a measurement of the number of state changes (from 0 to 1 or vice versa) per second on an *asynchronous* communications channel.

Baud rate is often mistakenly assumed to correspond to the number of bits transmitted per second, but because in modern high-speed digital communications systems one state change can be made to represent more than 1 data bit, baud rate and *bits per second* are not always the same. A rate of 300 *baud* is likely to correspond to 300 bits per second, but at higher baud rates, the number of bits per second transmitted can be higher than the baud rate as one state change can represent more than one data bit. For example, 2400 bits per

second can be sent at 1200 baud if each state change represents two bits of information.

On the PC, the *MODE* command is used to set the baud rate of a serial device, perhaps a modem or a printer. Both the sending and the receiving devices must be set to the same baud rate, and in times past, mismatched baud rates were one of the most common reasons for communications failures. These days, intelligent modems can lock onto one of a range of rates, and can even change rates in response to changing line conditions during the course of a transmission.

benchmark   A test that attempts to quantify hardware or software performance—usually in terms of speed, reliability, or accuracy. One of the major problems in determining performance is deciding which of the many benchmarks available actually reflects how you plan to use the system. For best results, you should evaluate performance using the same mix of *applications* and system commands that you expect to use in your day-to-day work.

Berg connector   A type of connector most commonly used in PC floppy drive power cables; it has four conductors arranged in a row.

Bernoulli box   An early data-storage device featuring a removable cartridge, developed by Iomega Corporation.

beta software   Software that has been released to a cross-section of typical users for testing before the commercial release of the package.

bias voltage   The high-voltage charge applied to the developing roller inside an EP cartridge.

binary Any scheme that uses two different states, components, conditions, or conclusions. In mathematics, the binary or base-2 numbering system uses combinations of the digits 0 and 1 to represent all values. The more familiar decimal system has a base of 10 (0–9).

Computers and other digital devices are designed to work with information (internally) in the form of binary numbers, because it is relatively simple to construct electronic circuits that generate two voltage levels ("on" and "off," corresponding to 1 and 0).

Unlike computers, people find binary numbers that consist of long strings of *0*s and *1*s difficult to read, so most people who work at this level use *hexadecimal* (base-16) numbers instead.

binary-coded decimal Abbreviated BCD. A simple system for converting decimal numbers into *binary* form, where each decimal digit is converted into binary and then stored as a single character.

In binary numbers, the largest value that can be stored in a single *8-bit byte* is 255, and this obviously represents a severe limitation to storing larger numbers. BCD is a way around this limitation that stays within the 8-bit storage format. For example, the decimal number 756 can be broken down so that the numbers 7, 5, and 6 are represented by one byte each. In BCD, each decimal digit occupies a byte, so three bytes are needed for a three-digit decimal number. There is no limit to the size of the stored number; as the number increases in size, so does the amount of storage space set aside to hold it.

BIOS Acronym for basic input/output system, pronounced "bye-os." In the PC, a set of instructions, stored in read-only memory (ROM), that prevents programs from fighting over hardware. The BIOS lets your computer's hardware and operating system communicate with *application programs* and peripheral devices such as hard disks, printers, and video adapters. These instructions are stored in non-volatile memory as a permanent part of your computer. They are always available at specific addresses in memory, so all programs can access them to perform their basic input and output functions.

IBM computers contain a copyrighted BIOS that only their computers can use; however, other companies such as *Phoenix*, *Award*, and *American Megatrends* have developed BIOSes for other manufacturer's computers that *emulate* or mimic the IBM instructions without using the same code. If you use a non-IBM computer, the BIOS company's copyright message and BIOS version number are displayed every time you turn on your computer.

BIOS CMOS setup program Program that modifies BIOS settings in the *CMOS memory*. This program is available at system startup time by pressing some key combination like Alt+F1 or Ctrl+F2.

BIOS extensions In the PC, extensions to the main *BIOS* (basic input/output system) that enable the computer to work with add-on devices such as hard disk controllers and EGA or VGA adapters. The *ROM* chips containing these extensions do not have to be located on the *motherboard*; they can also be on *expansion boards* plugged into the *expansion bus*. Any BIOS extensions needed to run these expansion boards are loaded automatically when you *boot* your computer.

BIOS parameter block   Abbreviated BPB. In the PC, a part of the *boot record* contained on every formatted disk, which contains information about the disk's physical characteristics. This information includes the version number of the operating system used to format the disk, the number of bytes per sector, the number of sectors per cluster, per track, and per disk, and is provided for use by *device drivers*.

BIOS shadow   A copy of the BIOS in memory.

bit   Contraction of BInary digiT. A bit is the basic unit of information in the *binary* numbering system, representing either 0 (for off) or 1 (for on). Bits can be grouped together to make up larger storage units, the most common being the 8-bit *byte*. A byte can represent all kinds of information including the letters of the alphabet, the numbers 0 through 9, and common punctuation symbols.

bit-mapped font   A set of characters in a specific style and size, in which each character is defined by a pattern of dots. The computer must keep a complete set of bitmaps for every font you use on your system, and these bitmaps can consume large amounts of disk space.

bit-mapped graphic   A graphic, created using a *paint program* like MacPaint or PC Paintbrush, composed of a series of dots, or *pixels*, rather than a set of lines or vectors. Resizing a bit-mapped image without distortion or *aliasing* is very difficult, and bit-mapped graphics consume large amounts of disk and memory space. Color bit-mapped graphics often require many times the amount of control information that a monochrome bit-map needs. *Scanners* and screen-capture programs may also produce bit-mapped images.

bits per inch   Abbreviated bpi. The number of *bits* (binary digits) that a tape or disk can store per inch of length.

bits per second   Abbreviated bps. The number of binary digits, or bits, transmitted every second during a data transfer. A measurement of the speed of operation of equipment such as a computer's data bus, or a modem connecting a computer to a transmission line.

blank   A piece of plastic or metal that covers a space where a device is going to be installed.

BNC connector   A small connector with a half-turn locking shell used with coaxial cable.

boot   The loading of an operating system into memory, usually from a hard disk, although occasionally from a floppy disk. This is an automatic procedure begun when you first turn on or reset your computer. A set of instructions contained in ROM begin executing, first running a series of power-on self tests (POST) to check that devices such as hard disks are in working order, then locating and loading the operating system, and finally, passing control of the computer over to that operating system.

The term is supposed to be derived from the expression "pulling yourself up by your own bootstraps."

boot record   That part of a formatted disk containing the operating system loading program, along with other basic information needed by the computer when it starts running.

bootable disk   Any disk capable of loading and starting the operating system, although most often used when referring to a floppy disk. In these days of larger and larger operating systems, it is less common to boot from a floppy disk. In some cases, all of the files needed to start the operating system will not fit on a single floppy disk, which makes it impossible to boot from a floppy.

BPS (bits per second)   A measurement of how much data (how many bits) is being transmitted in one second. Typically used to describe the speed of asynchronous communications (modems).

bridge   This type of connectivity device operates in the Data Link layer of the *OSI model*. It is used to join similar topologies (Ethernet to Ethernet, token-ring to token-ring) and to divide traffic on network segments. This device will pass information destined for one particular workstation to that segment, but will not pass broadcast traffic.

broadband network   In communications, a technique for transmitting a large amount of information, including voice, data, and video, over long distances.

The transmission capacity is divided into several distinct channels that can be used concurrently, normally by using *frequency-division multiplexing*, and these individual channels are protected from each other by guard channels of unused frequencies. A broadband network can operate at speeds of up to 20 megabits per second, and is based on the same technology used by cable television.

broadcasting   Sending a signal to all entities that can listen to it. In networking, it refers to sending a signal to all entities connected to that network.

brouter   In networking, a device that combines the attributes of a *bridge* and a *router*. A brouter can route one or more specific protocols, such as *TCP/IP*, and bridge all others.

brownout   A short period of low voltage often caused by an unusually heavy demand for power. A brownout may cause your computer to crash, and if your area experiences frequent brownouts, you should consider purchasing an *uninterruptable power supply* (UPS).

browser   An application program used to explore *Internet* resources. A browser lets you wander from node to node without concern for the technical details of the links between the nodes or the specific methods used to access them, and presents the information—text, graphics, sound, or video—as a document on the screen.

bubble jet printer   A type of sprayed ink printer, this type uses an electric signal that energizes a heating element, causing ink to vaporize and get pushed out of the pinhole and onto the paper.

buffer   An area of memory set aside for temporary storage of data, often until some external event completes. Many peripherals, such as printers, have their own buffers. The computer transfers the data for printing from memory into the buffer, and the printer then processes that data directly from the buffer, freeing the computer for other tasks.

bug A logical or programming error in hardware or software that causes a malfunction of some sort. If the problem is in software, it can be fixed by changes to the program. If the fault is in hardware, new circuits must be designed and constructed. Some bugs are fatal and cause the program to hang or cause data loss, others are just annoying, and many are never even noticed. The term apparently originates from the days of the first electro-mechanical computers, when a problem was traced to a moth caught between two contacts inside the machinery.

bug-fix A release of hardware or software that corrects known *bugs* but does not contain additional new features. Such releases are usually designated only by an increase in the decimal portion of the *version number*; for example, the revision level may advance from 2.0 to 2.01 or 2.1, rather than from 2.0 to 3.0.

bulletin board system Abbreviated BBS. A computer system, equipped with one or more modems, acting as a message-passing system or centralized information source, usually for a particular special interest group. Bulletin board systems are often established by software vendors and by different PC *user groups*.

bus A set of pathways that allow information and signals to travel between components inside or outside of a computer. In the PC, several buses are available:

• ISA

• EISA

• VL bus

• PCI

Because you may want to add a new function to your computer, most PC buses allow for this through one or more *expansion slots*; when you plug an *expansion board* into an expansion slot, you are actually plugging the board into the bus and making it part of the system.

bus clock A chip on the motherboard that produces a type of signal (called a clock signal) that indicates how fast the bus can transmit information.

bus connector slot A slot made up of several small copper channels that grab the matching "fingers" of the expansion circuit boards. The fingers connect to copper pathways on the motherboard.

bus mastering A technique that allows certain advanced bus architectures to delegate control of data transfers between the central processing unit (CPU) and associated peripheral devices to an add-in board. This gives greater system bus access and higher data-transfer rates than conventional systems. It also lets the NIC (network interface card) take temporary control of the computer's bus to bypass the CPU and move data directly to RAM.

More modern buses such as *MCA, EISA, VL bus*, and *PCI* all support some form of bus mastering, but older systems such as *ISA* do not.

bus mouse A *mouse* connected to the computer using an *expansion board* plugged into an *expansion slot*, instead of simply connected to a serial port as in the case of a *serial mouse*.

bus slot   A slot on the motherboard that allows the installation of expansion cards. These cards can interface directly with the bus and send their data on it.

bus topology   Type of physical topology that consists of a single cable that runs to every workstation on the network. Each computer shares that same data and address path. As messages pass through the trunk, each workstation checks to see if the message is addressed for itself. This topology is very difficult to reconfigure, since reconfiguration requires you to disconnect and reconnect a portion of the network (thus bringing the whole network down).

byte   Contraction of BinarY digiT Eight. A group of 8 bits that in computer storage terms usually holds a single character, such as a number, letter, or other symbol.

Because bytes represent a very small amount of storage, they are usually grouped into *kilobytes* (1,024 bytes), *megabytes* (1,048,576 bytes), or even *gigabytes* (1,073,741,824 bytes) for convenience when describing hard disk capacity or computer memory size.

bytes per inch   Abbreviated bpi. The number of *bytes* that a tape or disk can store per inch of length.

C: In the PC, the usual drive designation for the first *hard disk*.

cable access method   Defines a set of rules for how computers put data on a network cable and retrieve it from the cable.

cable   The medium used to physically transfer data from computer to computer.

cache   Pronounced "cash." A special area of memory, managed by a *cache controller*, that improves performance by storing the contents of frequently accessed memory locations and their addresses. When the processor references a memory address, the cache checks to see if it holds that address. If it does, the information is passed directly to the processor; if not, a normal memory access takes place instead. A cache can speed up operations in a computer whose RAM access is slow compared with its processor speed, because the cache memory is always faster than normal RAM.

cache controller   Pronounced "cash controller." A special-purpose processor, such as the Intel 82385, whose sole task is to manage *cache memory*. On newer processors, such as the *Intel Pentium*, cache management is integrated directly into the processor.

cache memory   Pronounced "cash memory." A relatively small section of very fast memory (often *static RAM*) reserved for the temporary storage of the data or instructions likely to be needed next by the processor. For example, the *Intel Pentium* has an 8K code cache as well as an 8K data cache.

caddy   The flat plastic container used to load a *compact disk* into a *CD-ROM drive*.

caliper   The thickness of an individual piece of paper.

Canon engine   The combination of laser mechanism and toner cartridge, first produced by Canon, used as the heart of Hewlett-Packard's popular line of laser printers.

capacitive keyboard   Keyboard designed with two sheets of semi-conductive material separated by a thin sheet of Mylar inside the keyboard. When a key is pressed, the plunger presses down and a paddle connected to the plunger presses the two sheets of semi-conductive material together, changing the total capacitance of the two sheets. The controller can tell by the capacitance value returned which key was pressed.

capacitive touch screen   Type of display monitor that has two clear plastic coating over the screen, separated by air. When the user presses the screen in a particular spot, the coatings are pressed together and the controller registers a change in the total capacitance of the two layers. The controller then determines where the screen was pressed by the capacitance values and sends that information to the computer in the form of X,Y coordinates.

capacitor   An electrical component, normally found in power supplies and timing circuits, used to store electrical charge.

card   A *printed circuit board* or *adapter* that you plug into your computer to add support for a specific piece of *hardware* not normally present on the computer.

card services   Part of the software support needed for *PCMCIA* hardware devices in a *portable computer*, controlling the use of system *interrupts*, *memory*, or power management.

When an application wants to access a *PC Card*, it always goes through the card services software and never communicates directly with the underlying hardware. For example, if you use a PCMCIA modem, card services establishes which communications port and which interrupts and I/O addresses are in use, not the applications program.

cardcage   An enclosure designed to hold *printed circuit boards* or *cards*. Most PCs have an area with edge connectors and mounting plates designed to receive *expansion boards*. The term originally referred to an external box that held rack-mounted cards.

carpal tunnel   A tunnel of bone and ligament from the forearm to the hand, containing nine tendons and the median nerve.

carpal-tunnel syndrome   A form of wrist injury caused by holding the hands in an awkward position for long periods of time. A narrow tunnel in the wrist—the carpal tunnel—contains tendons and the median nerve, which conducts sensation from the thumb, index, and middle fingers and parts of the hand up the arm to the central nervous system. Burning sensations and tingling occur when the median nerve is compressed as it passes through the narrow tunnel of bone and ligature at the wrist. Keyboard operators, musicians, dental hygienists, meat packers, and other workers who perform repetitive motions for long periods of time may be prone to this sort of injury. Improvements in the work environment, more frequent breaks, and even job modification can all help alleviate this problem, which is costing industry $805 million dollars each year, according to National Institute for Occupational Health figures.

carriage motor   Stepper motor that is used to move the print head back and forth on a dot-matrix printer.

carrier signal In communications, a signal of chosen frequency generated to carry data, often used for long-distance transmissions. The data is added to this carrier signal by *modulation*, and decoded on the receiving end by *demodulation*.

CBIOS Acronym for Compatibility Basic Input/Output System. Firmware service routines built into the IBM PS/2 series of computers with the Micro Channel Architecture (MCA), generally considered to be a super-set of the original IBM PC BIOS.

CCD (charge coupled device) A device that allows light to be converted into electrical pulses.

CCITT Acronym for Comité Consultatif Internationale de Téléphonie et de Télégraphie. An organization, based in Geneva, that develops world-wide data communications standards. CCITT is part of the ITU (International Telecommunications Union). The organization has been renamed ITU-T (ITU Telecommunications Standardization Sector).

Three main sets of standards have been established: *CCITT Groups 1–4* standards apply to facsimile transmissions; the *CCITT V series* of standards apply to modems and error detection and correction methods; and the *CCITT X series* standards apply to local area networks. Recently, the trend has been to refer to these standards as ITU standards rather than CCITT standards; you will see both.

Recommendations are published every four years, and each update is identified by the color of its cover; the 1988 edition was known as the Blue Book, and the 1992 update had white covers.

CCITT Groups 1–4 A set of four *CCITT* standards for facsimile transmissions.

- **Groups 1 and 2** defined analog facsimile transmissions, and are no longer used. Groups 3 and 4 describe digital systems, as follows:

- **Group 3** specifies a 9600 bps modem to transmit standard images of 203 dots per inch (dpi) horizontally by 98 dpi vertically in standard mode, and 203 dpi by 198 dpi in fine mode.

- **Group 4** supports images up to 400 dpi for high-speed transmission over a digital data network like *ISDN*, rather than a dial-up telephone line.

CCITT V Series A set of recommended standards for data communications over a telephone line, including transmission speeds and operational modes, issued by *CCITT*.

CCITT X Series A set of recommended standards issued by *CCITT* to standardize protocols and equipment used in public and private computer networks, including the transmission speeds, the interfaces to and between networks, and the operation of user *hardware*.

CD-I Acronym for Compact Disk-Interactive, pronounced "see-dee-eye." A *hardware* and *software* standard disk format that encompasses data, text, audio, still video images, and animated graphics. The standard also defines methods of encoding and decoding compressed data, as well as displaying data.

CD-R Abbreviation for CD Recordable. A type of CD device that brings *CD-ROM* publishing into the realm of the small business or home office. From a functional point of view, a CD-R and a CD-ROM are identical; you can read CD-R disks using almost any CD-ROM drive, although the processes that create the disks are slightly different. Low-cost CD-R drives are available from many manufacturers, including Kao, Kodak, Mitsui, Phillips, Ricoh, Sony, TDK, 3M, and Verbatim.

CD-ROM Acronym for Compact Disk–Read-Only Memory, pronounced "see-dee-rom." A high-capacity, optical storage device that uses *compact disk* technology to store large amounts of information, up to 650 MB (the equivalent of approximately 300,000 pages of text), on a single 4.72" disk.

A CD-ROM uses the *constant linear velocity* encoding scheme to store information in a single, spiral track, divided into many equal-length segments. To read data, the *CD-ROM disk drive* must increase the rotational speed as the read head gets closer to the center of the disk, and decrease as the head moves back out. Typical CD-ROM data access times are in the range of 0.3 to 1.5 seconds—much slower than a *hard disk*.

CD-ROM disk drive A disk device that uses *compact disk* technology for information storage. CD-ROM disk drives designed for computer use are much more expensive than audio CD players; this is because CD-ROM disk drives are manufactured to much higher tolerances. If a CD player misreads a small amount of data, the

human ear will probably not detect the difference; if a CD-ROM disk drive misreads a few bytes of a program, the program simply will not run. Many CD-ROM disk drives also have headphone jacks, external speaker jacks, and a volume control.

CD-ROM drives are available with several different data transfer rates—single-speed, double-speed, etc. all the way up to 16x.

The two most popular CD-ROM drive interface cards are *SCSI* or ATAPI (AT Attachment Packet Interface). ATAPI is part of the Enhanced *IDE* specification introduced by Western Digital in 1994, and lets you plug an IDE CD-ROM drive directly into an IDE connector on your system's *motherboard*. Other CD-ROM drives may use the computer's *parallel port* or a *PCMCIA* connection.

CD-ROM Extended Architecture Abbreviated CD-ROM/XA. An extension to the *CD-ROM* format, developed by Microsoft, Phillips and Sony, that allows for the storage of audio and visual information on compact disk, so that you can play the audio at the same time you view the visual data.

CD-ROM/XA is compatible with the *High Sierra specification* also known as ISO standard 9660.

central processing unit Abbreviated CPU. The computing and control part of the computer. The CPU in a *mainframe computer* may be contained on many *printed circuit boards*; the CPU in a *mini computer* may be contained on several boards; and the CPU in a PC is contained in a single extremely powerful microprocessor.

Centronics parallel interface   A standard 36-pin *interface* in the PC world for the exchange of information between the PC and a *peripheral* such as a printer, originally developed by the printer manufacturer Centronics, Inc. The standard defines 8 *parallel* data lines, plus additional lines for status and control information.

CGA   Acronym for Color/Graphics Adapter. A *video adapter* introduced by IBM in 1981 that provided low-resolution text and graphics. CGA provided several different text and graphics modes, including 40- or 80-column by 25 line 16-color text mode, and graphics modes of 640 horizontal *pixels* by 200 vertical pixels with 2 colors, or 320 horizontal pixels by 200 vertical pixels with 4 colors. CGA has been superseded by later video standards, including *EGA*, *VGA*, *SuperVGA*, and *XGA*.

charge-coupled device   Abbreviated CCD. A special type of memory that can store patterns of changes in a sequential manner. The light-detecting circuitry contained in many still and video cameras is a CCD.

charging step   The stage in the EP printing process when a special wire within the EP toner cartridge gets a high voltage from the HVPS. This high voltage is used to apply a strong, uniform negative charge to the surface of the photosensitive drum.

checksum   A method of providing information for error detection, usually calculated by summing a set of values.

The checksum is usually appended to the end of the data that it is calculated from, so that data and checksum can be compared. For example, *Xmodem*, the popular *file* transfer protocol, uses a 1-byte checksum calculated by adding all the *ASCII* values for all 128 data bytes, and ignoring any numerical overflow. The checksum is added to the end of the Xmodem data packet. This kind of checksum will not always detect all errors, and in later versions of the Xmodem protocol was replaced by a *cyclical redundancy check* (CRC) for more rigorous error control.

"chip creep"   The slow self-loosening of chips from their sockets on the system board as a result of the frequent heating and cooling down of the board (which causes parts of the board—significantly, the chip connector slots—to alternately expand and shrink).

circuit   A communications channel or path between two devices capable of carrying electrical current. Also used to describe a set of components connected together to perform a specific task.

Class A certification   An *FCC* certification for computer equipment, including mainframe and mini computers destined for use in an industrial, commercial, or office setting, rather than for personal use at home. The Class A commercial certification is less restrictive than the *Class B certification* for residential use because it assumes that most residential areas are more than 30 feet away from any commercial computer equipment.

Class B certification   An *FCC* certification for computer equipment, including PCs, laptops, and portables destined for use in the home rather than in a commercial setting. Class B levels of radio frequency interference (*RFI*) must be low enough so that they do not interfere with radio or television reception when there is more than one wall and 30 feet separating the computer from the receiver. Class B certification is more restrictive than the commercial *Class A certification*.

cleaning step Sixth and final step in the EP print process. A rubber blade inside the EP cartridge scrapes any toner that was not transferred to the paper into a used toner receptacle inside the EP cartridge, and a fluorescent lamp discharges any remaining charge on the photosensitive drum.

client A network entity that can request resources from the network or server.

client software The software that allows the computer to communicate with the network.

clock doubling Technology that allows a chip to run at the bus's rated speed externally, but still be able to run the processor's internal clock at twice the speed of the bus. This technology improves computer performance.

clock signal Built-in metronome-like signal that indicates how fast the components can operate.

clock speed Also known as clock rate. The internal speed of a computer or processor, normally expressed in *MHz*.

The faster the clock speed, the faster the computer will perform a specific operation, assuming the other components in the system, such as disk drives, can keep up with the increased speed.

The Intel *8088* processor used in the original *IBM PC* had a clock speed of 4.77 MHz; the *80286* first ran at 6 MHz but some processors are available that run at 25 MHz; the *80386* and *80486* processors run at clock speeds ranging from 16 to 66 MHz; and the *MIPS R4400* runs at 150 MHz. *Pentium II* processors currently run at clock speeds up to 400 MHz.

clock/calendar board An internal time-of-day and month-year calendar that is kept up-to-date by a small battery-backup system. This allows your computer to update the time even when turned off. Appointment scheduling programs and programs that start at specific times use the output from the clock/calendar board.

clock-multiplying A mechanism used in certain chips that allows the chip to process data and instructions internally at a different speed from that used for external operations. For example, the Intel *80486DX2* operates at 50 MHz internally, but at 25 MHz externally and when communicating with other system components; this is known as clock doubling. The Intel *DX4* chip uses clock-tripling technology, and the *PowerPC* 601 can run at 1, 2, 3, or 4 times the speed of the bus.

clone *Hardware* that is identical in function to an original. Usually used in the sense of, for example, an "AT clone," a PC that uses an 80286 microprocessor and functions in the same way as an IBM PC/AT computer. Although most clones do perform as intended, minor internal differences can cause severe problems in some clones that can only be solved by the intervention of the manufacturer.

Companies have offered clones of IBM-compatible computers for many years, but Apple waited until early 1995 to announce that they too would license the Macintosh operating system and related technology to other manufacturers.

cluster The smallest unit of *hard disk* space that *DOS* can allocate to a file, consisting of one or more contiguous *sectors*. The number of sectors contained in a cluster depends on the hard disk type.

CMOS Acronym for Complementary Metal-Oxide Semiconductor, pronounced "see-moss." A type of integrated circuit used in processors and for memory. CMOS devices operate at very high speeds and use very little power, so they generate very little heat. In the PC, battery-backed CMOS is used to store operating parameters such as *hard disk* type when the computer is switched off; in the *Macintosh* PRAM performs this same function.

coaxial cable Abbreviated coax, pronounced "co-ax." A high-capacity cable used in networking. It contains an inner copper conductor surrounded by plastic insulation, and an outer braided copper or foil shield. Coaxial cable is used for broadband and baseband communications networks, and is used by cable television because the cable is usually free from external interference, and it permits very high transmission rates over long distances.

cold boot The computer startup process that begins when you turn on power to the computer. A cold boot might be needed if a program or the *operating system* crashes in such a way that you cannot continue. If operations are interrupted in a minor way, a *warm boot* may suffice.

color printer A general term for all printers, including *dot-matrix*, *ink-jet*, thermal-transfer, and *laser printers* that can create colored as well as black and white output.

COM port In *DOS*, the device name used to denote a *serial communications* port. In versions of DOS after 3.3, four COM ports are supported, COM1, COM2, COM3, and COM4; prior to that, only COM1 and COM2 were available.

command processor Also called the command interpreter. The command processor is that part of the *operating system* that displays the command prompt on the screen, interprets and executes all the commands and *file names* that you enter, and displays error messages when appropriate.

The command processor also contains the *environment*, a memory area that holds values for important system definitions or defaults that are used by the system, and which can be changed by the user.

communication device Device that the computer uses to communicate with other computers.

compact disk Abbreviated CD. A nonmagnetic, polished, optical disk used to store large amounts of digital information. A CD can store approximately 650 MB of information, equivalent to over 1,700 low-density *floppy disks*. This translates into approximately 300,000 pages of text or 72 minutes of music, all on a single 4.72" disk.

Digital information is stored on the compact disk as a series of microscopic pits and smooth areas that have different reflective properties. A beam of laser light shines on the disk so that the reflections can be detected and converted into digital data.

compatibility The extent to which a given piece of *hardware* or *software* conforms to an accepted standard, regardless of the original manufacturer.

In hardware, compatibility is often expressed in terms of certain other widely accepted models, such as a computer described as IBM-compatible, or a modem as Hayes-compatible. This implies that the device will perform in every way just like the standard device.

In software, compatibility is usually described as the ability to read data file formats created by other vendors' software, or the ability to work together and share data.

complex instruction set computing   Abbreviated CISC, pronounced "sisk." A processor that can recognize and execute well over 100 different *assembly-language* instructions. CISC processors can be very powerful, but there is a price for that power in terms of the number of clock cycles these instructions take to execute.

This is in contrast to *reduced instruction set computing* processors, where the number of available instructions has been cut to a minimum. RISC processors are common in *workstations*, and can be designed to run up to 70 percent faster than CISC processors.

composite video   A method of combining all the elements of video information, including red, blue, and green components, horizontal synchronization, and vertical synchronization, into one signal. Televisions and video recorders require an *NTSC* composite-video signal.

CompuServe   One of the largest and most successful of the commercial online PC information services.

CompuServe provides a tremendous range of information and services, including online *conferences*, hundreds of vendor-specific *forums*, file *downloading*, weather and stock market information, *e-mail* and other messaging services, and travel and entertainment information. CompuServe also offers *Internet* access, as well as access to *USENET newsgroups*.

computation bound   A condition where the speed of operation of the processor actually limits the speed of program execution. The processor is limited by the number of arithmetic operations it must perform.

conditioning step   The step in the EP process where an electrically charged wire (called the charge corona) applies a uniform negative charge to the surface of the EP drum.

conductor   Any material having free electrons that allows electricity to flow.

CONFIG.SYS   In *DOS* and *OS/2*, a special *text file* containing settings that control the way that the *operating system* works. CONFIG.SYS must be located in the root directory of the default *boot* disk, normally drive C, and is read by the operating system only once as the system starts running.

Some *application* programs and *peripheral* devices require you to include special statements in CONFIG.SYS, while other commands may specify the number of disk-read buffers or open files on your system, how the *disk cache* should be configured, or load any special *device drivers* your system may need.

configuration   The process of establishing your own preferred setup for an *application* program or computer system. Configuration information is usually stored in a *configuration file* so that it can be loaded automatically next time you start your computer.

configuration file   A file, created by an *application* program or by the operating system, containing *configuration* information specific to your own computing environment.

Application program configuration files may have a *file-name extension* of CFG or SET; Windows configuration files use the INI filename extension. If you accidentally erase an application's configuration file, the program will return to using its default settings, and so will continue to function, but these settings may not be suitable for your use.

connectivity   In networking, the degree to which any given computer or *application* program can cooperate with other network components, either hardware or software, purchased from other vendors.

connector   Any component that "connects" two devices together. Also, the "slot" that an expansion card fits into.

constant angular velocity   Abbreviated CAV. An unchanging speed of rotation. *Hard disks* use a constant angular velocity encoding scheme, where the disk rotates at a constant rate. This means that *sectors* on the disk are at the maximum density along the inside *track* of the disk; as the *read/write heads* move outwards, the sectors must spread out to cover the increased track circumference, and therefore the *data transfer rate* falls off.

constant linear velocity   Abbreviated CLV. A changing speed of rotation. *CD-ROM disk drives* use a constant linear velocity encoding scheme to make sure that the data density remains constant. Information on a *compact disk* is stored in a single, spiral track, divided into many equal-length segments. To read the data, the CD-ROM disk drive must increase the rotational speed as the read head gets closer to the center of the disk, and decrease as the head moves back out. Typical CD-ROM data access times are in the order of 0.3 to 1.5 seconds; much slower than a *hard disk*.

conventional memory   The amount of memory accessible by *DOS* in PCs using an Intel processor operating in *real mode*, normally the first 640 K. The Intel *8086* and *8088* processors can access 1 MB of memory; the designers of the original *IBM PC* made 640 KB available to the *operating system* and *application* programs, and reserved the remaining space for internal system use, the *BIOS*, and video buffers. 640 KB may not seem like much memory space now, but it was ten times the amount of memory available in other leading personal computers available at the time. Since that time, applications have increased in size to the point where 640 K is woefully inadequate.

convergence   The alignment of the three electron guns (one each for red, blue and green) in a monitor that create the colors you see on the screen. When all three of the electron guns are perfectly aligned and used at full power, the result is pure white. Deviation from this alignment gives poor convergence, leading to white *pixels* showing some color at the edges, and to a decrease in image sharpness and resolution.

cooperative multitasking A form of *multitasking* in which all running *applications* must work together to share system resources. *Microsoft Windows 3.x* supports cooperative multitasking by maintaining a list of the active applications and the order in which they execute. When Windows transfers control to an application, other applications cannot run until that application returns control to Windows once again. Windows' cooperative multitasking system differs from a *preemptive multitasking* system such as that used in *OS/2, Windows 95, Windows NT*, and *Windows 98* where the *operating system* executes each application in turn for a specific period of time before switching to the next application, regardless of whether the applications themselves return control to the operating system.

coprocessor A secondary processor used to speed up operations by taking over a specific part of the main processor's work. The most common type of coprocessor is the math or *floating-point coprocessor*, designed to manage arithmetic calculations many times faster than the main processor.

corona roller Type of transfer corona assembly that uses a charged roller to apply charge to the paper.

corona wire Type of transfer corona assembly. Also, the wire in that assembly that is charged by the high voltage supply. It is narrow in diameter and located in a special notch under the EP print cartridge.

corporate culture Set of unwritten rules that become established over time within the workplace.

CPU (centralized processing unit) Controls and directs all the activities of the computer using both external and internal buses. The "brain" of the computer.

CPU Clock Type of clock signal that dictates how fast the CPU can run.

crash An unexpected program halt, sometimes due to a hardware failure, but most often due to a software error, from which there is no recovery. You will probably have to *reboot* your computer to recover after a crash.

crosstalk Problem related to electromagnetic fields when two wires carrying electrical signals run parallel and one of the wires induces a signal in the second wire. If these wires are carrying data, the extra, unintended signal can cause errors in the communication. Crosstalk is especially a problem in unshielded parallel cables that are longer than ten feet.

CRT Acronym for Cathode-Ray Tube. A display device used in computer monitors and television sets. A CRT display consists of a glass vacuum tube that contains one electron gun for a monochrome display, or three (red, green, and blue) electron guns for a color display. Electron beams from these guns sweep rapidly across the inside of the screen from the upper-left to the lower-right of the screen.

The inside of the screen is coated with thousands of *phosphor* dots that glow when they are struck by the electron beam. To stop the image from flickering, the beams sweep at a rate of between 43 and 87 times per second, depending on the phosphor persistence, and the scanning mode used—*interlaced* or *non-interlaced*. This is known as the *refresh rate* and is measured in Hz. The Video Electronics Standards Association (VESA) recommends a vertical refresh rate of 72 Hz, non-interlaced, at a resolution of 800-by-600 *pixels*.

CSMA/CA (Carrier-Sense Multiple Access with Collision Avoidance)   Media access technology in which the card "listens" to the wire to determine when there is no traffic, sends a small amount of data, and checks to determine if that data transmitted okay before sending the rest of the data. This media access method is most commonly used with the AppleTalk protocol.

CSMA/CD (Carrier-Sense Multiple Access with Collision Detection)   This media access technology tries to detect traffic before it tries to send all its data. If it detects that another machine is transmitting, it will wait until that machine is finished before sending. If no other machine is transmitting, the NIC will send the data. Once the NIC starts transmitting, it "listens" to see if another machine transmitted at the same time (a "collision"). If a collision is detected, both NICs back off for a random period of time and retransmit. This access method is most commonly used with Ethernet.

cylinder   A *hard disk* consists of two or more *platters*, each with two sides. Each side is further divided into concentric circles known as *tracks*; and all the tracks at the same concentric position on a disk are known collectively as a cylinder.

daisy-chaining   Pattern of cabling where the cables run from the first device to the second, second to the third, and so on. If the devices have both an "in" and an "out", the in of the first device of each pair is connected to the out of the second device of each pair.

daisy-wheel printer   An *impact printer* that uses a plastic or metal print mechanism with a different character on the end of each spoke of the wheel. As the print mechanism rotates to the correct letter, a small hammer strikes the character against the ribbon, transferring the image onto the paper. Changing to a different font is a matter of changing the daisy wheel; this means that you cannot change fonts in the middle of a document as you can with a *laser printer.* Daisy-wheel printers have two main drawbacks; they are relatively slow in printing, and they can be very noisy.

data   Information in a form suitable for processing by a computer, such as the *digital* representation of text, numbers, graphic images, or sounds. Strictly speaking, "data" is the plural of the Latin word "datum," meaning an item of information; but it is commonly used in both plural and singular constructions.

data area   In *DOS*, that part of a *floppy disk* or *hard disk* that is available for use after the *boot record, partition table, root directory,* and *file allocation table* have been established by the *formatting* program. This area is the largest part of a disk and is where programs and *data files* are located.

data bits   In asynchronous transmissions, the *bits* that actually comprise the *data;* usually 7 or 8 data bits make up the data word.

data bus   *Bus* used to send and receive data to the microprocessor.

data compression   Any method of encoding *data* so that it occupies less space than in its original form. Many different mathematical techniques can be used, but the overall purpose is to compress the data so that it can be stored, retrieved, or transmitted more efficiently. Data compression is used in facsimile and many other forms of data transmission, CD-ROM publishing, still image and video image manipulation, and *database management systems*.

data encoding scheme   The method used by a *disk controller* to store digital information onto a *hard disk* or *floppy disk*. Common encoding schemes used in the PC world include *modified frequency modulation* (MFM) encoding, *run-length limited* (RLL) encoding, and *advanced run-length limited* (ARLL) encoding.

Data Encryption Standard   Abbreviated DES. A standard method of encrypting and decrypting *data*, developed by the U.S. National Bureau of Standards.

DES is a block cipher that works by a combination of transposition and substitution, and was developed after years of work at IBM, rigorously tested by the National Security Agency, and finally accepted as being free of any mathematical or statistical weaknesses. This suggests that it is impossible to break the system using statistical frequency tables or to work the algorithm backwards using standard mathematical methods. DES has remained unbroken despite years of use; it completely randomizes the information so that it is impossible to determine the encryption key even if some of the original text is known. DES is used by the federal government and most banks and money-transfer systems to protect all sensitive computer information.

data packet   In networking, a unit of information transmitted as a discrete entity from one node on the network to another. More specifically, in *packet-switching networks*, a *packet* is a transmission unit of a fixed maximum length that contains a header, a set of *data*, and error control information.

data transfer rate   The speed at which a *disk drive* can transfer information from the drive to the processor, usually measured in megabits or megabytes per second. For example, a *SCSI* drive can reach a transfer rate of about 5 megabytes per second.

data type
1. The kind of *data* being stored or manipulated. In Paradox for Windows, for example, data types include numeric (numbers), *alphanumeric* (text characters), date, logical (true or false), memo (used for larger pieces of text), formatted memo, short number, currency, *OLE*, graphic, and *binary* (all other types of data). Once the data type has been specified for a *field*, it cannot be changed to another data type, and the type also determines the kind of operation that can be performed on the data. For example, you cannot perform a calculation on alphanumeric data, or separate the digits in a numeric field.

2. In programming, the data type specifies the range of values that a *variable* or *constant* can hold, and how that information is stored in the computer memory. For example, the *floating-point* data type can hold a different range of values from the *integer* data type, and should be manipulated differently; and the character or *string* data type is different again.

data-link layer   The second of seven layers of the *International Standards Organization*'s Open Systems Interconnection (ISO/OSI) model for computer-to-computer communications. The data-link layer validates the integrity of the flow of *data* from one node to another by synchronizing blocks of data, and by controlling the flow of data.

daughter board   A *printed circuit board* that attaches to another board to provide additional functions. For example, a multimedia PC *video adapter* may accept a *frame grabber* daughter board to add *freeze-frame* video processing.

DB connector   Any of several types of cable connectors used for *parallel* or *serial* cables. The number following the letters DB (for data bus) indicates the number of pins that the connector usually has; a DB-25 connector can have up to 25 pins, and a DB-9 connector up to 9. In practice, not all the pins (and not all the lines in the cable) may be present in the larger connectors. If your situation demands, for example, that all 25 lines of a serial cable be present, make sure you buy the right cable. Common DB connectors include DB-9, DB-15, DB-19, DB-25, DB-37, and DB-50.

DC-2000   A quarter-inch tape minicartridge used in some tape backup systems with a capacity of up to 250 MB when some form of *data compression* is used.

DCE   Abbreviation for Data Communications Equipment. In communications, any device that connects a computer or terminal to a communications channel or public network, usually a *modem*.

DCI   Abbreviation for Display Control Interface. A device-driver specification from Intel and Microsoft intended to speed up video playback in Microsoft Windows.

For this device driver to work, your hardware must support DCI; if it does, a Windows application can send video information directly to the screen and so bypass any holdups in the Windows *graphics device interface* (GDI).

Multimedia applications and programs that manage digital video can benefit from using DCI.

debouncing   A keyboard feature that eliminates unintended triggering of keystrokes. It works by having the keyboard controller constantly scan the keyboard for keystrokes. Only keystrokes that are pressed for more than two scans are considered keystrokes. This prevents spurious electronic signals from generating input.

DEC Alpha chip   A 64-bit *microprocessor* from Digital Equipment Corporation (DEC), introduced in 1992. The Alpha is a *superscalar* design, which allows the processor to execute more than one instruction per clock cycle. It has both an 8K data and an 8K instruction cache, and a *floating point processor.* Equivalent to 1.68 million transistors, the fastest Alpha at the time of this writing runs at an incredible 500 MHz.

decibel   Abbreviated dB. One tenth of a bel, a unit of measurement common in electronics that quantifies the loudness or strength of a signal.

decimal   The base-10 numbering system that uses the familiar numbers 0–9.

dedicated line   A communications circuit used for one specific purpose.

dedicated server   Server that is assigned to perform a specific application or service (for example, a mail server or a print server).

defragmentation   The process of reorganizing and rewriting *files* so that they occupy one large continuous area on your hard disk rather than several smaller areas.

When a file on your hard disk is updated, especially over a long period of time, it may be written into different areas all over the disk. This *file fragmentation* can lead to significant delays in loading files, but its effect can be reversed by defragmentation. The *Norton Utilities* and *PC Tools* packages both contain excellent defragmentation programs.

defragmenter   Any *utility* program that rewrites all the parts of a *file* into contiguous *clusters* on a hard disk. As you update your *data files* over time, they may become fragmented, or divided up into several widely-spaced pieces. This can slow down data retrieval if the problem becomes severe. Using a defragmenter (such as the *DOS* 6 utility *DEFRAG*) can restore that lost performance.

demand paging   A common form of *virtual memory* management where pages of information are read into memory from disk only when required by the program.

device   A general term used to describe any computer *peripheral* or *hardware* element that can send or receive *data*. For example, modems, printers, serial ports, disk drives, and monitors are all referred to as devices. Some devices may require special software, known as a *device driver*, to control or manage them.

device driver   A small program that allows a computer to communicate with and control a *device*. Each *operating system* contains a standard set of device drivers for the keyboard, the monitor, and so on, but if you add specialized *peripherals* such as a *CD-ROM disk drive*, or a *network interface card*, you will probably have to add the appropriate device driver so that the operating system knows how to manage the device. In *DOS*, device drivers are loaded by the *DEVICE* or *DEVICEHIGH* commands in *CONFIG.SYS*.

device name   The name used by the *operating system* to identify a computer-system component. For example, LPT1 is the *DOS* device name for the first *parallel port*.

device-dependence   The requirement that a specific hardware component be present for a program to work. Device-dependent *software* is often very difficult to move or *port* to another computer due to this reliance on specific hardware.

device-independence   The ability to produce similar results in a wide variety of environments, without requiring the presence of specific hardware.

The *Unix operating system* and the *PostScript page-description language* are both examples of device-independence. Unix runs on a wide range of computers, from the PC to a *Cray*, and PostScript is used by many different printer manufacturers.

diagnostic program   A program that tests computer *hardware* and *peripherals* for correct operation. In the PC, some faults are easy to find, and these are known as "hard faults"; the diagnostic program will diagnose them correctly every time. Others, such as memory faults, can be difficult to find; these are called "soft faults" because they do not occur every time the memory location is tested, but only under very specific circumstances.

Most PCs run a simple set of system checks when the computer is first turned on; in the IBM world these tests are stored in *ROM,* and are known as the *power-on self-tests* (POST). If the POST detects an error condition, the computer will stop, and you will see an error message on the screen. *DOS* 6 also includes the *Microsoft Diagnostics* program (MSD) for more complete system testing.

digital   Describes any device that represents values in the form of *binary* digits.

digital audio   Analog sound waves stored in a digital form; each digital audio file can be decomposed into a series of samples.

digital audio tape   Abbreviated DAT. A method of recording information in digital form on a small audio tape cassette, originally developed by Sony and *Hewlett-Packard.* Over a gigabyte of information can be recorded on a cassette, and so a DAT can be used as a backup media. Like all tape devices, however, DATs are relatively slow.

digital signal   A signal that consists of discrete values. These values do not change over time; in effect, they change instantly from one value to another.

Digital Video Interactive   Abbreviated DVI. A proprietary technique from *Intel Corporation* used to store highly compressed, *full-motion video* information onto compact discs.

DVI is usually available as a chip set, and uses a form of compression that saves only the changes between images, rather than saving each individual frame. This form of *data compression* can reduce memory requirements by a factor of 100 or more.

On a CD-ROM, DVI provides over 70 minutes of full-screen video, 2 hours of half-screen video, 40,000 medium-resolution images, or 7,000 *high-resolution* images.

digital-to-analog converter   Abbreviated DAC or D-A converter. A device that converts discrete digital information into a continuously varying *analog* signal.

Many modern *sound boards* can sample and play back at up to 44.1 KHz using a *16-bit* digital-to-analog converter that produces spectacular stereo sound. *Compact disc* players use a digital-to-analog converter to convert the digital signals read from the disc to the analog signal that you hear as music.

DIMM (Dual In-Line Memory Module)   Memory module that is similar to a SIMM (Single In-Line Memory Module), except that a DIMM is double-sided: there are memory chips on both sides of the memory module.

DIN-*n*   Circular type of connector used with computers. (The *n* represents the number of connectors.)

DIP (Dual In-Line Package)   Package for integrated circuits containing two rows of pins (usually black with markings on top to indicate their manufacturer and purpose). Most commonly used for memory chips.

DIP switch   A small switch used to select the operating mode of a *device*, mounted as a *dual in-line package*. DIP switches can be either sliding or rocker switches, and are often grouped together for convenience. They are used on *printed circuit boards*, *dot-matrix printers*, *modems*, and other *peripherals*.

direct access storage device   Abbreviated DASD, pronounced "daz-dee." A storage device such as a *hard disk*, whose *data* can be accessed directly, without having to read all the preceding data (as with a sequential device such as a tape drive).

direct current   Abbreviated DC. Electrical current that travels in one direction only and does not reverse the direction of flow. The PC's *power supply* converts AC line voltage from a wall outlet into the various DC voltages that the internal components of the computer need to operate.

direct memory access   Abbreviated DMA. A method of transferring information directly from a mass-storage device such as a *hard disk* or from an adapter card into *memory (or vice versa)*, without the information passing through the processor. Because the processor is not involved in the transfer, direct memory access is usually very fast.

DMA transfers are controlled by a special chip known as a DMA controller; the 8237A (or its equivalent) is used in most PCs. Generally, most PCs use two of these chips to provide eight DMA channels, numbered 0 through 7; only seven of these channels are available, as channel 4 is used to connect—or cascade—the two controllers together. Channels 0 through 3 are 8-bit channels, and can manage up to 64K of data in a single

DMA operation; channels 5 through 7 transfer data 16 bits at a time and can manage up to 128 K of data. Channel 3 is reserved for the floppy disk drive controller, and channel 5 is used by the hard-disk controller in PS/2 systems.

discrete component   Any electronic component or *hardware device* that can be treated as a separate and distinct unit.

disk cache   Pronounced "disk cash." An area of computer memory where *data* is temporarily stored on its way to or from a disk.

When an *application* needs *data* from a hard disk, it asks the operating system to find it. The data is read and passed back to the application. Under certain circumstances, such as when updating a database, the same information may be requested and read many times over. A disk cache mediates between the application and the hard disk, and when an application asks for information from the hard disk, the cache program first checks to see if that data is already in the cache memory. If it is, the disk cache program loads the information from the cache memory rather than from the hard disk. If the information is not in memory, the cache program reads the data from the disk, copies it into the cache memory for future reference, and then passes the data to the requesting application.

A disk cache program can significantly speed up most disk operations. *DOS* contains the disk cache driver *SMARTDRV.SYS*, and *OS/2* provides *CACHE* if you are using the *high performance file system*, or *DISKCACHE* if you are using the *file allocation table* system. Disk cache programs are also available from other third-party sources.

disk capacity The storage capacity of a *hard* or *floppy disk*, usually stated in kilobytes (KB or K), megabytes (MB), or gigabytes (GB).

disk controller The electronic circuitry that controls and manages the operation of *floppy* or *hard disks* installed in the computer.

A single disk controller may manage more than one hard disk; many disk controllers also manage floppy disks and compatible tape drives. In the *Macintosh*, the disk controller is built into the system. In IBM-compatible computers it may be a *printed-circuit board* inserted into the *expansion bus*, or may be part of the hard disk drive itself as in the case of an *IDE* drive.

disk drive A *peripheral* storage *device* that reads and writes magnetic or optical disks. When more than one disk drive is installed on a computer, the *operating system* assigns each drive a unique name—for example *A:* and *C:* in *DOS, Windows,* and *OS/2*.

Three types of disk drive are in common use; *floppy-disk* drives, *hard-disk* drives, and compact-disc drives. Floppy-disk drives accept removable 5.25″ or 3.5″ media. Hard-disk drives usually have much greater capacity and are considerably faster than floppy-disk drives, and they are contained inside a protective sealed case. Compact-disc drives can be either internal or external to the system unit, and accept compact discs loaded in special *caddies*.

disk duplexing In networking, a *fault-tolerant* technique that writes the same information simultaneously onto two different *hard disks*. Each of the hard disks uses a different *disk controller* to provide greater redundancy. In the event of one disk or disk controller failing, information from the other system can be used to continue operations. Disk duplexing is offered by most of the major *network operating systems*, and is designed to protect the system against a single disk failure; it is not designed to protect against multiple disk failures, and is no substitute for a well-planned series of disk *backups*.

disk mirroring In networking, a *fault-tolerant* technique that writes the same information simultaneously onto two different *hard disks*, using the same *disk controller*. In the event of one disk failing, information from the other can be used to continue operations. Disk mirroring is offered by most of the major *network operating systems*, and is designed to protect the system against a single disk failure; it is not designed to protect against multiple disk failures and is no substitute for a well-planned series of disk *backups*.

disk optimizer A utility program that rearranges *files* and *directories* on a disk for optimum performance.

As you work with files on your *hard disk*, over time they may become fragmented, or broken up into several small pieces. By fragmenting files, the operating system makes better use of the disk space available.

The problem with *file fragmentation* is that the disk heads have to move to different locations on the disk to read or write to a fragmented file. This takes more time than reading the file as a single piece. By reducing or eliminating file fragmentation, you can restore the original level of performance of your disk system. Also, it is usually easier to unerase an unfragmented file than it is to recover a badly fragmented file.

diskette   An easily removable and portable "floppy" disk that is 3.5" in diameter and enclosed in a durable plastic case that has a metal shutter over the media access window.

diskless workstation   A networked computer that does not have any *local disk* storage capability.

The computer boots up and loads all its programs from the network *file server*. Diskless workstations are particularly valuable when very sensitive information is processed; information cannot be copied from the file server onto a local disk, because there isn't one.

distributed processing   A computer system in which processing is performed by several separate computers linked by a communications network. The term often refers to any computer system supported by a network, but more properly refers to a system in which each computer is chosen to handle a specific workload, and the network supports the system as a whole.

DMA (Direct Memory Access)   Feature of a bus that allows devices to bypass the processor and write their information directly into main memory.

DMA channels   Dedicated lines that make DMA possible.

DMI   Abbreviation for Desktop Management Interface. A standard method of identifying PC hardware and software components automatically, without input from the user.

At minimum, DMI will identify the manufacturer, product name, serial number, and installation time and date of any component installed in a PC. DMI is backed by Digital Equipment Corporation, IBM, Intel, Microsoft, Novell, Sun, and more than 300 other vendors.

DNS   Abbreviation for Domain Name System. The method used when naming Internet *host* computers, and the directory services used when looking up those names. Each of these host names (such as pd.zevon.com) corresponds to a long decimal number known as the IP address (such as 199.10.44.8). These *domain names* are much easier to remember than the long IP addresses.

docking station   A hardware system into which a *portable computer* fits so that it can be used as a full-fledged desktop computer.

Docking stations vary from simple port replicators that allow you access to parallel and serial ports and a mouse, to complete systems that give you access to network connections, CD-ROMs, even a tape backup system or *PCMCIA* ports.

domain   The general category that a computer on the Internet belongs to. The most common high-level domains are:

   .com: a commercial organization

   .edu: an educational establishment

   .gov: a branch of the U.S. government

   .int: an international organization

   .mil: a branch of the U.S. military

   .net: a network

   .org: a non-profit organization

Most countries also have unique domains named after their international abbreviation. For example, .UK for the United Kingdom and .CA for Canada.

domain name   The easy-to-understand name given to an *Internet* host computer, as opposed to the numerical IP address.

DOS

1. Acronym for Disk Operating System, an *operating system* originally developed by *Microsoft* for the *IBM PC*. DOS exists in two very similar versions; *MS-DOS*, developed and marketed by Microsoft for use with *IBM-compatible* computers, and *PC-DOS*, supported and sold by IBM for use only on computers manufactured by IBM.

2. A DOS *CONFIG.SYS* command that loads the *operating system* into *conventional memory*, *extended memory*, or into *upper memory blocks* on computers using the Intel *80386* or later processor. To use this command, you must have previously loaded the *HIMEM.SYS device driver* with the *DEVICE* command in CONFIG.SYS.

DOS extender Program that allows certain programs to switch the processor to protected mode and access the memory above 1 megabyte—for example, MS-DOS's HIMEM.SYS.

DOS prompt A visual confirmation that the *DOS operating system* is ready to receive input from the keyboard. The default prompt includes the *current drive* letter followed by a greater-than symbol; for example, C>. You can create your own custom prompt with the PROMPT command.

dot pitch In a monitor, the vertical distance between the centers of like-colored phosphors on the screen of a color monitor, measured in millimeters (mm). As the dot pitch becomes smaller, the finer detail appears on the screen; straight lines appear sharper, and colors more vivid. Today's monitors often have a dot pitch of between 0.31 mm and 0.28 mm.

dot-matrix printer An *impact printer* that uses columns of small pins and an inked ribbon to create the tiny pattern of dots that form the characters. Dot-matrix printers are available in 9-, 18-, or 24-pin configurations, but they are very noisy and produce relatively low quality output.

dots per inch Abbreviated dpi. A measure of resolution expressed by the number of dots that a device can print or display in one inch. *Laser printers* can print at 300 or 600 dpi, while *Linotronic* laser imagesetters can print at resolutions of 1270 or 2450 dpi.

double-density disk A floppy disk with a storage capacity of 360 KB (twice the recording density and capacity of the earliest 5.25" floppy disks, which held only 180 KB). The name is now somewhat misleading, as 360 KB is the smallest disk capacity currently available.

downloading utility A utility program used to download font information from your *hard disk* into your printer's memory so that you can use the font. Many word processing and page layout programs can also download font information into the printer.

drawing tablet Pointing device that includes a pencil-like device (called a stylus) for drawing on its flat rubber-coated sheet of plastic.

drift In a monitor, any unwanted motion or undulation in a line drawn on the screen.

drive bay An opening in the *system unit* into which you can install a floppy disk drive, hard disk drive, or tape drive. Modern computers usually accommodate *half-height drive* bays.

drive geometry   Term used to describe the number of cylinders, read/write heads, and sectors in a hard disk.

drive hole   Hole in a floppy disk that is allows the motor in the disk drive to spin the disk. Also known as the hub hole.

drive letter   In *DOS, Windows,* and *OS/2,* a designation used to specify a particular hard or floppy disk. For example, the first floppy disk is usually referred to as drive A, and the first hard disk as drive C.

driver   See *device driver*

D-Shell   See *DB-nn connectors*

D-Sub   See *DB-nn connectors*

DSP   Abbreviation for Digital Signal Processor. A specialized high-speed chip, used for data manipulation in sound cards, communications adapters, video and image manipulation, and other data-acquisition processes where speed is essential.

DSR   Abbreviation for *data set* ready. A *hardware* signal defined by the *RS-232-C* standard to indicate that the device is ready.

DTE   Abbreviation for Data Terminal Equipment. In communications, any device, such as a terminal or a computer, connected to a communications channel or public network.

DTR   Abbreviation for data terminal ready. A *hardware* signal defined by the *RS-232-C* standard to indicate that the computer is ready to accept a transmission.

dual in-line package   Abbreviated DIP. A standard housing constructed of hard plastic commonly used to hold an *integrated circuit.* The circuit's leads are connected to two parallel rows of pins designed to fit snugly into a socket; these pins may also be soldered directly to a *printed-circuit board.* If you try to install or remove dual in-line packages, be careful not to bend or damage their pins.

dumb terminal   A combination of keyboard and screen that has no local computing power, used to input information to a large, remote computer, often a minicomputer or a mainframe. This remote computer provides all the processing power for the system.

duplex   In asynchronous transmissions, the ability to transmit and receive on the same channel at the same time; also referred to as full duplex. Half-duplex channels can transmit only or receive only.

Most dial-up services available to PC users take advantage of full-duplex capabilities, but if you cannot see what you are typing, switch to half duplex. If you are using half duplex and you can see two of every character you type, change to full duplex.

duplex printing   Printing a document on both sides of the page so that the appropriate pages face each other when the document is bound.

Dvorak keyboard   Pronounced "di-vor-ack." A keyboard layout invented by August Dvorak in 1936 as a faster alternative to the *QWERTY* typewriter keyboard. The Dvorak keyboard groups all vowels and punctuation marks on the left side of the keyboard, and common consonants together on the right. Studies have shown that typists make 70 percent of all keystrokes on the second or home row on the Dvorak keyboard compared with 32 percent on the QWERTY keyboard. The Dvorak keyboard, in spite of its advantages, has not found wide acceptance, mostly because of the retraining costs involved in switching.

DX4 A 32-bit chip, based on the *80486*, from Intel. Despite the name, the DX4 is not a clock-quadrupled chip; it is a clock-tripled chip. For example, the 75-MHz version of the chip completes three CPU cycles for each cycle of the 25 MHz motherboard. The DX4 is available in 75, 83, and 100 MHz versions, and fills the performance gap between the existing chips in the 80486 set and the Pentium processor.

Dynamic electricity See *electricity*

dynamic link library Abbreviated DLL. A program module that contains executable code and *data* that can be used by *application* programs, or even by other DLLs, in performing a specific task.

The DLL is linked into the application only when you run the program, and it is unloaded again when no longer needed. This means that if two DLL applications are running at the same time, and both of them perform a particular function, only one copy of the code for that function is loaded, making for a more efficient use of limited memory. Another benefit of using dynamic linking is that *.EXE* files are not as large, since frequently used routines can be put into a DLL rather than repeated in each EXE that uses them. This results in saved disk space and faster program loading.

DLLs are used extensively in *Microsoft Windows, OS/2*, and in *Windows NT*. DLLs may have *filename extensions* of .DLL, .DRV, or .FON.

dynamic RAM Abbreviated DRAM, pronounced "dee-ram." A common type of computer memory that uses capacitors and transistors storing electrical charges to represent memory states. These capacitors lose their electrical charge, and so need to be refreshed every millisecond, during which time they cannot be read by the processor.

DRAM chips are small, simple, cheap, easy to make, and hold approximately four times as much information as a *static RAM* (SRAM) chip of similar complexity. However, they are slower than static RAM. Processors operating at *clock speeds* of 25 MHz or more need DRAM with access times of faster than 80 nanoseconds (80 billionths of a second), while SRAM chips can be read in as little as 15 to 30 nanoseconds.

edge connector A form of connector consisting of a row of etched contacts along the edge of a *printed circuit board* that is inserted into an *expansion slot* in the computer.

EEPROM Acronym for Electrically Erasable Programmable Read-Only Memory, pronounced "ee-ee-prom," or "double-ee-prom." A memory chip that maintains its contents without electrical power, and whose contents can be erased and reprogrammed either within the computer or from an external source. EEPROMS are used where the application requires stable storage without power, but where the chip may have to be reprogrammed.

EGA   Acronym for Enhanced Graphics Adapter. A *video adapter* standard that provides medium-resolution text and graphics, introduced by IBM in 1984. EGA can display 16 colors at the same time from a choice of 64, with a horizontal resolution of 640 *pixels* and a vertical resolution of 350 pixels. EGA has been superseded by *VGA* and *SVGA*.

EISA   Acronym for Extended Industry Standard Architecture, pronounced "ee-sah." A PC *bus* standard that extends the traditional *AT-bus* to 32 bits and allows more than one processor to share the bus.

EISA was developed by the so-called Gang of Nine (AST Research, *Compaq Computer Corporation*, *Epson*, *Hewlett-Packard*, NEC, Olivetti, *Tandy*, Wyse Technology, and Zenith Data Systems) in 1988 in reply to IBM's introduction of their proprietary *Micro Channel architecture* (MCA).

EISA maintains compatibility with the earlier *Industry Standard Architecture* (ISA), and also provides for additional features introduced by IBM in the MCA standard. EISA accepts ISA *expansion cards*, and so, unlike the Micro Channel architecture, is compatible with earlier systems.

EISA has a 32-bit data path, and at a bus speed of 8 MHz, can achieve a maximum throughput of 33 megabytes per second.

electricity   The flow of free electrons from one molecule of substance to another. This flow of electrons is used to do work.

electromagnetic drawing tablets   Type of drawing tablet that has grids of wires underneath the rubberized surface. The stylus contains a small sensor that is sensitive to electromagnetic fields. At timed intervals, an electromagnetic pulse is sent across the grid. The sensor in the stylus picks up these pulses.

electromagnetic interference   Abbreviated EMI. Any electromagnetic radiation released by an electronic *device* that disrupts the operation or performance of any other device.

electron gun   The device that shoots electrons toward the back side of the monitor screen.

electrostatic discharge (ESD)   When two objects of dissimilar charge come in contact with one another, they will exchange electrons in order to standardize the electrostatic charge between the two objects. This exchange, or discharge, can sometimes be seen as a spark or arc of electricity. Even when it cannot be seen it is damaging to electronic components.

electrostatic plotter   A *raster device* in which special paper or film is charged as it passes a row of electrodes, and then toner is added to create the image. Electrostatic plotters can create black-and-white or color output, and those used in the automotive industry are capable of producing output on paper up to 6 feet wide.

e-mail   Also called electronic mail. The use of a network to transmit text messages, memos, and reports. Users can send a message to one or more individual users, to a predefined group, or to all users on the system. When you receive a message, you can read, print, forward, answer, or delete it.

emulator   A *device* built to work exactly like another device, either *hardware*, *software*, or a combination of both. For example, a *terminal emulation* program lets a PC pretend to be a terminal attached to a *mainframe computer* or to certain of the online services or *bulletin boards* by providing the *control codes* that the remote system expects to see.

Encapsulated PostScript Abbreviated EPS. The *file* format of the *PostScript page description language*. The EPS standard is *device independent*, so that images can easily be transferred between different *applications*, and they can be sized and output to different printers without any loss of image quality or distortion. Many high-quality *clip art* packages store images in EPS form.

The EPS file contains the PostScript commands needed to recreate the image, but the image itself cannot be displayed on a monitor unless the file also contains an optional preview image stored in *TIFF* or *PICT* format.

The EPS file can only be printed on a PostScript-compatible *laser* printer, and the printer itself determines the final printing resolution; a laser printer might be capable of 300 *dpi*, whereas a *Linotronic* printer is capable of 2450 dpi.

encoding Process by which binary information is changed into flux transition patterns on a disk surface.

encryption The process of encoding information in an attempt to make it secure from unauthorized access. The reverse of this process is known as decryption.

One of the most popular encryption programs is Pretty Good Privacy (PGP), written by Phil Zimmermann, available at no charge from certain Internet sites.

end user During the mainframe computer era, the end user was always a person who received output from the computer, and used that output in their work. They rarely, if ever, even saw the computer, much less learned to use it themselves.

Today, the term more often refers to the person who uses the *application* program to produce their own results. End users today often write *macros* to automate complex or repetitive tasks, and sometimes write procedures using command languages.

Enhanced Expanded Memory Specification Abbreviated EEMS. A revised version (4.0) of the original Lotus-Intel-Microsoft *Expanded Memory Specification* (LIM EMS), that lets DOS *applications* use more than 640 KB of memory space.

enhanced keyboard A 101- or 102-key keyboard introduced by IBM that has become the accepted standard for PC keyboard layout. Unlike earlier keyboards, it has 12 *function keys* across the top, rather than 10 function keys in a block on the left side, has extra *Ctrl* and *Alt* keys, and has a set of *cursor control keys* between the main keyboard and the numeric keypad.

Enhanced Small Device Interface Abbreviated ESDI. A popular *hard disk, floppy disk*, and tape drive interface standard, capable of a *data transfer rate* of 10 to 20 megabits per second. ESDI is most often used with large hard disks.

enterprise A term used to encompass an entire business group, organization, or corporation, including all local, remote, and satellite offices. Most often used with reference to large networked systems.

entry-level system A computer system that meets the basic requirements for a specific task. As computers become both cheaper and more capable, the definition of an entry-level system changes. Also, *application* developers continue to create new and more complex programs, which in turn demand more capability from the *hardware*.

EP print drum Device that is coated with a photosensitive material that can hold a static charge when not exposed to light. The drum contains a cleaning blade that continuously scrapes the used toner off the photosensitive drum to keep it clean.

EP printer (ElectroPhotographic printer) Printer that uses high voltage, a laser, and a black carbon toner to form an image on a page.

EP printer process Six-step process an EP laser printer uses to form images on paper. The steps, in order, are: charging, exposing, developing, transfer, fusing, and cleaning.

EPROM Acronym for erasable programmable read-only memory, pronounced "ee-prom." A memory chip that maintains its contents without electrical power, and whose contents can be erased and reprogrammed by removing a protective cover and exposing the chip to ultraviolet light.

erasable CD A standard format for an erasable CD which allows users to store and revise large amounts of data.

The standard is supported by Sony, Phillips, IBM, Hewlett-Packard, and other leading companies. One of the major advantages of this new standard is that it is completely compatible with existing compact discs, and makers of *CD-ROM disk drives* only have to make minor manufacturing changes to existing drives to meet the standard.

ergonomics Standards that define the positioning and use of the body to promote a healthy work environment.

error The difference between the expected and the actual. In computing, an error is not necessarily the same as a mistake, but is often the way that the computer reports unexpected, unusual, impossible, or illegal events. Errors range from trivial, like a disk drive that does not contain a disk, to fatal, as when a serious operating system bug renders the system useless.

error detection and correction A mechanism used during a *file* transfer to determine whether transmission errors have occurred, and to correct those errors, if possible. Some programs or transmission protocols request a retransmission of the affected block of *data* if such an error is detected. More complex protocols attempt to both detect and correct transmission errors.

error message A message from the program or the operating system, informing you of a condition that requires some human intervention to solve.

Error messages can indicate relatively trivial problems, like a disk drive that does not contain a disk, all the way to fatal problems, as when a serious operating system bug renders the system useless and requires a system restart.

ESD mat Preventive measure to guard against the effects of ESD. The excess charge is drained away from any item that comes in contact with it.

even parity A technique that counts the number of 1s in a binary number and, if the number of 1s total is not an even number, adds a digit to make it even. (See also *parity*)

exa-   Abbreviated E. A prefix meaning one quintillion, 10 to the 18th power. In computing, this translates into 1,152,921,504,606,846,976; the power of 2 closest to one quintillion (10 to the 60th power).

exabyte   Abbreviated EB. 1 quintillion bytes, or 1,152,921,504,606,846,976 bytes.

exit roller   Found on laser and page printers, the mechanism that guides the paper out of the printer into the paper-receiving tray.

expandability   The ability of a system to accommodate expansion. In *hardware*, this may include the addition of more memory, more or larger disk drives, and new adapters, and in *software* may include the ability of a network to add users, nodes, or connections to other networks.

expanded memory   A *DOS* mechanism by which *applications* can access more than the 640 KB of *memory* normally available to them.

The original IBM PC, based on Intel's 8088/8086 CPU, limited memory access to the first 640 K. A collaboration of Lotus, Intel, and Microsoft developed a technique for adding memory above the 640K limitation. A specification called the LIM Expanded Memory Specification, EMS, allowed applications to get around the current memory limitation by inserting a memory card into the PC. This memory card could store up to 32 MB of memory. There were two versions of the specification, LIM 3.2 and then LIM 4.0.

DPMI, the DOS Protect Mode Interface developed by Microsoft and used in Windows 3.x, Windows 95, and Windows NT, is the standard that applications use today.

expanded memory specification   Abbreviated EMS. The original version of the Lotus-Intel-Microsoft Expanded Memory Specification (LIM EMS), that lets DOS applications use more than 640 KB of memory space.

expansion bus   An extension of the main computer *bus* that includes *expansion slots* for use by compatible *adapters*, such as including memory boards, video adapters, hard disk controllers, and SCSI interface cards.

expansion card   A device that can be installed into a computer's expansion bus.

expansion slot   One of the connectors on the *expansion bus* that gives an *adapter* access to the system bus. You can add as many additional adapters as there are expansion slots inside your computer.

expansion unit   An external housing available with certain portable computers designed to contain additional *expansion slots* and maintain a connection to the main *expansion bus* in the computer's system unit.

exposing step   Second step in the EP print process. In this step, the laser turns on and shines on a section of the charged photosensitive drum. The laser scans from left to right, flashing on and off, reducing areas of the photosensitive drum's charge to a slight negative charge. As the drum rotates, a pattern of exposed areas are formed representing images to be printed.

extended ASCII character set   The second part of the *ASCII character set* from decimal code 128 to decimal code 255. This part of the ASCII character set is not standard, and will contain different characters on different types of computer. In IBM-compatible computers, it includes special mathematical symbols and characters from the PC line-drawing set. The Apple extended ASCII character set uses a different set of characters.

extended DOS partition   A further optional division of a hard disk, after the *primary DOS partition*, that functions as one or more additional *logical* drives. A logical drive is simply an area of a larger disk that acts as though it were a separate disk with its own *drive letter*. Creating an extended partition allows you to install a second operating system, such as OS/2; and in early DOS versions it is the only way to use disk space above 32 MB.

DOS partitions are created and changed using the *FDISK* command.

extended memory   Memory beyond 1 MB on computers using the Intel *80386* and later processors, not configured for *expanded memory*.

Computers based on the Intel *8086* and *8088* processors can only access 1 MB of memory, of which 640 KB is available for application programs, and the remaining 384 KB is reserved for *DOS*, the *BIOS*, and video settings.

Later processors can access more memory, but it was the *80386* with its ability to address 4 GB of memory that really made extended memory usable, along with the Windows memory manager *HIMEM.SYS* that lets Windows use all of the extended memory installed in your computer.

extended memory manager   A *device driver* that supports the *software* portion of the *extended memory specification* in an IBM-compatible computer.

extended memory specification   Abbreviated XMS. A standard developed by Microsoft, Intel, Lotus, and AST Research that has become the preferred way of accessing *extended memory* in the PC. *DOS* and Windows include the extended memory *device driver* HIMEM.SYS, and this command or an equivalent must be present in your *CONFIG.SYS file* before you can access extended memory successfully.

external bus   An external component connected though expansion cards and slots allows the processor to talk to other devices. This component allows the CPU to talk to the other devices in the computer and vice versa.

external cache memory   Separate expansion board that installs in a special processor-direct bus that contains cache memory.

external hard disk   A *hard disk* packaged in its own case, with cables and an independent power supply, rather than a disk drive housed inside and integrated with the computer's system unit.

external modem   A stand-alone modem, separate from the computer and connected by a serial cable. LEDs on the front of the chassis indicate the current modem status, and can be useful in troubleshooting communications problems. An external modem is a good buy if you want to use a modem with different computers at different times, or with different types of computer.

extremely low-frequency emission Abbreviated ELF. Radiation emitted by a computer monitor and other very common household electrical appliances such as televisions, hair dryers, electric blankets and food processors.

ELF emissions fall into the range from 5 Hz to 2000 Hz, and decline with the square of the distance from the source. Emissions are not constant around a monitor; they are higher from the sides and rear, and weakest from the front of the screen. Low-emission models are available, and *laptop computers* with an *LCD* display do not emit any ELF fields.

FAQ Abbreviation for frequently asked questions, pronounced "fack." A document, maintained as part of a newsgroup or Web site, that contains answers to questions that newcomers to the topic most often ask.

FAQs are posted to the newsgroup on a regular basis, weekly or monthly, and some grow so large that they are divided into sections; the designation 1/4 indicates that this section is the first of a total of four sections.

Also, a document like this for any group or software package.

fatal error An *operating system* or *application* program error from which there is no hope of recovery without rebooting (and thus losing any unsaved work).

fault tolerance A design method that ensures continued system operation in the event of individual failures by providing redundant elements.

At the component level, designers include redundant chips and circuits and add the capability to bypass faults automatically. At the computer system level, they replicate any elements likely to fail, such as processors and large disk drives.

Fault-tolerant operations often require backup or *UPS* power systems in the event of a main power failure, and may imply the duplication of entire computer systems in remote locations to protect against vandalism, acts of war, or natural disaster.

fax Abbreviation for facsimile. The electronic transmission of copies of documents for reproduction at a remote location.

The sending fax machine scans a paper image and converts the image into a form suitable for transmission over a telephone line. The receiving fax machine decodes and prints a copy of the original image. Each fax machine includes a scanner, fax modem, and printer.

fax modem An adapter that fits into a PC expansion slot providing many of the capabilities of a full-sized *fax* machine, but at a fraction of the cost.

FCC Acronym for Federal Communications Commission. A U.S. government regulatory body for radio, television, all interstate telecommunications services, and all international services that originate inside the U.S.

All computer equipment must be certified by the FCC before it can be offered for sale in the U.S. to ensure that it meets the legal limits for conductive and radio frequency emissions, which could otherwise interfere with commercial broadcasts.

FCC certification   Approval by the FCC that a specific computer model meets its standards for *radio frequency interference* emissions.

There are two levels of certification. *Class A* certification is for computers used in commercial settings, such as mainframes and minicomputers, and the more stringent *Class B* certification is for computers used in the home and in home offices, such as PCs, laptops, and portables.

female connector   Any cable connector with receptacles designed to receive the pins on the male part of the connector.

fiber distributed data interface   Abbreviated FDDI. A specification for fiber-optic networks transmitting at a speed of up to 100 megabits per second over a dual, counter-rotating, *token-ring* topology. FDDI is suited to systems that require the transfer of very large amounts of information, such as medical imaging, 3-D seismic processing, oil reservoir simulation, and full-motion video.

fiber optic cable   A transmission technology that sends pulses of light along specially manufactured optical fibers. Each fiber consists of a core, thinner than a human hair, surrounded by a sheath with a much lower refractive index. Light signals introduced at one end of the cable are conducted along the cable as the signals are reflected from the sheath.

Fiber optic cable is lighter and smaller than traditional copper cable, is immune to electrical interference, and has better signal-transmitting qualities. However, it is more expensive than traditional cables and more difficult to repair.

file   A named collection of *data* stored on disk, appearing to the user as a single entity. A file can contain a program or part of a program, may be a *data file*, or can contain a user-created document. Files may actually be fragmented or stored in many different places across the disk; the *operating system* manages the task of locating all the pieces when the file is read.

file allocation table   Abbreviated FAT, pronounced "fat." A table maintained by the *DOS* or *OS/2 operating systems* that lists all the *clusters* available on a disk. The FAT includes the location of each cluster, as well as whether it is in use, available for use, or damaged in some way and therefore unavailable.

Because files are not necessarily stored in consecutive clusters on a disk, but can be scattered all over the disk, the FAT also keeps track of which pieces belong to which *file*.

OS/2 supports a compatible version of the DOS FAT, sometimes known as the SuperFAT, which adds *32-bit* capabilities to increase speed, access to *OS/2 extended attributes*, and a free-space bitmap which results in much reduced allocation times.

file compression program   An *application* program that shrinks program or *data files*, so that they occupy less disk space. The file must then be extracted or decompressed before you can use it.

Many of the most popular file compression programs are *shareware*, like WinZIP, PKZIP, LHA, and StuffIt for the *Macintosh*, although utility packages like *PC Tools* from Central Point Software also contain file compression programs.

file fragmentation   The storage of a *file* in several noncontiguous areas of a disk, rather than as one single unit.

When you store a file on a disk, *DOS* looks for the first available free cluster on the disk, and stores the file there. If the file is too large for one cluster, the operating system looks for the next free cluster, and stores the next part of the file there. These clusters may not be next to one another, and may be widely scattered over the disk.

This fragmentation can slow down data retrieval if the problem becomes severe, but by using a *defragmenter*, you can restore that lost performance. The defragmented program removes file fragmentation by rewriting all files and *directories* into contiguous areas of your disk.

file locking   Software feature that allows more than one user at time to use a program or file.

file recovery   The process of recovering *deleted* or damaged *files* from a disk. In many operating systems, a deleted file still exists on disk until the space it occupies is overwritten with something else. A file can be deleted accidentally, or can become inaccessible when part of the file's control information is lost.

Many utility packages offer excellent file recovery programs that guide the user through the recovery process. In cases where damage is extreme, the program may only be able to recover some of the damaged file, and substantial editing may be necessary before the file can be used; indeed the best way to recover a damaged program file is to restore it from a *backup* copy. You must, of course, recover the deleted or damaged files before you add any new files or *directories* to the disk.

file server   A networked computer used to store *files* for access by other *client* computers on the network. On larger networks, the file server may run a special *network operating system*; on smaller installations, the file server may run a PC operating system supplemented by *peer-to-peer* networking software.

file sharing   In networking, the sharing of *files* via the network *file server*. Shared files can be read, reviewed, and updated by more than one individual. Access to the file or files is often regulated by password protection, account or security clearance, or file locking, to prevent simultaneous changes from being made by more than one person at a time.

file system   In an *operating system*, the structure by which *files* are organized, stored, and named.

Some file systems are built-in components of the operating system, while others are installable. For example, *OS/2* supports several different file systems, including the FAT file system, the high-performance file system, and the CD-ROM file system, which is installed by the ISF command when you attach a CD-ROM to your system.

file transfer protocol   In communications, a method of transferring one or more *files* from one computer to another, often over a *modem* and a telephone line.

The protocol divides the file into smaller units, and each unit is processed in sequence. The transfer protocol also handles *error detection and correction*, by one of several methods.

filespec   A contraction of file specification, commonly used to denote the complete drive letter, path name, *directory* name, and file name needed to access a specific *file*.

firewall   A method of preventing unauthorized access to a computer system, often found on networked computers.

A firewall is designed to provide normal service to authorized users, while at the same time preventing those unauthorized users from gaining access to the system; in reality, they almost always add some level of inconvenience to legal users, and their ability to control illegal access may be questionable. The Internet community has long favored unrestricted access to information, but as more and more commercial use is made of the Internet, the need for stricter controls is becoming increasingly apparent.

firmware   Any *software* stored in a form of read-only memory—*ROM, EPROM,* or *EEPROM*—that maintains its contents when power is removed. The *BIOS* used in IBM-compatible computers is firmware.

first in, first out   Abbreviated FIFO, pronounced "fi-foe." A method used to process information in which the first item in the list is processed first. FIFO is commonly used when printing a set of documents; the first document received in the queue is the first document to be printed.

fixed disk   A disk drive that contain several disks (also known as platters) stacked together and mounted through their centers on a small rod. The disks rotate as read/write heads float above the disks that make, modify, or sense changes in the magnetic positions of the coatings on the disk.

fixed resistor   Type of resistor that is used to reduce the current by a certain amount. Fixed resistors are color coded to identify their resistance values and tolerance bands.

fixed-frequency monitor   A monitor designed to receive an input signal at just one frequency. This is in contrast to a *multisynch monitor,* which can detect and adjust to a variety of different input signals.

flash memory   A special form of non-volatile *EEPROM* that can be erased at signal levels normally found inside the PC, so that you can reprogram the contents with whatever you like without pulling the chips out of your computer. Also, once flash memory has been programmed, you can remove the *expansion board* it is mounted on and plug it into another computer if you wish.

flatbed scanner   An optical device used to digitize a whole page or a large image.

flat-panel display   In laptop and notebook computers, a very narrow display that uses one of several technologies, such as electroluminescence, *LCD,* or thin film transistors.

flicker   On a monitor, any form of unwanted rapid fluctuation in the image that occurs when the refresh rate is too slow to maintain an even level of brightness.

floating-point calculation   A calculation of numbers whose decimal point is not fixed but moves or floats to provide the best degree of accuracy. Floating-point calculations can be implemented in *software,* or they can be performed much faster by a separate *floating-point processor.*

floating-point processor   A special-purpose secondary processor designed to perform *floating-point calculations* much faster than the main processor.

Many processors have matched companion floating-point processors; the 80386 and the 80387 for example, although a modern trend in processor design is to integrate the floating-point unit onto the main processor, as in the 80486 and the Pentium.

floppy disk   A flat, round, magnetically coated plastic disk enclosed in a protective jacket.

Data is written on to the floppy disk by the disk drive's read/write heads as the disk rotates inside the jacket. The advantage of the floppy disk is that it is removable, and so can be used to distribute commercial *software*, to transfer programs from one computer to another, or to *back up files* from a *hard disk*. But compared to a hard disk, floppy disks are also slower, offer relatively small amounts of storage, and can be easily damaged.

Floppy disks in personal computing are of two physical sizes; 5.25" or 3.5", and a variety of storage capacities. The 5.25" floppy disk has a stiff plastic external cover, while the 3.5" floppy disk is enclosed in a hard plastic case. IBM-compatibles use 5.25" and 3.5" disks, and the *Macintosh* uses 3.5" disks.

floppy disk controller   The circuit board that is installed in a computer to translate signals from the CPU into signals that the floppy disk drive can understand. Often it is integrated into the same circuit board that houses the hard disk controller; it can, however, be integrated into the motherboard in the PC.

floppy disk drive   A device used to read and write *data* to and from a *floppy disk*. Floppy-disk drives may be full-height drives, but more commonly these days they are *half-height* drives.

floppy drive cable   A cable that connects the floppy drive(s) to the floppy drive controller. The cable is a 34-wire ribbon cable that usually has 3 connectors.

floptical disk   A removable optical disk with a recording capacity of between 20 and 25 megabytes.

flux transition   Presence or absence of a magnetic field in a particle of the coating on the disk. As the disk passes over an area the electromagnet is energized to cause the material to be magnetized in a small area.

font cartridge   A plug-in module available for certain printers that adds new fonts to those already available in the printer. The font information for *bit-mapped* or *outline fonts* is stored in *ROM* in the cartridge.

footprint   The amount of desktop or floor space occupied by a computer or display terminal. By extension, also refers to the size of software items such as applications or operating systems.

foreground   In an *operating system*, a process that runs in the foreground is running at a higher level of priority than a *background* task.

Only *multitasking* operating systems support true foreground and background processing; however, some *application* programs can mimic background and foreground processing; many word processors will print a document while still accepting input from the keyboard.

form factors   Physical characteristics and dimensions of drive styles.

form feed   Abbreviated FF. A printer command that advances the paper in the printer to the top of the next page. This can be done by pressing the form feed button on the printer, or an *application* can issue the command. In the *ASCII character set* a form feed has the decimal value of 12.

formatter board   Type of circuit board that takes the information the printer receives from the computer and turns it into commands for the various components in the printer.

formatting

1. To apply the page-layout commands and font specifications to a document and produce the final printed output.

2. The process of initializing a new, blank *floppy disk* or *hard disk* so that it can be used to store information.

forum   A feature of *online services* and bulletin boards that allows subscribers to post messages for others to read, and to reply to messages posted by other users.

Most forums are devoted to a specific subject such as working from home or photography, while others are run by hardware and software vendors providing what amounts to online technical support.

free memory   An area of memory not currently in use.

freeware   A form of *software* distribution where the author retains copyright of the software, but makes the program available to others at no cost. Freeware is often distributed on *bulletin boards*, or through *user groups*. The program may not be resold or distributed by others for profit.

frequency modulation encoding   Abbreviated FM encoding. A method of storing digital information on a disk or tape. FM encoding is inefficient in its use of disk space and has largely been replaced by more efficient methods like *modified frequency modulation (MFM) encoding*, and the more complex methods of *run length limited (RLL) encoding* and *advanced run length limited (ARLL) encoding*.

friction feed   A paper-feed mechanism that uses pinch rollers to move the paper through a printer, one page at a time.

Friction feed is usually available on those printers that use paper with *pin-feed* holes or that use a *tractor feed*, so that they can also print on single sheets of paper. Manually loading more than just a few sheets of paper using friction feed can become tedious very quickly.

front-end processor   A specialized processor that manipulates *data* before passing it on to the main processor. In large computer-to-computer communications systems, a front-end processor is often used to manage all aspects of communications, leaving the main computer free to handle the data processing.

FRU (field replacement unit)   The individual parts or whole assemblies that can be replaced to repair a computer.

ftp   Abbreviation for file transfer protocol. The protocol used to access a remote *Internet host*, and then transfer files between that host and your own computer. Ftp is also the name of the program used to manage this protocol.

Ftp is based on *client/server architecture*; you run an ftp client program on your system, and connect with an ftp server running on the Internet host computer. The ftp program originated as a *Unix* utility, but versions are now available for almost all popular operating systems. The traditional Unix ftp program starts a text-based command processor; modern versions use a graphical user interface with pull-down menus instead. The general consensus seems to be that the graphical versions are easier to use, but once you get the hang of things, the command processor versions, while not as pretty, are usually faster.

full backup   A *backup* that includes all the *files* on your *hard disk*. If you have a large hard disk, this process can consume a lot of time and a large number of floppy disks, and one way to speed up the process is to use a tape drive system to help streamline and automate the process.

function keys   The set of programmable keys on the keyboard that can perform special tasks assigned by the current *application* program.

Most keyboards have 10 or 12 function keys, and they are used by an application as shortcut keys. For example, many programs use F1 to gain access to the help system; in other programs the use of function keys is so complex that special plastic key overlays are needed just so you can remember how to use them.

fuser   Device on an EP Printer that uses two rollers to heat the toner particles and melt them to the paper. The fuser is made up of a halogen heating lamp, a Teflon-coated aluminum fusing roller, and a rubberized pressure roller. The lamp heats the aluminum roller. As the paper passes between the two rollers, the rubber roller presses the paper against the heated roller. This causes the toner to melt and become a permanent image on the paper.

fusing assembly   See *fuser*

fusing step   Fifth step in the EP print process. The stage at which the toner image is made permanent. The fuser melts the elements in the toner and the image is pressed permanently into the paper.

G   Abbreviation for *giga-*, meaning 1 billion, or 10^9.

gateway   In networking, a shared connection between a *local area network* and a larger system, such as a mainframe computer or a large *packet-switching network*. Usually slower than a *bridge* or *router*, a gateway typically has its own processor and memory, and can perform protocol conversions. Protocol conversion allows a gateway to connect two dissimilar networks; data is converted and reformatted before it is forwarded to the new network.

gender changer   A special intermediary connector for use with two cables that both have male or both have female connectors.

general purpose interface bus   Abbreviated GPIB. A 24-pin parallel interface bus that conforms to the IEEE 488 interface definition standard, often used to connect scientific instruments together or to a computer. Originally developed by *Hewlett-Packard*, GPIB is also known as the Hewlett-Packard Interface Bus (HPIB).

genlocking   A contraction of generator lock. The synchronization and superimposition of computer-generated text or graphics onto a video signal, so that the two images can be combined onto the same signal and displayed at the same time.

In the PC, a board containing the circuitry required for genlocking often plugs onto the display adapter. It converts the *VGA* signal into a standard *NTSC* video signal, which it then synchronizes with an external video signal.

giga-   A prefix meaning 1 billion, or 10 to the ninth power.

gigabyte   Pronounced "gig-a-bite." Strictly speaking, a gigabyte would be one billion bytes; however, bytes are most often counted in powers of 2, and so a gigabyte becomes 2 the 30th power, or 1,073,741,824 bytes.

GPF (General Protection Fault)   Occurs when a Windows application runs out of usable memory and tries to take memory from another application. When this happens Windows will halt the misbehaving program and display this message.

graphical user interface   Abbreviated GUI, pronounced "gooey." A graphics-based user interface that allows users to select files, programs, or commands by pointing to pictorial representations on the screen rather than by typing long, complex commands from a *command prompt*.

Application programs execute in *windows*, using a consistent set of *pull-down menus*, *dialog boxes*, and other graphical elements such as *scroll bars* and *icons*. This consistency among interface elements is a major benefit for the user, because as soon as you learn how to use the interface in one program, you can use it in all other programs running in the same *environment*.

graphics accelerator board   A specialized *expansion board* containing a *graphics coprocessor* as well as all the other circuitry found on a *video adapter*. By offloading most of the graphics processing tasks from the main processor onto the graphics accelerator board, you can improve the performance of your system considerably, particularly if you are a *Microsoft Windows* user.

graphics coprocessor   A fixed-function graphics chip, designed to speed up the processing and display of high-resolution images. Popular graphics coprocessors include the *S3 86C9xx* accelerator chips.

gray-scale monitor   A monitor and *video adapter* that uses a set of gray shades from black to white instead of using colors. Gray-scale monitors are expensive and are used in medical and photographic imaging systems.

half-height drive   A space-saving drive bay that is half the height of the 3" drive bays used in the original IBM PC. Most of today's drives are half-height drives.

hand-held computer   A *portable* computer that is small enough to be held in one hand.

hand-held scanner   Type of *scanner* that is small enough to be held in your hand. Used to digitize a relatively small image or artwork, it consists of the controller, CCD, and light source contained in a small enclosure with wheels on it.

hard card   A single *expansion board* that contains a small *hard disk* and associated controller circuitry. A hard card allows you to add another hard disk, even when all your drive bays are occupied, as long as there is still a single *expansion slot* available. Hard cards were brought to prominence by Plus Development Corporation.

hard disk   The part of a *hard disk drive* that stores *data*, rather than the mechanism for reading and writing to it.

hard disk controller   An *expansion board* that contains the necessary circuitry to control and coordinate a *hard disk drive*. Many hard disk controllers are capable of managing more than one hard disk, as well as floppy disks and even tape drives.

hard disk drive   A storage device that uses a set of rotating, magnetically coated disks called *platters* to store data or programs. In everyday use, the terms "hard disk," "hard disk drive," and "hard drive" are all used interchangeably, because the disk and the drive mechanism are a single unit.

A typical hard disk platter rotates at up to 3600 rpm, and the read/write heads float on a cushion of air from 10 to 25 millionths of an inch thick so that the heads never come into contact with the recording surface. The whole unit is hermetically sealed to prevent airborne contaminants from entering and interfering with these close tolerances.

Hard disks range in capacity from a few tens of megabytes to several gigabytes of storage space; the bigger the disk, the more important a well-thought out *backup* strategy becomes. Hard disks are very reliable, but they do fail, and usually at the most inconvenient moment.

hard disk interface   A standard way of accessing the data stored on a hard disk. Several different hard-disk interface standards have evolved over time, including the *ST-506 interface, enhanced small device interface, integrated drive electronics interface*, and *small computer-system interface*.

hard disk system   A disk storage system containing the following components: the *hard disk controller, hard disk*, and *host adapter*.

hard memory error   Reproducible memory error that is related to hardware failure.

hard reset   A system reset made by pressing the computer's reset button, or by turning the power off and then on again. Used only when the system has crashed so badly that a Ctrl-Alt-Del *reboot* doesn't work.

hardware   All the physical electronic components of a computer system, including *peripherals*, printed circuit boards, displays and printers; if you can stub your toe on it, it must be hardware.

hardware interrupt   An *interrupt* or request for service generated by a *hardware device* such as a keystroke from the keyboard or a tick from the *clock*. Because the processor may receive several such signals simultaneously, hardware interrupts are usually assigned a priority level, and processed according to that priority.

hardware-dependence   The requirement that a specific *hardware* component be present for a program to work. Hardware-dependent *software* is often very difficult to move or *port* to another computer.

hardware-independence   The ability to produce similar results in a wide variety of environments, without requiring the presence of specific *hardware*.

The *Unix operating system* and the *PostScript page-description language* are both examples of hardware independence. Unix runs on a wide range of computers, from the PC to a *Cray*, and Post-Script is used by many printer manufacturers.

hardwired   Describes a system designed in a way that does not allow for flexibility or future expansion. May also refer to a device or computer connected directly to a network.

Hayes-compatible modem   Any modem that recognizes the commands in the industry-standard *AT-command set*, defined by Hayes Microcomputer Products, Inc.

head   The electromagnetic device used to read and write to and from magnetic media such as *hard* and *floppy disks*, *tape drives*, and *compact discs*. The head converts the information read into electrical pulses sent to the computer for processing.

head crash   An unexpected collision between a hard disk *head* and the rapidly rotating magnetic recording surface of the disk resulting in damage to the disk surface, and in some severe cases resulting in damage to the head itself.

A head crash in the *file allocation table* (FAT) area of a disk can be especially devastating, because the FAT contains instructions for the *operating system* on how to find all the other *directories* and *files* on the disk, and if it is damaged, the other files and directories may become completely inaccessible.

Recent hard disk design has done much to eliminate this problem.

hertz   Abbreviated Hz. A unit of frequency measurement; 1 hertz equals one cycle per second.

hexadecimal   Abbreviated hex. The base-16 numbering system that uses the digits 0 to 9, followed by the letters A to F (equivalent to the decimal numbers 10 through 15).

Hex is a very convenient way to represent the binary numbers computers use internally, because it fits neatly into the 8-bit byte. All of the 16 hex digits 0 to F can be represented in four bits, and so two hex digits (one digit for each set of four bits) can be stored in a single byte. This means that one byte can contain any one of 256 different hex numbers, from 0 through FF. Hex numbers are often labeled with a lower-case *h* (for example, 1234h) to distinguish them from decimal numbers.

HGC   Abbreviation for Hercules graphics card. A *video adapter* for DOS computers, introduced by Hercules Computer Technology. HGC provides monochrome graphics with 720 horizontal *pixels* and 348 vertical pixels.

high memory area   Abbreviated HMA. In an IBM-compatible computer, the first 64 K of *extended memory* above the 1 MB limit of 8086 and 8088 addresses. Programs that conform to the *extended memory specification* can use this memory as an extension of *conventional memory* although only one program can use or control HMA at a time; *DOS*, *Microsoft Windows*, or an *application*. If you load DOS into the HMA, you can recover approximately 50 K of conventional memory for use by your *applications*.

high performance file system   Abbreviated HPFS. A *file system* available in *OS/2* and *Windows NT 3.x* that supports long, mixed-case *file names* of up to 256 characters, up to 64 K of *extended attributes* per *file*, faster disk access with an advanced *disk cache* for caching files and *directory* information, highly contiguous file allocation that eliminates *file fragmentation*, and support for hard disks of up to 64 GB in size. *DOS* does not recognize the HPFS file structure.

You cannot use the HPFS on a floppy disk.

high resolution   In monitors and printers, a description of high-quality output; resolution refers to the sharpness and detail of the image.

What actually constitutes high resolution is in the eye of the beholder; high resolution to one person represents a bad case of the *jaggies* to another. On a 12-inch monitor, a realistic-looking display requires a grid of approximately 1,000 by 1,000 *pixels*. *Laser printers* can manage a resolution of 300 to 600 *dpi*, but Linotronic typesetters can print at up to 2540 dpi.

high voltage power supply (HVPS)   Provides the high voltages that are used during the EP print process. This component converts house AC currents into higher voltages that the two corona assemblies can use.

high-density disk   A floppy disk with more recording density and storage capacity than a *double-density disk*. In the *Macintosh*, high-density disks contain 1.44 MB. In IBM-compatible computers, high-density 5.25" floppy disks contain 1.2 MB, while high-density 3.5" floppy disks contain either 1.44 MB or 2.88 MB of storage space.

high-level format   The process of preparing a *floppy disk* or a *hard disk partition* for use by the *operating system*. In the case of *DOS*, a high-level format creates the *boot sector*, the *file allocation table* (FAT), and the *root directory*.

high-persistence phosphor   In a monitor, a phosphor that glows for a relatively long time after being energized by electrons. This can lead to ghost images on the screen.

HIMEM.SYS   The *DOS* and *Microsoft Windows device driver* that manages the use of extended memory and the high memory area on IBM-compatible computers. HIMEM.SYS not only allows your *application* programs to access extended memory, it also oversees that area to prevent other programs from trying to use the same space at the same time.

HIMEM.SYS must be loaded by a *DEVICE* command in your *CONFIG.SYS* file; you cannot use *DEVICEHIGH*.

home computer   Any computer designed or purchased for home use. Originally, home computers were often used for games, educational purposes, and financial management, and they were less powerful than their business counterparts. This gap has narrowed considerably in recent years as home users continue to demand the same level of power, speed, and convenience that they find in office systems. Often the home computer is used as an extension to an office system for after-hours work.

home page   On the *Internet World Wide Web*, an initial starting page. A home page, as shown in the illustration below, may be related to a single person, a specific subject, or to a corporation, and is a convenient jumping-off point to other pages or resources.

horizontal scanning frequency   In a monitor, the frequency at which the monitor repaints the horizontal lines that make up an image. Horizontal scanning frequency is measured in kHz, and is standardized at 31.5 kHz for a *VGA*. For *SuperVGA*, this frequency ranges from 35 to 48 kHz, depending on the refresh rate of the *video adapter*.

host   The central or controlling computer in a networked or *distributed processing* environment, providing services that other computers or terminals can access via the network.

Computers connected to the *Internet* are also described as hosts, and can be accessed using *ftp*, *telnet*, *Gopher*, or a *World Wide Web browser*.

host adapter   Translates signals from the hard drive and controller to signals the computer's bus can understand.

"house" AC current   The electricity that comes from most house wall outlets. The electricity is rated at 120 volts, 60 hertz.

HP LaserJet   A family of very popular desktop *laser printers* manufactured by *Hewlett-Packard Company*.

Hewlett-Packard virtually created the market for small, fast laser printers when they introduced the original LaserJet in 1984. Since that time, the LaserJet II, III, and IV series of printers have continued to dominate the market; each new generation of printer improves on the capabilities of the previous one.

HTML   Abbreviation for Hypertext Markup Language. A standardized *hypertext* language used to create *World Wide Web* pages and other hypertext documents.

When you access an *Internet* HTML document using a *World Wide Web browser*, you will see a mixture of text, graphics, and *links* to other documents. When you click on a link, the related document will open automatically, no matter where on the Internet that document is actually located. Normally, you don't see the individual elements that make up HTML when you view a document, although certain browsers have a special mode that displays both the text and the HTML in a document.

HTTP   Abbreviation for Hypertext Transport Protocol. The protocol used to manage the *links* between one *hypertext* document and another.

HTTP is the mechanism that opens the related document when you click on a hypertext link, no matter where on the Internet that related document happens to be.

hubs   A connectivity device used to link several computers together into a physical star topology. They repeat any signal that comes in on one port and copies it to the other ports.

hybrid topology   A mix of more than one topology type used on a network.

IAB   Abbreviation for Internet Architecture Board. The coordinating committee for the management of the *Internet*. Previously, the abbreviation IAB stood for Internet Activities Board.

IBM 3270   A general name for a family of IBM system components—printers, terminals, and terminal cluster controllers—that can be used with a *mainframe computer* by an *SNA* link. *Terminal emulation software* that emulates a 3270 terminal is available for both *DOS* and *Microsoft Windows*, as well as for *OS/2*.

IBM PC   A series of *personal computers* based on the *Intel 8088* processor, introduced by IBM in mid-1981.

The specifications for the IBM PC seem puny in comparison to current computer systems; the PC was released containing 16K of memory, expandable to 64K on the *motherboard*, and a monochrome *video adapter* incapable of displaying *bit-mapped graphics*. The floppy disk drive held 160K of data and programs. There was no hard disk on the original IBM PC; that came later with the release of the *IBM PC/XT*.

In 1983, IBM released an improved version of the PC, the IBM PC-2, which came with 64K of memory, expandable to 256K on the motherboard, and a double-density floppy disk drive capable of storing 360K of programs and *data*. The Color/Graphics Adapter (*CGA)* and an *RGB* color monitor were also introduced at the same time.

IBM PC/AT   A series of *personal computers* based on the *Intel 80286* processor, introduced by IBM in 1984.

The AT represented a significant performance increase over previous computers, up to 75 percent faster than the PC/XT, and the *AT bus* standard is used in many *clones* or *IBM-compatible computers*.

IBM PC/XT   A series of *personal computers* based on the *Intel 8088* processor, introduced by IBM in 1983.

The PC/XT was the first IBM personal computer to offer a built-in hard disk and the capability to expand memory up to a whopping 640 K on the *motherboard*. The original PC/XT used an Intel 8088 running at a *clock speed* of 4.77 MHz—very slow when compared with today's 266 and 300 MHz clock speeds.

IBM PS/2   A series of personal computers using several different *Intel* processors, introduced by IBM in 1987.

The main difference between the PS/2 line and earlier IBM personal computers was a major change to the internal *bus*. Previous computers used the *AT bus*, also known as *industry-standard architecture*, but IBM used the proprietary *micro channel architecture* in the PS/2 line instead. Micro channel architecture *expansion boards* will not work in a computer using ISA.

IBM RS/6000   A set of seven or nine separate 32-bit chips used in IBM's line of *RISC* workstations. With up to 7.4 million transistors depending on configuration, the RS/6000 uses a *superscalar* design with 4 separate 16K data cache units and an 8K instruction cache.

The joint venture announced between IBM, Apple, and Motorola in late 1991 specified the joint development of a single-chip version of the RS/6000 architecture called the *PowerPC*.

IBM ThinkPad   A series of innovative and popular notebook computers from IBM.

The ThinkPad first introduced the touch-sensitive dual-button pointing stick or TrackPoint, the pencil-eraser-like device between the G, H, and B keys that replaces the mouse, which is now found on many different portable computers.

The ThinkPad 701C, also known as "the Butterfly," introduced another innovative concept, that of the expanding keyboard. When the 701C case is closed, the TrackWrite keyboard is completely concealed inside the case; the right half sits above the left. When the case is opened, the two parts of the full-sized keyboard automatically unfold and overhang the edges of the case. The 701C, based on the *Intel DX2 50 MHz* processor, also contains an internal 14,400 bps fax/data modem with built-in speaker phone and digital answering machine, infrared wireless file transfer, and two *PCMCIA* Type I or Type II *PC cards* or one Type III card.

IBM-compatible computer   Originally, any personal computer compatible with the IBM line of personal computers.

With the launch of IBM's proprietary *micro channel architecture* in the PS/2 line of computers, which replaced the *AT bus*, two incompatible standards emerged, and so the term became misleading. Now, it is becoming more common to use the term "industry-standard computer" when referring to a computer that uses the AT or ISA bus, and the term "DOS computer" to describe any PC that runs DOS and is based on one of the *Intel* family of chips.

IC chip (integrated circuit chip)   Chip that integrates resistors and capacitors to larger assemblies that perform certain functions.

IC puller   "U" shaped tool used for pulling IC chips.

IDE (integrated drive electronics)   A hard disk technology that can connect multiple drives together. These drives integrate the controller and drive into one assembly. This makes them very inexpensive. Because of this, IDE drives are the most commonly used disk technology installed in computers today.

IEEE (Institute for Electrical and Electronics Engineers)   International organization that develops standards for electrical and electronics topics.

imagesetter   A large, professional-quality typesetter capable of *high-resolution* output on paper or film.

Linotronic imagesetters can print at resolutions of 1225 to 2450 dpi; compare this to the 300 to 600 dpi produced by most desktop laser printers.

impact printer   Any printer that forms an image on paper by forcing a character image against an inked ribbon. *Dot-matrix*, *daisy-wheel*, and *line printers* are all impact printers, whereas *laser printers* are not.

impedance   An electrical property of a cable that combines capacitance, inductance, and resistance. Impedance can be described as the apparent resistance to the flow of alternating current at a given frequency; mismatches in impedance along a cable cause distortions and reflections.

incremental backup   A *backup* of a hard disk that consists of only those *files* created or modified since the last backup was performed.

infection   The presence of a computer virus.

INI file   Text file that are created by an installation program when a new Windows application is installed. INI files contain settings for individual Windows applications as well as for Windows itself.

initialization commands   The commands sent to the modem by the communication's program to initialize (prepare) it. These commands establish things like on what ring to answer the call or the wait time between the last keystroke and disconnection.

ink   Liquid that is used to stain or imprint images on paper.

ink cartridge   A replaceable unit that holds the ink in an ink-jet printer. The cartridge contains several small chambers. At the top of each chamber is a metal plate and tube leading to the ink supply. At the bottom of the chamber is a small pinhole that is used to spray the ink on the page.

ink-jet printer   A printer that creates an image by spraying tiny droplets of ink from the print head. While many *dot-matrix printers* have 9 to 24 pins, most ink jets have print heads with somewhere between 30 and 60 nozzles, and this allows them to create *high-resolution* images in a single pass over the paper. Both color and black-and-white ink-jet printers are available.

input/output   Abbreviated I/O. The transfer of *data* between the computer and its *peripheral* devices, disk drives, terminals and printers.

input/output addresses   Lines on a bus used to allow the CPU to send instructions to the devices installed in the bus slots. Each device is given its own communication line to the CPU. These lines function like one-way (unidirectional) mailboxes.

input/output bound   Abbreviated I/O bound. A condition where the speed of operation of the I/O port limits the speed of program execution; getting the *data* into and out of the computer is more time-consuming than processing that same data.

install   To configure and prepare *hardware* or *software* for operation.

Many application packages have their own install programs—programs that copy all the required files from the original distribution floppy disks or CD into appropriate *directories* on your hard disk, and then help you to configure the program to your own operating requirements. *Microsoft Windows* programs are usually installed by a program called SETUP.

installation program   A program whose sole function is to install (and sometimes configure) another program.

The program guides the user through what might be a rather complex set of choices, copying the correct files into the right *directories*, decompressing them if necessary, and asking for the next disk when appropriate. This program may also ask for a person's name or a company name so that the startup screen can be customized.

Some older IBM-compatible installation programs may change your *CONFIG.SYS* or *AUTO-EXEC.BAT* files without letting you know; others will ask your permission and add their statements to the end of the existing commands.

Institute of Electrical and Electronic Engineers Abbreviated IEEE. Pronounced "eye-triple-ee." A membership organization, founded in 1963, including engineers, students, and scientists. IEEE also acts as a coordinating body for computing and communications standards, particularly the IEEE 802 standard for the physical and *data-link* layers of *local area networks*, following the *ISO/OSI model*.

insulative material Any material that does not conduct electricity.

integer A whole number, one in which there is no decimal portion.

integrated circuit Abbreviated IC, also known as a chip. A small semiconductor circuit that contains many electronic components.

integrated drive electronics interface Abbreviated IDE. A popular *hard-disk interface* standard, used for disks in the range of 40 MB to 1.2 GB, requiring medium to fast *data transfer rates*. IDE gets its name from the fact that the electronic control circuitry needed is actually located on the drive itself, thus eliminating the need for a separate *hard-disk controller* card.

integrated system boards A system board that has most of the computer's circuitry attached, as opposed to having been installed as expansion cards.

Intel OverDrive The original Intel OverDrive *microprocessor* was designed as a user-installable upgrade to an *80486SX* or *80486DX*-based computer, while the Pentium OverDrive chip is designed as a replacement for 486-based systems. OverDrive chips boost system performance by using the same *clock multiplying* technology found in the Intel *80486DX-2* and *DX4* chips. Once installed, an OverDrive processor can increase *application* performance by an estimated 40 to 70 percent.

intelligent hub A class of hub that can be remotely managed on the network.

interface That point where a connection is made between two different parts of a system, such as between two *hardware devices*, between a user and a program or *operating system*, or between two *application* programs.

In hardware, an interface describes the logical and physical connections used, as in *RS-232-C*, and is often considered to be synonymous with the term "port."

A *user interface* consists of all the means by which a program communicates with the user, including a *command line*, *menus*, *dialog boxes*, online *help* systems, and so on. User interfaces can be classified as *character-based*, *menu-driven*, or *graphical*.

Software interfaces are *application program interfaces*; the codes and messages used by programs to communicate behind the scenes.

interface standard Any standard way of connecting two *devices* or elements having different functions.

Many different interface standards are used in the PC world, including *SCSI*, *integrated drive electronics*, and the *enhanced small device interface* for hard disks, *RS-232-C* and the *Centronics parallel interface* for serial devices and parallel printers, and the *ISO/OSI model* for computer-to-computer communications over a network.

interlacing   A display technique that uses two passes over the *monitor* screen, painting every other line on the screen the first time, and then filling in the rest of the lines on the second pass. It relies on the physiological phenomenon known as *persistence of vision* to produce the effect of a continuous image. *Non-interlaced* scanning paints all the lines on the display in a single pass; and so, while more expensive, it reduces unwanted *flicker* and eyestrain.

interleave factor   The order in which the *sectors* were arranged on your hard disk by the initial *low-level format.*

Introduced as a compensation for slow computers, interleaving eliminates the delay that results when a drive is not ready to read or write the next sector as soon as it has read or written the previous one. With a 3:1 interleave factor, sequentially numbered sectors are located three sectors apart on the disk. An interleave that is either too high or too low can lead to a severe degradation in performance, because the computer spends its time waiting for the next sector to arrive at the read/write heads. Thanks to increases in PC speed, interleaving is obsolete, and most modern disks use a 1:1 interleave factor (which actually indicates a non-interleaved drive).

interleaved memory   A method of speeding up *data* access by dividing *dynamic RAM* (DRAM) memory into two separate banks so that the processor can read one bank while the other is being refreshed. DRAM requires that its contents be updated at least every thousandth of a second, and while it is being refreshed it cannot be read by the processor; interleaving memory speeds up access times. Of course, if the processor needs to read from the same bank

of RAM repeatedly, it must wait for the full DRAM cycle time.

The introduction of *static RAM* (SRAM) has removed the need for interleaved memory, because SRAM memory can retain its contents without the need for refreshment.

interleaving   A process that involves writing data to every other sector as the disk rotates, instead of sequentially to every sector. Interleaving evens out the data flow and allows the drive to keep pace with the rest of the system. Interleaving is given in ratios. A 1:1 ratio means that data is written to each sector. A 2:1 interleave means that data is written to every other sector.

internal cache memory   Cache memory for temporarily storing program instructions and data inside the processor.

internal hard disk   A *hard disk drive* housed inside the computer's system unit and integrated with it, rather than an external drive packaged with its own case, cables, and independent power supply.

internal modem   A *modem* that plugs into the expansion bus of a personal computer.

International Standards Organization Abbreviated ISO. An international standard-making body, based in Geneva, that establishes global standards for communications and information exchange. ANSI is the U.S. member of ISO.

The 7-layer International Standards Organization's Open Systems Interconnection (ISO/OSI) model for computer-to-computer communications is one of the ISO's most widely accepted recommendations.

internet   Abbreviation for internetwork. A set of computer networks, made up of a large number of smaller networks, using different networking protocols.

Internet   The world's largest computer network, connecting over 100 million users in almost every nation. The Internet is growing at a phenomenal rate—between 10 and 15 percent per month—so any size estimates are quickly out-of-date.

The Internet was originally established to meet the research needs of the U.S. Defense industry, but it has grown into a huge global network serving universities, academic researchers, commercial interests, and government agencies, both in the U.S. and overseas. The Internet uses *TCP/IP* protocols, and many of the Internet *hosts* run the *Unix* operating system.

Internet access can be via a permanent network connection or by dial-up through one of the many service providers.

Internet address   An *IP* or *domain* address which identifies a specific node on the Internet.

interprocess communication   Abbreviated IPC. A term that describes all the methods used to pass information between two programs running on the same computer running a *multitasking operating system,* or between two programs running on a network, including *pipes, shared memory, queues,* the Clipboard, *DDE* (Dynamic Data Exchange), and *OLE* (Object Linking and Embedding).

interrupt   A signal to the processor generated by a device under its control (such as the system clock) that interrupts normal processing.

An interrupt indicates that an event requiring the processor's attention has occurred, causing the processor to suspend and save its current activity, and then branch to an interrupt service routine. This service routine processes the interrupt, whether it was generated by the system clock, a keystroke, or a mouse click; and when it's complete, returns control to the suspended process. In the PC, interrupts are often divided into three classes; internal *hardware,* external hardware, and *software* interrupts. The Intel 80x86 family of processors supports 256 prioritized interrupts, of which the first 64 are reserved for use by the system *hardware* or by *DOS.*

interrupt controller   A chip, used to process and prioritize *hardware interrupts.* In IBM-compatible computers, the Intel 8259A Programmable Interrupt Controller responds to each hardware interrupt, assigns a priority, and forwards it to the main processor.

interrupt handler   Special *software* invoked when an *interrupt* occurs. Each type of interrupt, such as a clock tick or a keystroke, is processed by its own specific interrupt handler. A table, called the *interrupt vector table,* maintains a list of addresses for these specific interrupt handlers.

interrupt request lines   Abbreviated IRQ. Hardware lines that carry a signal from a device to the processor.

A *hardware* interrupt signals that an event has taken place that requires the processor's attention, and may come from the keyboard, the input/output ports, or the system's disk drives. In the PC, the main processor does not accept interrupts from hardware devices directly; instead interrupts are routed to an Intel 8259A Programmable Interrupt Controller. This chip responds to each hardware interrupt, assigns a priority, and forwards it to the main processor.

interrupt vector table   A list of addresses for specific *software* routines known as *interrupt handlers*. In a *DOS* computer, the interrupt vector table consists of 256 pointers located in the first megabyte of memory.

IP   Abbreviation for Internet Protocol. The underlying *communications protocol* on which the *Internet* is based. IP allows a data packet to travel across many networks before reaching its final destination.

IRC   Abbreviation for Internet Relay Chat. An Internet client/server application that allows large groups of users to communicate with each other interactively. Specific channels are devoted to one particular topic, from the sacred to the profane, and topics come and go regularly as interest levels change.

ISA   Abbreviation for industry-standard architecture. The *16-bit bus* design was first used in *IBM's PC/AT* computer in 1984. ISA has a bus speed of 8 MHz, and a maximum throughput of 8 megabytes per second. *EISA* is a *32-bit* extension to this standard bus.

ISDN   Abbreviation for Integrated Services Digital Network. A worldwide digital communications network emerging from existing telephone services, intended to replace all current systems with a completely digital transmission system.

Computers and other devices connect to ISDN via simple, standardized interfaces, and when complete, ISDN systems will be capable of transmitting voice, video, music, and data.

ISO/OSI model   Abbreviation for International Standards Organization/Open System Interconnection. In networking, a reference model defined by the ISO that divides computer-to-computer communications into seven connected layers, known as a "protocol stack."

ITU   Abbreviation for International Telecommunications Union. The United Nations umbrella organization that develops and standardizes telecommunications worldwide. The ITU also contains the *CCITT* (now called ITU-T), the International Frequency Registration Board (IFRB), and the Consultative Committee on International Radio (CCIR). Popular usage is starting to refer to the CCITT standards as ITU standards.

joystick   A popular multidirectional pointing device, used extensively in many computer games, as well as in certain professional applications such as computer-aided design (CAD).

jumper   A small plastic and metal connector that completes a circuit, usually to select one option from a set of several user-definable options. Jumpers are often used to select one particular hardware configuration rather than another.

kernel   The most fundamental part of an *operating system*. The kernel stays resident in memory at all times, often hidden from the user, and manages system memory, the file system, and disk operations.

keyboard   The typewriter-like set of keys used to input *data* and control commands to the computer. Most keyboards use a *QWERTY* layout, and may also have a calculator-like numeric keypad off to one side, as well as a set of *cursor-movement keys*.

keyboard buffer A small amount of system memory used to store the most recently typed keys, also known as the type-ahead buffer. Some utility programs let you collect a number of keystrokes or commands and edit or reissue them.

keyboard connectors The connector that carries the signals from the keyboard controller to the CPU.

keyboard layout Most computers use a keyboard based on the traditional *QWERTY* typewriter-like keyboard.

In the *IBM PC* and *DOS* computers, the most common keyboard currently used has 101 keys, with 12 function keys arranged over the top of all the other keys.

keyboard template A plastic card that fits over certain keys (usually the *function keys*) on the keyboard to remind you how to use them. These templates are specific to an *application*, and can be very useful if you are an occasional user, or you are learning to use the program.

keyswitch Type of keyboard that works by using an individual switch for each key. When a key is pressed, a plunger under the key cap moves down and makes a connection between two signal lines coming from the keyboard controller, sending a signal to the computer.

kilo- A prefix indicating 1000 in the metric system. Because computing is based on powers of 2, in this context kilo usually means 2 to the 10th power or 1024. To differentiate between these two uses, a lowercase *k* is used to indicate 1000 (as in kHz), and an uppercase *K* to indicate 1024 (as in KB).

kilobit Abbreviated Kb or Kbit. 1024 *bits* (binary digits).

kilobits per second Abbreviated Kbps. The number of *bits*, or binary digits, transmitted every second, measured in multiples of 1024 bits per second. Used as an indicator of communications transmission rate.

kilobyte Abbreviated K, KB, or Kbyte. 1024 *bytes*.

LAN See *local area network*

LAN Manager A *network operating system*, developed by *Microsoft* and 3Com, that runs on *80386*, 80486 (and better) computers. The *file-server software* is a version of *OS/2*; client PCs can be OS/2, *DOS*, *Unix*, or *Macintosh*-based. *Disk mirroring*, *disk duplexing*, and *UPS*-monitoring functions are all available, and the operating system supports *IPX/SPX*, *TCP/IP* and *NetBEUI* communications protocols.

laptop computer A small *portable computer* light enough to carry comfortably, with a *flat screen* and keyboard that fold together.

Laptop computers are battery-operated, often have a thin, backlit or sidelit *LCD* display screen, and some models can even mate with a *docking station* to perform as a full-sized desktop system back at the office. Advances in battery technology allow laptop computers to run for many hours between charges, and some models have a set of business applications built into ROM.

laser printer   A *high-resolution* non-impact printer that uses a variation of the electro-photographic process used in photocopying machines to print text and graphics onto paper.

A laser printer uses a rotating disc to reflect laser beams onto a photosensitive drum, where the image of the page is converted into an electro-static charge that attracts and holds the toner. A piece of charged paper is then rolled against the drum to transfer the image, and heat is applied to fuse the toner and paper together to create the final image.

laser scanner   The assembly in an EP process printer that contains the laser. This component is responsible for writing the image to the EP drum.

latency   The time that elapses between issuing a request for *data*, and actually starting the data transfer.

In a *hard disk*, this translates into the time it takes to position the disk's read/write *head* and rotate the disk so that the required *sector* or *cluster* is under the head. Latency is just one of many factors that influence disk access speeds.

layout   In *printed-circuit board* design, the arrangement of the individual components on the circuit board.

LCD monitor   A *monitor* that uses *liquid-crystal display* technology. Many *laptop* and *notebook computers* use LCD displays because of their low power requirements.

LED page printer   A type of EP process printer that uses a row of LEDs instead of a laser to expose the EP drum.

letter quality   A printer mode that produces text higher in quality than *draft mode*. As the name suggests, letter quality printing is supposed to be good enough to be used in business letters, and therefore comparable to typewriter output. *Laser printers*, some *ink-jet printers* and all *daisy-wheel printers* produce letter-quality output; certain high-end *dot-matrix printers* can produce letter-quality output, but most do not.

light pen   A light-sensitive input device shaped like a pen, used to draw on the computer screen or to make menu selections. As the tip of the light pen makes contact with the screen, it sends a signal back to the computer containing the x-y coordinates of the *pixels* at that point.

light-emitting diode   Abbreviated LED. A small semiconductor device that emits light as current flows through it. LEDs are often used as activity lights on computer peripherals such as hard disk drives and modems.

line adapter   In communications, a device such as a modem that converts a digital signal into a form suitable for transmission over a communications channel.

line printer   Any printer that prints a complete line at a time, rather than printing one character at a time (as a *dot-matrix* or *daisy-wheel printer* does), or one page at a time (as a *laser printer* does). Line printers are very high-speed printers, and are common in the corporate environment where they are used with *mainframe computers, minicomputers*, and networked systems.

line sharing device   A small electronic device that allows a fax machine and a telephone answering machine to share the same phone line. The device answers the call and listens for the characteristic high-pitched fax carrier signal. If this signal is detected, the call is routed to the fax machine; if it is not present, the call is sent to a telephone or answering machine instead.

liquid crystal display   Abbreviated LCD. A display technology common in *portable computers* that uses electric current to align crystals in a special liquid.

The rod-shaped crystals are contained between two parallel transparent electrodes, and when current is applied, they change their orientation, creating a darker area. Many LCD screens are also back-lit or side-lit to increase visibility and reduce the possibility of eyestrain.

local area network   Abbreviated LAN. A group of computers and associated *peripherals* connected by a communications channel capable of sharing files and other resources between several users.

local bus   A PC *bus* specification that allows peripherals to exchange data at a rate faster than the 8 megabytes per second allowed by the *ISA* (Industry Standard Architecture), and the 32 megabytes per second allowed by the *EISA* (Extended Industry Standard Architecture) definitions. Local bus can achieve a maximum data rate of 133 megabytes per second with a 33MHz bus speed, 148 megabytes per second with a 40MHz bus, or 267 megabytes per second with a 50MHz bus.

To date, the *Video Electronics Standards Association (VESA)* video cards have been the main peripheral to benefit from local bus use.

local disk   In networking, a disk attached to a *workstation* rather than to the *file server*.

local printer   In networking, a printer attached to a *workstation* rather than to the *file server* or a *print server*.

logical drive   The internal division of a large *hard disk* into smaller units. One single *physical drive* may be organized into several logical drives for convenience; *DOS* supports up to 23 logical drives on a system. On a single-floppy system, the disk drive can function as both logical drive A and logical drive B, depending on the exact circumstances.

logical topology   Defines how the network is laid out as far as how messages travel within the network.

logic board   The sturdy sheet or board to which all other components on the computer are attached. These components consist of the CPU, underlying circuitry, expansion slots, video components, and RAM slots, just to name a few. Also known as a motherboard or planar board.

long file name   The ability of a file system to take advantage of multiple-character file names. Several operating systems are not limited to the DOS "8.3" file-naming convention of eight characters before a period and three more optional characters forming the *filename extension*. Unix, Windows 95, Windows NT, OS/2, and the Macintosh file systems can all manage long file names, even those containing spaces, more than one period, and mixed upper- and lowercase letters.

long-haul   A *modem* or other communications device that can transmit information over long distances.

lost chain   A part of a *file*, consisting of one or more *clusters*, that no longer has an entry in the *file allocation table*, and so cannot be reconnected to the rest of the file. The *DOS* command *CHKDSK* detects these lost chains, optionally converting them into files so that you can delete them and recover the disk space they occupy. You can also examine the contents of these lost chains after CHKDSK has recovered them, but the chance of the contents being usable is very slim indeed.

lost cluster   A *cluster*, originally once part of a *file*, for which there is now no *file allocation table* entry. Use the *DOS* command *CHKDSK* to convert lost clusters into files. You can then examine the contents of the cluster, and decide if you want to keep it or delete it and recover the disk space that it occupies.

low resolution   In monitors and printers, a description of low-quality output, lacking sharpness or definition. *Resolution* is determined by the technology used to create the output.

What actually constitutes low resolution is in the eye of the beholder; what one person may consider to be low resolution may be quite acceptable to another.

low-level format   The process that creates the *tracks* and *sectors* on a blank *hard disk* or *floppy disk*; sometimes called the physical format. Most hard disks are already low-level formatted; however, floppy disks receive both a low- and a *high-level format* (or logical format) when you use the *DOS* or *OS/2* command *FORMAT*.

LPTx ports   In *DOS*, the device name used to denote a parallel communications *port*, often used with a printer. DOS supports three parallel ports: LPT1, LPT2, and LPT3, and *OS/2* adds support for network ports LPT4 through LPT9.

LSB (Least Significant Bit)   Rightmost bit in a binary number.

magnetic field   An area of magnetism created around a current-carrying wire.

magneto-optical drives   Abbreviated MO. An erasable, high-capacity, removable storage device similar to a *CD-ROM drive*.

Magneto-optical drives use both magnetic and laser technology to write *data* to the disk, and use the laser to read that data back again. Writing data takes two passes over the disk, an erase pass followed by the write pass, but reading can be done in just one pass and, as a result, is much faster.

main motor   The stepper motor that is used to drive the rollers in the paper path of a printer.

mainframe computer   A large, fast *multiuser* computer system, designed to manage very large amounts of *data* and very complex computing tasks. Mainframes are normally installed in large corporations, universities, or military installations, and can support hundreds, even thousands, of users.

maintenance release   A software upgrade that corrects minor *bugs* or adds a few small features, distinguished from a major release by an increase in only the decimal portion of the version number—for example, from 3.0 to 3.1, rather than from 3.1 to 4.0.

major release version Leftmost number in a version number of a software release. A major release introduces several new features and may completely alter the way the software operates; thus, versions 2.01 and 2.32 may be only marginally different from each other, but versions 2.32 and 3.01 will appear significantly different in the way they work or in the tasks they can accomplish.

male connector Any cable connector with pins designed to engage the sockets on the female part of the connector.

Maltron keyboard An alternative keyboard designed to eliminate *carpal tunnel syndrome* that arranges the keys in two concave areas conforming to the shape of the hand, allowing better alignment of the forearm and wrist.

math coprocessor An processor that speeds up the floating decimal point calculations that are needed in algebra and statistical calculations.

MBONE Abbreviation for Multicast Backbone. An experimental method of transmitting digital video over the *Internet* in real time.

The TCP/IP protocols used for Internet transmissions are unsuitable for real time audio or video; they were designed to deliver text and other files reliably, but with some delay. MBONE requires the creation of another backbone service with special hardware and software to accommodate video and audio transmissions; the existing Internet hardware cannot manage time-critical transmissions.

MCA Abbreviation for Micro Channel Architecture. A *32-bit* proprietary *expansion bus* first introduced by IBM in 1987 for the *IBM PS/2* range of computers, and also used in the RS/6000 series.

MCA is incompatible with expansion boards that follow the earlier *16-bit* AT bus standard, physically because the boards are about 50 percent smaller, and electronically as the bus depends on more proprietary integrated circuits.

MCA was designed for *multiprocessing*, and it also allows expansion boards to identify themselves, thus eliminating many of the conflicts that arose through the use of manual settings in the original bus.

MCGA Acronym for Multi-Color Graphics Array. A *video adapter* included with certain *IBM PS/2* computers, that provides 64 gray shades with a palette of 16 colors at a resolution of 640 by 350 *pixels*.

MDA Acronym for Monochrome Display Adapter. A *video adapter* introduced in 1981 that could display text but not graphics, in one color, at a resolution of 640 *pixels* horizontally by 350 vertically. MDAs were replaced in many cases by the Hercules Graphics Card (*HGC*).

mean time between failures Abbreviated MTBF. The statistically-derived average length of time that a system component operates before failing.

mean time to repair Abbreviated MTTR. The average length of time that it takes to repair a failed component.

Media Control Interface   Abbreviated MCI. A standard *interface* used for controlling *multimedia* files and devices. Each device has its own *device driver* that implements a standard set of MCI functions such as stop, play, or record.

meg   A common abbreviation for *megabyte*.

mega-   Abbreviated M. A prefix meaning one million in the metric system. Because computing is based on powers of 2, in this context mega usually means 2^{20} or 1,048,576; the power of 2 closest to one million.

megabit   Abbreviated Mbit. Usually 1,048,576 binary digits or bits of *data*. Often used as equivalent to 1 million bits.

megabits per second   Abbreviated Mbps. A measurement of the amount of information moving across a network or communications link in one second, measured in multiples of 1,048,576 bits.

megabyte   Abbreviated MB. Usually 1,048,576 bytes. Megabytes are a common way of representing computer *memory* or *hard-disk* capacity.

megahertz   Abbreviated MHz. One million cycles per second. A processor's *clock speed* is often expressed in MHz. The original IBM PC operated an *8088* running at 4.77 MHz, while the more modern *Pentium* processor runs at speeds of up to 300 MHz and higher.

Megahertz (MHz)   Millions of cycles per second.

membrane keyboard   A pressure-sensitive keyboard covered by a protective plastic sheet used in a hostile environment where operators may not always have clean hands. While it is very difficult to type quickly and accurately on a membrane keyboard, they are most often used for occasional *data entry* in factories or in fast-food restaurants.

memory   The primary random-access memory (*RAM*) installed in the computer.

The operating system copies *application* programs from disk into memory, where all program execution and *data* processing takes place; results are written back out to disk again. The amount of memory installed in the computer can determine the size and number of programs that it can run, as well as the size of the largest data *file*.

memory address   The exact location in memory that stores a particular *data* item or program instruction.

memory board   A *printed circuit board* containing *memory* chips. When all the sockets on a memory board are filled, and the board contains the maximum amount of memory that it can manage, it is said to be "fully populated."

memory cache   An area of high-speed *memory* on the processor that stores commonly used code or *data* obtained from slower memory, replacing the need to access the system's main memory to fetch instructions.

The Intel 82385 cache controller chip was used with fast *static RAM* on some systems to increase performance, but more modern processors include cache management functions on the main processor. The Intel *80486* contains a single 8K cache to manage both *data* and instruction caching; the *Pentium* contains two separate 8K caches, one each for data and instructions.

memory chip   A chip that holds *data* or program instructions. A memory chip may hold its contents temporarily, as in the case of *RAM*, or permanently, as in the case of *ROM*.

memory management   The way in which the computer handles memory. In the PC, you may find the following kinds of memory:

- *Conventional memory*. This is the area of memory below 640 KB.

- *Upper memory*. Also known as reserved memory. The 384 KB of memory between 640 KB and 1 MB. This space is used by system hardware such as your *video adapter*. Unused portions of upper memory are known as *upper memory blocks* (UMBs), and on an *80386* (or later) processor, you can use these UMBs for loading device drivers or terminate-and-stay-resident programs.

- *Extended memory*. That memory above 1MB on 80386 (or later) processors. Extended memory needs an extended-memory manager such as *HIMEM.SYS*.

- *High memory area*. The first 64K of extended memory.

- *Expanded memory*. Memory above conventional memory that can be used by certain *DOS* applications, usually found on an expansion board.

memory management unit   Abbreviated MMU. The part of the processor that manages the mapping of virtual memory addresses to actual physical addresses.

In some systems, such as those based on early *Intel* or *Motorola* processors, the MMU was a separate chip; however, in most modern processors, the MMU is integrated into the *CPU* chip itself.

memory map   The organization and allocation of memory in a computer. A memory map will give an indication of the amount of memory used by the *operating system*, and the amount remaining for use by *applications*.

memory optimization   The process of making as much conventional memory available to DOS programs as possible.

mesh topology   Type of logical topology where each device on a network is connected to every other device on the network. This topology uses routers to search multiple paths and determine the best path.

message channel   A form of *interprocess communication* found in *multitasking operating systems*. Interprocess communications allow two programs running in the same computer to share information.

metafile   A *file* that contains information about other files, particularly those used for *data* interchange. For example, a graphics metafile contains not only a graphical image of some kind, but also information on how the image should be displayed. This allows the image to be output to a variety of different display devices. Metafiles often have the *file-name extension* .MET.

metropolitan area network   Abbreviated MAN. A public high-speed network, operating at 100 megabits per second, capable of voice and *data* transmission over a distance of up to 50 miles. A MAN is smaller than a wide area network (WAN) but larger than a local area network (LAN).

MFM (Modified FM)   A method of encoding data onto a hard disk that uses frequency modulation to efficiently convert electrical signals into magnetic flux patterns.

microcomputer   Any computer based on a single-chip processor. Many modern microcomputers are as powerful or even more powerful than *mainframe computers* from a few years ago.

microkernel   An alternative *kernel* design developed by researchers at Carnegie-Mellon University and implemented in the Mac *operating system*.

Traditionally, the kernel has been a monolithic piece of the operating system, resident in memory at all times, taking care of operations as varied as *virtual memory* management, *file* input/output and task scheduling. The microkernel, on the other hand, is a kernel stripped down to the point where it is only concerned with loading, running, and scheduling tasks. All other operating system functions (virtual memory management, disk input/output, and so on) are implemented and managed as tasks running on top of the microkernel.

micron   A unit of measurement. One millionth of a meter, corresponding to approximately 1/25,000 of an inch. The core diameter of *fiber optic* network cabling is often specified in terms of microns, with 62.5 being a common size.

microprocessor   Abbreviated processor. A *CPU* on one single chip. The first microprocessor was developed by *Intel* in 1969. The microprocessors most often used in PCs are the Motorola 680x0 series used in the *Apple Macintosh* computers, and the Intel 80x86 family used in IBM and *IBM-compatible* computers.

Besides computers, microprocessors are used in applications ranging from microwave ovens, VCRs, and automobiles to pocket calculators and *laser printers*.

MIDI   Pronounced "middy." Acronym for musical instrument digital interface. A standard *protocol* that describes communications between computers, synthesizers, and musical instruments.

Instead of transcribing a composition by hand, a musician can play the piece at a piano-style keyboard and record it on a computer as a series of musical messages. These messages include the start of a note, its length, tempo, pitch, attack, and decay time. Once this information is recorded on disk, it can be edited very easily using appropriate software; for example, transposing a piece from one key to another is an easy task for a computer, and a long, laborious task to perform manually.

MIDI port   A port that allows the connection of a musical instrument digital interface (*MIDI*) device to a personal computer.

The three types of port described in the standard are MIDI In, MIDI Out, and MIDI Thru. A synthesizer receives MIDI messages via its MIDI In port, and forwards messages to other devices using the MIDI Thru port. A synthesizer can send its own messages to the computer using the MIDI Out port.

MIDI ports are standard on the Atari ST personal computer, but have to be added to the *IBM-compatible* and *Macintosh* computers.

milli-   Abbreviated m. A prefix meaning one thousandth in the metric system, often expressed as 10^{-3}.

millisecond   Abbreviated ms or msec. A unit of measurement equal to one thousandth of a second. In computing, *hard disk* and *CD-ROM* drive *access times* are often described in terms of milliseconds; the higher the number the slower the disk system.

Millivolt   Abbreviated mv. A unit of measurement equal to one thousandth of a volt.

MIME   Abbreviation for Multipurpose Internet Mail Extensions. A set of extensions that allows *Internet e-mail* users to add non-ASCII elements such as graphics, PostScript files, audio, or video to their e-mail. Most of the common e-mail client programs include MIME capabilities.

minicomputer   A medium-sized computer system capable of managing over 100 users simultaneously, suitable for use in a small company or single corporate or government department. Compare to *mainframe computer*.

minihard disk   A hard disk mounted on a Type III *PCMCIA* card.

MIPS   Acronym for million of instructions per second. A measure of the processing speed of a computer's *CPU*.

MIPS R4000 and R4400   A family of 64-bit *microprocessors* from MIPS Computer Systems. The R4000 has a 1.3 million *transistor* design, with both an 8K data *cache* and an 8K instruction cache, as well as a *floating point processor*. Internally, the R4000 runs at 100 MHz, double its external 50-MHz clock output. The R4400, with 2.2 million transistors, is based on the R4000, but has larger cache units (16K data cache and 16K instruction cache), and runs internally at 150 MHz, externally at 75 MHz. Silicon Graphics acquired MIPS in June of 1992.

modem   Contraction of modulator/demodulator, a device that allows a computer to transmit information over a telephone line.

The modem translates between the *digital* signals that the computer uses, and *analog* signals suitable for transmission over telephone lines. When transmitting, the modem *modulates* the digital *data* onto a carrier signal on the telephone line. When receiving, the modem performs the reverse process, and *demodulates* the data from the carrier signal.

Modems usually operate at speeds ranging from 2,400 to 28,800 bits per second over standard telephone lines, and can use even faster rates over leased lines. A suitable communications program is needed to operate the modem.

modified frequency modulation encoding   Abbreviated MFM encoding. The most widely used method of storing *data* on a hard disk. Based on an earlier technique known as frequency modulation (FM) encoding, MFM achieves a two-fold increase in data storage density over standard FM recording, but it is not as efficient a space saver as *run-length limited encoding*.

modulation   In communications, the process used by a *modem* to add the *digital* signal onto the *carrier signal*, so that the signal can be transmitted over a telephone line.

The frequency, amplitude, or phase of a signal may be modulated to represent a digital or *analog* signal.

Molex connector   See *standard peripheral power connector*

monitor   A video output device capable of displaying text and graphics, often in color.

monochrome monitor   A *monitor* that can display text and graphics in one color only. For example, white text on a green background, or black text on a white background.

Most Significant Bit (MSB)   The leftmost bit in a binary number.

motherboard   The main *printed circuit board* in a computer that contains the *central processing unit*, appropriate *coprocessor* and support chips, device controllers, *memory*, and also *expansion slots* to give access to the computer's internal *bus*. Also known as a logic board or system board.

mouse   A small input device with one or more buttons used as for pointing or drawing. As you move the mouse in any direction, an on-screen mouse cursor follows the mouse movements; all movements are relative. Once the mouse pointer is in the correct position on the screen, you can press one of the mouse buttons to initiate an action or operation; different user interfaces and *file* programs interpret mouse clicks in different ways.

MS-DOS   Acronym for Microsoft Disk Operating System, pronounced "emm-ess-dos." MS-DOS, like other *operating systems*, allocates system resources such as hard and floppy disks, the monitor and the printer to the applications programs that need them.

MS-DOS is a *single-user*, single-tasking operating system, with either a *command-line interface*,

or a *shell* interface. It is the most ubiquitous operating system ever written, running over 50,000 different applications programs on an estimated 100 million computers.

MSD (Microsoft Diagnostics)   A PC diagnostic and technical information program first released along with *MS-DOS* 6.

multilayer   A *printed circuit board* that contains several different layers of circuitry. The layers are laminated together to make a single board, onto which the other discrete components are added.

multimedia   A computer technology that displays information using a combination of *full-motion video*, *animation*, sound, graphics and text with a high degree of user interaction.

multimedia personal computer   Abbreviated MPC. The Multimedia PC Marketing Council, consisting of several hardware and software vendors, including Microsoft, Zenith Data Systems, Video Seven, Media Vision, and NEC Technologies, sets standards for multimedia PCs and the software that runs on them.

The Council's original Level 1 minimum requirements for a multimedia PC included an *80386SX* running at 16 MHz, 2 MB of memory, a hard disk with 30 MB of free space, a *CD-ROM* capable of a 150K/second transfer rate and an *8-bit sound card*.

The newer Level 2 requirements now specify an *80486SX* running at 25 MHz, 8 MB of memory, a hard disk with 160 MB of free space, a double-speed *CD-ROM XA* capable of a 300K/second transfer rate, and a *16-bit* sound card.

multimeter Electronic device used to measure and test ohms, amperes, and volts.

multiple DOS configurations *DOS 6* includes features that allow you to define different system *configurations* and choose the one you want to use at startup time. This can be very useful if several people share the same computer system, or if you want to be able to swap between several configurations.

To do this you define a startup menu in your *CONFIG.SYS file*, and then create configuration blocks for each selection in the startup menu. When your system starts, the menu is presented on the screen, you choose the selection you want to use, and your system is configured accordingly.

multiplexing In communications, a technique that transmits several signals over a single communications channel.

Frequency-division multiplexing separates the signals by modulating the *data* into different carrier frequencies. *Time-division multiplexing* divides up the available time between the various signals. *Statistical multiplexing* uses statistical techniques to dynamically allocate transmission space depending on the traffic pattern.

multiplexor Often abbreviated mux. In communications, a device that merges several lower-speed transmission channels into one high-speed channel at one end of the link. Another multiplexor reverses this process at the other end of the link to reproduce the low-speed channels.

multiprocessing The ability of an *operating system* to use more than one *CPU* in a single computer. Symmetrical multiprocessing refers to the operating system's ability to assign tasks dynamically to the next available processor, whereas asymmetrical multiprocessing requires that the original program designer choose the processor to use for a given task at the time of writing the program.

multisync monitor A monitor designed to detect and adjust to a variety of different input signals. By contrast, a *fixed-frequency monitor* must receive a signal at one specific frequency.

multitasking The simultaneous execution of two or more programs in one computer.

multithreading The *concurrent* processing of several *tasks* or *threads* inside the same program. Because several tasks can be processed in parallel, one task does not have to wait for another to finish before starting.

multiuser Describes a computer system that supports more than one simultaneous user.

DOS, OS/2, Windows, and *Windows NT* are all *single-user operating systems; Unix* and its derivatives are all multiuser systems.

nano- Abbreviated n. A prefix meaning one-billionth in the American numbering scheme, and one thousand millionth in the British system.

nanosecond Abbreviated ns. One-billionth of second. The speed of computer memory and logic chips is measured in nanoseconds.

Processors operating at *clock speeds* of 25 MHz or more need *dynamic RAM* with access times of faster than 80 nanoseconds, while *static RAM* chips can be read in as little as 10 to 15 nanoseconds.

narrowband In communications, a voice-grade transmission channel of 2,400 bits per second or less.

near letter quality A quality of print output that is not quite as good as that created with a typewriter.

NetBEUI Abbreviation for NetBIOS Extended User Interface. A network *device driver* for the *transport layer* supplied with *Microsoft's LAN Manager*.

NetBIOS Acronym for Network Basic Input/Output System. In networking, a layer of software, originally developed in 1984 by IBM and Sytek, that links a *network operating system* with specific network hardware. NetBIOS provides an *application program interface* (API) with a consistent set of commands for requesting lower-level network services to transmit information from node to node.

netiquette A contraction of network etiquette. The set of unwritten rules governing the use of *e-mail*, *USENET newsgroups*, and other *online services*.

network A group of computers and associated peripherals connected by a communications *channel* capable of sharing files and other resources between several users.

A network can range from a *peer-to-peer network* connecting a small number of users in an office or department, to a *local area network* connecting many users over permanently installed cables and dial-up lines, or to a *wide area network* connecting users on several different networks spread over a wide geographic area.

network architecture The descriptions and rules for defining the structure of the network, including hardware, software, and layer.

network file system Abbreviated NFS. A distributed file sharing system developed almost a decade ago by Sun Microsystems, Inc.

NFS allows a computer on a network to use the files and peripherals of another networked computer as if they were local. NFS is platform-independent, and runs on mainframes, minicomputers, *RISC*-based *workstations*, *diskless workstations*, and personal computers. NFS has been licensed and implemented by more than 300 vendors.

network interface card Abbreviated NIC. In networking, the PC expansion board that plugs into a personal computer or server and works with the *network operating system* to control the flow of information over the network. The network interface card is connected to the network cabling (*twisted pair*, *coaxial* or *fiber optic cable*), which in turn connects all the network interface cards in the network.

network layer The third of seven layers of the International Standards Organization's Open Systems Interconnection (ISO/OSI) model for computer-to-computer communications.

The network layer defines protocols for data routing to ensure that the information arrives at the correct destination node.

network media The media used to transfer data from one point to another on a network.

newsgroup A USENET e-mail group devoted to the discussion of a single topic. *Subscribers post articles* to the newsgroup which can then be read by all the other subscribers. Newsgroups do not usually contain hard news items.

NeXT   Originally a *Unix*-based *workstation* from NeXT Inc. using a 24 MHz *Motorola 68040* processor, a high-resolution color display, stereo sound, and an erasable optical disk.

NeXT computers had the reputation for being well manufactured and providing good value for money; however, the hardware part of the company was sold to Canon in 1993, and NeXT now concentrates on marketing the software development environment known as NeXTStep, a windowed, *object-oriented*, programming environment for creating graphics-based *applications*.

NIC   See *network interface card*

node   In communications, any device attached to the network.

noise   In communications, extraneous signals on a transmission channel that degrade the quality or performance of the channel. Noise is often caused by interference from nearby power lines, from electrical equipment, or from *spikes* in the *AC* line voltage.

non-conductor   Material that inhibits the flow of electricity. See also *insulator*.

non-dedicated server   A computer that can be both a server and a workstation. In practice, by performing the functions of both server and workstation, this type of server does neither function very well. Non-dedicated servers are typically used in peer-to-peer network.

non-impact printer   Any printer that creates an image without striking a ribbon against the paper.

Nonimpact printers include *thermal printers*, *ink-jet printers*, and *laser printers*. These printers are all much quieter in operation than *impact printers*, and their main drawback is that they cannot use multi-part paper to make several copies of the same printout or report.

non-integrated system board   System board characterized by having each major assembly installed as expansion cards.

non-interlaced   Describes a *monitor* in which the display is updated (*refreshed*) in a single pass, painting every line on the screen. *Interlacing* takes two passes to paint the screen, painting every other line on the first pass, and then sequentially filling in the other lines on the second pass. Non-interlaced scanning, while more expensive to implement, reduces unwanted *flicker* and eyestrain.

non-preemptive multitasking   Any form of multitasking where the operating system cannot preempt a running *task* and process the next task in the queue.

The *cooperative multitasking* scheme used in *Microsoft Windows* is non-preemptive, and the drawback to this method is that while programs are easy to write for this environment, a single badly-written program can hog the whole system. By refusing to relinquish the processor, such a program can cause serious problems for other programs running at the same time. Poorly-written non-preemptive multitasking can produce a kind of stuttering effect on running *applications*, depending on how well (or badly) programs behave.

nonvolatile memory Any form of *memory* that holds its contents when power is removed. *ROM*, *EPROM*, and *EEPROM* are all nonvolatile memory.

Norton Utilities A popular package of small *utility programs* from the Peter Norton Computing Group of Symantec Corporation that run on *DOS* computers, the *Macintosh*, and *Unix*-based systems.

The utilities include UnErase, the famous file-recovery program; Speed Disk, the disk *defragmenting* program; and Norton Disk Doctor, a program that finds and fixes both logical and physical problems on hard and floppy disks.

NOS (Network Operating System) Software that runs on the server and controls and manages the network. The NOS controls the communication with resources and the flow of data across the network.

notebook computer A small *portable computer*, about the size of a computer book, with a *flat screen* and a keyboard that fold together.

A notebook computer is lighter and smaller than a *laptop computer*, and recent advances in battery technology allow them to run for as long as 9 hours between charges. Some models use *flash memory* rather than conventional hard disks for program and data storage, while other models offer a range of business applications in *ROM*. Many offer *PCMCIA expansion slots* for additional *peripherals* such as *modems*, *fax modems*, or network connections.

NTSC Abbreviation for National Television System Committee, founded in 1941 to establish broadcast-television standards in North America.

NTSC originally defined a picture composed of 525 horizontal lines, consisting of two separate interlaced fields of 262.5 lines each, refreshed at 30 Hz, or 30 times a second. The modern broadcast signal carries more information including multichannel television sound (MTS) and second audio program (SAP). Many personal computer video controllers can output an NTSC-compatible signal in addition to or instead of their usual monitor signal.

null A character that has all the binary digits set to zero (*ASCII* 0), and therefore has no value.

In programming, a null character is used for several special purposes, including padding fields, or serving as delimiter characters. In the C language, for example, a null character indicates the end of a *character string*.

null modem A short *RS-232-C* cable that connects two personal computers so that they can communicate without the use of *modems*. The cable connects the two computers' serial ports, and certain lines in the cable are crossed over so that the wires used for sending data by one computer are used for receiving data by the other computer, and vice versa.

numeric keypad A set of keys to the right of the main part of the keyboard, used for numeric data entry.

object-oriented A term that can be applied to any computer system, *operating system*, *programming language*, *application program*, or *graphical user interface* that supports the use of *objects*.

octet The *Internet's* own term for eight bits or a *byte*. Some computer systems attached to the Internet have used a byte with more than eight bits, hence the need for this term.

odd parity   A technique that counts the number of *1*s in a binary number and, if the number of *1*s total is not an odd number, adds a digit to make it odd. See also *parity*.

OEM   Acronym for original equipment manufacturer. The original manufacturer of a *hardware* subsystem or component. For example, Canon makes the print engine used in many laser printers, including those from Hewlett-Packard; in this case, Canon is the OEM and HP is a value-added reseller (*VAR*).

offline   Describes a printer or other *peripheral* that is not currently in ready mode and is therefore unavailable for use.

off-the-shelf   Describes a ready-to-use hardware or software product that is packaged and ready for sale, as opposed to one that is proprietary or has been customized.

ohm   Unit of electrical resistance.

online

1. Most broadly, describes any capability available directly on a computer, as in "online *help* system"; or any work done on a computer instead of by more traditional means.

2. Describes a *peripheral* such as a printer or modem when it is directly connected to a computer and ready to operate.

3. In communications, describes a computer connected to another, remote, computer over a network or a modem link.

online service   A service that provides an *online* connection via *modem* for access to various services. Online services fall into four main groups:

- **Commercial services:** Services such as *America Online*, *CompuServe*, and *Netcom* charge a monthly membership fee for access to their own online *forums*, *e-mail* services, software libraries, and online *conferences*.

- **Internet:** The *Internet* is a worldwide network of computer systems located at government and educational institutions. The Internet is not always easy to access from a home PC, nor is it always easy to use, but the wealth of information available is staggering. The main problem for casual users is that there is no central listing of everything that is available.

- **Specialist databases:** Specific databases aimed at researchers can be accessed through online services such as *Dow Jones News/Retrieval* for business news, and Lexis and Nexis, the legal information and news archives.

- **Local Bulletin boards:** There are thousands of small, local *bulletin board systems* (BBS), often run from private homes, by local PC *Users Groups*, or by local schools. Some BBS offer software libraries, e-mail, online conferences, and games, while others may be devoted to a specific subject. Look for listings in local computer-related publications, or ask at your local PC Users Group.

Exploring the world of online services is a fascinating pastime that can eat up all your spare time; it can also quickly increase your phone bill.

open architecture   A vendor-independent computer design that is publicly available and well understood within the industry. An open architecture allows the user to configure the computer easily by adding *expansion cards*.

operating system Abbreviated OS. The software responsible for allocating system resources, including memory, processor time, disk space, and peripheral devices such as printers, modems, and the monitor. All *application* programs use the operating system to gain access to these system resources as they are needed. The operating system is the first program loaded into the computer as it *boots*, and it remains in memory at all times thereafter.

Popular PC operating systems include *DOS, OS/2, Windows 95, Windows 98, Windows NT,* and *Unix.*

optical character recognition Abbreviated OCR. The computer recognition of printed or typed characters. OCR is usually performed using a standard optical *scanner* and special software, although some systems use special readers. The text is reproduced just as though it had been typed. Certain advanced systems can resolve neat hand-written characters.

optical disk A disk that can be read from and written to, like a fixed disk, but, like a CD, is read with a laser.

optical drive A type of storage drive that uses a laser to read from and write to the storage medium.

optical mouse A mouse that uses a special mouse pad and a beam of laser light. The beam of light shines onto the mouse pad and reflects back to a sensor in the mouse. Special small lines crossing the mouse pad reflect the light into the sensor in different ways to signal the position of the mouse.

optical scanner An input peripheral that uses CCD devices and a light source to "read" an image and convert it into a stream of data.

optical touch screen A type of touch screen that uses light beams on the top and left side, and optical sensors on the bottom and right side to detect the position of your finger when you touch the screen.

option diskette A diskette that contains the device-specific configuration files for the device being installed into a MCA bus computer.

opto-mechanical mouse Type of mouse that contains a round ball that makes contact with two rollers. Each roller is connected to a wheel that has small holes in it. The wheel rotates between the arms of a U-shaped mechanism that holds a light on one arm and an optical sensor on the other. As the wheels rotate, the light flashes coming through the holes indicate the speed and direction of the mouse, and these values are transmitted to the computer and the mouse control software.

OS/2 A *32-bit multitasking operating system* for *Intel 80386* (or later) processors, originally developed by Microsoft and IBM, but now wholly supported by IBM.

Originally, OS/2 was developed jointly by Microsoft and IBM as the successor to DOS, while Windows was developed as a stop-gap measure until OS/2 was ready. However, Microsoft chose to back Windows, placing considerable resources behind the breakthrough release of Windows 3.0. IBM took control of OS/2 development, and in Spring 1992 released OS/2 version 2.0, which was widely hailed as a major technical achievement, winning several prestigious industry awards.

OSI (Open Systems Interconnection) model A protocol model, developed by the International Standards Organization (ISO), that was intended to provide a common way of describing network protocols. This model describes a seven-layered relationship between the stages of communication. Not every protocol maps perfectly to the OSI model, as there is some overlap within some the layers of some protocols.

output Computer generated information that is displayed on the screen, printed, written to disk or tape, or sent over a communications link to another computer.

packet Any block of data sent over a network. Each packet contains information about the sender and the receiver, and error-control information, in addition to the actual message. Packets may be fixed- or variable-length, and they will be reassembled if necessary when they reach their destination.

packet switching A data transmission method that simultaneously sends data packets from many sources over the same communications channel or telephone line, thus optimizing use of the line.

page description language Describes the whole page being printed. The controller in the printer interprets these commands and turns them into laser pulses or firing print wires.

page printers Type of printer that handles print jobs one page at a time instead of one line at a time.

paged memory management unit Abbreviated PMMU. A specialized chip designed to manage *virtual memory*. High-end processors such as the Motorola *68030* and *68040*, and the Intel *80386*, *80486*, and later, have all the functions of a PMMU built into the chip itself.

page-mode RAM A *memory-management* technique used to speed up the performance of *dynamic RAM*.

In a page-mode memory system, the memory is divided into pages by specialized dynamic RAM chips. Consecutive accesses to *memory addresses* in the same page results in a page-mode cycle that takes about half the time of a regular dynamic RAM cycle. For example, a normal dynamic RAM cycle time can take from 130 to 180 *nanoseconds*, while a typical page-mode cycle can be completed in 30 to 40 nanoseconds.

pages per minute Abbreviated ppm. An approximation of the number of pages that a laser printer can print in one minute. This number often represents the rate that the printer can reach when printing the simplest output; if you combine text with complex graphics, performance will fall.

palmtop computer A very small battery-powered *portable computer* that you can hold in one hand, often weighing about a pound. Most palmtop computers have small screens and tiny keyboards.

paper pickup roller A D-shaped roller that rotates against the paper and pushes one sheet into the printer.

paper registration roller A roller in an EP process printer that keeps paper movement in sync with the EP image formation process.

paper transport assembly The set of devices that moves the paper through the printer. It consists of a motor and several rubberized rollers that each perform a different function.

parallel communications The transmission of information from computer to computer, or from computer to a peripheral, where all the bits that make up the character are transmitted at the same time over a multiline cable.

parallel port An input/output port that manages information 8 bits at a time, often used to connect a *parallel printer*.

parallel printer Any printer that can be connected to the computer using the *parallel port*.

parallel processing A computing method that can only be performed on systems containing two or more processors operating simultaneously.

Parallel processing uses several processors, all working on different aspects of the same program at the same time, in order to share the computational load. Parallel processing computers can reach incredible speeds; the Cray X-MP48 peaks at 1000 million floating point operations per second (1000 MFLOP) using just four extremely powerful processors, while parallel-hypercube systems first marketed by Intel can exceed 65,536 processors with possible speeds of up to 262 billion floating point operations per second (262 GFLOPS). What is this mind-boggling speed used for? Applications such as weather forecasting where the predictive programs can take as long to run as the weather actually takes to arrive, 3-D seismic modeling, groundwater and toxic flow studies, and modeling full-motion dinosaur images used in movies.

parameter RAM Abbreviated PRAM and pronounced pee-ram. A small part of the Macintosh random-access memory (RAM) that holds information including the hardware configuration, the date and time, which disk is the startup disk, and information about the state of the Desktop. The contents of PRAM are maintained by a battery, and so the contents are not lost when the Mac is turned off or unplugged at the end of your session.

parity In communications, a simple form of error checking that uses an extra, or redundant, bit, after the *data bits* but before the *stop bit(s)*.

Parity may be set to odd, even, mark, space, or none. Odd parity indicates that the sum of all the 1 bits in the byte plus the parity bit must be odd. If the total is already odd, the parity bit is set to zero; if it is even, the parity bit is set to 1.

In even parity, if the sum of all the 1 bits is even, the parity bit must be set to 0; if it is odd, the parity bit must be set to 1.

In mark parity, the parity bit is always set to 1, and is used as the eighth bit.

In space parity, the parity bit is set to 0, and used as the eighth bit.

If parity is set to none, there is no parity bit, and no *parity checking* is performed.

The parity setting on your computer must match the setting on the remote computer for successful communications. Most *online services* use no parity and an eight-bit data *word*.

parity bit An extra or redundant bit used to detect transmission errors.

parity checking A check mechanism applied to a character or series of characters that uses the addition of extra or redundant bits known as *parity bits*. Parity checking is used in situations as diverse as asynchronous communications and computer memory coordination.

parity error A mismatch in *parity bits* that indicates an error in transmitted data.

park To move the hard disk read/write heads to a safe area of the disk (called a landing zone) before you turn your system off, to guard against damage when the computer is moved. Most modern hard disks park their heads automatically, and so you do not need to run a special program to park the heads.

partition A portion of a *hard disk* that the *operating system* treats as if it were a separate *drive*.

In *DOS*, a hard disk can be divided into several partitions, including a *primary DOS partition*, an *extended DOS partition*, and a non-DOS partition:

- The primary DOS partition contains important DOS files needed to start the computer running, and is generally assigned the drive letter C.

- The extended DOS partition can help organize that part of the hard disk not occupied by the primary DOS partition.

- The non-DOS partition is only needed if you want to use more than one operating system at a time on your computer; if you only plan to use DOS, you don't need to reserve disk space for a non-DOS partition.

Information about these partitions, including which of them is the *active partition*, is contained in the *partition table*. Partitions are created or changed using the *FDISK* command. Floppy disks cannot be shared between different operating systems, and so do not have partitions.

partition table In *DOS*, an area of the *hard disk* containing information on how the disk is organized.

The partition table also contains information that tells the computer which *operating system* to load; most disks will contain DOS, but some users may divide their hard disk into different *partitions*, or areas, each containing a different operating system. The partition table indicates which of these partitions is the *active partition*, the partition that should be used to start the computer.

passive hub Type of hub that electrically connects all network ports together. This type of hub is not powered.

passive-matrix screen An *LCD* display mechanism that uses a transistor to control every row of *pixels* on the screen. This is in sharp contrast to *active-matrix screens*, where each individual pixel is controlled by its own transistor. Passive-matrix displays are slower to respond, have weaker colors, and have a narrower viewing angle, but they are much cheaper to make than active-matrix displays.

patch A quick software "fix" used to resolve a problem until the next release of the software.

patch level Part of a (software) program's version identification number that indicates that this version of software has had some errors fixed, but that there are no new features. If there is a patch number, it follows the major release number and maintenance release number; in other words, it will be the third (or sometimes the third and fourth) digit of the version number.

PC Acronym for "personal computer." A computer specifically designed for use by one person at a time, equipped with its own *central processing unit*, *memory*, *operating system*, *keyboard* and display, *hard-* and *floppy disks*, as well as other *peripherals* when needed.

When written in capital letters, the acronym usually indicates a computer conforming to the IBM standard rather than a *Macintosh* computer. The spelled-out capitalized form, Personal Computer, indicates that the computer was made by IBM.

PC Card A term describing add-in cards that conform to the *PCMCIA* (Personal Computer Memory Card International Association) standard.

PC Card slot An opening in the case of a *portable computer* intended to receive a *PC Card*; also known as a *PCMCIA* slot.

PC Card Socket Services See *Socket Services*

PC Tools A popular set of *utility programs* offered by Central Point Software for IBM-compatible and Macintosh computers.

PC Tools has been called the Swiss army knife of utility packages, and the programs do cover an incredible range, including a DOS *shell*, word processing and database programs, complex calculators for financial and scientific use, *fax*, *modem*, and PC-to-PC communications, disk diagnostics, *file recovery*, file backup, *virus* detection and protection, and disk optimization and *file defragmentation* programs.

A *Microsoft Windows* version was released in 1993, and in 1994, Central Point Software was bought by Symantec.

PC-DOS The version of the *DOS operating system* supplied with PCs sold by IBM.

PC-DOS and *MS-DOS* started out as virtually identical operating systems, with only a few very minor differences in device driver names and file sizes, but after the release of MS-DOS 6, the two grew much further apart.

PC-DOS 7 was released by IBM in early 1995, and includes the *REXX* programming language, enhanced *PCMCIA* support, *Stacker* file-compression, and FILEUP, an application used to *synchronize* files between portable and desktop PCs.

PCI Abbreviation for Peripheral Component Interconnect. A specification introduced by *Intel* that defines a *local bus* that allows up to ten PCI-compliant expansion cards to be plugged into the computer. One of these ten cards must be the PCI controller card, but the others can include a video card, network interface card, SCSI interface, or any other basic input/output function.

The PCI controller exchanges information with the computer's processor as 32- or 64-bits, and allows intelligent PCI adapters to perform certain tasks concurrently with the main processor by using *bus mastering* techniques.

PCI can operate at a bus speed of 32 MHz, and can manage a maximum throughput of 132 megabytes per second with a 32-bit data path or 264 megabytes per second with a 64-bit data path.

PCMCIA Abbreviation for PC Memory Card International Association. A nonprofit association formed in 1989 with over 320 members in the computer and electronics industries that developed a standard for credit-card size plug-in adapters aimed at *portable computers*.

A PCMCIA adapter card, or *PC Card*, uses a 68-pin connector, with longer power and ground pins, so they always engage before the signal pins. Several versions of the standard have been approved by PCMCIA:

- **Type I:** The thinnest PC Card, only 3.3 mm thick; used for memory enhancements including *dynamic RAM*, *static RAM*, and *EEPROM*.

- **Type II:** A card used for *modems* or LAN adapters, 5 mm thick.

- **Type III:** A 10.5 mm card, used for *mini-hard disks* and other devices that need more space, including wireless LANs.

In theory, although space is always a major consideration, each PCMCIA adapter can support 16 PC Card sockets, and up to 255 adapters can be installed in a PC that follows the PCMCIA standard; in other words PCMCIA allows for up to 4080 PC Cards on the same computer.

The majority of PCMCIA devices are *modems*, *Ethernet* and *Token Ring* network adapters, dynamic RAM, and *flash memory* cards, although mini-hard disks, *wireless LAN* adapters, and *SCSI* adapters are also available.

PDA   Abbreviation for Personal Digital Assistant. A tiny *pen-based palmtop computer* that combines fax, *e-mail*, *PCMCIA* support, and simple word processing into an easy-to-use unit that fits into a pocket. PDAs are available from several manufacturers, including Apple's Newton, and others from Casio, Tandy, Toshiba, Motorola, Sharp, Sony, and AT&T.

peer-to-peer networks   Network where the computers act as both workstations and servers, and where there is no centralized administration or control.

pen-based computer   A computer that accepts handwriting as input. Using a pen-like stylus, you print neatly on a screen, and the computer translates this input using *pattern recognition* techniques. You can also choose selections from on-screen menus using the stylus.

Pentium   A 32-bit *microprocessor* introduced by *Intel* in 1993. After losing a courtroom battle to maintain control of the *x*86 designation, Intel named this member of its family the Pentium rather than the 80586 or the 586. The Pentium represents the continuing evolution of the *80486* family of microprocessors, and adds several notable features, including 8K instruction code and data *caches*, built-in *floating-point processor* and *memory management unit*, as well as a *superscalar* design and dual *pipelining* that allow the Pentium to execute more than one instruction per clock cycle.

Available in a whole range of clock speeds, from 60 MHz all the way up to 300+ MHz versions, the Pentium is equivalent to an astonishing 3.1 million *transistors*, more than twice that of the 80486.

Pentium Pro   The latest microprocessor in the 80*x*86 family from Intel. The 32-bit P6 has a 64-bit data path between the processor and cache, and is capable of running at clock speeds up to 200 MHz. Unlike the Pentium, the Pentium Pro has its secondary cache built into the CPU itself, rather than on the motherboard, meaning that it accesses cache at internal speed, not bus speed. The Pentium Pro contains the equivalent of 5.5 million transistors, and is aimed at the server and very high-end desktop markets.

peripheral   Any hardware device attached to and controlled by a computer, such as a monitor, keyboard, hard-disk, floppy-disk, CD-ROM drives, printer, mouse, tape drive, and joystick.

permanent swap file   A *swap file* that, once created, is used over and over again. This file is used in *virtual memory* operations, where *hard disk* space is used in place of random-access memory (*RAM*).

A permanent swap file allows *Microsoft Windows* to write information to a known place on the hard disk, which enhances performance over using conventional methods with a *temporary swap file*. The Windows permanent swap file consists of a large number of consecutive contiguous *clusters*; it is often the largest single file on the hard disk, and of course this disk space cannot be used by any other *application*. If you have plenty of unused hard disk space, consider a permanent swap file to boost performance. If disk space is at a premium, use a temporary swap file to conserve disk space, at the cost of a slight loss in performance.

peta-   Abbreviated P. A prefix for one quadrillion, or 10 to the 15th power. In computing, based on the binary system, peta has the value of 1,125,899,906,842,624, or the power of 2 closest to one quadrillion (thus, 2 to the 50th power).

petabyte   Abbreviated PB. Although it can represent one quadrillion bytes (10 to the 15th power), it usually refers to 1,125,899,906,842,624 bytes (2 to the 50th power).

PGA (Pin Grid Array)   A type of IC package that consists of a grid of pins connected to a square, flat package.

phosphor   The special electrofluorescent coating used on the inside of a *CRT* screen that glows for a few milliseconds when struck by an electron beam. Because the illumination is so brief, it must be refreshed constantly to maintain an image.

Photo CD   A specification from Kodak that allows you to record and then display photographic images on CD. Originally, only single-session recordings could be made, where the images were recorded during a single recording session. However, several CD-ROM players are now compatible with multi-session Photo CD, where images can be loaded onto the CD several times over several different recording sessions.

photosensitive drum   See *EP Drum*

physical drive   A real device in the computer that you can see or touch, rather than a *logical drive*, which is a part of the *hard disk* that functions as if it were a separate disk drive but is not. One physical drive may be divided into several logical drives.

physical layer   The first and lowest of the seven layers in the International Standards Organization's Open Systems Interconnection (*ISO/OSI*) model for computer-to-computer communications. The physical layer defines the physical, electrical, mechanical, and functional procedures used to connect the equipment.

physical topology   A description that identifies how the cables on a network are physically arranged.

pickup roller   See *paper pickup roller*

pin-compatible   A description of a chip or other electronic component with connecting pins exactly equivalent to the connecting pins used by a different device. This allows for easy system upgrade; you replace the older chip with a newer, more capable version.

pincushion distortion   A type of distortion that usually occurs at the edges of a video screen where the sides of an image seem to bow inwards.

pipelining

1. In processor architecture, a method of fetching and decoding instructions that ensures that the processor never needs to wait; as soon as an instruction is executed, another is waiting.

2. In parallel processing, the method used to pass instructions from one processing unit to another.

pits and lands   Refers to the indentations and spaces between them; the indentations are etched into a CD by the CD recorder's laser beam. When the CD is played, the read laser reflects off the CD's surface and onto a sensor, which detects the sequence of pits and lands and translates those patterns into sequences of *1*s and *0*s.

pixel   Contraction of picture element. The smallest element that display software can use to create text or graphics. A display *resolution* described as being 640 × 480 has 640 pixels across the screen and 480 down the screen, for a total of 307,200 pixels. The higher the number of pixels, the higher the screen resolution.

A monochrome pixel can have two values, black or white, and this can be represented by one bit as either zero or one. At the other end of the scale, *true color*, capable of displaying approximately 16.7 million colors, requires 24 bits of information for each pixel.

platter   The actual disk inside a *hard disk* enclosure that carries the magnetic recording material. Many hard disks have multiple platters, most of which have two sides that can be used for recording data.

plotter   A *peripheral* used to draw high-resolution charts, graphs, layouts, and other line-based diagrams, and often used with CAD (*computer aided design*) systems.

Plug-and-Play   Abbreviated PnP. A standard from Compaq, Microsoft, Intel, and Phoenix that defines automatic techniques designed to make PC configuration simple and straightforward. Currently, ISA expansion boards are covered by the specification, but the standard may soon also cover *SCSI* and *PCMCIA* buses.

PnP adapters contain configuration information stored in non-volatile memory, which includes vendor information, serial number, and checksum information. The PnP chipset allows each adapter to be isolated, one at a time, until all cards have been properly identified by the operating system.

PnP requires *BIOS* changes so that cards can be isolated and identified at boot time; when you insert a new card, the BIOS should perform an auto-configuration sequence enabling the new card with appropriate settings. New systems with flash BIOS will be easy to change; older systems with ROM BIOS will need a hardware change before they can take advantage of PnP.

Plug-and-Pray   What most of us will do when our *Plug-and-Play* systems do not work automatically.

plug-compatible   Describes any hardware device designed to work in exactly the same way as a device manufactured by a different company.

For example, external *modems* are plug-compatible, in that you can replace one with another without changing the cabling or connector.

polling   Method of media access that requires a central, intelligent device that asks every workstation in turn if it has any data to transmit. If the workstation responds in the affirmative, the controller allows the workstation to transmit its data.

port

1. A physical connection, such as a *serial port* or a *parallel port*.

2. To move a program or *operating system* from one hardware platform to another. For example, *Windows NT* portability refers to the fact that the same operating system can run on both *Intel* and *RISC* architectures.

3. A number used to identify a specific *Internet* application (location).

post   An individual *article* or *e-mail* message sent to a *USENET newsgroup* or to a *mailing list*, rather than to a specific individual. Post can also refer to the process of sending the article to the newsgroup.

POST   See *Power-On Self-Test*

posting   The process of sending an individual *article* or *e-mail* message to a *newsgroup* or to a *mailing list*.

PostScript   A *page-description language* developed by Adobe Systems, Inc., used when printing high-quality text and graphics. *Desktop publishing* or illustration programs that create PostScript output can print on any PostScript printer or imagesetter, because PostScript is *hardware-independent*. An *interpreter* in the printer translates the PostScript commands into commands that the printer can understand. This means that you can create your document, and then take it to any print shop with a PostScript printer to make the final printed output.

PostScript uses English-like commands to scale *outline fonts* and control the page layout; because of this, users have a great deal of flexibility when it comes to font specification.

PostScript printer   A printer that can interpret *PostScript page-description language* commands. Because the PostScript page-description language is complex and computer intensive, PostScript printers often contain as much computing power as the PC you originally used to create the output, and they are often much more expensive than standard printers.

potentiometer   See *variable resistor*

power supply   A part of the computer that converts the power from a wall outlet into the lower voltages, typically 5 to 12 volts DC, required internally in the computer. PC power supplies are usually rated in watts, ranging from 90 watts at the low end to 300 watts at the high end. If the power supply in your computer fails, nothing works, not even the fan.

The power supply is one of the main sources of heat in a computer and usually requires a fan to provide additional ventilation; it is also a sealed unit with no operator-serviceable parts, and you should make sure it stays that way.

power surge   A brief but sudden increase in line voltage, often destructive, usually caused by a nearby electrical appliance such as a photocopier or elevator, or when power is reapplied after an outage.

power user   A person who is proficient with many software packages, and who understands how to put the computer to work quickly and effectively. While not necessarily a programmer, a power user is familiar with creating and using *macros*, and other command languages.

power-on self test   Abbreviated POST. A set of *diagnostic programs*, loaded automatically from *ROM BIOS* during startup, designed to ensure that the major system components are present and operating. If a problem is found, the POST software writes an error message in the screen, sometimes with a diagnostic code number indicating the type of fault located. These POST tests execute before any attempt is made to load the operating system.

PowerPC   A family of *microprocessors* jointly developed by Apple, Motorola, and IBM. The *32-bit* 601 houses 2.8 million transistors, runs at 110 MHz, and is designed for use in high-performance, low-cost PCs. The 66MHz 602 is targeted at the consumer electronics and entry-level computer markets. The low-wattage 603e is aimed at battery-powered computers, the 604 is for high-end PCs and workstations, and the top-of-the-line 620 is designed for servers and very high performance applications. The 620 is a 64-bit chip.

PCs based on the PowerPC chip usually include a minimum of 16 MB of memory, a 540MB hard disk, PCI bus architecture including a local-bus based graphics adapter, and a CD-ROM.

PPP   Abbreviation for Point-to-Point Protocol. One of the most common protocols used to connect a PC to an *Internet* host via high-speed modem and a telephone line.

PPP establishes a temporary but direct connection to an Internet host, eliminating the need for connecting to an interim system. PPP also provides a method of automatically assigning an IP address, so that remote or mobile systems can connect to the network at any point.

preemptive multitasking   A form of *multitasking* where the operating system executes an application for a specific period of time, according to its assigned priority and need. At that time, it is preempted, and another task is given access to the *CPU* for its allocated time. Although an application can give up control before its time is up, such as during input/output waits, no task is ever allowed to execute for longer than its allotted time period. *OS/2*, *Unix*, *Windows 95*, *Windows 98*, and *Windows NT* all use preemptive multitasking.

presentation layer   The sixth of seven layers of the International Standards Organization's Open Systems Interconnection (*ISO/OSI*) model for computer-to-computer communications. The presentation layer defines the way that data is formatted, presented, converted, and encoded.

primary DOS partition   In *DOS*, a division of the *hard disk* that contains important *operating system* files.

A DOS hard disk can be divided into two partitions, or areas; the *primary DOS partition*, and the *extended DOS partition*. If you want to start your computer from the hard disk, the disk must contain an active primary DOS partition that includes the three DOS system files: *MSDOS.SYS*, *IO.SYS*, and *COMMAND.COM*. The primary DOS partition on the first hard disk in the system is referred to as drive C.

Disk partitions are displayed, created, and changed using the *FDISK* command.

print consumables   Items that are used up or are regularly worn out by a printer and thus need to be replaced.

print controller assembly   Large circuit board in the printer that converts signals from the computer into signals for the various parts in the laser printer.

print media   The material that is printed on when a printer is printing.

print server   Server that hosts printing services for users.

printed-circuit board   Abbreviated PCB. Any flat board made of plastic or fiberglass that contains chips and other electronic components. Many PCBs are *multi-layer* boards with several different sets of copper traces connecting components together.

printer   A computer *peripheral* that presents computer output as a printed image on paper or film.

Printers vary considerably in price, speed, *resolution*, noise level, convenience, paper-handling abilities, printing mechanism, and quality, and all of these points should be considered when making a selection.

printer emulation   The ability of a printer to change modes so that it behaves just like a printer from another manufacturer.

Many *dot-matrix printers* offer an *Epson* printer emulation in addition to their own native mode. This means you can use the printer as an Epson printer just by changing some switches; a useful feature if the software you are using does not have a *device driver* for your printer, but does have the appropriate Epson driver. Many non-HP laser printers support an HP LaserJet emulation.

printer ribbon   Cloth or polyester ribbon that is soaked in ink and coiled up inside a plastic case. Usually found in impact printers.

PRINTER.SYS   A *DOS device driver* that lets you use *code-page* switching with printers that support this capability. To activate it, load PRINTER.SYS using *CONFIG.SYS*.

printhead   That part of a printer that creates the printed image. In a *dot-matrix printer*, the printhead contains the small pins that strike the ribbon to create the image, and in an *ink-jet printer*, the printhead contains the jets used to create the ink droplets as well as the ink reservoirs. A laser printer creates images using an electrophotographic method similar to that found in photocopiers and does not have a printhead.

privileged mode   An operating mode supported in protected mode in *80286* (or later) processors, that allows the operating system and certain classes of *device driver* to manipulate parts of the system including memory and input/output ports.

PRN   In *DOS* and *OS/2,* the logical device name for a printer, usually the first parallel port, which is also known as LPT1.

process   In a *multitasking operating system,* a program or a part of a program. For example, in *OS/2* there are really no such things as programs; they are known as processes instead. All EXE and COM files execute as processes, and one process can run one or more other processes. Indeed, all full-screen *sessions* contain at least two processes, the *command processor* and the *application* running in that session.

processor direct slot   Slot used for adding higher-speed expansion cards, like memory or cache cards. Because it is a local bus slot it runs at the processor's rated speed.

program   A sequence of instructions that a computer can execute. Synonymous with *software.*

programmable   Capable of being programmed. The fact that a computer is programmable is what sets it apart from all other instruments that use microprocessors; it is truly a general-purpose machine.

PROM   Acronym for programmable read-only memory, pronounced "prom." A chip used when developing firmware. A PROM can be programmed and tested in the lab, and when the firmware is complete, it can be transferred to a ROM for manufacturing.

protected mode   In *Intel 80286* and higher processors, an operating state that supports advanced features.

Protected mode in these processors provides hardware support for *multitasking* and *virtual* *memory* management, and prevents programs from accessing blocks of memory that belong to other executing programs.

In *16-bit* protected mode, supported on 80286 and higher processors, the *CPU* can directly address a total of 16 MB of memory; in *32-bit* protected mode, supported on *80386* and higher processors, the CPU can address up to 4 GB of memory.

OS/2 and most versions of *UNIX* that run on these processors execute in protected mode.

protocol   In networking and communications, the specification that defines the procedures to follow when transmitting and receiving data. Protocols define the format, timing, sequence, and error checking systems used.

protocol stack   In networking and communications, the several layers of *software* that define the computer-to-computer or computer-to-network *protocol.* The protocol stack on a Novell *NetWare* system will be different from that used on a Banyan *VINES* network, or on a *Microsoft LAN Manager* system.

public-domain software   Software that is freely distributed to anyone who wants to use, copy, or distribute it.

puck   Mouse-shaped device used for drawing or specifying coordinates on a drawing tablet.

Pulse Code Modulation   Abbreviated PCM. A method used to convert an *analog* signal into noise-free *digital data* that can be stored and manipulated by computer. PCM takes an 8-bit sample of a 4kHz bandwidth 8,000 times a second, which gives 16 K of data per second. PCM is often used in multimedia applications.

QEMM 386   A memory-management program from QuarterDeck Office Systems for IBM-compatible computers.

QEMM 386 moves *terminate-and-stay resident programs* and *device drivers*, including network drivers, into *high memory*, leaving more *conventional memory* available for running *application* programs.

QEMM 50/60 is a special version of the program designed for use on *IBM PS/2* Model 50 and 60 computers.

QSOP (Quad Small Outline Package)   A type of IC package that has all leads soldered directly to the circuit board. Also called a "surface mount" chip.

quadrature amplitude modulation   A data-encoding technique used by modems operating at 2400 bits per second or faster.

Quadrature amplitude modulation is a combination of phase and amplitude change that can encode multiple bits on a single carrier signal. For example, the CCITT V.42 bis standard uses four phase changes and two amplitude changes to create 16 different signal changes.

quarter-inch cartridge   Abbreviated QIC. A set of tape standards defined by the Quarter-Inch Cartridge Drive Standards, a trade association established in 1987.

queue   Pronounced "Q." A temporary list of items waiting for a particular service. An example is the print queue of documents waiting to be printed on a network print server; the first document received in the queue is the first to be printed.

QWERTY keyboard   Pronounced "kwertee." The standard typewriter and computer keyboard layout, named for the first six keys at the top left of the alphabetic keyboard.

radio frequency interference   Abbreviated RFI. Many electronic devices, including computers and *peripherals*, can interfere with other signals in the radio-frequency range by producing electromagnetic radiation; this is normally regulated by government agencies in each country.

rag stock   A type of paper that mainly consists of cotton fibers.

RAID   Acronym for Redundant Array of Inexpensive Disks. In networking and truly critical applications, a method of using several hard disk drives in an array to provide *fault tolerance* in the event that one or more drives fail catastrophically.

The different levels of RAID, 0 through 5, are each designed for a specific use. The correct level of RAID for your installation depends on how you use your network.

RAM   Acronym for random access memory. The main system *memory* in a computer, used for the *operating system*, *application* programs, and *data*.

RAM chip   A semiconductor storage device, either dynamic RAM or static RAM.

RAM cram   A slang expression used to describe the increasing demands made upon limited memory space, especially the inability to run large *application* programs in a PC with 1 MB of RAM running *DOS*.

RAM disk   An area of *memory* managed by a special *device driver* and used as a simulated disk.

Because the *RAM* disk operates in memory, it works very quickly, much faster than a regular *hard disk*. Remember that anything you store on your RAM disk will be erased when you turn your computer off, so you must save its contents onto a real disk first. RAM disks may also be called *virtual drives*.

RAMDRIVE.SYS   The *DOS* device driver used to create a *RAM disk*. You must load this device driver using a *DEVICE* or *DEVICEHIGH* in your *CONFIG.SYS file*.

random access   Describes the ability of a storage device to go directly to the required *memory address* without having to read from the beginning every time *data* is requested.

There is nothing random or haphazard about random access; a more precise term is direct access. Unfortunately, the word "random" is used as part of the abbreviation RAM, and is obviously here to stay. In a random-access device, the information can be read directly by accessing the appropriate memory address. Some storage devices, such as tapes, must start at the beginning to find a specific storage location, and if the information is towards the end of the tape, access can take a long time. This access method is known as "sequential access."

raster device   A device that manages an image as lines of dots. Television sets and most computer displays are raster devices, as are some electrostatic printers and plotters.

read   To copy program or *data* files from a floppy or a hard disk into computer memory, to run the program or process the data in some way. The computer may also read your commands and data input from the keyboard.

read/write head   That part of a *floppy-* or *hard-disk* system that reads and writes *data* to and from a magnetic disk.

README file   A *text file* placed on a set of distribution disks by the manufacturer at the last minute that may contain important information not contained in the program manuals or online *help* system. You should always look for a README file when installing a new program on your system; it may contain information pertinent to your specific configuration.

The file name may vary slightly; READ.ME, README.TXT, and README.DOC are all used. README files do not contain any formatting commands, so you can look at them using any *word processor*.

read-only   Describes a *file* or other collection of information that may only be read; it may not be updated in any way or deleted.

Certain important *operating system* files are designated as read-only files to prevent you from deleting them by accident. Also, certain types of memory (*ROM*), and certain devices such as *CD-ROM* can be read but not changed.

read-only attribute   In *DOS* and *OS/2*, a *file attribute* that indicates the file can be read but cannot be updated or changed in any way; nor can you delete the file.

real mode   The mode of a 286 or higher processor that allows it to act as though it is a very fast 8086 processor. A processor will switch to this mode when it needs to run an older, DOS program that can't take advantage of the newer processor's features.

reboot   To restart the computer and reload the *operating system*, usually after a *crash*.

Red Book audio   The standard definition of compact disc digital audio as a *16-bit* stereo *pulse code modulation* waveform at 44.1 kHz. So called because of the cover color used when the definition was first published.

reduced instruction set computing   Abbreviated RISC, pronounced "risk." A processor that recognizes only a limited number of *assembly-language* instructions.

RISC chips are relatively cheap to produce and debug, as they usually contain fewer than 128 different instructions. *CISC* processors use a richer set of instructions, typically somewhere between 200 to 300. RISC processors are commonly used in *workstations*, and can be designed to run up to 70 percent faster than CISC processors.

reference disk   A special disk that is bootable and contains a program that is able to send special commands to MCA bus devices to configure their parameters.

reformat   To reinitialize a disk and destroy the original contents.

refresh

1. In a *monitor*, to recharge the phosphors on the inside of the screen and maintain the image.

2. In certain memory systems, *dynamic RAM* must be recharged so that it continues to hold its contents.

refresh rate   In a *monitor*, the rate at which the phosphors that create the image on the screen are recharged.

registration roller   See *paper registration rollers*

relative addressing   In programming, the specification of a memory location by using an expression to calculate the address, rather than explicitly specifying the location by using its address.

removable mass storage   Any high-capacity storage device inserted into a drive for reading and writing, then removed for storage and safekeeping. This term is not usually applied to floppy disks, but to tape- and cartridge-backup systems, and *Bernoulli boxes*.

removable media drive   Type of drive system that is similar to fixed disk drive, but the storage medium is removable.

rendering   In computer graphics, the conversion of an outline image into a fully-formed, three-dimensional image, by the addition of colors and shading.

repeater   In networking, a simple hardware device that moves all *packets* from one local area network segment to another. The main purpose of a repeater is to extend the length of the network transmission medium beyond the normal maximum cable lengths.

Repetitive Stress Injury   Abbreviated RSI. A common group of work-related injuries. Computer operators performing repetitive tasks can suffer pins-and-needles and loss of feeling in their wrists and hands, and pains in their shoulders and neck. *Carpal-tunnel syndrome*, common among people who use a keyboard all day, is one form of RSI.

reserved memory   In *DOS*, a term used to describe that area of memory between 640 K and 1 MB, also known as upper memory. Reserved memory is used by DOS to store system and video information. Some consider the term erroneous, as the memory could be used by memory management programs.

reserved word   Any word that has a special meaning and therefore cannot be used for any other purpose in the same context. For example, the words that make up a computer language (if, printf, putchar), and certain device names in an *operating system* (COM1, LPT1), are all different kinds of reserved word.

reset button   The small button on the front of many computers used to *reboot* the computer without turning off the power.

resistive drawing tablet   A drawing tablet that has a special resistive surface under the rubberized coating (instead of a grid of wires). The resistive surface has a current induced from each of the X and Y coordinate sides; the value of the current, which gets larger as it travels along one coordinate side, is sensed by the puck as an indication of relative position.

resistor pack   An assembly made up of several resistors.

resistor   An electronic component that is used to resist the flow of electricity up to a specific level. The resistance is dissipated as heat.

resolution   The degree of sharpness of a printed or displayed image, often expressed in *dpi*.

Resolution depends on the number of elements that make up the image, either dots on a laser printer or *pixels* on a monitor; the higher the number per inch, the higher the resolution of the image appears.

resource   Any part of a computer system that can be used by a program as it runs. This can include memory, hard and floppy disks, and printers.

In some programming environments, items like *dialog boxes*, bit maps, and *fonts* are considered to be resources, and they can be used by several different *application* programs without requiring any internal changes to the programs.

resource discovery expansion card   An expansion card that is used to tell the user or service technician what resources are being used in the computer and indicate possible conflicts. These cards are designed to be installed into any expansion slot.

response time   The time lag between sending a request and receiving the *data*. Response time can be applied to a complete computer system, as in the time taken to look up a certain customer record, or to a system component, as in the time taken to access a specific cluster on disk.

reverse engineering   The process of disassembling a hardware or software product from another company to find out how it works, with the intention of duplicating some or all of its functions in another product.

reverse video   In a monochrome monitor, a display mode used to highlight characters on the screen by reversing the normal background and foreground colors; for example, if the normal mode is to show green characters on a black background, reverse video displays black characters on a green background.

revision version   Indicated by the first number to the right of the decimal point in a software version identification number. A revision version is released when small number of features need to be introduced or when several errors need to be fixed.

RGB   Abbreviation for red-green-blue. A method of generating colors in a video system that uses the additive primaries method. Percentages of red, blue and green are mixed to form the colors; 0 percent of the colors creates black, 100 percent of all three colors creates white.

RGB monitor   A color monitor that accepts separate inputs for red, blue and green color signals, and normally produces a sharper image than composite color monitors, in which information for all three colors is transmitted together.

rheostat   See *variable resistor*

ring network   A *network topology* in the form of a closed loop or circle. Each *node* in the network is connected to the next, and messages move in one direction around the system. When a message arrives at a node, the node examines the address information in the message. If the address matches the node's address, the message is accepted; otherwise the node regenerates the signal and places the message back on the network for the next node in the system. It is this regeneration that allows a ring network to cover much greater distances than star and bus networks. Ring networks normally use some form of token-passing *protocol* to regulate network traffic.

ring topology   Type of physical topology in which each computer connects to two other computers, joining them in a circle and creating a unidirectional path where messages move from workstation to workstation. Each entity participating in the ring reads a message, then regenerates it, and hands it to its neighbor.

RJ-11/RJ-45   A commonly used modular telephone connector. RJ-11 is a four or six-pin connector used in most connections destined for voice use; it is the connector used on phone cords. RJ-45 is the eight-pin connector used for data transmission over *twisted-pair wiring*, and can be used for networking; RJ-45 is the connector used on 10Base-T Ethernet cables.

ROM   Acronym for read-only memory. A semiconductor-based *memory* system that stores information permanently and does not lose its contents when power is switched off. ROMs are used for *firmware* such as the *BIOS* used in the PC; and in some *portable computers*, *application* programs and even the *operating system* are being stored in ROM.

root directory   In a hierarchical *directory* structure, the directory from which all other directories must branch.

The root directory is created by the FORMAT command, and can contain files as well as other directories. It is wise to store as few files as possible in the root directory, because in DOS there is a limit to the number of entries (files or directories) that the root directory can hold. Also, you cannot delete the root directory.

The *backslash* (\) character represents the root directory, and you can use this character to make the root directory the current directory in a single step, if you type **CD** \ from the system prompt.

roping   In a *monitor*, a form of image distortion that gives solid straight lines a twisted or helical appearance. This problem is caused by poor *convergence*.

ROT-13   A simple *encryption* scheme often used to scramble *posts* to *newsgroups*. ROT-13 makes the article unreadable until the text is decoded, and is often used when the subject matter might be considered offensive. Many newsreaders have a built-in command to unscramble ROT-13 text, and if you use it, don't be surprised by what you read; if you think you might be offended, don't decrypt the post.

router   In networking, an intelligent connecting device that can send packets to the correct local area network segment to take them to their destination. Routers link local area network segments at the network layer of the International Standards Organization's Open Systems Interconnect (*ISO/OSI*) model for computer-to-computer communications.

RS-232-C   In *asynchronous transmissions*, a recommended standard interface established by the Electrical Industries Association. The standard defines the specific lines, timing and signal characteristics used between the computer and the *peripheral* device, and uses a 25-pin or 9-pin *DB connector*.

RS-232-C is used for *serial communications* between a computer and a peripheral such as a printer, *modem, digitizing tablet,* or *mouse*. The maximum cable limit of 50 feet can be extended by using very high quality cable, line drivers to boost the signal, or *short-haul modems*.

RS is the abbreviation for recommended standard, and the C denotes the third revision of that standard. RS-232-C is functionally identical to the CCITT V.24 standard.

RS-422/423/449   In *asynchronous transmissions*, a recommended standard interface established by the Electrical Industries Association for distances greater than 50 feet, but less than 1000 feet. The standard defines the specific lines, timing and signal characteristics used between the computer and the *peripheral* device.

RS (recommended standard) 449 incorporates RS-422 and RS-423; serial ports on *Macintosh* computers are RS-422 ports.

RTS   Abbreviation for request to send. A hardware signal defined by the *RS-232-C* standard to request permission to transmit.

run-length limited encoding   Abbreviated RLL encoding. An efficient method of storing information on a *hard disk* that effectively doubles the storage capacity of a disk when compared to older, less efficient methods such as *modified frequency modulation encoding* (MFM).

RXD Abbreviation for receive *data*. A *hardware* signal defined by the *RS-232-C* standard to carry data from one device to another.

S3 86Cxxx A family of fixed-function graphics accelerator chips from S3 Corporation. These chips, the 86C801, 86C805, 86C924, and 86C928, are used in many of the accelerated graphics adapters that speed up *Microsoft Windows'* video response.

save To transfer information from the computer's *memory* to a more permanent storage medium such as a *hard disk*.

As you work with your computer, you should save your work every few minutes. Otherwise, if you suffer a power failure or a severe program error, all your work will be lost because it is stored in memory, which is volatile, and when the power is removed, the contents of memory are lost.

scan code In *IBM-compatible computers*, a code number generated when a key on the keyboard is pressed or released. Each key and shifted key is assigned a unique code that the computer's *BIOS* translates into its *ASCII* equivalent.

scanner An optical device used to digitize images such as line art or photographs, so that they can be merged with text by a *page-layout* or *desktop publishing program* or incorporated into a *CAD* drawing.

SCSI Acronym for small computer system interface, pronounced "scuzzy." A high-speed, system-level *parallel interface* defined by the *ANSI* X3T9.2 committee. SCSI is used to connect a *personal computer* to several peripheral devices

using just one *port*. Devices connected in this way are said to be "daisy-chained" together, and each device must have a unique identifier or priority number.

SCSI is available on the IBM RS/6000, and the IBM PS/2 Model 65 and higher computers. It can also be installed in an IBM-compatible computer as a single *expansion board*, with a special connector extending through the back of the computer case. Today, SCSI is often used to connect *hard disks*, *tape drives*, *CD-ROM* drives, and other mass storage media, as well as scanners and printers.

There are several different SCSI interface definitions:

- **SCSI-1:** A 1986 definition of an *8-bit* parallel interface with a maximum data transfer rate of 5 megabytes per second.

- **SCSI-2:** This 1994 definition broadened the 8-bit data bus to *16-* or *32-bits* (also known as Wide SCSI), doubling the data transfer rate to 10 or 20 megabytes per second (also known as Fast SCSI). Wide SCSI and Fast SCSI can be combined to give Fast-Wide SCSI, with a 16-bit data bus and a maximum data-transfer rate of 20 megabytes per second. SCSI-2 is backward compatible with SCSI-1, but for maximum benefit, you should use SCSI-2 devices with a SCSI-2 controller.

- **SCSI-3:** This definition increased the number of connected peripherals from 7 to 16, increased cable lengths, added support for a *serial interface* and for a *fiber optic* interface. Data transfer rates depend on the hardware implementation, but data rates in excess of 100 megabytes per second are possible.

- **SCSI FAST:** Refers to a derivative of SCSI-2 that allows data transfer rates of 10 Mega-Transfers per second. (A "MegaTransfer" is the term used to describe the speed of the signals on the interface regardless of the width of the bus. For example, 10 MegaTransfers per second on one-byte-wide bus produces a data transfer of 10 megabytes/second. On a two-byte-wide bus, 10 MegaTransfers per second produces a data transfer of 20 megabytes/second.)

- **SCSI FAST-20:** Follows the SCSI standard and can ship data back and forth at 20 Mega-Transfers per second (see definition in the bulleted item directly above), which is twice as fast as SCSI FAST rates.

- **SCSI FAST-40:** The same as SCSI FAST-20, except that it handles data at 40 MegaTransfers per second.

- **SCSI WIDE:** is technically the term used to describe the two-byte-wide connector (68-pin) specified in the SCSI-3 Parallel Interface standard.

- **SCSI FAST-WIDE:** simply means a combination of FAST transfer rate with two-byte-wide connector, producing a data transfer rate of 20 megabytes/second.

SCSI adapter   Device that is used to manage all the devices on the SCSI bus as well as to send and retrieve data from the devices.

SCSI bus   Another name for the *SCSI* interface and communications *protocol*.

SCSI terminator   The *SCSI* interface must be correctly terminated to prevent signals echoing on the *bus*. Many SCSI devices have built-in terminators that engage when they are needed; with some older SCSI devices you have to add an external SCSI terminator that plugs into the device's SCSI connector.

second source   In computer hardware, an alternative supplier of an identical product. The fact that a second source for a product exists is a safety net for the buyer, because it means that there are at least two suppliers for this same product.

sector   The smallest unit of storage on a disk, usually 512 bytes. Sectors are grouped together into *clusters*.

seek time   Time it takes the actuator arm to move from rest position to active position for the read/write head to access the information. Often used as a performance gauge of an individual drive. The major part of a hard disk's *access time* is actually seek time.

segmented addressing   An addressing scheme used in *Intel* processors that divides the address space into logical pieces called segments.

To access any given address, a program must specify the segment and also an offset within that segment. This addressing method is sometimes abbreviated to segment:offset, and is used in Intel processors in *real mode*; most other processors use a single flat address space.

semaphore　In programming, an *interprocess communication* signal that indicates the status of a shared system resource, such as *shared memory*.

Event semaphores allow a *thread* to tell other threads that an event has occurred and it is safe for them to resume execution. Mutual exclusion (mutex) semaphores protect system resources such as files, data, and peripherals from simultaneous access by several processes. Multiple wait (muxwait) semaphores allow threads to wait for multiple events to take place, or for multiple resources to become free.

semiconductor　A material that is halfway between a conductor (which conducts electricity) and an insulator (which resists electricity), whose electrical behavior can be precisely controlled by the addition of impurities called dopants.

The most commonly used semiconductors are silicon and germanium, and when electrically charged they change their state from conductive to nonconductive, or from nonconductive to conductive. Semiconductor wafers can be manufactured to create a whole variety of electronic devices; in personal computers, semiconductors are used in the processor, memory, and many other chips.

Easily the most significant semiconductor device is the *transistor*, which acts like an on/off switch, and is incorporated into modern *microprocessors* by the million.

serial communications　The transmission of information from computer to computer, or from computer to a *peripheral*, one bit at a time.

Serial communications can be synchronous and controlled by a clock, or asynchronous and coordinated by *start* and *stop bits* embedded in the data stream. It is important to remember that both the sending and the receiving devices must use the same *baud rate*, *parity* setting, and other *communication parameters*.

serial mouse　A *mouse* that attaches directly to one of the computer's *serial ports*.

serial port　A computer input/output *port* that supports *serial communications*, in which information is processed one bit at a time.

RS-232-C is a common serial *protocol* used by computers when communicating with modems, printers, mice, and other peripherals.

serial printer　A printer that attaches to one of the computer's *serial ports*.

server　In networking, any computer that makes access to *files*, printing, communications, or other services available to users of the network. In large networks, a server may run a special *network operating system*; in smaller installations, a server may run a personal computer *operating system*.

server-based network　Network that uses a dedicated, centralized server to perform administrative functions and resource sharing.

service provider　A general term used to describe those companies providing a connection to the *Internet* for private and home users. Several of the online services such as CompuServe and America Online are providing access to more and more of the Internet as a part of their basic services.

session layer   The fifth of seven layers of the International Standards Organization's Open Systems Interconnection (*ISO/OSI*) model for computer-to-computer communications. The session layer coordinates communications and maintains the *session* for as long as it is needed, performing *security*, logging, and administrative functions.

settling time   The time it takes a disk's read/write head to stabilize once it has moved to the correct part of the disk. Settling time is measured in milliseconds.

setup string   A short group of text characters sent to a printer, *modem*, or *monitor*, to invoke a particular mode of operation.

SGML   Abbreviation for Standard Generalized Markup Language. A standard (ISO 8879) for defining the structure and managing the contents of any digital document. *HTML*, used in many *World Wide Web* documents on the *Internet*, is a part of SGML.

shadow memory   In PCs based on the *80386* (or later) processor, the technique of copying the contents of the *BIOS ROM* into faster *RAM* when the computer first boots up; also known as shadow RAM or shadow ROM.

RAM is usually two to three times faster than ROM, and the speedier access cuts down the time required to read a memory address so the processor spends more time working and less time waiting.

shared memory   An *interprocess communications* technique in which the same *memory* is accessed by more than one program running in a multitasking *operating system*. *Semaphores* or other management elements prevent the applications from "colliding," or trying to update the same information at the same time.

shareware   A form of software distribution that makes copyrighted programs freely available on a trial basis; if you like the program and use it, you are expected to register your copy and send a small fee to the program creator. Once your copy is registered, you might receive a more complete manual, technical support, access to the programmer's bulletin board, or information about upgrades. You can *download* shareware from many *bulletin boards* and *online services* including *CompuServe*, and it is often available from your local PC *user group*.

short-haul modem   A simple, low-cost modem that can only transmit information over short distances, such as from one side of a building to the other.

silicon   A *semiconductor* material used in many electronic devices. Silicon is a very common element found in almost all rocks and in beach sand, and when "doped" with chemical impurities, becomes a semiconductor. Large cylinders of silicon are cut into wafers, and then etched with a pattern of minute electrical circuits to form a silicon chip.

Silicon Valley   A nickname for the area around Palo Alto and Sunnyvale in the Santa Clara Valley region of Northern California, noted for the number of high-technology hardware and software companies located there.

single in-line memory module   Abbreviated SIMM. Individual *RAM* chips are soldered or surface mounted onto small narrow circuit boards called carrier modules, which can be plugged into sockets on the *motherboard*. These carrier modules are simple to install and occupy less space than conventional memory modules.

single in-line package   Abbreviated SIP. A plastic housing containing an electronic component with a single row of pins or connections protruding from one side of the package.

single-density disk   A floppy disk that is certified for recording with *frequency modulation encoding*. Single-density disks have been superseded by *double-density disks* and *high-density disks*.

SLIP   Abbreviation for Serial Line Internet Protocol. A communications protocol used over serial lines or dial-up connections. *SLIP* is a popular protocol used when connecting a PC to the Internet. Recently it has been overtaken in popularity by PPP.

SMARTDRV.SYS   The *DOS device driver* that provides compatibility for *hard-disk controllers* that cannot work with EMM386 and Windows running in enhanced mode. Use the *DEVICE* command to load this device driver in *CONFIG.SYS*.

This command does not load the DOS *disk cache*; use the *SMARTDRV* command for that.

socket services   Part of the software support needed for *PCMCIA* hardware devices in a *portable computer*, controlling the interface to the hardware.

Socket services is the lowest layer in the software that manages PCMCIA cards. It provides a BIOS-level software interface to the hardware, effectively hiding the specific details from higher levels of software. Socket services also detect when you insert or remove a PCMCIA card and identify the type of card it is.

soft memory error   Errors that occur once and disappear after the computer is rebooted, usually caused by power fluctuations or single bit errors. Also referred to as "phantoms."

software   An *application program* or an *operating system* that a computer can execute. Software is a broad term that can imply one or many programs, and it can also refer to applications that may actually consist of more than one program.

software setup programs   Programs that can be used to change the configuration of a hardware device. These setup programs often come on a disk in the same package as the hardware device.

SOHO   Abbreviation for small office/home office. That portion of the market for computer services occupied by small offices and home-based businesses rather than the large corporate buyers. SOHO is a small but growing market sector characterized by very well-informed buyers.

Solaris   A *Unix*-based *operating system* from SunSoft that runs on *Intel* processors and supports a *graphical user interface*, *e-mail*, the *Network File System*, and Network Information Service. Solaris brings a common *look-and-feel* to both *SPARC* and Intel platforms.

soldering iron   A tool that is used to melt solder. Solder is usually used to join two or more metallic surfaces to ensure an electrical connection (for example, between a wire and a component).

solenoid   A device that converts electromagnetic force into motion. Solenoids are used to move levers, for example inside a hard disk drive.

sound board   An add-in *expansion board* for the PC that allows you to produce audio output of high-quality recorded voice, music, and sounds through headphones or external speakers. In the *Macintosh*, digital stereo sound reproduction is built into the system.

Almost all *multimedia* applications take advantage of a sound board if one is present; the *MPC* Level 2 specification requires the inclusion of a *16-bit* sound card.

source   The disk, file, or document from which information is moved or copied.

source code   The original human-readable version of a program, written in a particular programming language, before the program is compiled or *interpreted* into a machine-readable form.

spaghetti code   A slang expression used to describe any badly designed or poorly structured program that is as hard to unravel (and understand) as a bowl of spaghetti.

SPARC   Acronym for Scalar Processor ARChitecture. A *32-bit RISC* processor from Sun Microsystems.

SPARCstation   A family of *Unix workstations* from Sun Microsystems, based on the *SPARC* processor. SPARCstations range from small, *diskless* desktop systems to high-performance, tower SPARCservers in *multiprocessor* configurations.

special interest group   Abbreviated SIG. A group that meets to share information about a specific topic; *hardware*, *application software*, *programming languages*, even *operating systems*. A SIG is often part of a larger organization like a *users group* or the *ACM*.

spin speed   An indication of how fast the platters on a fixed disk are spinning.

spindle   The rod that platters are mounted on in a hard disk drive.

ST506 interface   A popular *hard-disk* interface standard developed by Seagate Technologies, first used in *IBM's PC/XT* computer, and still popular today with disk capacities smaller than about 40 MB. ST506 has a relatively slow *data transfer rate* of 5 megabits per second. A later variation of ST506 called ST412 added several improvements, and because these two interfaces are so closely related, they are often referred to as ST506/412.

stack   A reserved area of *memory* used to keep track of a program's internal operations, including functions' return addresses, passed parameters, and so on. A stack is usually maintained as a "last in, first out" (LIFO) *data structure*, so that the last item added to the structure is the first item used.

stand-alone Describes a system designed to meet specific individual needs that does not rely on or assume the presence of any other components to complete the assigned task.

standard mode Historically, the most common *Microsoft Windows 3.x* operating mode, in which *application* programs in *16-bit protected mode* on *80286* run (and later) processors. Standard mode supported *task switching* and provided access to 16 MB of memory. It did not allow the *multitasking* of *non-Windows applications* found in *386-enhanced mode*.

standard peripheral power connector Type of connector used to power various internal drives. Also called a *Molex connector*.

star network A *network topology* in the form of a star. At the center of the star is a wiring *hub* or concentrator, and the *nodes* or *workstations* are arranged around the central point representing the points of the star. Wiring costs tend to be higher for star networks than for other configurations, as very little cable is shared; each node requires its own individual cable. Star networks do not follow any of the IEEE standards.

start bit In *asynchronous transmissions*, a start bit is transmitted to indicate the beginning of a new data *word*.

static electricity A result of a build-up of electrons on a surface. This type of electrical charge doesn't move on its own but can be carried or transferred to surfaces depending on the differences in the number of electrons on each surface (the relative difference in charges).

static RAM Abbreviated SRAM, pronounced "ess-ram." A type of computer *memory* that retains its contents as long as power is supplied;

it does not need constant refreshment like *dynamic RAM* chips. A static RAM chip can only store about one fourth of the information that a dynamic RAM of the same complexity can hold.

Static RAM, with access times of 15 to 30 nano-seconds, is much faster than dynamic RAM, at 80 nano-seconds or more, and is often used in *caches*; however, static RAM is four to five times as expensive as dynamic RAM.

static-charge eliminator strip The device in EP process printers that drains the static charge from the paper after the toner has been transferred to the paper.

stepper motor A very precise motor that can move in very small increments. Often used in printers.

stop bit(s) In *asynchronous transmissions*, stop bits are transmitted to indicate the end of the current *data* word. Depending on the convention in use, one or two stop bits are used.

STP (shield twisted-pair) Cabling that has a braided foil shield around the twisted pairs of wire to decrease electrical interference.

streaming tape A high-speed tape *backup* system, often used to make a complete backup of an entire *hard disk*.

A streaming tape is designed to optimize throughput so that time is never wasted by stopping the tape during a backup; this also means that the computer and backup software also have to be fast enough to keep up with the *tape drive*.

stylus A pen-like pointing device used in *pen-based* systems and *personal digital assistants*.

substrate   The inactive base material used in the construction of a disk, tape, *printed circuit board*, or *integrated circuit*.

supercomputer   The most powerful class of computer. The term was first applied to the *Cray-1* computer. Supercomputers can cost over $50 million each, and are capable of drawing and animating dinosaurs in a motion picture. They are also put to more mundane uses such as weather forecasting and complex, three-dimensional modeling, and oil reservoir modeling.

superscalar   A microprocessor architecture that contains more than one execution unit, or pipeline, allowing the processor to execute more than one instruction per clock cycle.

For example, the *Pentium* processor is superscalar, and has two side-by-side pipelines for integer instructions. The processor determines whether an instruction can be executed in parallel with the next instruction in line. If it doesn't detect any dependencies, the two instructions are executed.

SuperVGA   Abbreviated SVGA. An enhancement to the Video Graphics Array (*VGA*) video standard defined by the *Video Electronics Standards Association* (VESA).

SuperVGA *video adapters* can display at least 800 pixels horizontally and 600 vertically (the VESA-recommended standard), and up to 1600 horizontally and 1200 vertically; with 16, 256, 32,767, or 16,777,216 colors displayed simultaneously. Most SuperVGA boards contain several megabytes of *video RAM* for increased performance.

surface mount technology   Abbreviated SMT. A manufacturing technology in which *integrated circuits* are attached directly to the *printed circuit board*, rather than being soldered into predrilled holes in the board. This process also allows electronic components to be mounted on both sides of a board.

surge   A sudden and often destructive increase in line voltage. A regulating device known as a *surge suppressor* or surge protector can protect computer equipment against surges.

surge suppressor   Also known as a surge protector. A regulating device placed between the computer and the AC line connection that protects the computer system from power *surges*.

swap file   On a *hard disk*, a file used to store parts of running programs that have been swapped out of *memory* temporarily to make room for other running programs.

A swap file may be permanent, always occupying the same amount of hard disk space even though the *application* that created it may not be running, or is temporary, and only created as and when needed.

swapping   The process of exchanging one item for another. In a virtual memory system, swapping occurs when a program requests a virtual memory location that is not currently in memory; the information is then read from disk, and displaces old information held in memory.

Swapping may also refer to changing floppy disks as needed when using two disks in a single floppy disk drive.

synchronization The timing of separate elements or events to occur simultaneously.

1. In a *multimedia* presentation, synchronization ensures that the audio and video components are timed correctly, and so actually make sense.

2. In computer-to-computer communications, the hardware and software must be synchronized so that file transfers can take place.

3. The process of updating files on both a portable computer and a desktop system so that they both have the latest versions is also known as synchronization.

synchronous transmission In communications, a transmission method that uses a clock signal to regulate *data* flow. Synchronous transmissions do not use *start* and *stop bits*.

system area That part of a *DOS* disk which contains the *partition table*, the *file allocation table*, and the *root directory*.

system attribute In *DOS* and *OS/2*, the *file attribute* that indicates that the file is part of the *operating system*, and should not appear in normal directory listings. There are also further restrictions on a system file; you cannot delete, copy, or display the contents of such a file.

system board The sturdy sheet or board to which all other components on the computer are attached. These components consist of the CPU, underlying circuitry, expansion slots, video components, and RAM slots, just to name a few. Also known as a *logic board, motherboard,* or planar board.

system bus The expansion cards and slots that allow the processor to talk with other devices.

system connector Connector attached to the motherboard that services the electronic components on it.

system date The date and time as maintained by the computer's internal clock. You should always make sure that the system clock is accurate, because the *operating system* notes the time that files were created; this can be important if you are trying to find the most recent version of a document or spreadsheet.

system disk A disk that contains all the files necessary to *boot* and start the *operating system*. In most computers, the *hard disk* is the system disk; indeed, many modern operating systems are too large to run from floppy disk.

system file In *DOS* and *OS/2*, a file whose *system attribute* is set. In IBM's PC-DOS, the two system files are called IBMBIOS.COM and IBM-DOS.COM; in Microsoft's MS-DOS, they are called IO.SYS and MSDOS.SYS. These files contain the essential routines needed to manage devices, memory, and input/output operations.

system resources In reference to Windows troubleshooting, the amount of memory and hard disk space that are available for Windows to use.

system software The programs that make up the *operating system*, along with the associated utility programs, as distinct from an *application program*.

system time   The time and date maintained by the internal clock inside the computer.

This internal clock circuitry is usually backed up by a small battery so that the clock continues to keep time even though the computer may be switched off. The system time is used to date-stamp files with the time of their creation or revision, and you can use this date stamp to determine which of two files contains the latest version of your document. The system time can also be inserted into a document as the current time by a *word processor* or a *spreadsheet program*.

system unit   The case that houses the processor, *motherboard*, internal *hard-* and *floppy disks*, *power supply*, and the *expansion bus*.

SYSTEM.INI   In *Microsoft Windows*, an *initialization file* that contains information on your hardware and the internal Windows operating environment.

Systems Application Architecture (SAA)
A set of IBM standards, first introduced in 1987, that define a consistent set of interfaces for future IBM software. Three standards are defined:

- **Common User Access (CUA):** A *graphical user interface* definition for products designed for use in an *object-oriented* operating environment. The OS/2 desktop follows CUA guidelines in its design; Microsoft Windows implements certain CUA features, but by no means all of them.

- **Common Programming Interface (CPI):** A set of *Application Programming Interfaces (APIs)* designed to encourage independence from the underlying *operating system*. The standard *database query language* is *SQL*.

- **Common Communications Support (CCS):** A common set of *communications protocols* that interconnect SAA systems and devices.

tap
1. A connector that attaches to a cable without blocking the passage of information along that cable.

2. In communications, a connection onto the main transmission medium of the network.

tape backup device   See *tape drive*

tape cartridge   A self-contained tape storage module, containing tape much like that in a video cassette. Tape cartridges are primarily used to back up *hard disk* systems.

tape drive   Removable media drive that uses a tape cartridge with a long polyester ribbon coated with magnetic oxide and wrapped around two spools, with a read/write head in between.

T-connector   A T-shaped connector, used with coaxial cable, that connects two *thin Ethernet* cables and also provides a third connector for the *network interface card*.

T1   A long-distance, point-to-point 1.544-megabit per second *communications channel* that can be used for both digitized voice and data transmission; T1 lines are usually divided into 24 channels, each transmitting at 64 kilobits per second.

T3   A long-distance point-to-point 44.736-megabit per second communications service that can provide up to 28 *T1* channels. A T3 channel can carry 672 voice conversations, and is usually available over *fiber-optic cable*.

TCP   Abbreviation for Transmission Control Protocol. The connection-oriented, transport-level protocol used in the *TCP/IP* suite of communications protocols.

TCP/IP   Acronym for Transmission Control Protocol/Internet Protocol. A set of computer-to-computer *communications protocols* first developed for the Defense Advanced Research Projects Agency (DARPA) in the late 1970s. The set of TCP/IP protocols encompass media access, packet transport, session communications, file transfer, e-mail, and terminal emulation.

TCP/IP is supported by a very large number of hardware and software vendors, and is available on many different computers from PCs to mainframes. Many corporations, universities, and government agencies use TCP/IP, and it is also the foundation of the *Internet*.

telnet   That part of the *TCP/IP* suite of protocols used for remote login and *terminal emulation*; also the name of the program used to connect to *Internet* host systems.

Originally a Unix utility, telnet is available these days for almost all popular operating systems. You will find that most versions of telnet are character-based applications, although some contain the text inside a windowed system.

temporary swap file   A *swap file* that is created every time it is needed. A temporary swap file will not consist of a single large area of contiguous hard disk space, but may consist of several discontinuous pieces of space. By its very nature, a temporary swap file does not occupy valuable hard disk space if the *application* that created it is not running. In a *permanent swap file* the hard disk space is always reserved, and is therefore unavailable to any other application program. If hard disk space is at a premium, choose a temporary swap file.

tendinitis   Inflammation of tendons, which can lead to swelling and loss of movement. (An example of an *RSI*.)

tenosynovitis   A condition that manifests itself in the inflammation of the sheath around the tendons of the wrists. (An example of an *RSI*.)

tera-   Abbreviated T. A prefix meaning 10 to the 12th power in the metric system, 1,000,000,000,000; commonly referred to as a trillion in the American numbering system, and a million million in the British numbering system.

terabyte   Abbreviated TB. In computing, usually 2 to the 40th power, or 1,099,511,627,776 bytes. A terabyte is equivalent to 1,000 gigabytes, and usually refers to extremely large hard-disk capacities.

terminal   A monitor and keyboard attached to a computer (usually a *mainframe*), used for data entry and display. Unlike a personal computer, a terminal does not have its own *central processing unit* or *hard disk*.

terminate-and-stay-resident program   Abbreviated TSR. A *DOS* program that stays loaded in memory, even when it is not actually running, so that you can invoke it very quickly to perform a specific task.

Popular TSR programs include calendars, appointment schedulers, calculators and the like that you can invoke while using your word processor, spreadsheet, or other application. TSRs occupy *conventional memory* space that becomes unavailable for use by your applications programs; however, if you have a recent version of DOS and an *80386* (or later) processor, you can load your TSRs into *upper memory blocks*, and therefore recover that conventional memory for other uses.

terminating resistor pack A device installed at both ends of a bus to keep the signals "on the bus." Along with the data it is sending via the bus, this device also sends a signal that identifies the device that is sending the information in the first place.

terminator A device attached to the last *peripheral* in a series, or the last *node* on a network.

For example, the last device on a *SCSI bus* must terminate the bus; otherwise the bus will not perform properly. A resistor is placed at both ends of an *Ethernet* cable to prevent signals reflecting and interfering with the transmission.

text editor In computer programming, software used to prepare program *source code*. Text editors do not have all the advanced formatting facilities available in word processors, but they may have other features that particularly relate to programming like complex search and replace options, and multiple windows.

text file A *file* that consists of text characters without any formatting information. Also known as an *ASCII* file, a text file can be read by any word processor. The *README* file, containing late-breaking news about an *application*, is always a text file.

text mode One of the video modes of a video card. This mode displays characters to the monitor.

thermal printer A *nonimpact* printer that uses a thermal *printhead* and specially treated paper to create an image. The main advantage of thermal printers is that they are virtually silent; the main disadvantage is that they usually produce poor quality output that is likely to fade with time. They are used in calculators and in terminals to provide a local printing capability.

thick Ethernet Connecting *coaxial* cable used on an Ethernet network. The cable is 1 cm (approximately 0.4") thick, and can be used to connect network *nodes* up to a distance of approximately 3300 feet. Primarily used for facility-wide installations. Also known as 10Base5.

thin Ethernet Connecting *coaxial* cable used on an Ethernet network. The cable is 5 mm (approximately 0.2") thick, and can be used to connect network *nodes* up to a distance of approximately 1000 feet. Primarily used for office installations. Also known as 10Base2.

thrashing An excessive amount of disk activity in a *virtual memory* system, to the point where the system is spending all its time *swapping* pages in and out of memory, and no time executing the application. Thrashing can be caused when poor system *configuration* creates a *swap file* that is too small, or when insufficient memory is installed in the computer. Increasing the size of the swap file and adding memory are the best ways to reduce thrashing.

thread

1. A *concurrent* process that is part of a larger *process* or program. In a *multitasking operating system*, a program may contain several threads, all running at the same time inside the same program. This means that one part of a program can be making a calculation, while another part is drawing a graph or chart.

2. A connected set of *postings* to a *USENET newsgroup* or to an online *forum*. Many newsreaders present postings as threads rather than in strict chronological sequence.

TMS34020 A graphics chip from Texas Instruments used in *high-end* PC graphics adapters. The older 34010 uses a 16-bit data *bus* with a 32-bit data *word*, while the 34020 uses 32 bits for both.

Both are compatible with the Texas Instruments Graphical Architecture (*TIGA*) used in some IBM-compatible computers. TIGA video adapters and monitors display 1024 *pixels* horizontally, and 786 pixels vertically, using 256 colors.

token passing A media access method that gives every *NIC* equal access to the cable. The token is a special packet of data that is passed from computer to computer. Any computer that wants to transmit has to wait until it has the token, at which point it can add its own data to the token and send it on.

Token Ring network IBM's implementation of the *token-ring network* architecture; it uses a token-passing protocol transmitting at 4 or 16 megabits per second.

Using standard telephone wiring, a Token Ring network can connect up to 72 devices; with shielded *twisted-pair wiring*, the network can support up to 260 nodes. Although it is based on a closed-loop ring structure, a Token Ring network uses a star-shaped cluster of up to eight nodes all attached to the same wiring concentrator or MultiStation Access Unit (MSAU). These MSAUs are then connected to the main ring circuit. See the accompanying diagram.

A Token Ring network can include *personal computers*, *minicomputers*, and *mainframes*. The IEEE 802.5 standard defines token ring networks.

token-ring network A *local area network* with a ring structure that uses token-passing to regulate traffic on the network and avoid collisions.

On a token-ring network, the controlling computer generates a "token" that controls the right to transmit. This token is continuously passed from one node to the next around the network. When a node has information to transmit, it captures the token, sets its status to busy, and adds the message and the destination address. All other nodes continuously read the token to determine if they are the recipient of a message; if they are, they collect the token, extract the message, and return the token to the sender. The sender then removes the message and sets the token status to free, indicating that it can be used by the next node in sequence.

tolerance band Found on a *fixed resistor*, this colored band indicates how well the resistor holds to its rated value. (The values of the tolerance-band colors are given in a table earlier in this book. The higher the value, the lower the precision of the resistor.)

toner Black carbon substance mixed with polyester resins and iron oxide particles. During the EP printing process, toner is first attracted to areas that have been exposed to the laser in laser printers, and is later deposited and melted onto the print medium.

toner cartridge The replaceable cartridge in a *laser printer* or photocopier that contains the electrically charged ink to be fused to the paper during printing.

topology   A way of laying out a network. Can describe either the logical or physical layout.

touch screen   A special *monitor* that lets the user make choices by touching *icons* or graphical buttons on the screen.

Touch-screen systems are popular for interactive displays in museums and in automatic teller machines, where input is limited. They never achieved much popularity in the business world, because users have to hold their hands in midair to touch the screen, which becomes tiring very quickly.

tower case   A *system unit* case designed to stand on the floor rather than be placed on a desktop. Tower cases often have more *drive bays* and *expansion slots* than the desktop units, and are commonly used for *file servers* and *workstations*.

track   A concentric collection of *sectors* on a *hard disk* or *floppy disk*.

The outermost track on the top of the disk (or *platter*) is numbered track 0 side 0, and the outermost track on the other side is numbered track 0 side 1. Numbering increases inwards towards the center of the disk. Tracks are created during the disk *formatting* process.

On tapes, tracks are parallel lines down the axis of the tape.

trackball   An input device used for pointing, designed as an alternative to the *mouse*.

A trackball is almost an upside-down mouse; it stays still, and contains a movable ball that you rotate using your fingers to move the mouse cursor on the screen. Because a trackball

does not need the area of flat space that the mouse needs, trackballs are popular with users of *portable computers*; Apple PowerBook computers include a trackball as part of the keyboard case, and Microsoft has released a small trackball that clips onto the side of a laptop computer.

tracks per inch   Abbreviated TPI. The number of tracks of sectors on a hard or *floppy disk*. TPI is an indication of the density of data that you can store on any given disk; the larger the TPI, the more data the disk can hold. Among floppy disks, *high-density 5.25" disks* have 96 TPI, while most *3.5" disks* have 135 TPI.

track-to-track access time   An indication of *hard disk* speed; the amount of time it takes the disk's *read/write heads* to move from one track to the next adjacent track.

transfer corona assembly   The part of an EP process printer that is responsible for transferring the developed image from the EP drum to the paper.

transfer step   Fourth step in the EP print process. This is the step at which the image is transferred to the paper. With this step the corona wire has a strong positive charge and applies it to the paper. The toner, because it has an opposite charge, then sticks to the paper.

transistor   Abbreviation for transfer resistor. A semiconductor component that acts like a switch, controlling the flow of an electric current. A small voltage applied at one pole controls a larger voltage on the other poles. Transistors are incorporated into modern *microprocessors* by the million.

transport layer   The fourth of seven layers of the International Standards Organization's Open Systems Interconnection (*ISO/OSI*) model for computer-to-computer communications. The transport layer defines *protocols* for message structure, and supervises the validity of the transmission by performing some error checking.

Trojan horse   A type of *virus* that pretends to be a useful program, such as a game or a utility program, when in reality it contains special code that will intentionally damage any system onto which it is loaded.

troubleshooting   The process of identifying a computer problem so it can be fixed.

true color   A term used to indicate that a device, usually a video adapter, is capable of displaying 16,777,216 different colors; you will also see this number abbreviated to simply 16 million.

TSR program (Terminate and Stay Resident program)   A program that, once it is loaded into memory, keeps a portion of itself in memory once terminated so that it can be called up again very quickly, usually with a combination of keystrokes.

twisted-pair cable   Cable that comprises two insulated wires twisted together at six twists per inch. In twisted-pair cable, one wire carries the signal and the other is grounded. Telephone wire installed in modern buildings is often twisted-pair wiring.

TXD   Abbreviation for transmit data. A *hardware* signal defined by the *RS-232-C* standard that carries information from one device to another.

UART   Acronym for Universal Asynchronous Receiver/Transmitter. An electronic module that combines the transmitting and receiving circuitry needed for *asynchronous transmission* over a serial line.

Asynchronous transmissions use *start* and *stop bits* encoded in the data stream to coordinate communications rather than the clock pulse found in *synchronous transmissions*.

UART (Universal Asynchronous Receiver/ Transmitter)   The chip on the serial port interface that controls the data flow through the serial port. If you are going to use an external modem faster than 9600 Kbps, you must have a 16550 or 16650 UART on the serial port.

undelete   To recover an accidentally deleted *file*. *DOS* 5 (and later) provides the UNDELETE command, but many of the popular utility program packages also contain similar *undelete programs*, which often have a much better user interface and are therefore easier to use.

undelete program   A utility program that recovers *deleted* or damaged *files* from a disk. A file can be deleted accidentally, or can become inaccessible when part of the file's control information is lost.

Many utility packages offer excellent file recovery programs, including the *Norton Utilities* from Symantec, *PC Tools* from Central Point Software, and the Mace Utilities from Fifth Generation Systems. Even DOS, starting with version 5, offers the *UNDELETE* command.

These programs guide the user through the recovery process or, if damage is extreme, attempt to recover as much of the damaged file as possible. In this case, substantial editing may be necessary before the file can be used; indeed the best way to recover a damaged file is to restore it from a backup copy.

unformat   The process of recovering an accidentally formatted disk. *DOS* 5 (and later) provides the UNFORMAT command, but many of the popular utility program packages also contain similar programs, which often have a much better user interface and so are easier to use.

unformat program   A utility program that recovers files and directories after a disk has been formatted by accident.

Many utility packages offer excellent unformat programs, including the *Norton Utilities* from Symantec, *PC Tools* from Central Point Software, and the Mace Utilities from Fifth Generation Systems. Even *DOS* 5 (and later) offers the *UNFORMAT* command.

These programs guide the user through the recovery process, offering advice and assistance as they go. You must, of course, recover the original information on the disk before you add any new files or directories to the disk.

uninterruptible power supply   Abbreviated UPS, pronounced "you-pea-ess." An alternative power source, usually a set of batteries, used to power a computer system if the normal power service is interrupted or falls below acceptable levels.

A UPS can often supply power for just long enough to let you shut down the computer in an orderly fashion; it is not designed to support long-term operations.

Unix   Pronounced "you-nix." A *32-bit, multiuser, multitasking, portable operating system* originally developed by AT&T, now owned by *Novell*.

Unix was developed by Dennis Ritchie and Ken Thompson at Bell Laboratories in the early 1970s. It has been enhanced over the years, particularly by computer scientists at the University of California, Berkeley.

Networking, in the form of the *TCP/IP* set of protocols, has been available in Unix from the early stages. During the 1980s, AT&T began the work of consolidating the many versions of Unix. In January 1989, the Unix Software Operation was formed as a separate AT&T division, and in November 1989, that division introduced a significant new release, System V Release 4.0. In June 1990, the Unix Software Operation became known as Unix System Laboratories (USL), which was bought by Novell in 1993.

Unix is available on a huge range of computational hardware, from a *PC* to a *Cray*, and is also available in other, related forms. For example, *AIX* runs on IBM *workstations*; *A/UX* is a graphical version that runs on powerful *Macintosh* computers, and *Solaris* from SunSoft runs on *Intel* processors. Many of the computers that make up the *Internet* run Unix.

upgradable computer   A computer system specifically designed to be upgraded as technology advances.

Upgradable computers differ in how much of the PC's circuitry must be changed when you make the upgrade, and also in how you actually make the upgrade. At minimum, you must replace the processor; at most, some upgrades come close to changing all the circuitry installed in the computer.

upgrade

1. The process of installing a newer and more powerful version; for example, to upgrade to a newer and more capable version of a *software* package, or to upgrade from your current *hard disk* to one that is twice the size. In the case of *hardware*, an upgrade is often called an upgrade kit.

2. A new and more powerful version of an existing system, either hardware or software, is also known as an upgrade.

upload In communications, sending a *file* or files from one computer to another over a network or using a *modem*. For example, a file could be uploaded to a *bulletin board*. In this case, the remote computer stores the uploaded file on disk for further processing when the transmission is complete. Files can also be uploaded to a network *file server*.

upper memory blocks Abbreviated UMB. The memory between 640 KB and 1 MB in an IBM-compatible computer running *DOS* was originally reserved for system and video use; however, not all the space is used, and the unused portions are known as upper memory blocks.

If you have an *80386* (or later) processor, you can gain up to 200K of additional memory by accessing these UMBs, and you can use this space to load *device drivers* and *terminate-and-stay-resident* programs.

upward compatibility The design of *software* so as to function with other, more powerful, products likely to become available in the short term. The use of standards makes upward compatibility much easier to achieve.

URL Abbreviation for Uniform Resource Locator, pronounced "earl." A method of accessing *Internet* resources.

URLs contain information about both the access method to use and also about the resource itself, and are used by *Web browsers* to connect you directly to a specific document or page on the *World Wide Web*, without you having to know where that resource is located physically.

The first part of the URL, before the colon, specifies the access method. On the Web, this is usually *http* (for hypertext transmission protocol), but you might also see file, *ftp*, or *gopher* instead. The second part of the URL, after the colon, specifies the resource. The text after the two slashes usually indicates a *server* name, and the text after the single slash defines the directory or individual file you will connect to. If you are linking to a document, it will usually have the filename extension .html, the abbreviation for hypertext markup language.

URLs are always case-sensitive, so pay particular attention to upper- and lowercase letters, and to symbols as well.

USB An abbreviation for Universal Serial Bus, a peripheral bus "standard" that was jointly developed by Compaq, DEC, IBM, Intel, Microsoft, NEC, and Northern Telecom to allow computer peripherals to be automatically configured as soon as they are physically attached. USB will also allow up to 127 devices to run simultaneously on a computer, with peripherals such as monitors and keyboards acting as additional plug-in sites, or hubs. USB was specified to have a 12 megabit/second data rate and to provide a low-cost interface for Integrated Services Digital Network (ISDN) and digital PBXes.

One of the benefits of having Microsoft as part of the development effort is that Windows 95 can already let your PC recognize USB peripherals. Once you get the drivers installed for the new drive or whatever, Windows will take care of the rest. Almost all new PC designs from major vendors shipping today already have USB connections on the motherboard and the correct Win OS to make them work.

USB and FireWire (IEEE 1394) may appear similar in their goals of automatic configuration of peripherals (what FireWire calls "hotplugging") without the need to reboot or run SETUP, but they are not really the same, and the developers point out that they have different applications. USB is slower than FireWire but is supposed to address traditional PC connections, like keyboards and mice. Conversely, FireWire targets high-bandwidth consumer electronics connections to the PC, like digital camcorders, cameras, and digital videodisc players. The two technologies target different kinds of peripheral devices and are supposed to be complementary. USB proponents feel that future PCs probably will have both USB and FireWire connection ports.

user group   A voluntary group of users of a specific computer or *software* package, who meet to share tips and listen to industry experts. Some PC user groups hold large, well-attended monthly meetings, run their own *bulletin boards*, and publish newsletters of exceptional quality.

utility program   A small program, or set of small programs, that supports the *operating system* by providing additional services that the operating system does not provide.

In the PC world, there are many tasks routinely performed by utility programs, including *hard disk* backup, *disk optimization*, *file recovery*, *safe formatting*, and *resource* editing.

UTP   Unshielded twisted-pair cabling.

uudecode   Pronounced "you-you-de-code."

1. To convert a *text file* created by the *Unix uuencode* utility back into its original *binary* form. Graphical images and other binary files are often sent to USENET newsgroups in this form, because the newsgroups can only handle text and don't know how to manage binary files.

2. The name of the utility program that performs a text-to-binary file conversion. Originally a Unix utility, uudecode is now available for most operating systems.

uuencode   Pronounced "you-you-en-code."

1. To convert a *binary file* such as a graphical image into a *text file* so that the file can be sent over the *Internet* or to a *USENET newsgroup* as a part of an *e-mail* message. When you receive a uuencoded text file, you must process it through the *Unix uudecode* utility to turn it back into a graphical image that you can view.

2. The name of the utility that performs a binary-to-text file conversion. Originally a Unix utility, uuencode is now available for most operating systems.

vaccine   An *application* program that removes and destroys a computer *virus*.

The people who unleash computer viruses are often very accomplished programmers, and they are constantly creating new and novel ways of causing damage to a system. The *antivirus* and vaccine programmers do the best they can to catch up, but they must always lag behind to some extent.

vacuum tube   Electronic component that is a glorified switch. A small voltage at one pole switches on or off a larger voltage at the other poles.

vaporware   A sarcastic term applied to a product that has been announced but has missed its release date, often by a large margin, and so is not actually available.

VAR   Acronym for value-added reseller; a company that adds value to a system, repackages it, and then resells it to the public. This added value can take the form of better documentation, user support, service support, system integration, or even just a new nameplate on the outside of the box. For example, Canon makes the print engine used in many laser printers, including those from Hewlett-Packard; in this case, Canon is an original equipment manufacturer (*OEM*) and HP is the value-added reseller.

variable resistor   A resistor that does not have a fixed value, but rather can be changed. Typically the value is changed using a knob or slider.

VDT   Acronym for video display terminal. Synonymous with *monitor*.

vendor   The person or company that manufactures, supplies, or sells computer hardware, software, or related services.

version number   A method of identifying a particular *software* or *hardware* release.

The version number is assigned by the software developer, and often includes numbers before and after a decimal point; the higher the number, the more recent the release. The number before the decimal point indicates the major revision levels (DOS 5, DOS 6), while the part after the decimal indicates a minor revision level (DOS 6.1, DOS 6.2), which in some cases can produce a significant difference in performance.

vertical scanning frequency   In a *monitor*, the frequency at which the monitor repaints the whole screen; sometimes called the vertical refresh rate.

Vertical scanning frequency is measured in *Hz* (cycles per second), and higher rates are associated with less *flicker*. *VGA* has a vertical scanning frequency of 60 or 70 Hz, and *SuperVGA* rates vary from the *VESA* guidelines of 56 Hz (which is about the minimum tolerable) and 60 Hz, to the official recommended standard of 72 Hz.

very low-frequency emission   Abbreviated VLF. Radiation emitted by a computer monitor and other very common household electrical appliances such as televisions, hair dryers, electric blankets, and food processors. VLF emissions fall into the range from 2 kHz to 400 kHz, and decline with the square of the distance from the source. Emissions are not constant around a monitor; they are higher from the sides and rear, and weakest from the front of the screen.

VESA (Video Electronics Standards Association)   Group formed to set standards and make sure that the cards made for one vendor's slot will work in another vendor's computer.

VGA   Acronym for Video Graphics Array. A *video adapter* introduced by IBM along with the *IBM PS/2* line of computers in 1987.

VGA supports previous graphics standards, and provides several different graphics resolutions, including 640 *pixels* horizontally by 480 pixels vertically. A maximum of 256 colors can be displayed simultaneously, chosen from a palette of 262,114 colors.

Because the VGA standard requires an *analog display*, it is capable of resolving a continuous range of gray shades or colors, in contrast to a digital display which can only resolve a finite range of shades or colors.

VGA passthrough   A feature of certain high-resolution *video adapters* that lets a *VGA* signal literally pass through the board. This VGA signal might originate on a *motherboard-*mounted VGA adapter and go to a monitor connected to the high-resolution board. This feature lets you use one monitor for both VGA and high-resolution levels.

An expansion board installed in an expansion but slot telling it to display a particular graphic or character.

video adapter   An *expansion board* that plugs into the *expansion bus* in a *DOS* computer, and provides for text and graphics output to the monitor. The adapter converts the text and graphic signals into several instructions for the display that tell it how to draw the graphic.

Some later video adapters, such as the *VGA*, are included in the circuitry on the *motherboard*, rather than as separate plug-in boards.

Video CD   A compact disc format standard developed by Sony, Phillips, JVC, and Matsushita that allows up to 74 minutes of video to be stored on one compact disc.

Compact discs recorded in Video CD format can be played on *CD-I*, Video CD, and *CD-ROM drives*, and CD players that have digital output and an add-on video adapter.

video RAM   Abbreviated VRAM, pronounced "vee-ram." Special-purpose *RAM* with two data paths for access, rather than just one as in conventional RAM. These two paths let a VRAM

board manage two functions at once—refreshing the display and communicating with the processor. VRAM doesn't require the system to complete one function before starting the other, so it allows faster operation for the whole video system.

videodisk   An optical disk used for storing video images and sound. A videodisc player can play back the contents of the videodisc on a computer or onto a standard television set. One videodisc can contain up to 55,000 still images, or up to 2 hours worth of *full-frame video*.

virtual 8086 mode   A mode found in the *80386* and later processors that lets the processor *emulate* several *8086* environments simultaneously.

The *operating system* controls the external elements, such as *interrupts*, and input and output; and *applications* running in this mode are protected from the applications running in all the other virtual 8086 environments, and behave as though they have control of the whole 8086 environment. To the user, this looks like several 8086 systems all running side-by-side, but under the control of the operating system. Both *OS/2* and *Windows NT* use this feature of the processor to multitask multiple *DOS* sessions.

virtual DOS machine   Abbreviated VDM. A *DOS emulation* that takes advantage of the *virtual 8086 mode* of *80386* (or later) processors.

Operating systems including *OS/2, Windows NT,* and *Windows 95* use this feature of the processor to create multiple *multitasking* DOS and Windows sessions, and each VDM runs as a single-threaded, *protected-mode* process. OS/2 can go one step further and can boot a native, non-emulated version of DOS into a virtual DOS machine.

virtual machine　An environment created by the operating system that gives each executing *application* program the illusion that it has complete control of an independent computer, and can access all the system resources that it needs.

For example, the Intel *80386* (and higher) processor can run multiple *DOS* applications in completely separate and protected address spaces using a processor mode known as *virtual 8086 mode*.

virtual machine boot　Abbreviation VMB. A feature found in the *OS/2 operating system* that lets you boot a native, non-emulated version of *DOS* into a *virtual DOS machine*.

Support is provided for versions of DOS other than the *OS/2* emulation, including DOS 3.3, 4.0, 5.0, 6.0, *DR-DOS*, Concurrent DOS, and indeed, any other 8086 operating systems. Applications running in this mode are protected from the applications running in all the other *virtual 8086* environments, and behave as though they have control of the whole 8086 environment. To the user, this looks like several 8086 systems all running side-by-side, but all under the control of the OS/2 operating system.

virtual memory　A memory-management technique that allows information in physical memory to be swapped out to a *hard disk*. This technique provides *application* programs with more memory space than is actually available in the computer.

True virtual-memory management requires specialized *hardware* in the processor for the operating system to use; it is not just a question of writing information out to a *swap file* on the hard disk at the application level.

In a virtual memory system, programs and their data are divided up into smaller pieces called pages. At the point where more memory is needed, the operating system decides which pages are least likely to be needed soon (using an algorithm based on frequency of use, most recent use, and program priority), and it writes these pages out to disk. The memory space that they used is now available to the rest of the system for other application programs. When these pages are needed again, they are loaded back into real memory, displacing other pages.

virtual reality　Abbreviated VR. A computer-generated environment that presents the illusion of reality. The user may wear a head-mounted display (HMD) which displays a three-dimensional image of the environment, and use an instrumented glove to manipulate objects within the environment.

A whole range of applications are emerging to exploit VR; architects can present clients with a VR walk through of a proposed structure, and biologists can seem to get inside a human cell. Undoubtedly, the most lucrative avenues for VR will be computer games.

virus　A program intended to damage your computer system without your knowledge or permission.

A virus may attach itself to another program, or to the *partition table* or the boot track on your *hard disk*. When a certain event occurs, a date passes, or a specific program executes, the virus is triggered into action. Not all viruses are harmful; some are just annoying. The most famous virus of all is probably the Israeli or Jerusalem virus, also known as Friday the 13th, first seen on a computer at the University of Jerusalem in July 1987. This virus slows down your system and draws black boxes on the lower-left portion of the screen. If the virus is in memory on any Friday the 13th, every program executed is erased from your hard disk.

VL bus Also known as VL local bus. Abbreviation for the *VESA* local bus, a bus architecture introduced by the Video Electronics Standards Association (VESA), in which up to three adapter slots are built into the motherboard. The VL bus allows for *bus mastering*.

The VL bus is a 32-bit bus, running at either 33 or 40MHz. The maximum throughput is 133 megabytes per second at 33 MHz, or 148 megabytes per second at 40 MHz. The most common VL bus adapters are video adapters, hard-disk controllers, and network interface cards.

VLSI (Very Large Scale Integration) Technology used by chip manufacturers to integrate the functions of several small chips into one chip.

voice recognition Also known as speech recognition. Computer recognition and analysis of human language is a particularly difficult branch of computer science. Background noise, different voices, accents and dialects, and the ability to recognize and add new words to a computer vocabulary all contrive to complicate the problem.

Systems that work with just one speaker must be trained before they can be used, and systems that can work with any speaker have extremely restricted vocabularies. In the future, voice recognition will find wide applications from the phone companies to credit card authorizations to automatic voice-mail systems.

volatile memory Any memory system that does not maintain its contents when power is lost. Normal computer memory, whether *dynamic RAM* or *static RAM,* is volatile; *flash memory* and *ROMs* are not volatile.

volts Unit of electrical potential.

volume

1. A unit of physical storage, such as a *floppy disk,* a *hard disk,* or a *tape cartridge*. A volume may hold a number of complete files, or may just hold parts of files.

2. In networking, a volume is the highest level of the *file server directory* and file structure. Large hard disks can be divided into several different volumes when the *network operating system* is first installed.

volume serial number In *DOS* and *OS/2*, a unique number assigned to a disk during the formatting process, and displayed at the beginning of a directory listing.

In the *Macintosh*, System 7 assigns a similar number, known as a "volume reference number," that programs can use when referring to disks.

wafer A flat, thin piece of *semiconductor* material used in the construction of a chip. A wafer goes through a series of photomasking and etching steps to produce the final chip, which has leads attached and is finally packaged in a ceramic, plastic, or metal holder.

wait state   A clock cycle during which no instructions are executed because the processor is waiting for data from a device or from memory.

Static RAM chips and paged-mode RAM chips are becoming popular because they can store information without being constantly refreshed by the processor, and so eliminate the wait state. A computer that can process information without wait states is known as a *zero wait state* computer.

WAN (Wide Area Network)   Network that expands *LANs* to include networks outside of the local environment and also to distribute resources across distances.

warm boot   A *reboot* performed after the operating system has started running.

web browser   A *World Wide Web* client application that lets you look at *hypertext* documents and follow *links* to other *HTML* documents on the Web. When you find something that interests you as you browse through a hypertext document, you can click your mouse on that object, and the browser automatically takes care of accessing the Internet host that holds the document you requested; you don't need to know the IP address, the name of the host system, or any other details.

wideband   In communications, a channel capable of handling more frequencies than a standard 3 kHz voice channel.

WIN.INI   In *Microsoft Windows*, an *initialization file* that contains information to help customize your copy of Windows.

When Windows starts, the contents of WIN.INI are read from the *hard disk* into memory so that they are immediately available. WIN.INI contains sections that define the use of colors, fonts, country-specific information, the desktop, and many other settings.

Winchester disk   An early nickname for a *hard disk*. IBM developed a hard disk that was capable of storing 30 MB on each side of the *platter*, and so was called a 3030, and this reminded people of the Winchester 30-30 rifle.

window   In a *graphical user interface*, a rectangular portion of the screen that acts as a viewing area for *application* programs.

Windows can be *tiled* or *cascaded*, and can be individually moved and sized on the screen. Some programs can open multiple *document windows* inside their *application window* to display several word processing or spreadsheet *data files* at the same time.

Windows 95   The replacement for the DOS and Windows 3.1 operating systems, from Microsoft Corporation.

Windows 95 is a *32-bit*, *multitasking*, multi-threaded operating system capable of running DOS, Windows 3.1, and Windows 95 applications, supports *Plug and Play* (on the appropriate hardware), and adds an enhanced FAT file system in the Virtual FAT which allows *long file names* of up to 255 characters while also supporting the DOS 8.3 file-naming conventions.

Applets include WordPad (word processor), Paint, and WinPad (personal information manager), as well as System Tools such as Backup, ScanDisk, Disk Defragmenter, and DriveSpace. Access to *Microsoft Network* is available directly from the Windows 95 desktop. A new Start button and desktop TaskBar make application management easy and straightforward.

Windows 98   The newest home PC operating system released by Microsoft, as the successor to their popular Windows 95 operating system. Basically the same as Windows 95, it offers a few improvements. For example, Windows 98 improves upon the basic "look and feel" of Windows 95 with a new "browser-like" interface. It also contains bug-fixes and can support two monitors simultaneously. In addition to new interface features, it includes support for new hardware, including Universal Serial Bus devices.

Windows accelerator   An expansion card or a chip containing circuitry dedicated to speeding up the performance of PC video *hardware* so that *Microsoft Windows* appears to run faster. Standard display adapters do not handle the throughput required by Windows particularly well, and rapidly become *input/output bound*. An accelerator card specifically "tuned" for Windows can improve overall performance considerably.

Windows application   Any *application* program that runs within the *Microsoft Windows environment* and cannot run without Windows. All Windows applications follow certain conventions in their arrangement of menus, the use and style of *dialog boxes*, as well as keyboard and mouse use.

Windows NT   A *32-bit multitasking portable operating system* developed by Microsoft, and first released in 1993.

Windows NT is designed as a portable operating system, and initial versions run on Intel *80386* (or later) processors, and RISC processors such as the *MIPS R4000*, and the *DEC Alpha*.

Windows NT contains the *graphical user interface* from *Windows* 3.1, and can run Windows 3.1 and *DOS* applications as well as *OS/2* 16-bit character-based applications, and new 32-bit programs specifically developed for Windows NT.

Multitasking under Windows NT is *preemptive*, and applications can execute multiple *threads*. Security is built into the operating system at the U.S. Government- approved C2 security level. Windows NT supports the DOS *FAT file system*, the *OS/2 HPFS*, installable file systems such as *CD-ROM* systems, and a native file system called *NTFS*. Windows NT also supports *multiprocessing*, *OLE*, and *peer-to-peer* networking.

wireless networks   Connecting networks without traditional cabling methods. Transmissions are made through the air by infrared light, laser light, narrow-band radio, microwave, or spread-spectrum radio.

word   A computer's natural unit of storage. A word can be 8 bits, 16 bits, 32 bits, or 64 bits in size.

workgroup   A group of individuals who work together and share the same files and databases over a local area network. Special *groupware* such as *Lotus Notes* coordinates the workgroup and allows users to edit drawings or documents and update the database as a group.

workstation

1. In networking, any *personal computer* (other than the *file server*) attached to the network.

2. A high-performance computer optimized for graphics applications such as *computer-aided design*, *computer-aided engineering*, or scientific applications.

World Wide Web   Abbreviated WWW, W3, or simply the Web. A huge collection of *hypertext* pages on the *Internet*.

World Wide Web concepts were developed in Switzerland by the European Laboratory for Particle Physics (known as CERN), but the Web is not just a tool for scientists; it is one of the most flexible and exciting tools in existence for surfing the Internet.

Hypertext *links* connect pieces of information (text, graphics, audio, or video) in separate *HTML* pages located at the same or at different Internet sites, and you explore these pages and links using a *Web browser* such as NCSA *Mosaic*.

You can also access a WWW resource directly if you specify the appropriate *URL* (Uniform Resource Locator).

worm   A destructive program that reproduces itself to the point where a computer or network can do nothing but manage the worm. Eventually, your computer *memory* or *hard disk* will fill up completely. Compare to *WORM* (an acronym).

WORM   Acronym for Write Once Read Many. A high-capacity optical storage device that can only be written to once, but can be read any number of times. WORM devices can store from 200 to 700 MB of information on a 5.25" disk, and so are well-suited to archival and other non-changing storage. Compare to *worm* (lowercase).

write   To transfer information from the processor to memory, to a storage medium such as a *hard* or *floppy disk*, or to the display. In the PC world, the term usually refers to storing information onto disks.

write-back cache   A technique used in cache design for writing information back into main memory.

In a write-back cache, the cache stores the changed block of data, but only updates main memory under certain conditions, such as when the whole block must be overwritten because a newer block must be loaded into the cache, or when the controlling algorithm determines that too much time has elapsed since the last update. This method is rather complex to implement, but is much faster than other designs.

write-protect   To prevent the addition or deletion of *files* on a disk or tape. *Floppy disks* have write-protect notches or small write-protect tabs that allow files to be read from the disk, but prevent any modifications or deletions.

Certain *attributes* can make individual files write-protected so they can be read but not altered or erased.

write-through cache   A technique used in cache design for writing information back into main memory.

In a write-through cache, each time the processor returns a changed bit of data to the cache, the cache updates that information in both the cache and in main memory. This method is simple to implement, but is not as fast as other designs; delays can be introduced when the processor must wait to complete write operations to slower main memory.

XGA Acronym for Extended Graphics Array. A high-resolution *video adapter* introduced by IBM in 1991 to replace the *8514/A* standard.

XGA is only available as a *microchannel architecture expansion board*; it is not available in *ISA* or *EISA* form. XGA supports resolution of 1024 horizontal *pixels* by 768 vertical pixels with 256 colors, as well as a *VGA* mode of 640 pixels by 480 pixels with 65,536 colors, and like the 8514/A, XGA is *interlaced*. XGA is optimized for use with *graphical user interfaces*, and instead of being very good at drawing lines, it is a *bit-block transfer* device designed to move blocks of bits like windows or dialog boxes.

Yellow Book The definition of the standard storage format for compact disc data, also referred to as the *CD-ROM* format. So called because of the cover color used when the specification was first published.

zero wait state Describes a computer that can process information without *wait states*. A wait state is a clock cycle during which no instructions are executed because the processor is waiting for data from a device or from memory.

Static RAM chips and *paged-mode RAM* chips are becoming popular because they can store information without being constantly refreshed by the processor, and so they eliminate the wait state.

ZIF socket Abbreviation for Zero Insertion Force socket. A specially designed chip socket which makes replacing a chip easier and safer.

ZIP drives External or internal hard disk capable of storing approximately 100 MB of data on a removable disk.

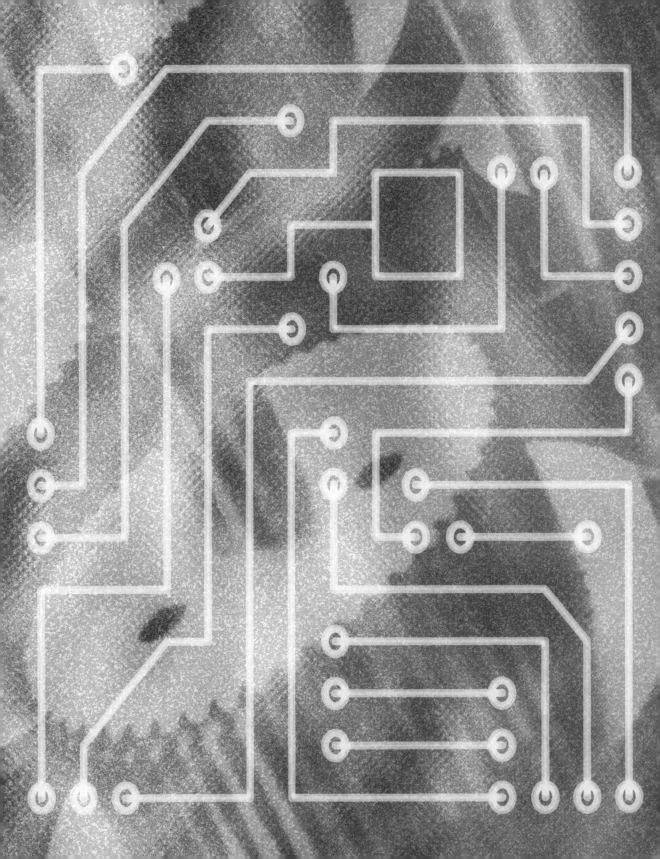

Computer Service Information Website Directory

Within this appendix are several tables of URLs for service information that can be found on the Internet (specifically, on the World Wide Web). Most of the URLs listed point to the companies' support websites. Where a support page was unavailable, we give the URL of the company's home page, where you can at least get an idea of how to contact the company for questions about their products or services.

In this appendix, we offer URLs for selected websites in the following categories:

- Computer Hardware Vendors
- Computer Software Vendors
- Third-Party Technical Support

Computer Hardware

Table C.1 is a listing of the service and support websites of some of the most popular computer hardware vendors. While this is not a comprehensive list, it includes most of the important manufacturers that have useful websites as of this writing.

TABLE C.1: Major Hardware Vendor Support Sites

Company	Address
3Dfx	http://www.3dfx.com/download/
Acer	http://www.aceramerica.com/aac/support/index.htm
Advanced Logic Research (ALR)	http://www.alr.com/service/service.htm
Apple	http://support.info.apple.com/tso/tsohome/tso-home.html

Continued on next page

TABLE C.1 CONTINUED: Major Hardware Vendor Support Sites

Company	Address
AST	http://www.ast.com/support/support.htm
ATI	http://support.atitech.ca/
Boca Research	http://www.bocaresearch.com/support/
Creative Labs *(Soundblaster multimedia equipment)*	http://www-nt-ok.creaf.com/wwwnew/tech/support/support.html
CTX	http://www.ctxintl.com/techsup.htm
Digital Equipment Corp.	http://www.dec.com/info/services/mcs/mcs_hardware.htm
DTK	http://www.dtkcomputer.com/tech.html
Epson	http://www.epson.com/connects/
ESS Technology	http://www.esstech.com/
Fujitsu	http://www.fujitsu.com/
Gateway 2000	http://www.gw2k.com/corp/support/cs_techdocs/
Hayes	http://www.hayes.com/support/index.htm
Hewlett-Packard (HP)	http://www.hp.com/wcso-support/Services/services.html
IBM	http://www.ibm.com/Support/
Leading Edge	http://www.primenet.com/~fwagner/le/
Logitech	http://support.logitech.com/
Matrox	http://www.matrox.com/mgaweb/techsupp/ftp.htm
Media Vision	http://www.svtus.com/new/new.html
Megahertz	http://www.support.3com.com/
Micron	http://www.micronpc.com/support/support.html
Midwest Micro	http://www.mwmicro.com/support/

Continued on next page

TABLE C.1 CONTINUED: Major Hardware Vendor Support Sites

Company	Address
Multi-Tech	http://www.multitech.com/support/support.htm
NCR	http://www3.ncr.com/service/
NEC	http://www.nec.com/support.html
Okidata	http://www.okidata.com/services/
Packard Bell	http://support.packardbell.com/
Panasonic	http://www.panasonic.com/host/support/index.html
PNY Technologies	http://www.pny.com/Tech/index.stm
Practical Peripherals	http://www.practical.com/support/
Quantum	http://support.quantum.com/
S3	http://www.s3.com/bbs/0main/topindex.htm
Samsung	http://www.sosimple.com/svcdir.htm
Seagate	http://www.seagate.com/support/supporttop.shtml
Sony	http://www.ita.sel.sony.com/support/
SUN Microsystems	http://www.sun.com/service/
Supermac	http://www.supermac.com/service/index.html
Toshiba	http://www.toshiba.com/tais/csd/support/
US Robotics	http://support.3com.com/
Viking Components	http://www.vikingmem.com/support/index.html
VisionTek	http://www.bsin.com/support.htm
Western Digital	http://www.wdc.com/support/
Zenith Data Systems	http://support.zds.com/default.asp

Computer Software

In addition to hardware vendors, we have compiled a list of some of the major software vendors (Table C.2). Again, it's not a comprehensive list, but should be useful for getting you the information you need.

TABLE C.2: Major Software Vendor Support Sites

Company	Address
Adobe	http://www.adobe.com/supportservice/main.html
Caldera	http://www.caldera.com/tech-ref/
Claris	http://www.claris.com/support/support.html
Corel	http://www.corel.com/support/index.htm
Lotus	http://www.support.lotus.com/
Microsoft	http://www.microsoft.com/support/
Netscape	http://home.netscape.com/comprod/products/support_programs/index.html
Novell	http://support.novell.com/

Other Technical Support Information

Of course, there are all sorts of sources for technical support information besides the websites of the vendors. In this table (Table C.3), we provide the URLs for some useful websites that are run, not by vendors, but by informed third parties.

TABLE C.3: Other Technical Support Sites

Description	Address
HealthyPC.com *Offers computing advice columns, and software patch downloads*	http://www.zdnet.com/hpc/
HelpMeNow.com *A free technical support forum and chat area*	http://www.HelpMeNow.com/
CMP Techweb *An e-zine for all aspects of the technical support industry. Check out the encyclopedia for a definition of almost any technical term.*	http://www.techweb.com/
PC Week *The magazine's website. Great for information on PC developments. Also, you can download the Ziff-Davis benchmarking utilities.*	http://www.pcweek.com/
Help Desk Institute *Great source of help desk resources*	http://www.HelpDeskInst.com
The Computer Technology Industry Association *Information on computer resources as well as information on the A+ certification*	http://www.comptia.org/
Ask the Geek *('nuf said?)*	http://www.geekman.com/askgeek.html
Software.net *A vendor directory that lists vendors offering technical support information*	http://www.software.net/directory.htm
Software Support Professionals Association *Provides support professionals a place to chat and exchange support information*	http://www.sspa-online.com/
The Technical Support Nightmare *A humorous look at technical support*	http://www.geocities.com/SiliconValley/Vista/9426/

Continued on next page

TABLE C.3 CONTINUED: Other Technical Support Sites

Description	Address
Scott's page o' Computer Literacy *Another technical support humor page*	http://www.center-net.com/8888/
Association of Support Professionals *Another professional support organization*	http://www.asponline.com/
SupportHelp.com *A database of technical support web-sites, addresses, phone numbers, and other support resources*	http://www.supporthelp.com/

INDEX

Note to the Reader: Throughout this index **boldfaced** page numbers indicate primary discussions of a topic. *Italicized* page numbers indicate illustrations.

(

E

F

I

J

M

Q

R

S

T

X

Y

Z

A+ TEST PREPARATION FROM THE EXPERTS

Sybex presents the most comprehensive study guides
for CompTIA's 1998 A+ exams for PC technicians.

ISBN 0-7821-2344-9
800 pp. 7½" x 9" $49.99
Hardcover July 1998

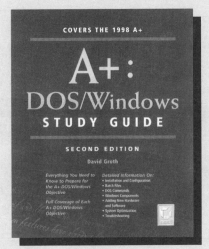

ISBN 0-7821-2351-1
688 pp. 7½" x 9" $49.99
Hardcover July 1998

ISBN 0-7821-2380-5
1,488 pp. 7½" x 9" $84.98
Hardcover 2-volume boxed set
August 1998

ISBN 0-7821-2345-7
304 pp. 5⅞" x 8¼" $19.99
Softcover August 1998

ISBN 0-7821-2346-5
304 pp. 5⅞" x 8¼" $19.99
Softcover August 1998

MCSE CORE REQUIREMENT STUDY GUIDES FROM NETWORK PRESS

Sybex's Network Press presents updated and expanded second editions
of the definitive study guides for MCSE candidates.

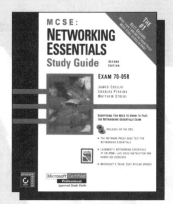

ISBN: 0-7821-2220-5
704pp; 7¹/₂" x 9"; Hardcover
$49.99

ISBN: 0-7821-2223-X
784pp; 7¹/₂" x 9"; Hardcover
$49.99

ISBN: 0-7821-2222-1
832pp; 7¹/₂" x 9"; Hardcover
$49.99

ISBN: 0-7821-2221-3
704pp; 7¹/₂" x 9"; Hardcover
$49.99

ISBN: 0-7821-2256-6
800pp; 7¹/₂" x 9"; Hardcover
$49.99

A $50.00 SAVINGS!

MCSE Core Requirements
Box Set
ISBN: 0-7821-2245-0
4 hardcover books;
3,024pp total; $149.96

Microsoft Certified
Professional
Approved Study Guide

NETWORK PRESS
SYBEX

STUDY GUIDES FOR THE MICROSOFT CERTIFIED SYSTEMS ENGINEER EXAMS

MCSE ELECTIVE STUDY GUIDES FROM NETWORK PRESS®

Sybex's Network Press expands the definitive study guide series for MCSE candidates.

MCSE: TCP/IP FOR NT SERVER 4 STUDY GUIDE

THIRD EDITION

EXAM 70-059

TODD LAMMLE
WITH MONICA LAMMLE
AND JAMES CHELLIS

ISBN: 0-7821-2224-8
688pp; 7^1/2" x 9"; Hardcover
$49.99

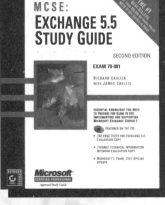

MCSE: EXCHANGE 5.5 STUDY GUIDE

SECOND EDITION

EXAM 70-081

RICHARD EASLICK
WITH JAMES CHELLIS

ISBN: 0-7821-2261-2
848pp; 7^1/2" x 9"; Hardcover
$49.99

MCSE: INTERNET INFORMATION SERVER 4 STUDY GUIDE

SECOND EDITION

EXAM 70-087

MATTHEW STREBE
CHARLES PERKINS

ISBN: 0-7821-2248-5
704pp; 7^1/2" x 9"; Hardcover
$49.99

MCSE: SQL SERVER 6.5 ADMINISTRATION STUDY GUIDE

LANCE MORTENSEN
RICK SAWTELL
MICHAEL LEE

ISBN: 0-7821-2172-1
672pp; 7^1/2" x 9"; Hardcover
$49.99

MCSE: PROXY SERVER 2 STUDY GUIDE

EXAM 70-088

ERIK ROZELL
AND TODD LAMMLE
WITH JAMES CHELLIS

ISBN: 0-7821-2194-2
576pp; 7^1/2" x 9"; Hardcover
$49.99

MCSE: EXCHANGE 5 STUDY GUIDE

RICHARD EASLICK
WITH JAMES CHELLIS

ISBN: 0-7821-1967-0
656pp; 7^1/2" x 9"; Hardcover
$49.99

Microsoft® Certified
Professional
Approved Study Guide

NETWORK PRESS®
SYBEX

STUDY GUIDES FOR THE MICROSOFT CERTIFIED SYSTEMS ENGINEER EXAMS

The A+ Core Module Objectives

Domain 1.0: Installation, Configuration, and Upgrading (30%)

1.1: Identify basic terms, concepts, and functions of system modules, including how each module should work during normal operation. — Chapters 2, 4, 5

1.2: Identify basic procedures for adding and removing field replaceable modules. — Chapter 7

1.3: Identify available IRQs, DMAs, and I/O addresses and procedures for configuring them for device installation. — Chapter 7

1.4: Identify common peripheral ports, associated cabling, and their connectors. — Chapter 1

1.5: Identify proper procedures for installing and configuring IDE/EIDE devices. — Chapter 4

1.6: Identify proper procedures for installing and configuring SCSI devices. — Chapter 4

1.7: Identify proper procedures for installing and configuring peripheral devices. — Chapter 6

1.8: Identify concepts and procedures relating to BIOS. — Chapter 2

1.9: Identify hardware methods of system optimization and when to use them. — Chapter 3

Domain 2.0: Diagnosing and Troubleshooting (20%)

2.1: Identify common symptoms and problems associated with each module and how to troubleshoot and isolate the problems. — Chapter 12

2.2: Identify basic troubleshooting procedures and good practices for eliciting problem symptoms from customers. — Chapter 11

Domain 3.0: Safety and Preventive Maintenance (10%)

3.1: Identify the purpose of various types of preventive maintenance products and procedures, and when to use/perform them. — Chapter 10

3.2: Identify procedures and devices for protecting against environmental hazards. — Chapter 10

3.3: Identify the potential hazards and proper safety procedures relating to lasers and high-voltage equipment. — Chapter 10

3.4: Identify items that require special disposal procedures that comply with environmental guidelines. — Chapter 10

3.5: Identify ESD (Electrostatic Discharge) precautions and procedures, including the use of ESD protection devices. — Chapter 10